148789
P9-AGL-058

STEFFAN, Truman Guy, comp. Lord Byron's Cain; Twelve Essays and a Text with Variants and Annotations. Texas, 1969 (c1968). 509p tab bibl (Tower Bibliographical Studies) 68-56131. 15.00

CHOICE *MAR.'70*
Language & Literature
English & American

PR
4356
S81

First new edition in 65 years of Byron's dramatic poem which was regarded by the Lord Chancellor as legally indefensible because of its "mischievous" theology and which, more recently, has come to be seen as a subtle, intricate and profound work of art. Steffan was coeditor of the Variorum *Don Juan* and wrote a careful study of that poem, "The Making of a Masterpiece." Here he has prepared 12 essays to accompany a more accurate text of Byron's most intriguing example of "mental theatre" than we have had hitherto. He traces the history of its composition and discusses the poet's intentions, as well as they can be determined from letters and reported comments, and describes the controversial reception of the work. Then he examines its content and technique: its religious ideas, the ideological and psychological conflicts among the characters, Byron's use of sources, his imagery, diction and versification. He analyzes the manuscript and earlier printed versions. Finally there is a fully evaluated survey of *Cain* criticism from 1821 to the present. The careful editing and abundant critical apparatus make this an indispensable addition to any collection of the major English poets. Thorough index and bibliography.

TRUMAN GUY STEFFAN

This important work stands not only as a valuable addition to Byron scholarship but also as an illuminating record of the changing critical and cultural attitudes from the early nineteenth century to the present. Professor Steffan has done a remarkable job in bringing together and synthesizing an enormous body of material.

He is now professor of English at The University of Texas at Austin. A specialist in English Romantic Literature, he has published numerous articles, is the author of *The Making of a Masterpiece,* and is coeditor of Volumes II and III of *Byron's Don Juan,* published in 1957.

LORD BYRON'S
CAIN

TWELVE ESSAYS AND A TEXT WITH VARIANTS AND ANNOTATIONS BY

TRUMAN GUY STEFFAN

UNIVERSITY OF TEXAS PRESS
AUSTIN & LONDON

202159

Standard Book Number 292–78388–4
Library of Congress Catalog Card No. 68–56131
Copyright © 1968 by Truman Guy Steffan
All Rights Reserved
Printed by the University of Texas Printing Division, Austin
Bound by Universal Bookbindery, Inc., San Antonio

FOR MY PARENTS

ACKNOWLEDGMENTS

I WISH TO THANK the following authors and publishers for their permission to print extracts from the books designated in the following list: George Allen and Unwin, Ltd., for selections from Stopford Brooke's "Byron's *Cain*" in *The Hibbert Journal,* XVII (October, 1919–July, 1920); and J. M. Dent & Sons, Ltd., and E. P. Dutton & Co., Inc., for the same selections from Brooke's essay reprinted in *Naturalism in English Poetry,* copyright 1920; J. M. Dent & Sons, Ltd., for selections from Henry Crabb Robinson's *Books and Their Writers*, edited by Edith J. Morley, copyright 1938; the Council of The English Goethe Society for J. G. Robertson's translation of Goethe's essay on *Cain* and other selections from "Goethe and Byron" in *Publications of the English Goethe Society* (1925); the Columbia University Press and Hoxie Neale Fairchild for selections from Volume 3 of *Religious Trends in English Poetry,* copyright 1949; William Heinemann, Ltd., and the Macmillan Company for selections from Volume 4 of George Brandes' *Main Currents in Nineteenth Century Literature* (1905); the Macmillan Company for selections from Volume 2 of Oliver Elton's *Survey of English Literature, 1780–1830,* copyright 1924; and for selections from Solomon Francis Gingerich's essay "Byron" in *Essays in the Romantic Poets,* copyright 1924; Sir John Murray, for some of E. H. Coleridge's notes in Volumes 2, 4, 5, and 7 of *The Works of Lord Byron, Poetry*; for some of R. E. Prothero's notes in Volumes 5 and 6 of *The Works of Lord Byron, Letters and Journals*; and for parts of two letters in Volume 2 of *Lord Byron's Correspondence,* copyright 1922; the Modern Language Association and Edward E. Bostetter for selections from "Byron and the Politics of Paradise," *PMLA,* LXXV (1960), 571–576; the University of Oklahoma Press and Frederick L. Jones for parts of two letters from *The Letters of Mary W. Shelley,* copyright 1944; the Clarendon Press, Oxford, and Professor

Jones for parts of four letters from Volume 2 of *The Letters of Percy Bysshe Shelley,* copyright 1964; the University of Pennsylvania Press and William H. Marshall for selections from *The Structure of Byron's Major Poems,* copyright 1962; Putnam's and Coward-McCann for selections from Nayán Louise Redfield's translation of Antoine Fabre d'Olivet's *Cain,* copyright 1923; *The University Review* of The University of Missouri at Kansas City and Constantine N. Stavrou for selections from "Milton, Byron, and the Devil," XXI (March, 1955), 155–159; John Harrison for selections from his dissertation, "The Imagery of Byron's Romantic Narratives and Dramas" (University of Colorado, 1958); Frank Rainwater for selections from his dissertation, "Lord Byron: A Study of the Development of His Philosophy, with Special Emphasis upon the Dramas" (Vanderbilt University, 1949).

I am indebted to a host of other writers for abundant information and interpretation that were indispensable to this volume. The books and articles of the following authors were especially useful: Samuel C. Chew, Ernest De Selincourt, Manfred Eimer, Richard Ellmann, Stuart Gilbert, H. J. C. Grierson, P. P. Howe, Ian Jack, Michael K. Joseph, G. Wilson Knight, Ernest J. Lovell, Jr., Leslie A. Marchand, Edward W. Marjarum, Sir Arthur Quiller-Couch, Maximilian Rudwin, Paul Siegel, Allan Lang Strout, Peter L. Thorslev, Jr., and Wallace Wood. The names of many other people from whom I gathered data and insights have, I trust, been recorded in appropriate places throughout the book. My disagreement with a few ideas of some scholars does not detract from their value to a study of *Cain.* This poem has long stimulated the expression of divergent opinion.

Two benefactions were basic: the permission of The University of Texas Library at Austin and of the late Sir John Murray to publish Byron's manuscript of *Cain*, and a grant by The University of Texas Research Institute that enabled me to purchase photocopies and microfilm of materials for Part III.

I am appreciative of the innumerable services accorded me over a prolonged period by the library of The University of Texas at Austin—the exceptional accommodations made by Miss Lorena Baker, Miss Kathleen Blow, Mrs. June Moll, and their staffs, the prompt attention given my requests by the order and duplicating departments, and the efficiency of Mr. Charles Lee Dwyer and Mrs. Jean Herold in locating books and periodicals in other libraries. The National Central Library in England procured for me photocopies of items I could not obtain in this country, and the photographic department of the British Museum was also helpful. Dr. Oscar José Santucho kindly offered me the benefit of his extensive bibliographical research.

It is impossible to specify the daily assistance that one person rendered at every stage of research, composition, revision, checking, and proofing—through it all my wife was a devoted and indefatigable collaborator. Without her the project would never have been completed.

CONTENTS

ILLUSTRATION

TABLES

ABBREVIATIONS

The following abbreviations are used in this book:

Bayle: *A General Dictionary, Historical and Critical.* Trans. the Reverend M. John Peter Bernard, the Reverend M. Thomas Birch, Mr. John Lockman, *et al.* 10 vols. London: J. Bettenham, 1734–1741.

Blumenthal: *Lord Byron's Mystery "Cain" and Its Relation to Milton's "Paradise Lost" and Gessner's "Death of Abel."* Oldenburg: Gerhard Stalling, 1891.

Bostetter: "Byron and the Politics of Paradise," *PMLA*, LXXV (1960), 571–576.

Brandes: *Main Currents in Nineteenth Century Literature.* Vol. IV. London: William Heinemann, 1901–1905.

Brooke: "Byron's 'Cain'," *The Hibbert Journal. A Quarterly Review of Religion, Theology, and Philosophy,* XVIII (October, 1919–July, 1920), 74–94. Reprinted in 1920 as Chapter XII of *Naturalism in English Poetry.* London: Dent & Sons.

Chew: *The Dramas of Lord Byron.* Gottingen: Vendenhoeck and Ruprecht, 1915; Baltimore: The John Hopkins Press.

Correspondence: *Lord Byron's Correspondence.* Ed. John Murray. 2 vols. London: John Murray, 1922.

Courthope: *A History of English Poetry.* Vol. VI. London: Macmillan & Co., 1910.

De Selincourt: "Byron" in *Wordsworthian and Other Studies.* New York: Russell & Russell, 1947.

Eimer: *Byron und der Kosmos. Ein Beitrag Zur Weltanschauung des Dichters und den Ansichten seiner Zeit.* Anglistische Forschungen, XXXIV. Heidelberg: Carl Winter, 1912.

Elton: *Survey of English Literature, 1780–1830.* Vol. II. New York: The Macmillan Company, 1924.

Elze: *Lord Byron, a Biography with a Critical Essay on His Place in Literature.* London: John Murray, 1872.

Fabre d'Olivet: *Cain a Dramatic Mystery in Three Acts by Lord Byron Translated into French Verse and Refuted in a Series of Philosophical and Critical Remarks Preceded by a Letter Addressed to Lord Byron, upon the Motives and the Purpose of This Work.* [Paris]: 1823. Trans. Nayán Louise Redfield. New York and London: C. P. Putnam's Sons, 1923.

Fairchild: *Religious Trends in English Poetry.* Vol. III: *1780–1830, Romantic Faith.* New York: Columbia University Press, 1961.

Gerard: *Byron Re-studied in His Dramas; Being a Contribution towards a Definitive Estimate of His Genius.* London: F. V. White & Co., 1886.

Gillardon: *Shelley's enwirkung auf Byron.* Karlsruhe: M. Gillardon, 1898.

Gingerich: "Byron" in *Essays in the Romantic Poets.* New York: The Macmillan Company, 1929.

Harrison: "The Imagery of Byron's Romantic Narratives and Dramas." Dissertation, University of Colorado, 1958.

Harroviensis: *A Letter to Sir Walter Scott, Bart., in Answer to the Remonstrance of Oxoniensis on the Publication of Cain, a Mystery by Lord Byron.* London: Rodwell and Martin, 1822.

Havens: *The Influence of Milton on English Poetry.* Cambridge: Harvard University Press, 1922.

Joseph: *Byron the Poet.* London: Victor Gollancz, Ltd., 1964.

Kennedy: *Conversations on Religion, with Lord Byron and Others, Held in Cephalonia, a Short Time Previous to his Lordship's Death.* London: John Murray, 1830.

LJ: *The Works of Lord Byron. Letters and Journals.* Ed. Rowland E. Prothero. 6 vols. Revised and enlarged edition. London: John Murray, 1898–1901.

Lovell: *Byron: The Record of a Quest.* Austin: University of Texas Press, 1949.

Marchand: *Byron's Poetry. A Critical Introduction.* Boston: Houghton Mifflin Co., 1965.

Marshall: *The Structure of Byron's Major Poems.* Philadelphia: University of Pennsylvania Press, 1962.

Medwin: *Journal of the Conversations of Lord Byron: Noted during a Residence with His Lordship at Pisa in the Years 1821 and 1822.* London: Printed for Henry Colburn, 1824.

Moore: Thomas Moore. *Letters and Journals of Lord Byron.* 6 vols. in *The Works of Lord Byron.* 17 vols. London: John Murray, 1832.

Moorman: "Byron" in *The Cambridge History of English Literature.* Eds. A. W. Ward and A. R. Waller, XII, Chap. 2. New York: The Macmillan Co., 1933.

Noel, *Essays*: "Lord Byron and His Times" in *Essays on Poetry and Poets.* London: Kegan Paul, Trench & Co., 1886.

Noel, *Life*: *Life of Lord Byron.* London: Walter Scott, 1890.

PL: John Milton. "Paradise Lost" in *The Poems of John Milton.* Ed. James Holly Hanford. Second edition. New York: Ronald Press Co., 1953.

Poetry: *The Works of Lord Byron. Poetry.* Ed. Ernest Hartley Coleridge. 7 vols. Revised and enlarged edition. London: John Murray, 1904–1905.

Rainwater: "Lord Byron: A Study of the Development of His Philosophy, with Special Emphasis upon the Dramas." Dissertation, Vanderbilt University, 1949.

Rudwin: *The Devil in Legend and Literature.* Chicago: The Open Court Publishing Co., 1931.

Stavrou: "Milton, Byron, and the Devil," *The University of Kansas City Review,* XXI (March, 1955), 153–159.

Thorslev: *The Byronic Hero.* Minneapolis: University of Minnesota Press, 1962.

Wenzel: "Miltons und Byrons Satan," *Archiv für das Studium der neueren Sprachen und Litteraturen,* LXXXIII (1889), 67–90.

Wright: *The Works of Lord Byron.* Vols. VII–XVII. London: John Murray, 1832–1833.

PART I

CHRONICLE, ART, AND THOUGHT

HISTORY AND ARGUMENT

Publication

SHELLEY REGRETTED that he could claim no credit for the inception of *Cain* and declared that Byron had conceived it many years before 1821.[1] A fondness for the stories of the Old Testament and an indoctrination of Calvinism had begun during his Scottish childhood. Several allusions to the first murderer in his earlier poetry show that Byron had previously thought of him as the prototype of three emotional experiences: the propensity to violence; the corrosive torment of guilt; and that congenital moral and physical evil which is an hereditary curse.[2] These were never deeply buried in his mind and had often emerged in his writing, from "The Prayer of Nature" (1806) through the tales, *Childe Harold,* and *Manfred* to *Marino Faliero* (1820).

The active incubation of *Cain* had started by January 28, 1821. On that

[1] Letter to Horace Smith, April 11, 1822, *Letters of Percy Bysshe Shelley*, II, 412.

[2] Two poems referred to the mark on the criminal's brow: *The Giaour,* 1058; *Childe Harold*, I, st. 83. See also *The Bride of Abydos*, II, st. 12; *Manfred*, I, i, 249; *Childe Harold*, IV, st. 149; and *Marino Faliero*, IV, ii, 54–60. Most of the early allusions to Eve refer humorously to the temptation, her frailty, and her wantonness.

day, six months before he began writing, Byron recorded in a journal that he was ruminating the topics of four tragedies, and Cain was one of them. Shortly thereafter in the same diary he wrote three lines under the heading *Thought for a Speech of Lucifer, in the Tragedy of Cain:*

> Were *Death* an *evil,* would *I* let thee *live?*
> Fool! live as I live—as thy father lives,
> And thy son's sons shall live for evermore.

Lucifer's implication that life was misery for Adam, for Cain, and for all his descendants indicated that Byron already considered the never-ending unhappiness of mortal life as one of the ideas of the play and one of the clubs Lucifer was to use on Cain.[3]

According to the dates on the MS, he began writing on July 16, 1821, finished the poem September 9, 1821, and the next day scrawled the Preface.[4] During these seven weeks, a change occurred in one of Byron's familiar habits. From April, 1820, when he began *Marino Faliero,* to July, 1821, when he finished *The Two Foscari,* he had regularly reported to London or noted in his diary the progress he was making. I found no such reports for *Cain.* Furthermore, he kept going until he had five acts for the other plays, but he wrote only three for *Cain,* although back in January he had planned on five. This reduction may have been due to Byron's discouragement over the poor reception of the preceding plays,[5] and that blow may also be the reason for his silence on *Cain* during its composition from July to September. *Faliero* had not sold well, the critical reception had been unfavorable, the performance was a sad business, and his friends were lukewarm when they read the MSS of *Sardanapalus*

[3] *LJ,* V, 189, 191. This statement in the journal was preceded by a paragraph on the inevitable commingling of pleasure and pain. At the height of pleasure there is sorrow, fear of the future, "a doubt of what *is.*" Man can possess no good thing longer than sixteen minutes. Nor does such pessimistic knowledge "make men better or wiser. During the greatest horrors of the greatest plagues, . . . men were more cruel and profligate than ever. It is all a mystery." Such gloomy reflections on man's wretched life and character were typical of the mood of *Cain* and were frequent in Byron's meditations, in *Don Juan,* in *Childe Harold,* and elsewhere.

[4] Byron told J. J. Coulmann that he wrote *Cain* when he was drunk. "When I reread it later, I was astonished" (Ernest J. Lovell, Jr., *His Very Self and Voice: Collected Conversations of Lord Byron,* p. 342).

[5] David Erdman discussed this possibility in "Byron's Stage Fright," *ELH,* VI (1939), 219–243.

and *The Two Foscari.* Byron was writing *Cain* for himself, and he informed no one about the composition until he had finished it.

In one other way Byron was negligent about *Cain* and the other dramas of 1821. He had spent a month copying and correcting *Faliero*, and he had also given some weeks to cleaning up and revising the original drafts of the first five cantos of *Don Juan.* Mary Shelley wrote the fair copies of the remaining cantos, and then Byron read them over and made some changes. But he sent the original MSS of the three plays to Murray and directed that a copy of *Sardanapalus* be prepared in London and that his friends, John Cam Hobhouse or Douglas Kinnaird, or his sister, Augusta Leigh, who were familiar with his hand, be asked to decipher the script for the printer. The very day he wrote the Preface to *Cain,* he hurried the poem off in three packets to his publisher and requested acknowledgment of its receipt and proof "by return of post." Two days later he sent the three final lines of Eve's curse.[6]

During October he waited impatiently for proofs, informing Murray tartly that he had stayed in Ravenna an extra week for them. They finally came and by November 3 had been corrected. When he noticed that the addition to Eve's speech was missing, he tried to supply it from memory and suggested that William Gifford, Murray's editor, choose between the two versions. He did not want them to send revised proofs; "it is only losing time."[7]

Earlier in the year there had been some bargaining over the first three historical plays, and in September Byron had refused an offer Kinnaird had from Murray. Since the Londoners did not then know about *Cain,* it was not mentioned in the letters that reported these financial negotiations. Ultimately Murray paid £1,100 for *Sardanapalus, The Two Foscari,* and *Cain.*[8]

[6] Letters to Murray, Moore, Hobhouse, and Kinnaird, May 30, June 14, September 10, 12, 19, 20, 27, 1821. *LJ*, V, 301–302, 308, 360–361, 367–368, 373, 377; September 13, October 16, 1821, *Correspondence*, II, 197, 202.

[7] Letters to Murray and Moore, October 26, 28, November 3, 1821, *LJ*, V, 396, 398, 469–470. Mary Shelley had read *Cain* by November 2 (*Mary Shelley's Journal*, p. 161). She probably used the proof sheets, since the original MS had been sent to London in September and the book did not reach Pisa until January.

[8] Murray in his little pamphlet, *Notes on Captain Medwin's Conversations of Lord Byron,* itemized all the payments he had made for Byron's works (p. 8). Smiles and Coleridge stated that Murray paid £2,710 for the three tragedies, but this was an error. Leslie A. Marchand wrote that Murray paid 2,500

Our dramatic poem was advertised separately in the *Morning Chronicle* on November 24, 1821, "for the purpose of exciting the greater curiosity." Six thousand copies of the volume of three plays were issued on December 19, 1821, and a month later Murray told Hobhouse that they were not selling. Byron on January 23, 1822, wrote that he had received a copy. He complained that the dedication to Goethe had been omitted and that there were misprints.[9]

In October, 1822, after he had failed to persuade Murray to print *Heaven and Earth* and was making unusual concessions about changes in that "oratorio," he wrote his publisher that he had no objection to the omission of a passage in *Cain*, possibly the three and a half lines on Christ (I, 163–166), that Murray or Gifford a year earlier may have censored without consulting the author.[10]

Byron's View of His Play

Early in 1821, Byron had jotted in his diary that the story of Cain was a metaphysical subject, and later he so designated the drama in letters to his friends. His use of this epithet was partly jocose, partly serious, and quite elastic. Stopford Brooke and most interpreters before and after him assumed that Byron meant simply that he had written a philosophical

---

guineas for the plays and Cantos III–V of *Don Juan* (*Byron. A Biography*, III, 953 and n.). Murray's pamphlet listed £1,525 for the three *Don Juan* cantos. If we add this to the £1,100 for the plays we get £2,625 for the two books.

[9] John Watkins made the remark about the advertisement (*Memoirs of the Life and Writings of the Right Honourable Lord Byron, with Anecdotes of Some of His Contemporaries*, p. 383). See John Cam Hobhouse's *Recollections of a Long Life*, II, 179, for the report on the sale. On January 24, 1822, E. E. Williams recorded the arrival in Pisa of Byron's personal copy of the dramas (*Maria Gisborne and Edward E. Williams, Shelley's Friends: Their Journals and Letters*, pp. 126–127). See also Byron's letter, *LJ*, VI, 8. The volume was in print in late November or early December. Sir Walter Scott received a copy on December 13 (John Gibson Lockhart, *Memoirs of the Life of Sir Walter Scott*, V, 150–151).

[10] Gifford probably censored the Manichean sentences of the Preface. The last two paragraphs of this foreword, which do not appear on the Stark MS, must have been sent after September 10 and accepted by Murray at some stage of publication.

Ethel Mayne and Leslie Marchand have related the main facts about the composition of *Cain*, and R. C. Babcock wrote a hectic article on the subject in 1927. I have assembled the data for this section and the next one from the journals and correspondence of Byron and his contemporaries.

drama, concerned with theological doctrine. But he had also applied the label to *Lara,* to the third canto of *Childe Harold,* and to *Manfred.* In 1815 he felt that *Lara* was "too little narrative, and too metaphysical to please the greater number of readers." In 1817 he distinguished between Cantos III and IV of *Childe Harold* by stating that the latter had no metaphysics in it, treated "more of works of art than of Nature," and was "not a continuation of the Third. I have parted company with Shelley and Wordsworth. Subject matter and treatment are alike new."[11] Apparently he regarded the nature passages of Canto III, in which he was indebted to some of the ideas of Wordsworth and Shelley, as metaphysical. We may deduce that he called *Lara,* Canto III of *Childe Harold, Manfred,* and *Cain,* metaphysical because all four were freighted with a certain kind of abstract meditation—psychological analysis, introspection and speculation on the nature of God and the individual's relationship to divinity and to society, and on the baffling problems of mortality, eternity, and human destiny.[12]

The adjective had other connotations for him. His gay metaphysical

[11] *LJ,* III, 201; IV, 153, 155. *Poetry,* II, 311. The sentences about *Childe Harold* that Coleridge attributed to letters of July 20 and August 7, 1817, do not appear in the Prothero edition.

[12] Byron's distinction between the third and fourth cantos of *Childe Harold* was too simple and misleading. There were differences, but the last canto is easily lodged within the boundaries of his unprofessional metaphysics. He loaded it with cogitation on the "taint of sin" and predestination, the freedom and creativity of the imagination, the limitations of reason, the subconscious activity of grief, the prejudice caused by compulsory education, the tyranny of infatuation, nemesis, the deterioration of nations, and the power of the eternal spirit of Nature. Even his aesthetic comments on statues and buildings could be called metaphysical.

Since *Lara, Manfred,* and *Cain* had some attributes of the Zeluco story, Ernest J. Lovell, Jr. conjectured that Byron might have considered such elements metaphysical. He noted that the three heroes "rejected a God of love and each sought after knowledge forbidden" (Lovell, p. 208 n.). These characteristics do not pertain to *Childe Harold,* III.

The word was common in *Don Juan,* where its occurrences had a jocular kinship and little flexibility. Coleridge's lectures on metaphysics were incomprehensible. Lambro did not know why he was cheerful, because he knew no metaphysics (psychology). Byron's own remarks on Cuvier's theory of cyclical destruction, on idealism, on the fluctuations of truth, and the uncertainty of knowledge—all these he termed metaphysical (Ded. st. 2; I, st. 91; III, st. 26; IX, sts. 37–41; XI, sts. 1–5; XII, sts. 52, 71–72; XIII, st. 87; XV, 89–92).

style was a sober rhetoric, often an agitated declamation, or a ragged rhapsody, stilted and clangorous. *Manfred, Cain, Heaven and Earth,* and *The Deformed Transformed*—the quartet that Marchand called speculative—were perhaps also linked in Byron's mind with the lofty clouds of metaphysical heights because they had celestial and infernal beings, miraculous events, and preternatural situations: spiritual essences of the natural elements, evil entities and agents of destruction, amorous angels and avenging furies, a colloquy in a hall that had a globe of fire, the metamorphosis of a hunchback into an Achilles, a flight among the stars to a realm of gigantic phantoms, a column of fire ascending to heaven, a whirlwind, and a flood of annihilation.

As soon as Byron had mailed the *Cain* MS to Murray, he began puffing it and asked for Gifford's judgment. He had "a good opinion of the piece, as poetry" and lauded the clinchers to Eve's tirade. He was also pleased with the facility and the variety of his production in the past fifteen months, in spite of many mundane distractions. One jesting comment to Moore hinted at his habitual uneasiness about public opinion: *Cain* was entitled "a mystery" in honor of what it would remain to the reader.[13]

Before he received anyone's verdict on the drama, he did what was unusual for him: he wrote an explication for Thomas Moore of the fantasy of Act II:

> . . . I have sent him [Murray] another tragedy—*Cain* by name—making three in MS. now in his hands, or in the printer's. It is in the *Manfred* metaphysical style, and full of some Titanic declamation;—Lucifer being one of the *dram. pers.*, who takes Cain a voyage among the stars, and afterwards to "Hades," where he shows him the phantoms of a former world, and its inhabitants. I have gone upon the notion of Cuvier, that the world has been destroyed three or four times, and was inhabited by mammoths, behemoths, and what not; but *not* by man till the Mosaic period, as, indeed, is proved by the strata of bones found;—those of all unknown animals, and known, being dug out, but none of mankind. I have, therefore, supposed Cain to be shown, in the *rational* Preadamites, beings endowed with a higher intelligence than man, but totally unlike him in form, and with much greater strength of mind and person. You may suppose the small talk which takes place between him and Lucifer upon these matters is not quite canonical.

[13] Letters to Murray and Moore, September 12, 19, 1821, *LJ*, V, 361, 368. See textual notes, III, 441–443.

> The consequence is, that Cain comes back and kills Abel in a fit of dissatisfaction, partly with the politics of Paradise, which have driven them all out of it, and partly because (as it is written in Genesis) Abel's sacrifice was the more acceptable to the Deity.[14]

Six weeks later he explained to Murray the effect on the mind of Cain of the journey outward into space and backward in time. He analyzed, better than anyone has done, the cause of the murder and Cain's emotion thereafter:

> Cain is a proud man: if Lucifer promised him kingdoms, etc., it would *elate* him: the object of the Demon is to *depress* him still further in his own estimation than he was before, by showing him infinite things and his own abasement, till he falls into the frame of mind that leads to the Catastrophe, from mere *internal* irritation, *not* premeditation, or envy of *Abel* (which would have made him contemptible), but from the rage and fury against the inadequacy of his state to his conceptions, and which discharges itself rather against Life, and the Author of Life, than the mere living.
>
> His subsequent remorse is the natural effect of looking on his sudden deed. Had the *deed* been *premeditated,* his repentance would have been tardier.[15]

This exposition was a reply to Murray's letter that had informed him of Gifford's unfavorable view. During October he was piqued because no one wrote him about *Cain.* Now that London boggled over it, he was mortified and began a vigorous defense. He predicted that the world would come to see that *Cain* had "the vital principle of permanency within it" and that the whole volume of plays eventually would be preferred to his other writings.[16] He was vexed when Gifford and Murray wanted him to omit or alter some of Lucifer's audacious speeches on God's destruction of many past worlds and their inhabitants. "The two passages cannot be altered without making Lucifer talk like the Bishop of Lincoln—which would not be in the character of the former." His notation that the source of this pessimism was Cuvier did not soothe his publisher or anyone who was disturbed by radical notions. He covered his chagrin with a show of levity: "The other passage is also in character: if *nonsense*—so much the

[14] Letter of September 19, 1821, *LJ,* V, 367–368.

[15] Letter of November 3, 1821, *LJ,* V, 470.

[16] Letters of September 20, 1821, May 17, 29, 1822, *LJ,* V, 371–372; VI, 64, 75.

better, because then it can do no harm, and the sillier Satan is made, the safer for every body."[17]

He was annoyed by Jeffrey's comment that *Cain* seemed elaborate, which to Byron implied that he had worked long and hard at it. This he denied, for the plays "were written as fast as I could put pen to paper, and printed from the *original* MSS., and never revised but in the proofs" and thus they were the most carelessly composed of his writings. Their faults were those of negligence, not of labor.[18]

Another plea was the argument from precedent that he had tried when *Juan* was condemned for indecency: "If *Cain* be 'blasphemous'; *Paradise Lost* is blasphemous." His people were not more impious than Satan or Mephistopheles or the Prometheus of Aeschylus.[19]

His most logical defense stressed three views. Readers should recognize the creative objectivity of an author and should not assume that the opinions of people in a play were the author's own opinions. *Cain* was a drama, not a religious tract, and he avouched in it "no creed nor personal hypothesis."

> With respect to "Religion," can I never convince you that *I* have no such opinions as the characters in that drama, which seems to have frightened every body. . . . My ideas of a character may run away with me: like all imaginative men, I, of course, embody myself with the character while I *draw* it, but not a moment after the pen is from off the paper. I am no enemy to religion. . . . I incline, myself, very much to the Catholic doctrines.[20]

He could recall nothing in the play that denied immortality.

Almost no critic in 1822 or thereafter was willing to allow Byron's claim to dramatic objectivity. The only contemporaries who did so were

[17] Letter to Murray, November 3, 1821, *LJ*, V, 469.

[18] Letters to Murray and Moore, June 6 and 8, 1822, *LJ*, VI, 76–77, 81. Perhaps Byron protested too much; formerly he had made a similar comment about the haste with which he had written some of the verse tales.

[19] Letters to Murray, November 3, 1821, February 8, 1822, *LJ*, V, 469–470; VI, 13–17.

[20] *Ibid.*, and letters to Moore, February 20, March 4, 1822, *LJ*, VI, 23–24, 31–32. "Nor can I conceive why people will always mix up my own character and opinions with those of the imaginary beings which, as a poet, I have the right and liberty to draw" (Kennedy, p. 162). "Some call me an Atheist, others a Manichaean. . . . I am taxed with having made my drama a peg to hang on it a long, and some say tiresome, dissertation on the principle of Evil; and, what is worse, with having given Lucifer the best of the argument" (Medwin, p. 127).

the liberals, and some of them tipped their hand by approving of the attack on despotic and outworn notions. Both conservatives and liberals, from the Tory reviewers and Leigh Hunt to Brandes and twentieth-century scholars, have identified Cain's and Lucifer's unorthodox views and rebellious personalities with Byron's own Promethean temperament and sympathies.[21]

A second literary vindication was that the impious opinions of Cain and Lucifer were consistent with a biblical and traditional conception of their characters.

> . . . if I am to write a drama, I must make my characters speak as I conceive them likely to argue.
>
> . . . if Lucifer and Cain speak as the first Murderer and the first Rebel may be supposed to speak, surely all the rest of the personages talk also according to their characters—and the stronger passions have ever been permitted to the drama.[22]

It would be absurd to expect piety and submission from Cain and Lucifer. He reminded his critics that he had given talk to Adam, Abel, and Adah that was as pious as the catechism.

Finally Byron relied on common sense and his own doubt about the tangible influence one piece of literature could have on human belief and behavior. "I really thought *Cain* a speculative and hardy, but still a harmless, production." Fictional people never led anybody astray. How could a mere drama be injurious in any practical way? Surely "Gifford is too wise a man to think that such things can have any *serious* effect; *who* was ever altered by a poem?"[23]

[21] An unnamed person reported to Byron that the liberals liked *Cain,* but that "the Ultraists" were making a terrible outcry (Medwin, p. 127). See "The Major Periodicals and Pamphlets."

[22] Letters to Murray, Moore, November 3, 1821, February 8, 20, 1822, March 4, *LJ,* V, 470; VI, 13–17, 23–24, 32. "Have I not a right to draw the characters with as much fidelity, and truth, and consistency, as history or tradition fixes on them?" (Kennedy, p. 159). "I could not make Lucifer expound the Thirty-nine Articles, nor talk as the Divines do: that would never have suited his purpose. . . . I have made Lucifer say no more in his defence than was absolutely necessary. . . . I was forced to keep his dramatic character. *Au reste,* I have adhered closely to the Old Testament, and I defy any one to question my moral" (Medwin, p. 128).

[23] Letters to Murray and Moore, November 3, 1821, and March 8, 1822. *LJ*, V, 469–470; VI, 38. Kennedy told Byron about a distressed man who read *Cain* and

Byron, disturbed by the embarrassment he had caused his publisher, wrote a long letter that Murray released to the London press.[24] He named several writers whose works he thought more unorthodox than his drama: Priestley, Hume, Gibbon, Bolingbroke, Drummond, and Voltaire had been published, and the courts had not deprived the booksellers of their rights. If Murray lost money because of *Cain,* Byron would refund whatever Murray had paid him. He enjoined this prudent tradesman to announce that since all wise counsellors had been opposed to publication, the author alone was responsible for it, and if Murray were prosecuted, the proceedings should be transferred to Byron, who would come to England for the trial.

In time Byron so wearied of the commotion that he wrote Murray to send him no more periodicals and returned one issue of the *Quarterly* unopened. Though in *Don Juan* (XI, st. 56) Byron wrote that *Cain* was his Waterloo, he soon reaffirmed his independence. He was not to be deterred by the hubbub; "they shall not interrupt the march of my mind, nor prevent me from telling the tyrants who are attempting to trample upon all thought, that their thrones will yet be rocked to their foundation."[25]

---

next morning shot himself. Byron wanted very much to read the account in the newspaper (Kennedy, pp. 161, 250).

[24] Few of Byron's letters have had such a wide circulation as this one of February 8, 1822. He urged Murray to make any use of it he wanted to. *The Examiner* printed it on March 10, 1822 (p. 152) and *The Literary Gazette* on March 16 (pp. 166–167). Other magazines picked it up and several reviewers were soon answering some of its arguments. A wag ("Ensign O'Doherty," probably J. G. Lockhart) published a clever rhyming of the letter in *Blackwood's* (March, 1822). Watkins knew that Murray had given it to the press (pp. 387–388). Leigh Hunt heard about it as soon as he arrived in Pisa. Medwin wrote that Byron let him make a copy in Pisa and he used it in his *Conversations* (pp. 129–131). By this time it had become standard fare. The introductions to the 1833 and 1837 editions printed it. Smiles in his brief 1891 account of the *Cain* controversy quoted part of it (I, 427–428) and so did Coleridge. Prothero included all of it (VI, 13–18). Quennell in his collection of letters omitted it. See also a letter to Moore, February 28, 1822, *LJ*, VI, 27–28.

[25] May 2, 1822, *Correspondence,* II, 223. Some of Byron's acquaintances—Fletcher (his valet), Colonel Stanhope, J. J. Coulmann, and Henry Edward Fox—stated that Byron repented and recanted or at least regretted that he had ever written *Cain* and *Don Juan* and thought that he would one day make a retraction. Hobhouse, *Recollections,* III, 59–60; Lovell, *His Very Self,* pp. 342, 352.

Cain *in Chancery*

The prevailing view that *Cain* was blasphemous encouraged piracy. Publishers like Benbow guessed that the Chancellor, Lord Eldon, would not issue an injunction to sustain Murray's copyright of a wicked book. When Benbow's cheap reprint appeared soon after the December publication of *Cain,* Murray employed Counsellor Lancelot Shadwell to protect his copyright and stop Benbow's piracy. Shadwell agreed with Byron that Lucifer spoke in character, often very absurdly, and that the poem could harm no reasonable mind.

On February 7, 1822, Shadwell applied to the Court of Chancery for an injunction to restrain Benbow from printing *Cain,* but the Lord Chancellor was reluctant to grant it. Though he had not read the book, he believed "from what he had heard, that it was of a nature to preclude his interference in protecting the plaintiff's property." But upon the Counsellor's urging that the case be heard, "his Lordship assented."[26]

When Shadwell appeared before Lord Eldon on February 9, his defense of the morality of *Cain* borrowed some of Byron's arguments. He defined the primary purpose of the drama as the presentation of the causes of the first murder and stressed Lucifer's influence on Cain as the decisive force. He called the court's attention to Adah's piety and to the criminal's remorse and punishment. Finally he leaned heavily on the similarity to *Paradise Lost.*

Lord Eldon, in his reply to Shadwell's petition, doubted that Byron's purpose was the same as his predecessor's—the promotion of reverence for Christianity. He refused to grant the injunction and wryly admitted that he thereby allowed the wide, pirated dissemination, at low cost, of a mischievous book. Some people have interpreted Lord Eldon's opinions about *Don Juan* and *Cain* as typical of the Tory government's opposition to a free press and of its fear of Byron's prestige. But as Paul M. Zall has explained, the Chancellor's unfavorable views on Southey's *Wat Tyler,* Shelley's *Queen Mab,* and the works of other authors sprang from moral and legal principles.[27]

Shadwell's plea was printed by Wright (XIV, 5–6):

> This work professes . . . to represent the state of Cain's mind when it

[26] *The Examiner* (February 11, 1822), 90.

[27] Paul M. Zall, "Lord Eldon's Censorship," *PMLA,* LXVIII (June, 1953), 436–443.

received those temptations which led him to commit the murder of his brother. . . . The book only does that which was before done by Milton, and adheres more closely to the words contained in Scripture. The book, in the commencement, represents Cain in a moody, dissipated disposition, when the Evil Spirit tempts him to go forth with him to acquire knowledge. After the first act, he leads him through the abyss of space; and, in the third, Cain returns with a still more gloomy spirit. Although the poet puts passages into his mouth, which of themselves are blasphemous and impious; yet it is what Milton has done also, both in his Paradise Lost, and Regained. But those passages are powerfully combated by the beautiful arguments of his wife, Adah. . . . the book represents what Scripture represents,—that he is, notwithstanding, instigated to destroy the altar of his brother, whom he is then led on to put to death; but then the punishment of his crime follows in the very words of the Scripture itself. Cain's mind is immediately visited with all the horror of remorse, and he goes forth a wanderer on the face of the earth. I trust I am the last person in the world who would attempt to defend a blasphemous or impious work; but I say that this poem is as much entitled to the protection of the court, in the abstract, as either the Paradise Lost or the Paradise Regained. So confident am I of this, that I would at present undertake to compare it with those works, passage by passage, and show that it is perfectly as moral as those productions of Milton. Every sentence carries . . . its own balsam. The authority of God is recognised; and Cain's impiety and crime are introduced to show that its just punishment immediately followed. I repeat, that there is no reason why this work, taken abstractedly, should not be protected as well as either of the books I have mentioned. I therefore trust that your Lordship will grant this injunction *in limine,* and then the defendants may come in and show cause against it.

The following is a composite report of Lord Eldon's judgment on the case of "Murray v. Benbow and Another." The bracketed part was taken from *The Quarterly Review* (XXVII, [April, 1822], 129–130) and is a portion of an article on several similar cases, which the anonymous author wrote to show how British law encouraged the inexpensive promulgation of wicked works. The Lord Chancellor for many years consistently refused to take measures to check piracy when he deemed a book immoral, subversive, or blasphemous. The author of this article stated that he derived his account of "Murray v. Benbow" from Messrs. Jacob and Walker, "the able reporters in the Court of Chancery." The unbracketed portions below were taken from a briefer article in *The Examiner* (February 17, 1822, p. 111).[28]

* * *

Saturday, Feb. 9

Mr. Shadwell said, when he moved for an injunction in this case on a former day, his Lordship was of opinion that he could not grant it without notice of the motion being served on the Defendants, which had since been done.—His Lordship at the same time doubted whether he could interfere, on account of the nature and tendency of the book.

The Lord Chancellor.—"I gave no opinion of my own as to its merits; I had never seen it. I only spoke of what I had heard. . . . Although the Defendants do not appear, it is my duty to see that the work is of such a nature that the Court ought to interfere. Hand me the book up, and I will read it."

The book was accordingly handed to his Lordship.

Tuesday, Feb 12

The Lord Chancellor.—This Court, like every other Court of Justice, holds Christianity to be a part of the law of the land. Its jurisdiction in protecting literary property I take to be founded on this:—Where an action of damages will lie in a Court of Law for the piracy of a work, it will lend its assistance to aid the defective remedy which such a proceeding affords; for it is obvious that publication after publication might take place, which you could never otherwise hunt down [by proceeding in the other courts]. But when the work is of such a nature that an action for piracy will not lie, then this Court will not grant an injunction to protect the copyright. [Now this publication, if it is one intended to vilify and bring into discredit that portion of scripture history to which it relates, is a publication with reference to which . . . the party could not recover any damages in respect of a piracy of it. . . . You have alluded to Milton's immortal work; it did happen in the course of last long vacation, amongst the solicitae jucunda oblivia vitae, I read that work from beginning to end; it is therefore quite fresh in my memory, and it appears to me that the great object of its author was to promote the cause of Christianity; there are undoubtedly a great many passages in it, of which, if that were not its object, it would be very improper by law to vindicate the publication; but taking it all together, it is clear that the object and effect were not to bring into disrepute but to promote the rever-

28 See also Smiles, *A Publisher and His Friends*, I, 428.

ence of our religion. Now the real question is, looking at the work before me, its preface, the poem, its manner of treating the subject, particularly with reference to the fall and the atonement, whether its intent be as innocent as that of the other with which you have compared it; or whether it be to traduce and bring into discredit that part of sacred history.] This question I have no right to determine. It is one which is only fitted for the consideration of a jury. All I am now called upon to say is, whether I entertain a reasonable doubt on the character of the book; and I trust I shall not be considered unreasonable when I say I do entertain such a doubt. [There is a great difficulty in these cases, because it appears a strange thing to permit the multiplication of copies, by way of preventing the circulation of a mischievous work, which I do not presume to determine that this is, but that I cannot help: and the singularity of the case, in this instance, is more obvious because here is a defendant who has multiplied this work by piracy, and does not think proper to appear. If the work be of that character which a court of common law would consider criminal, it is pretty clear why he does not appear, because he would come confitens reus, and for the same reason the question may perhaps not be tried by an action at law, and if it turns out to be the case I shall be bound to give my own opinion. That opinion I express no further now than to say that, after having read the work, I cannot grant the injunction . . . It is true that this mode of dealing with the work, if it be calculated to produce mischievous effects, opens a door for its wide dissemination, but the duty of stopping the work does not belong to a court of equity, which has no criminal jurisdiction and cannot punish or check the offence. If the character of the work is such that the publication of it amounts to a temporal offence, there is another way of proceeding, and the publication of it should be proceeded against directly as an offence; but whether this or any other work should be so dealt with it would be very improper for me to form or intimate an opinion.]

Mr. Shadwell.—Then, my Lord, I suppose the result is, that I take nothing by my present motion.

The Lord Chancellor.—Just so. Injunction refused.

In a few minutes after his Lordship had pronounced the decision, an officer of the Court gave Mr. Shadwell the copy of the work which he had upon a former day handed up to the bench.

Mr. Shadwell.—I was almost afraid, my Lord, after what your Lordship had said, to claim a property in this book.

The Lord Chancellor.—I have no wish to claim a property in it, I assure you.

Though most reviewers joined Lord Eldon in deprecating the encouragement that his decision gave to the proliferation of a wicked book, the press was not unanimous in sharing his scruple. In a short laudatory notice of *Cain,* the *Rambler's Magazine* was pleased that the Lord Chancellor had declined to prohibit Benbow's cheap publication of the poem. The high price of books had too long excluded poor people from the gates of knowledge. The *Rambler* hoped that many more inexpensive editions of "dear and valuable works" would "rapidly proceed from the press, in spite of threats and animadversions."[29] R. Carlile, H. Gray, J. Smith, and M. Price soon brought out at least five piratical editions of *Cain* in London in 1822. In the same year Galignani published it in Paris and William Gilley in New York. At a later date, Murray was granted an injunction, but this did not deter Benbow from reprinting the poem in 1824, nor W. Dugdale in 1826.

Colonel Leicester Stanhope recorded Byron's wrath at Lord Eldon, whom he called "The Demon of the Law." The decision, the poet said, was unjust because it "had robbed him of his property, and had cast it away in the public market, to be scrambled for and divided among the breakers and defyers of the law . . . it had lowered the price of the work, . . . and had thereby increased its sale ten-fold.[30] Byron inveighed against the English legal code as "voluminous and undefined, contradictory and bloody." One abuse was that the Lord Chancellor had arbitrary power and "contrary to every wise principle of justice [was] also the highest political functionary in the realm." Under Lord Eldon, lawsuits incurred prolonged delays and great expense, put justice "beyond the reach of the mass of the people and enabled the rich, right or wrong, to triumph."[31]

A later episode of this legal comedy, in which neither Murray nor Benbow nor Byron figured, occurred in 1823. In a court presided over by one Mr. Minshull, Thomas Price, another pirate, asked that the court require Benjamin Johnson to turn over to him nine hundred copies of *Cain* that Price, a year earlier, had contracted with Johnson to print for him. Price had not paid Johnson for the work and so the court dismissed the complaint. Minshull had never read the play, but had heard about it and agreed with the printer that it ought to be used as waste paper. He would

[29] *Rambler's Magazine,* I (March 1, 1822), 119.

[30] Leicester F. C. Stanhope, *Greece in 1823 and 1824,* p. 541.

[31] *Ibid.,* pp. 541–542.

never help Price "disseminate" it, and he wished he had the power to "order every copy of it to be burnt."[32]

Byron's Dramatic Theory

For a year and a half (from April, 1820, to September, 1821) while Byron was working on four plays,[33] his letters reveal that he was following a few general dramatic principles. He never wrote a systematic exposition of them, but from time to time, beginning in September, 1820, he sent random and redundant comments to London. One group of opinions was a vigorous opposition to both the past and the present British theatre. Though he conceded that Shelley's *Cenci* had "power and poetry," it belonged to the Elizabethan tradition, which did not offer good models. "I deny that the English have hitherto had a drama at all." He had a low opinion of the absurd trash of those "turbid mountebanks," "our mad old dramatists" with their intricate confusion of plot, bustle, and extravagant rhetoric. As a member of the Drury Lane Committee in 1815 he had read many plays, found most of them impossibly bad, and even those that he approved for production were pompous and implausible.[34] In his own plots he wanted to avoid coincidental discoveries and mistakes and ranting villains. When he described the differences between *Marino Faliero* and the British plays that were popular on the stage in his day, he explained that *Faliero* was not melodramatic, had "no surprises, no starts, no trap-doors, nor opportunities 'for tossing their heads and kicking their heels'."[35]

One other principle that differed from contemporary fashion was his belief that love was not a suitable emotion for tragedy, unless it were "*furious, criminal,* and *hapless.*" Since Count Cenci's assault on his daughter was furious and criminal, Byron might have had other circumstances in mind when he wrote that the subject of Shelley's play was "essentially *un*dramatic." One might suppose that he considered

[32] "Police, Bow-Street," *The Examiner* (October 19, 1823), 684.

[33] *Marino Faliero, Sardanapalus, The Two Foscari, Cain.*

[34] For his reminiscences of his Drury Lane experience, see *LJ*, V, 442–444, and pertinent letters of 1815, III, 201–248.

[35] Letters to Murray and Shelley, January 4, February 16, April 26, 1821, *LJ*, V, 217–218, 243–244, 268. Extracts from a diary, January 12, 1821, *LJ*, V, 167. He approved of Ben Jonson, who, he wrote, was a scholar and a classic (*LJ*, V, 218). *Werner* conformed to the melodramatic fashion, and in the nineteenth century it had a more popular theatrical history than Byron's other plays.

as tragic the passion of Manfred and Astarte, but he thrust their calamity into the past and dealt with the hero's failure to escape the remorse caused by that guilty passion. He was faithful to his dramatic code in *Marino Faliero* and boasted that it had at least one distinction—no love scenes, "the grand ingredient of a modern play." Teresa Guiccioli disagreed with his axiom that "love was *not the loftiest* theme for true tragedy, and having the advantage of her native language, and natural female eloquence, she overcame my fewer arguments. I believe she was right. I must put more love into *Sardanapalus* than I intended."[36] He did not, however, make love the cause of the king's downfall. Although he permitted his men and women to be affectionate, as in the dialogue with Adah in *Cain,* he used illicit passion only in *Heaven and Earth* to trap the women and the angels in a ruinous dilemma.[37]

He also advertised his positive aims. His "regular drama," as he termed it, proposed "to dramatize, like the Greeks . . . striking passages of history," to show "*suppressed* passion," and to maintain a strict simplicity of plot. *Sardanapalus,* he thought, was "writ according to Aristotle—all, save the chorus—I could not reconcile me to that."[38]

In the last paragraph of the Preface to *Marino Faliero* Byron mentioned his desire to preserve "a nearer approach to unity than the irregularity, which is the reproach of the English theatrical compositions, permits." In the third paragraph of the Preface to *Sardanapalus* he stated his classical aims most fully:

> The Author has in one instance attempted to preserve, and in the other to approach, the "unities"; conceiving that with any very distant departure from them, there may be poetry, but can be no drama. He is aware of the unpopularity of this notion in present English literature; but it is not a system of his own, being merely an opinion, which, not very long ago, was the law of literature throughout the world, and is still so in the more civilised parts of it. . . . The writer . . . preferred the more regular formation of a structure, however feeble, to an entire abandonment of all rules whatsoever. Where he has failed, the failure is in the architect,—and not in the art.

Byron thus compressed the time span of the legends about Sardanapalus

[36] Extracts from a diary, January 13, 1821, *LJ*, V, 173.

[37] In *The Deformed Transformed* love as human need is a psychological topic.

[38] Letters to Murray and Moore, June 22, July 14, and September 20, 1821, *LJ*, V, 310, 323, 371–372. Coleridge wrote that Byron's predilection for regular drama was an infatuation (*Poetry*, V, 3).

and represented the rebellion as occurring in one day "by a sudden conspiracy, instead of the long war of the history." In his correspondence he often pointed with satisfaction to his careful observation of the unities, "which are my great object of research," and explained how he restricted the time and location of the first two historical plays.[39]

Jeffrey and the other reviewers strongly objected to these artificial restrictions, and Goethe was amused by Byron's classical discipline:

> Goethe agreed with me, and laughed to think that Lord Byron, who, in practical life, could never adapt himself, and never even asked about a law, finally subjected himself to the stupidest of laws—that of the *three unties.*
>
> "He understood the purpose of this law," said he, "no better than the rest of the world. *Comprehensibility* is the purpose, and the three unities are only so far good as they conduce to this end. If the observance of them hinders the comprehension of a work, it is foolish to treat them as laws, and to try to observe them."[40]

E. H. Coleridge surmised that Byron may have tried by the regularity of his plays to achieve the

> discomfiture of the romantic school, with its contempt for regularity, its passionate appeal from art to nature. If he was minded to raise a "Grecian temple of the purest architecture" . . . it was not without some thought and hope of shaming, by force of contrast, the "mosque," the "grotesque edifice" of barbarian contemporaries and rivals. Byron was "ever a fighter," and his claim to regularity, to a closer preservation of the "unities," was of the nature of a challenge.[41]

F. W. Moorman and others saw in the dramas the "same alternation of the romantic and classical mode which can be traced in his early poems." The lyrical, supernatural, and emotional turbulence of *Manfred, Cain,* and *Heaven and Earth* encouraged a freer form. But the classical impulse also drew him to Alfieri's tragedies and accounted for his attempt to impose the unities on the historical plays. C. T. Goode has showed that the

[39] He noted in his diary that the action in *Marino Faliero* was limited to twenty-four hours and that the change of place was infrequent (*LJ*, V, 167). See also letters to Murray and Moore, May 25, 30, June 4, July 22, 1821, *LJ*, V, 299, 301, 304, 324.

[40] Johann Wolfgang Goethe, *Conversations with Eckermann*, p. 95.

[41] *Poetry*, IV, 327–328.

poet experimented with the unities, not out of contrariness, but because they were one of several techniques that might simplify and bring order and reality to British drama that tried to surpass the Elizabethans in confusion and bombast. John Morley believed that Byron's sanity and balance accounted for his formal effort to check the "barbarism" to which the English were prone. Roden Noel in his *Life of Byron* complained that the poet was in bondage to the unities and that they were "unadapted to the spirit and circumstances of modern drama"; but in an earlier essay he surmised that Byron may have felt that these laws were helpful restraints on his desultory, intense genius. W. J. Courthope suggested that the application of the unities was suitable to Byron's introspective drama that was less concerned with plot and action than with motive and the lengthy discussion of situations.[42]

After Byron had written three historical dramas, his allegiance to the rules began to waver. When he turned to the Bible and to fantasy in *Cain,* he broke away from his regular practice. He did superficially maintain the unity of time, for the clock span is much less than twenty-four hours. The play begins with the family prayers at sunrise. These are followed by a long discourse between Cain and Lucifer, which leads to a trip that requires but two hours. After his return Cain has a brief scene with Adah, and then comes the climax—the sacrifices of the two brothers, the quarrel, and the murder. The ensuing family agitation does not take long. The departure of Cain and Adah at the end of the drama occurs near sunset. Byron confines the location of Acts I and III to the "Land without Paradise." However, in Act II he undertakes an imaginative expansion of both time and space, for the journey covers tremendous regions of the universe and remote eras of cosmic history. Cain thinks he has been absent from home for years. The most significant unity in *Cain* is that of plot, and here perhaps Byron was more successful, less artificial than in some of his other plays. The physical and psychological line of action concentrates on the inner and outer pressures that drive Cain to his crime, and almost everything in the play is strictly germane to this single development.

To most modern readers Byron's theoretical purposes in playwriting seem to be close to those of the seventeenth-century French classical theatre. Though he referred once or twice to the French, he mentioned much

[42] F. W. Moorman, XII, 51–54; C. T. Goode, *Byron as Critic*, pp. 106–117; John Morley, "Byron" in *Critical Miscellanies*, pp. 145–146; Noel, *Life*, p. 160; Noel, *Essays*, p. 103; Courthope, VI, 261.

oftener the Italians and especially Alfieri.[43] One of the little group in the Pisan circle, Edward E. Williams, was for this reason much disappointed in *Faliero.* "Alfieri affords no model for the English Drama, with which Lord B. seems to find great fault, without promising to mend it."[44] Williams might have been influenced by Shelley, who knew what Byron was trying to do and disapproved of his principles. In two letters Shelley explained his objections.

> He [Byron] affects to patronize a system of criticism fit only for the production of mediocrity, & although all his fine poems & passages have been produced in defiance of this system: yet I recognize the pernicious effects of it in the "Doge of Venice," & it will cramp & limit his future efforts however great they may be unless he gets rid of it.[45]

> He is occupied in forming a new drama, and, with views which I doubt not will expand as he proceeds, is determined to write a series of plays, in which he will follow the French tragedians and Alfieri, rather than those of England and Spain, and produce something new, at least, to England. This seems to me the wrong road; but genius like his is destined to lead and not to follow. He will shake off his shackles as he finds they cramp him. I believe he will produce something very great; and that familiarity with the dramatic power of human nature, will soon enable him to soften down the severe and unharmonising traits of his "Marino Faliero."[46]

Byron professed to follow Alfieri in simplicity of style. In his attempt to avoid the bombast of the current theatre, he tried to break down poetry to "common language."[47] In practice, he did soar, as in certain passages of *Cain.* He rarely achieved conciseness, and he sometimes fell into barren-

[43] In September, 1820, in one of his earliest commentaries on the nature of his plays, he explained that *Faliero* was too long, too regular, the persons too few, "the *unity* too much observed," more "like a play of Alfieri's than of your stage" (letters to Murray, September 28 and October 8, 1820, *LJ*, V, 81, 90). Medwin, p. 92.

[44] *Maria Gisborne and Edward E. Williams, Shelley's Friends,* entry for October 22, 1821, p. 104.

[45] Letter to Mary Shelley, August 7, 1821, P. Shelley, *Letters*, II, 317.

[46] Letter to Horace Smith, September 14, 1821, *ibid.*, II, 349.

[47] Letter to Murray, July, 14, 1821, *LJ*, V, 323.

ness that the reviewers found dull. The various levels of diction that he mingled in *Cain* will be described in a later section.

One concomitant of the vocabulary of ordinary speech was a kind of versification that many readers called prose-poetry. The metrical characteristics of the drama will also be analyzed in a separate essay. For the moment we may note that both the diction and the prosody of *Cain* were techniques by which he tried to achieve his general dramatic purposes.

One other tenet that had little bearing on plays like *Manfred, Cain,* and *Heaven and Earth,* but did apply to *Faliero* and the *Foscari* was the value Byron placed on factual accuracy. This scruple seemed to be carried over from his interest in the travel data of *Childe Harold,* in the physical settings of the tales, and in the descriptive parts of *Don Juan* like the storm and the details of life on Haidée's island. He named his sources for *Marino Faliero,* asked that one of these be translated and published with the play, wrote some expository notes, and strove to be "strictly historical." "I want to be as near truth as the Drama can be."[48] This desire to be factual was related to his impatience with the wild fictions of the current theatre.

More important and more useful was his interest in psychological realism, which was also an implicit and conscious goal. This he re-enforced with analytical remarks on the conduct of a few characters. In reply to a criticism by Foscolo of the spitting episode in *Faliero,* he sent Murray an interpretation of Calendaro's behavior and feelings toward Bertram and a justification of the Doge's repetitions. Byron showed that he aimed at psychological realism in *Cain* when he explained to his correspondents the emotional consequence of the great journey and the motivation for the murder.[49]

More than one literary historian has wondered how Byron planned to clean away the corruption of public taste and reform the excesses of the contemporary theatre by writing plays that he declared were never designed for performance and that could be truly appreciated only by remote posterity. In the Preface to *Faliero* Byron stated, "I have had no view to the stage; in its present state it is, perhaps, not a very exalted object of ambition." This he affirmed emphatically in the Preface to his next

[48] Letters to Murray, July 17, 24, August 31, September 11, October 12, 1820; July 14, 1821, *LJ*, V, 52, 62, 67, 75, 95–96, 323.

[49] Letters to Murray and Moore, October 8, 1820; September 19, November 3, 1821, *LJ*, V, 89–90, 367–368, 470. See "Byron's View of His Play."

volume of three plays: "In publishing the following Tragedies, I have only to repeat, that they were not composed with the most remote view to the stage." In his correspondence he repeatedly insisted that his plays were for a "mental theatre," and that the kind of drama he was trying to write was as opposite to the English theatrical tradition "as one thing can be to another." "They might as well act the Prometheus of Aeschylus" as perform *Faliero*.[50] David Erdman was probably right in his subtle analysis of Byron's complex feelings about the theatre.[51] Byron would no doubt have delighted in the applause of a stage performance, but he also dreaded the humiliation of failure. He was candid about his sensitivity to an unfavorable response from an audience:

> And I cannot conceive any man of irritable feeling putting himself at the mercies of an audience. The sneering reader, and the loud critic, and the tart review, are scattered and distant calamities; but the trampling of an intelligent or of an ignorant audience on a production which, be it good or bad, has been a mental labour to the writer, is a palpable and immediate grievance, heightened by a man's doubt of their competency to judge, and his certainty of his own imprudence in electing them his judges. Were I capable of writing a play which could be deemed stage-worthy, success would give me no pleasure, and failure great pain. It is for this reason that, even during the time of being one of the committee of one of the theatres, I never made the attempt, and never will.[52]

Thus when Byron heard that *Faliero* was being performed in London he protested vigorously, and he suffered acutely when a Milanese newspaper erroneously reported that the play had been hissed. Both before and after this embarrassment, whatever his secret aspiration may have been, he consistently opposed stage presentation of his plays.

Just as popular taste and current fashion had challenged Byron to make a dramatic innovation and to defend and describe it, so his susceptibility to public opinion chilled his enthusiasm for playwriting and caused him

[50] Letters to Murray, January 20, August 23, September 20, 1821, *LJ*, V, 229, 347, 371–372. Even when he wrote *Manfred* several years earlier (1817), he declared that he had rendered it "*quite impossible* for the stage, for which my intercourse with D[rury] Lane has given me the greatest contempt" (Letter to Murray, February 15, 1817, *LJ*, IV, 55).

[51] Erdman, "Byron's Stage Fright."

[52] Preface to *Marino Faliero, Poetry,* IV, 337–338. Byron apparently repeated these views in his conversation with Medwin (p. 89).

to abandon it as a serious enterprise. Byron's reaction to his public had always been a mixture of concern and indifference. He would declare that he never coveted fame, that, except for the tales, none of his work was in a popular style, that he would have his say in spite of public disfavor, and that posterity would appreciate the merit of his plays. On the other hand, while he was writing the third act of *The Two Foscari* he wanted to know what the response to *Marino Faliero* had been.

> It is proper that you should apprize me of this, because I am in the *third* act of a *third* drama; and if I have nothing to expect but coldness from the public and hesitation from yourself, it were better to break off in time. I had proposed to myself to go on, as far as my Mind would carry me, and I have thought of plenty of subjects. But *if* I am trying an impracticable experiment, it is better to say so at once.

When he read the cold reviews of *Faliero*, he was discouraged and felt even more depressed about the hostile reception of the later volume of three plays. Thereafter he ceased to wage a theoretical campaign in his letters.[53]

[53] Letters to Murray, June 29 and July 22, 1821, *LJ*, V, 313, 325; "Detached Thoughts," *LJ*, V, 467. Though I have assembled the material for this section myself, I have added little to Goode's *Byron as Critic*, the most painstaking exposition of the subject that I know.

THE DEVOUT STOCKADE

The God of This World

IN 1813 BYRON WROTE William Gifford that he had early been "disgusted with a Calvinistic Scotch School," where he was "cudgelled to Church" for the first ten years of his life. This coercion during his boyhood and his later view of the paltriness of man and his world, which was only an atom in the universe, were, he said, the origins of the skepticism about immortality in Canto II of *Childe Harold.* This doubt he called a malady of the mind, like other kinds of hypochondria.[1] The theological malaise recurred in later cantos of *Harold,* in *Cain,* and in *Don Juan.*

Byron selected for his critical drama only a small part of the corpus of Calvinist and orthodox belief. (1) A primary premise was divine omnipotence and omniscience. The former was absolute, the latter infallible, and both were eternal and not to be questioned, because it was impossible to think of a creative and directive deity without them. (2) A

[1] *LJ*, II, 221–222. For earlier expressions of heterodoxy (1807, 1811), see letters to Long and Hodgson, II, 18–23, 35–36, 72–73. Ten years later, January 25, 1821, he wrote in a diary that no one was certain of salvation. But immortality was such "a *grand peut-être*" that the stupidest and wickedest men clung to it (V, 187). See also an entry a few days later (V, 190). After he finished *Cain*, he took an intuitive and semirational stand and insisted on immortality, though he could not accept resurrection and the "menace of Hell" (V, 456–459).

corollary was human impotence and ignorance. The more the preachers glorified the greatness of God the more they decried mankind and proclaimed its weakness and utter dependence on the Almighty Lord. Man could do and learn nothing by his own meager talent and puny effort, and so whatever he accomplished he owed to God's assistance. Human diminution, while it encouraged humility, magnified divine power and also gave opportunity for the exercise of (3) its benevolence and providence, another axiom inherent in the concept of deity. God, having created all things was tenderly solicitous about his weak creatures and eager to help them. (4) In partial recompense for such watchful care, he required obedience to his authority and grateful worship of his benefaction. Acquiescence to the celestial will and veneration of its power, glory, and perfection were pristine obligations.

God's impeccable goodness was betrayed by a toxin in man's soul, more baneful than impotence and ignorance—(5) a confounding and incurable depravity that caused man to will and do evil and to deserve punishment. So the benevolent deity had to be (6) an agent of wrath and justice. He must chastise his erring creature and reduce (7) mortal life to a vale of tears. (8) Fear and pain would persuade man to rectify his conduct or at least deter him from future infraction of divine law. Since he was wholly and irretrievably bad, there was no hope that he could purge evil from his nature.

Among the various explanations of the origin and purpose of iniquity, Byron cited one that combined divine omniscience and benevolence with human frailty, short-sightedness, and the necessity of faith. Bayle and other skeptical rationalists, whom Byron had read, denied that human weakness, ignorance, depravity, the origin and continuance of evil, divine wrath and punishment, and human misery could all be accounted for without discredit to the deity. These conditions could not be logically reconciled with the first and third premises—omnipotence and omniscience, benevolence and providence. One must instead trust to infinite wisdom and goodness and rejoice because God moved in mysterious ways his wonders to perform. (9) To dim-witted or corrupt man, the divine design was inexplicable, but a devout person was certain (10) that apparent evil would eventually turn out to be good. Byron did not in *Cain* allude to the argument that man's freedom of will permitted both good and bad decisions without interference from the deity and that any man, originally good and endowed with judgment, was responsible for his own conduct.

To the preceding ten ideas we may add three more to complete the creed that Byron assailed or rejected in his drama. (11) Sinfulness, guilt, punishment, and sorrow—the essence of human life—were endlessly transmitted from one generation to another. (12) The duality of man's nature alleviated the severity of the system, because it blessed him with a divine spirit, and so immortality was a reality for the soul, vastly superior (at least potentially) to the wretched state of the frail and wicked flesh. (13) The evangelical sects believed that salvation and immortality had been vicariously ensured by Christ's atonement, through his crucifixion for the sins of the whole world.

In this poem, Byron either ignored or minimized certain other popular doctrines: He did almost nothing with predestination and the foreordained division of all souls into the elect and the damned, which could lead to conceit, smugness, and intolerance among the blessed, and to desperation among the doomed, and which Burns satirized in "The Twa Herds," "The Kirk's Alarm," and "Holy Willie's Prayer," and Browning in "Johannes Agricola in Meditation." Abel was favored by the Lord, but no one implied that he was elect. Cain, moreover, had not been damned by predestination, though Byron had the Angel scold him for having been contumacious since the day he was born, and Cain complained that the fall had, in the womb, spoiled his disposition, but these remarks on his distemper were applications of the fifth and eleventh tenets. If, as Gingerich, Fairchild, and other critics maintained, Cain was fated to kill his brother, the universal pollution or original sin, and not individual predestination, determined this dire necessity. In *Heaven and Earth,* however, predestination was a rigid truth. Noah and his sons were God's chosen people. Japhet's love and pity for Anah could not cancel his own election or prevent her damnation.

Two concomitants of predestination were also absent from *Cain*. There was no residue of seventeenth- and eighteenth-century enthusiasm, no conviction of a zealot that he was divinely inspired and therefore an indisputable prophet of truth and an unerring and autocratic guide in practical conduct. At the other extreme, Byron did not in this drama revel in the tortures of the damned in hell, that Milton and Dante described and that Burns had his wildest preachers rant about. The Hades of Act II was a dark historical tomb of wrecked worlds and gigantic phantoms, and not a den of eternal punishment and wailing sufferers. The agonized contortions of the defeated Titans in *Hyperion* were closer to the infernal tradition than was Byron's realm of the dead. He combined the old myths about giants and the Homeric concept of the Stygian shadows with an imaginary extension of Cuvier's geological theory to portray a process of endless deterioration and demolition.

The most conspicuous omissions in this negative poem were the wonderful operations of infinite mercy that one segment of evangelical orthodoxy acclaimed: the grace of forgiveness, the miracle of redemption after repentance, and the ultimate union with God's saints and martyrs in the Kingdom of Heaven. Finally there was no place for the sacraments and institutional functions in the situation that Byron wrote his drama about.

A few of these omissions, as well as the description of Hades, indicate that among the ancestors of *Cain* were several who were not of the Calvinist covenant and who did not accede to contemporary religious conventions. The ironic skepticism of Bayle and Voltaire, the biblical commentary of Bishop Warburton, who was anathema to many proper clergymen, and a rational judgment that Byron found in Gibbon and in other eighteenth-century writers made him critical of a rigorous theology. Then the political revolutions of the recent past, a repugnance for absolute authority, and a compassion for the vanquished likewise turned him against dogmas that seemed arbitrary and restrictive of individual rights. To dramatize his aversion and his pessimism, he drew from two disparate areas of thought: (1) the speculations in geology, cosmology, and astronomy of such scientists as Fontenelle and Cuvier and (2) a bifurcation in ontology that went back to Plato and Zoroaster. These provided him with a cosmic stage, with pre-adamite worlds, and with an everlasting warfare between body and soul, between good and evil spirits. Rational skepticism, social unrest, and Byron's scientific and heretical machinery became the weapons that the protagonists in *Cain* used to disrupt the settled order and to tear asunder the god of this world.

The Orthodox Family

Byron included in his drama a small group of satisfied people, the conformists who accepted authority and convention—quiet, resigned folk who asked few questions, required fewer answers, and represented a sector of eighteenth-century rationale that advocated faith in established institutions and opposed change and innovation.

Since today we are willing to grant literature the right to deal with any subject, from any point of view, we do not demand, as the reviewers and pamphleteers did, that Byron should have given the family a cogent dialectic that would have outmatched the criticism made by Cain and Lucifer. Though Byron massed the heaviest guns on the devil's ramparts, he also sketched for us what the insurrectionists were shooting at. Most of the orthodox position was concentrated in the sunrise hymn, in Abel's address at the altar, and in five scenes of conflict—the skirmish following the hymn, Adah's opposition to Cain and Lucifer in the last 225 lines of Act I, her soothing ministration of her distracted husband in the first third of Act III,[2] Abel's exhortation of his brother and resistance to his sacrilege, and finally the counterattack of the family and the Angel against the malefactor.

In the hymn and in Abel's summation, the family praised the traditional attributes of the creator and organizer of the universe and its phenomena: his infinity, wisdom, and charity. Adam had drilled these fundamentals into them, and Abel had learned also about the ethical value of divine guidance in practical conduct and was grateful because God's presence, and this alone, could ward off evil, and because under His control nothing could err, except to some good end. Abel implied that some events seemed unfortunate, but these did not sadden or perplex him. Though God's will was inscrutable, Abel trusted that its intention and its ultimate attainment were benign.[3]

The family conformed to all divine precepts. Adam had been tamed down, Eve was no longer inquisitive, and they went cheerfully to their daily tasks, which they found easy to do. Their morning thanksgiving was no doubt a habit. Zillah usually got up before the birds to sing her canticles, and Abel performed his sacrifices with dutiful regularity.[4]

He and his parents calmly and humbly assumed that they were sinful and that God had been easy on them, for they had deserved extermination. Lucifer and Adah referred to Eve's folly in Eden and she herself, though repentant, was self-conscious about her sin, and blurted out her explanation of Cain's refusal to pray. "The fruit of our forbidden tree begins / To fall." Adam faced the repetition as inexorable. "And we must gather it again." The mother and father at the outset sighed over

[2] Adah shared the family's conventional views, but since Byron interwove her traits and feelings with those of Cain and Lucifer, her functional characterization can be most effectively discussed after a consideration of the rebels.

[3] I, 1–18; II, ii, 311; III, 223–244. Writers like Noel, Dowden, Hancock, Brandes, and Bostetter read *Cain* as an attack on political tyranny and stressed Byron's disapproval of the family.

[4] I, 47–51, 179–187.

one of the theological mottoes of the play: the infamy of mankind is perpetual. Adam accepted it as part of the doom they must bear as a faithful servant of God would do.[5]

The family shared a common dread of death. The parents had told the children that it was their "hideous heritage," and Adam's long homilies about the realm of the dead had made it so repugnant that when Cain mentioned it, everyone was aghast: Eve wept, Abel and Zillah prayed, and Adah stared at him speechless.[6] Had Byron been completely fair to Christian idealism, the family's trust in providence would have overcome their fear of death and offset the terror of the faithless Cain. But Byron chose to treat this fear as a natural human feeling, experienced by all members of the family.

They were united in their anxious endeavor to bring the black sheep back into the fold, but their efforts were ineffective, for they could meet his objections only by a monotonous reiteration of their belief in divine omnipotence and benevolence. Adam, with the best of fatherly intentions, trying to explain to his dubious son the origin of pain in the world, had seemed illogical in his faith that good would miraculously spring from suffering, which might better not have occurred at all. He was distressed when Cain did not join in matins and would not thank God for the gift of life. Both parents feared that his rebuke of them for not snatching the fruit of eternal life was a perilous resurgence of their disobedience, and so they chided his blasphemy. Eve did not understand the reason for her son's complaint, and spoke for all conservatives when she urged him to be contented with things as they were, for she knew that discontent had caused her transgression. Abel too had done his best to draw his brother to the straight path, had often implored him to make the customary sacrifices, and in the opening scene had warned him that rebellion would be futile because it would only arouse God's wrath.[7]

His prudence and constancy were unadventurous, but Byron, with perhaps too little variation, tried to convince us that Abel's goodness was genuine and pleasant. He was his mother's favorite, was beloved by Adam, God, and the angels, and his sacrifices were always acceptable. His platitudes dulled the ring of his sincerity, but they did not deaden it. His formulae ("The peace of God be on thee") were warm and friendly.

[5] I, 29–52; III, 226–231, 415–418.

[6] I, 251–256; II, i, 60–64; II, ii, 16–18.

[7] I, 22–55, 74–77, 312–313, 328–329; II, ii, 285–305.

Beneath his polite questions about the journey was an apprehension that Cain was in peril because his companion might be the enemy of God. Cain's fleering mimicry of the common title "Most High" and then the ugly symptoms of extreme agitation alarmed the peaceable lad, and he earnestly hoped that their devotions would calm his brother. Abel's decorum in urging Cain, as the elder, to proceed with the first offering, might seem a little fussy, but it had biblical precedent and was intended to be respectful.[8]

Byron gave Abel more gumption and higher stature than most readers have allowed him. The younger man's persistence, along with Adah's pleading, finally pushed Cain out of his negligence and into open revolt. After the offender's altar was demolished, Abel valiantly strove to make Cain relent and regain the Lord's favor, offered his own altar for a second sacrifice, and steadfastly opposed Cain's destructive frenzy. Abel resisted because he believed as resolutely in his principles as Cain had doubted them, and because he actually did love God more than physical life. He forgave his slayer, who he thought had been swept by madness. These grand clichés do not nullify his strength and nobility, nor the poignancy of his pity for Zillah and of his final request that Cain comfort her.[9] He may have stood serenely on the proper side and always said the correct things, but he was also a man of integrity and compassion. Roden Noel was right in praising Byron's portrayal of Abel during the entire catastrophic episode.

Byron left Zillah a very minor voice. In the song at sunrise he began a contrast between the sisters that he did not pursue. After the four proper quatrains from her kin, she dared to remind the loving Creator that he had permitted the serpent to creep in and drive her father from Paradise.[10] Though she prayed God to keep them from further evil, she has foreshadowed the heresy of the rebels, and Byron glided on this transition to her brother's aloofness from the family ritual. In Act III he appropriately had Zillah, bewildered and incredulous, discover the murder of her husband, rebuke the stronger Cain for his cruelty in not defending Abel from his assailant, and then sound the alarm: "Death is in the world!" The

[8] I, 63–64; II, ii, 338–353; III, 162–203.

[9] III, 208–214, 280–337.

[10] I, 18–21. Samuel C. Chew thought that Byron at first planned to contrast them in the same way he did Anah and Aholibamah in *Heaven and Earth* (p. 133 n.).

force and irony of her exclamation rank it high among the many fine speeches of the last act. Her two final remarks are the natural requests of a bereaved wife.[11]

Byron treated Eve more roughly than he did the four milder members of the family. Though Cain condemned Adam for yielding to Eve, plucking the wrong fruit, and bequeathing death to him, and even cursed his father for giving him birth,[12] he was more often severe with Eve than with Adam. She had blundered first, and had then lured her husband, and so was the prime offender. It was to her that all men were indebted for death. And now her smugness was worse than Adam's, because she had "forgot the mind / Which made her thirst for knowledge at the risk / Of an eternal curse." Adah complained that her mother in the "most flushed / And heedless, harmless wantonness of bliss" had committed the sin that brought more harm to her children than it did to her. Lucifer indirectly called Eve reckless, and when he mentioned her favoritism for Abel, Cain's retort was scathing: "Let him keep / Her favour, since the serpent was the first / To win it."[13]

Adam, shocked when he saw Abel dead, held Eve responsible for that grievous loss; he was otherwise temperate in his language during the crisis and disowned Cain quietly.[14] Eve, however, was furious and vindictive, and Adam and Adah were unable to check her rage. In a long series of ferocious variations, she made two demands that were more severe than the Angel's decree: all things in the world were to injure, spurn, and isolate Cain, and he must suffer unceasing and excruciating physical and mental anguish.[15]

With the many reproaches cast upon Eve by Adam, Adah, Lucifer, and especially Cain, and then with the wild and ugly slashing at her son, Byron was castigating Eve. His harsh portrait of her probably sprang from his mixed feelings about his ill-tempered mother, his wife ("the moral

[11] III, 358–370, 450, 453–454. Recall Cain's reference to her piety, I, 186–187.

[12] I, 33–34, 69–70, 294–297; II i, 191–195; II, ii, 22–25, 365; III, 118.

[13] I, 107–108, 180–182, 395–405; II, ii, 203–204, 342–345,408—409; III, 44.

[14] III, 382, 413–418, 444–450. According to Stopford Brooke (p. 89), Byron, after the murder, showed how the dogma of original sin flamed out in the hot emotions of the family. Brooke referred to Adam's reproach of Eve and to her imprecation as "the fiery brood of the incarnate sin." He might also have noted Zillah's indignation.

[15] III, 382–449. As Bostetter observed, Adam and Eve, as well as the Angel, drove Cain into exile (p. 575).

Clytemnestra"), and his cynicism about the malice of women in general.[16] But autobiographical projection does not completely explain Eve's behavior. Byron's social purpose required that she be an implacable leader among the forces of traditional authority, which have been responsible for the unhappiness and the banishment of the rebellious individual.

Since Cain and Lucifer dominated most of the dialogue, the orthodox people usually seem inconspicuous. Their normal mildness and patience, their attention to duty and obedience to law, and their placid contentment were not lively qualities, and some readers have scanted these virtues. This family did not often have an invigorating kind of goodness, and their limitations were never so dynamic as any vice would be. Their language was usually commonplace, and their submissiveness, their adherence to convention, and their lack of originality could not compete for our attention with the perfervid negation of the rebels. But we cannot ignore them. Byron needed these ordinary folk in his design of conflict, and he succeeded in giving Abel and Eve their own personal energy.

The family's interaction with Cain constitutes a double psychological pattern of warring opposites and derivative parallels. Cain and his kin encompass the normal discords of divided humanity: their faith and his doubt, their contentment and his discontent, their resignation and his rebellion, their docility and his intensity. They were not, however, entirely at variance with him, for they have endowed him with part of themselves. Eve, as she, Adam, and Cain all testify, was the progenitor of her son's inclinations and his destiny. But if she transmitted to him her former curiosity and intransigence and her present harshness, Adam and his other children shared with him their softness. Abel was Cain's brother and Adah his sister in spirit as well as in flesh. He embraced them even as he turned against and away from them.

[16] See the vigorous and jesting stanzas on Gulbeyez and the fury of an aroused woman, *Don Juan,* V, sts. 131–137; VI, 101–110.

AN APOLOGY FOR REVOLT

Cain

BYRON COULD NOT BLACKEN his hero; he could not make the murderer a hardened criminal. Common sense, his social purpose, and the classical theory of tragedy required that he make out an excellent case for the rebel, to convince us that the rebellion was justified and unavoidable. We must not dismiss Cain as a grouch nor detest him as vicious or monstrous. We must not even look at him through the eyes of his parents. We are to be as generous as Abel and Adah were at the end, and if we conclude, as his brother did, that Cain was for the moment crazed, we must understand why and how that aberration happened. Byron wanted us to take Cain seriously, to heed his many complaints, and to respect him as a virtuous man, neither completely right nor wrong, and far from unreasonable. His dramatic intention was to show that the ruin of this struggling worthy man was an ironic tragedy: his good qualities were partly the cause of his troubles and of the crime he committed. External circumstances contributed to his downfall, but the honesty of his attitude and the intensity of feeling toward his world and its authority also propelled him toward a catastrophe.

We cannot, however, forget that Cain was a murderer, and Byron did not absolve him entirely. Moreover, most of us would have found him fractious, moody, and immoderate, almost impossible to please, and very hard to work and live with. When this hero, with his difficult temperament, his faults, and misgivings met Lucifer, his ruin was inevitable, and therefore his career was tragic in that sense too.

We may start with the most amiable qualities that arouse our sympathy. Cain apologized when he saw that his behavior at the morning prayers had hurt his brother and sisters. Later he told Lucifer that he could not bear to see Adah cry, and so he had yielded to her pleading and Abel's and consented to make an offering to God. Adah loved the gentleness that she knew was inherent in his nature and implored him to let it prevail. The broadest expression of this kindliness was his desire for cosmic harmony, for the concord of the two eternal forces that now jarred the universe with their unending warfare.

Byron gave even more attention to Cain's domestic affections. His love for Adah "was born with him" and was an essential part of his life: "What should I be without her." He turned from all other beautiful things in the world to gaze on her face and never for an instant believed that his love would diminish when her beauty faded. His devotion to his children was one cause of his anxiety about their future. In the first part of Act III, Byron alternated this devotion with Cain's anger in a paradoxical pattern. After the catastrophe, he returned to Cain's gentleness, fused it again with his domestic affection in a reminiscence of boyhood experience, and with grief over his inability to perform the burial rites it should have been his fraternal duty to attend to. The most profound treatment of this sentiment was Byron's version of the Socratic and Shelleyean definition of love as altruistic, a permanent outgoing beyond self. Cain loved "What makes my feelings more endurable / And is more than myself because I love it." Byron thus differentiated him from the egoistic Lucifer, whom Cain pitied because he was unable to love anyone.[1]

Cain's capacity for affection was allied with his passionate response to beauty. Byron gave some of his most lyrical writing to Cain's sensuous praise of Adah and Enoch and to his awed exclamations on the stars and

[1] Cain's expressions of gentleness and family affection occurred six times in Act I: 56–61, 187–188, 300–333, 347, 432–433, 451–455, of which the last was his most ardent exclamation on sexual and parental love. On the space flight Byron reminded us of these traits five more times: II, ii, 251–273, 305–309, 320–322, 332–338, 377–379 (the last two were general utterances of all-embracing love and altruism, which was not dependent on the stimulus of sensuous beauty). In Act III, expressions of affection for Enoch occurred in 10–12, 17–36, 156, and 161 and for Abel in 534–540. Elze, p. 416; Gerard, pp. 94, 98–99; Chew, p. 130; Thorslev, p. 180; Marchand, p. 90.

the other marvels of space. "Pleasant tears" filled his eyes when he looked at a sunset. Byron merged three of Cain's most appealing qualities—his gentleness, his delight in beauty, and his idealism. Neither death nor any evil must ever touch the magnificence of the stars nor his sister's loveliness, and this urgent desire rose at one point to a firm faith in the permanence of love and beauty. Another ecstatic outburst was his only expression of cosmic optimism. He surmised that an unseen force guided the firefly in its flight and the star on its course.[2] The manner of presenting this deistic thought was romantic. Cain arrived at the idea via his aesthetic sensitivity, his personal observation, and his intuition. It was for him an emotional, empirical truth that was not the result of parental instruction, of individual ratiocination, nor a dictum from authority.

Cain's most aggressive ardor was his intellectual aspiration. Eve and Lucifer thought that he had inherited his mother's curiosity. Thirsting for knowledge, he asked Lucifer, "Wilt thou teach me all?" There was nothing that the devil could speak about that Cain did not long to know. Even a sinful mortal had a right to universal knowledge, and so he deplored man's ignorance and the narrowness of his ken. Eager to solve the mystery of his being and of life and death, he tried to grasp the concept of immortality and became intoxicated with eternity and the possibility of unlimited growth. When his horizon was expanded and he was exposed to an approximation of infinity in the tremendous distances of space and the eons of time, he boasted that his thoughts were not unworthy of these marvels, which were beyond his faculties, but still inferior to his desires and conceptions. Like Faust, he was a man of boundless intellectual longing. He was naïvely hopeful that knowledge would be the road to happiness. His confidence sometimes matched his aspiration, and then, sublimely conscious only of the capabilities of mind, he asserted that pure thought could master all things. Thus he accepted Lucifer's theory that placed time under the control of individual mind. But he also reached beyond his grasp and demanded to see what was impossible for mortal eyes—the dwelling places of God and Lucifer.[3]

[2] I, 281–284; II, i, 98–117, 123–132; II, ii, 242–245, 255–262, 327–332; III, 10–12, 25–30. Blumenthal, p. 7; Chew, p. 130; Brooke, p. 85.

[3] I, 246–249, 301, 321–322, 458–462, 535–539; II, i, 49–50, 80–83, 90–94, 115–116; II, ii, 126–129, 161–163, 230–238, 366–368, 397–408; III, 53–62. Chew stressed Cain's skeptical independence, the right to use his mind freely (p. 133), but, he did not support his statement. Gerard (p. 98), Moorman (p. 52), C. H. Herford

The biblical narrative about this man, whom the poet has elevated to a pinnacle of idealism, was a legend of crime that was a mystery only because the motivation was obscure. Byron wrote his drama to show us *why* Cain killed Abel. Cain's troubles derived from the virtues we have been praising, from certain other qualities and flaws we need to examine, from the environment, and from the painful interaction of these realities. The poet let his unhappy hero expound his discontent at length, complain about conditions he found intolerable, and disclose those attitudes and feelings that finally led to murder. Some maintain that the tragedy was the result of a conflict between love and Cain's desire for knowledge. His choice of knowledge over love, his decision to leave Adah and follow Lucifer was then the turning point that led to his downfall. But even before Lucifer's arrival, Byron showed how intellectual ambition contained the seeds of disappointment and disaster. Cain had been accustomed to using his mind critically, and he had arrived at some skeptical and discouraging notions.[4] He thought his family complacent and unreflective as they went through their routine rituals. He was unable to reconcile certain tribulations in the world with their disciplined parables about serpents, trees, and fruits, which told him to accept impediments as part of God's wise design. Unlike them, he could not resign himself to constraints. He hated his inability to profit, untoiling, from the earth and to gratify with knowledge his thousand swelling thoughts.[5]

By relying on talk, Byron did not render us proof that Cain's life was a hard one. He showed no scenes of Cain hard at work and never let him act or talk like a tired man, but he did make the necessity of physical toil, whose produce was scanty, a continual vexation for one whose main interests were mental and not material. Adah echoed her brother's attitude and Lucifer also referred to their life of toil.[6]

(*The Age of Wordsworth*, p. 231), Rainwater (p. 123), and others commented on Cain's intellectual aspiration. Noel (*Essays*, pp. 98–99) and Fairchild (III, 429) discounted it.

[4] As Constantine N. Stavrou (p. 154) and others have noted, Byron enlisted Cain in the "Devil's Party at the outset." His soliloquy expressed "militant and Promethean disbelief."

[5] I, 168–189; II, ii, 125–129.

[6] I, 65, 174–175, 185, 359; II, ii, 125, 416; III, 109–113, 217–218. Byron was following Genesis, 3:17–19, where God decreed that Adam must toil and sweat to get food from the earth. Furthermore this was traditional. The mystery plays on

Byron burdened his hero with a gloomy temperament that was prone to look on the worst side of things. In the very first scene, Cain said that he was sick at heart, and Adah in the final act declared that he had often been despondent. Lucifer confirmed Cain's dismal prospect of earthly life: war with all things, pain, disease, fear, and sorrow, with only a few brief moments of pleasure, and then finally death.[7]

Cain's dejection was usually a result of his feeling of insignificance, which in turn led to frustration. He who aspired to great heights sank, as Faust did, to extreme depths when he was disappointed and concluded that he was nothing, knew nothing, and could hope for nothing. Cain was dissatisfied with the cosmic journey and repeatedly complained that he had not learned much about death after all, for everything seemed dim and shadowy. He did see enough to intensify his conviction of his own littleness, and thus after the trip he was more downcast over it than he had ever been before. The vision of the cosmos and of eternity and of the earth's temporal and spatial minuteness, the historical vista of many worlds, all vanished, and of superior creatures, now mere wraiths, battered his ego and in despair he cried out to Adah that the devil had been right —man was nothing.[8]

Cain's low spirits were almost as much the result of injured pride as of thwarted ambition. "I will have nought to do with happiness / Which humbles me and mine." He was annoyed by Abel's docile conformity and the "base humility of worship that seemed a token of fear.[9] In the past Cain had haughtily refused to offer a sacrifice to God, and he boasted that he had never bowed to anyone, nor would he bow to Lucifer. He considered himself worthy to consort with spirits, but he smarted under Lucifer's arrogance and retaliated with disdain.[10]

---

the expulsion of Adam in all four British cycles included the punishment of hard work, and Caym (Cayn) grumbled about it in two plays on the killing of Abell. In the Towneley play, Cayn's labor with the soil brought only poor harvest. Nevertheless a few critics have seen no justification for Cain's complaint.

[7] I, 53–58, 454–457; II, ii, 149–151, 416; III, 37, 45–46.

[8] II, i, 116, 167–176; II, ii, 77–78, 108–109, 126–129, 161–168, 175–176, 228–232, 417–424; III, 67–74, 113–115.

[9] I, 465–466; III, 99–102. Cain in anger repeated Lucifer's jeer at Adam's cringing reverence (I, 431).

[10] I, 34, 179–187, 191, 310–318; II, i, 83–86; II, ii, 341–342, 424–426. His pride was sometimes dissipated by spasms of self-contempt and frustration and miti-

Byron was logical in isolating his hero. As a proud and restless seeker of knowledge, he was a nonconformist, at odds with his environment. He had no intellectual companion, no one who understood his problems or sympathized with his skepticism. At the end of the drama, he paid the usual penalty for excessive and criminal individualism—rejection by nature and society. In one respect Cain's career followed a Byronic pattern: a malcontent, isolated from his fellow men, rebelled against authority and became an outcast.[11]

One minor trait that Byron associated with Cain's pride was irritability. Lucifer needed only to commend Cain's love of Abel as "meekly done" to provoke him. When he asked Cain to repeat his resolution not to bend a knee, Cain was sarcastic: "Have I not said it? Need I say it? / Could not thy mighty knowledge teach thee that?" In Act I he had scoffed at Lucifer's unhappiness. "And thou, with all thy might, what art thou?" When Lucifer pressed too heavily on the text of man's feebleness, Cain was imperti-

---

gated by his gentleness and his love of Adah. Most commentators enrolled Cain among the throng of Byron's haughty aristocrats (Harold, Conrad, Lara, Hugo, Alp, Manfred, Lambro, Faliero, and Werner). Byron in a letter of November 3, 1821 (*LJ*, V, 470) wrote that "Cain is a proud man." Arthur Symons grounded the revolt and the final illumination in conceit. *Cain* was "a long, restless, proud, and helpless questioning of the powers of good and evil." Though his pride equaled Lucifer's, he could also humbly admit failure. " 'Obstinate questionings,' resolving themselves into nothing except that pride and that humility of despair, form the whole drama . . ." (*The Romantic Movement in English Poetry*, p. 261). Bertrand Russell likewise thought that aristocratic and satanic arrogance was inextricable in the Byronic psychology of self-assertion, revolt, and guilt ("Byron and the Modern World," *Journal of the History of Ideas*, I [1940], 27–28). Fairchild wrote that Cain's skepticism was based on "the flinty rock of pride" (p. 430).

[11] I, 188–191; III, 422–448, 475–476. Giuseppe Mazzini, "Byron and Goethe" in *Life and Writings*, VI, 68–73. Paul Siegel: "Even before [Cain] is sent forth an exile, he is isolated from the rest of human society by his spirit of revolt; even his beloved Adah does not understand him" (" 'A Paradise within Thee' in Milton, Byron, and Shelley," *Modern Language Notes*, LVI [December, 1941], 617). Russell also thought that the solitary impulse was an essential component of the revolt of the self-assertive individualist. He had to *feel* solitary even if he must depend on others to survive and continue his work and even if he fell in love ("Byron," pp. 34–35). Edward Dowden (*The French Revolution and English Literature*, p. 264), A. E. Hancock ("Byron" in *French Revolution and the English Poets*, pp. 90–91), and others noted that all of Byron's aristocratic rebels were aloof and solitary (see n. 10).

nent and told the fallen angel that he was not so much either. Once he tartly said that Lucifer could have no fellowship with man. Cain was annoyed because the devil had spurned domestic ties and offended Cain's own instincts and also because Lucifer had denied the existence of beauty and had insisted that Cain's perception of Adah's beauty was self-delusion. Again he reproached the devil for malignant hypocrisy because, though claiming the power to do man good, he certainly had not done him any favors in the past. Byron had more friction between the two rebels than most readers have noticed. Cain was a touchy, even testy, hero and struck back six times when Lucifer was insolent.[12]

One of the strong feelings in the stormy texture of Cain's passionate life was his antipathy to his parents. He was displeased with their mental deterioration and their smugness, but it was their haste and folly in the past that he could not forgive. Four times he imputed the cause of his unhappiness to them—they were responsible for *his* loss of Paradise. Thrice he fumed over their fatal blunder in not plucking the fruit of the tree of life, for thereby they had bequeathed to him and everyone else the heritage of death. Once he gibed at Eve's partiality to Abel and the serpent, but he was also relentless and wanted her and Adam alone to die, for they, and only they, were the sinners. In a fit of depression, he raged at his parents for begetting him, and at the end he was petulant in blaming them for his recalcitrance.[13]

Cain's dejection, his prickly irritation with Lucifer over slights to his pride, and his animus toward his parents were all evidences of an acute, almost neurotic, sensitivity to pain. Byron demonstrated that this mordant sensibility could not be separated from his enjoyment of beauty and his capacity for love and that it also greatly increased his unhappiness. The man who loved Adah and Enoch and who thrilled to the splendors of space was a tenderhearted man who suffered with the lamb that had been stung by a reptile, who dwelt on the cruelty of blood-sacrifice with intense aversion, and who grieved for the death of animals and for the mighty

[12] I, 125, 315–316; II, i, 85–88; II, ii, 275, 341–342, 393–397, 424–426.

[13] I, 33–34, 69–70, 105–108, 179–182, 210–211, 294–297, 434–435, 444–447; II, i, 61–65, 191–195; II, ii, 14–26, 203–204, 343–345, 365; III, 22–24, 42–44, 75–76, 118, 506–508. B. H. Lehman, though he gave no proof, wrote that Cain accused his parents of egoistically serving themselves, "with no eye, no love for their offspring. Their rights, not their duties guided them" (" 'Leadership' in the Romantic Poets," *PMLA*, XXXVII [1922], p. 659). I, 434–435 and 444–449 may touch on this idea.

phantoms of demolished worlds. His sharpest pangs came from his anticipation of the sorrow that was in store for Enoch and his descendants.[14]

Excitability was a concomitant of Cain's other qualities. A sensitive man, yearning for attainment, for spiritual power over material circumstance, often discouraged by failure and hurt by the world's pain, would be unstable, given to moods of despair and to outbursts of rage, followed promptly by remorse. Byron tried to make this trait derivative by having Lucifer declare that mother and son were alike in their impetuosity. Cain's nerves broke soon after he reached Hades, and he railed against Adam, God, and life itself. He frightened Adah when he exclaimed in agitation that it would be better to dash Enoch against the rocks than to let him inherit a life of suffering. Before the sacrifices, as Cain told his brother about his journey, he felt tension mounting within him that he could not control and he begged to be left alone for a while. When Abel tried to quiet him, Cain replied, "Nothing can calm me. . . . Never / Knew I what calm was in the soul." This instability, which kept him on the edge of frenzy, was one more emotional force in the total complex that toppled him into passionate homicide.[15]

[14] I, 286–287, 440–450; II, i, 68–71; II, ii, 152–159, 281–305; III, 23–24, 32, 82–84, 122–136.

Shelley's madman in *Julian and Maddalo* had Cain's vicarious susceptibility: he could moan

> For woes which others hear not, and could see
> The absent with the glance of phantasy,
> And with the poor and trampled sit and weep,
> Following the captive to his dungeon deep;
> *Me*—who am as a nerve o'er which do creep
> The else unfelt oppressions of this earth,
>
> 445–450

[15] II, ii, 18–25, 408–409; III, 122–127, 185–187, 202–205, 280–316. Byron may have intended this excitability to be a source of Cain's jealousy. Heber and Chew thought Byron had not given his hero this ignoble feeling, and Chew also considered the passage in which Lucifer stimulated it to be a mistake (II, ii, 338–356). Byron had Lucifer dwell on Abel's popularity for almost thirty lines and then state that Cain had thought about it previously. His victim began a confession, stopped in the middle of his exclamation, and abruptly changed the subject. Byron here interpolated one of his rare stage directions: "he pauses, as agitated." This natural surge of feeling need not contradict Byron's portrayal of Cain as a normally affectionate man. Cain's envy of Abel was mixed with anger at God, for he lost control only after Lucifer declared that God and the angels smiled on Abel and accepted his offerings. There was also a hint of jealousy in III, 191–194, where Cain's in-

We might ascribe his melancholy and his nervousness simply to discontent with futile toil, to his feeling of insignificance and frustration. These grievances he had thrown at Adam and Eve, but that animosity was only a bridge to his rebellion against God, the ultimate source of man's troubles. Byron, as all writers must do, worked within the bias and boundaries of his experience, and these included his Scottish childhood, the intellectual currents of his era, and the dynamic forces of his temperament. The popular distortions of Augustinian and Calvinistic theology, fulminated by the Scottish clergy and echoed by the nurse Catherine Gordon hired for her son, had left their mark on Byron's soul. Though he never seemed emotionally free of their influence, his mind did repudiate their dogmas. Hence, in solving the mystery of Cain's motivation, Byron assigned as one source of his hero's exasperation those doctrines that we reviewed earlier and that, he thought, thrust man into wretched desperation, from which there was no escape. His expository and critical aim was to show why this was sadly true, and his psychological aim was to demonstrate how these doctrines could drive man to despair, madness, and crime.

Cain had doubted his parent's assumption that divine power had always been used for man's benefit. They had not soothed his sense of injury by bidding him trust to God's wisdom and benevolence, which Cain's experience had not verified. He could not credit his father's faith that future good would proceed from present evil. He had no proof of infinite mercy and could not envisage an all-embracing atonement and ultimate redemption. It was impossible for him to foresee that the expulsion from Eden might be a fortunate fall, which would eventually be transformed into a miraculous ascension. Cain was therefore willing to listen to Lucifer's aspersions and to agree that God's misuse of power accounted for all adversity on earth.[16]

God had granted man a glimpse of Paradise and eternity, but then the Almighty Judge barred his prisoner from these supreme boons and confined him to earth. Adah knew that the loss of a golden age of ease and peace and unlimited expansion of the spirit had been one of her brother's chronic complaints.[17] God had reduced man to wretched impotence, had inflicted mortality on him—the limitations of the flesh that hurt his pride,

---

sistence that he was indifferent might imply that he did care about God's preference for Abel.

[16] I, 74–79; II, ii, 280–305; III, 245–247.

[17] III, 37–40, 70–79.

clogged spiritual aspiration, and were a continual cause of defeat. When vistas of space exhilarated him, his thoughts might be able to encompass eternity and infinity, but he realized with chagrin that his dust was finite and unworthy.[18] The conflict between mind and body was central in this drama, in *Manfred, Sardanapalus,* and Cantos II and V of *Don Juan,* and symbolic in *Heaven and Earth.*

Just as Cain saw no fairness or kindness in the affliction of mortality, so he was puzzled, depressed, and enraged by its history: God's arrangement of the fall, the beginning and continuance of innate depravity, and the persecution of future generations. God should not have planted the tree if he meant to forbid it. How could the human desire for knowledge be wrong? How could Cain be considered wicked for a deed he did not commit? Though he had heard the answers to the questions preached at him so often that he seemed at times to take them for granted, man's sinfulness remained a mystery, an abuse, a cause of woe and indignation. Even more cruel were the everlasting punishments. Since the desire for knowledge was good, his parents should not have been expelled from Eden. Thereafter the imposition of toil, pain, and guilt on Cain and on millions of unborn innocents, as penalties for an offense committed by Adam and Eve, was the action of an irrational and ruthless tyrant.[19]

The most abominable crime of this tyrant was the penalty of death. Dread of this termination had poisoned Cain's whole life. At the beginning of the drama the reason he gave Adam for refusing to join in the family's thanksgiving was this inescapable blight on the human state. He who must die had nothing to thank Jehovah for. He has been a frightened man, trembling as he hunted for the mysterious foe that might be skulking in the night shadows of the walls of Eden. He has observed how strangely every member of his family acted when death was mentioned. Ignorance exaggerated his terror, and, unable to allay his "thousand fears," he could not talk about them without agitation. They were the topic of one of the longest discussions that Cain and Lucifer engaged in, and within forty lines he confessed his fright five times and just as often questioned Lucifer about the nature of the Unknown. A desire to know

[18] I, 174–178; II, i, 80–83, 115–116; II, ii, 126–129; III, 72–74, 109–116. Cain kept the wound sore by hitting himself many times with the insulting epithets of *clay* and *dust,* e.g., I, 100, 292; II, i, 166; II, ii, 109, 370; III, 511, 541.

[19] I, 64–79, 286–287, 434–455; II, i, 68–71, 193–195; III, 23–25, 83–92, 118–124, 522.

more about this fearful reality became one objective of the journey into the region of the phantoms.

Upon the entrance into Hades, he cursed the inventor of a life that led only to death. He was profoundly shaken when Lucifer showed him the destruction of entire worlds, and, though he exclaimed over its hideous mystery, he said that Hades had lessened his fear, "Now that I know it leads to something definite." In Act I, he had also momentarily accepted Lucifer's simple statement that death was a return to earth. But he gained no lasting relief. The most severe strain, that was never alleviated and that broke his self-control, was the dread that he, by fathering Enoch, had become an agent of death. Since he could not endure the responsibility for this calamity, he condemned his parents for it, but finally shifted the onus of his fear on the Eternal Destroyer.

In Act III, as Cain rendered his tribute to this destroyer, the daily dread merged with scorn and hatred. Before the altar, in several slurring suppositions about the harm Jehovah might do to him, Cain indirectly and impudently drew together most of his charges: the Almighty was an arbitrary judge and dispenser of good and evil, who acted according to the simple expedient that might made right. He was a vengeful deity who required propitiation and who loved bloodshed. Cain's horror of death and his loathing of ceremonial gore provided the final exasperation that drove him to demolish his brother's altar, the symbol of man's honor of a savage power, and then to strike at Abel, who had intervened, as a defender of despotic authority. Cain's fury was discharged, not against his brother, but against a life plagued with pain and human impotence, and against "the Author of Life," who was also the author of wrong and of death.[20]

Byron involved Cain's fear with its opposite—the death wish. The desire not to live was a desire to escape the burdens that seemed to the sensitive man too heavy to bear: insignificance, mortality, frustration, toil, pain, and the responsibility for the unhappiness of posterity. When he lamented, "I am nothing," he also wanted to be nothing. Early in the play he spurned the instinct for life as loathsome, twice wished he had

[20] I, 29, 108–110, 250–299, 457; II, i, 60–64, 72–75, 137–149, 191–196; II, ii, 14–21, 35–38, 74, 81–82, 85, 95, 129–130, 150–153, 162–163, 171–172, 363–365, 411–413; III, 44, 255–279, 285, 292–293, 299–303, 310, 371–374. *LJ*, V, 470. We should recall that Cain's fear of death was also a family trait; his parents, Abel, and Zillah encouraged it, just as they were responsible for much of the discontent.

never been born, and repeatedly cried, "let me die." He told Lucifer that to be resolved into the dust would be a good thing, and later he wanted to remain in Hades because he was sick of earthly existence. The suicidal impulse became most intense when the prospect of an endless chain of death loomed large in his imagination, and in angry confusion he thought he must kill his son to save him from continuing this chain. He and Adah for a moment were willing to die in order to save others from death, but he soon decided that such a sacrifice would be an act of injustice against the innocent. After the murder, the death wish, aggravated by remorse and the revulsion of others, became a desperate and hopeless demand for extinction, repeated four times.[21]

Many of Cain's remarks implied two or more traits, emotions, and attitudes, and thus, in trying to cover the whole constitution of his mind and heart, we had to revert to the same speeches in different parts of the exposition.[22] This interlocking was true of many positive and negative traits too; no one of them could be separated from the others, nor from the state of the world and the authority controlling it. All merged and interacted: pride, an habitually gloomy outlook, emotional instability, an obsession with death, and a suicidal tendency were so entwined with his gentleness, his devotion to his wife and child, his enjoyment of beauty, his curiosity and idealism, his altruism and his imaginative capacity to share the suffering of unborn generations that they all served as both cause and effect; and then discontent, failure, and the galling sense of his own weakness and of mortal restrictions, his impatient and hostile awareness of his isolation among people who misunderstood and disapproved of him, and finally his bitter resentment at divine injustice, irrationality, tyranny, and atrocity—these internal pressures finally exploded into violence and left him a shattered man.

Byron's characterization of his tragic hero was more paradoxical near the end of the drama. During the denouement he combined new attitudes with habitual ones. He used the shocks that followed Cain's violence to induce a radical change in feeling and outlook. Cain's frantic realization of his brother's death and Zillah's horror jolted him into anguished self-illumination: "I am awake at last—a dreary dream / Had maddened

[21] I, 112–115, 290–291; II, i, 68, 113, 117; II, ii, 108–109; III, 44, 79–81, 125–136, 347–348, 483, 500, 509–515.

[22] E.g., Cain's anticipation of Enoch's tribulation was evidence of his own kindliness, affection, sensitivity to pain, and guiltiness, as well as an impeachment of his parents for their mistake and of God for his injustice.

me." In his confusion, he renounced the dream, the idealism that now seemed dreary, and the longing for infinite life and knowledge, for freedom from sin, guilt, death, and tyranny—all this had been madness.

Byron then staggered Cain with Adam's stricken rejection, Eve's ferocious vengeance, and the Angel's stern judgment. This triple repudiation, together with the awareness that his wild act of destruction had caused an irretrievable loss, wrung from him a few piercing utterances of remorse. The Angel's seal burned within the criminal's brain and nothing could expunge the guilt. Neither God nor his own soul would forgive him. Why did Adah not shrink from dwelling with a murderer? How in future years could Enoch bear to look at him?[23] Cain who had formerly resented man's sinfulness now in desolation accepted it as his due.

In this mood of self-abasement, his scornful impatience with Abel was replaced by painful recollection of the childhood they had shared and by a rueful acknowledgment of the benefits that Abel might have brought to posterity and that Cain had demolished. He had been so proudly occupied with complaints about God's injustice and the unsatisfactory conditions it caused on earth that he had not reflected on his own shortcomings. Now he tormented himself with his neglect of obligations never to be fulfilled. The burial duty was the only one he mentioned, but this might stand for a lifetime of responsibilities he had severed. The most poignant admission of guilt and futility was his earnest willingness to yield up his own unwanted existence if thereby he could restore Abel to life.[24]

In the midst of these changes were repetitions of the old sullen resentment and belligerence. These erupted in the hostile question, "Am I then / My brother's keeper," in his gruff fatalistic refusal to assume responsibility for his faults. "That which I am, I am. I did not seek / For life nor did I make myself," and in the ignoble rationalization about prenatal determinism: he owed his erratic and waspish temperament to his parents. "After the fall too soon was I begotten, / Ere yet my mother's mind subsided from / The serpent, and my sire still mourned for Eden." Cain thus retained his habitual antagonism toward his parents and God, and the Angel rebuked him, "Stern hast thou been and stubborn from the womb." Even at the very end Cain ruefully referred to his intractable temper.[25]

[23] III, 336–446, 461–462, 471–476, 521–523, 531–533, 561.

[24] III, 510–514, 535–540, 556–560.

[25] III, 468–469, 503, 506–510, 559. Although Chew conceded that the question "Am I my brother's keeper" was traditional and too familiar for the poet to dis-

Some readers have been so impressed by the outbreak of rancor that they slighted the many speeches of remorse after the murder and so averred that Byron made no change in Cain in Act III. Other critics, aware of the contradiction between the old and new feelings, found it implausible and attributed it to Byron's confusion, to the sway that traditional morality and religion exercised over his judgment. Still others who respected the traits that Byron developed before the catastrophe—Cain's intellectual curiosity, skepticism, and aspiration, his dissatisfaction with the trammels of his nature and his environment, and above all his independence and his resistance to an unjust authority—these readers have been displeased with Byron's final resolution, with Cain's awakening, humility, and repentance, which they regarded as weak and illogical, a surrender to Adamical piety and conformity.[26]

Though one may not be able to reconcile the contradictions, he may accept them as the tragic ironies that were involved with Cain's rebellion and downfall and with the ensuing and inevitable illumination. In the last two hundred lines of the drama, several logical expectations were overturned by the psychological consequences of his fatal deed. When we remember what the hero had been, what he formerly had felt and thought and said, then the catastrophe and its aftermath have some disparities that we may object to as inconsistent but that we may also regard as emotionally credible and tragically true.

Cain, who had been terrified by death, has brought it to mankind in anger and by recourse to the very bloodshed he had denounced in the Conqueror. He who had stalked the Unknown at night in the purlieus of Eden and who had been appalled in Hades by the ghostly multitudes of the dead now could not recognize the stark fact of death in Abel's pallor, silence, and breathless immobility. He wanted to believe that his brother was asleep or pretending. "This is mockery," and so it was in a grim sense that Cain did not understand. A son who had scolded his parents for their haste and folly has yielded his soul to be alternately so dejected and incensed by a crafty insurgent that he has acted more im-

---

regard, he thought that this "flash of defiance" did not fit Cain's remorse (p. 120). Thorslev agreed that Byron's retention of the biblical words was "a blot on the drama" and inconsistent with the hero's "new-found realization of the primacy of love" (p. 182).

[26] For various opinions on the characterization of Cain at the end of the drama see "Annotations."

petuously, if no less destructively, than his parents had done. An intellectual idealist, who had been irked by the fleshly barrier, has been swept by mortal passion to ruin. The spasm of fury and the very act of killing were the degrading triumph of the flesh over the mind and will.

A husband and father who was naturally gentle and affectionate and who had fervently desired human betterment has darkened Earth and impeded its progress by depriving the future of his brother's meliorating influence. A lonely man who had felt himself cut off from human sympathy and understanding has by one blow thrust himself into criminal isolation. The iconoclast who had protested the stigma of undeserved sinfulness has admitted his personal guilt and conceded that there have been too many threats and too much harshness. The death wish that had been motivated by common discouragement was now stimulated by intense remorse and a longing for an atonement that he had denounced less than an hour ago.[27]

As Cain turned with Adah eastward to the wilderness, the many ironic realities of his transformation and self-discovery were less a betrayal of his former rebellion than the unavoidable experience of a sensitive intelligence trapped and goaded by intolerable circumstance. Byron, who had, for two and a half acts, given a sympathetic presentation of the causes and complexities of revolt, with its wrath, distress, confusion, and justification, did not invalidate nor compromise that revolt in the last two hundred lines. For men like Byron, Lucifer, and Cain, rebellion against the social, political, and theological system was imperative. The outcomes of the struggle—calamity and then anguish over the fratricide and a crushing rejection by the system and a confession of immoderation—these too were inevitable.

The awakening from the dreary dream of madness need not therefore be taken as a renunciation of principle and protest. If the homicide was the result of terrible pressures on a certain kind of soul, then the remorse and the illumination were the consistent aftermath of that crime—for that kind of man. Byron in the denouement exposed its inescapable complexities, just as he had laid bare those that had driven the hero to catastrophe. Now there were other sharp fears and pains, a punitive and more rigorous

[27] The ironies began with the murder, but most of them were concentrated on Cain's final speeches: III, 342–357, 371–377, 444–446, 475–476, 482–484, 509–515, 521–525, 556–560. Elze (p. 417), Noel (*Life*, p. 161), and Bostetter (p. 575) pointed out two of these ironies.

exile, a broader, deeper knowledge of self and the world and its ruler, certainly just as sad as the previous groping had been. These were the bitter fruits of revolt, different and yet like the old ones, and in this harsh system a necessity.

Lucifer

A major criticism has been that Byron did not differentiate Cain and Lucifer and so weakened his play by not devising a conflict, or at least a contrast, between them. This objection oversimplified the relationship that Byron designed between his hero and his villain. They shared common grievances and a common rebellion, but Cain had several traits that Lucifer did not, and Lucifer differed from Cain not only in degree but in certain attitudes and abilities, and most of all in his immediate goals and intentions.

Since in some speeches Byron used the devil as his *raisonneur,* he was careful to do for him what he had done for Cain—make clear his sympathy with and admiration of this Spirit of denial, while at the same time retaining some traditional qualities. Lucifer did not look as if he were the epitome of repellent iniquity, degenerate vice, or gross destructiveness. Unlike Milton's Satan, who was physically ugly, Lucifer's appearance evoked praise from both Cain and Adah. He was a fallen angel "of a sterner and a sadder aspect" than other angels and not "as beautiful / As he hath been"; yet Cain once and Adah twice said that he was more wonderful than the cherubim that guarded Paradise: "thou seemest / Like an ethereal night."[28]

From this splendid prince came an emanation of magnetism, and Adah paid a timorous tribute to his fascination. Both mortals were also drawn to him because sorrow seemed "half of his immortality." Lucifer frankly admitted his unhappiness, which was so obvious that it brought tears to Adah's eyes.[29]

Just as compelling was his might, which surpassed that of the angels Cain and Adah had seen. Lucifer's courage and volitional strength, and his defiance of the Conqueror appealed to Cain's own rebellious impulse. There was one complication, because Byron was ambiguous about Lucifer's conception of his relationship with Jehovah. Soon after he met Cain, he said that he had been defeated in warfare. Six times in his first

[28] I, 80, 93–95, 392–393, 507–517.

[29] I, 81–82, 95–96, 122, 408–413, 517–519; II, i, 87–88.

long speech he granted that his foe was invincible: "let him reign on." He denied that he himself was a god and continued at intervals, with acrid resentment, to refer to the Almighty Victor. Half way through Act I, however, Byron began to apply the Manichean doctrine and alternated these avowals of God's power with a succession of announcements by Lucifer of his equal might. He now by inference claimed divinity for himself, when he mentioned "the edict of the other God." He insisted that he had not been subdued, denied that Jehovah was superior, and boasted that they had divided the universe between them, that he still maintained sway over half of it, commanded many subjects, and was determined to battle forever against his opponent. By a climactic display of belligerence just before he departed, he perhaps hoped that Cain would disregard the earlier grudging acknowledgments of failure. At least these tend to recede because Byron made the proclamation of power his farewell impression of Lucifer.[30]

The second form of his might was intellectual and wielded greater influence over Cain's mind. Byron represented Lucifer as the embodiment of knowledge, comprising both the substance and the processes of science in its broadest application. He claimed omniscience and warned that human ignorance was contemptible and dangerous, for it did not save anyone from evil. He therefore condescended to serve as tutor and guide for the uninformed, inexperienced, but insatiably curious young man. This then was one relationship between the two minds. Lucifer, knowledgeable and articulate, could express what Cain had strongly felt and dimly thought, clarify that which had confused Cain, supply him with information about life and death that he could not garner by himself, and offer some unpleasant notions that lay beyond Cain's present capacity for cynical negation and that he was unable to accept.[31]

One salient factor of Lucifer's intellectual strength was his idealism. Lucifer, like an expert Platonist, affirmed that thought was the immortal part of man and could never be quenched, that it could transcend and

[30] I, 93, 128–163, 237–239, 305–310, 384–388, 487–508, 529–532, 546–554; II, i, 6–7; II, ii, 35, 88, 154, 375–376, 388–392, 404, 426–442.

[31] I, 300–301, 558–559; II, i, 22–25; II, ii, 101–102, 230–237. Almost all critics since Jeffrey have stated that Lucifer merely enunciated Cain's discontent and confirmed his apostasy. The following have commented on Lucifer's intellectuality: Brandes (IV, 315), Edward Wayne Marjarum (*Byron as Skeptic and Believer*, p. 35), Lehman ("Leadership," p. 659), Fairchild (III, 430–431), Stavrou (p. 159), and Marchand (pp. 87–88).

control external matter, was the governor of emotion, dispelled fear and offered man more satisfaction than love could, and above all, provided the road to truth, to discovery and evaluation of self and nature, the inner and outer worlds.[32] He argued for the use of mind in analytic, critical, and synthetic activity. Byron put into Lucifer's closing lecture in Act II a fusion of eighteenth-century rationalism and nineteenth-century romanticism. Lucifer urged Cain to be independent in using his judgment, never to submit to arbitrary authority, and to strive to create his own inner reality.[33] Though Adah also coaxed Cain to stop regretting their lost Paradise and to build a new one by and for themselves, Cain was not yet strong enough to perform heroic feats of creative idealism. In his conversation with her and Lucifer he looked resentfully back to the ruined past, and when he and Adah entered the wilderness he was too shaken by the catastrophe to be other than gloomy and negative.[34]

Lucifer was more successful in teaching Cain a simpler phase of idealism—the notion of subjective or psychological time. Before the journey, Lucifer told him about his control of time, his ability to compress eternity into minutes and to stretch minutes into eternity. After the trip, as Cain and Adah talked about the brevity of his absence, Cain adopted his mentor's theory: years of experience had been crowded into a short two-hour span, for the mind measured time "by that which it beholds, / Pleasing or painful, little or almighty."[35]

So far we have been considering those qualities that Byron clearly regarded as sympathetic and attractive in Lucifer. When he followed the tradition that has given us the cliché, "proud as Lucifer," Byron, from an aristocratic point of view, was not contaminating him with one of the

[32] I, 102–104, 213–216, 300–301, 423–430; II, ii, 230–232, 418–422. Lucifer once ominously said that death led to the highest knowledge (II, ii, 164–166), but Byron did not have him develop this Platonic idea nor Cain respond to it.

[33] II, ii, 450–466. One minor idealistic surprise that Byron casually put into a Lucifer speech was a belief in the reliability of an innate moral sense that contradicted God's dispensation (Bostetter, p. 572). In view of our later discussion, this naïve belief might seem incongruous with Lucifer's exalted confidence in the powers of the mind and also with his effort to reverse the roles of himself and the deity. Another unusual exception was the lyrical imagery (I, 489–496) that followed this trust in moral intuition and that Byron usually gave only to Cain and Adah.

[34] I, 171–174; II, i, 72–74; III, 31–40, 72–74, 347, 526, 544, 552–553.

[35] I, 535–538; III, 53–62.

seven deadly sins. Pride was another trait that he and Cain shared, and though it was more sharply accentuated in Lucifer, it was presented in both as preferable to abject humility. As we noticed, pride aggravated Cain's unhappiness, because failure to fulfill his potentiality and consciousness of his inadequacy were painful blows to his ego. But pride had mitigated Lucifer's wretchedness, because it prevented him from even thinking of submission or admitting inferiority or paying homage to a victor. Hence three times in the play he scorned the abasement of the obsequious angels, who hymned their praises of God and did what they were bidden because of their timidity.[36]

More interesting were Byron's mutations of the guile that has always been the devil's supreme talent. The first was Lucifer's endeavor to ingratiate himself with Cain. Cain's readiness to join Lucifer's rebellion was neatly turned to a flattering assertion of their spiritual kinship. Lucifer came to earth because of their mutual opposition to the tyrant and also because of Cain's special fitness for lofty companionship. He then declared that he and Cain were fellow sufferers, and twice allied himself with the mortifying limitations of humanity. He told Cain that he knew the disappointments of men and felt for them, and ruefully complained that he was doomed to the same kind of endless ignominy as Cain. This bond of discontent was a poignant reality that Lucifer cleverly exploited to gain the confidence of the unhappy man.[37]

Another disarming ruse was the pretense that he was Cain's benefactor. Upon his arrival, he promptly encouraged the dispirited youth by informing him of his immortality, which Cain had not heard of before.[38] Lucifer freely discussed the nature of death, which was of gravest importance to Cain, promised to satisfy his thirst for knowledge, to show him many wonders, and to do all these favors without extorting any kind of vasselage

[36] I, 134–135, 228, 236–238, 383–390; II, i, 7–12, 85–87; II, ii, 424–430.

[37] I, 100–101, 124, 135–140, 157–161, 192–195; II, i, 149–150. Some readers, who skipped too many of Byron's lines, saw no guile in Lucifer. For them he was man's sincere helpmate, Byron's critical replacement for the God of evangelical theology.

[38] I, 103–119. See "Annotations" for the Preface, line 41. John Galt saw fine subtlety in this revelation: "The poet rises to the sublime in making Lucifer first inspire Cain with the knowledge of his immortality—a portion of truth which hath the efficacy of falsehood upon the victim, for Cain, feeling himself already unhappy, knowing that his being cannot be abridged, has the less scruple to desire to be as Lucifer, 'mighty' " (*The Life of Lord Byron*, pp. 241–242).

or homage, as God would do with the man he enabled to walk on the waters.[39] In avouching his own generosity, he traduced that of Jehovah.

Lucifer expanded the scope of his benevolent intentions and like a politician assured Cain, in retrospect, that had he won the battle in heaven, he would have arranged affairs in Eden for man's benefit. He would have given man knowledge, happiness, and eternal life, have made him a god, would never have planted a forbidden tree, and never have burdened man with toil and pain and mortality. At the same time he emphatically exonerated himself of all responsibility for the trouble in Eden. He insisted that he had had nothing whatever to do with the temptation of Eve or the fall of man.[40]

By portraying Lucifer as a shrewd and ingratiating friend, Byron hurried him down the road that a seducer usually led his victim. The devil's promises of the good he might have done really did Cain harm. They aggravated his discontent with past and present hardships. Furthermore, the gift of knowledge that Lucifer bestowed during the journey had the insidious objective of driving Cain to his downfall. Lucifer, still posing as a benefactor, adroitly used the infinite regions of space and time to cast man and his earth into a new finite perspective that shrank them, badly

[39] I, 301–302, 322–323, 558–561; II, i, 13–25.

[40] I, 126–127, 196–210, 216–245. Byron by puffing the devil with these artful claims of kindness and wisdom, which we have discussed in the preceding three paragraphs, reversed the Manichean doctrine, debased and impaired Jehovah, reformed and elevated Lucifer.

We therefore have three reasons why Byron divorced Lucifer from the serpent in the Genesis story. Though perhaps consistent with the devil's guile, the serpentine role was incompatible with his pride, his dignity and might, and his role as benefactor. The prince who divided the universe with Jehovah would not stoop to assume the guise of serpent. Moreover, it was important to free him of all responsibility for man's unhappiness, to have the serpent, not Lucifer, lure Eve to the ruin of mankind. If God was to be the persecutor, then Lucifer, as the honest, helpful friend of man, could not be an insidious snaky foe.

Byron's knowledge of man's egoistic habit of rationalizing his mistakes was the origin of Lucifer's clever explanation of the confusion between himself and the serpent (I, 221–223, 233–237). Man's fear and vanity will make him "cast upon the spiritual nature / His own low failing." Adam's descendants will "array / Their earliest fault in fable," invest Lucifer with the reptile shape that he and they scorned, and thereby make him the villain and extenuate their own misdemeanor.

damaged Cain's self-esteem, and stirred the inner turmoil that erupted four times in Hades, twice more with Adah and Enoch, and rose ominously to the surface again when Abel urged him to make a sacrifice.[41] By the end of Act II Byron completed his version of Satan and Mephistopheles and their manipulation of Eve and Faust. Lucifer, exploiting a youthful bias against authority and a zest for knowledge, and assuming the plausible guise of patron, fellow sufferer, and teacher, has accomplished his ruinous purpose more subtly and quickly, but with less diversity, than did his diabolical predecessors.

Lucifer's wily prudence did not keep him from making a few mistakes. He struck too soon at Cain's independence, by asking him to bow, was rebuffed, then tried to catch the lad in an inconsistency by quizzing him about some knee-bending to Jehovah, and got a huffy denial and a rebuke. This he twisted into a canny and complacent triumph: "He who bows not to him has bowed to me! . . . / Thou art my worshipper; not worshipping / Him makes thee mine. . . ." In Act II, as we have seen, Lucifer resumed his cordial manner and promised that his princely generosity entailed no conditions. He handled Adah with less suavity and less success. When she admired the morning star—his own planet—he quickly asked her to adore it, and she, of course, refused. Since he never could quiet her alarm and since they were at odds over the value of love and the forthcoming journey, he finally responded to her wonder and pity with malice and tormented her with the prediction that she would be the mother of suffering millions.[42]

The effect of the great journey on Cain implied a second pernicious tactic. Even while Lucifer was posing as a companion in misery and as a friendly instructor, he was also beating at Cain's self-confidence, which had been unsettled even before Lucifer's arrival. In Act II he mounted to a position of superiority, disparaged all of man's capacities, and jeered at his frailty, ignorance, vanity, and fearfulness. Man was no better than the reptiles and not so intelligent as the serpent. He refused to show Cain the dwelling places of the two cosmic principles because mortal eyes dared not gaze on eternity. Cain must learn to limit his ambition to the

[41] II, ii, 106–109, 125–130, 279–285, 420–421; III, 63–74, 109–126, 177–207.

[42] I, 302–320, 497–525; II, i, 13–22. Harroviensis also gave Lucifer sly credit for concealing from Adah his boldest blasphemy—the request for man's worship—because he saw that it would have horrified her (pp. 28–29).

narrow scope of his humanity and reconcile himself to one barren truth: the sum of human knowledge was nothingness.[43] The diabolical use of the ancient tradition of the dichotomy between body and soul and of Byron's favorite materialistic theme—the dominion of flesh—in the passage on lechery was aimed to spatter Cain's aspiration, and also to vilify God's design of procreation as crafty and brutal.[44] Not the least odious of the devil's upbraiding was his forceful assertion that man's sinfulness and sorrow were an incurable plague of all human life, present and future. Though he blamed God for this scourge, he also spoke of it to deepen Cain's dejection.[45] Hoping to demoralize the man completely, he dwelt spitefully on the irksome fact of mortality. When the devil kept referring to clay and dust, his scorn was a mirror of Cain's self-contempt.[46] Half of Lucifer's insults expressed what Cain himself had bitterly thought and felt.

Not all of this belittling of humanity could be truly applied to Cain. His aspiration was not a sham. He was proud of his own worth and of his lofty yearning, and not arrogant in Lucifer's manner nor vain about petty abilities and possessions. He feared death, but he was not a craven coward.

Though some of the smears were false, the campaign was effective deviltry, and Cain, who had long been disconsolate, now became wild with dismay. We have already observed that the educational tour, undertaken under the guise of beneficence, was Lucifer's most theatrical strat-

[43] II, ii, 67–74, 91–98, 145, 401–407, 421–424. John William Harrison thought that Byron let Lucifer have three allusions to the New Testament (I, 163–166, 540–542; II, i, 16–20) to display his foreknowledge and thereby to abase Cain, who, hearing them, would feel ignorant (pp. 101–102). Byron, however, did not show that these allusions discouraged Cain. One might with equal plausibility infer that Lucifer inflated Cain's ego by telling him that only one other would enter Hades and return.

[44] II, i, 49–60. The most succinct expression of Byron's dualism and of the constraint pressed on the soul by the body came in II, i, 115–116. Cain had spoken of the same discouragement in lines 80–83. Plato, Zoroaster, Bayle, and others were the ancestors and corroborators of this, one of the most cherished ideas in Byron's writing.

[45] II, ii, 148–152, 220–227.

[46] I, 100–101, 217; II, i, 27–28, 83–85, 145–166; II, ii, 273–274, 406. Cain often abused himself with the same derogatory epithets that Lucifer used on him (see n. 18).

agem to humiliate his proud novice and to intensify his discouragement over the littleness of mortal life. We should also recall that Lucifer's assault on man's pride and his harping on man's insignificance had a social and theological as well as a psychological and dramatic purpose. It was part of Byron's attack on religious ideas that demeaned man's powers and rendered him despondent.

On too few occasions this sober abuse was lightened by the kind of mockery that Mephistopheles used, and Byron, too, in the editorials of *Don Juan*. Once it was aimed at man's conceit: "Must no reptiles / Breathe save th' erect ones?" Not so rough was the taunt that man was too paltry to make temptation of him interesting. The most graceful witticism was a mischievous warning about future guile. Lucifer was amused by his candor that was contrary to his professional interests, but then man was too stupid to heed good counsel. The joke was wasted on the humorless Cain. We have already noted the three sneers at the obsequious worship of the timid angels. He did not hesitate to scoff at divine benevolence as a sham and thrice derided the niggardliness of the "indulgent Lord / And bounteous planter of barred Paradise." God might be the author of happiness, but he kept it a secret. At the end of the tour Lucifer invited Cain to return to earth to try the rest of Jehovah's "boons to you and yours."[47]

These three mockeries of God's generosity remind us that Byron was disturbed by the discrepancy between orthodox theory and empirical conditions. (1) With Lucifer as spokesman, he argued that conventional beliefs made God ungodlike, robbed Him of dignity, integrity, and mercy, and turned Him into an envious, malicious, and savage autocrat. If one accepted this inversion of the deity, he could explain the origin of evil as a logical emanation from an Evil Power. But pious people insisted that God was forever, and in all his deeds, good. (2) Byron, Cain, and Lucifer observed the widespread existence of evil in the human state—disease, misfortune, warfare, and death, ignorance, folly, crime, and injustice, and the many rigid restrictions imposed on man's desires by his own frail body, by the finite horizon of mortal life, as well as by the regulations of external power. All three maintained that such evil was an undeniable fact and could not be dismissed as an illusion or as a transitory appearance. Could

[47] I, 134–135, 242–245, 266–268, 386–390, 485–489; II, i, 7–12, 172–173; II, ii, 205–214, 347–348, 449–451. Stavrou (p. 153). Thorslev thought that Lucifer had "more wit and sophistication than Milton's Satan" (p. 112). This was probably true, but he was not so urbane as Lucifer in "The Vision of Judgment" nor so acrimonious as Caesar in *The Deformed Transformed.*

one reconcile this abundant evil with a conception of a supremely Good Spirit? This paradox was a subject of repeated indignation and lamentation in the drama and was one cause of confusion, gloom, resentment, and ultimate violence.

Man's unhappiness in the modern world could also be attributed in part to social and political abuses. Byron may have thought of Jehovah as an oppressive contemporary government and also as the collective force of conservative opinion, the dictator of decrees and conventions that obstructed the activity and growth of the individual, enslaved his mind and will, exhausted him with fruitless labor, and kept him mentally stagnant and emotionally depressed. Cain's restive discomfort in his physical and mental world and Lucifer's assaults against Jehovah resembled the uneasiness and the remonstrance of romantic individualists, of jealous guardians of personal prerogative and social justice, and especially of idealists who wanted to believe in perfectability but who have been roiled by the obstacles created by entrenched authority, timid custom, and human infirmity.

We must keep in mind Lucifer's dual role: on the specific and literal level, he was Cain's teacher and irritant, tormenting the unhappy boy, arousing his wrath, and playing the familiar role of a master of guile. On a broadly social and abstract level, Lucifer was a vigorous intellectual critic of religious dogma that Byron detested and of the abuses of tyrannic authority. The two levels merge, for this criticism intensified Cain's dissatisfaction with himself, his world, and his God, and so motivated the murder and rendered it an impulsive act of social protest and indignation.

Lucifer's third campaign developed Byron's social thesis. His notorious rebellion, a denunciation of the many vices of the Conqueror, was delivered with force but with little subtlety. He reviled God's omnipotence, which he condemned as a despotism that ruled by fear. He thrashed at the concept of providence as contrary to the facts: God's perverse mismanagement of human affairs, his interdiction of knowledge, his trapping man into disobedience, the dire penalties that were out of all proportion to the offense, the wretchedness of mortal existence, and the shame of depravity. In Act II, Lucifer pointed to the systematic deterioration and demolition of one world after another as proof of God's wanton brutality. He even questioned the divine creativity. He thus not only vigorously spelled out what Cain had felt and thought about Jehovah, but added his own ferocious accusations.[48]

[48] I, 126–127, 137–166, 197–210, 266–267, 388–390, 487–489, 559–561; II, i,

Lucifer tried two maneuvers that tampered with a family relationship that had long existed in Cain's life. One succeeded, at least momentarily, but the other failed completely. When he turned the screw on Cain's jealousy, he pressed hard on a weakness that Byron indicated had been bothering Cain. The devil, once more acting as an irritant, brought into the open a resentment that had disturbed Cain ever since he noticed how much affection, human and divine, was being lavished on Abel.[49]

Lucifer's cynicism about human lust, however, was utterly wasted. Cain was so devoted to Adah that he ignored the devil's charge that concupiscence was a trick played by God to insure the reproduction of bodies, all doomed to a life of misery. Cain would not agree that man's love of woman marked the dominion of body over mind and was further evidence of God's cunning.

Lucifer failed almost as completely when he advanced three cynical propositions about love and beauty. He denied the existence of earthly beauty and reduced man's perception of it to self-delusion. If one came close to an object, he said, and looked at it clearly, it no longer appeared to be beautiful. This was contrary to Cain's experience with Adah and he said so with passionate eloquence. Then Lucifer argued that since love depended on beauty, it would vanish when beauty faded. Cain was an incredulous platonist and would not apply the law of mutability to his love for Adah or to her beauty. Lucifer's cynicism scored only once. Cain turned from the hypothesis about the transience of beauty to a criticism of God. If Adah's beauty did fade, God would be the loser "on seeing perish such a work."

Lucifer's third attempt to discredit love was his witty use of the distinction between the wise cherubim and the loving seraphim. This antithesis, he said, proved that love was ignorance, that knowledge was superior to love, and that Cain must choose between them. His sophistry disturbed Adah, but not Cain, who declared that his love had been born with him

---

16–25, 44–49, 57–60; II, ii, 40–43, 79–88, 101–102, 148–152, 219–227; 347–348, 393–396, 443–458.

Bostetter: The devil's main purpose in Act I was "to turn Cain's questions into the conviction that God's actions are evil, and that Lucifer with his exceptional and defiant spirit stands for the Good" (p. 572). Stavrou: The only conflict between Cain and Lucifer was that between doubt and denial (p. 157). He did not cite much evidence. One could pair I, 76–78 and 140–147; 104–108 and 197–205, 298–301. This conflict was nominal because Cain was willing to be convinced.

[49] II, ii, 338–356.

and was not a matter of choice. Although Lucifer could not undermine Cain's love of Adah, he still won a victory. He proved that knowledge was more powerful than love, for his promise to gratify Cain's curiosity drew him away from Adah.[50]

Except for Lucifer's pessimism about love and beauty and a few specific attacks on both Cain and Jehovah, he was a proponent of most of Cain's unhappy attitudes and emotions. As a fellow intellectualist, more sophisticated than his pupil, Lucifer formulated and converted Cain's amorphous thought into an elaborate strategy of psychological incitement. Lucifer's negation was abrasive, aggravating internal lesions and tensions, intensifying doubts, fears, and grievances, and always pounding at Cain's frustration and the shame of mortal triviality, pushing him ever deeper into dejection and goading him to furious rebellion.

Byron created a complex individuality for his social and theological critic. This master rebel was a compound of several devilish paradoxes. Here was a sorrowful and defeated power, who was still splendid and confident of his ability to continue the battle forever; an idealist, staunchly confident of the capacities of mind, proffering an arcane and coveted enlightenment, but evasive and either unwilling or unable to vouchsafe the ultimate truth; a plausible altruist, apparently responsive to the human plight, but really indifferent to it and utterly selfish, consumed by hatred and given to malice, incapable of love and cynical about its brevity and its carnality; a disarming diplomat, adroit in winning compliance and ruthless in manipulating emotion; a sly sadist, using his favors to augment his victim's depression and scoffing at his weakness; a spirit of wit and wisdom who made some serious errors; and finally an arrogant champion of liberty, an abusive opponent of autocracy, and a keen analyst of its destructiveness, who was himself a paragon of negation.

Adah

Byron developed his antithesis between Cain and Adah in two long scenes and more briefly in the opening and closing situations. Two details suggest the basic difference in their minds. (1) To Adah the cypress was

[50] I, 322–323, 423–433, 558–559; II, i, 50–60; II, ii, 249–252, 269–272, 323–336. Thorslev: Lucifer's inability to love was the one difference between him and Cain (p. 180). Cain did not, however, as Thorslev said, "continually" recur to the question: "Dost thou love nothing?" He first asked this in 310, repeated it in 319, and expressed his disapproving pity in 338. For Thorslev's interpretation, see "*Cain* in the Twentieth Century."

a convenient tree that cast a dense shade over her sleeping boy. To Cain the cypress was a symbol of the child's heritage of death that would darken its whole life. (2) When Cain first saw Lucifer, he realized at once that an unusual spirit approached him. When Adah met him, she greeted him casually, and like a hospitable housewife, invited him to be their guest and share their siesta as other angels had done.[51] Here was an ordinary mind, concerned with practical matters of daily routine, and she was neither blessed with the gift of imaginative perception nor afflicted with morbid foreboding.

She was steeped in the orthodoxy of her family, and theological questions never puzzled her. She knew that "Omnipotence / Must be all goodness," that the serpent lied, that her parents did wrong, and that their punishment, though severe, was just. She disapproved of, but could not answer, Lucifer's criticism of God. She did not understand, though she was worried by, Cain's skeptical rebellion. Her trust in God's kindness made it impossible for her to believe that He had punished innocent people or that He had shrunk her husband to nothing.[52]

Her kindliness was almost angelic. Cain's frowns hurt her and she coaxed him to be as gentle as she knew he could be. She would not let him awaken Enoch, even with a kiss. Violence was alien to her nature, and she was horrified when Cain talked about dashing Enoch against the rock, and was dazed by the murder of Abel.[53]

The key to her gentleness was her dedication to love.[54] She therefore was as optimistic in her view of the world as Cain and Lucifer were pessimistic. The two intellectuals were agitated by their strenuous negation. Adah was clear-eyed and confident in her choice of love over knowledge and in equating its altruistic activity with happiness. "What else can joy be, but the spreading joy?" God, she knew, was happy because he diffused joy among angels and mortals. Her own happiness consisted of the pleasures of parenthood and of her devoted service to her family. Her tenderness embraced even the sorrowful Lucifer, and she could weep for him too. Adah's altruism, like Cain's, extended to all humanity, and she was willing to die to save others. She accepted what he could not—the

[51] I, 80–97, 340–345; III, 2–9. See Brandes (p. 335) and the comments on Adah in Part III of this book.

[52] I, 352–353, 390–391, 404–407, 556–557; III, 74–75, 93–94.

[53] I, 56; III, 13–17, 126–137, 143–148, 396.

[54] The reviewer in *The Examiner* wrote that Adah made "a god of her affection" (June 2, 1822, p. 341).

logic of a single vicarious atonement that would redeem all mankind. Her devotion exposed her to pain, as Cain's sensitivity also did for him. She was distressed to learn that her children could not love each other as she and Cain had, and was sorely wounded when Lucifer told her that she was to be the mother of suffering millions.[55]

Byron stressed the creative and harmonizing power of her altruism. In Act I he introduced her as a votary of love, chanting in her stanza of the hymn that beauty was made to be loved. She was thereafter eager to praise and serve all the beauty that came within her ken and that soared above it —her family, the natural world, the Invisible and his angels. She willingly performed Cain's gardening chores. She worked for harmony when she tried to quiet him after his return from Hades and urged him to make an offering with Abel. It was she who suggested that he offer to God the beautiful blooms and fruits of the earth, and she who made an important subjective distinction: these fruits would be an acceptable peace offering if "Giv'n with a gentle and a contrite spirit."[56]

Her love was a protective force. She was confident that it had the power to avert the serpent's subtlety, and, after the crime, her love struggled to defend her husband. She begged him to clear himself of the charge of murder, tried to stop Eve from cursing him, pleaded with Adam not to

[55] I, 364–375, 431, 437, 478–481, 518–525; III, 79, 85–86, 137–139, 153–154. Chew thought Adah tried to domesticate Cain, to draw him away from "verity and freedom," with its hardship and despair to comfort, conformity, and the "little joys of common life" (p. 133). A few passages (I, 361–363; III, 36–38, 46–50) might support his view, but these speeches were not an effort to make Cain "renounce the vision of infinity."

[56] I, 14–17, 337–338; III, 104–108, 140–159.

Coleridge (*Poetry*, p. 260): Adah suggested "the disastrous compromise," not a burnt offering, but the fruits of the earth, "which would cost the giver little or nothing." Her suggestion was proof of Lucifer's cynical prediction that "there/Are some things still which woman may tempt man to" (II, ii, 209–211).

Coleridge's little joke and masculine bias overlooked III, 107–108. Adah's suggestion was sincere; it was not an error of judgment, not a pampering of her husband's recalcitrance. She saw that the important part of the offering was the state of mind with which it was given. What Coleridge called a lazy man's offering, the fruits of the earth, would be acceptable if given with "a gentle and a contrite spirit." Had Cain presented a whole zoo to the Lord, it would have been unwelcome so long as he was resentful. Moreover, Byron followed the biblical distinction between the occupation of the brothers. Since Cain was a farmer, Adah's suggestion was a logical one.

part in anger from his son, and interceded for him with the Angel, protesting that banishment and the peril of murderous retaliation were intolerable.[57]

The creativeness of her love enabled her not to mourn, as Cain did, for lost Eden. Like her father, she was resigned to bear what must be borne, but she also knew that they could build another Eden anywhere at any time, as long as they were united. At the end, she calmly decided that her office was to dry the tears, share the burden, and stabilize the family, and so she gently urged Cain to lead the way into the wilderness.[58]

Byron gave her the intuition that the opposite of love was separation. Happiness was not possible in isolation, and solitude was a sin. She endured absence only by thinking how soon she would next see her family, and she told Cain at the begnning of the drama that if he did not promptly follow her, she would seek him, and in a short time she returned to interrupt his conversation with Lucifer. She soon perceived that the latter was a dividing force, stepping "between heart and heart," and so she implored Cain not to leave with Lucifer, and then she wanted to accompany her husband on the journey. Even before the murder, she said she could endure anything, even death, if she could be with her family. In the crisis she would not leave Cain lonely with the dead. "Let us depart together." To the love-centered woman, isolation was the only intolerable disaster.[59]

Although Byron kept Adah out of most of the theological discussion, he gave her a dramatic function in relation to Lucifer that resembled the artistic use Goethe made of Gretchen, who was able to penetrate the evil reality of Mephistopheles. Adah quickly arrived at an intuitive and emotional definition of the nature of evil. She listened only a short while to Lucifer's negative criticism and declared flatly that he was as false as the serpent and asked, "Are you of heav'n?" Byron then let her describe Lucifer's psychological purpose and method in dealing with mortals: "we . . . / Art girt about by demons, who assume / The words of God and tempt us with our own / Dissatisfied and curious thoughts . . ." She recognized the identity Cain shared with Lucifer, and after Cain's return from the journey, she noticed how badly Lucifer had depressed her husband. Above all, she instinctively realized that Lucifer was the antipode of love and she rejected him as decisively as Cain had welcomed him. One com-

[57] III, 157–161, 396, 400–407, 447–448, 477–488.

[58] I, 362; III, 35–43, 547–555.

[59] I, 62–63, 347–351, 361, 375–376, 466–476; III, 94–95, 462–463, 527–528.

plication was that she also recognized Lucifer's splendor, and since she was an altruist and responsive to others, she was frightened by his mesmerism.[60]

Adah was a credible parallel or echo of her husband's traits, perceptions, and worries. Perhaps Byron implied that as a devoted and dependent wife, who did not think for or of herself, she had absorbed a part of Cain's personality. The most pleasant parallel was her aesthetic sensibility. Her delight in the beauty of the stars and of her child equaled Cain's. She anticipated his exposition of subjective time; the two hours of his absence had seemed a long two hours. Some of her comments were so typical of Cain that they were uncharacteristic of her. She once deplored her mother's error and lamented that it brought the children more trouble than it did Eve. Then Byron had her repeat Cain's description of their hardships —the exile, the sorrow and toil and dread, the remorse for the past, and the hopelessness about the future. She too was ignorant of death, though she did not fear it. But she reflected Cain's habitual inner tension when she admitted that her heart was not tranquil, though she was not wretched.[61]

One of her lines may be too far out of character. When Cain thought that Enoch would not look at his guilty father, she exclaimed: "If I thought that he would not, I would—." This impulsive hint of violence was more characteristic of Cain before the crime than it was of Adah. Since she would never punish Enoch, we may surmise that Byron was mainly intent on making his point about Cain's illumination and repentance. He gave vehemence to Adah in order to elicit from Cain a reply that revealed the change in him: "No more of threats, we have had too many of them.[62]

Except for that one outburst, Adah's characterization was consistent and not so simple as some readers have maintained. Byron gave her several ideas about devotion and separation, ranging from loyal solicitude for in-

[60] I, 375–376, 392–393, 400–422, 485, 510–516; III, 45–51.

[61] I, 357–361, 396–405, 466–471, 483–484, 511–517; III, 54–55, 140–141, 149–154. William H. Marshall wrote that Adah's view of time was fixed and absolute, measured by the sun, which is itself part of Creation and thereby the work of the material Principle [God]." He thought that Cain's view of time was intellectual and not emotional and hence he made it an aspect of the intellectual principle [Lucifer] (p. 152). One flaw in this dichotomy is that both Cain and Adah took an emotional view of time.

[62] III, 524–525.

dividuals to universal altruism, and presented a relationship with Lucifer that was peculiar to her and unlike Cain's. The harmony and disharmony of her life with her brother created a reciprocal design similar to that in some of Byron's other poems. Angiolina's tolerance and reasonableness were countered by Marino Faliero's pride and fury. Then his reluctance to slay his friends showed some of his wife's compassion. Myrrha shared the love and revelry of Sardanapalus, but she was also a stern critic of his frivolity. After circumstances drove him into action she vigorously applauded and matched his heroic effort. The masculine and feminine foils and interchanges were implicit in these and other pairs. Manfred made the dual relationship explicit. He told the Witch of the Alps about the resemblances and differences between himself and Astarte. Her voice, hair, and physical features were like his, but "tempered into beauty." She had the same "lone thoughts and wanderings, / The quest of hidden knowledge, and a mind / To comprehend the Universe"; but she was favored with virtues he lacked—pity, cheerfulness, tenderness, and humility (II, ii, 105–116). Just as Astarte, Myrrha, and Angiolina were the extensions, the complements, and the opposites of their men, so Adah was Cain's domestic twin and softer counterpart. She was both like and unlike him, and resided within his mind and heart as intimately as Lucifer did. She must oppose Cain and Lucifer, but she will marvel at the Prince of Darkness, be attracted to and repelled by him, and serve his disciple; at one time chide her brother and then echo him, now plead against his wildness and then defend him. Adah was not Byron's fullest portrait of a woman, but she was convincing and adequately involved with the principal subjects of the drama.

THE RE-CREATION OF GENESIS

CONSERVATIVE CLERGYMEN AND LAITY in 1821 insisted on a literal reading of the Eden story because they maintained that the Scriptures were God's revelation of historical fact and truth. A second influence on the contemporary view of Genesis was the prestige of Milton's epic expansion of the Eden episode and the development of his religious thesis. Milton and the literalists adopted one variation to relate Genesis consistently to later books in the Bible: the serpent was the devil in disguise. This suited Milton's narrative purpose, too, because the episode then became part of a contest between Jehovah and Satan, in which the former crushed his foe ignominiously. The brevity of the biblical account encouraged literal readers to speculate reverently about the reasons for Jehovah's interdiction of the trees, the temptation, the disobedience, and the murder.

Milton's invention of long speeches for the serpent and the guilty pair and his full exposure of their thoughts and emotions were orthodox in basic concept and devout in tone. Some sticklers for the unadorned word did not approve of Milton's fiction, but Byron and Shelley not only accepted his development as a prerogative of poetry but also regarded Satan as the hero of *Paradise Lost.* This interpretation was their invention, for Milton had made it clear that the devil was a villain who had beguiled Eve into disobedience. He also carefully explained that our first parents had not been bullied into their trespass, but were voluntary sinners, who deserved the penalties meted out to them.

Milton concisely narrated the murder of Abel as a prophecy made by Michael to Adam, and did not enrich it with psychological detail. He assigned to Cain the motive of envy and connected the crime with the pollution incurred by the original fall. Byron assimilated into his poem both of these traditions.

Some reviewers and pamphleteers scolded him for daring to distort the holy scripture.[1] Later critical opinion (e.g., Chew and Calvert) held that the first two and a half acts of the play had almost nothing to do with the Bible,[2] and more recent scholarship has usually taken this view for granted. As Byron might have remarked, "Some millions must be wrong, that's pretty clear: / Perhaps it may turn out that all were right" (*DJ*, XV, st. 90).

In making enormous additions to the biblical story, he borrowed some thoughts and emotions from Milton's characterization, and a few other things from Gessner, and worked in his own fanciful elaboration of a nineteenth-century scientific theory. But, as we have observed in the preceding essay, he departed radically from Milton and the conservatives in his conception of all the actors, including God. He sometimes did use the biblical words, as he stated he had done in his Preface, and altered them only to fit the meter. More significant was the consummate skill with which he adapted the data of Genesis in every act of the play for his own purposes. Without encroaching too often on our analysis of Byron's ideas and people, we can identify the content of his biblical adaptation and make a few conjectures about the many forces behind it and the artistic methods it revealed.

An exacting and tenacious formalist may require that Byron's management of his biblical resources be directed by a single controlling idea. The opposite is true and Byron's genius and his creative habits cannot be forced into the kind of structure that pleases some modern analysts. We are not now watching the young Keats endeavor and fail to discipline a horror

[1] Matthews, Jeffrey, Watkins, and others. See "The Major Periodicals and Pamphlets."

[2] Chew, pp. 119–120; William J. Calvert, *Byron, Romantic Paradox,* p. 175. Byron's use of his main sources, Milton, Gessner, and Bayle, will be recorded in appropriate places in the Annotations. For other possible influences, see "Some Possible Sources and Parallels for Act II."

tale by Boccaccio into a lucid aesthetic unity, nor observing Tennyson, with opulent serenity, adapt an Arthurian legend to nineteenth-century morality. And yet Byron's wrath and protest in the experience of Cain and Lucifer bear the same relation to Genesis as Wordsworth's passion and stoicism in the narrative of Laodamia and Protesilaus have to the ancient myth and Browning's hopefulness and affirmation with David, Saul, and Lazarus have to their biblical ancestors. Byron's baffled hero and cynical devil, the purlieus of Paradise, and the flight to Hades are as much the poet's private dream as Bernard Shaw's civilized Caesar and barbarous Egypt are the intimate and legitimate offspring of that strong-minded individualist. Byron plundered and transformed Genesis as boldly as Shaw did Plutarch, and both thought that literary precedent and their own genius and serious objectives entitled them to a liberal and flexible manipulation of their sources.

Many personal, religious, and social ideas and certain definite and complex functions that he wanted his people to serve explain Byron's handling of the substance of Genesis. One pundit wrote that if Milton's purpose in *Paradise Lost* was to justify the ways of God to man, then Byron's aim was to justify the ways of man to God. But this epigram is not a master key that will unlock all doors that lead from Genesis into *Cain*. Byron's difficulties with his mother and his wife, the audacities of Caroline Lamb and the tantrums of La Fornarina, his love of paradox and shocking, theatrical effects, his egoism and individualism, his anger at autocracy, his critical and skeptical temper, his reading of certain rationalists and scientists like Bayle, Warburton, Voltaire, and Cuvier, his revulsion from Calvinist dogmas, and, contrariwise, his helpless, unhappy absorption of some of them, his own sense of guilt, his fatalism, pessimism, self-pity, and confusion, these and perhaps a dozen other urgencies, and some that would entertain the Freudians, and, above all, his artistic competence controlled his re-creation of Genesis. These circumstances and emotions erected over the old story a superstructure of theology, political allegory, fantasy, rhetoric, and psychology. In this essay we will try to deduce some of the artistic and dramatic principles that governed the poet's retention, modification, and omission of biblical incident, speech, and detail and that accounted for the arrangement of the superstructure in patterns of conflict, contrast, parallel, and themal variation.

Byron, following the Bible, divided the story of Adam's family into two parts, the first being much larger than the second: (1) the creation, the dialogue between Eve and the serpent, the eating of the fruit, the

Lord's assessment of penalties to the guilty parties, and his justification of them, the exile, and the birth of Cain and Abel (1, 2, 4:1–2); (2) the offerings the two brothers made to the Lord, his reaction to them and his lecture to Cain, the murder, the second talk between Cain and God, and the banishment (4:3–16). In both sections the family suffered a calamity. Byron staged only the shorter part, the second disaster.

His decision to begin his drama in the Greek fashion, as near the catastrophe as possible—the morning on which the murder occurred[3]—obliged him to glimpse the first and larger part of the story in retrospect, piecemeal and redundantly, during the family talk, the hero's rumination, and his discourse with Lucifer.

At the very start of the play, Byron introduced the biblical past into the hymn, where five members of the family lauded some of the acts of creation and recalled the serpent and the expulsion. Then the two trees and the plucking of the fruit were the subject of disagreement between Cain and his parents, and Byron let the clashing attitudes toward this fleeting intrusion of past history portend the temperamental and ideological conflict that later pervaded the drama. Cain in his soliloquy pondered the first disaster, its cause and results, and five minutes later brought the topic up with Lucifer. Thereafter both of them returned intermittently to three biblical events: (1) the ban that God placed on the tree of knowledge, (2) God's threat that if man ate the fruit, he would perish, and (3) the banishment from Eden and the explanation that God gave for it. Since man, aspiring to be godlike, ate the fruit of the tree of life in order to gain immortality, God therefore had to drive Adam from Paradise. These three incidents in the first part of the biblical story and the emotions they engendered in Cain and Lucifer permeated their conversation.[4] Thus, though Byron did not directly dramatize the first main part of the Eden story, he gave it crucial psychological value. It supplied the object and tenor of Cain's skepticism and animosity and much of Lucifer's censure and invective. Byron continuously made past history not only molest and discompose their present life but also darken the future of the hero.

[3] He further compressed the time span by eliminating the biblical pause between the quarrel of the brothers and the crime and by having Cain's anger precipitate immediate violence. Theatrical expedience accounted for this alteration of the biblical story.

[4] For Byron's typical use of biblical phrasing about these three events, see Annotations I, 203–205. The views of Cain and Lucifer about the past were discussed in the preceding essay.

His removal of the devil from the biblical temptation made a great stir among his contemporaries because it was contrary to Milton and popular tradition. Twice in the Preface and four times in the play he insisted that only a snake and not the devil talked with Eve. When we discussed Byron's characterization of Lucifer, we saw that it suited his dramatic and psychological intentions to be more baldly literal in his reading of Genesis than the strictest literalists had been.

Though Byron did not restate the biblical colloquy between Eve and the serpent, he wove it into the drama by constantly implying a parallel between the past and present situations, between the serpent's seduction of Eve and Cain's entanglement with Lucifer. He began with the parental alarm after Cain's question in line 33. "Wherefore plucked ye not the tree of life?" Adam and Eve promptly connected his challenge with their crisis in Eden. Near the end of the drama, Adam again darted back to the past with the reproach that Cain's crime was the work of Eve and the serpent.[5] Between these two somber misgivings Byron distributed throughout the drama at least thirty allusions to the fatal dialogue in Eden and to Adam's collusion. Most of the time he underlined the parallel by means of Cain's bitter and persistent memory of the parental blunder.[6] In no other psychological area was Byron a more careful artist than in this spectral evocation of a remote, calamitous decision, which Cain, by listening to Lucifer, was himself duplicating. The poet let the devil forge the parallel chain by his taunts about the temptation,[7] by his endorsement of the promises made by the serpent and by his crafty tampering with Cain's mind and heart. Thus Byron re-enacted the biblical temptation scene, substituting Cain and Lucifer for Eve and the serpent and freely borrowing from Book IX of *Paradise Lost.* The irony of this prolonged parallelism is that Cain was not conscious that his role was similar to his mother's, that his willing association with Lucifer incorporated his mother's succumbing to the blandishment of the serpent, and that his yearning

[5] I, 33–41; III, 382.

[6] For Cain's continuous recollection of his mother's encounter with the serpent, of his father's yielding to her, and of the consequences, see "An Apology for Revolt," n. 13. Even during the flight and in Hades, Cain's mind kept returning to the snake and the fall: II, i, 63–65, 72–75, 171, 193–195; II, ii, 24–25, 152–163, 195–204, 232–235, 344–345. Lucifer contributed his share of reminders: II, ii, 101–102, 145–157, 196–207, 324, 348, 408–409, 459.

[7] I, 194–196, 216–242, 559–561. See note 6; lines 408–409 were a pointed comparison of mother and son.

for wisdom and his eagerness to travel were variants of her curiosity about the new life and knowledge the serpent had offered her.[8] Here Byron made Adah a timid and alert foil to her reckless husband. She was afraid that history was being repeated, that he and she might be slipping into the same delusion that snared their parents.[9]

When Cain doubted that Enoch could elude the serpent's subtlety, Byron hinted that a third generation, and all thereafter, because of the very nature of man, might be caught by the old trickery.[10] Byron's echoing method gave the old story a universal extension. Just as Cain and Enoch were twice more Eve, so Byron and his successors were many times Cain, dreaming and fighting under the same captivating tree, lulled or incited by the cajolery or demagoguery of the voices who told them what they wanted to hear, undertaking their quest or rebellion anew, and perhaps also ending in wreckage or rough awakening.

Byron did not absorb into the play all of the first part of the Genesis narrative. The Bible, the old Mystery plays, Milton, and popular tradition used the nakedness of Adam and Eve and their differing attitudes toward it before and after the disaster as an indicator of a great change in man's state. Innocence was replaced by an embarrassed and shameful self-consciousness. Byron ignored these emotions, the fig-leaf aprons, and the clothing of animal skin. When Adam and Eve felt that nudity was a disgrace and covered themselves, they thereby tacitly and symbolically admitted their guilt. This sense of obloquy was contrary to Byron's conception of Cain's mind and moral problem. If Byron had put these biblical details into his hero's meditation, Cain would have doubted that man should be ashamed of knowledge, or be held culpable for gaining it, or that modesty had any relevance to truth. Byron knew the significance of the biblical nakedness and its connection with the family disaster. Once Cain sadly applied the symbol to the sleeping Enoch: "Thine are the hours and days when both are cheering / And innocent. Thou has not plucked the fruit. / Thou know'st not that thou art naked" (III, 21–23).

Byron also disregarded four penalties that God inflicted on Eve and the serpent. Nothing is said in the play about the pain of childbirth, wom-

[8] The closest he came to seeing the relationship was his complaint that his mother had lost the curiosity that made her risk an eternal curse (I, 180–182).

[9] She worried about it several times: I, 351, 375–376, 392–393, 401–405, 556–557.

[10] Enoch will succumb to the serpent's subtlety because Cain will transmit his own weakness to the child (III, 158–160).

an's subjection to man, the endless enmity between woman and the serpent, and the curse on the latter, doomed to crawl on its belly and to eat dust forever (3:14–16). One can surmise the reason for the last of these omissions. Milton transformed Satan and his fallen angels into hissing snakes and baited the parched and hungry horde with the fruit of an illusory tree of knowledge, that turned to cinders and bitter ashes in their mouths. Byron, careful to maintain the power and dignity of Lucifer, made not the slightest allusion to such a degradation. As we noted in an earlier discussion, Lucifer acknowledged but did not whine about Jehovah's victory. He admitted that he was unhappy, but Byron only hinted at the biblical humiliation: the earth and its dust were an eternal part of humanity and of the devil, too (II, i, 148–150).

The nearest he came to the enmity between womankind and the serpent was (1) Adah's recognition of the resemblance between Lucifer's blasphemy and that of the serpent and her continuous fright thereafter, and (2) Eve's hectic demand that the creatures she obviously loathed should hurt her son: may "snakes spring up in his path" and "the leaves / On which he lays his head to sleep be strewed / With scorpions!" Byron transferred the dust that the biblical and Miltonic serpent ate to Cain: "[May] Earth's fruits be ashes in his mouth" (III, 427–430).

Why did Byron omit the two other afflictions that God decreed for all women? Cain might have grieved over the pangs of childbirth, since he was racked by the future pain of Enoch and his progeny. But if we can judge from Byron's letters, the verse tales, and some of the dramas, he accepted one penalty—woman's subjection to man—as her normal status.[11] He felt no need to deplore it in *Cain.*

Byron emphasized three penalties and had his hero condemn them as too rigorous: the loss of Paradise; the necessity of constant sweat to wrest from the earth its fruit—Byron's substitute for the thorn and thistle of the Bible (3:18–19); and mortality.

The broadest expansion of the punishment episode in Genesis appeared

[11] In *Don Juan* he wrote that the pain of parturition was no worse than man's daily discomfort of shaving, but then in the same stanzas he sympathized with woman's sad and helpless subordination in man's world, a view he returned to elsewhere: XIV, sts. 23–24; I, sts, 193–194; II, sts. 200–201; XVI, sts. 64–67. Gulnare, Myrrha, Marina, and Aholibamah were not subservient and at least spoke out or acted against their bondage.

in Byron's treatment of the guilty pair. The Bible condemned both the man and the woman and chastised them with equal severity. Although Byron also assumed that the two were jointly at fault, he bore down harder on Eve than on Adam, possibly, as we have previously surmised, because of his personal bias.

We come now to Byron's modification of the second part of the story. In Genesis, Cain's wife and children were mentioned only after he went to the land of Nod (4:16–17). Byron followed Gessner's *Death of Abel,* set the biblical clock backward, and created a fuller domestic environment for his hero. Byron's exploitation of this simple change was many-sided. It permitted a religious and temperamental contrast between husband and wife and the expression of softer traits in the criminal hero. It also provided an emotional scene at the beginning of Act III and rendered the attack on the axiom of heredity personal by means of a father's anxiety over the fate of his children.

The poet took advantage of the biblical distinction between Abel the shepherd and Cain the farmer, just as the Mysteries and Gessner had done. Cain's labor with the earth was one cause of his discontent. In the climax, it determined the difference in the offerings to the Lord. In Genesis, the shepherd brought "the firstlings of his flock and of the fat thereof" (4:4). Byron liked this phrasing and used it in part or as a whole three times, once as early as I, 184. He was even more partial to "the fruit of the ground" that farmer Cain offered to God, and gave it an important role in his complex treatment of that image.

In the sacrificial scene, the Bible did not give Byron much to work with in developing the criminal's emotional state:

> And the Lord had respect unto Abel and to his offering: But unto Cain and to his offering he had not respect. And Cain was very wroth, and his countenance fell. And the Lord said unto Cain, Why art thou wroth? and why is thy countenance fallen? If thou doest well, shalt thou not be accepted? and if thou doest not well, sin lieth at the door. And unto thee shall be his desire, and thou shalt rule over him. And Cain talked with Abel his brother: and it came to pass, when they were in the field, that Cain rose up against Abel his brother, and slew him. (4:4–8)

The two unmistakable emotions in this biblical situation were disappointment and anger. Jealousy may also be implied, and this has become a traditional assumption. The Mystery plays and Gessner's *Death of Abel* stressed the rivalry between the brothers and Cain's envy of the more prosperous Abel. The tiller of the soil customarily suffered a harder lot than the shepherd. Byron, catching the bare hint in the Bible and following tradition, merged jealousy with the other feelings that he invented to motivate the crime. Since Byron and the literalists assumed that Abel's animal-sacrifice was a biblical custom, the poet used this ceremony to aggravate Cain's antagonism toward the deity.[12]

Byron reversed the biblical order of the offerings. According to Medwin, he said that "one mistake crept in[to the biblical narrative]—Abel's should have been made the first sacrifice."[13] Byron's change had the dramatic value of following pious convention with the impious revolt that started a rapid succession of events: God's tornadic sign of displeasure, Cain's anger at God's preference of Abel's offering, his attempt to overthrow Abel's altar, his brother's resistance, and then the fatal blow. After the careful preparation of Acts I and II, and of lines 1–210 of Act III, in which Cain's ideas and feelings had been thoroughly presented, Byron's final sequence seems inevitable. Had he followed the biblical order of the two sacrifices (putting Cain's first and Abel's second), he would have stumbled into an awkward regression and halted the momentum he had designed.

In the conversation between Jehovah and Cain, Byron substituted the Angel, that both Gessner and one of the Mysteries had used. After the parsons had been very noisy against *Cain,* Byron wrote Murray:

> I have even avoided introducing the Deity, as in Scripture, (though Milton does, and not very wisely either); but have adopted his Angel as sent to Cain instead, on purpose to avoid shocking any feelings on the subject by falling short of what all uninspired men must fall short in, viz. giving an adequate notion of the effect of the presence of Jehovah. The Old Mysteries introduced him liberally enough, and all this is avoided in the New one.[14]

This was a necessary deviation from the biblical situation. After the abundant criticism of the deity in the preceding fifteen hundred lines, the

[12] Cain referred angrily to animal sacrifice six times: III, 214–219, 255–258, 266–267, 284–285, 291–293, 298–304.

[13] Medwin, p. 126.

[14] *LJ,* VI, 16. Byron could not have known the fragmentary York Mystery, "Cayme and Abell," that used the Angel.

poet could not bring God late into the play and allow him only the peremptory remarks of Genesis, 3:9–22. Had he tried to imitate Milton, and compose for the Lord at this point a copious defense of his treatment of man, Byron would not only have failed to give a credible illusion "of the presence of Jehovah," but might have dissipated the dramatic unity and effectiveness that he had achieved in Act III. The substitution of the angelic messenger, who could be curt, saved the play from becoming what the contemporary reviewers wanted it to be—a religious tract, a debate between good and evil.

Byron retained the insolent question, "Am I my brother's keeper?" as evidence of Cain's continuing truculence, an apparent contradiction in the midst of his penitence. He also saw the advantage of keeping God's charge to the culprit. Since Cain had complained about the futility of hard work, one prediction now became ironic: "When thou tillest the ground, it shall not henceforth yield unto thee her strength" (4:12). Byron lifted it almost verbatim (III, 474–475).

A major change was the transfer from Cain to Adah of the lament that the punishment was greater than he could bear and the fear that he might be slain by other mortals. This anxiety naturally belonged to the solicitous wife that Byron had created earlier in the play. Furthermore, the transfer preserved the heroic stature that Byron wanted Cain to have in the closing moments of the poem. He did not let him be unnerved by the Angel's sentence of banishment or by the dread that his children might kill him. Cain would have welcomed death. As he entered the wilderness, it was not fear but nobler and more desolate emotions that tortured him.[15]

Finally there was the device that God used to protect Cain from retaliation—the mark and the threat of sevenfold vengeance on "whosoever slayeth Cain." In the drama the Angel granted this dispensation after Adah's grievous plea and after he had frightened her with the warning that Cain might be killed by his own children. In the Angel's speech, Byron faithfully reproduced the biblical text.[16] His further use of it we will consider in the next essay.

As we have seen, the poet retained most of the incidents and the dia-

[15] The transfer of Genesis 4:13–14 occurred in III, 477–488. Brandes saw this transfer as central in Byron's portrait of "the first loving woman." He did not consider its significance for the characterization of the hero.

[16] Genesis 4:15; III, 493–500.

logue of the original narrative. He retold more than half of it through recollection, omitted some matters, and modified others. His re-creation of Genesis, directed by the emotions and ideological purposes we glanced at near the beginning of this section, was a literary artifice in the best sense of that word, with an eye to structural relationships and dramatic and poetic techniques. This was notably true in the expert manipulation of concrete objects, biblical images, and symbols, that merit a separate essay.

IMAGES FROM PARADISE AND BEYOND

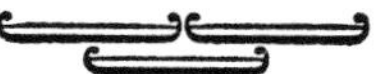

THE EDEN *trees* and their *fruits,* that God banned shortly after he placed them and man in the garden and that soon became the objects of temptation and sin, provided Byron with a variable symbol. They were the core of the regret and dismay of the devout family and of the rebels' criticism of God. Lucifer praised their potential value, but Cain was puzzled and disgruntled about them. Reason told him that they were benign, but experience had proved them deadly. He called the tree of knowledge a cheat and was vexed because his parents did not choose the tree of life. Byron adjusted the emotional content of the image to the speaker, and thus at different times the trees were salutary or harmful, mystifying or obstructive.[1]

Byron also gave the fruit four figurative meanings that were germane to his expansion of the Genesis narrative. He made it a symbol of human depravity and of the sorrow and manifold wretchedness that imprisoned

[1] I, 30–38, 72–74, 105–108, 171, 197–204, 232–233, 296, 352–353, 434–435, 444–445, 457–462, 559–560. There are six references to the original trees and fruits in Act II and one in Act III. The image disappeared during the space journey but returned in Hades: II, ii, 24–25, 151–152, 161–167, 201–202, 233–234, 409; III, 22. Here Byron also referred to nonsymbolic trees, stripped of bark and branches and to the "deep woods of earth," when Cain compared the ghosts of primeval monsters to animals he had seen (II, ii, 135–142).

the soul and that mortal man could never escape. Adam and Eve thought that their son's blasphemy at dawn was the result of their sin: the forbidden fruit had fallen and they had to gather it. But for Cain, it signified the frustration and the injustice of mortal existence: "I judge but by the fruits—and they are bitter— / Which I must feed on for a fault not mine." In Adah's lament, Byron merged the original and the hereditary meanings: "Oh my mother! thou / Hast plucked a fruit more fatal to thine offspring / Than to thyself." Lucifer turned the symbol into a paradox and added a new figurative meaning to convince Cain that an advantage could accrue from the debacle. "One good gift has the fatal apple giv'n— / Your reason."[2]

In Act III Byron drew from trees a connotation that was pertinent to the immediate downfall and that also retained some of the old tragic feeling. The gloomy cypress was a symbol of death. When Eve demanded that the woods give no shelter to Cain and when he entered the wilderness, Byron devised two more variations on the old tree image and made them part of the rejection and isolation that Cain must suffer for his guilt. They were new bitter fruit for him.[3]

Against the sad and deleterious fruits, within Eden and outside it, in both the literal and figurative sense, Byron placed the healthy, natural fruits that Cain and Adah enjoyed in the landscape around them. Byron had them refer five times to these good fruits. In Act I Adam spoke of the fruits that glow "as the light which ripens." In Act III she urged Cain to offer God "The fruits of the earth, the early beautiful / Blossom and bud and bloom of flow'rs and fruits."[4] Before, during, and after the offering to the Lord, Cain warmly expressed his admiration for the earth-fruits. Here, in the crisis of Cain's life, in the midst of anger and defiance and rejection by God, the allusions to "fresh fruit," "in their various bloom and ripeness," and to the "sweet and blooming fruits of earth / And milder seasons" were brief, cheerful sounds, barely heard in the emotional

[2] I, 30–31, 78–79, 395–397; II, ii, 459–460. In the remainder of Adah's speech (398–413), she supported her charge against her mother by first comparing Eve's misfortune with her children's worsened condition and then by comparing the hypnotic effect Lucifer has on her with the serpent's temptation of Eve. For similar figurative uses of the fruit, see I, 108, 444–445; II, ii, 148–152, 457–458.

[3] III, 3–9, 28, 423, 441–442, 455–459, 544.

[4] I, 338–339; III, 105–108. In I, 325, there is a neutral reference to the tree-fruits, which Cain plans to cull to please Adah. This may be Byron's attempt to balance Abel's biblical "firstlings of the flock" in I, 184.

storm. These were moments of natural beauty and goodness among many despondent recollections of their gloomy polarities: the tree-fruits of the Eden calamity, the fruits of man's evil nature, a continual harvest of misdemeanors, and the punitive fruits of toil, pain, disappointment, and death. At the end of the drama, even the glad fruits of the earth were transformed. Eve shrilly begged that "Earth's fruits be ashes" in her son's mouth, and Cain's farewell suggested that Eve's wish had already been granted: "Oh earth! / For all the fruits thou hast rendered to me, I / Give thee back this [the corpse of Abel]."[5]

Byron's cultivation of the biblical trees and fruits was directed by many themal and psychological aims. These images were associated with diverse traits and moods—convention, doubt, and revolt, yearning and failure, eternal vision and daily reality, joy and sadness, natural health and moral sickness, mortal weakness and spiritual power, guilt and vengeance. Each separate use seemed appropriate and the total impression is not inartistic confusion, but a pliant, fertile, and imaginative adaptation of limited material.

Since the scheme of the *serpent* was sly and disruptive and since its character has ever been invidious, it gave the poet a broad symbolic range, stretching from the tricky and the abhorrent to the bizarre and the virulent. Everyone in the play spoke of the snake as the original tempter and destroyer, beginning with Zillah's bare and naïve statement of the basic paradox: "Oh God! who loving, making, blessing all, / Yet didst permit the serpent to creep in / And drive my father forth from Paradise."[6] Near the end of the drama Adam thought the serpent embodied human corruption, and he saw its work as the cause of the murder. Eve also felt the venom of a sequent evil that now brought new grief in the loss of Abel: "The serpent's fangs / Are in my heart." Then with the same image Byron showed that Eve was more than ever vitiated by the rudimental taint, for she converted the symbol into an instrument of vengeance: "May th' eternal serpent's curse be on him. . . . snakes spring up in his path."[7]

Between these two extremes, the archetypal serpent in Eden and the ineradicable depravity of the human heart, Byron worked out a number of variations with the serpentine image. Lucifer twisted it into ridicule. He

[5] III, 218–219, 259–260, 283, 428, 542–544.

[6] I, 18–20, 35–44, 69–70, 194–196, 224–226, 240–242, 351, 392–393, 403–405, 556–557; II, ii, 204, 208–209, 343–344; III, 157–160.

[7] III, 382–384, 402–427.

jested about the existence of snakes on other planets, jeered at man's kinship with the reptile, and later phrased a vicious comparison: "The rest / Of your poor attributes is such as suits / Reptiles engendered out of the subsiding / Slime . . ." Byron allowed the susceptible Adah to see the magnetic and hypocritical facet of the image. She identified the beautiful fiend with the "fair serpent," called them both liars, and dreaded their power. The sensations that Lucifer aroused in her implied the hypnotic power that legend has bestowed on the snake. But love gave her the confidence that "a father's blessing may avert / A reptile's subtlety." Cain was not so sure.[8]

His attitude toward the serpent was very unstable. He regarded it with curiosity, wonder, doubt, hatred, and contempt. The image reflected his confusion and several other traits. Personal experience had once connected it with common pain. He remembered how a reptile's sting had been the cause of a lamb's suffering and how he had been moved more by compassion for the lamb and the ewe than by horror at the reptile. Even after the lamb was cured, Cain recalled the harrowing episode as empirical refutation of Adam's ethical optimism. Here the image combined the hero's sensitivity and skepticism. Earlier it had entered his scornful dismissal of a pious explanation of the human predicament. His parents had preached to him of "serpents and of fruits and trees." "What need of snakes and fruits to teach us" that we are miserable? Byron linked the crafty foe with Cain's animosity toward his parents. He condemned them for yielding to it and relied on his mother's temptation as an excuse for his own violence. Eve had conceived him while she was overwrought by the serpent. In Hades the image touched upon Cain's quest of reality. He recognized the kinship of the coiling monster to the snake that had basked under the Eden tree, but the latter, he felt, must have had "more of beauty." The fantastic vision magnified, in Miltonic fashion, the simple essence of evil as a hideous distortion, but Cain surmised that in human experience it assumed a more subtle and dangerous form and often wore a pretty mask.[9]

[8] I, 351, 392–393, 406–413, 556–557; II, i, 171–173; II, ii, 95–98; III, 158–160.

[9] I, 69–70, 170–171, 461–462; II, ii, 190–199, 280–305; III, 506–508. It is connected again with his hostility toward his mother in II, ii, 343–345.

G. Wilson Knight saw in the serpent-image something I cannot: a reflection of Byron's "strong feeling for sexual guilt," that attained "gigantic proportion in the

Byron's exploitation of the serpent was as persistent as his use of the tree-fruits and manifested the same artistic principle of involving it with thought and feeling and symbolizing his themes with flexible and even contradictory variety.

For a third themal image, Byron did not need to recall the first three chapters of Genesis, where God formed Adam out of "the dust of the ground," and where he told the culprits that they must return to the earth. *Dust, clay,* and *earth* had long been Byron's favorite images of mortality, and he used them often to express some of Cain's most powerful emotions and also a few relationships between him and other people. Abel calmly accepted his dust, but Cain always spurned it as the inferior part of his nature, unworthy of his mind and of the beauty he saw in space. Since he was earth-bound, the image vented his frustration, imposed by a tantalizing deity, who "after flatt'ring dust with glimpses of / Eden and immortality resolves / It back to dust again—for what?"[10]

Byron gave the image to Lucifer for two contrary purposes. When Cain wondered why a spirit would deign to "walk with dust" and Lucifer replied, "I know the thoughts / Of dust and feel for it and with you," the image was a gesture of sympathy. Lucifer's repetition of this consolation became a grim admission that he shared the destiny of mortals: "Thou / Shalt soon return to earth and all its dust; / 'Tis part of thy eternity and mine." Most of the time Lucifer wielded the symbol as a weapon for battering Cain's confidence. He overwhelmed his companion with two images of the vast accumulation of dust, one in the past, the other in the future, each pointing to deterioration, misery, and destruction. Then in a direct attack on Cain's self-respect, he turned the image into a contemptuous epithet: "Dust! Limit thy ambition." To see either of the two

---

immense serpent" ("The Two Eternities: An Essay on Byron" in *The Burning Oracle,* p. 223).

Lura Nancy and Duilio T. Pedrini covered so much territory in their two-part article that they could do little more than make a few generalizations about the attitudes of the author and the characters toward the serpent ("Serpent Imagery and Symbolism in the Major English Romantic Poets: Blake, Wordsworth, Coleridge, Byron, Shelley, Keats," *Psychiatric Quarterly Supplement,* XXXIV [1960], 240–241; XXXV [1961], 54–55).

For Harrison's interpretation see "*Cain* in the Twentieth Century."

[10] II, i, 115–116; III, 72–74. See also I, 100; II, ii, 109, 370; III, 114–115.

eternal principles would be fatal to a fragile child of earth. When Byron iterated the word *clay* four times in four lines, his object was to wound Cain's pride. "Poor clay!" said Lucifer, with a mixture of pity and scorn, "What are they which dwell / So humbly in their pride as to sojourn / With worms in clay?"[11]

Byron, following the Bible, also identified the image with physical death. Cain's despondency over mortality, i.e., over spiritual defeat—"being dust and grov'ling in the dust" until he returned to dust—made him prefer death to life. He was sick of all that dust had shown him and wanted to remain in Hades. Thus Byron connected the symbol with Cain's death wish. When Lucifer defined death as a resolution into the earth, that seemed to Cain to be a desirable consummation: "Were I quiet earth / That were no evil. Would I ne'er had been / Aught else but dust!" Finally, Byron varied the emotional gamut of the image by associating it with two opposite death desires—vengeance and penitence. Eve wanted the dust to refuse her son a grave. Cain was willing to die if that would redeem Abel from the dust.[12]

The fourth and fifth principal images form a pair—*light* and *darkness*. These two were the object of God's second action in Genesis and have been traditionally attached to concepts of good and evil, life and death, creation and destruction. Byron accepted these connotations and, as other poets had done, also fused the pair with differences in emotion (love and hate, benevolence and malevolence), in awareness (illumination and ignorance), in aesthetic values (beauty and ugliness, attraction and repulsion), and in temperament and outlook (cheer and gloom, optimism and pessimism). In disposition Abel and Adah were light people, Cain and Lucifer dark, though it was also Byron's intention that his hero be a seeker of light, and Lucifer, a genuine light-bringer, as his name signifies.

Byron introduced the pair in the hymn that concerned some of God's attributes and acts of creation and that was a forecast of the primary notions, conflicts, and images of the drama. Light and its kindred words—fire, day, sunrise, morning, illuminate—occurred eight times and were counterpointed by darkness and its associates—night, shadow, serpent, and evil (15 times). Allied with darkness were the nine statements or implications of division, both positive and negative: God's separation of

[11] I, 99–101, 123, 217; II, i, 28, 43–48, 83–85, 148–150, 163–166; II, ii, 224–226, 403–410.

[12] I, 288–292; II, ii, 108–109; III, 114–115, 442–443, 510–511. Byron had used *earth, clay,* and *dust* with the same significance in *Childe Harold* and other poems.

chaotic elements into new forms and his later separation of the family from Paradise. Darkness, evil, and destructive division were tempered by an alternating stress on divine creativeness (6 times), the refrain, "all hail" (9), eternity (2), and the insistence on love and blessing (4). Intermingled too were the opposed materials of earth, sky, and water (5 times).

One of Cain's contradictions, curiosity that was hindered by fear of death, was presented in a scene of darkness, penetrated by light. He related how he lingered at twilight outside Eden and later amid gigantic shadows searched for the unknown, while the only light came from the stars and the fire-armed guards. Fire was a suitable medium for Cain's fear: unspeakable thoughts about death burned his breast.[13]

Since Byron turned the Prince of Darkness into a Light-Bearer, it was fitting that Adah conveyed her impression of him by distinguishing between degrees of light. His beauty was not the dazzling sunny noon of the other angels but the endearing light of the stars, which might be suns. Lucifer naturally claimed the morning star for himself and proudly called it the leader of the host of heaven. When he said that there was a "wisdom in the spirit which directs / To right"—and to resistance of Jehovah—, he compared this force to the attraction that his morning star had for human eyes. And when he announced his perpetual belligerence, he promised to dispute God's power, star by star.[14]

The most fervid tribute to light came from Cain's inventory of beautiful experiences. The moon and stars seemed to be a spirit's world, and the hues of twilight, of sunrise and sunset, transported him out of the body and floated his soul with the sun among the clouds. The imagery of light expressed, with Shelleyean motion and excitement, Cain's aesthetic rapture and idealism—an adoration of beauty that proved the existence of soul—and led to a zenith of ardor inspired by Adah's lovely face.[15]

Just as Cain had twice admired the stars and hoped that they were indestructible, so on the great flight their ethereal glints enabled him to encompass eternity, and he for once hailed God (or the gods) and his works (or accidents). His unexpected intuition of a cosmic force that guided both a star and a firefly was also stimulated by a light image.[16]

[13] I, 84–91, 256–258, 270–281.

[14] I, 489–501, 507–516; II, ii, 437. Recall that in the opening lines Adam and Eve had spoken of Jehovah as the creator of light.

[15] II, ii, 255–269.

[16] Cain's paean to the stars in II, i, 98–132 was only the most excited of his

On the journey through space Byron attenuated the light from the earth to create his narrative perspective, the impression of increasing distance, and to deepen his hero's pessimism, to discourage him with a sense of the littleness of the world and its inhabitants. The light of the earth and its moon diminished to a blue circle and circlet, and as he and Lucifer travelled outward like sunbeams, the earth-light waned, gathered a halo, became a tiny star, and was almost lost among the multitude of other specks. Lucifer had to point out its single sparkle, no brighter than a glow worm at dusk. Three references then followed to the lights that faded until they were gone entirely as they reached Hades. The innumerable lights had kindled a longing to know more, but they also reminded Cain of his mortality. The rapid dwindling of the earth-light had astonished him. "Is yon our earth? . . . Can it be? . . . Where is it? . . . I cannot see it."[17] Later, in retrospect, this shrinking all but maddened him.

The poet complicated the movement from far to farthest, from small to smallest, from substance to phantoms by shifting from images of diminishing light to those of darkness. Marking the transition from the marvellous regions of space to the realm of the dead, he repeated the image of dim shadows several times as the travellers approached and entered Hades. Cain was awed by the dreary twilight of an area that had no sun or moon or star. The obscurity was a disappointment, because he could see and learn little, and then he sank to the nadir of his despair—his death wish. He asked that he be allowed to dwell forever in the shadows.[18]

---

many comments on them in Act II: i, 31–32, 37–43, 181–189; ii, 3–6, 242–246, 255, 360–363. There were three star passages in Act I: 280–284, Lucifer's assurance that they were eternal; 494–502, a joint tribute by Adah and Lucifer; and 512–517, Adah's recollection that their beauty had moved her to tears.

Stars were a common image in Byron's poetry. Since they were the residences of the angels, they were often mentioned in *Heaven and Earth,* e.g., i, 38–40, 80, 87; ii, 3–5, 38, 75–77. In *Sardanapalus* Byron's conception of the hero's character and of the Chaldean religion made allusions to the stars appropriate there: I, ii, 10–11, 122–123, 556–558; II, 5–7, 47–48, 63–70, 169, 243–244, especially 251–268, 346–349. See also Lioni's speech in *Marino Faliero,* IV, i, 68–70, and "Detached Thoughts," *LJ,* V, 458. In *Childe Harold,* III, sts. 88 ff., Byron wrote his most renowned early oration on the stars, with some Wordsworthian intuitions.

[17] II, i, 27–132, 144–145, 167, 173, 176.

[18] II, i, 177–180, 190, 196; II, ii, 1, 11–13, 109 (Adah had used the same biblical image of the shadow of death, I, 470, 167, 175–176).

The most arresting variations in the realm of darkness were Cain's four recollections of the spectacular vistas of light: the "bright populace" of an unimaginable heaven, worlds begirt with light, some emitting sparks, some with luminous belts, brilliant orbs in the sky, too beautiful to have death in them. These radiant memories sustained the wonder of the journey but also intensified the eerie and depressing blackness of Hades. Near the end of the great tour, juxtaposing in his mind the myriads of starry worlds and the appalling murk of death, and tensed by these diametric marvels, Cain made his audacious request that would be the next advance in knowledge: he must look at the residences of Lucifer and Jehovah. Byron thus linked the image-chain of light and darkness to Cain's aspiration.[19]

Back on Cain's troubled little earth, Byron added two more light-dark recollections and electrified both with emotion. When Cain told Adah that he had flown near the sun and plunged into everlasting darkness, had "skirred extinguished worlds," and beheld the "immemorial works / Of endless beings," he drew the inexorable conclusion of his own nothingness. As he recounted for Abel the vision of suns and moons, a light image warned the listener of the turbulence within Cain: his flashing eyes were a dangerous sign.[20]

The double image differentiated husband and wife. Cain felt the gloom under the cypress as a foreboding of death, whereas Adah thought that its shade merely enabled her child to sleep. After an outburst that soon followed, Byron, with his only pseudocolloquial phrasing of a light image, suggested that Cain had partially recovered his control: not for all the stars would he hurt Enoch.[21]

In Act III Byron thrust his dual image into each big situation and aimed it at some consistent attitude or emotion. During the sacrifices Abel's epithet, "Sole Lord of light," was typical of his piety, whereas Cain brought the image down to the natural processes of earth. He offered fruits that had been ripened in the broad sun. Abel's ascending fire signified divine approval, but since it had burned flesh, it enraged Cain, and his wrath burst with a light image: he would not let the bloody record stand in the sun to shame creation. A fire image expressed the murderer's bewilderment: he could not believe that life could be quenched so easily.

[19] II, i, 181–188; II, ii, 3–6, 242–245, 358–368.

[20] III, 56–69, 177–185.

[21] III, 3–8, 128–130. Both Cain and Adah used the word *shadows*.

For Eve's fury, Byron used his favorite lightning: "a livid light / Breaks through as from a thunder cloud." She demanded as retribution that the sun deny Cain its light. When sorrow was the dominant mood, Byron returned to the night cycle. Cain lamented that his crime had darkened the earth. Banishment sent the sinner into an alien and black unknown, and Adah urged that they leave before sunset, since she did not want to walk through the wilderness at night. One glimmer was a solace. Adah, appealing for mercy to the celestial agent of doom, addressed him as "Angel of light," and he granted them a guarantee of safety.[22]

The morning song, which germinated several poetic ideas, might also prepare us for *water* imagery throughout the play. Adam and Eve worshipped the Creator who drew light on the waters out of the darkness of the deep and divided wave from wave. Twice on the great journey, water was a phenomenon that startled a lad who had never seen a large body of it. He flew over the enormous liquid plains of some worlds, and in Hades saw an august apparition of an ocean, that he lamely compared with a stream from Paradise. Byron may have tried to expand Cain's finite eye to an infinite horizon by rocketing from the mundane river to the immeasurable sea of "glorious azure." Comprehension of magnitude was also the purpose of an inept and homely simile: the stars rolled by like leaves along the limpid streams of Eden. More intimately allied with the fundamental ideas of the drama were four psychological water images. Lucifer, foretelling the episode of the apostle who would walk the waters, insinuated that God was a hard bargainer, whereas Lucifer would be magnanimous and conduct his pupil through the air gratuitously. A reader might expect Eve to include a nasty water miracle as a vengeful horror for the murderer (it must turn to blood). With less strain, Byron had Cain, brooding about his guilt, lament that the four rivers of Eden could not cleanse his soul. At the very end, a water image expressed his awareness of the ravage he had done to the future: he had dried up the fountain of a gentle race that might have softened man's soul.[23] Although the water imagery was scattered, the three panoramas were relevant to Cain's education, and the first image in the song and the last four we mentioned were connected with dominant matters—the nature of the two opposed powers and the hero's guilt.

[22] III, 231, 260–262 (a repetition of I, 339), 279–304, 351–352, 390–392, 443, 457–459, 486 ff.

[23] I, 2–7; II, i, 16–22, 99–104, 186–187; II, ii, 178–183; III, 432–433, 522, 557.

The imagery of *division* was more numerous, more powerful, and thoroughly integrated with the dramatic thought and conflict. Again the morning hymn started the sequence: the first three singers chanted about God's manifold divisive work during the creation. Thereafter the image was actively destructive. Zillah's quatrain in the sunrise hymn recalled the expulsion; and six more times in Act I, Cain, Adah, and Lucifer, with sorrow and resentment, stressed the violence of this divorce, which had deprived the family of happiness and eternity. When Cain called Enoch his *disinherited* boy, the sundering image was implicit. It appeared in a different form, still violent and still integral, in Lucifer's boast that he had divided the universe with Jehovah and would continue the battle to sustain that dichotomy. In a more peaceable mood, Cain regretted the split between the two powers, which jarred all elements, and wondered how the incorrigible cleavage had ever occurred. Adah feared that the devil was stepping between her and her husband; separation was the one misfortune she could not endure. Near the end of the fatal day, Eve became a fierce orator of division, calling for her son's complete severance from nature and society. As the outcast departed, Byron came back to positive action: Adah will henceforth divide Cain's burden.[24]

Two minor details in the biblical scene of banishment supplied the imagination of the poet with a spectacle that he firmly related to a single major idea: God had placed the *cherubim* guards at the eastern border of Eden and the "*flaming sword* which turned every way, to keep the way of the tree of life" (3:24). Byron did not alter the biblical story, as one of the old Mysteries had done, and have a cherub drive Adam and Eve out of Eden with flaming sword. Instead he put it into Eve's stormy prophecy of Cain's punishment: "May the swords / And wings of fi'ry cherubim pursue him / By day and night." Here and on five occasions when Cain remembered the "fire-armed angels," Byron retained their biblical significance. Cain always thought of them as instruments of God's power and wrath and his rejection of sinners. They were the barrier God placed between mortal man and eternity (the tree of life). Even when Cain was astounded by the size of the creatures in Hades, taller than the cherub-*guarded* walls of Eden, and by the strangeness of their eyes, "flashing like the fi'ry swords" that *fenced* Paradise, he slipped in a double reference to the obstructive function of these angels and their brilliant weapons.[25]

[24] I, 20, 65–66, 174, 203–205, 348–349, 358, 435, 464–475, 482, 547–554; II, ii, 376–381, 431–440; III, 551.

[25] I, 84–85, 90–91, 173, 274; II, i, 32–33; II, ii, 138–140; III, 425–427. In I,

Byron added the *gate,* the *walls,* and the *battlements* around Eden, which were not biblical, but Miltonic and traditional. These were not ornaments, for they too belonged to the conception of a restrictive deity and became one more grievance, a constant reminder of the prohibition against man's liberty and an obstacle to his aspiration for knowledge and immortality. Cain hated these walls and feared their guardians so intensely that he fancied that he might see, lurking in their shadows, "chequered / By the far-flashing of the cherubs' swords," the great Unknown—Death (I, 270–277).[26]

In the concluding pages of the drama, Byron took three images from the biblical story and merged them with Cain's guilt and remorse. He retained the rebuke that God delivered to Cain: "the voice of thy brother's blood crieth unto me from the ground. And now art thou cursed from the earth, which hath opened her mouth to receive thy brother's blood from thy hand" (4:10–11). To this, the most extraordinary image that Byron lifted from Genesis, he added only a few words (slain, late, drink, rash):

> The voice of thy slain brother's blood cries out
> Ev'n from the ground unto the Lord. Now art thou
> Cursed from the earth, which opened late her mouth
> To drink thy brother's blood from thy rash hand.
>
> III, 470–73

This passage has the sixteenth and seventeenth variations on *blood* that Byron wrote in the last 300 lines of the play. Four more followed—twenty-one in all. The longest stretch without this image of violence comes in the 37 lines from 433 to 470. Several references were to synonyms: "sanguinary incense," "altar without gore," "hands/Incarnadine,"

232–233, the cherubim appeared without their swords but in their prohibitive service. In I, 416–425, they and the seraphim were used for the purpose of contrasting love and knowledge and were here related to another themal conflict. When Adah spoke of the childless cherubs (III, 153) she was thinking as a mother of the human joys of parenthood.

In *Heaven and Earth,* Raphael threatened Azaziel: "the flaming sword, / Which chased the first-born out of Paradise, / Still flashes in the angelic hands" (I, iii, 785–787).

[26] There are at least a half-dozen memories of these guarded walls: I, 85–90, 273; II, i, 32–33; II, ii, 139–140, 266.

and "red" (twice). Only Adah and Abel were not given bloody words. Beginning with line 255 ("If thou lov'st blood"), Cain's first allusions to it were the sinister outbursts of a man revolted by the sacrifice: "How heav'n licks up the flames when thick with blood" of lambs and kids. After the murder, the emotional variations on the image were ingeniously involved with Cain's dazed and gradual realization of his deed, with Zillah's and Adam's cries of shock and horror, with Eve's demand for vengeance ("May the clear rivers turn to blood as he / Stoops down to stain them with his raging lip"), with the Angel's charge of guilt, and finally with Cain's remorse and self-condemnation ("Blood darkens earth and heav'n").[27]

The second remorseful image we have already mentioned—the failure of the four *rivers* to provide ablution of guilt. The symbol that Byron liked best was the *seal* that God stamped on Cain: "The mark that was put upon Cain is a sublime and shadowy act: Goethe would have made more of it than I have done." Byron did do more than quote it. He first associated the mark with Cain's remorse. When the Angel explained that the sign carried exemption "from such deeds as thou hast done," Cain in despair cried, "No, let me die!" Then Byron used the external mark to point to an intense and enduring inner reality. The brand burned Cain's forehead, but the pain was less severe than his mental agony.[28]

Though we have been considering only the patterns of recurrent and interrelated imagery, one isolated metaphor was so conspicuous and so strongly phrased that it merits more than cursory attention. As Cain with

[27] III, 285, 292, 321, 344–346, 361–362, 391–393, 432–433, 491, 521, 530, 559.

[28] III, 493–501, 522. Byron's comment on the mark was recorded by Medwin (p. 129). Though his reports that are not corrobroated by other sources cannot always be trusted, this statement and the one referred to in the preceding essay (n. 13) seem plausible.

Brandes interpreted the mark as a sign of the suffering and immortality of humanity (p. 317).

Chew thought that the episode did not fit Byron's plan and that he or Goethe could have handled it successfully only by "altering the catastrophe so as to bring out the full force of the symbolism behind the act. As it is, the 'seal' of the angel is rather of an anti-climax to Eve's curse" (p. 120). Chew did not explain what he thought the "full force of the symbolism" was or how the catastrophe would have to be altered to bring it out.

W. Paul Elledge's thoughtful article, "Imagery and Theme in Byron's *Cain*," appeared in May, 1966, after I had completed my essay.

his usual excitement told his brother about his journey, Byron drew an auditory image from astronomical lore—the *music* made by the rotating planets—to communicate the impact of a distant ether, which persisted on earth and rendered life there unimportant. The whirlwind of overwhelming earths, moons, and suns, and the loud-voiced spheres, thundering around him, had made Cain unfit for mortal converse (III, 181–184).

The restriction of most of the imagery to the everyday environs that Cain was familiar with and to the tales he had heard from his parents entailed some loss in richness and variety. Since he had seen little of the world and since the action of the drama, until the space flight, was limited, the images were commonplace. Only three were memorable: the cherubim waving their swords, the thunderous music of the spheres, the crying of Abel's blood and the mouth of the earth that opened to drink it. Did Byron confine his imaginative range because he wanted to or because he was lacking in poetic talent? Clouds, the high coloring of sunrise and sunset, and the song of birds entered two speeches of Adah and Cain to show their sensitivity. Another brief mention of bird songs was suggested by Zillah's piety. No one could say, moreover, that Byron neglected the sky and stars. But except for the generic and symbolic trees and fruits, the cypress, the wilderness, and the produce of Cain's offering, Byron ignored the plants and flowers that Cain might have known, and even overlooked the thorn and thistle of the Bible. The animals and insects that Cain spoke of—the glow worm, the firefly, the ewe and its lamb, the stinging scorpion, the lion he wrestled with, Abel's firstlings of the flock, the unforgettable serpent, the ancestors of the mammoth in Hades, the leviathans and other prehistoric monsters—all these were ample for his purpose. Fog, sleet, ice, and wintry gales Cain had never seen. Byron, with an ingenuity he did not repeat, had Lucifer forecast that snow would be a future hardship.

If the imagery was sparse, it was not haphazard, but almost entirely the subject of the hero's thought and feeling, of his observation and memory, or a poetic comment on them, and was therefore merged with his problems and personality. All the pervasive or intermittent images were either thematic or psychological in function, related to the theology (e.g., the doctrines of depravity, punishment, and inherited sin) or to the skeptical indignation about them, to the hero's love of his family and natural beauty, to his aspiration and many dissatisfactions, and to his crime and remorse.

A MEDLEY OF LANGUAGE

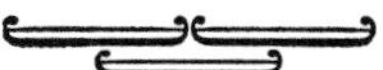

IN THE PREFACE to Cantos I and II of *Childe Harold* Byron stated that, in the manner of James Beattie, he planned to use the Spenserian stanza for different moods. He did try a few lighthearted and satiric passages, excluded most of them from publication, but retained "two stanzas of a buffooning cast on London's Sunday" (I, 68–69).[1] Thomas Moore did not like such interruptions of "a prolonged tone of solemnity by [a] descent into the ludicrous or burlesque." He thought Byron was convinced that the experiment was a failure and did not repeat it in the following cantos of *Childe Harold.*[2] When Byron revived the antithetical design in *Don Juan,* where his intention required an abrupt and systematic alternation of tone, from frivolous or mocking to sober or sentimental and back again, Francis Cohen spoke for those who objected to the mixture of styles, and then Byron defended it on the grounds of realism.[3]

In 1820–1821, as he worked on three historical dramas, he proposed a plain language that was simpler than the rhetoric of *Harold* and the versatility of *Don Juan* and that he thought would create a stylistic unity appropriate to his austere purpose in tragedy. But in *Cain,* he neither

[1] *LJ,* I, 335; *Poetry,* II, 38–40 n., 78–80 n. Some of the phrasing in I, 25–26 and in I, 71–80 on the bullfight was sardonic.

[2] Moore, VIII, 48 n. But see the mockery of art critics in Canto IV, st. 53.

[3] Letter to Murray, August 12, 1819, *LJ,* IV, 341–342.

aimed at nor achieved a homogeneous style. Instead, he mixed various levels of vocabulary and different degrees of structural complexity in his sentences. These levels were so divergent that they did not blend together. Several emotions and conditions may have caused the motley of styles: the disfavor that had doused the verve of 1820 and relaxed the discipline that had tried to forge a neoclassical drama; the religious confusion that had begun in Aberdeen, that made him chafe against the fetters he also felt he must resign himself to, and that ruffled an even flow of expression; the oratorical mode of past centuries and his own linguistic bondage, which tightened his poetic hand whenever he broached a solemn subject; and naturally the haste, mobility, and humor of his daily self that must speak out from time to time.

Titanic Declamation

Of the various manners in *Cain,* the most impressive was the elevated utterance that Byron contrived in the long speeches and that won the plaudits of most reviewers, even those who disapproved of other aspects of the play. The censure of religious doctrine, the revolt against tyranny, and the journey into the tremendous regions of space and past eras required formal, dignified, and massive expression. This style derived from Milton and his imitators and from Byron's own rhetoric in *Manfred* and the last two cantos of *Childe Harold.* Occasionally he tortured a sentence, as he did in Lucifer's crabbed homily on Cain's sinfulness and the misery he would transmit to future generations. The verse is jerky in movement and awkward in phrasing and construction, in spite of Byron's attempt to work out a balanced comparison:

First-born of the first man,
Thy present state of sin—and thou art evil—
Of sorrow—and thou sufferest—are both Eden
In all its innocence compared to what
Thou shortly may'st be; and that state again
In its redoubled wretchedness, a Paradise
To what thy sons' sons' sons, accumulating
In generations like to dust (which they
In fact but add to), shall endure and do.
II, ii, 219–227

The syntax is more obscurely involved than most of the sentence structure of Byron's orotund manner. He did not often use much subordination, but preferred parallelism and a loose chain of coordinate phrases and clauses.

The subject matter of the drama encouraged the declamatory use of polysyllabic diction. The fall of man and its unhappy effects on posterity loaded the poem with many onerous words: *denunciation, prohibited, expulsion, disinherited, destruction, degeneracy, degradation, heaviness, wretchedness, burthensome, miserable, inexorable, inevitable, accumulating, propagating.* The hostility of Cain and Lucifer toward Jehovah and the prevailing negation of the whole drama produced a fund of cumbrous epithets: *omnipotent, independency, immortality, indissoluble, inexplicable, insatiable, inscrutable, irrevocable, extinguished, nothingness, unchangeable, unconscious, unfathomable, unimaginable, unparticipated, unspeakable, unutterable.* The journey in Act II contributed another reservoir of hefty words referring to large quantities and to vast extents of time and space: *myriads, innumerable, unnumbered* (these are three favorites), *boundless, immemorial, enormous, inordinate, immeasurable, immensity, interminable, multitude, magnitude, overpowering, overwhelming.*

Cain's report to Abel about his trip briefly represented at its best the soaring declamation that was a majestic match for the awesome experience he described:

The dead,
Th' immortal, the unbounded, the omnipotent,
The overpow'ring mysteries of space,
Th' innumerable worlds that were and are,
A whirlwind of such overwhelming things,
Suns, moons, and earths, upon their loud-voiced spheres
Singing in thunder round me, as have made me
Unfit for mortal converse.

III, 177–184

A few other excerpts will show how Byron at intervals inflated his vocabulary for stupendous occasions:

And all the unnumbered and innumerable
Multitudes, millions, myriads, which may be,
To inherit agonies accumulated
By ages—

I, 447–450

Oh ye interminable gloomy realms
Of swimming shadows and enormous shapes,
Some fully shown, some indistinct, and all
Mighty and melancholy—

II, ii, 30–33

By a most crushing and inexorable
Destruction and disorder of the elements,

II, ii, 80–81

Of thine omnipotent benevolence,
Inscrutable, but still to be fulfilled

III, 235–236

Byron's endeavor to represent Cain's hysterical confusion after the murder (III, 321–357) resulted in a different kind of rhetoric. No stateliness, no rumbling array of polysyllables, no coherent vehemence, but an explosion, with neurotic shifts of thought and feeling, fractured syntax, stark questions, and wild exclamations.

Since eloquence is best appreciated or depreciated in a capacious and resplendent panoply, the reader is referred to several impassioned speeches: Lucifer's first proclamation of opposition to God, his climactic harangue and final exhortation, Adah's praise of his beauty, the visions of space and of the dead, Cain's angry survey of universal unhappiness, his lament on the plight of future generations, the addresses of the brothers to the Lord, and Eve's malediction.[4]

One could compile another anthology of passages that are more personal and tread less pompously in Byron's public manner, though most of them are as vehement as the first group: Cain's first soliloquy, the criticism of his life and his family and his search for death, Lucifer's disavowal of the Eden temptation and his derision of God's conditional favors, Adah's consternation about human discontent and the devil's captivation, Cain's ardent recollection of beautiful experiences, and his remorseful farewells.[5]

[4] I, 137–166; 438–462, 506–519; II, i, 98–117, 177–190; II, ii, 1–13, 44–62, 132–142, 426–466; III, 17–34, 109–126, 223–279 (two speeches), 419–443.

[5] I, 64–98, 167–191, 218–246, 268–281, 395–413; II, i, 5–25; II, ii, 255–269; III, 506–515, 528–544. The average length of the twenty-three speeches listed here and in note 4 is only about twenty-one lines. The longest—Lucifer's forty lines at the end of Act II—is broken into two parts by Cain's single verse. The next longest

Repetition and Parallelism

The most conspicuous artifice in *Cain* was the iteration of words to underscore parallel structure. Although this pattern was noisy and wooden, Byron associated it with emotional intensity. Passion was channelled into the fixed movement of anaphora, like that of a classical ballet:

Thine eyes are flashing with unnatural light,
Thy cheek is flushed with an unnatural hue,
Thy words are fraught with an unnatural sound.

III, 185–187

Curse him not mother, for he is thy son.
Curse him not mother, for he is my brother
And my betrothed.[6]

III, 405–407

Repetition could become blatant and bulky when the echoes came too close together: "The million millions, / The myriads, the all-peopled earth, / The unpeopled earth, and the o'erpeopled Hell" (I, 521–523). Fortunately such devices were infrequent.[7] Byron was less obtrusive when he fitted a series of similar details or ideas into a parallel design but did not accentuate it by hammering at the same words.

And the unfathomable gulfs of Hades
And the interminable realms of space
And the infinity of endless ages,

II, ii, 433–435

---

is Cain's soliloquy in Act I—thirty-five lines. Since the list is only representative of the declamation in the poem, not every long speech is included; e.g., II, ii, 44–62, 88–105, are omitted.

[6] In II, ii, 23–25, he used the verb *curse* again in similar repetition. See also II, ii, 158–159, for a more quietly phrased parallelism. One of Byron's attempts to use a double Miltonic turn, a special kind of parallelism, was enfeebled by diction that was too banal for unusual treatment: "Mighty yet and beautiful / As the most beautiful and mighty which / Live and yet so unlike them that I scarce / Can call them living" (II, ii, 59–62). More successful was a shorter turn: "Which struck a world to chaos, as a chaos / Subsiding has struck out a world" (II, ii, 82–83).

[7] See III, 114–116, 276–279, and I, 157–163, where Byron's duplication of five words was hard driven. Sometimes repetition lost epigrammatic force because of the sheer weight of the words: "Might satiate the insatiable of life" (III, 81).

The design was a perfect outlet for Cain's impatience. After Lucifer had worked on his jealousy, Cain tried both to conceal and to release his agitation by a counterattack. Lucifer has withheld secret information. In a hurried succession of five parallel statements he reviewed the shattering revelations of the past hour: "[1] Thou hast shown me wonders; [2] thou hast shown me those / Mighty pre-Adamites . . . [3] thou hast pointed out / Myriads of starry worlds . . .; / [4] thou hast shown me shadows / Of . . . Death; [5] thou hast shown me much, / But not all." The structured iteration conveyed the nervousness he was laboring to control and built to the sharp break, *But not all,* that confronted Lucifer with evasiveness. The repetition was a symptom of the urgency that forced Lucifer to face Cain's demand, "Show me where Jehovah dwells." To mask the mechanics Byron placed between the parallel elements four subordinate clauses and three phrases, omitted in our quotation (II, ii, 358–367).

Another natural and convincing exploitation of parallel design for the expression of intensity was Cain's reply to Adah's plea that he make an offering with "a gentle and a contrite spirit." Cain's hot resentment propelled the angry questions: "For what should I be gentle? . . . / . . . For what must I be grateful? / . . . For what should I / Be contrite . . .?" This contrivance was better disguised than that in Cain's earlier excitement with Lucifer because other questions intervened to give Cain's view of living conditions that made gentleness, gratitude, and contrition seem irrational (III, 111–118).

Byron used this technique of dispersion to underplay the mechanics of parallelism in Eve's imprecation (III, 419–443). Here was passionate redundance, in which the specific details were all compulsive variations on a single thought or feeling, which must be vented again and again in different ways until the pressure was released and utterly spent. Eve heaped up a dozen and a half optatives but concentrated on her single furious wish that Cain suffer physical and psychological torment and misfortune. At the end, the desire for his isolation was the unifying base for six concrete variations.

A skeletal rendition of Cain's altar speech will show how Byron sustained the parallel artifice for many lines and involved it elaborately with other matter here omitted. The "inasmuch" clause is retained to illustrate the kind of structure that he used to break the monotony of seven conditional clauses followed by the insolent imperatives:

If thou must be propitiated with prayers,
Take them. If thou must be induced with altars
And softened with a sacrifice, receive them....
If thou lov'st blood, the shepherd's shrine...
... hath shed it for thy service,...
Or if the sweet and blooming fruits... /... may seem
Good to thee, inasmuch as they have not
Suffered in limb or life...
... if a shrine without victim
And altar without gore may win thy favour,
Look on it....
... If he's evil, / Strike him....
... If he be good, / Strike him or spare him as thou wilt, ...

III, 251–273

Inversion

We might expect Byron to use inversion, for this device would be consistent with other aspects of his formal declamation. But the contrary is true. Inversion was so rare as to be exceptional. He occasionally transposed the noun and adjective, especially when the latter was polysyllabic: "Thoughts unspeakable," "lights innumerable," "fruit forbidden." That his purpose was rhythmical is apparent if the inversion is read in its context: ". . . He hangs his guilty head / And covers his ferocious eye with hands / Incarnadine." Even less common was the inversion of subjet and verb: "Never till / Now met I aught to sympathise with me."[8]

One kind of inversion Byron did like—the use of *not* after a verb, especially with imperatives. In Act I there were over twenty like these: blaspheme not, tarry not, shrink not, tempt me not, sinned not, he who bows not. Another minor formality was a hortatory cliché that he seldom used: ". . . let me not see renewed / My misery in thine. . . . / Let me not see my offspring fall. . . . / . . . let us hence, . . ." (I, 40–47). These formal constructions had a terse, archaic vigor that hurried us away from some of the heavier lines.

Biblical Imitation

Byron's major stylistic blunder in *Cain* was his abundant use of bibli-

[8] The inversions quoted in this paragraph are to be found, in the order mentioned, in I, 256; II, i, 178; II, ii, 25; III, 397–399; II, ii, 303–305; I, 189–190.

cal archaisms. Modern as he could be in *Beppo* and *Don Juan* and in parts of *Cain* and other plays, he seemed bound by the tradition that there must be at least an intermittent display of biblical forms in a serious literary work dealing with a sacred situation. His *thou's, thee's, thy's,* and *thine's* are tiresome enough, but the biblical verbs are an ungainly irritation. Since dialogue requires the use of the second person when people are talking to each other, *art, dost, hast, canst, didst, wouldst, wert,* and *wilt* turn up everywhere, along with *doth, hath,* and too many dissonant verbs ending in *st* and *est—beholdest, steppest, pretendest, saidst, sufferest*—and a scattering of third person verbs that use *eth* or *th—commandeth, dresseth, saith, soundeth.* He did not often put together such ugly combinations as "This spirit curseth us."[9] Byron may have felt that he was conscientious in his scriptural usage, but occasionally one suspects that a biblical suffix was convenient padding when he needed an extra syllable. In the following line, *lieth* seems an affectation that merely filled out the verse: "And he who lieth there was childless. I / Have dried. . . ." (III, 556–557).

In the first 205 lines of Act I Byron used forty-five archaic pronouns and thirty-three archaic verb forms. Three such words turn ten monosyllables, which step along with a fair degree of ease, into a plodding and thick-sounding verse:

> And had you not been fit by your own soul
> And *hadst thou* not been fit by *thine* own soul
> (I, 192, italics mine)

There could be no compromise. Having decided to use the jargon, he could not avoid a clumsy phrase even when making the simplest statement: "You had never bent" or "You ne'er had bent" must become "Thou ne'er hadst bent" (I, 327). When the archaic form occurred with an inversion, then the awkwardness was compounded: "Saidst thou not," "seest thou not," "Thou hast laboured not," "where dwellest thou."

[9] I, 525. Such phrasing does set our teeth on edge. In a fine paragraph on Byron's language in *Cain,* Bostetter surmised that the scriptural subject tempted the poet into Miltonic and biblical imitation: "he couched his revolt against the traditional order in the most traditional of styles." Bostetter thought that the verbal formulas comprised Byron's "indictment of the tyrant-god" and that both the pseudoclassical rhetoric and the biblical jargon were unsuitable media for a poem of revolt (p. 575).

Worst of all was his compression of many biblical verbs: "look'st almost," "what mean'st thou," "thou breath'st" (see the section on contraction).

At times he either forgot or reduced his scriptural machinery. In the first 205 lines, three descriptive and reflective speeches (64–97, 136–191) are a relief. This kind of natural oasis recurred throughout the play, and stylistic alternation happened on a small scale too, every few lines in some places. He continued to use the common pronominal and verbal forms: "you have forgotten" instead of "thou hast forgotten," "you know," "he seems." One can find lines that contain the antique and the modern side by side: "Our father / *Saith* that he *has* beheld" (I, 502–503, italics mine).

Colloquialism

The ordinary speech and familiar idiom, which Byron intermingled with formal elevation and biblical archaism, were perhaps the spontaneous result of three impulses: (1) a semiconscious levity that well accorded with the spirit, if not with the language, of his earnest flouting of reverent canons; (2) his personal identification with the emotional experience that he created for his people; and (3) his intention to present this experience as relevant to contemporary life. The simplicity that he strove for in the historical plays and the conversational mode of *Beppo* and *Don Juan,* that was his natural and most trenchant medium, kept breaking into the dialogue of *Cain* and alternating with magniloquence and the unwieldy biblical forms.

Byron rarely sustained this plain talk for long. It appeared most of the time in single lines—low sinkings that some reviewers did not like:

> I'm glad of that. I would not have them die . . .
> I'm sorry for it . . .
> Say, what have we here? . . .
> What is that / To us? They sinned, then let them die! . . .
> I'm sick at heart, but it will pass . . .
> 'Twere better that he never had been born . . .
> But we who see the truth must speak it . . .
> Many of the same kind, at least so called . . .[10]

A single word, like a conversational *why* and *what,* can suddenly take us from the environs of Eden to London parks and streets: "Why, I have

[10] I, 283; II, ii, 332; III, 95, 75–76; I, 58; III, 136; I, 240; II, ii, 200.

seen the fireflies," "Why, what are things?" "His lips too are apart; why then he breathes."[11]

Just as Byron at times shifted within a verse from an archaic to a modern verb form, so too he could follow a speech idiom with a phrase that he had heard only from the pulpit: "*What if* I show *to thee* things which have died" (II, i, 141, italics mine). Sometimes it is the colloquial word and not the antiquated one that seems to be a mistake. In one of the lines where he stayed close to the phrasing in Genesis, his biblical diction is harmonious:

> Genesis: ". . . it shall come to pass that every one that findeth me shall slay me" (4:14).
> Byron: "'Twill come to pass that whoso findeth him / Shall slay him" (III, 481–482).

Byron's *findeth,* which he retained, and *whoso,* which he added, blend with the scriptural formula, "it shall come to pass that," but here metrics probably caused him to use a bookish contraction that sounds wrong in the context: "'Twill come to pass . . ."

Byron relied on simplicity of sentence structure more often than on vocabulary to convey a realistic effect, to speed up the movement of his verse, and to counteract the sluggishness imposed by heavy and archaic diction. As Cain soliloquized (I, 64–98) about his discontent with past and present circumstance and then about his wonder at the approach of Lucifer he used short predications, abrupt questions, and exclamations. The clauses became longer when he described the angels that guarded Paradise. In Act III the gasping segments were a perfect medium for Cain's bewilderment after the murder.

An oral pattern was valuable when it lightened some theological discussion, where the subject and language were general and abstract. In the following passage, note the short predications and interrogations, the natural speech order and syntax, the simple coordination of clauses with *and,* the detached verbal unit, *he being good,* and the ellipsis *Strange good that*:

[11] II, i, 123, 137; III, 339. The scattered colloquial phrases are appropriate to the "levity and flippancy" that Stavrou found in Byron's preface and that he thought made *Cain* "a Bayle-like polemic against that part of Christianity which was anathema to Byron . . ." (p. 153).

Why do I exist?
Why art *thou* wretched? Why are all things so?
Ev'n he who made us must be, as the Maker
Of things unhappy! To produce destruction
Can surely never be the task of joy,
And yet my sire says he's omnipotent.
Then why is evil, he being good? I asked
This question of my father, and he said,
Because this evil only was the path
To good. Strange good that must arise from out
Its deadly opposite.

II, ii, 279–289

Some formal literary elements remained: the inversion, *Of things unhappy*; the infinitive phrase as subject of the verb, *To produce destruction;* and the customary *art thou.*

More effective was the application of colloquial structure to concrete topics. In one fine passage, Cain brought the mystery of death down to the domestic circle and told how his family reacted to its terror. Here he was talking seriously about common behavior, and Byron achieved a perfect blend of tangible matter, specific, monosyllabic diction, and the coordination of short clauses. In this setting, the final inversion does not seem unnatural:

My father
Says he is something dreadful, and my mother
Weeps when he's named, and Abel lifts his eyes
To heav'n and Zillah casts hers to the earth
And sighs a prayer, and Adah looks on me
And speaks not.

I, 251–256

A few lines later, when Cain remembered a childhood incident, Byron again, both in sentence pattern and in diction, matched the colloquial style to the subject: "Could I wrestle with him? / I wrestled with the lion when a boy / In play till he ran roaring from my gripe" (I, 259–261). Another pastoral episode is too long to quote—the suffering and cure of the suckling lamb stung by a reptile (II, ii, 289–305). In the narrative, Byron used the straightforward structure and sensory words of plain talk, flawed by some sentimental and literary adjectives (*poor* suckling, *vain* and *piteous* bleating, *helpless* wretch, *tremulous* mother). Characteristic of his sudden variation are the last three lines of the passage that rise to the rolling manner of the public orator: "Purchase renewal of its little life / With agonies unutterable, though / Dispelled by antidotes."

Just as successful is the often praised discourse of Adah over the sleeping Enoch (III, 137–156). The words are simple and many are sensory, and the sentences move in parallel coordinates. There are only four brief subordinate clauses, eight biblical forms, and one imperative inversion (*talk not*).

The exclamation *Oh God* was reverential in the opening prayer and in Adam's "Oh God! why didst thou plant the tree of knowledge?" (I, 32). But the following were expletives, devoid of religious feeling (three by Adah and one by Cain), that Byron himself might have uttered in moments of alarm, distress, or irritation:[12]

Oh my God! / Shall they not love . . .
Alone! Oh my God! / Who could be happy and alone . . .
Oh my God! / Touch not the child . . .
Oh God, I dare not think on't . . .[13]

Byron's oral style in *Cain* was best when he achieved a lean dignity with a large proportion of monosyllables:

Nor hand it down to those who spring from him . . .
And from the face of God shall he be hid . . .
I must not, dare not touch what I have made thee . . .[14]

Many lines had only one ordinary dissyllable:

All bonds I break between us, as he broke . . .
And now that it begins let it be borne . . .
And I who have shed blood cannot shed tears . . .
I will not leave thee lonely with the dead. . . .[15]

When Byron swelled into formal rhetoric with an inverted order of archaic words, the monosyllables simplified the verse: "Stern hast thou been and

[12] Cain's "Oh God! Oh God!" in III, 333, after the murder is a dubious instance. It may be an appeal, but I doubt that Byron so intended it.

[13] I, 367–368, 472–473; III, 126–127; II, ii, 18.

[14] III, 84, 479, 534.

[15] III, 410, 416, 521, 527.

stubborn from the womb" (III, 503). In the last 118 lines of the play, 23 were completely monosyllabic and 48 others were predominately so, with no more than one polysyllable (*brother, father, upon, within, return, taken*).[16]

In our discussion of Byron's formal style, we stressed the long declamations, but these take up only 759 lines. Three-fifths of the drama (58% or 1035 lines) is a dialogue with short speeches, none of which exceed 8 lines. These give the impression that the people are conversing and not haranguing each other. In these quick exchanges, even with biblical words, the tone is colloquial because the sentence structure is direct and often fragmentary and elliptical. The first of these occasions comes near the beginning of the play when Adam chides his son for not joining in the family prayer (I, 22–35). After Lucifer's arrival, there are patches of talk where no speech is longer than 3 lines.[17] In Act II, i, 118–205, except for two speeches of 12 and 15 lines, the dialogue is again broken into many questions and brief replies and exclamations.[18] The splitting of a single verse among two or three speakers is another artifice that resembles the natural interruptions of talk.[19]

Contraction

Metrics account for some of Byrons' vagaries:

> I pity thee who lovest what must perish.
> And I thee who lov'st nothing. And thy brother . . .
> II, ii, 337–338

[16] The proportion increases in some parts; sixteen of the twenty-five lines of Eve's curse (419–443) and twenty-seven of the thirty-five lines of Cain's two distracted speeches after the murder (321–333, 336–357) are mainly monosyllabic. This is true also of the first sixty of Act III, and of twenty in another passage from line 75 to line 115. In all these lines, the polysyllables are commonplace.

[17] I, 98–104, 109–136, 288–357, 519–529.

[18] At intervals in Act II, ii, Byron interrupts the longer declamations with brief exchanges: 62–87, 142–177, 337–355, 388–400. Arthur M. Norman ("Dialogue in Byron's Dramas," *N&Q*, n.s. I [July, 1954], 304–306) and Oliver Elton (II, 165) liked the staccato effect of such animated talk. Norman thought it would be effective in the theatre. Elton: "And the action is kept moving by the device of quick and instantaneous retorts, which ricochet in the dialogues with Lucifer and Abel." Such conversation "shows no failure in dignity, and it is more satisfactory than the grandiose visions of the pre-Adamite inhabitants of Earth."

[19] See "A Metrical Heresy" for data on this technique.

In line 337, he was able to use *lovest* and have one of his main patterns—the eleven-syllable verse with feminine ending. In order to repeat this pattern in 338, he shortened on the MS the same verb (*lov'st*) that he had used in its full form in 337; and all editors have retained this inconsistency, which apparently was determined only by metrical law.[20]

One can find on the MS and in various editions both the contracted and the uncontracted forms of the biblical second person of many verbs: *livest, look'st, sayest, say'st, show'st, madest, mad'st, seemest, seem'st.* Prosodic concern always seemed to cause this inconsistency. Byron's rhythmic pulse was demanding, but he was sometimes either deaf to, or careless about, euphony. Some contractions that were made for metrical reasons have an ugly sound that must be hard on keen ears: *know'st, think'st, speak'st, slew'st.* These words were a strange and unsuccessful fusion of two styles—the starched and solemn unworldliness of biblical archaism and the short cuts of modern speech—whenever he wanted to curtail a line.

A large number of pronominal contractions that are common in ordinary talk were more suitable for *Don Juan* than for some of the formal contexts of *Cain.* The first and third person singular pronouns merged with *will, would,* and forms of *to be*: *I'll, I'm, I'd, he'll, he'd, he's, 'tis* (by far the most common), *'twas, 'twere, 'twill, 'twould.* The full forms also occurred, because rhetoric and metrics could check the colloquial habit. In the rare incongruity of *thou'lt,* Byron tried to impose a colloquial form on an archaic expression (*thou wilt*).

Some compressions he never did use. Those with *have* (*I've, you've*) were not part of his vocabulary: "Of which I have heard," "I have done this," "I have heard it said." Such combinations sound clumsy beside their oral equivalents (I've heard, I've done this, I've heard it said) and beside some relaxed phrasing that Byron did use: "I'm sick at heart," "he'd have us so," "I'll not believe it." There was again little consistency. He wrote *is't*, but not *we're*, though the latter seems metrically preferable to *we are* in the following line: "For then we are [we're] all alike, is't not so, Cain?"[21]

[20] Line 337 is completely iambic. The metrical variations in the second and third feet of 338 are common in *Cain.* Had Byron used *lovest* in 338, he would have had a twelve-syllable line with variation in three feet. This kind of line, though not frequent in *Cain,* is not unusual.

[21] The quotations in this paragraph can be found in II, i, 62; II, ii, 250; I, 420, 58, 143; II, ii, 238; III, 143.

Other reductions—*o'er, e'er* (*ne'er*) and all of its compounds, *whate'er, whatso'er, where'er, whene'er*—appeared so frequently on the MS that their full form was a rarity (except for *never*). *There's, on't* and *'twixt* occurred at least once and *'gainst* twice.[22]

In another category of contractions, also directed by Byron's metrical and colloquial interest, the vowel *e* was sloughed before suffixes of certain groups of nouns, adjectives, and verbals. The manuscript offered no guidance here, but the first edition did. One numerous group ends in *ering, eling,* and *ening*. The first edition printed *cov'ring, grov'ling,* and *off'ring*. But this and later editions frequently did not so spell these words even in similar metrical circumstances. For instance, *offering,* the most common of this group, if pronounced *off'ring*, almost always gave a better scansion, but the editions did not often contract it.[23]

Another group omitted *e* in a final unaccented *er* and *en*, and before *ry*: *bow'r flow'rs, pow'r, driv'n, giv'n, heav'n, sev'n, fall'n, ev'ry, fi'ry, myst'ry, slav'ry.*[24] The first edition pointed to the shortening with sporadic apostrophes: *giv'n* and *heav'n*. One word was contracted in two ways, *e'en, ev'n,* and was always a monosyllable, though it usually appeared as *even*. The 1821 printing of *flatt'rer* was unpleasant, but most editors have kept it. We should keep in mind that these were exceptional mark-

[22] II, ii, 18, 26, 214; III, 125, 462. Byron always spelled *e'er, ne'er, o'er* without an apostrophe, which, however, he did consistently use in biblical contractions that are spelled without an apostrophe: *ar't, can'st, could'st, did'st, do'st, had'st, ha'st.* Another idiosyncrasy was that he almost always misplaced it, putting it between the *s* and *t*: *cans't, dos't.* His editors, of course, omitted it entirely in these words, although they sometimes did print *could'st.* Byron also wrote *it's* when he meant the possessive *its.*

[23] See I, 117, 292; III, 284. Others are *flutt'ring* (I, 411), *flatt'ring* (III, 72), *suff'ring* (II, i, 96), and *wand'ring* (III, 164). None of these have been so printed, however. Exceptions are *suffering* (I, 158), *fastening* (I, 410), and *offering's* (III, 286), for which in the cited lines the meter requires full measure. Since *reddening* (III, 26) and *widening* (II, i, 203) are usually dissyllabic, contraction need not be indicated.

[24] There are some exceptions: *misery* seems to be given full measure in I, 41, 156, 179, and III, 123, and *mystery* likewise in I, 460; II, i, 140; III, 179. *Sullen* in I, 239 is not contracted. Most of the time the metrical reading gives *Eden* two syllables (e.g., II, i, 170; III, 73), but it could be monosyllabic in II, ii, 149, and be read as either one or two syllables in the terminal position, e.g., I, 66, 391; II, i, 104; III, 40. Some past participles ending in *en* are not usually contracted: *begotten* (III, 506), *forgotten* (II, ii, 148), and *forbidden* (II, ii, 25, 152; III, 34).

ings. The informal pronunciation seemed called for almost every time the words in this group occurred, but the editions did not indicate it. At least once the 1821 edition used an apostrophe when it was not needed to indicate a customary monosyllabic reading: *pray'rs.*[25]

Then there is a group of concealed (unmarked) contractions. In words with certain suffixes, syllabic shortening occurs in speech and in the scansion of Byron's verse, but the apostrophe is unsuitable because no vowel is dropped. In these words the unaccented *e* or *i* before the suffix is transmuted, as in the pronunciation of *brilliant,* into something like the *y sound* in *young*: *beauteous, bounteous, curious, glorious, impious, various.* All these become dissyllabic. The following with different suffixes have in common with the preceding list of words a transmutation of the vowel sound when the final two syllables are fused: *aërial, continual, ethereal, inferior, superior, material, mutual, unnatural. Myriad,* one of Byron's favorite words in *Cain,* is always telescoped into two syllables when the verse is scanned.

An associated group comprises the comparative and superlative degrees of adjectives ending in *y*: *earlier, earliest, mightier, happier, loftier, loveliest.*[26] All these could be dissyllabic in the cited lines, though the slurring of the unstressed *i* may be uncouth to some ears.

There are limits to the submersion of unaccented mid-vowels. One reader has suggested that the *e* is silent in *innumerable,* cutting that word to four syllables and in II, i, 178 giving us an iambic pentameter verse. Such shortening is unsatisfactory in I, 159, and in other places, where it results in nine-syllable lines.[27] It might seem possible to pronounce some analogous words like *interminable, unimaginable, inexorable,* and *unutterable* as if they were contracted: *interm'nable, unimag'nable, inex'rable, unutt'rable*; but with one exception this truncates the verse and does not improve the scansion.[28] Metrics can thus be a guide to the feasibility of contraction. Shortening of *innumerable* and similar words is inadvisable if it creates an unnecessary irregularity.

Elision is a related practice, common in earlier poetry, but the *Cain* MS and the editors ignore this possibility. Yet in nine lines a rhythmic

[25] III, 374, 285, 360; II, ii, 281; III, 290, 291. See Variants for I, 44.

[26] I, 186, 236, 93, 145, 417–418; II, ii, 251.

[27] This happens in I, 457, and II, i, 120. Contraction of *innumerable* is possible in II, ii, 41 and 243, but of doubtful usefulness in II, i, 41 and III, 180, where it can be shortened only if the elision of *the* is omitted.

[28] The words occur in II, i, 102; II, ii, 6, 30, 80, 304, 434; III, 377.

reading merges the definite article *the* with an unaccented syllable beginning with a vowel, especially *e*: *Th' Eternal, th' erect, th' Invisible, th' immortal.*[29]

The many oral and metrical compressions, the clumsy shortening of the biblical second-person form of the present tense, the pronominal contractions, the dropping of mid *e* before several suffixes and in some final syllables, the elisions, and the numerous unmarked and hidden reductions, especially those that used a *y* sound—all these had a definite effect on the pronunciation of Byron's language in *Cain.* Sometimes they harshened the sound, but often they lightened and speeded up the cadence, and varied the tone with the familiar mode and idiom of common talk.

Energy

Both the colloquial and the oratorical styles used active verbs. The biblical legend of the tree-fruits gave Byron one group that he drew upon repeatedly: *plant, till, toil, ripen, cull, feed upon,* and his two favorites, *pluck* and *snatch.* The two disastrous crimes provided him with another vigorous group—verbs of violence, expulsion, punishment, and destruction. Then since Byron included a conflict between two eternal principles and rebellion in two of his characters, and since he conceived of both of them as dynamic personalities, and one as intensely emotional, we can see why energetic verbs animate a large number of lines. Lucifer's description of the successive destruction of worlds also contributed its share of violence in Act II.[30]

Byron's ardent temperament and his customary manner of impassioned expression inevitably directed the activity of the phrasing in this drama. Both Byron and Cain would see things *swim* in visions and feel that thoughts were *crowding* and *burning* within them. Byron and his fictional people were proud and could not endure *grov'ling,* and so he will use *bow* five times in seven lines (I, 311–317) and *bend* twice in the next ten (318, 327).

We have observed that some of Byron's formal and abstract theological

[29] I, 55, and III, 402; II, i, 173; I, 499, 500; II, ii, 92. Other elisions are *th' innumerable,* II, i, 178; III, 180; *th' exemption,* III, 247.

[30] In addition to the nine mentioned earlier in the paragraph, the following are typical of Byron's verbs in *Cain: assail, battle, blow, break bonds, burn, cast down, crush, dash against, depart, destroy, drive, extinguish, fall, go or carry forth, jar, madden, pursue, quail, quake, quench, scatter, scorch, shake, shun, shut out, smite, sting, strew, strike, thrust, torture, tremble, war, wreck.*

discussion is almost torpid and that archaic words stiffen many a line. But the vigor of his nouns and verbs and his stylistic variations tend to submerge these demerits. The energy inherent in the social rebellion and in Byron's conception of Cain and Lucifer is expressed not only through single words but through the total treatment of the dialogue and the situations. In the passages that are notable for vigor, in the fervid declamations, from Cain's soliloquy of dissatisfaction and surprise to his frenzy after the murder, in the many short conversational exchanges, and in the several recollections of physical circumstance, the energy is the composite result of the substance (physical, emotional, or intellectual) and of the particular forms of expression: the vibrant questions and exclamations, the vocabulary of common talk, the contractions, the broken sentences, the firm march of monosyllables, the sonority of the polysyllables, and the rugged rhythms.

A METRICAL HERESY

THE FEW CONTEMPORARY REVIEWERS who commented on the language and verse of *Cain* and of Byron's other plays disparaged them. Some critics conceded that in the best passages of *Cain,* Byron's verse had "harmony," "great weight and energy," but Jeffrey complained that it lacked "the sweetness of versification for which [Byron] used to be distinguished," and that its movement was gauche and unmusical.[1] *The Monthly Magazine* surmised that the poet might have made prose drafts, which he then turned, "by a summary process, into blank verse." His roughness was inadmissible in "any composition which purports to be governed by even the loosest laws of poetical rhyme."[2] Oxoniensis, *The British Review,* and the *Quarterly* also thought that the verse often read like prose chopped into lines of ten syllables. John Matthews in *Blackwood's* specified one mannerism: "We continually meet with lines terminating most unhappily in some miserable conjunction or preposition—with some feeble auxiliary of a verb, or by some presuming adjective, which usurps this post in the verse, and suffers its tardy substantive lamely to limp behind in the follow-

[1] *The Edinburgh Review,* XXXVI, 419–420.

[2] *The Monthly Magazine,* LIII (February, 1822), 15.

ing line."[3] Bishop Reginald Heber found this practice so frequent as to be systematic and thought that it enfeebled Byron's verse.[4]

The same objection was argued by George Darley in one of a series of six articles he wrote in 1823 for *The London Magazine.* Byron, he charged, had demolished the identity of the single line.[5] He reproduced eleven lines from *The Two Foscari* and let the coincidence of a major pause and a strongly stressed word determine the length of a verse. The result was that he printed only four lines as Byron wrote them and jumbled the rest together as prose sentences. Darley defined two technical lapses that produced this muddle: "the neglecting [of] final emphases and pauses." He recalled that Beaumont, Fletcher, and Massinger had been earlier offenders. Massinger's habit of varying the length of his lines also irritated Darley: "speeches [were] often wholly indivisible into pentameters by any device of printing or capitals, unless lines could be divided in the middle of a word." He quoted a passage from *A New Way to Pay Old Debts* (I, 2) as an illustration of an "awkward medley of verse and prose."

Halfway through his article, Darley enunciated the prosody that he and his contemporaries accepted as essential for blank verse, and then he described the current violations that he detested:

> If the standard poetry of our nation be examined, it will be found that, for the most part, there is a pause of greater or less duration at the end of every line, whether indicated by a stop or not. It will also be found that a sounding word generally closes each verse. And it is the due attention to make

[3] *Blackwood's Edinburgh Magazine,* "Lord Byron," XI (February, 1822), 215. Matthews scolded Byron again for the same habit and quoted III, 240–242, as a sample (p. 217). See also Oxoniensis (*A Remonstrance Addressed to Mr. John Murray, Respecting a Recent Publication,* p. 10). The censure of *The British Review* was directed at the verse of *Sardanapalus,* but the writer made it clear that his criticism could be applied to the other plays. He wrote that he had always doubted the correctness of Byron's poetic ear (XIX [December, 1822], 78–82).

[4] *The Quarterly Review,* XXVII (July, 1822), 490. For these and other opinions on Byron's prosody see "The Major Periodicals and Pamphlets."

[5] Though he briefly deprecated Byron's "prose-poetry" and "false method of versification" in his second letter (*The London Magazine,* VIII [August, 1823], 130–131), he developed his criticism fully in the "Fifth Letter" ([November, 1823], 533–538). For these articles George Darley used the pseudonym of "John Lacy." Josephine Bauer, *The London Magazine, 1820–29,* I, 89, 269, 310; Elmer L. Brooks, "Byron and the *London Magazine,*" *K-SJ,* V (1956), 56–58.

> these pauses of a certain perceptible duration, and to introduce these sounding closes, which confers dignity, grandeur, and strength on the verse. In contradistinction to this, if the prevailing poetry of the day be inspected, we shall find that the lines perpetually run into one another without any pause at all, the final word of this line not being disjoined by any perceptible division of time from the first word of the succeeding; and also, that the verses frequently end with words neither emphatic nor sonorous. So that no difference whatever exists between such versification and sweet weak prose, but a certain superfluity of capital letters squandered over the page. (p. 534)

Although Darley took credit for being the first to discover that "the majesty of English verse depends on final *pauses* as well as final emphatic syllables," the few quotations I gave at the beginning of this essay show that he only voiced the prevailing bias of his time and phrased it more precisely than the major reviewers did. He noted two refinements that others missed: (1) "the most insignificant words, such as *on, of, which,* may properly enough end our most heroic lines, if followed by a pause of perceptible duration." He quoted a few lines from *Othello* (III, iii, 453–456) to illustrate this possibility. (2) "The most significant and sounding words may close our lines improperly, i.e. when *not* followed by a pause in recitation." He then quoted from *Sardanapalus* and explained how the lack of a pause after the word *strong* (I, ii, 503) deadened one's awareness of the metrics. Darley quoted from four of Byron's dramas to illustrate his views, but not a single line from *Cain.*

The most abusive and entertaining part of Darley's essay was his impeachment of Byron as "the arch-patron and propagator of this degenerate system" of prose-poetry, "this un-British school of versification," that undermined "our energetic laws of verse." Since he could not convict Byron of being a disciple of the Jacobean dramatists, he became a metrical chauvinist and traced the origin of Byron's deterioration to a foreign land. Standing steadfast on the theory that terminal stress-and-pause was native to British prosody and gave British verse its manly strength, its "firm and stately tread of numbers," Darley accused Byron of unpatriotically following an Italian fashion. Byron's fame and talent had given currency to a soft, suave, and languid effeminancy that depraved the British ear and debased its "numbers." So he became "the greatest enemy of its poetry [our] country ever had," and had "given *that* a blow [from] which I fear it will never recover" (p. 536).

Darley's six long articles covered a large number of plays and a wide area of subjects—credibility of plot and character, naturalness and eloquence of language, as well as firmness of versification. His conservative criteria reflected the ordinary literary judgment of Byron's day. He did not quote from *Manfred,* and had he looked carefully at it, he might have praised the steadier pace of its lines and opined that since Byron had finished it soon after he settled in Venice, the lazy Italian disease had not yet infected Byron's poetry. Samuel Chew wrote in 1915 that he had scanned the entire play, and though he backed his conclusions with almost no evidence, he reported that the results of his examination were "what one would expect from a poet unaccustomed to blank verse"—all lines were quite regular except for three that were fragmentary and one that was hypermetric (III, 3, 9) and that Chew misread, for Byron often treated "wandering" as dissyllabic. Chew's generalizations would have pleased the reviewers of 1822–1823: "harsh and irregular enjambment is avoided, there are very few double feminine endings and weak endings, and the employment of syllabic substitution is very timid" (pp. 84–85 n.).

Chew's observations, however, were probably inexact and misleading. For instance, five of the last eight lines of the Abbot's final speech in the first scene of Act III have eleven syllables and light endings, and three of them are run-on. Though the blank verse of *Manfred* certainly did not crumble into the looseness of Massinger and Fletcher, I suspect that it was less monotonous than Chew asserted. In the historical play, as contemporary readers noticed, Byron broke away from the moderate formality of the *Manfred* prosody. In *Cain* he was even more sophisticated in his metrical variety than in the earlier dramas. But the reviewers, who did not consider this variety sophisticated, and who advocated a solid tread, that they insisted was indigenous to British verse, began a tradition that has continued to the present time. Critics and literary historians of the later nineteenth and early twentieth centuries—Swinburne, Roden Noel, John Nichols, W. P. Trent, Stephen Phillips, Arthur Symons, John Churton Collins, F. W. Moorman, Sir Arthur Quiller-Couch, Oliver Elton, C. H. Herford, and R. D. Havens—even though most of them praised some aspects of Byron's poetry, all abominated his blank verse. It had neither verve nor grace nor flexibility nor melody nor resonance. It was inept, defective, loose-jointed, halting, and discordant—their favorite words for it were *slipshod* and *execrable*—and it was generally indistinguishable from his prose. Like their predecessors, they shook their heads over the lines that ended with "the awkwardest of monosyllabic parts of speech, 'ands,' 'ofs,' etc.," (Noel), and Quiller-Couch accused Byron of having no sense for the slide of the cesura. Noel deprecated the verse of Byron's drama as "the worst ever written by a great poet," and Herford asserted that no one of comparable stature ever stammered over verse "so unutterably blank as his." Byron had a poor metrical ear, or none at all, and no technical capacity for the form. He had broken down the language of poetry so thoroughly that it sank to a level "not even that of good prose" (Symons).

Courthope, however, declared that the "free movement" of his verse proved "his acquaintance with the best models of English dramatic writing." Saintsbury, who usually disapproved of Byron on all scores, wrote that "his blank verse . . . could be very fine" and was an interesting variety of "an unrimed heroic with a certain, but not large, admixture of the newer style." Perhaps Saintsbury was thinking only of "The Dream," "Darkness," or parts of *Manfred.* Oliver Elton was more judicious in stating that, although Byron at times marred and mauled this measure and used it for a "dreary kind of rhetoric," nevertheless his blank verse had been underrated, and in *Cain,* he on occasion caught Milton's ring and also in some of the impassioned declamations composed a music of his own.[6]

The most recent verdicts have reiterated the older opinion. Paul West called the versification sloppy, "careless prose put in layers," and he too objected to lines that ended with prepositions.[7] G. Wilson Knight turned

[6] Algernon Charles Swinburne, *The Complete Works,* 1866 essay, XV, 127; 1884 essay, XIV, 177–178, where he wrote a parody of Byron's verse; Noel, *Essays,* pp. 96, 103; Noel, *Life,* p. 164; John Nichol, *Byron,* p. 207; W. P. Trent, "The Byron Revival" in *The Authority of Criticism,* p. 231; Stephen Phillips, "The Poetry of Byron," *The Cornhill,* LXXVII (January, 1898), 24; Arthur Symons, *The Romantic Movement in English Poetry,* p. 255; J. Churton Collins, "The Collected Works of Lord Byron" in *Studies in Poetry and Criticism,* pp. 90, 120; Moorman, XII, 49; Sir Arthur Quiller-Couch, "Byron" in *Studies in Literature,* pp. 12–13; C. H. Herford, *The Age of Wordsworth,* p. 230; Havens, p. 232; Courthope, VI, 270; George Saintsbury, "The Prosody of the Nineteenth Century" in *The Cambridge History of English Literature,* XIII, 261 (he made no comment on Byron's dramatic verse in Vol. III of *A History of English Prosody*); Elton, II, 159, 163–165.

[7] Paul West, *Byron and the Spoiler's Art,* pp. 108–109.

such venerable censure to an advantage by recommending that the verse be read as prose.[8] Though this worked fairly well with some parts of the plays, I believe that it would do Byron an unpoetic disservice with large portions of *Cain.*

In 1812 Byron wrote Caroline Lamb that blank verse was his abhorrence. Ten years later, according to Medwin, he considered it to be the most difficult of all meters, "because every line must be good." He also told Medwin that "good prose resolves itself into blank-verse." We perhaps should not take these remarks too seriously. The last one implied that he felt a rhythmic kinship between good prose and blank verse, and this feeling, as well as his oft-stated intention of trying to write in a plain dramatic style, may partly account for the prosody that has been so long decried. An analysis of the metrical characteristics of *Cain* reveals that Byron had fashioned a form that well might disturb the educated readers of his day, who expected poets to follow more or less rigidly a set of conventions. Byron modified some of these freely and thus exposed himself to charges of slovenliness and inartistic anarchy.[9]

Two of his deviations from the rules were to vary the length of his lines and at the same time avoid a steady insistence on strong endings by an abundant use of terminal light syllables. If we do some finger counting that it is impossible to conceive of Byron's ever doing, we find that the line lengths of *Cain* fall into three unequal groups: the decasyllables, most of which have masculine endings; the eleven-syllable lines, most of which have feminine endings; and a sprinkling of freakish verse of eight, nine, twelve, and thirteen syllables. About 70 per cent of the 1,794 lines of *Cain* have ten syllables, ending with an accent, which can sometimes be secondary:

> The son of her who snatched the apple spáke
> II, ii, 409

[8] G. Wilson Knight, *The Times Literary Supplement,* February 20, 1959, p. 97. Knight quoted II, ii, 148 ff. as a typical section of the dialogue in *Cain* that might be read more effectively with a prose intonation.

[9] *LJ, II,* 119–120; Medwin, pp. 137, 237. *The British Review* charged that "some conceit about varying the cadence, and dissipating the monotony of blank verse" had induced Byron "so to fritter and torment it, so to break up its continuity, by the interruptions . . . of the dialogue" that he destroyed the rhythm and "stately modulation" of blank verse (XIX [December, 1822], 78).

And dread and toil and sweat and heavinèss
I, 359

The reviewers who wrote that Byron arbitrarily counted off the correct number of ten syllables did not realize that in about 30 per cent of his verse he deviated from that convention.

The major variation was the eleven-syllable line with a slack ending (21% or 380 lines):

Oh God! why didst thou plant the tree of knówlĕdge?
I, 32

A related minor irregularity was the decasyllabic verse with a slack ending:

And tusks projecting like the trees strípped ŏf
II, ii, 141

And after flatt'ring dust with glímpsĕs ŏf
III, 72

Thou art my worshipper; not wórshĭppĭng
I, 319

If we add the twenty-eight times he did this to the 380 eleven-syllable lines we see that these slack-ending lines were numerous enough to irritate those critics who preferred blank verse with a sturdy final beat and who therefore protested that Byron had blundered into an unpoetical measure.

Before looking at other variables, we might pay more attention to Byron's light endings. In Act III, four-fifths of the eleven-syllable lines that have a feminine ending got it by means of a dissyllable that gave Byron a falling cadence:[10] e.g., *ages, altar, apple, conquered, daring, essence, father, happy, peopled, perish, purpose, serpent, shadows, victim, winter, wretches*. Occasionally Byron closed a line with a polysyllable like *nourishing* that gave him a pair of slacks for his sinking rhythm.

The light endings that offended the critics were those monosyllables that both in verse and prose were regarded as unemphatic words. Byron used these just often enough to make them conspicuous: *show me, shed*

[10] Seven of the light-ending ten-syllable lines have similar dissyllables.

them, made ye, share it, beyond us, pursue him, die with. The effect was again a falling cadence.

Associated with these light endings was the terminal occurrence of an ambiguous secondary stress. In a moderate number of ten- and eleven-syllable lines, Byron used polysyllables that end with a secondary stress or without any stress, depending on the context, and either choice resulted in a downward metrical slope: *beautiful, benevolence, endurable, ineffable, inheritor, humility, immensity, immortality, paradise, sacrifice, wilderness.*[11]

With such intermediate stress the tendency was still away from verse with a final thump and toward what Byron's detractors called limpness. But one could also say that the final slack syllables or secondary stresses contributed metrical variety and lightness of movement, especially when combined with certain other prosodic techniques.

Although Byron seemed to prefer to let his eleven-syllable lines decline lightly, he did end them with a strong or secondary stress seventy-one times. The compensation in almost all these lines was the single or double occurrence of two or more successive slack syllables within the line:

Of the sad ignorant victims underneath
III, 302

In the vast desolate night in search of him
I, 271

Next in order of frequency among the verse of irregular length is the twelve-syllable line (38 times). Many of these are less noticeable than the eleven-syllable variants since they differ from the regular pattern only by the addition of another iamb:

Bequeathed/ to me?/ I leave/ them my/ inher/itance
II, ii, 29
And star/ by star/ and u/niverse/ by u/niverse
II, ii, 437

In some twelve-syllable lines Byron broke away from a firm alternation of stresses and slacks and resorted to secondary accents or to a concentration of slacks, or to other kinds of metrical substitution.

[11] In Act III fourteen ten-syllable lines and two eleven-syllable lines end with such words.

Their swel/ling in/to pal/pable/ immen/sity
II, ii, 9

Destruc/tion and/ disor/der of/ the el/ements
II, ii, 81

Souls who/ dare look/ the om/nipo/tent tyr/ant in
I, 138

To in/herit / ago/nies ac/cumu/lated
I, 449

A small group of lines have eight, nine, or thirteen syllables:

8: To us? They sinned, then let them die!
III, 76

9: And yet thou seest. 'Tis a fearful light!
II, i, 177

13: But how? By a most crushing and inexorable
II, ii, 80

The rarity of the eight-, nine-, and thirteen-syllable verse (only eleven in the play) suggests that some of these were careless accidents.

As we noticed in the preceding essay, metrics and contraction were interrelated, especially when an unaccented mid-vowel was dropped or slurred, but not marked with an apostrophe, as in *happier*, which can usually be read as a dissyllable. Observance or disregard of this shortening alters the rhythm. For instance, the following line loses its iambic identity if *haughtiest* is pronounced as a trisyllable. The line then has two spondees, one pyrrhic, and one trochee in twelve syllables:

Head ten/ times high/er than/ the haugh/tiest/ cedar
II, ii, 192

But when the unaccented vowels are merged and the word becomes a dissyllable, *haughtiest,* the verse is less irregular, has eleven syllables with slack ending, three iambs, and two spondees:

Head ten/ times high/er than/ the haugh/tiest ce/dar

If words like *happier* and *haughtiest* are given full syllabic value, the number of lines that have more than ten syllables increases;[12] and so does

[12] In Act I, fifteen lines are so affected (e.g., 15, 93, 94, 145, 186, 201). If we

the number of lines containing a succession of slack syllables (e.g., *mightiest, beauteous*). Elision, a less frequent means of dropping an unaccented vowel, affected the scansion of nine lines in *Cain.*

Table 1 summarizes what we have been describing and indicates the freedom with which Byron departed from the standard line length. The rather large statistical differences from scene to scene encourage the speculation that there may be some relationship between matter and manner here. The percentage of ten syllable lines was unusually high in the first scene of Act II (82%) and much lower in the second scene (63%).

The first scene is mainly descriptive of the journey through space, and Byron was careful with description that he hoped to make impressive. The conscious formality was reflected in the large number of lines of conventional length and in the scarcity of the eleven-syllable variation (only 12%). There was only one line of twelve syllables here.

TABLE 1

Lines of Varying Length

Act	Total Lines	Numer of Syllables									
		10	10S	10L	11	11L	11S	12	8	9	13
I	562	423 75%	418 75%	5	124	105	19	11	0	3	1
II, i	205	168 82%	164	4	35	28	7	1	0	1	0
II, ii	466	295 63%	288	7	150	130	20	17	0	1	2
III	561	408 72%	396	12	142	117	25	9	1	1	1
Totals	1,794	1,294 72%	1,266 70%	28	451 25%	380 21%	71	38	1	6	4

KEY S = stressed ending; *L* = light or slack ending. Table I may be read thus: In Act I, out of the 562 lines, 423 (or 75%) have ten syllables, and of these, 418 have a stressed ending, 5 a light ending, etc.

---

also give full syllabic value to many words in which contraction is marked in the text (*pow'rful, fi'ry, cov'ring, heav'n's, grov'ling, myst'ry,* 11, 77, 84, 117, 131, 292, 322), eighteen more lines in Act I would have an additional syllable and slightly altered rhythm. If we reduce one of Byron's favorite words, *innumerable,* to four syllables, *innum'rable,* we change the scansion of eight lines and not always for the better. See textual notes, II, i, 178.

Scene Two takes place in the realm of the dead where Cain's distress and agitation became acute. With the rise in excitement, there was an increase in stylistic irregularity. The proportion of eleven-syllable lines rose to 32 per cent; there were also seventeen with twelve syllables and two with thirteen syllables.

Some of the quoted samples of eleven- and twelve-syllable lines were notable for irregularities other than length. Scansion of a consecutive swatch from the play reveals in detail certain technical habits that created the general effects deplored by Byron's contemporaries.

The first two-thirds of Act III provides four sections that are typical of the different kinds of dialogue, of the different moods of the play, and of the metrical variations.

1. Lines 1–223. The conversation between Cain and Adah, later joined by Abel, gives a fair specimen of the emotional gamut of the whole play. The speeches are short or of moderate length. Cain's feelings range from calm restraint to agitation.
2. Lines 223–279. Here occur the two long oratorical addresses of the brothers to the Lord. Since these differ greatly in content and versification, the statistics on them have been tabulated separately.
3. Lines 280–357. This section—the quarrel, the murder, and Cain's lamentation—has maximum excitement.
4. Lines 419–443. Eve's curse is a fusion of passionate and formal discourse.

In addition to these 382 lines, about 100 others scattered through the play were scanned because they provided some interesting irregularities.

The basic pattern was iambic pentameter:[13]

> What need/ of snakes/ and fruits/ to teach/ us that?
>
> I, 462

[13] I preferred to use the terminology and principles of the classical system of prosody. A newer system, based on linguistic principles, as explained and advocated by Terence Hawkes in his excellent essay, is subtler but its application is complicated. According to this system there is only one primary stress in "an intonation pattern" (a group of words bounded by pauses). "The Problems of Prosody," *A Review of English Literature,* III (April, 1962), 32–49.

The system also recognizes four degrees of stress, whereas my ear was able to distinguish only three degrees in Byron's verse: primary, secondary, and weak or slack.

> The fumes/ of scorch/ing flesh/ and smok/ing blood
> III, 299

Relatively few lines were thus regularly stressed. Had more of them been so, the reviewers might have applauded, but the rhythmic march of the play would have been stiffer than it now is. Byron often lightened the flow of his verse by interspersing one or two secondary accents and leaving only three or four primary stresses for each line:

> With ruder greeting than a father's kiss
> III, 130

> And gazing on eternity methought
> III, 65

Even when he further lightened the pace by adding an extra slack syllable at the end, the basic pattern was otherwise the same:

> Accept/ from out/ thy hum/ble first/ of shep/herd's
> III, 237

> And wings/ of fi'/ry cher/ubim/ pursue/ him
> III, 426

More common than the use of secondary stress and much more effective in muting the basic regularity was the variation he achieved by the substitution of one or more trochees. This change is especially noticeable when, in conjunction with an iamb, it brought together two stresses or two slacks.

> Thine are/ the hours/ and days/ when both/ are cheer/ing
> III, 21

> His eq/ual? No,/ I have/ nought in/ common/ with him
> I, 305

The initial trochee is quite common. Many lines begin with such words as *Fitting, Kiss him, Lashes, Visions, Pleasing, Flutters, Suffered, Done that, Take them.* Occasionally Byron went to trochees for almost an entire verse, and then the intrusion of one iamb again brought together two slacks—one of his favorite means of loosening the meter:

> I had/ borrowed/ more by/ a few/ drops of/ ages
> III, 66

More frequent than trochaic substitution was the use of spondees, which often resulted in a slow drag of three or more stresses:[14]

> Suns, moons,/ and earths,/ upon/ their loud-/voiced spheres
> III, 182
>
> The ser/aphs love/ most; cher/ubim/ know most
> I, 421
>
> To cast/ down yon/ vile flatt'/rer of/ the clouds
> III, 290

In the preceding two lines and in the following four the concentration of stresses impeded the pace and almost obliterated the basic pattern.

> Cain, that/ proud spir/it who/ withdrew/ thee hence
> III, 45
>
> Wilt thou/ frown ev'n/ on me?/ No A/dah, no.
> I, 56
>
> He is/ all-pow'r/ful, must/ all-good,/ too, fol/low?
> I, 77
>
> Eat, drink,/ toil, trem/ble, laugh,/ weep, sleep,/ and die
> II, ii, 416

The eight stresses in this last verse were a notable exception and placed it in a select company of the heavily accented lines by Milton, Keats, and Wordsworth. One of the distinctive cadences of *Cain* was the use of three or more successive stresses. It seemed to be as frequent here as in the

[14] My retention of this term and of "pyrrhic" violates one tenet of the new system. Hawkes stated, "The pyrrhic foot and the spondee cannot exist . . . if two stresses of the same degree occur side by side, the second must be stronger than the first" (*ibid.,* 40). He therefore treated the spondee and the pyrrhic as iambs. Though I can hear slightly different degrees of stress in some of the feet in *Cain* that I call spondaic and pyrrhic, these subtle distinctions would render tabulation extremely complex and would not alter the generalities I have drawn about Byron's practice of accumulating successive stresses and slacks.

Eve of St. Agnes. There are dozens of weighty and slow-moving accumulations:

make death hateful	I, 111
man's vast fears	I, 221
same sole womb	I, 371
first-born son	I, 483
God's own image	I, 506
Yon small blue circle	II, i, 29
dear-bought knowledge	II, ii, 160
Head ten times higher	II, ii, 192
scarce-born mortals	II, ii, 447
rose leaves strewn	III, 12
snakes spring up	III, 427
where long white clouds/ Streak the deep purple	I, 511–512

Though Byron used spondees more often within a line than at the initial or terminal positions, the following are typical beginnings that break the iambic pattern and start a verse with either an emphatic or a leisurely beat: *Hush, tread; Half open; Sound impious; Give way; No, he; Smite not; Thus quickly; Yes, death; Two altars; Eyes flashing.*

One would expect to find pyrrhics that counteracted a deliberate spondaic movement. In the following line a pyrrhic hurried the verse to the two stresses on the derogatory epithet:

In hymns/ and harp/ings and/ self-seek/ing prayers
I, 387

Two pairs of slacks that derived from a pyrrhic and a trochee speeded up one verse that started slowly with two stresses:

Might sa/tiate/ the in/sati/able/ of life
III, 81

One rhythmical habit was associated with the eleven-syllable lines that end strongly. Almost always Byron balanced this final stress with an anapest:

No sun, no moon, no lights innum/erable
II, i, 178

My disinher/ited boy/ 'Tis but a dream
III, 32

Hast plucked a fruit more fat/al to thine/ offspring
I, 396

Thou liv/est and must/ live forever./ Think not
I, 116

Some of the lines we have quoted have demonstrated Byron's penchant for compounding irregularity. If he broke the iambic pattern, he was likely to abandon it altogether. Thus many lines had several substitutions of more than one kind. Byron's italics, punctuation, and capitalization on the manuscript pointed the saliency of one irregular verse, that had a trochee, a pyrrhic, and two spondees:

To the/ great doub/le Mys/t'ries!—the/ *two Prin/ciples*!—
II, ii, 404 (MS)

Two trochees, one spondee, and one pyrrhic in twelve syllables give two pairs of slacks:

Ere the/ night clos/es o'er/ the in/hibi/ted walls
I, 88

The last three feet here could be scanned as two anapests: the inhib/ited walls. Such alternative scansion was not uncommon when Byron disrupted the iambic pattern. The following arrangement of pyrrhic, anapest, trochee, and two iambs gave Byron three groups of scanted syllables:

Distant/ and dazz/ling and/ innu/mera/ble
II, ii, 243

In one eleven-syllable line two trochees and two spondees were combined with the only dactyl I found in the play:

Own and be/loved,/she too/ under/stands not
I, 188

The following are typical of his treatment of eleven-syllable lines:

A lamb/ stung by/ a rep/tile. The/ poor suck/ling
(two trochees, one spondee) II, ii, 290

And al/tar with/out gore/ may win/ thy fa/vour
(one pyrrhic, one spondee) III, 267

Such specimens barely suggest the rhythmic variety in *Cain.* A few figures mark its extent (see Table 2). Note, for instance, that in the 382 scanned lines of Act III, only one-fourth of the ten-syllable lines were fully iambic, and many of these had secondary accents, not here tabulated.[15]

Over three-fourths of the lines had metrical substitution, and more than one-fourth of the feet were irregular, that is, there was more than one irregular foot per line. Table 2 records the number of the four kinds of rhythmic variation in each of the scanned sections of Act III. Half of the irregular feet were spondees and one-third trochees.

Table 3 shows the surprising fact that the beginning of the lines got most of the metrical variation. In the scanned portion of Act III, the first foot was irregular in 149 lines (41%) while the fifth foot was irregular in less than half as many lines—67 (18%). The amount of irregularity decreased from foot to foot, as if Byron were intuitively more prone to vary his pattern in the first two feet, but seemed just as bound to assert the basic pattern in the last two feet.

If we study the statistical differences in Table 3, we realize that those sections of Act III in which the emotional tone was most restrained (e.g., Abel's address to the Lord) or in which the tone was generally kept at the same pitch (e.g., the quarrel scene and Eve's curse), the distribution of irregular feet was relatively stable. In those sections where there was more variety of emotional tone and greater range of high and low pitches, the amount of metrical substitution increased, especially in the first foot. The statistical differences in Table 3 roughly parallel those of Table 2. There was, for instance, a greater percentage of irregular lines and feet in Cain's highly emotional address to the Lord and in the stormy murder episode than in Abel's tame prayer. Thus when Byron

[15] Twenty-five of the eleven-syllable lines were regularly iambic, with the exception of the final extra light syllable.

TABLE 2

Metrical Irregularities

Scanned Lines of Act III	Total Number Lines	Number Irregular Lines[a]	Per Cent of Number Irregular Lines	Number of Regular Lines[b]	Trochees	Spondees	Pyrrhics	Anapests	Number of Irregular Feet	Per Cent of Irregular Feet
1–223 Dialogue between Cain, Adah, Abel	223	163	73	60	113	138	23	7	281	25
224–244 Abel's address	21	14	67	7	8	9	6	0	23	22
245–279 Cain's address	35	30	86	5	17	17	9	2	45	26
280–357 Quarrel, murder, lament	78	65	83	13	28	83	19	3[c]	133	34
419–443 Eve's curse	25	19	76	6	7	14	13	1	35	28
Totals	382	291	76	91	173	261	70	13	517	27

[a] This figure includes lines that have metrical substitution for the iamb.
[b] This figure includes only iambic pentameter lines.
[c] One dactyl is counted here.

TABLE 3

*Number of Times in Act III Each Foot Is Irregular**

Line Numbers	First Foot	Second Foot	Third Foot	Fourth Foot	Fifth Foot
1–223	86	56	59	43	34
224–244	5	5	5	4	4
245–279	14	14	8	3	6
280–357	37	30	22	25	18
419–447	7	9	8	5	5
Totals	149 (41%)	114 (30%)	102 (27%)	80 (21%)	67 (18%)

* The irregularities in the sixth foot of the twelve- and thirteen-syllable lines are not included.

dealt with fluctuating emotions, he increased his metrical irregularity. This marriage of substance and style appeared even in single lines:

> Touch not/ the child—/ my child—/ thy child—/ Oh Cain
> III, 127

Adah's terror was expressed in verse so fragmented by three pauses and so heavily spondaic that the two iambs could not preserve more than a hint of the basic rhythm. Extreme metrical irregularity was appropriate to extreme emotional intensity. In extended sections we can detect a similar relationship. There were more spondees and other substitutions in Cain's taut and scornful reproach of the Lord than in Abel's quiet and reverent thanksgiving. In the quarrel and murder sections, there were eighty-three spondees in seventy-eight lines; and 34 per cent of all feet were irregular. Less than a fifth of the lines in this passionate episode were fully regular.

Another technique that contributed, perhaps more obviously than the others we have been observing, to those characteristics that critics have disliked was enjambment. Table 4 indicates that in the scanned sections, 46 per cent of the lines were run-on. Much of this enjambment was achieved by placing at the end of one verse and at the beginning of the next verse parts of verbs or of other closely related structural units:[16]

[16] Several reviews, among them *The British Review* (XIX [December, 1822],

TABLE 4

Run-On Lines in Act III

Total Number of Lines Used	Total Run-on	Per Cent
223 (lines 1–223)	101	*45*
21 (lines 224–244)	13	*62*
35 (lines 245–279)	18	*51*
78 (lines 280–357)	27	*35*
25 (lines 419–443)	15	*60*
Totals 382	174	*46*

He may be / A foe . . . III, 168–169
recall thee / To peace . . . III, 175–176
For what should I / Be contrite . . . III, 117–118
expiated by / The ages . . . III, 120–121

This typographical splitting of word groups naturally, or as some insist, unnaturally, separated adjectives and dependent phrases from their nouns and sometimes put pronouns and link words in the visually emphatic terminal position. As we have seen, such a practice met with consistent disapproval. However, it usually seems to be an intentional method of speedy enjambment. The following passage is typical of his gliding, though he rarely used so many as five consecutive run-ons:

. . . (as what off'ring can be
Aught unto thee?) but yet accept it for
The thanksgiving of him who spreads it in
The face of thy high heav'n, bowing his own
Ev'n to the dust, of which he is, in honour
Of thee and of thy name for evermore!
III, 239–244

Byron's enjambment in *Cain* was functional. As an integral part of his versification, it merged with the irregularity of syllabic count and with the copious substitution to minimize our awareness of the iambic

81–82) and *Blackwood's* ("Lord Byron," XI [February, 1822], 215), rebuked Byron for devising enjambment by dividing between two lines a noun and its adjective or a preposition and its object.

meter and to bring the verse closer to prosaic movement. Moreover, there was again a broad connection between purpose, content, and metrics. The highest level of enjambment—62 per cent and 60 per cent (see Table 4)—occurred in Abel's prayer and in Eve's curse. Though Abel's placidity may seem to have little in common with Eve's ferocity, both speeches were formal and conventional, and in both Byron aimed at fluency. Cain's sullen address at the altar was also a formal piece, but had slightly less enjambment, because, as almost always with his talk, the uneven pressure of feeling interrupted the flow. This fragmentation became extreme in the section on the quarrel, murder, and lament, and here the proportion of run-ons dropped to 35 per cent. The excitement reduced the sentence structure to short units, and a larger number of lines were therefore end-stopped.

Also related to the variable flow and to the sporadic increase of segmented structure was Byron's handling of cesuras. On his MS he indicated his pauses with dashes, which editors have usually changed to other marks of punctuation. There remained much internal punctuation and thus many cesuras.

As Table 5 shows, 60 per cent of the lines of Act III that I examined had a single cesura. It fell near the middle (after the fourth, fifth, or sixth syllable) in only 38 per cent of the 178 lines. Almost a third of the verses had two pauses and sixteen had three or four. In 111 lines (62%) Byron

TABLE 5

Cesuras in Act III

	Lines 1–100	Lines 280–357	Totals
2 pauses	30	25	55
3 pauses	5	5	10
4 pauses	1	5	6
1 pause	64	43	107
After second syllable	5	4	9
After third syllable	1	7	8
After fourth syllable	12	7	19
After fifth syllable	12	8	20
After sixth syllable	20	8	28
After seventh syllable	11	6	17
After eighth syllable	3	2	5
After ninth syllable	0	1	1

used multiple cesuras or placed a single pause near the beginning or the end of a line.[17] He did not permit us to feel that an internal hesitation was occurring at any one place or with any regularity; but with a roving cesura he clipped his rhythmic phrasing and forced us to move forward, not smoothly or steadily but nervously, in spurts. During the crisis, the second passage of Table 5 (280–357), the number of lines with multiple cesuras rose from 36 per cent to 45 per cent; and at the same time the single pause often came near the extremities, in 47 per cent as compared to 31 per cent, of those verses that had but one cesura.

One minor habit accentuated the pause and braced the metrical beat: the high incidence of the masculine cesura: 185 occurred after a primary or secondary stress; only 68 followed a slack syllable. Had the contrary happened, the many drops before a pause would have enervated the rhythm and left it flabby.

The location of the cesura was influenced by Byron's habit of frequently dividing a verse among two or more speakers. One of the early reviewers objected to Byron's excessive "subdivisions of the dialogue," which rendered it "absolutely devoid of all pretensions to rhythm."[18] One-fifth of the lines of the play were so divided (see Table 6).

Since any change of speaker within a line required a pause and at least

TABLE 6

Divided Lines

Act	Total Lines	Two Divisions	Three Divisions	Four Divisions	Total Number of Divided Lines
I	562	98	25	2	125
II, i	205	38	7	0	45
II, ii	466	89	12	1	102
III	561	72	11	0	83
Totals	1,794	297	55	3	355 (*20%*)

[17] Although one can clearly distinguish at least three (if not four) degrees of juncture or pause in the *Cain* verse, these degrees seemed less meaningful than the number of cesuras, their location, and the stress that preceded them.

[18] *The British Review,* XIX (December, 1822), 78.

momentarily checked the rhythmic movement, this practice tended to dissipate the metrical pattern. The following line is divided into four parts (the two brothers alternating the speeches). It may be scanned and is no more irregular than scores of undivided lines (2 spondees, 1 trochee, 2 iambs, and an extra scant syllable). Still the divisions, the pauses, the rapid diversion of our attention to different speakers expunge a sense of rhythmic advance and prevent our perception of the line as a metrical unit:

> And stone. // Choose thou. // I have/ chosen. // 'Tis/ the high/est
> III, 212

The following is more typical of the divided lines, breaking between the two speakers near the middle, with customary metrical substitution (2 trochees, 1 spondee):

> Though thy / God left / thee. // Say, / what have/ we here
> III, 95

Sometimes the regular alternation of stresses and slacks cushioned the splintering effect of pauses, as in the following line, which Byron divided into three speeches:

> The last of these. // And what are they? // That which
> Thou shalt be. . . .
> II, ii, 66–67

* * * * *

Byron did not ignore his conventional metrical pattern, for almost three-fourths of the feet in Act III were iambs. But he used so many devices that subdued, disguised, and embellished the prevailing pattern that we can see why some of his contemporaries chided him for technical negligence and artistic failure.

In *Cain* he liked falling cadences. These he achieved (1) by means of secondary stress, both at the end of a line and within it, often with polysyllables that had a single strong accent and a terminal weaker stress, (2) by a large number of feminine endings, most of the time gracefully done with polysyllables, but sometimes dependent on unemphatic monosyllables, and (3) by trochaic substitution not only in the first foot but often extended over whole lines.

One of his favorite methods of diminishing iambic rigidity was to concentrate two, three, and even four stresses (primary or secondary) and then in the same or other lines to compensate for these (and also for an accented ending in the eleven- and twelve-syllable lines) by a generous distribution of double slacks. By merging these effects with an occasional stress of weak monosyllables,[19] with his practice of splitting a verse among different speakers, with an eccentric use of pauses, and with abundant enjambment, Byron extensively modified the standard concepts of blank verse and shaped a medium, distinguished by its extreme flexibility, and expertly adjusted to his dramatic requirements.

Though we should not amplify an echo of sense in the rhythm, we can maintain that Byron's metrical variations were functional. He was systematic with his irregularities and gained thereby an enlivened variety; and then in a general way at least he adapted the meter to personalities, to changing emotional tensions, and to the differing language styles of the characters.[20]

[19] Only 40 of the 406 masculine endings in Act III used such words and most of these were pronouns (personal and interrogative) that seemed to me to receive structural or rhetorical as well as metrical stress. However, fourteen ten-syllable lines did use the so-called weak terminal words with secondary stress (*and, which, it*).

[20] The prosody of *Cain* is related to Byron's general dramatic theory, to the vocabulary levels that constantly vary in the play, and to the rhetoric that he was addicted to.

THE MANUSCRIPT AND THE TEXT

Description

THE OWNER OF THE MS is the Miriam Lutcher Stark Library of The University of Texas. The MS is bound in green morocco (done by Roger de Coverly), and the volume is entitled "Cain / Lord Byron's Original / Manuscript." The manuscript pages have been tipped and sewed in.

The MS is dated in three places. Byron wrote at the upper right top of page 1 of the play, "Ra[venna] July 16th. 1821," and at the bottom of the last page, "Ravenna Septr 9th. 1821." Here his "N" signature appears twice. (For a description of this symbol see *Byron's Don Juan, The Making of a Masterpiece,* I, 363 n. 1.) He dated the upper right top of page 1 of the Preface, "Ra[venna] Septr 10th. 1821." The *0* was written over a *9*.

The Preface has four pages, comprising two leaves, 7¼″ x 9¾″, each numbered and written on both sides. The drama has eighty-six pages, each measuring 9½″ x 14¾″. Originally these were probably twenty-two large leaves, 19″ x 14¾″, each of which was folded to make four pages. Byron numbered the first page of each leaf (1st, 2^{d}, etc.) in the upper left corner. Hence he numbered every fourth page, but used only half (i.e., two pages) of the twenty-second leaf. In the upper right corner of the numbered pages he wrote the act number.

The leaves of the Preface are watermarked "Sub Umbra Alarum Tuarum" without a date. Each leaf of the drama is watermarked twice with a fleur-de-lis and the initials "VB," but without a date. The leaves placed by the binder before and after the MS are watermarked "Van Gelder"; three of these also have a figure of a man with a rope poised on a sphere with a base.

The Preface contains a passage ("I am prepared to be accused of Manicheism. . . . [Waverly]") that was omitted from the first edition (see the textual notes on lines 29–35). The MS lacks the last two paragraphs—those on Cuvier and Alfieri—printed in the first and all other editions.

The MS of the drama does not have the last three lines of Eve's curse (see the textual notes, III, 441–443). Otherwise it is complete, though there are some verbal differences. There are revisions, made during or shortly after initial composition. The MS contains 3½ lines that were omitted from the first edition (see the textual notes, I, 163–166). Act I occupies the first seven leaves and the first page of leaf 8. Act II, Scene i, starts on the second page of leaf 8 and ends on the last page of leaf 10. Act II, Scene ii begins there and ends in the middle of the second page of leaf 16. Act III starts on leaf 16 and ends on the second page of leaf 22.

Handwriting

The handwriting is not unusual for Byron and is easier to read than many parts of the early *Don Juan* MSS. At the beginning and on certain later pages it is easily legible. He started *Cain* in a leisurely fashion, spacing his words and lines evenly for about a dozen pages, and making few revisions and no insertions. Corrections begin on page 10, where the script is still fairly regular. The first insertion occurs on page 14 (I, 260–261).

The different color of the ink and a much smaller script indicate that the revisions and insertions were usually made at some time after the initial writing. They were squeezed between lines already written. This interlinear crowding caused a normal degree of difficulty in reading the cancellations.

Shortcuts in the formation of letters are characteristic of Byron's writing. Lower case *w* usually looks like *u* or *v*; *d* and *ch* and various ascending and descending consonants resemble each other. His *m*'s and *n*'s are indistinguishable. Four of the vowels—*a, e, o, u*—often look alike. *Whom* was written as if it were *whan, forth* was usuualy spelled *futh, some* became *sune,* and *flash* and *flush* (III, 185–186) could be easily confused, and without the context one exchanged for the other. He hardly ever formed a second *l* in *will.*

One puzzling letter is an apparent double *s* when it follows a letter that he finished high (*o, w, r*). At first glance it may seem as if Byron wrote *dosst, mosst, cursst, waterss.* But what appears to be a second *s* is only a flourish on his first one. His genuine double *s* he formed in the usual mode of the day with a vertical stroke that made the letter resemble the *p* in modern script.

Did the printer set type from this MS? Although it is not difficult to read, still the revisions, some of the badly crowded insertions, and many of his barely formed letters made it a risky document to give to a printer. The context usually gives enough clues to enable one to read a doubtful word, but not always. For a printer to have deciphered *convulsion* in II, ii, 121, and *pervade* in I, 244, would have been an astonishing feat. When Byron received the proofs of *Sardanapalus,* he thought that the printer had "done wonders; he has read what I cannot—my own handwriting" (*LJ,* V, 301, 324). It seems unlikely that anyone in London made fair copies of the three 1821 plays for the printer.

One minor example of the influence of his handwriting on the establishment of the text may be cited. The 1821 and 1831 editions printed in II, i, 122, "What, yonder!" The 1833, 1837, and 1905 editions printed "That!—yonder!" Since Byron's *th* and *wh* are sometimes so similar as to be interchangeable, it is easy to see why we have different readings here.

Capitalization

Byron's capitalization was eccentric. For certain religious and biblical words he was consistent: the synonyms of the Deity and the Devil and their associates—*Cherub, Seraph, Angel, Eternity, Spirit, Spiritual, Serpent,* and *Snake.* With several common nouns he was inconsistent, sometimes capitalizing and sometimes not: *Death, Heaven, Earth, Sin, Night.* Occasionally he liked to elevate abstractions: *Virtue, Goodness, Good* and *Evil, Sorrow, Joy, Cause, Right, Gentleness, Mind*; some words of kinship: *Son, my Boy, Brother, Sister, Father,* but not *mother* in I, 170; and a large number of words, perhaps for emphasis, perhaps by whim: *Gates, Humanity, Clay, One, Orb on Orb, Sacrifice, Shepherd, Bird's Matins, Lion, Azure, Equal, Guests, Star, Noon, Morn, Millions.* If one of the words in the last group occurred a second time, it was likely not to be so honored. If the capitals had been more frequent, one might guess that they were rhythmic indicators, finger tapping the beat of the verse. Byron rarely capitalized an unstressed syllable (except for such words as *Eternity* and *Omnipotent*). But since in scores of lines he gave a capital only to the first word, and since he left hundreds of stressed syllables in lower case, the connection between rhythm and capitalization was fortuitous.

The 1821 and 1833 editions used capitals sparingly, not lending that distinction to *cherub, seraph, serpent, heaven,* nor even to some of the synonyms and epithets that referred to the deity (e.g., *conqueror*). The 1905 edition, edited by E. H. Coleridge, was consistent with *Cherub, Seraph,* and all synonyms of the deity, even the uncomplimentary ones (*Omnipotent tyrant, Indissoluble Tyrant, Destroyer, Conqueror, Invisible*), and most of the words referring to Lucifer (*Spirit, Demon, Prince*). Coleridge, in his treatment of other words, surpassed Byron's eccentricity. He gave capitals to *Eden Trees* and frequently, but not always, to *Knowledge* and *Life.* He capitalized *Knowledge* even when it did not refer to *the* tree, and also *Death, Heaven, Love, Earth, Good, Evil,* but not every time he met these words in the text. He upper-cased *Serpent* but almost never *snake.* The chief oddity of the 1905 edition was that it did not follow Byron's MS, for Coleridge sometimes capitalized words when Byron had not done so, and sometimes neglected to use capitals when Byron had clearly used them. For instance, he capriciously printed *Twilight, Truth, Men,* and *Time,* none of which Byron had capitalized (I, 86, 355, 157, 548).

Neither Byron nor any editor was reverential with pronouns referring to the deity. In Act I, *He* was capitalized only twice among the many times it was so used, but never *his* or *him.*

On rare occasions, the MS and all editions were in agreement, e.g., *Death, Immortality, Paradise* (II, ii, 365, 386; III, 73).

Punctuation

Byron stroked the MS with dashes, about two hundred in the first two hundred lines. Most of these he placed not at the end of the verses but within them.[1] One clear purpose was to mark the cesuras as he felt them while he was writing. Unfortunately the MS is not everywhere a guide to Byron's rhythmic intentions because he was not methodical and omitted the dashes in many lines that have internal pauses.

[1] Dashes used in conjunction with periods, question marks, and other punctuation were not counted.

As one might expect from the emotionalism of the play, the exclamation point was also conspicuous. In the first two hundred lines, not a passage of great excitement, he marked thirty-three exclamations. Because of the carelessness of his handwriting, many of Byron's other marks are hard to distinguish, especially the colon and semicolon. He made neither a logical nor a legible distinction between them. In 1813 Byron had admitted that he was "a sad hand at your punctuation" and did not know where to place a comma. He asked Murray to have someone "stop" or "point" his verse, and so Francis Hodgson punctuated a revised copy of the *Bride of Abydos* (*LJ*., III, 252, 283–284).

Murray's editors pruned most of the dashes from *Cain* and some of the exclamations and substituted more rational and more subdued pointing. The punctuation of the first edition (1821) was too sparse and sometimes at fault. John Wright in the 1833 edition added many commas and some periods that had been omitted in 1821. Some differences between these two editions were speculative, as when the 1833 editor changed semicolons to colons and vice-versa.

Italics

Although all editors changed Byron's punctuation and most of them scanted his capitalization, they respected his many italics, even when these seemed unnecessary. Their few omissions appear to be an oversight. Byron's italics were more functional than his other typographical devices. He underlined words whenever he raised his voice or wanted to change the rhythm. His italics thus affected the scansion, for he frequently used them to indicate a stress where it would not otherwise have come, for instance, on a pronoun or an auxiliary like *hath*. Some italics had psychological or rhetorical significance. Byron tried to make them imply a variety of attitudes or emotions: awe, impatience, fear, grief, anger, indignation, pleading, surprise, sarcasm and contempt (e.g., I, 161, 450; II, ii, 161–163; 403–404; III, 297–298, 386, 419, 438, 561). Occasionally he hoped that the italics would clarify his meaning (I, 225). A number of MS italics have been removed from the text because the normal fall of the accents in the verse seemed to convey the poet's psychological intention (e.g., I, 179, 421; III, 76, 146–147, 171, 204).

Insertions

Byron made seventeen MS insertions, totaling forty-two lines. One more insertion of three lines does not appear on the MS. Act III drew eleven additions, seven in the last seventy lines of the play. Only two went into Act I and none into the first scene of Act II (see Table 7).

Most of these additions were improvements and were motivated by a variety of considerations. The most valuable ones enriched the intellectual or psychological content of the play, gave Lucifer a witty thrust, some new ideas, and two climaxes for his last speech. A few tried to illuminate and refine the complexity of Cain's emotions. Others were directed by a craftsman's concern for clarity or emphasis, for simplification or expansion of material already in the text, and here Byron was willing to be repetitious to gain certain literary advantages. When the new lines made concrete and particular a previous generality or abstraction or when they contributed a strong image, then the insertions were rewarding.

The following discussion of particular additions speculates about Byron's intentions and the varied effects of the new lines. All quotations have been taken directly from the MS and use its capitalization and punc-

TABLE 7

MS Insertions

	Act	Line Number	Total Number of Lines
1.	I	260–261	2
2.	I	425–426	2
3.	II, Sc. ii	7	1
4.	II, Sc. ii	262, 264	2
5.	II, Sc. ii	440–442	3
6.	II, Sc. ii	452–458	7
7.	II, Sc. ii	459–466	8
8.	III	179, 182	2
9.	III	348	1
10.	III	362	1
[11.]	[III]	[441–443 not on MS]	[3]
12.	III	489	1
13.	III	506–508	3
14.	III	513–515	3
15.	III	521–522	2
16.	III	530	1
17.	III	541	1
18.	III	558, 560	2
		Total	45

tuation. Wherever it seemed feasible to quote the insertion in its context, the new lines have been printed in bold face. For the longer additions, the reader should refer to the text of the drama. I do not here discuss Byron's revision of words or phrases; this has been recorded in the textual notes.

1. I, 260–261

> I wrestled with the Lion when a boy
> In play till he ran roaring from my gripe.

The first insertion was made in the interest of homely realism. Cain, who has had difficulty imagining what death is like, wondered if it was a tangible creature that he could grapple with. The two new lines gave Cain a childlike and quasi-humorous reminiscence.

2. I, 425–426

> Since the all-knowing Cherubim love *least*
> The Seraphs' love can be but Ignorance.

This insertion is a sophistical witticism suitable to Lucifer's argument. Adah has stated that the cherubim were noted for their wisdom and the seraphim for their love. Since she perceived that Lucifer was loveless, she identified him as a cherub. Byron added two lines to Lucifer's reply that cleverly turned Adah's comment to the devil's advantage. As a consistent intellectualist, he used her distinction between the wise cherubim and the loving seraphim to sneer at love as the opposite of wisdom.

3. II, ii, 7

> I / Had deemed them rather the bright populace
> Of some all unimaginable Heaven—
> **Rather than things to be inhabited;**
> But that on drawing near them I beheld

This insertion was Byron's attempt to correct a faulty sentence. Line 5 began a comparison that he forgot to finish, as we can see by skipping line 7 and reading line 8 after line 6. His patching was also faulty because he repeated *rather* in the new line. Before publication either he or his editors made another weak and awkward revision, getting rid of *rather* and tacking onto the end of the line a pointless reflexive pronoun: "Than things to be inhabited themselves."

4. II, ii, 262, 264

. . . the Sun's gorgeous coming,
His Setting indescribable which fills
My eyes with pleasant tears as I behold
Him sink and feel my heart float softly with him
Along that Western Paradise of Clouds,
The forest shade—the Green bough—the bird's voice⟨s⟩—
The vesper bird's which seems to sing of love—
⟨Which⟩ mingles with the song of Cherubim
And

This kind of insertion Byron made often in *Don Juan*—descriptive amplification. Cain was recalling a number of sensory experiences that he considered beautiful. Any list of parallel items in Byron's verse invited an expansion. In line 262 he added the "Western Paradise of Clouds" to the sunset he already had. Then he moved from the general to the particular. The bird's voice, mentioned in line 263, became "The vesper bird's which seems to sing of love." Since the whole passage culminated in a tribute to Adah, this line on the bird's song of love began the transition that related the list of beautiful experiences to Cain's love of his wife, whose face excelled all other beautiful objects.

5–7. II, ii, 440–442, 452–458, 459–466 (see the text for these additions).

These three additions strengthened the conclusion of Act II. Rhetorical emphasis seems to be the purpose of the first insertion. Lucifer has been proclaiming his eternal hostility to God. Three new lines explained why his warfare with God will be endless. Since the opponents were immortal, neither one could destroy the other, and since their hatred will endure as long as they do, the conflict can have no end. In lines 431–439 Lucifer had insisted on the eternity of this struggle; the new lines provided the climax of the belligerent part of his last speech.

Lucifer then proceeded to a new and more intellectual topic—the nature of good and evil. He implied that ethical judgments were arbitrarily imposed by the victor in any contest; that is, by whoever had the power to enforce his decrees (443–446). He reiterated an opinion, expressed earlier in the play, that the gifts to mankind that the Eternal Victor called good had actually been few and bitter (446–448). The original ending of Act II then came abruptly, with Lucifer's suggestion that Cain go back to earth to try the rest of God's so-called good gifts.

Dissatisfied with this ending, Byron wrote an addition of seven lines (552–558) that reverted to the nature of good and evil, and offered a different kind of subjective definition. Good and evil were inherent qualities of reality, independent of social power. Lucifer implied that it was possible for an individual to determine for himself what was good and bad. Byron had Lucifer appeal to Cain's rational sense, bidding him to evaluate good and evil by the fruits of his own experience.

The word *fruits* suggested the Eden *apple,* and the preceding mention of *gifts* merged with it to start the third addition, which finally gave Byron the strong conclusion he had been trying for. It was a thoughtful insertion, consistent with one aspect of Byronic individualism. In Act I Lucifer had praised knowledge as superior to passion. Now he bade Cain use his mind, independently of authority, to resist tyrannic imposition, never to submit to autocratic dogmas that were contrary to empirical or intuitive testimony, and above all to use his mind to create his own spiritual world. This addition enabled Byron, after a long pessimistic survey of dead worlds, to end Act II with a hearty affirmation of romantic idealism. The last two additions were the most significant that Byron made to *Cain.*

8. III, 179, 182

The dead—
The Immortal—the Unbounded—The Omnipotent—
The overpowering mysteries of Space.
The innumerable Worlds that were and are—
A Whirlwind of such overwhelming things
Suns Moons and Earths upon their loud-voiced spheres
Singing in thunder round me . . .

In Act III Cain gave Abel a brief account of his travels, written in the polysyllabic manner of the descriptions in Act II. Into this list of the marvels Cain had seen, Byron inserted two sonorous extensions and treated them as appositives of nouns already in the text. In giving us more of what is already there, Byron followed two of his customary procedures. He made an original generality—"overwhelming things / Singing"—

more specific with a traditional image of cosmic music: the loud voices of the spheres were singing in thunder round him. He also tried to increase the emotional implications of the physical experience. Line 179 was one of many in this part of the play that prepared us for later violence. Byron reminded us again that the journey in Act II had both excited and depressed Cain. Having already used *overwhelming,* he had Cain tell Adah of the *overpowering* effect the *mysteries of Space* have had on him.

9–10. III, 348, 362

> Since I have taken life from my own flesh 348
> It is not blood—for who would shed his blood? 362

These were repetitions of matter already in the text. Byron probably used them for clarity. The first merely underscored Cain's realization of guilt and the second identified the "stream" (361) that horrified Zillah.

[11.] [III, 441–443]

> May the Grass wither from thy foot! the Woods 441
> Deny thee shelter! Earth a home! the Dust 442
> A Grave! the Sun his light! and Heaven her God![2] 443

This was the well-known insertion that Byron praised when he sent it in a letter to Murray. Beginning with lines 402–404 and continuing in lines 409–423, 425–427, 434, and 439–440, Eve intermingled her demands that Cain suffer physical and psychological pain with an insistence that part of his punishment must be the severance of all bonds with family, with humanity, and with the very forms of nature. These last three lines of her curse developed with specific variation the generality in line 434: "May every element shun—or change to him!" The transformation idea of line 441 also appeared in lines 428 and 432–433.

12. III, 489

> Thus he would but be what his father is.

This line, added at the beginning of one of the Angel's speeches, was a simple reinforcement of his prediction of future crime. Already in the text was Adah's fear that Enoch might murder Cain and also the Angel's

[2] See textual notes and variants. The lines are quoted from the letter as printed by Prothero, V, 361, and Quennell, II, 667.

ponderous logic: fratricide might engender parricides (492). Byron's insertion restated the gloomy forecast in plain, monosyllabic terms.

13. III, 506–508

> After the fall too soon was I begotten
> Ere yet my Mother's Mind subsided from
> The Serpent, and My Sire still mourned for Eden.

The Angel has declared that Cain had been stern and stubborn ever since he was born. Then Byron wrote this insertion to give his hero a rationalization of his intractable disposition. The psychology was an odd mixture of Calvinism and the theory of prenatal influences. The new lines made Cain one of Byron's doomed heroes, blighted before birth, even at the moment of conception, by the emotional turbulence of his parents. These three lines elucidated the fatalism of a clause that Byron had already written, "That which I am—I am" (509).

A possible criticism is that this explanation of Cain's temperament came too late in the play. It might have been more suitable in Acts I or II, where Cain told Lucifer about his life, and where he also revealed his unstable temper.

14. III, 513–515

> And I lie ghastly!—so shall be restored
> By God the life to him he loved; and taken
> From me a being I neer loved to bear.—

These three lines were a repetition of the death wish expressed in lines 509–512. In Acts I and II Cain made it clear that he has not loved life and will not take the responsibility for being alive. The change here was that remorse turned the death wish into a fervent desire to give up his own unwanted life in order to restore Abel to life. Since the new lines retraced the preceding four, perhaps Byron wanted to stress again not only Cain's remorse but also that unhappy man's consistent aversion to life itself.

15. III, 521–522

If we read line 520 and the first version of line 523, we see the original continuity:

> . . . Ah—little knows he [Enoch] what he weeps for—
> Think'st thou that he will bear to look on me?

Between these two lines, Byron inserted lines 521–522:

> And I who have shed blood cannot shed tears!
> But the four rivers would not cleanse my soul

At first glance the insertion does not seem to be related to the thought of the original lines. Byron made a superficial verbal connection: the child's weeping reminded Cain of his own inability to weep. The main purpose of the two new lines, however, was to point out the paradox of Cain's emotional state: the murderer could not release his grief in tears while he was tormented by guilt. Thus Byron implied a psychological connection between the original and the new lines: the criminal feared that his son would shrink from him because of the crime. Then Byron drew an image from Cain's environment—the Eden rivers—to express the intensity of his feeling of guilt that he could never cleanse away. Enoch's weeping and Cain's grief and guilt and anxiety over his child's regard for him all fitted into the total emotional situation, which was dominated by the criminal's remorse. For Byron's revision of line 523 see the textual notes.

16. III, 530

Byron began Cain's farewell to his brother thus:

> Oh! thou dead
> And everlasting witness!—⟨what thou art⟩
> I know not! 528, 529, 531

After one fragmentary trial he added an image:

> And everlasting witness! whose unsinking
> Blood darkens Earth and Heaven! what thou *now* art—

Byron had begun during the offering scene (255) a persistent series of blood images. By the time of the Angel's arrival he had used the image fifteen times. Then he gave to the Angel two personifications from the Bible: Abel's blood cried out from the earth that has opened her mouth to drink it from Cain's hand (470–473). After two intervening references to blood (491 and the inserted 521) and still another that he cancelled (513), Byron added to the sequence a grim cry of remorse (529–

530). Cain imagined that Abel's blood had not vanished into the ground but remained to darken heaven and earth. The insertion adapted a recurring image to Cain's distress.

17. III, 541

The first grave yet dug for Mortality.

The original lines 540 and 542 read thus: " . . . composed thy limbs into their Grave—/ But I have dug that Grave." The new line projected the single action of burial beyond the immediate occasion to all posterity. *Mortality* was the new key word. If Cain, who brought death to mankind, dug a grave for Abel, he would have performed a symbolic ritual that attested to the mortality of all men. Although the idea was thoughtful and sensitive, the insertion increased the repetition (*grave* was used three times and *dug* twice) and made the sentence seem labored. The whole speech had a jolting movement that was suitable to Cain's mood.

18. III, 558, 560

And *he* who lieth there was childless—I
Have dried the fountain of a gentle race—
Which might have graced his recent marriage Couch.
⟨Which⟩ might have tempered this stern blood of mine—
And
Uniting with our children Abel's offspring—

As Cain looked for the last time at his brother's corpse, he thought that when he killed the childless Abel he removed the possibility of mitigating the harshness that Cain's descendants would inherit from him (556–557, 559). The first new line (558) tells us that Abel had recently married. Byron might have thought that this fact and the probability that Abel would have had children increased the pathos of his death. It seems more likely, however, that Byron's main reason for the addition of both lines was to clarify the imagery of lines 557 and 559: murder dried the fountain of a gentle race that might have tempered Cain's stern blood. The new lines were redundant. The first one made explicit who the gentle race would have been: Abel's children. The second explained how the character of Cain's progeny could have been tempered: by a union of Cain's and Abel's offspring. Neither line added any implication that was not in the original.

A Printing Custom

The first edition and most of its successors followed one fashion of the day and indulged in a naïve and pointless deception. They created an appearance of colloquialism by the use of a superfluous apostrophe in the past tense or past participle of many verbs. With one possible exception, Byron did not do this on his MS.[3] The contracted printing is not a guide to pronunciation. *Work'd, sinn'd,* and *seem'd* are pronounced no differently from *worked, sinned, seemed.*[4] As I compiled a miscellaneous list of these popular spellings and rearranged them into groups, a pattern emerged. The editor or printer did not use the apostrophe with all verbs nor select at random some verbs for whimsical contraction. He did follow certain rules in the game:

1. The first group contained monosyllabic verbs ending in the following consonants: *g, k, l, m, n, p, r, s, ch, sh.* All verbs of this group were treated alike and got an apostrophe.

clogg'd
—
ask'd
bask'd
link'd
look'd
pluck'd
walk'd
work'd
—

call'd
fail'd
roll'd
still'd
till'd
toil'd
—
arm'd
deem'd

doom'd
form'd
seem'd
—
chain'd
deign'd
drain'd
mourn'd
sinn'd

[3] He wrote *betrothed* with both the apostrophe and the *e* in III, 407.

[4] According to E. De Selincourt, (*The Poems of John Keats,* pp. v–vi), Keats used this superfluous apostrophe purposefully though not consistently. De Selincourt thought that he and Keats heard some distinction in sound between the alternate spelling. "But it is often impossible to decide whether Keats wished the syllable to be dropped entirely, or whether he desired a slightly dissyllabic effect as a variation of his metre, or even whether, as is quite possible, by the retention of the *e* he wished to indicate that the previous syllable should be slightly lingered over in reading." De Selincourt therefore disliked the practice of Forman, an earlier editor of Keats' poetry, who changed the spelling of sixty past tenses in *Endymion.* Coleridge, who prepared his edition of Byron at about the same time Forman brought out his Keats, systematically used *ed.* Byron on his manuscript of *Cain* gave him ample precedent. He saw the *Cain* proofs and did not object to the 1821 apostrophes, and probably did not care about such minor subtleties.

unstain'd	—	quench'd
turn'd	barr'd	snatch'd
—	jarr'd	watch'd
wing'd	skirr'd	—
—	—	crush'd
clasp'd	pass'd	dash'd
stepp'd	toss'd	flush'd
stripp'd	—	wish'd

2. Seven monosyllabic verbs ending in diphthongs were treated in the same way: *show'd, sow'd, bow'd, pray'd, sway'd, strew'd, view'd.*

3. Fourteen polysyllabic, prefixed verbs, that are accented on the final syllable, have roots with the same consonant or diphthong endings as the preceding groups: *approach'd, intercheck'd, assail'd, dispell'd, fulfill'd, reveal'd, proclaim'd, resign'd, incurr'd, besmear'd, bequeath'd, betroth'd, destroy'd, renew'd.*

4. The pattern is likewise clear with polysyllabic verbs accented on the penultimate syllable. Most of these end in *en* or *er*: *harden'd, listen'd, madden'd, open'd, poison'd, ripen'd, sadden'd, soften'd, chequer'd, conquer'd, engender'd, gather'd, hinder'd, labour'd, render'd, scatter'd, suffer'd, temper'd, (un)enter'd, unnumber'd.* A subgroup of three verbs end in a diphthong: *borrow'd, follow'd, hollow'd. Extinguish'd* is a solitary member of its own group.

One characteristic these four groups have in common is that their present tense does not end in *e*; and this fact gives us a clue to the reason why the 1821 editor carefully withheld the apostrophe from as large a number of verbs as he gave it to. His inconsistency had its own logic. A final *e* indicates a long vowel in the verb-root: *name, hope, spare, induce, aspire.* The 1821 editor perhaps thought that to contract the past participle of verbs ending in *e* might not only look odd but might also give the misleading appearance of shortening the root vowel: *nam'd, hop'd, spar'd, induc'd.*[5]

The editor might have contracted some polysyllabic verbs that are accented on the first syllable, for here the final *e* has no effect on the

[5] I am indebted to my late colleague, Professor E. Bagby Atwood, for this suggestion. During the last conversation I had with him, he was kind enough to scrutinize my grouped listings of contracted and uncontracted verbs, and confirmed my speculations about the rules of the game.

vowels: *measure, measur'd, promise, promis'd*. However, one readily sees how appearance influenced him not to contract *dried, multiplied,* and *prophesied* to the absurd *dri'd, multipli'd, prophesi'd.*

We should remember that the contracted printing we have been discussing was a matter of spelling and had no effect on pronunciation or rhythm. All the care expended in following the implicit editorial rules for using or not using the apostrophe was idle play.

Characteristics of the Present Text

The present text is based on a collation of the following editions: 1821, 1831, 1833, 1837, 1904 (Oxford), 1905 (Coleridge), and 1905 (More). It corrects the misprints of the 1821 edition, includes a prefatory passage and a few lines of the play that the first edition had omitted, follows its practice of eschewing most of Byron's MS capitalization and further reduces the number of 1821 capitals (see the section on this topic), simplifies and omits some of the 1821 punctuation, which later editors generally tended to increase and alter. The 1821 and following editions retained scores of Byron's dashes and changed others to colons. Many of these mark independent clauses that are in reality short sentences, loosely and sometimes awkwardly strung together by such punctuation. Periods are substituted here for a moderate number of these dashes and colons. The visual effect seems to shorten Byron's sentences, but one should recall that Byron's structure in *Cain* is rather simple, except in some long and formal addresses. He and his editors were not always logical in joining these short segments by dashes and colons.

Italics, which Byron and all editors used lavishly, have here been diminished, but they have been retained wherever they affect the rhythm or serve a psychological purpose. I have adopted Coleridge's innovation of avoiding the superfluous apostrophes, which I discussed in "A Printing Custom," but have used contractions and elisions that reflect pronunciation and that are metrically functional.

There are a few deviations in words from the 1821 text, and on these occasions I used the MS version, because it seemed preferable.

The Content of the Textual Notes and Variants

The notes record MS cancellations, insertions, and undeleted variants. Cancellations have been enclosed within angle brackets. Whatever Byron wrote underneath another version has been presented as a cancellation. Wherever there are successive deletions, the second and third are printed below the first. The final version is not given in the notes. The reader can see what Byron substituted for a cancellation or for an uncanceled variant by looking at the present text. Ellipsis marks indicate that the omitted part of a quotation from the MS is the same as the present text. Doubtful transcriptions are followed by [*?*]; illegible deletions are indicated by [*xx*]. Brief interlinear MS insertions are preceded by the abbreviation [*ins.*].

No entry has been made solely to call attention to Byron's punctuation and capitalization, or to his odd use of the apostrophe. These were included as incidentals in notes made for another purpose.

Byron's MS repetitions—that is, his writing a word or phrase, deleting it, and writing the original a second time, without alteration—have not been noted. There is not a great deal of this unprofitable deletion, e.g., <men> Men, I, 136; <the they> they plucked, I, 444; <stretch> stretches, III, 149; reptile's <subtilty> subtlety (the latter is only a spelling correction), III, 160.

The variants from sundry editions include differences in words, in spelling, and in hyphenation, a selection of unusual capitalization, and a few changes in punctuation that affect the meaning. Where later editions agree with the first in these matters, this unanimity is shown by the tag *1821 et al.*

The italics on Byron's MS and in other editions of *Cain* that I have not retained have been put into the notes. These are distinguished from the editorial matter by a bracketed abbreviation [*ital.*].

The presence or absence of the superfluous contraction of the past tenses and participles of many verbs created a striking difference among the editions and so it has been noted. When I introduced a contraction or an elision that altered the pronunciation and the rhythm, I recorded the corresponding form used by other editions.

Included also are comments on the reading of certain words as dissyllabic or trisyllabic, because these too affect scansion. Since text and metrics are intimately connected, a limited number of entries have been made on lines where the versification is associated with elision or contraction or where it is unusual for some reason.

Quotations from the MS and Byron's letters, from the several editions, and from the critics appear in roman type. My own editorial identification and comment are printed in italics.

References in the textual notes to the various editions are abbreviated as indicated below. References to other books and articles can be identified in the Abbreviations or in the Bibliography.

1821=*Sardanapalus, The Two Foscari, Cain.* London: John Murray, 1821.

The characteristics of this first edition have been mentioned in the preceding sections.

1831=*The Works of Lord Byron.* 6 vols. London: John Murray, 1831.

Cain appeared in Volume III. Murray's 1829, 1830, and 1831 editions were mainly successive printings of the 1828 edition, with some additions in 1831. I chose the 1831 from this series because this was the one that E. H. Coleridge reported he had used in his 1903–1905 edition. It has the same textual omissions as the first edition.

1833 = *The Works of Lord Byron: With His Letters and Journals, and His Life*, by Thomas Moore. London: John Murray, 1832–1833. Coleridge identified the editor of Volumes 6–17 as John Wright.

Cain appeared in Volume XIV, and since this volume was published in 1833, that year has been used as the identifying date in the notes. In punctuation this edition seems closer to the first edition than the 1831 was. Its distinguishing feature was the inclusion of some contemporary opinions about the play. It also recorded in the notes the lines and the prefatory paragraphs omitted in 1821 and 1831, and cited a few MS variants (one of them inaccurately).

1837=*The Works of Lord Byron. Complete in One Volume.* London: John Murray, 1837.

This is based on Wright's 1833 edition. Collation of the 1833 and 1837 editions revealed some differences in punctuation, but otherwise the texts were almost identical. It may be assumed that any variant found in 1833 also appeared in 1837 unless otherwise indicated. The major difference was a considerable reduction of the passages from contemporary critics.

1904=*The Poetical Works of Lord Byron.* London & New York: Oxford University Press, 1904, reprinted 1945.

No editor was named and the derivation of the text was not stated. Collation did not clearly establish its relation with the other editions. On three occasions it offered a unique reading: II, ii, 328; III, 360, 478.

Three times it agreed with only 1905-C (I, 326; III, 285, 374). This suggests that the two editors might have used the same earlier edition, which was certainly not in these instances 1831. Three times 1904 agreed with only 1905-M (I, 35; II, ii, 242; III, 349), but there was no other evidence that it followed 1833. Its frequent agreement with 1837, especially when that edition differed from 1821 or 1831 or others, may be significant: I, 26, 223, 292, 397, 485; II, i, 171; II, ii, 113, 447; III, 114. I doubt, however, that the 1904 editor consulted 1837. It seems more likely that he followed one of the more recent Murray reissues or some other edition of the 1880's or 1890's. The Murray editions from 1855 to 1883, though sometimes labelled "new editions" were usually reissues of 1837 or 1833. That 1904 was based on one of these later reissues would account for its deviation from 1837 in the nine lines already mentioned and in I, 250.

1905-C=*The Works of Lord Byron. Poetry.* Edited by Ernest Hartley Coleridge. 7 vols. 2nd ed. London: John Murray, 1904–1905.

Volume V, which has *Cain,* was published in 1905. A collation with the 1831 text indicated an enormous number of differences in punctuation and capitalization. Coleridge's punctuation and capitalization were excessive and the latter was erratic (see the section on capitalization). He cited some of Wright's MS variants, omitted four from Act III that Wright had noted, added a few that Wright did not use, discarded almost all of the 1833 quotations from the critics, and added a few annotations of his own.

1905-M=*The Complete Political Works of Byron.* Edited by Paul Elmer More. Boston: Houghton, Mifflin and Co., 1905, reprinted 1933.

More stated that for his text he used the 1833 edition, which he preferred to the 1831. He retained the pointless apostrophes and observed the 1821 textual omissions, not even putting them in the notes, as Wright had done. In spite of these limitations, his text is preferable to that of Coleridge.

PART II

TEXT, VARIANTS, AND ANNOTATIONS

CAIN

A MYSTERY

"Now the Serpent was more subtil than any beast of the field which the Lord God had made."—*Gen.* 3:1.

Dramatis Personae

Men—ADAM
CAIN
ABEL

Spirits—ANGEL OF THE LORD
LUCIFER

Women—EVE
ADAH
ZILLAH

TO

SIR WALTER SCOTT, BART.

THIS MYSTERY OF CAIN

IS INSCRIBED,

BY HIS OBLIGED FRIEND,

AND FAITHFUL SERVANT,

THE AUTHOR.

PREFACE

THE FOLLOWING SCENES are entitled "A Mystery," in conformity with the ancient title annexed to dramas upon similar subjects, which were styled "Mysteries or Moralities." The author has by no means taken the same liberties with his subject which were common formerly, as may be seen by any reader curious enough to refer to those very profane productions, whether in English, French, Italian, or Spanish.* The author has endeavoured to preserve the language adapted to his characters;* and where it is (and this is but rarely) taken from actual *Scripture,* he has made as little alteration, even of words, as the rhythm would permit. The reader will recollect that the book of Genesis does not state that Eve was tempted by a demon, but by "the serpent"; and that only because he was "the most subtil of all the beasts of the field."* Whatever interpretation the Rabbins and the Fathers may have put upon this, I take the words as I find them and reply with Bishop Watson upon similar occasions, when the Fathers were quoted to him as Moderator in the schools of Cambridge, "Behold the Book!"—holding up the Scripture.* It is to be recollected that my present subject has nothing to do with the *New Testament,* to

* *An asterisk indicates an entry among the Annotations that have been placed after the text of the poem.*

At the top of page 1 of the Preface, Byron wrote, "R.^{a} [*Ravenna*] Septr 10.th 1821." *Byron wrote* "10" *over* "9." *He began the Preface the day after he finished the original draft of the play.*

2 *MS* antient
5 *MS* [*ins.*] very profane
7 *MS* language <of> adapted . . .
8 *MS* it is <rarely> <b> and. *MS* [*ins.*] actual . . .
9 *MS* rythm
12 *MS* subtile; [*ins.*] all
13 *1821* I must take; *MS and other editions* I take . . .
15 *MS* [*ins.*] of Cambridge

which no reference can be here made without anachronism.* With the poems upon similar topics I have not been recently familiar. Since I was twenty I have never read Milton; but I had read him so frequently before that this may make little difference. Gesner's *Death of Abel* I have never read since I was eight years of age, at Aberdeen.* The general impression of my recollection is delight; but of the contents I remember only that Cain's wife was called Mahala, and Abel's Thirza. In the following pages I have called them "Adah" and "Zillah," the earliest female names which occur in Genesis. They were those of Lamech's wives; those of Cain and Abel are not called by their names. Whether, then, a coincidence of subject may have caused the same in expression, I know nothing, and care as little.* I am prepared to be accused of Manicheism* or some other hard name ending in *ism,* which makes a formidable figure and awful sound in the eyes and ears of those who would be as much puzzled to explain the terms so bandied about as the liberal and pious indulgers in such epithets. Against such I can defend myself, or, if necessary, I can attack in turn. "Claw for claw, as Conan said to Satan, and the deevil take the shortest nails" (Waverley).*

The reader will please to bear in mind (what few choose to recollect) that there is no allusion to a future state in any of the books of Moses nor indeed in the Old Testament. For a reason for this extraordinary omission

18 *MS* [*ins.*] here

25 *1831* Zilla

26 *MS* which occur in <Scripture> Genesis.—They were those of <Lameth's> Lamech's wives . . .

27 *MS* not named by their names.

29–35 I am prepared . . . (Waverley). *This passage was omitted from the 1821 and 1831 editions, probably censored by the publisher or his consultants. Cf. I, 163–166 n. It was printed in a note in the 1833 and 1837 editions, introduced with the statement*: "Here follows, in the original draught." *The quotation from Scott, however, was omitted. The passage was printed in full as a part of the Preface in 1905-C. The 1904 and 1905-M editions omitted it, nor did they refer to it in their notes.*

30 *MS and notes in 1833 and 1837 editions* make a formidable; *1905-C* makes . . .

32 *MS* Indulgers <of> in . . .

33 *MS* [*ins.*] I can . . .

he may consult Warburton's *Divine Legation*; whether satisfactory or not, no better has yet been assigned. I have therefore supposed it new to Cain, without, I hope, any perversion of Holy Writ.*

With regard to the language of Lucifer, it was difficult for me to make him talk like a clergyman upon the same subjects; but I have done what I could to restrain him within the bounds of spiritual politeness. If he disclaims having tempted Eve in the shape of the serpent, it is only because the book of Genesis has not the most distant allusion to anything of the kind, but merely to the serpent in his serpentine capacity.

Note.—The reader will perceive that the author has partly adopted in this poem the notion of Cuvier, that the world had been destroyed several times before the creation of man. This speculation, derived from the different strata and the bones of enormous and unknown animals found in them, is not contrary to the Mosaic account, but rather confirms it; as no human bones have yet been discovered in those strata, although those of many known animals are found near the remains of the unknown.* The assertion of Lucifer that the pre-Adamite world was also peopled by rational beings much more intelligent than man and proportionably powerful to the mammoth, etc., etc., is, of course, a poetical fiction to help him to make out his case.

I ought to add that there is a "tramelogedia" of Alfieri, called *Abele.* I have never read that nor any other of the posthumous works of the writer, except his Life.*

39 he may <read> consult

47 *Below the words* "in his Serpentine capacity" *Byron drew a line across the page and wrote,* "Motto to the title page. / 'Now the Serpent was more subtil / than any beast of the field which the / Lord God had made.' / Genesis / Chapter 3.^{d} verse 1.st."

48–61 *The last two paragraphs are not on the MS.*

59 *MS, 1821, 1831* Tramelogedie; *1833 et al.* tramelogedia. *MS, 1821, 1831* Abel; *1833 et al.* Abele.

61 *MS and 1821 have no terminal date; 1833 et al. print* "Sept. 20, 1821," *which may be the date Byron sent Murray the last two paragraphs.*

ACT I

Scene I

The Land without Paradise. Time, Sunrise

ADAM, EVE, CAIN, ABEL, ADAH, ZILLAH, *offering a Sacrifice*

ADAM. God the Eternal! Infinite! All-wise!
Who out of darkness on the deep didst make
Light on the waters with a word—all hail!
Jehovah, with returning light, all hail!

EVE. God! who didst name the day and separate
Morning from night, till then divided never,
Who didst divide the wave from wave and call
Part of thy work the firmament—all hail!

ABEL. God! who didst call the elements into
Earth, ocean, air, and fire, and with the day
And night and worlds, which these illuminate
Or shadow, madest beings to enjoy them
And love both them and thee—all hail! all hail!

ADAH. God, the eternal parent of all things,
Who didst create these best and beauteous beings

MS Title: Cain ⟨a Tragedy⟩ in three Acts.

1 *MS* All Wise; *1821* All-Wise; *other editions* All-wise

3–4 *MS, 1905-C* All Hail; *other editions* all hail. *Same Variants in lines 8, 13, 17, 21.*

10 *MS* and ⟨out of⟩ day

11 *MS* World; *1821 et al.* worlds

14 *1905-C* God! the Eternal parent of . . .; *other editions* God, the Eternal! Parent of . . .; *MS* God! the eternal parent . . .

15 *MS* beauteous ⟨things⟩. *If* beauteous *is read as a dissyllable, the line has eleven syllables, five iambs with a feminine ending.* Beauteous *is dissyllabic also in line 94.*

To be belovèd, more than all, save thee,
Let me love thee and them—all hail! all hail!

ZILLAH. Oh God! who loving, making, blessing all,
Yet didst permit the serpent to creep in
And drive my father forth from Paradise,
Keep us from further evil—hail! all hail!

ADAM. Son Cain, my first-born, wherefore art thou silent?

CAIN. Why should I speak?

ADAM. To pray.

CAIN. Have ye not prayed?

ADAM. We have, most fervently.

CAIN. And loudly. I
Have heard you.

ADAM. So will God, I trust.

ABEL. Amen.

ADAM. But thou, my eldest born, art silent still.

16 *The 1905-C-M editions seem to be the first to use the accent on* belovèd, blessèd, *and* cursèd; *this occurs in lines 55, 188, 347, 419. Since the MS and early editions never use the accent, their printing will not be noted hereafter.*

19 *1821, 1831* serpent; *MS, 1833, 1837, 1905-C-M* Serpent. *1905-C usually capitalized this and other epithets for Lucifer (Demon, Spirit, etc.). The first two editions rarely did so, and others differed. This variant will not be noted hereafter. See the section on capitalization.*

23 *MS, 1905-C* prayed; *1821, 1831, 1833, 1837, 1904, 1905-M* pray'd. *Since this verb is consistently so printed, it will not be noted hereafter. Moreover, when this variation appears with other verbs, the division among the editions remains constant. "1821 et al." will indicate that six other editions are included. See the section "A Printing Custom."*

26 *MS* but ⟨you⟩ my . . . *This line provides an example of both slight and extreme differences in punctuation among the editions. 1821, 1831* But thou, my eldest-born, art silent still. *1833, 1837, 1904, 1905-M* But thou, my eldest born, art . . . *1905-C* But thou my eldest born? art silent still? *Note the shift in meaning here.*

CAIN. 'Tis better I should be so.

ADAM. Wherefore so?

CAIN. I have nought to ask.

ADAM. Nor aught to thank for?

CAIN. No.

ADAM. Dost thou not live?

CAIN. Must I not die?

EVE. Alas!
The fruit of our forbidden tree begins
To fall.

ADAM. And we must gather it again.
Oh God! why didst thou plant the tree of knowledge?

CAIN. And wherefore plucked ye not the tree of life?
Ye might have then defied him.

ADAM. Oh my son,
Blaspheme not; these are serpent's words.

CAIN. Why not?
The snake spoke truth. It *was* the tree of knowledge;

27 *1837, 1905-M* 'T is *These are the only editors to separate such contractions consistently, e.g., line 75* 'T was; *line 154* 'T were.

28 *Had Byron used* I've, *he would have had an iambic verse. As it stands he has an eleven-syllable line with an accented ending and with a clumsy anapest in the first foot.*

29 *MS, 1905-C live* [*ital.*]; *1821 et al.* live. *See the section on italics.*

33 *MS, 1905-C* plucked; *1821 et al.* pluck'd *Since this verb, which appears many times in the play, is consistently so printed, this variant will not be noted hereafter.*

35 *1821, 1831, 1833, 1837* serpents'; *MS, 1905-C* Serpent's; *1904, 1905-M* serpent's.

36 *MS, 1821 et al. truth* [*ital.*]

36–38 *1905-C* Tree of Knowledge . . . Tree of Life . . . Life; *but not capitalized in lines 30 and 32. Since this edition was inconsistent and since earlier editions usually did not capitalize these words, these variants will not be noted hereafter. See the section on capitalization.*

It *was* the tree of life. Knowledge is good,
And life is good, and how can both be evil?

EVE. My boy, thou speakest as I spoke, in sin,
Before thy birth; let me not see renewed
My misery in thine. I have repented.
Let me not see my offspring fall into
The snares beyond the walls of Paradise,
Which ev'n in Paradise destroyed his parents.
Content thee with what is. Had we been so,
Thou now hadst been contented. Oh my son!

ADAM. Our orisons completed, let us hence,
Each to his task of toil—not heavy, though
Needful. The earth is young and yields us kindly
Her fruits with little labour.

EVE. Cain, my son,
Behold thy father cheerful and resigned,
And do as he doth.

(*Exeunt* ADAM *and* EVE.

ZILLAH. Wilt thou not, my brother?

ABEL. Why wilt thou wear this gloom upon thy brow,
Which can avail thee nothing, save to rouse

38–40 *MS* how ⟨could⟩ [*?*] both . . . I spoke in ⟨vain⟩ / ⟨Long ere⟩ thy birth . . .

40 *1821 et al.* renew'd; *since the MS and 1905-C always spelled out such verb forms, their printing will generally not be noted hereafter.*

44 *MS, 1905-C* even . . . destroyed . . .; *1821 et al.* e'en . . . *destroy'd . . .; The first edition contraction* e'en *gives a verse with eleven syllables and a feminine ending. In 1813 Byron had ordered Murray always to print* even. "I utterly abhor 'een'— if it must be contracted, be it 'ev'n' " (*LJ, III, 278*).

45 *MS, 1821 et al. is* [*ital.*]

49 *MS* Earth is ⟨kind⟩—& yields . . .

51 *1821 et al.* resign'd

52 *1821* Exit Adam and Eve. *MS, 1831 et al.* Exeunt . . . *The same variants occur in line 64.*

Th' Eternal anger?

ADAH. My belovèd Cain,
Wilt thou frown ev'n on me?

CAIN. No Adah, no.
I fain would be alone a little while.
Abel, I'm sick at heart, but it will pass.
Precede me, brother; I will follow shortly.
And you, too, sisters, tarry not behind.
Your gentleness must not be harshly met.
I'll follow you anon.

ADAH. If not, I will
Return to seek you here.

ABEL. The peace of God
Be on your spirit, brother!

(*Exeunt* ABEL, ZILLAH, *and* ADAH.

CAIN (*solus*). And this is*
Life. Toil! And wherefore should I toil? Because
My father could not keep his place in Eden?
What had *I* done in this? I was unborn;*
I sought not to be born; nor love the state
To which that birth has brought me. Why did he
Yield to the serpent and the woman? Or
Yielding, why suffer? What was there in this?
The tree was planted, and why not for him?
If not, why place him near it, where it grew,
The fairest in the centre? They have but

55 *1821 et al.* The Eternal. *Elision gives the verse ten syllables; five iambs, and a masculine ending.*

56 *MS, 1821 et al.* even. *Without the contraction the line has eleven syllables, an anapest in the third foot, and a masculine ending. This variant also occurs in line 203.*

64 *1821* Exit Abel . . .

65 *MS* [*ins.*] and

One answer to all questions, " 'Twas *his* will
And he is good." How know I that? Because
He is all pow'rful, must all-good, too, follow?
I judge but by the fruits—and they are bitter—
Which I must feed on for a fault not mine.
Whom have we here? A shape like to the angels,
Yet of a sterner and a sadder aspect
Of spiritual essence. Why do I quake?
Why should I fear him more than other spirits,
Whom I see daily wave their fi'ry swords*
Before the gates, round which I linger oft
In twilight's hour to catch a glimpse of those
Gardens which are my just inheritance,
Ere the night closes o'er the inhibited walls
And the immortal trees, which overtop
The cherubim-defended battlements?
If I shrink not from these, the fire-armed angels,
Why should I quail from him who now approaches?
Yet he seems mightier far than them, nor less*
Beauteous, and yet not all as beautiful

76 *MS, 1821 et al. he* [*ital.*]

77 *MS, 1821 et al.* powerful. *Byron always seemed to regard* power *as a monosyllable* pow'r, *as in line 210; hence* pow'rful *here and in line 508 is dissyllabic.*

82 *Here and in line 222* spiritual *can be read as trisyllabic.*

84 *MS, 1821 et al.* fiery. *Here and in line 173 scansion seems to make contraction feasible.*

86 *MS* ⟨At⟩ twilight's; *1905-C* Twilight's. *Only this edition capitalized it.*

88 *MS* oer. *Since the MS consistently omitted the apostrophe in this word and in* eer, neer, whateer, *this MS spelling will not be noted hereafter. This verse is one of the infrequent twelve-syllable lines. Others in Act I are 138, 222, 225, 305, 447, 449, 457, 472, 499, 558.*

89–90 *MS* which ⟨oer⟩ top /The⟨ir⟩ Cherubim . . .

90 *MS, 1905-C* Cherubim; *1821 et al.* cherubim. *Early editions never capitalized* cherub *and* seraph; *the MS and 1905-C almost always did. This difference will not be noted hereafter.*

91 *1821 et al.* fire-arm'd

93 *MS* [*ins.*] far. *If* mightier *is dissyllabic, we have a regular iambic line.*

94 *MS* Beauti⟨ful⟩ and ⟨yet as if⟩ yet not . . .

As he hath been, and might be. Sorrow seems
Half of his immortality. And is it
So? And can aught grieve save humanity?
He cometh.

Enter LUCIFER.

LUCIFER. Mortal!

CAIN. Spirit, who art thou?

LUCIFER. Master of Spirits.

CAIN. And being so, canst thou*
Leave them and walk with dust?

LUCIFER. I know the thoughts
Of dust and feel for it and with you.

CAIN. How!
You know my thoughts?

LUCIFER. They are the thoughts of all
Worthy of thought. 'Tis your immortal part
Which speaks within you.

CAIN. What immortal part?
This has not been revealed. The tree of life
Was withheld from us by my father's folly,
While that of knowledge, by my mother's haste,
Was plucked too soon; and all the fruit is death.

LUCIFER. They have deceived thee; thou shalt live.

CAIN. I live,*
But live to die. And living, see no thing

96 *MS* ⟨Part⟩ of his . . .

97 *MS, 1905-C* Humanity

100 *MS* ⟨Design⟩ Leave them . . .

105 *1821 et al.* reveal'd

108 *1905-C* Death; *1821 et al.* death. *This frequent variant will not be noted hereafter. 1905-C is inconsistent; it does not capitalize the word in line 111.*

110 *MS, 1821, 1831, 1837, 1904, 1905-C-M* no thing; *1833* nothing. *1904 and 1905-M, which usually followed 1833, did not do so here. Perhaps Byron deliberately wanted the accent to fall on* thing, *giving him a regular iambic verse.*

To make death hateful, save an innate clinging,
A loathsome and yet all invincible
Instinct of life, which I abhor, as I
Despise myself, yet cannot overcome.
And so I live. Would I had never lived!

LUCIFER. Thou livest and must live forever. Think not*
The earth, which is thine outward cov'ring, is
Existence; it will cease, and thou wilt be
No less than thou art now.

CAIN. No less! and why
No more?

LUCIFER. It may be thou shalt be as we.

CAIN. And ye?

LUCIFER. Are everlasting.

CAIN. Are ye happy?

LUCIFER. We are mighty.

CAIN. Are ye happy?

LUCIFER. No. Art thou?

CAIN. How should I be so? Look on me!

LUCIFER. Poor clay!
And thou pretendest to be wretched! Thou!

CAIN. I am. And thou, with all thy might, what art thou?

113 *MS* which I ⟨despise⟩—as I

116 *MS* forever; *1821 et al.* for ever. *This consistent variant will not be noted hereafter.*

117 *MS, 1905-C* Earth; *1821 et al.* cov'ring. *This is the first time such a contraction was indicated in all editions. Similar words,* grov'ling, off'ring, flutt'ring *(292, 329, 411), though not contracted by earlier editions, should be so treated.*

119 *MS, 1821 et al.* No *less!* [*ital.*] and why

LUCIFER. One who aspired to be what made thee, and
Would not have made thee what thou art.

CAIN. Ah!
Thou look'st almost a god; and—

LUCIFER. I am none,
And having failed to be one, would be nought
Save what I am. He conquered; let him reign!

CAIN. Who?

LUCIFER. Thy sire's Maker and the earth's.

CAIN. And heav'n's
And all that in them is. So I have heard
His seraphs sing; and so my father saith.

LUCIFER. They say what they must sing and say on pain
Of being that which I am and thou art—
Of spirits and of men.

CAIN. And what is that?

LUCIFER. Souls who dare use their immortality,*
Souls who dare look the omnipotent tyrant in
His everlasting face and tell him that
His evil is not good! If he has made,
As he saith—which I know not nor believe—
But if he made us, he cannot unmake.

126 *MS* be What made ⟨you⟩—and

127 *One of the rare nine-syllable lines. Others in Act I are 367 and 463.*

129–130 *MS* to be ⟨none⟩—would . . .; *1821 et al.* fail'd, conquer'd

131 *MS* ⟨The⟩ Sire's . . .; *1821, et al.* sire's Maker, and the earth's. [Cain] And heaven's; *MS, 1905-C* Sire's maker . . . Earth's. *Although no edition here contracted* heaven's, *Byron consistently used it as a monosyllable (lines 254, 485, 502, 549–550).*

133 *MS* so ⟨our⟩ father⟨s⟩ saith.

138 *MS, 1821 et al.* Omnipotent

139 *MS* tell him ⟨not⟩ [?]

We are immortal! Nay, he'd have us so,
That he may torture. Let him! He is great,
But in his greatness is no happier than
We in our conflict. Goodness would not make*
Evil, and what else hath he made? But let him*
Sit on his vast and solitary throne,
Creating worlds, to make eternity
Less burthensome to his immense existence
And unparticipated solitude.
Let him crowd orb on orb, he is alone
Indefinite, indissoluble tyrant.
Could he but crush himself, 'twere the best boon
He ever granted. But let him reign on
And multiply himself in misery.
Spirits and men, at least we sympathise
And, suffering in concert, make our pangs
Innumerable, more endurable
By the unbounded sympathy of all
With all! But *He*, so wretched in his height,
So restless in his wretchedness, must still
Create and re-create. Perhaps he'll make
One day a Son unto himself, as he

143 *MS* he'de. *Byron did not add* e *to as many pronominal contractions on this MS as he did on* DON JUAN. *This variant will not be noted hereafter. MS, 1821 et al. have* [*ital.*].

145 Happier *may be dissyllabic.*

153 *MS, 1905-C* Indissoluble Tyrant

157 *1833, 1905-C* Men. *But in a similar phrase in line 136 these editions did not capitalize it. MS* sympathize; *1821 et al.* sympathise. *This consistent variant will not be noted hereafter.*

159 *MS* ⟨yet⟩ endurable

163 *MS* Create and ⟨create⟩ recreate . . .

163–166 *Three and a half lines were omitted entirely in the 1821 and 1831 editions. 1833 printed them in a note with the label* "In MS." *Coleridge (1905) restored them to the text, but 1904 and 1905-M did not. The 1833 note and the 1905 text are identical. The 1821 omission was no doubt intentional since Murray and his advisors probably regarded as blasphemous*

Gave you a father, and if he so doth,
Mark me! that Son will be a sacrifice.

CAIN. Thou speak'st to me of things which long have swum
In visions through my thought. I never could
Reconcile what I saw with what I heard.
My father and my mother talk to me
Or serpents and of fruits and trees. I see
The gates of what they call their Paradise
Guarded by fi'ry-sworded cherubim,
Which shut them out, and me. I feel the weight
Of daily toil and constant thought. I look
Around a world where I see nothing, with
Thoughts which arise within me, as if they
Could master all things; but I thought alone
This misery was mine. My father is
Tamed down; my mother has forgot the mind
Which made her thirst for knowledge at the risk
Of an eternal curse. My brother is
A watching shepherd boy, who offers up
The firstlings of the flock to him who bids
The earth yield nothing to us without sweat.
My sister Zillah sings an earlier hymn
Than the birds' matins; and my Adah, my
Own and belovèd, she too understands not

Lucifer's comment on God's motive for the creation of Christ. Though Byron protested the expurgation of DON JUAN, *the published correspondence contains no rebuke for this excision in* CAIN. *Almost a year later, on October 9, 1822, he wrote his publisher that he had no objection to the omission of a "passage in* CAIN," *that he did not identify (LJ, VI, 120).*

165 *MS* ⟨Made⟩ you ⟨your father's son⟩—and if he ⟨does⟩—

179 *MS, 1821 et al. mine [ital.]*

183–186 *MS* A ⟨drudging husbandman⟩ who offers up
The ⟨first fruits of the earth⟩ to him who ⟨made⟩
⟨That earth⟩ . . . / . . . ⟨the⟩ earlier . . .
It is possible that Byron read earlier *as a dissyllable, giving him a regular iambic verse.*

188 *This irregular eleven-syllable line can be scanned without a single iamb.*

The mind which overwhelms me. Never till
Now met I aught to sympathise with me.
'Tis well. I rather would consort with spirits.

LUCIFER. And hadst thou not been fit by thine own soul
For such companionship, I would not now
Have stood before thee as I am. A serpent
Had been enough to charm ye, as before.

CAIN. Ah! didst *thou* tempt my mother?

LUCIFER. I tempt none,
Save with the truth. Was not the tree, the tree
Of knowledge? And was not the tree of life
Still fruitful? Did *I* bid her pluck them not?
Did *I* plant things prohibited within
The reach of beings innocent, and curious
By their own innocence? I would have made ye
Gods; and ev'n He who thrust ye forth, so thrust ye*
Because "ye should not eat the fruits of life
And become gods as we." Were those his words?

CAIN. They were, as I have heard from those who heard them
In thunder.

LUCIFER. Then who was the demon? He
Who would not let ye live, or he who would*
Have made ye live forever in the joy
And pow'r of knowledge?

CAIN. Would they had snatched both

194–195 *MS* as I am;—but ⟨chosen⟩
⟨sent⟩
⟨The Serpent's charming Symbol—as before—⟩
⟨charming Serpent to you⟩

201 Curious *may be used as a dissyllable here and in line 403.*

203 *MS* he; *1821 et al.* He

204 *MS* ye ⟨might⟩ not ⟨cull⟩ eat . . .

205 *MS* were these his words? *1821 et al.* those

207 *MS, 1905-C* Demon

210 *MS, 1821 et al.* power, snatch'd. *Since this verb, which is almost as com-*

The fruits, or neither!

LUCIFER. One is yours already;
The other may be still.

CAIN. How so?

LUCIFER. By being
Yourselves in your resistance. Nothing can*
Quench the mind if the mind will be itself
And centre of surrounding things; 'tis made
To sway.

CAIN. But didst thou tempt my parents?

LUCIFER. I?*
Poor clay! What should I tempt them for, or how?

CAIN. They say the serpent was a spirit.

LUCIFER. Who
Saith that? It is not written so on high.
The proud One will not so far falsify,
Though man's vast fears and little vanity
Would make him cast upon the spiritual nature
His own low failing. The snake was the snake—
No more; and yet not less than those he tempted,
In nature being earth also, *more* in *wisdom,*
Since he could overcome them and foreknew
The knowledge fatal to their narrow joys.

---

mon in CAIN *as* pluck'd, *is always contracted in these editions, it will not be noted hereafter.*

217 *MS* tempt ⟨thee⟩ thee for or ⟨to⟩? *1821 et al.* tempt them for . . .

220 *MS* One ⟨does⟩ not . . .

221 *MS* Man's ⟨poor⟩ fears . . .

222 *MS*[*ins.*] the. *If* spiritual, *as in line 82, is trisyllabic, the line has twelve syllables and may be scanned thus:*

Wŏuld máke/ hĭm cást/ ŭpòn / thĕ spír / ĭtùal / nátŭre.

223 *MS* own ⟨vile⟩ failing—*MS, 1821, 1831* was; *1833, 1837 1904, 1905-C-M was* [*ital.*]

Think'st thou I'd take the shape of things that die?

CAIN. But the thing had a demon?

LUCIFER. He but woke one
In those he spake to with his forky tongue.
I tell thee that the serpent was no more
Than a mere serpent. Ask the cherubim
Who guard the tempting tree. When thousand ages
Have rolled o'er your dead ashes and your seed's,
The seed of the then world may thus array
Their earliest fault in fable and attribute*
To me a shape I scorn, as I scorn all
That bows to him who made things but to bend
Before his sullen, sole eternity.
But we who see the truth must speak it. Thy
Fond parents listened to a creeping thing
And fell. For what should spirits tempt them? What
Was there to envy in the narrow bounds
Of Paradise, that spirits who pervade
Space—but I speak to thee of what thou know'st not,*
With all thy tree of knowledge.

CAIN. But thou canst not
Speak aught of knowledge which I would not know
And do not thirst to know and bear a mind
To know.

LUCIFER. And heart to look on?

CAIN. Be it proved.

228–229 *MS* thou ⟨that I would⟩ take . . . / . . . ⟨No—he⟩ but . . .
234 *MS* rolled ⟨away⟩ oer you dead ashes & you Seed's; *1821 et al.* roll'd
235 *MS* world ⟨shall⟩ may . . .
236 Earliest *may be dissyllabic.*
237 *1905-M* To them a shape . . . *Probably a misprint.*
240 *MS* speak it;—⟨you⟩
241 *1821 et al.* listen'd
248 *MS* and ⟨have⟩ a mind

LUCIFER. Dar'st thou to look on Death?
CAIN. He has not yet
Been seen.
LUCIFER. But must be undergone.
CAIN. My father
Says he is something dreadful, and my mother
Weeps when he's named, and Abel lifts his eyes
To heav'n, and Zillah casts hers to the earth
And sighs a prayer, and Adah looks on me
And speaks not.
LUCIFER. And thou?
CAIN. Thoughts unspeakable
Crowd in my breast to burning when I hear
Of this almighty Death, who is, it seems,
Inevitable. Could I wrestle with him?
I wrestled with the lion when a boy
In play till he ran roaring from my gripe.
LUCIFER. It has no shape but will absorb all things
That bear the form of earth-born being.
CAIN. Ah!
I thought it was a being. Who could do
Such evil things to beings save a being?

250 *MS, 1821* Dar'st thou to look; *1833, 1837, 1905-M* Darest thou to look; *1904, 1905-C* Darest thou look. *The MS, 1821, 1904, and 1905-C* versions *seem better than the 1833, 1837, 1905-M, which has eleven syllables and a masculine ending. All editions capitalize* Death, *though Byron did not do so. MS* ⟨It⟩ has not yet

252 *MS* Says ⟨it⟩ is . . .

253 *MS* when ⟨his⟩ named—*1837* when he is named. *Other editions correspond to the present text.*

255 *MS* Adah ⟨casts⟩ on me

258 *MS* Death ⟨which⟩ is . . .

260–261 *These lines are the first inserted ones, crowded in the small script usual for such additions between the first line of Lucifer's speech (262) and the original last line of Cain's (259).*

264 *MS* who ⟨should⟩ could do

LUCIFER. Ask the Destroyer.

CAIN. Who?

LUCIFER. The Maker. Call him*
Which name thou wilt, he makes but to destroy.

CAIN. I knew not that, yet thought it. Since I heard*
Of death, although I know not what it is,
Yet it seems horrible. I have looked out
In the vast desolate night in search of him,
And when I saw gigantic shadows in
The umbrage of the walls of Eden, chequered
By the far-flashing of the cherubs' swords,
I watched for what I thought his coming; for
With fear rose longing in my heart to know
What 'twas which shook us all, but nothing came.
And then I turned my weary eyes from off
Our native and forbidden Paradise,
Up to the lights above us in the azure,
Which are so beautiful. Shall they too die?

LUCIFER. Perhaps, but long outlive both thine and thee.

CAIN. I'm glad of that. I would not have them die,
They are so lovely. What is death? I fear,
I feel, it is a dreadful thing, but what,
I cannot compass. 'Tis denounced against us,
Both them who sinned and sinned not, as an ill.
What ill?

LUCIFER. To be resolved into the earth.

268–270 *Earlier editions print these lines as one sentence.*
270, 273, 275, 278 *1821 et al.* look'd, chequer'd, watch'd, turn'd
273 *MS* Eden ⟨lit⟩ checquered
276 *MS* fear ⟨was⟩ longing . . .
287 *MS* Both ⟨they⟩ who . . .; *1821 et al.* sinn'd. *Since this verb is always so printed, it will not be noted hereafter.*

CAIN. But shall I know it?

LUCIFER. As I know not death,
I cannot answer.

CAIN. Were I quiet earth
That were no evil. Would I ne'er had been
Aught else but dust!

LUCIFER. That is a grov'ling wish,
Less than thy father's, for he wished to know.

CAIN. But not to live, or wherefore plucked he not
The life-tree?

LUCIFER. He was hindered.

CAIN. Deadly error!
Not to snatch first that fruit. But ere he plucked
The knowledge, he was ignorant of death.
Alas! I scarcely now know what it is
And yet I fear it—fear I know not what!

LUCIFER. And I who know all things fear nothing; see
What is true knowledge.

CAIN. Wilt thou teach me all?

LUCIFER. Aye, upon one condition.

CAIN. Name it.

LUCIFER. That
Thou dost fall down and worship me, thy Lord.

289 *MS* know ⟨it⟩ not . . .

292 *MS* That⟨s⟩ a groveling; *1821, 1831* grov'ling; *1833* groveling; *1837, 1904, 1905-M* grovelling; *1905-C grovelling* [*ital.*]. *The 1821, 1831 contraction seems metrically justifiable. There is no precedent for the 1905-C italics.*

293, 295 *1821 et al.* wish'd, hinder'd; *MS, 1905-C* Life-tree

296 *MS* eer. *Byron's spelling was typical of his haste, but he did not always make this mistake. 1821 et al.* ere

302 *MS, 1905-C* Aye; *1821 et al.* Ay. *Since this variation is consistent in these editions (e.g., I, 347, 353, 419; II, i, 171), it will not be noted hereafter.*

303 *MS* worship ⟨thee⟩ . . .

CAIN. Thou art not the Lord my father worships.

LUCIFER. No.

CAIN. His equal?

LUCIFER. No, I have nought in common with him,
Nor would. I would be aught above, beneath,
Aught save a sharer or a servant of
His power. I dwell apart, but I am great.
Many there are who worship me, and more
Who shall. Be thou amongst the first.

CAIN. I never*
As yet have bowed unto my father's God,
Although my brother Abel oft implores
That I would join with him in sacrifice.
Why should I bow to thee?

LUCIFER. Hast thou ne'er bowed
To him?

CAIN. Have I not said it? Need I say it?
Could not thy mighty knowledge teach thee that?

LUCIFER. He who bows not to him has bowed to me!*

CAIN. But I will bend to neither.

LUCIFER. Ne'er the less
Thou art my worshipper; not worshipping
Him makes thee mine the same.

CAIN. And what is that?

304 *This eleven-syllable line can be scanned as trochaic with an extra accent:*
Thou art/ not the/ Lord my/ father/ worships. [Lucifer] No.

306 *MS* [*ins.*] aught

309 *MS* Many ⟨sha⟩ there . . .; *intended to write* shall [*?*].

311, 314, 317 *1821 et al.* bow'd

318 *MS* But I will ⟨kneel⟩ . . .

320 *MS* Him—makes ⟨me thine⟩ mine . . .

LUCIFER. Thou'lt know here and hereafter.

CAIN. Let me but
Be taught the myst'ry of my being.

LUCIFER. Follow
Where I will lead thee.

CAIN. But I must retire
To till the earth, for I had promised—

LUCIFER. What?

CAIN. To cull some first-fruits.

LUCIFER. Why?

CAIN. To offer up
With Abel on an altar.

LUCIFER. Saidst thou not*
Thou ne'er hadst bent to him who made thee?

CAIN. Yes,
But Abel's earnest prayer has wrought upon me.
The off'ring is more his than mine—and Adah—

LUCIFER. Why dost thou hesitate?

CAIN. She is my sister,*
Born on the same day of the same womb, and
She wrung from me with tears this promise, and

322 *MS, 1821 et al.* mystery. *If* mystery *is trisyllabic, this irregular verse has twelve syllables. With a contraction,* myst'ry, *the eleven-syllable line may be scanned as iambic with feminine ending. See lines 460, 539.*

325 *MS, 1821, 1831* first fruits; *1833, 1837, 1904, 1905-C-M* first-fruits.

326 *MS* altar ⟨as the⟩ [*?*]. *MS, 1904, 1905-C* Said'st; *other editions print* Saidst.

329 *MS, 1821 et al.* offering. *Byron always seemed to regard this as dissyllabic. MS* than ⟨his⟩ mine . . .

331 *MS* day—⟨and I love her⟩—and

Rather than see her weep, I would, methinks,
Bear all and worship aught.

LUCIFER. Then follow me.

CAIN. I will.

Enter ADAH.

ADAH. My brother, I have come for thee.
It is our hour of rest and joy, and we
Have less without thee. Thou hast laboured not
This morn, but I have done thy task. The fruits
Are ripe and glowing as the light which ripens.
Come away.

CAIN. Seest thou not?

ADAH. I see an angel.
We have seen many. Will he share our hour
Of rest? He is welcome.

CAIN. But he is not like
The angels we have seen.

ADAH. Are there then others?
But he is welcome as they were. They deigned
To be our guests. Will he?

CAIN *(to Lucifer)*. Wilt thou?

LUCIFER. I ask
Thee to be mine.

CAIN. I must away with him.

334 *MS* worship ⟨all⟩—
337 *MS* Have ⟨none⟩ without thee—*1821 et al.* labour'd
339 *MS* Are ripe and ⟨lovely⟩ as the ⟨Sun⟩ which ripens.
340 *MS, 1821, 1831, 1833, 1837* See'st; *1905-C-M* Seest. *With two exceptions (II, i, 177; II, ii, 130) this variation is consistent and will not be noted hereafter. It occurs four times: II, ii, 113, 207; III, 491, 531.*
341 *MS* ⟨would⟩ he share . . .
344 *1821 et al.* deign'd

ADAH. And leave us?
CAIN. Aye.
ADAH. And me?
CAIN. Belovèd Adah!
ADAH. Let me go with thee.
LUCIFER. No, she must not.
ADAH. Who
Art thou that steppest between heart and heart?
CAIN. He is a god.
ADAH. How know'st thou?
CAIN. He speaks like
A god.
ADAH. So did the serpent, and it lied.
LUCIFER. Thou errest, Adah. Was not the tree that*
Of knowledge?
ADAH. Aye, to our eternal sorrow.
LUCIFER. And yet that grief is knowledge. So he lied not,
And if he did betray you, 'twas with truth;
And truth in its own essence cannot be
But good.
ADAH. But all we know of it has gathered
Evil on ill: expulsion from our home
And dread and toil and sweat and heaviness,
Remorse of that which was, and hope of that
Which cometh not. Cain, walk not with this spirit.

347 *MS, 1821 et al. me* [*ital.*]
349 *MS* that ⟨walkest⟩ between heart . . .
350–351 *MS, 1905-C* God; *1821 et al.* god. *The sense makes the latter more appropriate.*
355–356 *1905-C* Truth
357 *1821 et al.* gather'd
361 *1905-C* Spirit; *but Coleridge did not capitalize it in line 376. He usually did so when it referred to Lucifer.*

Bear with what we have borne, and love me. I
Love thee.

LUCIFER. More than thy mother and thy sire?*

ADAH. I do. Is that a sin too?

LUCIFER. No, not yet.
It one day will be in your children.

ADAH. What!
Must not my daughter love her brother Enoch?

LUCIFER. Not as thou lovest Cain.

ADAH. Oh my God!
Shall they not love and bring forth things that love
Out of their love? Have they not drawn their milk
Out of this bosom? Was not he, their father,
Born of the same sole womb in the same hour
With me? Did we not love each other? And
In multiplying our being multiply
Things which will love each other as we love
Them, and as I love thee, my Cain? Go not
Forth with this spirit. He is not of ours.

LUCIFER. The sin I speak of is not of my making
And cannot be a sin in you, whate'er
It seem in those who will replace ye in
Mortality.

ADAH. What is the sin which is not
Sin in itself? Can circumstance make sin
Or virtue? If it doth, we are the slaves
Of—

LUCIFER. Higher things than ye are slaves, and higher
Than them or ye would be so, did they not

381 *MS* [*ins.*] in

383–384 THE GENTLEMAN'S MAGAZINE *(XCI* [*December, 1821*]*, 615) and* THE LITERARY GAZETTE *(No. 257* [*December, 1821*]*, 811) called this bad grammar.*

Prefer an independency of torture
To the smooth agonies of adulation,
In hymns and harpings and self-seeking prayers,
To that which is omnipotent, because
It is omnipotent, and not from love,
But terror and self-hope.

ADAH. Omnipotence
Must be all goodness.

LUCIFER Was it so in Eden?

ADAH. Fiend, tempt me not with beauty. Thou art fairer
Than was the serpent, and as false.

LUCIFER. As true.
Ask Eve, your mother. Bears she not the knowledge
Of good and evil?

ADAH. Oh my mother! thou*
Hast plucked a fruit more fatal to thine offspring
Than to thyself. Thou at the least hast passed
Thy youth in Paradise, in innocent
And happy intercourse with happy spirits.
But we, thy children, ignorant of Eden,*
Art girt about by demons, who assume
The words of God and tempt us with our own
Dissatisfied and curious thoughts, as thou
Wert worked on by the snake in thy most flushed

386–387 *MS* To the ⟨long⟩ agonies . . . / . . . and ⟨obedient⟩ prayers

390 *On the MS Byron's hesitation at this point is indicated by his twice deleting* Adah *and by a sudden diminution of the script in the first half of line 390, as if it were an afterthought, and by the curving line he drew across the page separating the two halves of line 390.*

393 *MS* and ⟨more⟩ false—[Lucifer] ⟨How false?⟩ As true.

394 *MS* knows [*?*] she not the knowledge; *1821 et al.* bears she not . . .

397–398 *MS* hast ⟨known⟩ / ⟨A⟩ Thy youth ⟨of⟩ Paradise—⟨an⟩ innocent
MS, 1821, 1831 past; *1833, 1837, 1904, 1905-M* pass'd; *1905-C* passed

400 *MS* ignorant of ⟨this⟩—

404 *1821 et al.* work'd, flush'd

And heedless, harmless wantonness of bliss.
I cannot answer this immortal thing
Which stands before me. I cannot abhor him.
I look upon him with a pleasing fear
And yet I fly not from him. In his eye*
There is a fastening attraction which
Fixes my flutt'ring eyes on his. My heart
Beats quick, he awes me, and yet draws me near,
Nearer, and nearer. Cain, Cain, save me from him!

CAIN. What dreads my Adah? This is no ill spirit.

ADAH. He is not God, nor God's. I have beheld
The cherubs and the seraphs; he looks not
Like them.

CAIN. But there are spirits loftier still—
The archangels.

LUCIFER. And still loftier than the archangels.

ADAH. Aye, but not blessèd.

LUCIFER. If the blessedness
Consists in slav'ry—no.

ADAH. I have heard it said,
The seraphs love most; cherubim know most.*

407 *MS, 1837* can not

411 *MS, 1821 et al.* fluttering. *The metrics suggest that this should be dissyllabic. It is clumsy here but a typical contraction. See line 117 n.*

412 *MS* he awes ⟨him⟩ & yet . . . *One of the many heavily accented monosyllabic lines in* CAIN. *Its rhythmic irregularity and that of the next verse seem appropriate to Adah's agitation.*

414 *MS* This is no⟨th⟩ ill Spirit.

417–418 *In both lines* loftier *may be dissyllabic. Even so, 418 has thirteen syllables. Though elision may also be twice possible here,* th' archangels, *it does not improve sound or rhythm.*

420 *MS, 1821 et al.* slavery. *Contraction* (slav'ry, I've) *permits a regular iambic scansion. However, Byron never did contract* I have, *and so the line remains awkward.*

421 *MS* The Seraphs *love most* [*ins.*]—⟨the⟩ Cherubim *know most—All four words are ital on MS and in 1821 et al.*

And this should be a cherub, since he loves not.

LUCIFER. And if the higher knowledge quenches love,
What must he be you cannot love when known?
Since the all-knowing cherubim love least,
The seraphs' love can be but ignorance.
That they are not compatible, the doom
Of thy fond parents, for their daring, proves.
Choose betwixt love and knowledge, since there is
No other choice. Your sire has chosen already.
His worship is but fear.

ADAH. Oh Cain, choose love.

CAIN. For thee, my Adah, I choose not; it was
Born with me, but I love nought else.

ADAH. Our parents?

CAIN. Did they love us when they snatched from the tree
That which hath driv'n us all from Paradise?

ADAH. We were not born then, and if we had been,
Should we not love them and our children, Cain?

CAIN. My little Enoch! and his lisping sister!
Could I but deem them happy, I would half

424–426 *MS, 1821 et al. he be* [*ital.*] . . . *All editions ignored Byron's italics of* least. *Lines 425–426 were inserted on the MS, and at the same time a revision was made in the second half of line 424. The original sequence ran thus (423, 424, 427):*
And if the higher knowledge quenches love
What must *he be* [*ital.*] ⟨who places love in ignorance?⟩—
That they are not compatible . . .
1833 and 1905-C erroneously printed the MS version of line 424:
What can *he be* [*ital.*] . . .

428 *1831 added a period after* proves, *that 1821 had omitted.*

429 *1905-C* Love and Knowledge. *Neither the MS nor the early editions provide a precedent. Coleridge also capitalized* Love *in line 431.*

432 *MS* I chose not—; *1821 et al.* choose . . .

435 *MS* from ⟨Ed⟩ Paradise? *MS, 1821 et al.* driven

Forget—but it can never be forgotten
Through thrice a thousand generations. Never*
Shall men love the remembrance of the man
Who sowed the seed of evil and mankind
In the same hour. They plucked the tree of science
And sin, and not content with their own sorrow,
Begot me, thee, and all the few that are
And all the unnumbered and innumerable
Multitudes, millions, myriads, which may be,
To inherit agonies accumulated
By ages—and *I* must be sire of such things!
Thy beauty and thy love, my love and joy,
The rapturous moment and the placid hour,
All we love in our children and each other,
But lead them and ourselves through many years
Of sin and pain, or few, but still of sorrow,
Interchecked with an instant of brief pleasure,
To death, the unknown. Methinks the tree of knowledge
Hath not fulfilled its promise. If they sinned,
At least they ought to have known all things that are

440 *MS* can never ⟨can⟩ be . . . *It makes little difference if* forgotten *is contracted here or not; either gives us one of Byron's usual metrical patterns.*

443, 447, 456, 458 *1821 et al.* sow'd, unnumber'd, Intercheck'd, fulfill'd, sinn'd. *Since the second of these appears several times, it will not be noted hereafter.*

444 *MS same* [*ital.*]

446 *MS, 1821 et al.* Begot *me—thee* [*ital.*]

446–448 *MS* the few that are ⟨and all⟩
⟨The⟩ unnumbered & innumerable ⟨multitudes⟩
⟨Of beings that may be—⟩

448 *Here and in 522* myriads *is dissyllabic.*

452 *If* rapturous *is read as a dissyllable, the line has ten syllables and is iambic.*

454–455 *MS* ourselves ⟨unto long⟩ years
Of sin & pain—⟨or short of pain & sin⟩

457 *MS* ⟨And⟩ Death . . .; *1821 et al.* Death. *It is not however capitalized in lines 460, 468, except by 1905-C.*

Of knowledge—and the mystery of death.
What do they know? That they are miserable?
What need of snakes and fruits to teach us that?

ADAH. I am not wretched, Cain, and if thou
Wert happy—

CAIN. Be thou happy then alone.
I will have nought to do with happiness
Which humbles me and mine.

ADAH. Alone I could not,*
Nor would be happy; but with those around us,
I think I could be so, despite of death,
Which, as I know it not, I dread not, though
It seems an awful shadow, if I may
Judge from what I have heard.

LUCIFER. And thou couldst not
Alone, thou say'st, be happy?

ADAH. Alone! Oh my God!
Who could be happy and alone, or good?
To me my solitude seems sin, unless
When I think how soon I shall see my brother,
His brother and our children and our parents.

LUCIFER. Yet thy God is alone, and is he happy,
Lonely, and good?

ADAH. He is not so; he hath
The angels and the mortals to make happy,
And thus becomes so in diffusing joy.
What else can joy be, but the spreading joy?

460 *MS* Of knowledge—⟨but it was a lie no doubt⟩—
461 *MS* miserable? *1821 et al.* miserable.
465 *1837 misprint* naught. *This edition did not use this spelling elsewhere.*
467, 472 *MS, 1821 et al. would; Alone* [*ital.*]
477–478 *MS* And ⟨he is⟩ happy?—/ . . . ⟨for⟩ he hath
481 *MS* What else ⟨is⟩ Joy?—but ⟨in⟩ spreading Joy?
What else can be Joy but the . . . *1821 et al.* What else can joy be . . .

LUCIFER. Ask of your sire, the exile fresh from Eden,
Or of his first-born son. Ask your own heart,
It is not tranquil?

ADAH. Alas no, and you—
Are you of heav'n?

LUCIFER. If I am not, enquire
The cause of this all-spreading happiness
(Which you proclaim) of the all-great and good
Maker of life and living things. It is
His secret and he keeps it. We must bear,
And some of us resist, and both in vain,
His seraphs say; but it is worth the trial,
Since better may not be without. There is
A wisdom in the spirit which directs
To right, as in the dim blue air the eye
Of you young mortals lights at once upon
The star which watches, welcoming the morn.

ADAH. It is a beautiful star; I love it for
Its beauty.

LUCIFER. And why not adore?

ADAH. Our father

483 *MS* first born . . . heart⟨s⟩; *1821 et al.* first-born
484 *MS* tranquil? *1821 et al.* tranquil
485 *MS, 1833, 1905-C-M* enquire; *1821, 1831, 1837, 1904* inquire
489 *1821* We. *One of the few times the printer omitted Byron's italic; 1833 and 1905-C restored it.*
491 *MS* ⟨Perhaps it may be⟩—it is worth the trial—
492 *MS* [*ins.*] not
493 *MS* Spirit⟨s⟩
494 *MS* To Right, ⟨as in the twilight⟩ air the eye
⟨vast dim⟩
⟨obscure⟩ [*?*]
495–496 *MS* ⟨soo⟩ lights at once . . .
The Star which ⟨risest earliest of⟩ the Morn.
⟨sits up⟩ welcoming . . .

Adores th' Invisible only.

LUCIFER. But the symbols
Of th' Invisible are the loveliest
Of what is visible; and yon bright star
Is leader of the host of heav'n.

ADAH. Our father
Saith that he has beheld the God himself
Who made him and our mother.

LUCIFER. Hast *thou* seen him?

ADAH. Yes, in his works.

LUCIFER. But in his being?

ADAH. No,
Save in my father, who is God's own image,
Or in his angels, who are like to thee
And brighter, yet less beautiful and pow'rful
In seeming. As the silent sunny noon,
All light they look upon us, but thou seemest
Like an ethereal night, where long white clouds
Streak the deep purple, and unnumbered stars
Spangle the wonderful mysterious vault

499–500 *MS, 1821 et al.* The Invisible. *Even with elision, line 499 has twelve syllables.*

500 *MS* are the ⟨most⟩ [?] ⟨loveliest⟩
⟨loveliest⟩

505–506 *MS* But in his ⟨person?⟩/ . . . who is ⟨his⟩ God's . . .

507 *MS* ⟨and⟩ in his . . .

507–517 *John Nichol thought that Adah's impression of Lucifer's beautiful attraction for her was written* "more after the style of Shelley than anything else in Byron" (BYRON, *p. 143*).

508 *MS* ⟨Though⟩ brighter—yet less beautiful—⟨thou seemest⟩

510 *MS* seemest; *1821 et al.* seem'st. *The MS, which seems preferable, gives us an eleven-syllable verse with a feminine ending and a fluent run-on with the next verse, which begins with a trochee.*

511 *MS* ⟨A most⟩ etherial Night . . .; *1821 et al.* ethereal. *This consistent variant will not be noted hereafter. Byron generally used this word as a trisyllable.*

513 *Byron probably regarded* mysterious *as trisyllabic.*

With things that look as if they would be suns,
So beautiful, unnumbered, and endearing,
Not dazzling and yet drawing us to them,
They fill my eyes with tears, and so dost thou.
Thou seem'st unhappy; do not make us so,
And I will weep for thee.

LUCIFER. Alas, those tears!
Couldst thou but know what oceans will be shed.

ADAH. By me?

LUCIFER. By all.

ADAH. What all?

LUCIFER. The million millions,
The myriad myriads, the all-peopled earth,
The unpeopled earth, and the o'erpeopled Hell,
Of which thy bosom is the germ.

ADAH. Oh Cain!
This spirit curseth us.

CAIN. Let him say on.
Him will I follow.

ADAH. Whither?

LUCIFER. To a place
Whence he shall come back to thee in an hour,
But in that hour see things of many days.

ADAH. How can that be?

LUCIFER. Did not your Maker make
Out of old worlds this new one in few days?
And cannot I, who aided in this work,

520 *MS, 1833* Could'st; *1821, 1905-C-M* Couldst. *This is the only time in Acts I and II that 1833 used an apostrophe in this word or in* shouldst. *See III, 368.*

523 *MS, un*peopled, *oer*-peopled; *1821 et al. omitted the MS italics.*

524 *MS, 1821 et al.* O Cain

527 *MS, 1821 et al. Whence* [*ital.*]

Show in an hour what he hath made in many
Or hath destroyed in few?

CAIN. Lead on.

ADAH. Will he
In sooth return within an hour?

LUCIFER. He shall.
With us acts are exempt from time, and we
Can crowd eternity into an hour
Or stretch an hour into eternity.
We breathe not by a mortal measurement,
But that's a myst'ry. Cain, come on with me.

ADAH. Will he return?

LUCIFER. Aye, woman, he alone*
Of mortals from that place (the first and last
Who shall return, save ONE) shall come back to thee
To make that silent and expectant world
As populous as this. At present there
Are few inhabitants.

ADAH. Where dwellest thou?

LUCIFER. Throughout all space. Where should I dwell? Where are*
Thy God or Gods, there am I. All things are
Divided with me; life and death and time,
Eternity and heav'n and earth and that
Which is not heav'n nor earth, but peopled with

533 *1821 et al.* destroy'd

537 *MS* Or ⟨spin⟩ stretch . . .

539 *MS, 1821 et al.* mystery. *Whereas in line 460* mystery *was given full measure and in line 322 might be read as either contracted or not, it seems better here to read it as a dissyllable and to scan the line with five iambs.*

540 *MS* ⟨He will⟩ return.

546 *MS* where ⟨in⟩

548 *1905-C* Life and Death—and Time. *This edition is unique in its capitalization, for not even Byron capitalized these words. In 549 and 550 it inconsistently used lower case for* heaven.

Those who once peopled or shall people both—
These are my realms! So that I do divide
His, and possess a kingdom which is not
His. If I were not that which I have said,
Could I stand here? His angels are within
Your vision.

ADAH. So they were when the fair serpent
Spoke with our mother first.

LUCIFER. Cain, thou hast heard.
If thou dost long for knowledge, I can satiate
That thirst, nor ask thee to partake of fruits
Which shall deprive thee of a single good
The conqueror has left thee. Follow me.

CAIN. Spirit, I have said it.

(*Exeunt* LUCIFER *and* CAIN.

ADAH (*follows, exclaiming*). Cain! my brother! Cain!

551 *MS* ⟨and⟩ shall . . .
553–554 *MS, 1821 et al. His, His* [*ital.*]
558 *MS* If thou do'st ⟨seek⟩ for . . .
561 *MS, 1905-C* Conqueror

ACT II

Scene I

The Abyss of Space

CAIN. I tread on air and sink not; yet I fear
To sink.

LUCIFER. Have faith in me, and thou shalt be
Borne on the air, of which I am the prince.*

CAIN. Can I do so without impiety?

LUCIFER. Believe and sink not; doubt and perish. Thus
Would run the edict of the other God,
Who names me demon to his angels. They*
Echo the sound to miserable things,
Which, knowing nought beyond their shallow senses,
Worship the word which strikes their ear and deem
Evil or good what is proclaimed to them
In their abasement. I will have none such.
Worship or worship not, thou shalt behold
The worlds beyond thy little world, nor be
Amerced for doubts beyond thy little life
With torture of *my* dooming. There will come*

3, 7, 26 *MS, 1905-C* Prince, Demon

7 *MS* Angels; ⟨echo⟩

10 *MS* Worship the ⟨sound⟩ which . . .; *1905-C word* [*ital.*]. *There is no precedent for the italics.*

11, 17 *1821 et al.* proclaim'd, toss'd

13 *MS* [*ins.*] not

An hour when, tossed upon some water-drops,
A man shall say to a man, "Believe in me
And walk the waters"; and the man shall walk
The billows and be safe. *I* will not say,
"Believe in *me*," as a conditional creed
To save thee; but fly with me o'er the gulf*
Of space an equal flight, and I will show
What thou dar'st not deny—the history
Of past and present and of future worlds.

CAIN. Oh God or demon or whate'er thou art,
Is yon our earth?

LUCIFER. Dost thou not recognise
The dust which formed your father?

Can it be?*
Yon small blue circle, swinging in far ether,
With an inferior circlet purpler still,

17 *MS* An hour—⟨when walking on a petty lake⟩ . . . *Wilkinson:* "Nothing but a mixture of ignorance, folly, and extravagance could imagine a man being tossed on some water drops" (CAIN, A POEM, *p. 80*). *He regarded as inaccurate or obscure much of the diction in this scene:* conditional creed, *line 21;* a swinging planet, *line 29;* the roundest of the stars, *line 38;* stars that rolled like leaves along the Eden Streams, *lines 103–104;* cleave the blue, *line 144; and the clumsy sentence in lines 192–196 (pp. 80–89).*

22 *MS* but ⟨wing⟩ with me . . . *MS* Gulph; *all editions use* gulf. *This will not be noted hereafter.*

24 *MS dare'st; 1821 et al.* dar'st. *In line 133 Byron wrote* dar'st.

26 *MS, 1905-C* God! or Demon!

27 *MS, 1821* recognize; *1831 et al.* recognise

28 *MS* dust which ⟨made⟩ your father? *1821 et al.* form'd

29 *MS* Yon round blue . . .; *all editions print* Yon small blue . . .

30 *MS* Circlet ⟨dimmer⟩ purpler still; *1821 et al.* circlet near it still; *1905-C* circlet purpler it still. *This line on the moon is one of the few cruxes of the* CAIN *text. The earlier editions did not follow the MS because of a change made during publication. Coleridge decided to go back to the MS, but a pronoun,* it, *got into his version, probably a misprint. The MS seems to offer the better version, though it is far from graceful in rhythm or pleasant in sound.* Inferior, *as usual, is trisyllabic here and in 82; II, ii, 91, 133, 185.*

Which looks like that which lit our earthly night?
Is this our Paradise? Where are its walls
And they who guard them?

LUCIFER. Point me out the site
Of Paradise.

CAIN. How should I? As we move*
Like sunbeams onward, it grows small and smaller,
And as it waxes little and then less,
Gathers a halo round it like the light
Which shone the roundest of the stars when I
Beheld them from the skirts of Paradise.
Methinks they both, as we recede from them,
Appear to join th' innumerable stars
Which are around us and as we move on
Increase their myriads.

LUCIFER. And if there should be
Worlds greater than thine own, inhabited
By greater things, and they themselves far more
In number than the dust of thy dull earth,
Though multiplied to animated atoms,
All living and all doomed to death and wretched,
What wouldst thou think?

CAIN. I should be proud of thought*

33 *MS* ⟨Dost⟩ Point me out . . .

37–38 *MS* ⟨Moon⟩ light / Which ⟨was⟩ the roundest . . .

41 *MS, 1821 et al.* the innumerable . . .

43 Myriads *is dissyllabic here and in II, ii, 42, 144, 361. MS* And if ⟨they⟩ should be . . .

44–45 *Wilkinson rebuked Byron for his inexact and immoderate use of* things *(*CAIN, A POEM, *pp. 58, 85). The word occurs at least seventeen times in Act I and thirty-six times in Act II, but apparently not at all in Act III. It was more frequent in some parts of the poem than in others, e.g., II, i, 45, 50, 52, 61, 137, 138, 141, 155, 156, 159; ii, 210, 237, 249, 254, 280, 306, 311, 315.*

47 *MS* multiplied ⟨in⟩to . . .

48, 51, 53, 59 *1821 et al.* doom'd, link'd, chain'd, foredoom'd

Which knew such things.

LUCIFER. But if that high thought were
Linked to a servile mass of matter, and
Knowing such things, aspiring to such things
And science still beyond them, were chained down
To the most gross and petty paltry wants,
All foul and fulsome, and the very best
Of thine enjoyments a sweet degradation,
A most enervating and filthy cheat
To lure thee on to the renewal of
Fresh souls and bodies, all foredoomed to be
As frail and few so happy—

CAIN. Spirit! I
Know nought of death, save as a dreadful thing
Of which I have heard my parents speak, as of
A hideous heritage I owe to them
No less than life, a heritage not happy,
If I may judge, till now. But spirit, if
It be as thou hast said (and I within
Feel the prophetic torture of its truth),
Here let me die, for to give birth to those
Who can but suffer many years and die
Methinks is merely propagating death
And multiplying murder.

LUCIFER. Thou canst not
All die; there is what must survive.

CAIN. The Other

58 *MS* ⟨Although⟩ To lure . . .

62 *Another of the many lines in which Byron did not contract the auxiliary* I have *to* I've *and so wrote a clumsy verse.*

63 *If* hideous *is read as a dissyllable, the verse is iambic with ten syllables. If it is trisyllabic, the line has eleven syllables with a stressed ending and an anapest in the second foot.*

67 *MS (a)* [*ins.*] the *(b)* prophetic ⟨anguish⟩ . . .

72 *MS, 1821 et al. All* [*ital.*]*;* Other. *One of the few places at which the MS and all editions agree on capitalization.*

Spake not of this unto my father when
He shut him forth from Paradise with death
Written upon his forehead. But at least
Let what is mortal of me perish that
I may be in the rest as angels are.

LUCIFER. *I* am angelic. Wouldst thou be as I am?

CAIN. I know not what thou art. I see thy pow'r
And see thou show'st me things beyond *my* pow'r,
Beyond all pow'r of my born faculties,
Although inferior still to my desires
And my conceptions.

LUCIFER. What are they which dwell
So humbly in their pride as to sojourn
With worms in clay?

CAIN. And what art thou who dwellest
So haughtily in spirit and canst range
Nature and immortality and yet
Seem'st sorrowful?

LUCIFER. I seem that which I am,
And therefore do I ask of thee if thou
Wouldst be immortal?

CAIN. Thou hast said I must be
Immortal in despite of me. I knew not
This until lately, but since it must be,
Let me, or happy or unhappy, learn
To anticipate my immortality.

LUCIFER. Thou didst before I came upon thee.

CAIN. How?

74 *Byron on the MS hurriedly wrote* futh *for* forth. *He wrote it the same way again in III, 555.*

77 *MS* be in ⟨my⟩ rest. . . .

79–81 *MS, 1821 et al.* power

86 *Byron in haste wrote* haughity.

93 *MS* Let me—⟨unhappy or⟩ or happy or unhappy learn

LUCIFER. By suff'ring.

CAIN. And must torture be immortal?

LUCIFER. We and thy sons will try. But now behold!
Is it not glorious?

CAIN. Oh thou beautiful*
And unimaginable ether and
Ye multiplying masses of increased
And still increasing lights! What are ye? What
Is this blue wilderness of interminable
Air where ye roll along, as I have seen
The leaves along the limpid streams of Eden?
Is your course measured for ye? Or do ye
Sweep on in your unbounded revelry
Through an aërial universe of endless
Expansion, at which my soul aches to think,
Intoxicated with eternity?
Oh God! Oh Gods! or whatsoe'er ye are!
How beautiful ye are! how beautiful
Your works or accidents or whatso'er
They may be! Let me die as atoms die
(If that they die), or know ye in your might
And knowledge! My thoughts are not in this hour
Unworthy what I see, though my dust is.
Spirit, let me expire or see them nearer.

96 *MS, 1821 et al.* suffering

98 *If* glorious *is read as a dissyllable, the line can be scanned thus:* Is it/ not glor/ ious? Oh/ thou beau/ tiful. *It is dissyllabic also in II, ii, 68, 78, 179, 242.*

101 *MS, 1821, 1905-C* still-increasing; *1831, 1833, 1837, 1904, 1905-M* still increasing

102 *MS* blue ⟨Ocean⟩ of . . .

104 *MS* the limpid ⟨brooks⟩ of Eden—

107 *MS, 1821, 1831* aerial; *1833 et al.* aërial. *If this word is read as a dissyllable, the line is trochaic.*

LUCIFER. Art thou not nearer? Look back to thine earth.*

CAIN. Where is it? I see nothing save a mass
Of most innumerable lights.

LUCIFER. Look there.

CAIN. I cannot see it.

LUCIFER. Yet it sparkles still.

CAIN. That yonder?

LUCIFER. Yea.

CAIN. And wilt thou tell me so?
Why, I have seen the fireflies and fireworms
Sprinkle the dusky groves and the green banks
In the dim twilight, brighter than yon world
Which bears them.

LUCIFER. Thou hast seen both worms and worlds,
Each bright and sparkling. What dost think of them?

CAIN. That they are beautiful in their own sphere
And that the night, which makes both beautiful,
The little shining firefly in its flight*
And the immortal star in its great course,
Must both be guided.

LUCIFER. But by whom or what?

120 THE GENTLEMAN'S MAGAZINE *objected to Byron's phrasing. The reviewer declared that degrees of comparison are not applicable in describing* "an innumerable number" *(XCI [December, 1821], 615).*

122 *MS* That yonder? *1821, 1831* What, yonder! *1833 et al.* That!—yonder! *For the cause of these variants see the section on handwriting. I prefer the MS punctuation here.*

123, 130 *MS, 1821 et al.* fire-flies, fire-worms, fire-fly

127 *MS* Both bright . . .; *1821 et al.* Each bright . . .

128–132 *One of Byron's faulty sentences. If the following words were omitted, the syntax would be correct:* the night, which makes both beautiful. *When he reached line 132, he forgot that the subject of* must both be guided *was* night. *He thought that the* firefly *and the* star *were the subjects of* must both be guided.

129 *MS* ⟨Since⟩ And that . . .

CAIN. Show me.

LUCIFER. Dar'st thou behold?

CAIN. How know I what
I *dare* behold? As yet thou hast shown nought
I dare not gaze on further.

LUCIFER. On then with me.
Wouldst thou behold things mortal or immortal?

CAIN. Why, what are things?

LUCIFER. *Both* partly, but what doth
Sit next thy heart?

CAIN. The things I see.

LUCIFER. But what
Sate nearest it?

CAIN. The things I have not seen
Nor ever shall—the mysteries of death.

LUCIFER. What if I show to thee things which have died,
As I have shown thee much which cannot die?

CAIN. Do so.

LUCIFER. Away then on our mighty wings!

CAIN. Oh how we cleave the blue! The stars fade from us.
The earth! where is my earth? Let me look on it,
For I was made of it.

LUCIFER. 'Tis now beyond thee,
Less in the universe than thou in it;
Yet deem not that thou canst escape it. Thou
Shalt soon return to earth and all its dust;
'Tis part of thy eternity and mine.

135 *MS* dare not ⟨lo⟩ gaze . . .; *intended to write* look.

139 *MS, 1821 et al. Sate* [*ital.*]

140 *MS* Th⟨y⟩ Mysteries . . .; *No contraction here, but see II, ii, 404.*

CAIN. Where dost thou lead me?

LUCIFER. To what was before thee,
The phantasm of the world, of which thy world
Is but the wreck.

CAIN. What! Is it not then new?

LUCIFER. No more than life is; and that was ere thou
Or I were, or the things which seem to us
Greater than either. Many things will have
No end, and some which would pretend to have
Had no beginning have had one as mean
As thou; and mightier things have been extinct
To make way for much meaner than we can
Surmise, for moments only and the space
Have been and must be all unchangeable.
But changes make not death except to clay.
But thou art clay and canst but comprehend
That which was clay, and such thou shalt behold.

CAIN. Clay, spirit, what thou wilt, I can survey.

LUCIFER. Away then!

CAIN. But the lights fade from me fast,
And some till now grew larger as we approached
And wore the look of worlds.

LUCIFER. And such they are.

CAIN. And Edens in them?

LUCIFER. It may be.

CAIN. And men?

151 *MS* To what ⟨was⟩ before thee
⟨lived⟩
153 *MS* [*ins.*] it
155 *MS, 1821 et al.* *I* [*ital.*]
159 Mightier *may be dissyllabic, giving an iambic pentameter.*
161–162 *MS, 1821 et al. moments, space, unchangeable* [*ital*]
166–167 *MS* I can ⟨behol⟩ survey / . . . But the ⟨Stars⟩ lights . . .
168 *1821 et al.* approach'd

LUCIFER. Yea or things higher.

CAIN. Aye, and serpents too?

LUCIFER. Wouldst thou have men without them? Must no reptiles
Breathe save th' erect ones?

CAIN. How the lights recede!
Where fly we?

LUCIFER. To the world of phantoms, which*
Are beings past and shadows still to come.

CAIN. But it grows dark and dark, the stars are gone

LUCIFER. And yet thou seest.

CAIN. 'Tis a fearful light!
No sun, no moon, no lights innumerable—
The very blue of the empurpled night
Fades to a dreary twilight; yet I see
Huge dusky masses, but unlike the worlds
We were approaching, which begirt with light
Seemed full of life ev'n when their atmosphere
Of light gave way and showed them taking shapes
Unequal, of deep valleys and vast mountains,

171 *MS* And with Serpents too? *1821, 1833, 1837, 1904.* Ay? and serpents too? *1905-M* Ay, and . . .; *1905-C* Aye! and serpents too?

173 *MS, 1821 et al.* the erect

174 *MS* To the world of ⟨Ha⟩ . . .; *intended to write* Hades.

175 *MS* ⟨Were⟩ beings . . .

177 *1821 et al.* seest. *This is the only time the early editions omitted the apostrophe in this verb. Byron here spelled it* seeest, *possibly aware that the line needed the extra syllable. With* seest, *the verse has only nine syllables.*

178 *If the* e *is silent in innumerable* (innum'rable) *we have an iambic pentameter. Such contraction is also possible in II, ii, 243, with the same effect, and in II, ii, 41, it would give a twelve-syllable verse. But in II, i, 41, and III, 180, it seems less useful, and is most unsatisfactory in I, 159, 447, and II, i, 120, where it results in nine- or eleven-syllable lines.*

183–184 *1821 et al.* seem'd, show'd. *MS, 1821 et al.* even; *the same variant occurs in II, ii, 22, 115, 202, 212, 329. See also II, ii, 281.*

And some emitting sparks and some displaying
Enormous liquid plains and some begirt
With luminous belts and floating moons, which took
Like them the features of fair earth. Instead,
All here seems dark and dreadful.

LUCIFER. But distinct.
Thou seekest to behold death and dead things?

CAIN. I seek it not, but as I know there are
Such and that my sire's sin makes him and me
And all that we inherit liable
To such, I would behold at once what I
Must one day see perforce.

LUCIFER. Behold!

CAIN. 'Tis darkness.

LUCIFER. And so it shall be ever, but we will
Unfold its gates.

CAIN. Enormous vapours roll
Apart. What's this?

LUCIFER. Enter.

CAIN. Can I return?

LUCIFER. Return! Be sure. How else should death be peopled?
Its present realm is thin to what it will be
Through thee and thine.

CAIN. The clouds still open wide
And wider and make widening circles round us.

186–187 *Byron's handwriting of the three* some's *is typical of his haste. Each* m *is written* n, *and once the word is clearly* sune.

188–190 *MS* With luminous ⟨rings⟩ belts . . . / . . . of fair ⟨Worlds⟩ . . . / seems dark & ⟨doubtful⟩—

195 *MS* I would ⟨now⟩ behld . . . *Byron omitted the* o.

203 *Since* widening *is generally pronounced* wid'ning, *the contraction is not indicated.*

LUCIFER. Advance.

CAIN. And thou?

LUCIFER. Fear not. Without me thou
Couldst not have gone beyond thy world. On! on!

(*They disappear through the clouds.*

204 *After* thou *was deleted in line 205,* thou *was inserted at the end of 204.*

205 *MS* ⟨Thou⟩ could'st not have ⟨been here—On—On—⟩

Scene II

Hades

Enter LUCIFER *and* CAIN

CAIN. How silent and how vast are these dim worlds!
For they seem more than one and yet more peopled
Than the huge brilliant luminous orbs which swung
So thickly in the upper air that I
Had deemed them rather the bright populace
Of some all unimaginable heav'n
Than things to be inhabited themselves;
But that on drawing near them I beheld
Their swelling into palpable immensity
Of matter, which seemed made for life to dwell on
Rather than life itself. But here all is
So shadowy and so full of twilight that
It speaks of a day past.

LUCIFER. It is the realm
Of death. Wouldst have it present?

CAIN. Till I know
That which it really is, I cannot answer.

5 *MS* [*ins.*] them

5, 10 *1821 et al.* deem'd, seem'd

6 *1837, 1905-M* heaven; *MS and other editions* Heaven. *Capitalization of this word is always erratic.* Heaven *is not contracted by earlier editions in this line or in lines 255, 268, 426, 432.*

7 *MS* Rather than things to be inhabited. *This line was inserted in smaller script at the top of the page. Byron did not notice that his insertion had given him a superfluous* rather *(see line 5). Before publication the blunder was corrected. All editions have the present text.*

9 *A twelve-syllable line. Others in Act II are i, 102; ii, 22, 29, 81, 84, 221, 224, 269, 363, 380, 389, 404, 413, 422, 437.*

10–12 *MS* life to ⟨live⟩ [*?*] / . . . here all's ⟨s [*xx*]de⟩ is / . . . so ⟨twilight⟩ full of . . .

But if it be as I have heard my father
Deal out in his long homilies, 'tis a thing—
Oh God, I dare not think on't! Cursèd be
He who invented life that leads to death!
Or the dull mass of life that being life
Could not retain, but needs must forfeit it,
Ev'n for the innocent!

LUCIFER. Dost thou curse thy father?

CAIN. Cursed he not me in giving me my birth?
Cursed he not me before my birth, in daring
To pluck the fruit forbidden?

LUCIFER. Thou say'st well.
The curse is mutual 'twixt thy sire and thee.
But for thy sons and brothers?

CAIN. Let them share it
With me, their sire and brother. What else is
Bequeathed to me? I leave them my inheritance.
Oh ye interminable gloomy realms
Of swimming shadows and enormous shapes,
Some fully shown, some indistinct, and all
Mighty and melancholy—what are ye?
Live ye or have ye lived?

LUCIFER. Somewhat of both.

19 *MS* that ⟨led⟩ to ⟨it⟩ [*?*]—
26 Mutual *is dissyllabic here and in 442.*
29 *1821 et al.* Bequeath'd
32 *MS* indistinct! & ⟨some⟩
33–34 THE LITERARY GAZETTE *thought that this series of verbs was nonsensical or incomprehensible (No. 257 [December, 1821], 811);* THE GENTLEMAN'S MAGAZINE, *misquoting the lines, called them* "neither rhyme nor reason" *(XCI [December, 1821], 615).*

CAIN. Then what is death?

LUCIFER. What? Hath not he who made ye
Said 'tis another life?

CAIN. Till now he hath
Said nothing, save that all shall die.

LUCIFER. Perhaps.
He one day will unfold that further secret.

CAIN. Happy the day!

LUCIFER. Yes, happy! when unfolded
Through agonies unspeakable and clogged
With agonies eternal to innumerable
Yet unborn myriads of unconscious atoms,
All to be animated for this only!

CAIN. What are these mighty phantoms which I see*
Floating around me? They wear not the form
Of the intelligences I have seen
Round our regretted and unentered Eden,
Nor wear the form of man as I have viewed
In Adam's and in Abel's and in mine
Nor in my sister-bride's nor in my children's;
And yet they have an aspect which, though not
Of men nor angels, looks like something which,
If not the last, rose higher than the first,
Haughty and high and beautiful and full
Of seeming strength, but of inexplicable
Shape, for I never saw such. They bear not
The wing of seraph nor the face of man

38 *MS* will ⟨deign to⟩ unfold ⟨his⟩ further secret.
40, 47, 48 *1821 et al.* clogg'd, unenter'd, view'd
41 *A thirteen-syllable line; others are 80 and possibly 251.*
42 *MS* ⟨And⟩ unborn . . .
46 *MS, 1905-C* Intelligences
53 *MS* was higher than . . .; *1821 et al.* rose higher than . . .

Nor form of mightiest brute nor aught that is
Now breathing. Mighty yet and beautiful
As the most beautiful and mighty which
Live and yet so unlike them that I scarce
Can call them living.

LUCIFER. Yet they lived.

CAIN. Where?

LUCIFER. Where
Thou livest.

CAIN. When?

LUCIFER. On what thou callest earth
They did inhabit.

CAIN. Adam is the first.

LUCIFER. Of thine, I grant thee, but too mean to be
The last of these.

CAIN. And what are they?

LUCIFER. That which
Thou shalt be.

CAIN. But what *were* they?

LUCIFER. Living, high,*
Intelligent, good, great, and glorious things,
As much superior unto all thy sire,
Adam, could e'er have been in Eden as
The sixty-thousandth generation shall be
In its dull damp degeneracy to

58 Mightiest *may be dissyllabic.*
59 *MS* ⟨Like them—yet⟩ mighty ⟨and⟩ and . . .
60 *MS* ⟨And⟩ As . . .
64 *MS* Adam ⟨was⟩ the first.
66 *MS* And what ⟨were⟩ they?
69 Superior *is trysllabic and also in lines 103, 158, 426, 429.*
71–72 *MS* ⟨They⟩ sixty . . ./ In it's dull damp⟨ed⟩ . . .

Thee and thy son; and how weak they are, judge
By thy own flesh.

CAIN. Ah me! and did *they* perish?

LUCIFER. Yes, from their earth as thou wilt fade from thine.

CAIN. But was mine theirs?

LUCIFER. It was.

CAIN. But not as now.
It is too little and too lowly to
Sustain such creatures.

LUCIFER. True, it was more glorious.

CAIN. And wherefore did it fall?

LUCIFER. Ask him who fells.

CAIN. But how?

LUCIFER. By a most crushing and inexorable
Destruction and disorder of the elements,
Which struck a world to chaos, as a chaos
Subsiding has struck out a world. Such things,
Though rare in time, are frequent in eternity.
Pass on and gaze upon the past.

CAIN. 'Tis awful!

72, 80–83, 96–102 *Wilkinson ridiculed the language as affected and tormented:* struck a world, chaos subsiding, poor attributes, engendered out of subsiding slime, scarcely yet shaped planet. *Why was* degeneracy damp? (CAIN, A POEM, *pp. 56–58*).

76 *MS, 1821 et al. mine* [*ital.*]

79 *Coleridge:* "Compare the 'jingle between king and kine,' in *Sardanapalus*, Act V, Sc. I, lines 483–484. It is hard to say whether Byron inserted and then omitted to erase these blemishes from negligence and indifference, or whether he regarded them as permissible or even felicitous" (POETRY, *V, 243*). THE LITERARY GAZETTE *complained that the phrasing was* "a poor conceit, or a blundering misuse of words" (*No. 257* [*December, 1821*], *811*).

80 *MS* By a most ⟨sweeping⟩ . . .

84 *MS* ⟨Are⟩ Though ⟨rare⟩ in time . . .

LUCIFER. And true. Behold these phantoms. They were once
Material as thou art.
CAIN. And must I be
Like them?
LUCIFER. Let He who made thee answer that.
I show thee what thy predecessors are*
And what they were thou feelest, in degree
Inferior as thy petty feelings and
Thy pettier portion of th' immortal part
Of high intelligence and earthly strength.
What ye in common have with what they had
Is life, and what ye shall have—death. The rest
Of your poor attributes is such as suits
Reptiles engendered out of the subsiding
Slime of a mighty universe, crushed into
A scarcely-yet shaped planet, peopled with
Things whose enjoyment was to be in blindness—

87 *MS* ⟨As⟩ Material as; Material *is trisyllabic.*

88 *MS* he; *1821 et al.* He. *Many, from the early reviewers to Courthope (p. 271), commented on the bad grammar.*
Coleridge: "There is no doubt that [*sic*] Byron wrote, or that he should have written, 'Let Him' " (POETRY, *V, 243*). *More:* "Byron apparently had a genius for bad grammar. The curious thing is that Gifford and Murray should have let such solecisms slip through the press" (THE COMPLETE POETICAL WORKS, *p. 1032*). *Otto Jespersen:* "The feeling that some word is notionally the subject of the verbal idea, is sometimes strong enough to make a speaker or writer put it in the nominative in spite of the grammatical construction which requires the objective; thus after *let:* Let He who made thee answer that (Byron)" (ESSENTIALS OF ENGLISH GRAMMAR, *p. 134*).

89 *MS* thy ⟨things⟩ predecessors . . .

90 *MS, 1821 et al. were* [*ital.*]

92 *Perhaps* pettier *may be dissyllabic. MS, 1821 et al.* the immortal . . .

95 *MS, 1821 et al. shall* [*ital.*]

97, 98 *1821 et al.* engender'd, crush'd

99 *MS* scarcely yet-shaped . . .; *1821 et al.* scarcely-yet shaped . . .

100 *MS* enjoyment ⟨was placed in bonds⟩
⟨prescribed to⟩ [*?*] blindness—

A Paradise of Ignorance, from which
Knowledge was barred as poison. But behold
What these superior beings are or were;
Or if it irk thee, turn thee back and till
The earth, thy task. I'll waft thee there in safety.

CAIN. No, I'll stay here.

LUCIFER. How long?

CAIN. Forever. Since
I must one day return here from the earth,
I rather would remain. I am sick of all
That dust has shown me; let me dwell in shadows.

LUCIFER. It cannot be. Thou now beholdest as
A vision that which is reality.
To make thyself fit for this dwelling, thou
Must pass through what the things thou seest have past
The gates of death.

CAIN. By what gate have we entered
Ev'n now?

LUCIFER. By mine. But, plighted to return,
My spirit buoys thee up to breathe in regions

101–103 *MS* ⟨And⟩ Paradise of Ignorance ⟨to⟩ which ⟨knowledge⟩
⟨Was⟩ barred . . . hehold ⟨it!—look⟩
⟨At⟩ What these Superior . . .
In 103 these *was an insertion.*

102 *1821 et al.* barr'd

108 *Had Byron used the contraction* I'm *he would have avoided a clumsy anapest in the fourth foot.*

109 *MS* shadow; *1821 et al.* shadows. *Comparison with* shadows *in line 131 makes a terminal* s *in 109 doubtful.*

111 *MS* A Vision—⟨what is a⟩ reality;—

113 *MS* thou see'st have past; *1821, 1833, 1837, 1904* thou see'st have pass'd; *1905-C* thou seest have passed; *1905-M* seest have pass'd

114 *1821 et al.* enter'd

115 *MS* but ⟨on condition⟩ to return

116 *1904 misprint* to bathe in regions

Where all is breathless save thyself. Gaze on,
But do not think to dwell here till thine hour
Is come.

CAIN. And these too, can they ne'er repass
To earth again?

LUCIFER. *Their* earth is gone for ever,
So changed by its convulsion they would not
Be conscious to a single present spot
Of its new scarcely hardened surface. 'Twas—
Oh what a beautiful world it *was*!

CAIN. And is.
It is not with the earth, though I must till it,
I feel at war, but that I may not profit
By what it bears of beautiful, untoiling,
Nor gratify my thousand swelling thoughts
With knowledge, nor allay my thousand fears
Of death and life.

LUCIFER. What thy world is, thou seest
But canst not comprehend the shadow of
That which it was.

CAIN. And those enormous creatures,*
Phantoms inferior in intelligence
(At least so seeming) to the things we have passed,
Resembling somewhat the wild habitants
Of the deep woods of earth, the hugest which
Roar nightly in the forest, but ten-fold
In magnitude and terror, taller than
The cherub-guarded walls of Eden, with

123 *MS* new-scarcely . . .; *1821 et al.* harden'd . . .

130 *MS, 1821 et al.* see'st. *This is the only time that 1905-C used the apostrophe in this word. 1905-M did not do so here.*

134, 141, 147. *1821 et al.* pass'd, stripp'd, destroy'd

134–136 *MS* At least ⟨of⟩ . . . / Resembling ⟨something⟩ . . . / Of the ⟨most mass⟩ [*?*] deep . . . hugest ⟨in⟩ which

Eyes flashing like the fi'ry swords which fence them,
And tusks projecting like the trees stripped of
Their bark and branches—what were they?

LUCIFER. That which
The mammoth is in thy world, but these lie
By myriads underneath its surface.

CAIN. But
None on it?

LUCIFER. No, for thy frail race to war
With them would render the curse on it useless;
'Twould be destroyed so early.

CAIN. But why *war?*

LUCIFER. You have forgotten the denunciation*
Which drove your race from Eden: war with all things
And death to all things and disease to most things
And pangs and bitterness. These were the fruits
Of the forbidden tree.

CAIN. But animals—
Did they too eat of it, that they must die?

LUCIFER. Your Maker told ye, they were made for you
As you for him. You would not have their doom
Superior to your own? Had Adam not
Fall'n, all had stood.

CAIN. Alas, the hopeless wretches!
They too must share my sire's fate like his sons,
Like them too without having shared the apple,

140 *MS, 1821 et al.* fiery
142–143 *MS* Their ⟨branches⟩; what . . . / The ⟨Elephant⟩ is . . . but ⟨they⟩ lie; *MS, 1821 et al.* Mammoth . . .
145 *MS* thy ⟨feeble⟩ race . . .
⟨pious⟩ [*?*]
151 *MS* bitterness—⟨and⟩ these . . .
154 *MS* maker; *1821 et al.* Maker, *they* [*ital.*]
157 *MS, 1821 et al.* Fallen

Like them too without the so dear-bought knowledge.
It was a lying tree, for we *know* nothing.
At least it promised knowledge at the price
Of death, but knowledge still; but what *knows* man?

LUCIFER. It may be death leads to the highest knowledge,*
And being of all things the sole thing certain
At least leads to the surest science; therefore
The tree was true though deadly.

CAIN. These dim realms?
I see them but I know them not.

LUCIFER. Because
Thy hour is yet afar, and matter cannot
Comprehend spirit wholly, but 'tis something
To know there are such realms.

CAIN. We knew already
That there was death.

LUCIFER. But not what was beyond it.

CAIN. Nor know I now.

LUCIFER. Thou knowest that there is
A state and many states beyond thine own,
And this thou knewest not this morn.

CAIN. But all
Seems dim and shadowy.

LUCIFER. Be content; it will
Seem clearer to thine immortality.

160–166 *MS, 1821 et al. The following were italicized:* Knowledge (*3 times*), know (*twice*), promised, price, highest, surest. *The present text retained only those italics that affected the rhythm.*

162 ⟨but⟩ at the *price* [*ital.*]

163 What *know* ⟨we⟩ [*?*]
knows Man? [*ital.*]

165 *MS* the sole thing sure—;*1821 et al.* the sole thing certain

173 *MS, 1821* know'st; *1831 et al.* knowest. *Since the contraction resulted in a nine-syllable line, the 1831 spelling made a better verse.*

CAIN. And yon immeasurable liquid space
Of glorious azure, which floats on beyond us,
Which looks like water, and which I should deem
The river which flows out of Paradise
Past my own dwelling, but that it is bankless
And boundless and of an ethereal hue—
What is it?

LUCIFER. There is still some such on earth,
Although inferior, and thy children shall
Dwell near it; 'tis the phantasm of an ocean.

CAIN. 'Tis like another world, a liquid sun.
And those inordinate creatures sporting o'er
Its shining surface?

LUCIFER. Are its habitants,
The past leviathans.

CAIN. And yon immense
Serpent, which rears his dripping mane and vasty
Head ten times higher than the haughtiest cedar
Forth from the abyss, looking as he could coil
Himself around the orbs we lately looked on—

180 *MS* Which seems like . . .; *1821 et al.* Which looks like . . .

186 *MS, 1905-C* Ocean.

188 THE LITERARY GAZETTE: "the misapplication of the epithet 'inordinate,' *irregular* instead of *vast,* as the writer meant, does not improve the specimen. But it would be tedious to particularise the trivial blemishes which abound in this composition" (*No. 257* [*December, 1821*] *811*).

189 *MS, 1821, 1831, 1833, 1905-M* habitants; *1837, 1904, 1905-C* inhabitants. *There seems to be no precedent for the 1837 change, which two later editions used. The additional syllable is not a metrical requirement. Byron had used both forms earlier in the play*: inhabitants *in I, 545*; habitants *in II, ii, 135. In these two places the editions were in agreement with the MS.*

190 *1905-C* Leviathans

192 *MS* ⟨palm⟩ Cedar; haughtiest *may be dissyllabic.*

194, 195, 200 *1821 et al.* look'd, bask'd, call'd

Is he not of the kind which basked beneath
The tree in Eden?

LUCIFER. Eve, thy mother, best
Can tell what shape of serpent tempted her.

CAIN. This seems too terrible. No doubt the other
Had more of beauty.

LUCIFER. Hast thou ne'er beheld him?

CAIN. Many of the same kind, at least so called,
But never that precisely which persuaded
The fatal fruit, nor ev'n of the same aspect.

LUCIFER. Your father saw him not?

CAIN. No, 'twas my mother
Who tempted him; she tempted by the serpent.

LUCIFER. Good man, whene'er thy wife or thy sons' wives
Tempt thee or them to aught that's new or strange,
Be sure thou seest first who hath tempted *them*.

CAIN. Thy precept comes too late; there is no more
For serpents to tempt woman to.

LUCIFER. But there
Are some things still which woman may tempt man to,
And man tempt woman. Let thy sons look to it.
My counsel is a kind one, for 'tis ev'n
Giv'n chiefly at my own expense. 'Tis true,
'Twill not be followed, so there's little lost.

195 *MS* kind which ⟨lay around⟩ . . .

197 *MS* what ⟨kind⟩ of Serpent . . .

204 *1905-C.* serpent. *Here and in line 197 and a few other lines Coleridge did not follow the MS. Since the reference in 204 is specific, we would expect him to capitalize it as he often did. The early editions never capitalized it.*

207 *MS* first ⟨what⟩ hath . . .

213 *MS* Given at my ⟨spiritual⟩ expence; *1821 et al.* Given, expense; *MS* [*ins.*] chiefly.

214 *1821 et al.* follow'd

CAIN. I understand not this.

LUCIFER. The happier thou.
Thy world and thou are still too young. Thou thinkest
Thyself most wicked and unhappy. Is it
Not so?

CAIN. For crime, I know not; but for pain,
I have felt much.

LUCIFER. First-born of the first man,
Thy present state of sin—and thou art evil—
Of sorrow—and thou sufferest—are both Eden
In all its innocence compared to what
Thou shortly may'st be; and that state again
In its redoubled wretchedness, a Paradise
To what thy sons' sons' sons, accumulating
In generations like to dust (which they
In fact but add to), shall endure and do.
Now let us back to earth.

CAIN. And wherefore didst thou
Lead me only to inform me this?

LUCIFER. Was not thy quest for knowledge?

CAIN. Yes, as being
The road to happiness.

LUCIFER. If truth be so,
Thou hast it.

CAIN. Then my father's God did well
When he prohibited the fatal tree.

215 *If* happier *is read as a dissyllable, the verse is iambic pentameter.*

221 *A rough twelve-syllable verse. An ugly contraction* suff'rest *would not help the limping meter. Since Byron often used cacophonous contractions, we cannot say that considerations of sound deterred him here.*

227 *MS* shall ⟨do and⟩ endure . . .

229 *A nine-syllable line.*

230 *MS* quest ⟨the⟩ [*?*] for . . .

232–233 *MS* Then ⟨the⟩ my . . . / ⟨In⟩ When he . . .

LUCIFER. But had done better in not planting it.
But ignorance of evil doth not save
From evil; it must still roll on the same,
A part of all things.

CAIN. Not of all things. No,
I'll not believe it, for I thirst for good.

LUCIFER. And who and what doth not? Who covets evil
For its own bitter sake? None—nothing! 'Tis
The leaven of all life and lifelessness.

CAIN. Within those glorious orbs which we beheld,*
Distant and dazzling and innumerable,
Ere we came down into this phantom realm,
Ill cannot come; they are too beautiful.

LUCIFER. Thou hast seen them from afar.

CAIN. And what of that?
Distance can but diminish glory; they
When nearer must be more ineffable.

LUCIFER. Approach the things of earth most beautiful
And judge their beauty near.

CAIN. I have done this.
The loveliest thing I know is loveliest nearest.

LUCIFER. Then there must be delusion. What is that
Which being nearest to thine eyes is still
More beautiful than beauteous things remote?

CAIN. My sister Adah. All the stars of heav'n,*

239–240 *MS, 1821 et al. Who, None* [*ital.*]
241 *MS* ⟨as⟩ lifelessness.—⟨things⟩—
242 *1833, 1837, 1905-C* behold; *MS, 1904, 1905-M* beheld.
250 *MS* have done ⟨so⟩—
251 *This thirteen-syllable line may be reduced by two syllables if* loveliest *is twice read as dissyllabic, but this slurring gives an unpleasant reading.*
254 Beauteous *is dissyllabic.*
255–269 *This passage is a good sample of the caprice of 1905-C capitalization. Coleridge did not follow the MS, where Byron had sprinkled many*

The deep blue noon of night, lit by an orb
Which looks a spirit or a spirit's world,
The hues of twilight, the sun's gorgeous coming,
His setting indescribable, which fills
My eyes with pleasant tears as I behold
Him sink and feel my heart float softly with him
Along that western paradise of clouds,
The forest shade, the green bough, the bird's voice,
The vesper bird's, which seems to sing of love
And mingles with the song of cherubim,
As the day closes over Eden's walls—
All these are nothing to my eyes and heart
Like Adah's face. I turn from earth and heav'n
To gaze on it.

LUCIFER. 'Tis fair as frail mortality,
In the first dawn and bloom of young creation
And earliest embraces of earth's parents,

---

capitals: Noon of Night, Orb, Spirit, Spirit's World, Sun's Setting, Western Paradise of Clouds, Green bough. *Coleridge retained* Eden *and* Adah *and* Cherubim, *but among the remaining twelve chose only* Sun's. *Had he added some that he often used elsewhere*—Heaven *(255, 268)*, Love *(264)*, Earth *(268)—the picture of his practice would have been complete, for he often capitalized* Spirit, Twilight, Love.

256 *MS* Noon of Night ⟨shown girding an or⟩; *intended to write* orb.

258 *MS* gorgeous ⟨birth⟩.

261 *MS* heart ⟨sink⟩ softly . . .

262, 264 *Two inserted lines. The passage originally ran on the MS as follows (259–261, 263, 265)*:

His Setting indescribable which fills
My eyes with pleasant tears as I behold
Him sink and feel my heart sink softly with him—
The forest shade—the Green bough—the bird's voice⟨s⟩—
Which mingles with the song of Cherubim

265 *MS* ⟨Which⟩ mingles . . .

270–271 *MS* In the first ⟨vigour and vigour of⟩ Creation / And ⟨first⟩ embraces . . .

271 *It seems better to read* earliest *as a trisyllable here, giving us one of Byron's main patterns, an eleven-syllable line with a slack ending.*

Can make its offspring; still it is delusion.

CAIN. You think so, being not her brother.

LUCIFER. Mortal,
My brotherhood's with those who have no children.*

CAIN. Then thou canst have no fellowship with us.

LUCIFER. It may be that thine own shall be for me.
But if thou dost possess a beautiful
Being beyond all beauty in thine eyes,
Why art thou wretched?

CAIN. Why do I exist?
Why art *thou* wretched? Why are all things so?
Ev'n he who made us must be, as the Maker*
Of things unhappy! To produce destruction
Can surely never be the task of joy,
And yet my sire says he's omnipotent.
Then why is evil, he being good? I asked
This question of my father, and he said,
Because this evil only was the path
To good. Strange good that must arise from out
Its deadly opposite. I lately saw
A lamb stung by a reptile. The poor suckling
Lay foaming on the earth beneath the vain
And piteous bleating of its restless dam.
My father plucked some herbs and laid them to

273 *MS* ⟨In you—to because you are not⟩ her brother.

281 *MS* Even, Maker; *1821 et al.* Ev'n, maker. *On the MS this was a twelve-syllable line; 1821 shortened it by means of a contraction. Cain's bitter reference to the deity is not capitalized in any edition.*

285, 287, 288 *1905-C* Evil, Good. *Also capitalized in lines 298, 299, but Coleridge did not do so in lines 235, 238, 239.*

285 *1821 et al.* ask'd

289 *MS* ⟨Grown out it's⟩ opposite . . .

290 *MS* the poor ⟨creature⟩

291 *MS* earth ⟨and⟩ beneath the vain

292 Piteous *can be read as a dissyllable.*

The wound, and by degrees the helpless wretch
Resumed its careless life and rose to drain
The mother's milk, who o'er it tremulous
Stood licking its reviving limbs with joy.
Behold, my son, said Adam, how from evil
Springs good.

LUCIFER. What didst thou answer?

CAIN. Nothing, for
He is my father, but I thought, that 'twere
A better portion for the animal
Never to have been stung at all than to
Purchase renewal of its little life
With agonies unutterable, though
Dispelled by antidotes.

LUCIFER. But as thou saidst
Of all belovèd things thou lovest her
Who shared thy mother's milk and giveth hers
Unto thy children.

CAIN. Most assuredly.
What should I be without her?

LUCIFER. What am I?

CAIN. Dost thou love nothing?

LUCIFER. What does thy God love?

CAIN. All things, my father says, but I confess
I see it not in their allotment here.

LUCIFER. And therefore thou canst not see if *I* love

294–296 *MS* by ⟨the⟩ degrees . . . wretch⟨ed⟩
. . . and ⟨ran⟩ to drain
⟨stood⟩
⟨It's⟩ Mother's milk—⟨which⟩ oer . . .

299 *MS* Springs Good!—⟨and I⟩ What . . .

301 *MS* portion ⟨neer to have⟩

302 *MS, 1821 et al. stung at all* [*ital.*] . . .

305 *1821 et al.* Dispell'd

Or no, except some vast and gen'ral purpose,
To which particular things must melt like snows.

CAIN. Snows! what are they?

LUCIFER. Be happier in not knowing
What thy remoter offspring must encounter,
But bask beneath the clime which knows no winter.

CAIN. But dost thou not love something like thyself?

LUCIFER. And dost thou love thyself?

CAIN. Yes, but love more*
What makes my feelings more endurable
And is more than myself because I love it.

LUCIFER. Thou lovest it because 'tis beautiful,
As was the apple in thy mother's eye;
And when it ceases to be so, thy love
Will cease like any other appetite.

CAIN. Cease to be beautiful! how can that be?

LUCIFER. With time.

CAIN. But time has past, and hitherto
Ev'n Adam and my mother both are fair;
Not like fair Adah and the seraphim,
But very fair.

LUCIFER. All that must pass away
In them and her.

CAIN. I'm sorry for it, but
Cannot conceive my love for her the less.
And when her beauty disappears, methinks

314 *MS, 1821 et al.* general . . .
316 Happier *may be dissyllabic.*
320–321 *MS, 1821 et al. thyself* [*ital.*]. *MS* ⟨No⟩—but ⟨I⟩ love more / What makes ⟨me⟩ my . . .
328 *MS, 1821, 1831, 1833, 1837, 1905-M* past; *1904* pass'd; *1905-C* passed. *See lines 113, 134.*
330 *MS* ⟨or⟩ the Seraphim

He who creates all beauty will lose more
Than me in seeing perish such a work.

LUCIFER. I pity thee who lovest what must perish.

CAIN. And I thee who lov'st nothing.

LUCIFER. And thy brother—*
Sits he not near thy heart?

CAIN. Why should he not?

LUCIFER. Thy father loves him well; so does thy God.

CAIN. And so do I.

LUCIFER. 'Tis well and meekly done.

CAIN. Meekly!

LUCIFER. He is the second born of flesh
And is his mother's favourite.

CAIN. Let him keep
Her favour, since the serpent was the first
To win it.

LUCIFER. And his father's?

CAIN. What is that
To me? Should I not love that which all love?

LUCIFER. And the Jehovah, the indulgent Lord
And bounteous planter of barred Paradise—
He too looks smilingly on Abel.

CAIN. I
Ne'er saw him, and I know not if he smiles.

LUCIFER. But you have seen his angels.

CAIN. Rarely.

LUCIFER. But

339 *MS* Sit⟨'st⟩ he . . .
340 *MS* ⟨Your⟩ father . . . ⟨your⟩ God.
348, 359 *1821 et al.* barr'd, walk'd; *348* bounteous *may be read as dissyllabic.*
349 *MS* on Abel ⟨and⟩

Sufficiently to see they love your brother;
His sacrifices are acceptable.

CAIN. So be they. Wherefore speak to me of this?

LUCIFER. Because thou hast thought of this ere now.

CAIN. And if
I *have* thought, why recall a thought that—(*he pauses, as agitated*)—Spirit,
Here we are in thy world; speak not of mine.
Thou hast shown me wonders; thou hast shown me those
Mighty pre-Adamites who walked the earth
Of which ours is the wreck; thou hast pointed out
Myriads of starry worlds, of which our own
Is the dim and remote companion in
Infinity of life; thou hast shown me shadows
Of that existence with the dreaded name
Which my sire brought us—Death; thou hast shown me much,
But not all. Show me where Jehovah dwells
In his especial Paradise, or thine.
Where is it?

LUCIFER. Here and o'er all space.

CAIN. But ye
Have some allotted dwelling, as all things.
Clay has its earth, and other worlds their tenants;
All temporary breathing creatures their
Peculiar element; and things which have

356 *MS* thought that ⟨pauses⟩ . . .
357 *MS, 1821 et al. Here, thy, mine* [*ital.*]
359 *MS, 1821, 1905-C* Pre-Adamites; *1831 et al.* pre-Adamites.
361 *MS* our⟨s⟩ own
362 *MS* [*ins.*] the
364 *MS* existence ⟨which⟩ with . . .
365 *MS* Sire ⟨shrinks from⟩—Death; *1821 et al.* Death.
367–368 *MS, 1821 et al. thine, Here* [*ital.*]
372–373 *MS* which ⟨as thou say'st⟩ / ⟨Have⟩ ceased . . .

Long ceased to breathe *our* breath have theirs, thou say'st;
And the Jehovah and thyself have thine.
Ye do not dwell together?

LUCIFER. No, we reign
Together, but our dwellings are asunder.

CAIN. Would there were only one of ye! Perchance
An unity of purpose might make union
In elements which seem now jarred in storms.
How came ye, being spirits wise and infinite,
To separate? Are ye not as brethren in
Your essence and your nature and your glory?

LUCIFER. Art thou not Abel's brother?

CAIN. We are brethren
And so we shall remain, but were it not so,
Is spirit like to flesh? Can it fall out,
Infinity with immortality?
Jarring and turning space to misery—
For what?

LUCIFER. To reign.

CAIN. Did ye not tell me that
Ye are both eternal?

LUCIFER. Yea.

CAIN. And what I have seen,
Yon blue immensity, is boundless?

LUCIFER. Aye.*

CAIN. And cannot ye both reign then? Is there not
Enough? Why should ye differ?

LUCIFER. We both reign.

379 *1821 et al.* jarr'd
380 *MS, 1905-C* Spirits; *capitalized also in line 457.*
381 *MS* [*ins.*] as
386 *MS, 1821 et al.* Immortality
391–392 *MS, 1821 et al. reign, both* [*ital.*]

CAIN. But one of you makes evil.

LUCIFER. Which?

CAIN. Thou! For
If thou canst do man good, why dost thou not?

LUCIFER. And why not he who made? *I* made ye not;
Ye are his creatures and not mine.

CAIN. Then leave us
His creatures, as thou say'st we are, or show me
Thy dwelling or his dwelling.

LUCIFER. I could show thee
Both, but the time will come thou shalt see one
Of them for evermore.

CAIN. And why not now?

LUCIFER. Thy human mind hath scarcely grasp to gather
The little I have shown thee into calm
And clear thought, and *thou* wouldst go on aspiring
To the great double myst'ries, the *two principles,*
And gaze upon them on their secret thrones.
Dust! limit thy ambition, for to see
Either of these would be for thee to perish.

CAIN. And let me perish, so I see them.

LUCIFER. There
The son of her who snatched the apple spake.

393–394 *MS* Thou! ⟨it⟩ for / If thou ⟨can'st do us good why do'st thou not?⟩

396–398 *MS, 1821 et al. his, His, his* [*ital.*]

399 *MS.* (a) [*ins.*] come; (b) see ⟨bot⟩ one.

403–404 *Matthew Arnold quoted these lines twice in his essay on Byron, along with I, 137 ff., to illustrate the poet's negligence. Arnold did not specify the defects but only stated that such verse was inferior in thought and phrasing to that of Milton and Leopardi. Byron's unconcern about the* "management of words" *showed* "the insensibility of the barbarian" (*"Byron," pp. 103–104*).

404 *MS, 1821 et al.* Mysteries! the *two Principles* [*ital.*]

409 *MS* who ⟨plucked⟩ the Apple . . .

But thou wouldst only perish and not see them;
That sight is for the other state.

CAIN. Of death?

LUCIFER. That is the prelude.

CAIN. Then I dread it less,
Now that I know it leads to something definite.

LUCIFER. And now I will convey thee to thy world,
Where thou shalt multiply the race of Adam.
Eat, drink, toil, tremble, laugh, weep, sleep, and die.

CAIN. And to what end have I beheld these things
Which thou hast shown me?

LUCIFER. Didst thou not require*
Knowledge? And have I not, in what I showed,
Taught thee to know thyself?

CAIN. Alas! I seem
Nothing.

LUCIFER. And this should be the human sum
Of knowledge, to know mortal nature's nothingness.
Bequeath that science to thy children, and
'Twill spare them many tortures.

CAIN. Haughty spirit,
Thou speak'st it proudly, but thyself, though proud,
Hast a superior.

LUCIFER. No! by heav'n, which He*
Holds, and the abyss and the immensity
Of worlds and life, which I hold with him—No!

411 *MS* ⟨an⟩ other state—
413–414 *MS* it ⟨led⟩ [?] leads . . . / . . . th⟨e⟩ World.
416 *MS* laugh ⟨&⟩ weep ⟨and⟩ die. *Probably the heaviest accented line in* CAIN—*eight stresses in ten syllables.*
419 *1821 et al.* show'd
422 *MS* know ⟨human⟩ Nature's . . .
425 *MS* thyself ⟨alt⟩ [?] though proud; *intended to write* although [?].
426 *MS, 1821 et al.* He; *1905-C* he

I have a victor, true, but no superior.
Homage he has from all, but none from me.
I battle it against him, as I battled
In highest heav'n. Through all eternity
And the unfathomable gulfs of Hades
And the interminable realms of space
And the infinity of endless ages,
All, all, will I dispute. And world by world
And star by star and universe by universe
Shall tremble in the balance, till the great
Conflict shall cease, if ever it shall cease,
Which it ne'er shall, till he or I be quenched.
And what can quench our immortality
Or mutual and irrevocable hate?
He as a conqueror will call the conquered*
Evil, but what will be the good he gives?
Were I the victor, his works would be deemed
The only evil ones. And you, ye new
And scarce-born mortals, what have been his gifts
To you already, in your little world?

CAIN. But few and some of those but bitter.

LUCIFER. Back
With me then to thine earth and try the rest
Of his celestial boons to you and yours.

429, 432 *MS, 1905-C* Victor, Eternity; *1905-C* Heaven

436 *MS* All ⟨will I⟩ All will I . . .

440, 443, 445 *1821 et al.* quench'd, conquer'd, deem'd

440–442 *These three inserted lines were written in different ink and with finer quill, the last two in the right margin.*

444, 452 *MS, 1905-C Evil, Good* [*ital.*], Evil, Good. *All editions used the MS italics here.*

445 *MS, 1821 et al. his* [*ital.*]

446 *MS* & you—ye ⟨newborn Mortals⟩

447 *MS, 1821, 1831, 1833, 1905-C-M* scarce-born; *1837, 1904* scarce born

450 *MS* [*ins.*] and

451 *MS, 1821* to ye and yours; *1833 et al.* to you and yours. *This was originally the last line of the act. Beneath it Byron wrote and later canceled,*

Evil and good are things in their own essence
And not made good or evil by the giver;
But if he gives you good, so call him. If
Evil springs from him, do not name it mine,
Till ye know better its true fount; and judge
Not by words, though of spirits, but the fruits
Of your existence, such as it must be.
One good gift has the fatal apple giv'n—*
Your reason; let it not be over-swayed
By tyrannous threats to force you into faith
'Gainst all external sense and inward feelings.
Think and endure and form an inner world
In your own bosom, where the outward fails.
So shall you nearer be the spiritual
Nature, and war triumphant with your own.

(*They disappear.*

End of Act second. *To the right he wrote and did not cancel,* They disappear.

452–458 *These lines were the first addition Byron made at the end of Act II, and were written in very small script and different ink. He had already started Act III on the lower half of the page before he made this addition and also before he crowded lines 459–466, a second addition, into the left margin. Beneath line 458 he again wrote and later canceled* End of Act second.

453 *MS, 1905-C* Giver

454 *MS* ⟨Then⟩ if he . . .

455 *MS, 1821 et al. him, mine* [*ital.*]

459–460 *MS, 1821 et al. One good,* given, *reason* [*ital.*]

460 *1821 et al.* over-sway'd

465 Spiritual *is trisyllabic.*

466 *Beneath line 466 in the margin Byron wrote* End of Act second.

ACT III

Scene I

The Earth near Eden, as in Act I

Enter CAIN *and* ADAH

ADAH. Hush, tread softly, Cain.

CAIN. I will, but wherefore?

ADAH. Our little Enoch sleeps upon yon bed
Of leaves beneath the cypress.

CAIN. Cypress! 'tis
A gloomy tree, which looks as if it mourned
O'er what it shadows. Wherefore didst thou choose it
For our child's canopy?

ADAH. Because its branches
Shut out the sun like night and therefore seemed
Fitting to shadow slumber.

CAIN. Aye, the last
And longest, but no matter, lead me to him.
(*They go up to the child.*
How lovely he appears! His little cheeks*

3 *MS* ⟨yon⟩ Cypress.
4, 7 *1821 et al.* mourn'd, seem'd

In their pure incarnation vying with
The rose leaves strewn beneath them.

ADAH. And his lips too,
How beautifully parted! No, you shall not
Kiss him, at least not now. He will awake soon,
His hour of mid-day rest is nearly over,
But it were pity to disturb him till
'Tis closed.

CAIN. You have said well, I will contain*
My heart till then. He smiles and sleeps. Sleep on
And smile, thou little young inheritor
Of a world scarce less young. Sleep on and smile.
Thine are the hours and days when both are cheering
And innocent. Thou hast not plucked the fruit.
Thou know'st not that thou art naked. Must the time
Come thou shalt be amerced for sins unknown,
Which were not thine nor mine? But now sleep on,*
His cheeks are reddening into deeper smiles,
And shining lids are trembling o'er his long
Lashes, dark as the cypress which waves o'er them.
Half open, from beneath them the clear blue

11–12 *MS* incarnation ⟨the rose leaves⟩ / ⟨They press⟩ [*?*]
⟨vying⟩
The NED *gives* flesh colour *as one meaning of* incarnation, *labels this usage obsolete, and quotes the line in* CAIN. *Two years later Byron used* carnation *in* DON JUAN, *XVI, st. 93*: And Juan grew carnation with vexation. *The* NED, *quoting this line, gives almost the same meaning for this variant form*: the colour of human flesh or skin, a light rosy pink, but sometimes used for a deeper crimson colour as in the carnation flower.

13–14 *MS* you shall not ⟨kiss him⟩—/ ⟨Not now it will⟩

22 *MS, 1821 et al. thou* [*ital.*]

26–27 *MS* His ⟨litt⟩ cheeks . . . / And ⟨the snow⟩ lids . . . his ⟨eye⟩ long. *Since* reddening *is generally pronounced* redd'ning, *the contraction is not indicated.*

28 *MS* Cypress which ⟨bows⟩ oer them—

29 *MS* [*ins.*] them

Laughs out, although in slumber. He must dream—
Of what? Of Paradise! Aye, dream of it,
My disinherited boy. 'Tis but a dream;
For never more thyself, thy sons, nor fathers
Shall walk in that forbidden place of joy.

ADAH. Dear Cain! Nay, do not whisper o'er our son
Such melancholy yearnings o'er the past.
Why wilt thou always mourn for Paradise?
Can we not make another?

CAIN. Where?

ADAH. Here or
Where'er thou wilt. Where'er thou art, I feel not
The want of this so much regretted Eden.
Have I not thee, our boy, our sire, and brother,
And Zillah, our sweet sister, and our Eve,
To whom we owe so much besides our birth?

CAIN. Yes, death too is amongst the debts we owe her.

ADAH. Cain, that proud spirit who withdrew thee hence
Hath saddened thine still deeper. I had hoped
The promised wonders which thou hast beheld,
Visions, thou say'st, of past and present worlds
Would have composed thy mind into the calm
Of a contented knowledge; but I see

33 *MS* ⟨Now⟩—never more . . .
35 *MS* [*ins.*] nay, oer
36 *MS* melancholy ⟨longings of⟩ the past.
37 *MS* thou ⟨ever⟩ mourn . . .
39 *MS art* [*ital.*]
44 *MS* [*ins.*] amongst
45 *MS, 1905-C* Spirit; *capitalized also in lines 68, 78, 165.*
46, 56, 59, 64, 66 *1821 et al.* sadden'd, approach'd, roll'd, skirr'd, extinguish'd, borrow'd; *1905-M* borrowed. *This seems to be the only time that More did not follow the 1821, 1833, 1837 practice.*
49 *MS* mind ⟨to⟩ into . . .

Thy guide hath done thee evil. Still I thank him
And can forgive him all, that he so soon
Hath giv'n thee back to us.

CAIN. So soon?

ADAH. 'Tis scarcely*
Two hours since ye departed, two long hours
To me, but only hours upon the sun.

CAIN. And yet I have approached that sun and seen
Worlds which he once shone on and never more
Shall light, and worlds he never lit. Methought
Years had rolled o'er my absence.

ADAH. Hardly hours.

CAIN. The mind then hath capacity of time
And measures it by that which it beholds,
Pleasing or painful, little or almighty.
I had beheld the immemorial works
Of endless beings, skirred extinguished worlds,
And gazing on eternity methought
I had borrowed more by a few drops of ages
From its immensity, but now I feel
My littleness again. Well said the spirit
That I was nothing.

ADAH. Wherefore said he so?

53 *MS, 1821 et al.* given. *This variant recurs in lines 108, 374, where some editions did contract it.*

54–55 *MS, 1821 et al. long, me, hours* [*ital.*]

58 *MS* never ⟨saw⟩ . . .

63–64 *MS* beheld the ⟨works of ages—and⟩
⟨Immortal⟩ beings;—⟨and⟩ extinguished worlds—
⟨skirred⟩
Immemorial *should be given four syllables.*

66 *MS* borrowed more ⟨from it's⟩ by . . . *Had Byron contracted the auxiliary* I'd borrowed *in this twelve-syllable line, he would have had a better verse. Other twelve-syllable lines are 81, 167, 178, 189, 430, 455, 492, 525.*

69 *MS* ⟨Why⟩ said he so?

Jehovah said not that.

CAIN. No, he contents him
With making us the nothing which we are
And after flatt'ring dust with glimpses of
Eden and immortality resolves
It back to dust again—for what?

ADAH. Thou know'st,
Ev'n for our parents' error.

CAIN. What is that
To us? They sinned, then let them die!

ADAH. Thou hast not spoken well, nor is that thought
Thy own, but of the spirit who was with thee.
Would I could die for them so *they* might live.

CAIN. Why, so say I, provided that one victim
Might satiate the insatiable of life,
And that our little rosy sleeper there
Might never taste of death nor human sorrow
Nor hand it down to those who spring from him.

ADAH. How know we that some such atonement one day*
May not redeem our race?

CAIN. By sacrificing
The harmless for the guilty? What atonement
Were there? Why, *we* are innocent; what have we
Done that we must be victims for a deed
Before our birth, or need have victims to

70 *MS* ⟨He⟩ No—*he* [*ital.*]. 70–71 *MS, 1821 et al. he, nothing* [*ital.*]
72 *MS, 1821 et al.* flattering
73 *MS, 1821 et al.* Immortality
75 *MS, 1821 et al.* Even; *this variant recurs in lines 243, 471.*
76–79 *MS they* [*ital.*]; *MS, 1821 et al. let them, I, they* [*ital.*] *The eight-syllable line 76 is unique in* CAIN.
81 *MS, 1905-C* Insatiable
84 *MS* spring from ⟨them⟩—
89 *MS* must ⟨so⟩ victims . . .

Atone for this mysterious, nameless sin,
If it be such a sin to seek for knowledge?

ADAH. Alas! thou sinnest now, my Cain; thy words
Sound impious in mine ears.

CAIN. Then leave me.

ADAH. Never,
Though thy God left thee.

CAIN. Say, what have we here?

ADAH. Two altars, which our brother Abel made
During thine absence, whereupon to offer
A sacrifice to God on thy return.

CAIN. And how knew he that I would be so ready*
With the burnt off'rings, which he daily brings
With a meek brow, whose base humility
Shows more of fear than worship as a bribe
To the Creator?

ADAH. Surely 'tis well done.

CAIN. One altar may suffice, *I* have no off'ring.

ADAH. The fruits of the earth, the early beautiful
Blossom and bud and bloom of flow'rs and fruits,
These are a goodly off'ring to the Lord,
Giv'n with a gentle and a contrite spirit.

91 Mysterious *can be read as a trisyllable and the line scanned as iambic.*
94 *MS* in ⟨my⟩ ears. *If* impious *is read as a dissyllable, the verse has eleven syllables and irregular meter.*
98 *MS* on ⟨your⟩ return.
99 *MS, 1821 et al. he* that *I* [*ital.*]
100 *MS, 1821 et al.* offerings. *With two exceptions (238, 286), this word is consistently used as a dissyllable (104, 107, 214, 216, 239, 284).*
101 *MS* brow ⟨which⟩ whose . . .
102 *MS* worship—⟨to present⟩
103 *MS, 1821 et al.* Creator
106 *MS, 1821 et al.* flowers

CAIN. I have toiled and tilled and sweaten in the sun
According to the curse; must I do more?
For what should I be gentle? For a war
With all the elements ere they will yield
The bread we eat? For what must I be grateful?
For being dust and grov'ling in the dust
Till I return to dust? If I am nothing,
For nothing shall I be an hypocrite
And seem well-pleased with pain? For what should I
Be contrite? For my father's sin, already
Expiate with what we all have undergone,
And to be more than expiated by
The ages prophesied, upon our seed.
Little deems our young blooming sleeper there,
The germs of an eternal misery
To myriads is within him. Better 'twere
I snatched him in his sleep and dashed him 'gainst*
The rocks than let him live to—

ADAH. Oh my God!
Touch not the child—my child—thy child—Oh Cain!

109 *1821 et al.* toil'd, and till'd. *Again, contraction* I've toiled *would have improved the rhythm. As it now stands two scansions seem possible; in both the first foot is clumsy.* I have toiled / and tilled / and sweat / en in / the sun. I have / toiled and / tilled and / sweaten / in the sun.

114 *MS, 1821, 1831, 1833* groveling; *1837, 1904, 1905-C-M* grovelling. *As in I, 292, contraction seems preferable.*

118 *MS* sins; *1821 et al.* sin

119 *MS* [*ins.*] all

123–124 germs . . . is. *Uhlemayr*: "An irregular agreement of subject and verb occurs rather often in Byron's works" (*Lord Byron,* CAIN, *p. 22*).

124 *MS* ⟨Of⟩ Myriads. *As always,* myriads *should be read as a dissyllable here and in 439.*

125 *1821 et al.* dash'd

127 *MS* ⟨Hurt⟩ not the Child—⟨thy⟩ child—⟨my⟩ child . . . *MS, 1821 et al.* *thy* [*ital.*]

CAIN. Fear not, for all the stars and all the pow'r
Which sways them, I would not accost yon infant
With ruder greeting than a father's kiss.

ADAH. Then why so awful in thy speech?

CAIN. I said
'Twere better that he ceased to live than give
Life to so much of sorrow as he must
Endure and, harder still, bequeath; but since
That saying jars you, let us only say
'Twere better that he never had been born.

ADAH. Oh do not say so! Where were then the joys,
The mother's joys of watching, nourishing,
And loving him? Soft, he awakes. Sweet Enoch!

(She goes to the child.

Oh Cain, look on him, see how full of life,
Of strength, of bloom, of beauty, and of joy,
How like to me, how like to thee, when gentle,
For then we are all alike, is't not so, Cain?
Mother and sire and son, our features are
Reflected in each other, as they are
In the clear waters when they are gentle, and
When thou art gentle. Love us then my Cain!
And love thyself for our sakes, for we love thee.
Look, how he laughs and stretches out his arms
And opens wide his blue eyes upon thine,
To hail his father, while his little form
Flutters as winged with joy. Talk not of pain.
The childless cherubs well might envy thee

128 *MS, 1821 et al.* power; *this variant also occurs in 275.*
135 *MS* saying ⟨shock⟩ jars . . .
143, 146, 147 *1821 et al. then, all, they, gentle, thou, gentle* [*ital.*]
145 *MS* ⟨The mirror of⟩ each other . . .
151 *MS* father, ⟨with⟩ while . . .
152 *MS* ⟨Quivers⟩ with joy;—⟨Oh do not⟩ talk of pain! *1821 et al.* wing'd

The pleasures of a parent. Bless him, Cain.
As yet he hath no words to thank thee, but
His heart will, and thine own too.

CAIN. Bless thee, boy.
If that a mortal blessing may avail thee
To save thee from the serpent's curse.

ADAH. It shall.
Surely a father's blessing may avert
A reptile's subtlety.

CAIN. Of that I doubt,
But bless him ne'er the less.

ADAH. Our brother comes.*

CAIN. Thy brother Abel.

Enter ABEL.

ABEL. Welcome, Cain. My brother,
The peace of God be on thee!

CAIN. Abel, hail.

ABEL. Our sister tells me that thou hast been wand'ring
In high communion with a spirit far
Beyond our wonted range. Was he of those
We have seen and spoken with, like to our father?

CAIN. No.

ABEL. Why then commune with him? He may be
A foe to the Most High.

CAIN. And friend to man.
Has the Most High been so, if so you term him?

ABEL. Term him! Your words are strange today, my brother.
My sister Adah, leave us for awhile.

160 *1821 misprint* reptile
164 *MS, 1821 et al.* wandering
171 *MS, 1821 et al. Term him* [*ital.*]
172 *MS, 1821* a while; *1831 et al.* awhile

We mean to sacrifice.

ADAH. Farewell, my Cain,
But first embrace thy son. May his soft spirit
And Abel's pious ministry recall thee
To peace and holiness.

(*Exit* ADAH *with her child.*

ABEL. Where hast thou been?

CAIN. I know not.

ABEL. Nor what thou hast seen?

CAIN. The dead,
Th' immortal, the unbounded, the omnipotent,
The overpow'ring mysteries of space,
Th' innumerable worlds that were and are,
A whirlwind of such overwhelming things,
Suns, moons, and earths, upon their loud-voiced spheres*
Singing in thunder round me, as have made me*
Unfit for mortal converse. Leave me, Abel.

ABEL. Thine eyes are flashing with unnatural light,
Thy cheek is flushed with an unnatural hue,
Thy words are fraught with an unnatural sound.
What may this mean?

CAIN. It means—I pray thee, leave me.

ABEL. Not till we have prayed and sacrificed together.

CAIN. Abel, I pray thee, sacrifice alone.

175 *MS Abel's* ⟨gentle⟩ ministry . . .

178 *MS* The Immortal—the ⟨Immense⟩ . . . *MS, 1905-C* The Immortal, the Unbounded, the Omnipotent. *Other editions have the same text without capitalization. Even with elision, this is a twelve-syllable line.*

179 *This and line 182 were insertions. MS, 1821 et al.* overpowering

180 *MS, 1821 et al.* The innumerable

182 *A seven-stressed verse with only three slacks.*

185, 186, 187 Unnatural *may be read as a trisyllable.*

186 *1821 et al.* flush'd

189 *A twelve-syllable trochaic verse.*

Jehovah loves thee well.

ABEL. Both well, I hope.

CAIN. But thee the better; I care not for that.
Thou art fitter for his worship than I am;
Revere him then, but let it be alone—
At least without me.

ABEL. Brother, I should ill
Deserve the name of our great father's son,
If as my elder I revered thee not,
And in the worship of our God called not
On thee to join me and precede me in
Our priesthood; 'tis thy place.

CAIN. But I have ne'er
Asserted it.

ABEL. The more my grief; I pray thee
To do so now. Thy soul seems labouring in
Some strong delusion; it will calm thee.

CAIN. No,
Nothing can calm me more. Calm, say I? Never
Knew I what calm was in the soul, although
I have seen the elements stilled. My Abel, leave me
Or let me leave thee to thy pious purpose.

ABEL. Neither; we must perform our task together.
Spurn me not.

CAIN. If it must be so—well then,
What shall I do?

ABEL. Choose one of those two altars.

191 *MS, 1821 et al. Both [ital.]*
195 *MS me [ital.]*
198, 206 *1821 et al.* call'd, still'd
201 *MS* ⟨thy⟩ grief . . .
204 *MS, 1821 et al. Calm [ital.]*
206 *MS* stilled; ⟨Abel⟩ leave me—

CAIN. Choose for me; they to me are so much turf
And stone.

ABEL. Choose thou.

CAIN. I have chosen.

ABEL. 'Tis the highest
And suits thee as the elder. Now prepare
Thine off'rings.

CAIN. Where are thine?

ABEL. Behold them here,
The firstlings of the flock, and fat thereof—
A shepherd's humble off'ring.

CAIN. I have no flocks;
I am a tiller of the ground and must
Yield what it yieldeth to my toil—its fruit.
(*He gathers fruits.*
Behold them in their various bloom and ripeness.

(*They dress their altars and kindle a flame upon them.*

ABEL. My brother, as the elder, offer first
Thy prayer and thanksgiving with sacrifice.

CAIN. No, I am new to this; lead thou the way
And I will follow, as I may.

ABEL. (*kneeling*). Oh God,
Who made us and who breathed the breath of life
Within our nostrils, who hath blessed us

212 *Since* chosen *is monosyllabic, contraction is unnecessary in this eleven-syllable line with a slack ending.*

215 *MS* ⟨& the⟩ fat . . .

219 Various *may be read as a dissyllable.*

221 *MS* with ⟨this thy offering⟩—

223 *The stage direction is not on the MS, but was printed in 1821.*

224 *MS* & who ⟨placed⟩ the breath of life

225 *1905-M* blessèd. *Even with More's addition of* èd, *it is a rough verse. With* blessed, *it is a nine-syllable line.*

And spared, despite our father's sin, to make
His children all lost, as they might have been,
Had not thy justice been so tempered with
The mercy which is thy delight as to
Accord a pardon like a Paradise
Compared with our great crimes—Sole Lord of light,
Of good and glory and eternity,
Without whom all were evil and with whom
Nothing can err, except to some good end
Of thine omnipotent benevolence,
Inscrutable, but still to be fulfilled,
Accept from out thy humble first of shepherd's
First of the first-born flocks an offering,
In itself nothing (as what off'ring can be
Aught unto thee?) but yet accept it for
The thanksgiving of him who spreads it in
The face of thy high heav'n, bowing his own
Ev'n to the dust, of which he is, in honour
Of thee and of thy name for evermore!

(CAIN *standing erect during this speech.*

CAIN. Spirit, whate'er or whosoe'er thou art,
Omnipotent, it may be, and if good,
Shown in th' exemption of thy deeds from evil.
Jehovah upon earth and God in heav'n,

226 *MS* And ⟨deigned not for⟩ our father's . . .; *1833 misread the deletion*: And despised not for . . .

228, 236 *1821 et al.* temper'd, fulfill'd

231 *MS* ⟨Thou⟩ Lord . . .

237 *1905-C* shepherds'

238 *This is the first time that* offering *should be read as a trisyllable. In the next line, which is rhythmically irregular, it is better pronounced* off'ring, *as usual in the play.*

242 *MS, 1821 et al.* heaven. *This variant recurs in lines 248, 443, 530. See also 285 and 360, where some editions did contract it.*

245 *The stage direction does not appear on the MS, but was printed in 1821.*

247 *MS, 1821 et al.* the exemption

And it may be with other names because
Thine attributes seem many, as thy works,
If thou must be propitiated with prayers,
Take them. If thou must be induced with altars
And softened with a sacrifice, receive them.
Two beings here erect them unto thee.
If thou lov'st blood, the shepherd's shrine, which smokes*
On my right hand, hath shed it for thy service
In the first of his flock, whose limbs now reek
In sanguinary incense to thy skies.
Or if the sweet and blooming fruits of earth
And milder seasons, which the unstained turf
I spread them on now offers in the face
Of the broad sun which ripened them, may seem
Good to thee, inasmuch as they have not
Suffered in limb or life and rather form
A sample of thy works than supplication
To look on ours; if a shrine without victim
And altar without gore may win thy favour,
Look on it. And for him who dresseth it,
He is such as thou mad'st him and seeks nothing
Which must be won by kneeling. If he's evil,
Strike him. Thou art omnipotent and may'st,

251 *If* propitiated *is given four syllables the line may be scanned thus*:
˘ / \ / ˘ / / ˘ ˘ /
If thou / must be / propi/tiated / with prayers

253, 260, 262, 264 *1821 et al.* soften'd, unstain'd, ripen'd, suffer'd

258–260 *MS* In ⟨carnal⟩ incense . . . ⟨or if⟩
The sweet . . . of ⟨milder⟩ Earth
And ⟨softer⟩ Seasons . . .

259 *MS* [*ins.*] Or if

262 *MS* the ⟨fair⟩ broad . . .; [*ins.*] them

264–265 *MS* ⟨to⟩ and rather ⟨are⟩
A ⟨show of⟩ thy ⟨best⟩ works . . .

269 *Byron's script reads* as thy mad'st him; *he intended to write* they.

270 *MS* won with prayers—if he be evil . . . *All editions have the present text.*

For what can he oppose? If he be good,
Strike him or spare him as thou wilt, since all
Rest upon thee; and good and evil seem
To have no pow'r themselves, save in thy will.
And whether that be good or ill I know not,
Not being omnipotent nor fit to judge
Omnipotence, but merely to endure
Its mandate, which thus far I have endured.

(*The fire upon the altar of* ABEL *kindles into a column of the brightest flame and ascends to heaven, while a whirlwind throws down the altar of* CAIN *and scatters the fruits abroad upon the earth.*) *

ABEL (*kneeling*). Oh brother, pray! Jehovah's wroth with thee

CAIN. Why so?

ABEL. Thy fruits are scattered on the earth.

CAIN. From earth they came, to earth let them return;
Their seed will bear fresh fruit there ere the summer.
Thy burnt flesh-off'ring prospers better; see
How heav'n licks up the flames when thick with blood.

ABEL. Think not upon my offering's acceptance,*
But make another of thine own before

272 *MS* For what ⟨he⟩ can he . . .

274 *1905-C* Good and Evil. *Again there is no precedent in the MS or earlier editions for the capitalization.*

279 *MS stage directions*: The ⟨flame⟩ . . . brightest ⟨fire⟩ . . .

281 *1821 et al.* scatter'd

284 *1821 et al.* flesh-offr'ing. *For the first time these editions indicated the contracted pronunciation.*

285 *MS* when ⟨mixed⟩ with blood! *1821 et al.* heav'n. *Although Byron always used this word in* CAIN *as a monosyllable, this is the first time some editions contracted it; 1904 and 1905-C did not contract it.*

286 *1821* off'ring's; *MS, 1831 et al.* offerings.
Without the contraction the line has eleven syllables with feminine ending.

287 *MS* another of thy own . . .; *1821 et al.* thine own . . .

It is too late.

CAIN. I will build no more altars,
Nor suffer any.

ABEL (*rising*). Cain, what meanest thou?

CAIN. To cast down yon vile flatt'rer of the clouds,
The smoky harbinger of thy dull prayers,
Thine altar, with its blood of lambs and kids,
Which fed on milk, to be destroyed in blood.

ABEL (*opposing him*). Thou shalt not. Add not impious works to impious
Words. Let that altar stand. 'Tis hallowed now
By the immortal pleasure of Jehovah
In his acceptance of the victims.

CAIN. *His*!
His pleasure! What was his high pleasure in
The fumes of scorching flesh and smoking blood,
To the pain of the bleating mothers which
Still yearn for their dead offspring? Or the pangs
Of the sad ignorant victims underneath

290, 291 *1821 et al.* flatt'rer, pray'rs. *In this part of the play, the 1821 editor was suddenly conscious of the need of contracted readings. Since* prayers *is always pronounced as a monosyllable, its contraction is superfluous. 1904* flatt'rer, prayers; *MS, 1905-C* flatterer, prayers. *Line 290 is notable for its concentration of five successive stresses.*

293, 295 *1821 et al.* destroy'd, hallow'd

294 Impious *may again be read as dissyllabic. Here is a concentration of six heavy accents.*

296 *Prosody does not seem to require an elision here.*

298–300 *MS* pleasure in ⟨the fumes⟩
Of scorching flesh . . . blood ⟨unto⟩
⟨The⟩ pain of the ⟨poor⟩ bleating . . .
When Byron noticed that he had two extra syllables in line 298, he crossed out the fumes, *which he now added to the beginning of line 299. This change required the deletion of* unto *in line 299 and the addition of* To *and the excision of* poor *in line 300.*

Thy pious knife? Give way! This bloody record
Shall not stand in the sun to shame creation.

ABEL. Brother, give back! Thou shalt not touch my altar
With violence. If that thou wilt adopt it
To try another sacrifice, 'tis thine.

CAIN. Another sacrifice! Give way or else
That sacrifice may be—

ABEL. What mean'st thou?

CAIN. Give—
Give way! Thy God loves blood! Then look to it!
Give way, ere he hath more!

ABEL. In his great name
I stand between thee and the shrine which hath
Had his acceptance.

CAIN. If thou lov'st thyself,
Stand back till I have strewed this turf along
Its native soil; else—

ABEL (*opposing him*). I love God far more*
Than life.

CAIN (*striking him with a brand, on the temples, which he snatches from the altar*). Then take thy life unto thy God
Since he loves lives.

ABEL (*falls*). What hast thou done, my brother?

309 *1821, 1831* meanest; *MS, 1833 et al.* mean'st. *The first edition gives us a line of eleven syllables with a final accent. Did the editor prefer the less ugly sound?* What mean'st thou *is typical of Byron's harsh imitation of biblical language.*

311 *MS, 1821 et al. more, his* [*ital.*]

312 *MS* thee ⟨be hi⟩ and . . .

314 *MS* turf ⟨upon⟩; *1821 et al.* strew'd

315–316 *MS* I love ⟨my⟩ God—⟨more than⟩/ ⟨My My⟩ life—.
⟨my⟩ ⟨than⟩

CAIN. Brother!

ABEL. Oh God, receive thy servant and
Forgive his slayer, for he knew not what*
He did. Cain, give me—give me thy hand, and tell
Poor Zillah—

CAIN (*after a moment's stupefaction*). *My* hand! 'Tis all red, and with
What? (*A long pause. Looking slowly round.*)
Where am I? Alone! Where's Abel? Where
Cain? Can it be that I am he? My brother,
Awake! Why liest thou so on the green earth?
'Tis not the hour of slumber. Why so pale?
What hast thou? Thou wert full of life this morn.
Abel, I pray thee, mock me not. I smote
Too fiercely, but not fatally. Ah, why
Wouldst thou oppose me? This is mockery,
And only done to daunt me. 'Twas a blow,
And but a blow. Stir—stir—nay, only stir!
Why, so—that's well—thou breath'st—breathe upon me.
Oh God! Oh God!

ABEL (*very faintly*). What's he who speaks of God?*

CAIN. Thy murd'rer.

ABEL. Then may God forgive him. Cain,

327–328 *MS* mock me not—⟨I struck⟩
Too ⟨hard—but it was not my purpose—why⟩

329 *MS, 1821, 1831* Would'st; *1833 et al.* Wouldst. *Here 1821, which in Acts I and II had printed* wouldst *and* couldst *is inconsistent. It used the apostrophe again in III, 368, 498, 539.*

330 *1831 misprint* as a blow—

331 *MS* Stir—⟨only⟩ Stir—

332 *1821 et al.* breath'st; *MS, 1905-C* breathest. *The ugly contraction gave the line ten syllables. Even with the MS, 1905-C expansion, it is a roughly accented verse, appropriate to the context here.*

334 *MS, 1821 et al.* murderer. *This variant recurs in 488.*

Comfort poor Zillah. She has but one brother
Now. (ABEL *dies*.

CAIN. And I none! Who makes me brotherless?
His eyes are open. Then he is not dead.
Death is like sleep, and sleep shuts down our lids.
His lips too are apart; why then he breathes.
And yet I feel it not. His heart! his heart!
Let me see, doth it beat? Methinks—No—no.
This is a vision, else I am become
The native of another and worse world.
The earth swims round me. What is this? 'Tis wet,

(*Puts his hand to his brow, and then looks at it.*)

And yet there are no dews. 'Tis blood—my blood—
My brother's and my own and shed by me.
Then what have I further to do with life,
Since I have taken life from my own flesh?
But he cannot be dead. Is silence death?
No, he will wake; then let me watch by him.
Life cannot be so slight as to be quenched
Thus quickly. He hath spoken to me since.
What shall I say to him? My brother? No,
He will not answer to that name, for brethren
Smite not each other. Yet—yet—speak to me.
Oh for a word more of that gentle voice

336 *MS* ⟨and⟩ who makes . . .
337 *MS* eyes are ⟨gl⟩ open . . .
338 *MS* shuts ⟨bot⟩ down . . .
342 *MS* else ⟨this is⟩ I am become
345 *MS my* [*ital.*] blood—*Here the editors did not use Byron's italics.*
348 *This line is an insertion.*
349 *MS, 1821 et al., except 1904 and 1905-M* can not. *In line 351 all editions have* cannot.
350–351 *MS* [*ins*] wake, so
351 *1821 et al.* quench'd
352 *MS* spoken to me ⟨once⟩—

That I may bear to hear my own again!

Enter ZILLAH.

ZILLAH. I heard a heavy sound. What can it be?
'Tis Cain, and watching by my husband. What
Dost thou there, brother? Doth he sleep? Oh heav'n!
What means this paleness and yon stream? No, no!
It is not blood, for who would shed his blood?
Abel, what's this? Who hath done this? He moves not.
He breathes not, and his hands drop down from mine
With stony lifelessness. Ah, cruel Cain!
Why camest thou not in time to save him from
This violence? Whatever hath assailed him,
Thou wert the stronger and shouldst have stepped in
Between him and aggression. Father! Eve!
Adah! Come hither! Death is in the world!

(*Exit* ZILLAH, *calling on her parents, etc.*

357 *MS* hear my own ⟨once more⟩

360 *1821, 1831, 1833, 1837, 1905-M* heav'n. *MS, 1905-C* Heaven. *Coleridge capitalized it even when it was used as an expletive; 1904 did not contract it.*

361 *MS* stream ⟨? of—Abel!⟩

362 *This line is an insertion that involved revision of the end of line 361. The original ran thus (361, 363):*
What means this paleness—& yon stream? of—Abel!
Abel!—what's this—

365 *MS* ⟨Like⟩ With stoney . . .

366 *MS (a)* ⟨And⟩ came'st; *(b)* [*ins.*] Why. *1821 et al.* cam'st; *1905-C* camest; *On the MS Byron first seems to have written* cam'st *and then inserted* e *but did not strike through his apostrophe. The 1821 editor could have made the contrary interpretation, especially since his contraction gave an iambic pentameter.*

367 *1821 et al.* assail'd

368 *MS* should'st have ⟨gone⟩in; *1821, 1831, 1833, 1837* should'st . . . stepp'd; *1905-C* shouldst . . . stepped. *This is apparently the only time that 1833 and 1837 concur with 1821 and 1831 in the use of the apostrophe in* shouldst *or* wouldst. *1904, 1905-M* shouldst.

370 *In the stage direction MS, 1821* parents; *1831 et al.* Parents

CAIN (*solus*). And who hath brought him there? I, who abhor
The name of death so deeply that the thought
Empoisoned all my life before I knew
His aspect, I have led him here and giv'n
My brother to his cold and still embrace,
As if he would not have asserted his
Inexorable claim without my aid.
I am awake at last—a dreary dream*
Had maddened me; but he shall ne'er awake.

Enter ADAM, EVE, ADAH, *and* ZILLAH.

ADAM. A voice of woe from Zillah brings me here.*
What do I see? 'Tis true! My son, my son!
Woman, behold the serpent's work, and thine,* (*To* EVE.

EVE. Oh, speak not of it now. The serpent's fangs
Are in my heart. My best belovèd, Abel!
Jehovah, this is punishment beyond
A mother's sin, to take *him* from me.

ADAM. Who
Or what hath done this deed? Speak, Cain, since thou
Wert present. Was it some more hostile angel,
Who walks not with Jehovah? Or some wild
Brute of the forest?

EVE. Ah, a livid light

371 *MS* who ⟨first⟩ hath . . .
372 *MS, 1821 et al.* Death
373 *1821 et al.* empoison'd
374 *MS, 1904, 1905-C* given; *1821, 1831, 1833, 1837, 1905-M* giv'n
379 *MS* ⟨Hath⟩ maddened . . .; *1821 et al.* madden'd
380 *1821 misprint.* wo
384 *1821 et al.* beloved. *The only time 1905-C-M did not use the accent, possibly because the editors wanted to keep the line to ten syllables. If we use* belovèd *here, as 1905-C-M did elsewhere, we have an eleven-syllable line with the customary feminine ending.*
390 *MS* ⟨Savage⟩ Brute of the forest? [Eve] Ah—a ⟨hideous⟩ light

Breaks through as from a thunder cloud. Yon brand,
Massy and bloody, snatched from off the altar
And black with smoke and red with—

ADAM. Speak, my son!
Speak and assure us, wretched as we are,
That we are not more miserable still.

ADAH. Speak, Cain, and say it was not thou.

EVE. It was.
I see it now. He hangs his guilty head
And covers his ferocious eye with hands
Incarnadine.

ADAH. Mother, thou dost him wrong.
Cain, clear thee from this horrible accusal,
Which grief wrings from our parent.

EVE. Hear, Jehovah!
May th' eternal serpent's curse be on him,
For he was fitter for his seed than ours.
May all his days be desolate! May—

ADAH. Hold!
Curse him not mother, for he is thy son.
Curse him not mother, for he is my brother
And my betrothed.

EVE. He hath left thee no brother,
Zillah no husband, me no son. For thus*

391 *1821 et al.* thunder-cloud
396 *MS, 1821 et al. thou* [*ital.*]
401 *MS* ⟨Now⟩—Hear Jehovah!
402 *MS, 1821 et al.* the eternal*; the elision gives a trochaic verse.*
404 *MS* desolate! ⟨his⟩ may . . .
406 *MS* him ⟨for⟩ not . . .
407 *Byron first wrote* betrothed *and then added an apostrophe in different ink later. Thus he used the pointless contracted spelling of past participles that was common in the first edition. 1821 et al.* betroth'd
408 *MS, et al. no son* [*ital.*]

I curse him from my sight for evermore!
All bonds I break between us, as he broke
That of his nature in yon—Oh death! death!
Why didst thou not take me, who first incurred thee?
Why dost thou not so now?

ADAM. Eve, let not this,
Thy natural grief, lead to impiety.
A heavy doom was long forespoken to us,
And now that it begins let it be borne
In such sort as may show our God that we
Are faithful servants to his holy will.

EVE (*pointing to Cain*). *His* will! The will of yon incarnate spirit
Of death, whom I have brought upon the earth
To strew it with the dead. May all the curses
Of life be on him; and his agonies
Drive him forth o'er the wilderness, like us
From Eden, till his children do by him
As he did by his brother! May the swords
And wings of fi'ry cherubim pursue him
By day and night, snakes spring up in his path,
Earth's fruits be ashes in his mouth, the leaves
On which he lays his head to sleep be strewed
With scorpions! May his dreams be of his victim!

411 *1905-C in yon* [*ital.*]—Oh Death! Death! *There are no italics in earlier editions.*

412 *MS, 1821 et al. me* [*ital.*]; *1821 et al.* incurr'd

414 Natural *may be dissyllabic here.*

417 *MS* our God that ⟨he⟩ we

419 *MS, 1821 et al. His will* [*ital.*]; *MS, 1905-C* Incarnate Spirit

420 *MS* brought ⟨into⟩ this ⟨world⟩

423–424 *MS* Drive him ⟨forth oer the world—as we were driven/ . . . ⟨may⟩ his Children . . .

426 *MS, 1821 et al.* fiery

427 *MS* spring ⟨upon⟩ . . .

429 *1821 et al.* strew'd

430 *MS (a)* [*ins.*] May; *(b)* dreams ⟨of⟩ be . . . Scorpions *may be dissyllabic, giving an eleven-syllable line with a feminine ending.*

His waking a continual dread of death!
May the clear rivers turn to blood as he
Stoops down to stain them with his raging lip!
May ev'ry element shun or change to him!
May he live in the pangs which others die with!
And death itself wax something worse than death
To him who first acquainted him with man!
Hence, fratricide! Henceforth that word is *Cain*
Through all the coming myriads of mankind,
Who shall abhor thee though thou wert their sire.
May the grass wither from thy feet, the woods
Deny thee shelter, earth a home, the dust
A grave, the sun his light, and heav'n her God! (*Exit* EVE.

ADAM. Cain, get thee forth; we dwell no more together.
Depart and leave the dead to me. I am
Henceforth alone. We never must meet more.

ADAH. Oh part not with him thus, my father! Do not
Add thy deep curse to Eve's upon his head.

431 *MS* waking ⟨of⟩ . . .; continual *may be read as trisyllabic.*

434 *MS, 1821 et al.* every

436 *MS* itself ⟨be⟩ something . . .

438 Fatricide *is one of Byron's few misspellings on this MS. He had trouble with it again in line 492.*

441–443 *These lines are not on the MS but were printed in 1821 et al. Byron sent them in a letter to Murray, September 12, 1821:* "To the last speech of *Eve,* in the last act (*i.e.* where she curses Cain), add these three lines to the concluding one—[*the three lines follow*]. There's as pretty a piece of Imprecation for you, when joined to the lines already sent, as you may wish to meet with in the course of your business. But don't forget the addition of the above three lines, which are clinchers to Eve's speech" *(LJ, V, 361).*

441 *The letter version of this line as printed by Prothero and Quennell:* foot; *1821 et al.* feet. *The former capitalized* Grass, Woods, Earth, Dust, Grave, Sun, Heaven, *none of which 1821 et al. capitalized, except 1905-C* Heaven. *No edition contracted the latter word.*

ADAM. I curse him not; his spirit be his curse.
Come, Zillah.

ZILLAH. I must watch my husband's corse.

ADAM. We will return again when he is gone
Who hath provided for us this dread office.
Come, Zillah.

ZILLAH. Yet one kiss on yon pale clay
And those lips once so warm—my heart—my heart!

(*Exeunt* ADAM *and* ZILLAH, *weeping.*

ADAH. Cain, thou hast heard, we must go forth. I am ready,
So shall our children be. I will bear Enoch,
And you his sister. Ere the sun declines,
Let us depart nor walk the wilderness
Under the cloud of night. Nay, speak to me,
To me, thine own.

CAIN. Leave me.

ADAH. Why, all have left thee.

CAIN. And wherefore lingerest thou? Dost thou not fear
To dwell with one who hath done this?

ADAH. I fear
Nothing except to leave thee, much as I
Shrink from the deed which leaves thee brotherless.

450 *Coleridge commented on the cacophony.* "If Byron had read his plays aloud, or been at pains to revise the proofs, he would hardly have allowed 'corse' to remain in such close proximity to 'curse'" (POETRY, *V, 271 n. 3*).

452 *MS* provided ⟨her with⟩ this . . .

459 *MS* the ⟨shade⟩ of Night . . .

460 *MS, 1821 et al. me—thine own* [*ital.*]

461 *Contraction*—ling'rest—*might improve the rhythm but not the euphony.*

463 *MS* [*ins.*] thee

I must not speak of this; it is between thee
And the great God.

(*A Voice from within exclaims*, Cain! Cain!)

ADAH. Hear'st thou that voice?

(*The Voice within.* Cain! Cain!)

ADAH. It soundeth like an angel's tone.*

Enter the ANGEL *of the Lord.*

ANGEL. Where is thy brother Abel?

CAIN. Am I then
My brother's keeper?

ANGEL. Cain, what hast thou done?
The voice of thy slain brother's blood cries out
Ev'n from the ground unto the Lord. Now art thou
Cursed from the earth, which opened late her mouth
To drink thy brother's blood from thy rash hand.
Henceforth when thou shalt till the ground, it shall not
Yield thee her strength. A fugitive shalt thou
Be from this day, and vagabond on earth.

ADAH. This punishment is more than he can bear.*
Behold, thou driv'st him from the face of earth,
And from the face of God shall he be hid.
A fugitive and vagabond on earth,
'Twill come to pass that whoso findeth him
Shall slay him.

CAIN. Would they could! But who are they

465 *MS* it ⟨lie⟩ [*?*] between thee

472 *MS* [*ins.*] late; *MS* Curst; *1821 et al. Cursed; 1821, 1831, 1837, 1904, 1905-M* open'd*; 1833* opened.

473 *MS* ⟨To take⟩ thy brother's . . .

478 *1904* driv'st. *This is the only edition that used a contraction and thus printed a regular ten-syllable line. All others that used* drivest *have an eleven-syllable line with masculine ending. Byron was ambiguous on the MS with* drive'st.

Shall slay me? Where are these on the lone earth
As yet unpeopled?

ANGEL. Thou hast slain thy brother,
And who shall warrant thee against thy son?

ADAH. Angel of light! be merciful, nor say
That this poor aching breast now nourishes
A murd'rer in my boy and of his father.

ANGEL. Then he would but be what his father is.
Did not the milk of Eve give nutriment
To him thou now see'st so besmeared with blood?
The fratricide might well engender parricides.
But it shall not be so. The Lord thy God*
And mine commandeth me to set his seal
On Cain so that he may go forth in safety.
Who slayeth Cain, a sev'nfold vengeance shall
Be taken on his head. Come hither.

CAIN. What
Wouldst thou with me?

ANGEL. To mark upon thy brow
Exemption from such deeds as thou hast done.

CAIN. No, let me die!

ANGEL. It must not be.
(*The* ANGEL *sets the mark on* CAIN'S *brow.*

CAIN. It burns

485 *MS* ⟨And⟩ who ⟨then⟩ shall . . .
486 *MS, 1821 et al.* Angel of Light!
489 *MS* [*ins*] ⟨Even thus he would be that which his father is.⟩—
[*ins.*] ⟨what his⟩
[*ins.*] Thus he would but be what his father is.
491 *1821 et al.* besmear'd
496 *MS* ⟨On whosoeer⟩ [*?*] Cain. *MS, 1821 et al.* sevenfold. *The contraction seems to give a better verse.*
498 *MS* To mark ⟨up⟩on . . . *Byron left the line short by one syllable. 1821 et al.* upon. *MS, 1821, 1831* Would'st; *1833 et al.* Wouldst . . .
500 *MS stage direction:* sets the ⟨seal⟩ on . . .

My brow, but naught to that which is within it.
Is there more? Let me meet it as I may.

ANGEL. Stern hast thou been and stubborn from the womb,
As the ground thou must henceforth till; but he
Thou slew'st was gentle as the flocks he tended.

CAIN. After the fall too soon was I begotten,*
Ere yet my mother's mind subsided from
The serpent, and my sire still mourned for Eden.
That which I am, I am. I did not seek
For life nor did I make myself. But could I
With my own death redeem him from the dust—
And why not so? Let him return today,
And I lie ghastly! So shall be restored
By God the life to him he loved; and taken
From me a being I ne'er loved to bear.

ANGEL. Who shall heal murder? What is done is done.
Go forth. Fulfill thy days and be thy deeds
Unlike the last. (*The* ANGEL *disappears.*

ADAH. He's gone, let us go forth.

503 *MS* ⟨since⟩ the womb

506–508 *There are three inserted verses, crowded in fine script and separated by a line from the Angel's speech. As an indication of his hesitation, Byron wrote* Cain *three times and deleted them.*

508 *1821 et al.* mourn'd

512 *MS, 1821 et al.* to day*; 1905-M* to-day

513–515 *That these lines are also insertions is suggested by the fact that Byron wrote and canceled* Angel*; i.e., he had started the next speech and then he went back to Cain's speech. The last line of the insertion runs across the deleted* Angel. *Byron drew a line below the insertion.*
MS And I lie ⟨bloody⟩ . . .
⟨To⟩ God the life ⟨of⟩ him . . .
. . . I neer ⟨sought⟩ to bear.

517 *MS* fulfill*; 1821 et al.* fulfil

518 *MS Stage direction (a)* ⟨Exit⟩ Angel; *(b)* The Angel disappears; *MS* ⟨Again⟩—let us go forth—

I hear our little Enoch cry within
Our bow'r.

CAIN. Ah, little knows he what he weeps for;
And I who have shed blood cannot shed tears.
But the four rivers would not cleanse my soul.
Think'st thou my boy will bear to look on me?

ADAH. If I thought that he would not, I would—

CAIN (*interrupting her*). No.
No more of threats, we have had too many of them.
Go to our children, I will follow thee.

ADAH. I will not leave thee lonely with the dead.
Let us depart together.

CAIN. Oh thou dead
And everlasting witness, whose unsinking

520 *MS* [*ins.*] he. *MS, 1821 et al.* bower.

521–522 *These two inserted parenthetical lines disrupted the continuity of the original lines (520, 523):*

Ah—little knows he what he weeps for.—
Thinks't thou that he will bear to look on me?

The insertion of 521–522 made the pronoun in line 523 obscurely remote from its antecedent in line 520, and so Byron cancelled his first version of 523 and clarified the subject of the clause by substituting my boy *for* he: Thinkest thou my boy will bear . . . *He also substituted* Thinkest *for* Thinks't, *got rid of one of his ugly contractions, but gained an irregular line of eleven syllables with masculine ending. 1821 et al., however, printed* Thinks't.

522 *MS Note* [*ins.*] The "four rivers" which flowed round Eden and consequently the only waters with which Cain was acquainted upon the earth.

526 *MS* Go to ⟨thy boys⟩ I will . . .

528–531 *Line 530, its preliminary trial, and the revision of line 529 were insertions. The composition went through these stages:*

1. *(528, 529, 531)*

Oh! thou dead
And everlasting witness!—⟨what thou art⟩
I know not!

Blood darkens earth and heav'n, what thou now art
I know not, but if thou see'st what I am,
I think thou wilt forgive him, whom his God
Can ne'er forgive, nor his own soul. Farewell.
I must not, dare not touch what I have made thee.
I, who sprung from the same womb with thee, drained
The same breast, clasped thee often to my own,
In fondness brotherly and boyish, I
Can never meet thee more nor even dare
To do that for thee, which thou shouldst have done
For me—compose thy limbs into their grave,
The first grave yet dug for mortality.
But who hath dug that grave? Oh earth! Oh earth!
For all the fruits thou hast rendered to me, I
Give thee back this. Now for the wilderness.

(ADAH *stoops down and kisses the body of* ABEL.

---

2. *Then Byron tried to make an insertion but could not complete it and fit it into the lines already written (528, 529, 530 fragment):*

Oh! thou dead
And everlasting witness!—whose unsinking ⟨blood⟩
⟨Blood flows around to the ey⟩ . . .

3. *The final version (528–531):*

Oh! thou dead
And everlasting witness!—whose unsinking
Blood darkens Earth and Heaven! What thou *now* art
I know not!

530–532 *MS, 1821 et al. now, thou, I* [*ital.*]. *MS also italicized* thou *in line 531 but all editions ignored this.*

535–536 *MS* from the ⟨same b⟩; *intended to write* breast. *See line 536. 1821 et al.* drain'd, clasp'd.

539 *MS, 1821, 1831* should'st; *1833 et al.* shouldst

540 *MS* For me—compose⟨d⟩ thy limbs . . .

541 *This line is an insertion in the right margin. MS* grave ⟨ever⟩ dug . . .

542 *MS* But ⟨I have⟩ dug . . .

543 *MS* For ⟨th⟩ all; *1821 et al.* render'd

544 *MS stage direction* kisses the ⟨dead⟩ body . . .

ADAH. A dreary and an early doom, my brother,
Has been thy lot. Of all who mourn for thee
I alone must not weep. My office is
Henceforth to dry up tears and not to shed them.
But yet of all who mourn none mourn like me,
Not only for thyself, but him who slew thee.
Now Cain, I will divide thy burden with thee.

CAIN. Eastward from Eden will we take our way;
'Tis the most desolate and suits my steps.

ADAH. Lead! Thou shalt be my guide, and may our God
Be thine. Now let us carry forth our children.

CAIN. And he who lieth there was childless. I
Have dried the fountain of a gentle race,
Which might have graced his recent marriage couch
And might have tempered this stern blood of mine,
Uniting with our children Abel's offspring.
Oh Abel!

ADAH. Peace be with him.

CAIN. But with *me*!

(*Exeunt.*

(*The End*)

549 *MS* mourn like ⟨thee⟩
551 *MS* burthen; *1821 et al.* burden
552 *MS* from Eden⟨'s⟩ . . .
555 *MS* let ⟨bring out⟩ our children.
556 *MS, 1821 et al. he* [*ital.*]
558, 560 *These lines are the final MS insertion. The original version ran thus (556, 557, 559, 561):*
And he who ⟨lies⟩ there—⟨he is⟩ childless—I
Have dried the fountain of a gentle race—
⟨Which⟩ might have tempered ⟨the rash⟩ blood of mine—
⟨Oh Abel⟩
560 *MS* children ⟨ere we died;⟩
561 *MS* Oh . . . Me! ! ! *1821 et al.* O . . . *me!* [*ital.*]
After the last line Byron wrote End of Act third and of the drama.—*Below this he scrawled his signature symbol twice and* Ravenna Septr 9th 1821.

ANNOTATIONS

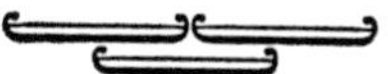

SINCE THE ESSAYS PROVIDE an exposition and evaluation of the content and technique of the poem and a survey of the views of past critics, this section for the most part eschews such matters. Seven-eighths of the annotations comprise a selection of analogues in the writings of Byron and other authors. We should not consistently regard a similarity of idea, detail, or language in the works of Byron's predecessors as evidence of his deliberate borrowing. He heard his biblical echoes, but I doubt that he was aware of all the parallels in *Cain* to *Paradise Lost, Faust*, Bayle's *Dictionary*, and other books. Some of these must have been the coincidental product of common interests. Others probably were reading memories that had transfused his own thoughts.

The slight remainder of the annotations identify some allusions and offer commentary (1) on three subjects that have elicited unusual disagreement of interpretation (see III, 286–316, 333–357, 506–561) and (2) on a few examples of Byron's artistry not discussed at length in other parts of the book.

Detailed comment on the text of the poem has been placed with the variants.

PREFACE

6 See "*Cain* and the Mysteries."

7 This dramatic principle, which is repeated in lines 42–43, was

more energetically expressed in Byron's letters to Murray. See "Byron's View of His Play."

12 Byron circled back to this point in lines 44–47. He also gave Lucifer an emphatic iteration of the denial that he was the serpent in I, 216–244. Byron took the idea from two sources: (1) William Warburton: "In the *History of the Fall,* it is to be observed that he mentions only the *Instrument* of the *Agent*, the *Serpent*; not the *Agent* himself, the *Devil* . . ." (*The Divine Legation of Moses*, II, pt. ii, 449–450). (2) Pierre Bayle:

> [Eve] suffered herself to be deceived by the lies and fair promises of the Serpent, and then she sollicited her husband to the same disobedience. . . . The truest opinion, *viz.* that Eve was seduced by the Devil, concealed under the body of a serpent, has been tacked to a thousand suppositions by the liberty which human invention had taken.

Bayle related many fictions about the serpent that he had found in literature (V, 119–120 and n. A).

16 Richard Watson (1737–1816), a man of remarkable energy, shrewdness, and versatility, in 1764 was elected professor of chemistry at Cambridge, and though he "had never read a syllable on the subject, nor seen a single experiment," he worked hard and delivered a popular series of lectures. He was ambitious to hold the chair of divinity, though he held no degree to qualify him for it. He maneuvered a doctorate for himself by royal mandate and was elected to the coveted chair in 1771. He wrote many religious tracts, his most successful being an *Apology for the Bible.*

His principles were a mixture of the liberal and the conservative. He favored the income tax, worked on agricultural reforms and for the abolition of the slave trade, supported Roman Catholic emancipation, and vindicated the right of revolution, but also held that every church should "require uniformity of doctrinal profession." His favorite topic was the defense of revealed religion, and he recognized no theological authority except the New Testament. It is this conventional position that Byron referred to in the Preface.

John Wright (XIV, 12 n.) quoted from the *Anecdotes of the Life of Richard Watson* (I, 63):

> I never troubled myself with answering any arguments which the opponents in the divinity-schools brought against the Articles of the Church

> . . . but I used . . . to say to them, holding up the New Testament in my hand, "En sacrum codicem! Here is the fountain of truth; why do you follow the streams derived from it by the sophistry, or polluted by the passions, of man?"

E. H. Coleridge made the sardonic comment that Bishop Watson's authority "as a school Divine" was "on a par with that of the author of *Cain*" (*Poetry*, V, 208 n.). John Genest thought Byron misleading. Though Watson always maintained that scriptural authority was paramount, "it does not by any means follow from thence, that he preferred the literal sense of the first chapters of Genesis to the more rational interpretation of them . . ." (*Some Account of the English Stage from the Restoration in 1660 to 1830*, IX, 137).

18 Byron was anachronistic, for he did allude to some New Testament matters: Lucifer's prophecy that God will create a Son who will become a sacrifice (I, 163–166); Lucifer's prediction that Cain will be the only mortal, except Christ, who will journey to the realm of the dead and return (I, 540–542); Lucifer's taunt that he will not require of Cain the same condition of belief that Christ will demand of Peter before he will let him walk upon the waters (II, i, 16–22, see Annotations); and the discussion Adah and Cain have about the cruelty and injustice of sacrificing one innocent victim for the guilt of others (III, 79–92). Many writers noted Byron's inconsistency. There are also echoes of New Testament phrasing in I, 317–320; II, i, 3; III, 319–320.

22 Byron told Medwin that Gessner's *Death of Abel* was one of the first books his German Master read to him. Although Byron in the Preface stated that he enjoyed it, his comment to Medwin mocked at Gessner's sentimentality: while the German Master "was crying his eyes out over its pages, I thought that any other than Cain had hardly committed a crime in ridding the world of so dull a fellow as Gessner made brother Abel" (Medwin, p. 125). Byron repeated the jest to Hobhouse in Pisa on September 20, 1822 (*Recollections of a Long Life*, III, 7).

Both Coleridge and Chew found Byron disingenuous in his casual nod at Gessner and both mentioned that "his recollections of Gessner's 'Death of Abel' . . . were clearer than he imagined" (*Poetry*, V, 200). They, however, along with Thorslev and others, found the indebtedness insignificant. Byron borrowed from Gessner the whirlwind demolition of Cain's altar, the substitution of the Angel for God, "the Teutonic domesticities of Cain and Adah," and "the evangelical piety of Adam and Abel" (*Poetry*, V, 201). Chew and Thorslev found more differences than resemblances.

Blumenthal made a concise comparison of Gessner's *Death of Abel* and Byron's *Cain.* A more recent criticism of Gessner's book has been written by Thorslev (pp. 94–98).

29 Byron's efforts to disclaim indebtedness to Milton, Gessner, and Alfieri deserved Hazlitt's twitting in his review of *Heaven and Earth.* "We are aware that it is hazardous and idle to accuse Lord Byron of plagiarism. He will swear that he never saw the picture [one by Poussin], or that it is so long ago that he has quite forgot it" (*Complete Works*, XVI, 415). *The Monthly Magazine*, *The Literary Gazette*, and others cited yards of borrowings that would have bothered a man less sensitive than Byron. After one scans some of these tiresome articles, he does not wonder that Byron ordered Murray to stop sending him periodical trash. Hazlitt in one of his essays on Byron admired the brilliant and talented use Byron made of borrowed materials.

A month after Byron sent Murray the MS of *Cain*, he wrote his publisher that he had read the Old Testament "through and through before I was eight years old" (*LJ*, V, 391).

29 Coleridge:

> The Manichaeans (the disciples of Mani or Manes, third century A.D.) held that there were two co-eternal Creators—a God of Darkness who made the body, and a God of Light who was responsible for the soul—and that it was the aim and function of the good spirit to rescue the soul, the spiritual part of man, from the possession and grasp of the body, which had been created by and was in possession of the spirit of evil. (*Poetry,* V, 209 n.)

Byron was familiar with the discussions of Manicheism in Bayle's *Dictionary.* There were several eighteenth-century translations, and Byron had a set but sold it before he left England (*LJ,* III, 73 and n.). Chew surmised from one of the notes to the fourth canto of *Childe Harold* that in Italy, Byron used a French edition. Though Hobhouse wrote these notes (and not Byron, as Chew said), Byron probably knew that his friend used Bayle.

A month after he finished *Cain* (October 9, 1821) he wrote Murray, "I want a Bayle, but am afraid of the carriage and the weight, as also of folios in general." Murray a few weeks later wrote that he had sent all the books Byron had requested (*LJ*, V, 391–392 and n.).

Bayle's discussions of Manichean doctrines were in the articles on Manicheans, Marcionites, Paulicians, Xenophanes, and Zoroaster. Byron also knew the articles on Adam, Eve, Abel, and Cain. As Roy Edwin Aycock in a good thesis on "Lord Byron and Bayle's Dictionary" explained, the sources of Byron's dualism and skepticism were many; three of Byron's favorite authors, Frederick the Great, Voltaire, and Gibbon all admired and knew Bayle thoroughly.

35 Coleridge:

> Conan the Jester, a character in the Irish ballads, was "a kind of Thersites, but brave and daring even to rashness. He had made a vow that he would never take a blow without returning it; and having . . . descended to the infernal regions, he received a cuff from the arch-fiend, which he instantly returned, using the expression in the text ('blow for blow')." Sometimes the proverb is worded thus: " 'Claw for Claw, and the devil take the shortest nails,' as Conan said to the devil."—*Waverley Novels*, 1829 (notes to chap. xxii. of *Waverley*), i. 241, note 1; see too, *ibid.*, p. 229. (*Poetry*, V, 209 n.)

41 Some relevant passages from Warburton (*Divine Legation*) run as follows:

> . . . *future Rewards and Punishments*, which were not the Sanction of the *Mosaic* Dispensation, were not taught in it *at all*: and that, in Consequence of the Omission, the PEOPLE had not this Doctrine for many ages. . . . No *Deist*, that I know of, ever pretending that the Doctrine of a future State was there to be found [II, pt. 2, 446]. And in no one Place of the *Mosaic* Institutes is there the least Mention, or any intelligible Hint of the Rewards and Punishments of another Life (p. 447). . . . the Doctrine of Life and Immortality was not yet known to a People *sitting in Darkness, and in the Region and Shadow of Death* . . . (p. 449)

Warburton marshalled a heavy list of texts to support his contention. *The British Review*, Britannicus, and Uriel surpassed other commentators with their array of biblical texts proving that the ancient Hebrews did know about immortality. Uriel had a low opinion of Warburton.

54 The translations of Cuvier's *Discours sur les revolutions de la surface du globe*, by Robert Kerr, appeared in a first edition in 1813. Early in his discussion Cuvier cited much evidence to show that numerous sudden geological revolutions had occurred before the existence of living beings (sections 4–7). ". . . none of the large species of quadrupeds,

whose remains are now found imbedded in regular rocky strata, are at all similar to any of the known living species" (p. 96). After citing more proofs of this generalization, Cuvier stated in section 32 that "it is quite undeniable that no human remains have been hitherto discovered among the extraneous fossils; and this furnishes a strong proof that the extinct races which are now found in a fossil state, were not varieties of known species." This latter statement could have given Byron some scientific basis for the fantasy of preadamite beings. Near the end of the book Cuvier drew his most sweeping conclusions:

> I am of opinion, then, with M. Deluc and M. Dolomieu,—That, if there is any circumstance thoroughly established in geology, it is, that the crust of our globe has been subjected to a great and sudden revolution, the epoch of which cannot be dated much farther back than five or six thousand years ago; that this revolution had buried all the countries which were before inhabited by men and by the other animals that are now best known; . . . Yet farther,—That the countries which are now inhabited, and which were laid dry by this last revolution, had been formerly inhabited at a more remote era, if not by man, at least by land animals; that, consequently, at least one previous revolution had submerged them under the waters; and that, judging from the different orders of animals of which we discover the remains in a fossil state, they had probably experienced two or three irruptions of the sea. (pp. 166–67)

61 See "Byron's Dramatic Theory." Coleridge (*Poetry*, V, 211) found no indebtedness to *Abele.* He quoted from E. A. Bowring's edition of Alfieri's *Tragedies* (1876), II, 472, on the coinage of "tramelogedy." Alfieri put "melo" in the middle of "tragedy" in an attempt to classify his plays.

Act I

64–79 Just as Goethe demonstrated that Mephistopheles invaded Faust's study when the discouraged scholar was emotionally ready for the devil's negation (I, Sc. 4), so Byron made clear that his hero's discontent with himself, his world, and his God anticipated most of Lucifer's negation.

67–79 Compare 67–69 and III, 509–510. Milton's Adam, despondent over his punishment and the ill will that he anticipated from posterity, exclaimed, "Did I request thee, Maker, from my clay / To mould me

Man? . . . Why hast thou added / The sense of endless woes? Inexplicable / Thy justice seems." He foresaw his son's reproach, "Wherefore didst thou beget me? I sought it not!" *PL,* X, 743–755, 762.

84–85 Milton had elaborated on Genesis, 3:24. As Adam and Eve left Eden, the "brandished sword of God before them blazed." When they looked back they saw a "flaming brand" waving over the gate (*PL,* XII, 632–644). In the "Fall of Man" of the Coventry cycle of mystery plays, the seraphim with a flaming sword drove Adam and Eve from Paradise.

93–96 In this description Havens (p. 231) thought the resemblance to Satan the strongest in the entire poem. Stavrou (p. 155) was more specific in pointing out the similarity to *PL,* I, 591–594: "his form had yet not lost / All her original brightness, nor appeared / Less than Archangel ruined, and the excess / Of glory obscured. . . ." Lucifer's sadness was a "conscious recall of [Satan's] 'baleful (i.e., full of sorrow or woe) eyes' " (*PL*, I, 56).

Wenzel (pp. 72–73) strayed into some passages of remote resemblance, discussed Milton's portrait of Satan's prodigious size, that Byron ignored, and also referred to Satan's dazzling disguise when he deceived Uriel in *PL*, III, 634–644.

99–135 Lucifer's entrance elicited many contemporary comparisons with Satan. *The British Critic* contrasted (1) Satan's evil destructiveness to Lucifer's apparent generosity and (2) Satan's occasional acknowledgment of God's creative power to Lucifer's denial of it. This reviewer anticipated Stavrou's later view that Byron's poem was a criticism of Miltonic concepts: "parallel or contrast?" Is it "Milton *versus* Byron" (pp. 534–537)?

Coleridge was impressed by the affinity between Lucifer and Satan and mentioned a few common elements. Both were repulsed but unvanquished Titans, "marred by a demonic sorrow." They admitted God's omnipotence and rivaled it (*Poetry,* V, 201). Havens' reaction to Lucifer was inconsistent. He approved of the resemblances to Satan but disapproved of certain differences. Lucifer had "the dignity, the pride, the love of freedom, the scorn of homage to the Almighty, which distinguished Milton's Satan." Though "more complex and more modern," Lucifer was "less admirable and impressive," "the spirit of negation and doubt; he does not fight, he sneers" (p. 231). It is odd that Havens found no negation in Satan. He also did not see that Byron had endowed his fallen archangel with "glory obscured," with courage, and determination to continue the battle (e.g., I, 93–96, 429–442, 489–491, 508–516). See the essay on Lucifer.

Stavrou, who saw the similarities between Satan and Lucifer, also defined their basic differences:

> Milton's Devil is distinguished principally by his self-conscious utterance of blasphemies; Byron's Devil abstains from heroics and contents himself with the Socratic questioning and examination of all creation. Milton's Devil recognizes that he has been worsted by one who is greater than he is; Byron's Lucifer calls all in doubt, and his nihilistic dialectic seeks to reduce all life and being to an absurdity. The salient differences between the two devils, in fact, underscore the divergencies in outlook of the two poets. (p. 154)

Milton made Satan heinous and despicable, the "antithesis of God," who was the epitome of "reason, order, wisdom, and love." Satan embodied "unreason, disorder, passion, and hatred." Byron made his devil a Promethean protagonist, who also resembled the hero-villain described in *Lara,* I, sts. 17–19, and in the other verse tales (pp. 155–156).

Edward E. Bostetter, without implying that Byron was indebted to Blake, thought that Lucifer had much in common with the older poet's devils (p. 575 n.). He did not pursue the comparison.

109–115 Milton had given Adam a strong suicidal desire after the expulsion. "As my will / Concurred not to my being, it were but right / And equal to reduce me to my dust . . . How gladly would I meet / Mortality my sentence, and be earth / Insensible. . . ." (*PL, X,* 746–751, 771–782).

A conflict between the death wish and the instinct of self-preservation was not uncommon in Byron's poetry. Manfred was torn by it: "We live, / Loathing our life, and dreading still to die." We can count few days "wherein the soul / Forbears to pant for death, and yet draws back / As from a stream in winter, though the chill / Be but a moment's" (II, ii, 165–176). In Act I he wanted to leap from the precipice but long hesitated (ii, 14–24). Cf. I, ii, 74–79, 92–100, 103–109; II, ii, 134–144; iv, 126–129.

116–119 See "Annotations," Preface, line 41.

137–166 Several critics have seen a resemblance between Arimanes, who ruled and crushed the world in *Manfred,* and Lucifer's conception of Jehovah. Though there were many allusions in II, iii, and iv, to the powerful destructiveness of Arimanes, see especially iv, 1–16, the Manicheism of *Manfred* was traditional. The evil power, Arimanes, was inferior to the "overruling Infinite." Astarte's spirit belonged to this higher power (II, iv, 46–49, 113–116). The cruel and despotic enemy of Prometheus in Byron's short poem on the Titan was a member of the same hierarchy.

Harroviensis (pp. 13–16) cited four of Satan's speeches that rivaled Lucifer's attack on Jehovah: *PL,* I, 116–124; II, 54–64; V, 853–869; IX, 135–151. These passages had a few ideas in common with Lucifer's declamation, which Harroviensis did not define: (1) Lucifer and Satan admitted that Jehovah reigned as a cruel tyrant and tortured his enemies. (2) Both doubted that Jehovah created the angels. Satan declared that the angels were self-created, their power self-derived and eternal. Lucifer declared that his immortality made him indestructible. (3) Both aspersed the divine creativity. Satan said that God, wanting to repair the losses he suffered during the civil strife and unable to make new angels, created earth and its inhabitants and so robbed Satan of part of his dominion. Lucifer said that Jehovah must continue the process of creation to make endurable his solitude, restlessness, boredom, and wretchedness. Harroviensis did not observe that there were also many differences. Satan was proud of having freed half of the angels and of being able to destroy in one day what God needed six to make. Satan scorned subservience and urged renewal of warfare. Lucifer stressed God's wickedness, loneliness, and unhappiness. Byron's devil sought to enlist the alliance of a mortal man by showing how Cain and Lucifer were united and strengthened by their suffering.

Heinrich Gillardon (pp. 24–26) saw more resemblance than I can between Lucifer's onslaught on Jehovah and the diatribe of Ahasuerus in Shelley's *Queen Mab,* who made the deity an Oriental despot, a sadistic persecutor, eager to make himself dreaded, crushing the world with woe and enjoying it, reducing all people by violence to slavery, rendering men capable only of sensual deeds, incapable of courage and of honest indignation, and therefore forestalling revolution (VII, 85, 91–96, 120, 125). Chew referred to this parallel without further explanation.

Maximilian Rudwin in two excellent chapters, "The Devil in Literature" and "The Salvation of Satan in Modern Poetry," made several generalizations that can be used to relate Lucifer to some of the main streams of Romanticism. (1) Since social and political upheavels compelled men to realize that evil controlled their affairs, poets revived the

Devil during periods of revolution. (2) Most of the re-creators of the Devil were exiled or ostracized because of their opposition to convention, authority, or tyranny. (3) Since the Devil advanced with civilization, he became an agent of progress, for the spirit of denial spurred the quest for truth. (4) When Byron and Shelley made the Devil a Promethean victim and rebel and a benefactor of mankind, they were sharing their era's compassion for the sufferer, its love of liberty, hatred of despotism, courageous self-sufficiency, and aspiration for infinite growth. Rudwin traced this rehabilitation of Satan among the French, beginning with Alfred de Vigny's *Eloa* in 1823 (pp. 271 ff.).

146–147 The account that James Kennedy wrote of Byron's opinion on this paradox was a personal expansion of the generalization in *Cain*:

> He said one of the greatest difficulties which he had met with, and which he could not overcome, was the existence of so much pure and unmixed evil in the world, as he had witnessed; and which he could not reconcile to the idea of a benevolent Creator. He added, that wherever he had been, he had found vice and misery predominant, and that real happiness and virtue were rarely, if ever, to be seen. He had made it, he said, his business to converse with, and inquire, into, the history of many wretched and deformed creatures with whom he had met, and he generally found their history a record of unvarying misery from their very birth. "How had these offended their Creator, to be thus subjected to misery?" (pp. 55–56)

Bayle had also found it rationally impossible to reconcile divine goodness and human evil.

> It is inconceivable, how evil could creep into the world, under the government of a sovereign Being, infinitely good . . . and infinitely powerful. . . . For if we depend . . . only on an almighty cause, infinitely good, we ought never to feel any evil. . . . If the Author of our Being is indefinitely beneficent, he ought to take a continual delight in making us happy, and in preventing all that could interrupt or lessen our pleasures. . . . Zoroaster, Plato, Plutarch, the Marcionites, the Manicheans, and in general all those who admit a principle naturally good, and a principle naturally bad, both eternal, and independent, all these, I say, pretend that it is impossible to account otherwise for the origin of evil. You answer, it comes from man himself; but how can that be, since, according to you, man is created by a Being infinitely holy, and infinitely powerful? Must not the work of such a Being be good? Can it be otherwise than good? . . . this is a subject which puts

> philosophy to a nonplus. . . . he should have proved by the word of God, that there is but one Creator of all things, who is infinite in goodness, . . . that man came innocent and good from his hands, but lost his innocence and goodness by his own fault. This is the origin of moral evil, and of natural evil. (Paulicians, Note E, VIII, 214–216)

147–156 In these lines Bostetter (p. 572) saw a mockery of the doctrine of "plentitude" and quoted Bishop King's *Essay on the Origin of Evil.* "God might, indeed, have refrained from creating, and continued alone, self-sufficient and perfect to all eternity; but his infinite Goodness would by no means allow it; this obliged him to produce external things; which things since they could not possibly be perfect, the Divine Goodness preferred imperfect ones to none at all." Bostetter found this quotation in Arthur Lovejoy, *The Great Chain of Being* (Cambridge, Mass.: Harvard University Press, 1936), p. 215.

203–205 These lines illustrate Byron's method of adapting the original Genesis dialogue. Byron here gave to Lucifer a condensed fusion of two speeches from Genesis and made them an accusing insinuation: Eve told the serpent, "But of the fruit of the tree which is in the midst of the garden, God hath said, Ye shall not eat of it, neither shall ye touch it, lest ye die. And the serpent said unto the woman, Ye shall not surely die: For God doth know that in the day ye eat thereof, then . . . ye shall be as gods, knowing good and evil" (3:3–5). Later the Lord, in his closing rebuke to Adam, echoed the earlier warning: "And the Lord God said, Behold, the man is become as one of us, to know good and evil: and now, lest he put forth his hand, and take also of the tree of life, and eat, and live for ever: Therefore the Lord God sent him forth from the garden of Eden . . ." (3:22–23).

208–210 Rudwin: Medieval priests often regarded the devil as "the incarnation of human reason in contrast to the Saviour, who represented faith." The church condemned skeptical inquiry and independent thought as the work of the devil. Goethe, Heine, Anatole France, Rapisardi, and Chekhov all presented the devil as the exponent of reason (pp. 246–247).

Stavrou differentiated the meanings that Milton and Byron gave to *knowledge*: "To Milton, 'knowledge' meant the acceptance of God's infallibility and justness without questioning, whereas, to Byron, 'knowledge' meant the rejection of a capricious God and his arbitrary justice in favor of the more bleak yet less chimerical philosophy of creative idealism" (p. 159).

213–216 Several commentators have noted the resemblance to *PL,* I, 254–255: "The mind is its own place, and in itself / Can make a Heaven of Hell, a Hell of Heaven." This subjectivity is "Lucifer's most important relationship with Milton's Satan" (Thorslev, p. 179).

The thought of these lines and of II, ii, 459–466, resembles Byron's "Prometheus" and Manfred's assertion of the power of the individual mind to control its own life (III, iv, 129–136). Several passages in Cantos III and IV of *Childe Harold* (e.g., III, st. 12; IV, sts. 5, 36, 49, 127, 163) expressed a similar idealism, counterbalanced by pessimism (Ward Pafford, "Byron and the Mind of Man," pp. 105–127).

216–244 For Byron's view that Lucifer and the serpent were different beings see the Preface, lines 9–12, 44–47, and "Annotations."

236–238 Wenzel, Stavrou, and Byron's contemporaries recognized that Lucifer's proud refusal to acknowledge God's authority resembled Satan's scornful refusal to bend his knee: "... To bow and sue for grace / With suppliant knee, and deify his power / Who from the terror of this arm so late / Doubted his empire, that were low indeed, / That were an ignominy and shame beneath / This downfall ... (*PL,* I, 111–116). Wenzel: Byron maintained this trait in the Lucifer of the "Vision of Judgment" (pp. 88–90).

245–249 Just as Mephistopheles took advantage of Faust's thirst for infinite growth and infinite variety of experience (I, Prologue in Heaven and Sc. 4), so Lucifer planned to exploit Cain's curiosity. Cf. I, 301, 558–559.

266–267 Cf. I, 144, 207–208, 532–533; II, ii, 39–43, 79–85, 298–304. *Cain* was not the only expression of Byron's troubled concept of a destructive deity. The foe in "Prometheus" was "the inexorable Heaven / ... / The ruling principle of Hate, / Which for its pleasure doth create / The things it may annihilate" (18–22). The deluge in *Heaven and Earth* was decreed by "the Omnipotent who makes and crushes" (iii, 62). Faliero near the beginning of his prophecy called upon a God who "kindlest and who quenchest suns" (V, iii, 38–39). Lady Byron deplored her husband's view of God as an avenger (*LJ,* VI, 262 n.). The Countess Teresa Guiccioli concurred: one mystery, founded on revelation, pained him: "the dogma of eternal punishment, which he could not reconcile with the idea of an omnipotent Creator, as omnipotence implies perfect goodness and justice ..." (*My Recollections of Lord Byron*, p. 154).

268–269 Jeffrey (*Edinburgh Review,* XXXVI, No. 72 [February, 1822], 440) and Heber (*The Quarterly Review,* XXVII [July, 1822], 524) remarked on the inconsistency here and in I, 298; II, i, 61; II, ii, 14–18, 35, where Byron made Cain ignorant of the nature of death. Since the first family had been accustomed to animal sacrifices, they must have been acquainted with the death of animals. In I, 183–184, 313–334; III, 255 ff., Cain spoke of Abel's blood-offerings. These ceremonies must have demonstrated to him the physical extinction of life. The contradiction may be resolved by assuming that Cain's ignorance and dread derived from the primitive fantasy that death was a hostile power, a tangible monster, and also from his uncertainty about the state of the mind after the cessation of bodily existence.

310–314 Frank Rainwater compared Cain's independence to "Manfred's refusal to give obeisance to Arimanes (II, iv, 28–49) and to "the Promethean's defiance of the false Jupiter" (p. 122).

317–320 "He that is not with me is against me," Matt. 12:30.

326–327 Mephistopheles liked to catch Faust in an inconsistency (I, Scenes 4, 11, 14, 23). Similarly, as soon as Cain referred to his promise to make an offering, Lucifer reminded him of the boast that he had never bowed to God (310–315).

330–331 Byron had Gessner's precedent for giving Cain and Abel sisters. Bayle recorded a legend that Eve "lay-in every year, and every time of a boy and a girl" (Eve, V, 121). "We cannot tell precisely how many brothers and sisters he had, when he killed Abel; however . . . those who say there were then no more than four persons in the world, are mistaken; for though it were true, as some suppose, that Cain was but thirty years old when he committed that murder, there would be no room to doubt but that Eve had already lain in several times" (Cain, IV, 18–19). Bayle cited several exotic names of Cain's and Abel's twin sisters, none of which Byron took (Eve, Note D, V, 121).

352–357 Harroviensis (pp. 24–25) saw some resemblance between the "sophistry" that Lucifer used on Adah and the "equally pernicious and more successful arguments" Satan used on Eve (*PL,* IX, 684–690, 725–730). Cf. Wenzel, pp. 81, 84–85.

363–379 William H. Marshall thought that Adah's "rejection of the possibility that love such as hers and Cain's shall someday be regarded as evil dramatizes her conceptual incapacity: she cannot comprehend that her anthropomorphic image of Godhead or of Creation is not enduring and therefore less than perfect." She cannot "distinguish between myth and reality" (pp. 142–144). This interpretation does not seem implicit in the text.

395–405 Harroviensis traced the similarities of the psychological assaults that Milton's and Byron's devils made on the minds of mother and son. In *PL,* IX, 538–732, the serpent had aroused Eve's interest by flattering her beauty, had by "glozing" argument persuaded her "to a disbelief of 'God's rigid threats of death'," had led her to question the justice of God's prohibition of the fruit, had excited her appetite for the knowledge that had been forbidden, and had convinced her that she and Adam possessed "as fit capacity for that knowledge as Gods." Harroviensis, commenting on a group of Lucifer's speeches (I, 99–166, 192–210; II, ii, 452–466), saw him flattering Cain with the assurance that his "immortal part" spoke "when he doubted Heaven's goodness," inducing him to regard God as a tyrant, tempting him to undertake an adventure that "would place him beyond the reach of fear," "exciting his desire to know more than is permitted for mortals to know," and confirming "Cain's pride and presumptuous confidence in himself" by urging him to exercise his reason in making moral judgments and in creating "an inner world." Finally, Harroviensis compared the readiness with which both Eve and Cain accepted as true what the devils told them (pp. 17–18, 36–39, 50–53). Wenzel traversed the same ground (pp. 81–85).

400 ff. In Faust (I, Sc. 16, Marthe's Garden), Gretchen tells her lover that the presence of Mephistopheles filled her with secret fear, stifled and overpowered her, and paralyzed her love for Faust and her ability to pray. Goethe also had the naïve girl define the egoistic, negative, and destructive aspects of evil; she perceived that the sneering devil had no interest in anything and was incapable of love.

409–413 The "fastening attraction" of Lucifer's eye and Adah's susceptibility to it were similar to the power of Coleridge's lamia or snake-woman, Geraldine, who with her evil eye subdued Christabel. Like Lucifer, she also used deception—a fair appearance, an unhappy plight, and a pretense of injury—to dominate the innocent girl and Sir Leoline. In the large family of such occult influences were the vampire fad, the tricks of Gothic fiction, and that precursor of hypnotism, the mystical Austrian physician, Friedrich Anton Mesmer (1734–1815), who caused a stir in Paris and was denounced as an imposter by some doctors. He believed that his magnetism, by physical contact, could affect a patient's nervous system and cure illness.

421 One distinction that the *NED* made between the seraphim and the cherubim was the same as Byron's: the seraphim were distinguished by fervor of love; while the cherubim excelled in knowledge (VIII, 490).

441–450 Cain often returned to this injustice, e.g., II, i, 60–71; III, 23–25, 82–84, 88–90, 118–124. Perhaps Byron's earliest expression of this lament in verse was in the 1806 "Prayer of Nature," st. 6: "Tell us that all, for one who fell, / Must perish in the mingling storm?" See also a letter to Hodgson, September 3, 1811, *LJ.*, II, 21.

In *Heaven and Earth* an unnamed mother and Japhet protested the punishment of the innocent. But in that play Byron also gave an uncritical exposition of orthodox views to several characters.

Harroviensis (pp. 56–58) and Blumenthal (p. 7): Cain's altruistic torment is a repetition of the distress that Milton gave Adam: ". . . in me all / Posterity stands cursed. . . . / . . . Ah, why should all mankind / For one man's fault thus guiltless be condemned, / If guiltless? But from me what can proceed / But all corrupt, both mind and will depraved. . . . / On me, me only, as the source and spring / Of all corruption, all the blame lights due" (*PL*, X, 817–834; XI, 500–507).

Adam had also felt the same apprehension that Cain uttered in 441–444: ". . . for what can I increase / Or multiply, but curses on my head? / Who of all ages to succeed, but feeling / The evil on him brought by me, will curse / My head?" (*PL*, X, 731–735).

466–481 Adah's dread of solitude and Lucifer's second insistence on Jehovah's isolation (cf. I, 148–152) resembled Adam's complaint: "In solitude / What happiness? Who can enjoy alone. . . ." He was not content with the animals but wanted human fellowship. God replied that he was "alone / from all eternity," talked only with inferiors, but was happy (*PL*, VIII, 363–411). Havens recorded the parallel (p. 232 n.).

540–542 Acts 2:27, 31–32; Eph. 4:9–10.

546–554 Cf. I, 305–310, 375–392; II, ii, 425 ff. Milton (*PL*, IV, 111–112), had Satan claim "divided empire with Heaven's king . . . / . . . and more than half perhaps . . ." (Wenzel, p. 79; Blumenthal, p. 6). Byron's contemporaries, however, charged that Byron was indebted to Bayle for this heresy.

Bayle quoted many authorities to show that it was rationally impossible to explain the origin of evil without assuming the existence of an Evil Spirit:

> If a man is the work of one only principle, sovereignly good, supremely holy, and all powerful, is it possible he could have so many wicked inclinations, or could commit so many crimes? . . . if man was the work of an infinitely good and holy principle, he would have been created not only without any actual wickedness, but without any inclination to it . . . (Manicheans, Note D, VII, 400)
>
> Their fundamental Doctrine was that of two coeternal Principles, independent on each other . . . it is so difficult to answer all the objections concerning the origin of Evil, that we ought not to wonder the Hypothesis of two Principles, the one good, the other bad, seduced several antient Philosophers, and got so many followers amongst the Christians . . . (Paulicians, VIII, 213–215)

Gillardon (pp. 22–25): Shelley also dabbled with the Manichean war between two hostile powers in his "Essay on Christianity" and in *The Revolt of Islam*, I, 24–27.

ACT II, Scene i

3 Coleridge: "According to the prince of the power of the air," Eph. 2:2.

7–12 Harroviensis (pp. 10–12) quoted three scornful speeches by Satan and Mammon that cast slurs on the obsequiousness that Jehovah required from the angels: *PL,* II, 237–257; V, 775–788; VI, 165–170. See also *PL,* I, 110–116.

Lucifer's sneer at the servility of the angels was consistent with his assertiveness in I, 237–239; II, ii, 429–430. It resembled Mephistopheles' taunt in the Prologue in Heaven, where he called the angels lackeys.

16–22 Matt. 14:22–33. Byron had Lucifer appropriately garble the biblical account. As Peter walked on the sea toward Jesus, the wind was boisterous, Peter became frightened, began to sink, and cried, "Lord, save me. And immediately Jesus stretched forth his hand, and caught him, and said unto him, O thou of little faith, wherefore didst thou doubt?"

22–25 Michael Joseph thought that one of the *Hebrew Melodies,* "When Coldness Wraps This Suffering Clay," anticipated the flight in *Cain* (p. 120). In that lyric, the soul, after it left the dead body, traces "each planet's heavenly way" or fills "the realms of space, / A thing of eyes." The soul sees everything on earth and in the sky. It recalls the chaos before earth was peopled, and the birth of "the farthest heaven." "Fixed in its own Eternity," it foresees the future quenching of the sun and the cataclysm of the universe. The resemblance between the subject of this lyric and Act II of *Cain* is very slight.

Eimer's citation (p. 216) from Pope's *The Temple of Fame* likewise bore little resemblance to the experience of Cain and Lucifer. In Pope's poem, the dreamer from a point in space surveyed all creation. On the globular earth that hung below him, he saw circling oceans, mountains, deserts, forests, cities, ships, and temples (11–20).

At the end of Part II, I have discussed a few sources or parallels that have been suggested for the journey—Fontenelle's *Entretien*, Shelley's *Queen Mab,* Ariosto's *Orlando Furioso*, and Laurence's translation of the *Book of Enoch.*

For the comments of many writers on the purposes, techniques, contents, and results of the flight through space to Hades, the reader is referred to various essays in this book: "The Opinions of Byron's Social and Literary Circle" for the remarks of Scott and Goethe; "The Major Periodicals and Pamphlets" for the generally adverse criticism of Heber, *The Monthly Magazine,* Harroviensis, Fabre d'Olivet, Wilkinson, and others; "The Victorian Approach to *Cain*" for the ideas of Arnold, Phillips, Blumenthal, and Dowden; and "*Cain* in the Twentieth Century" for the differing views of recent critics.

28–31 Chew (p. 125): This distant view of the earth and its moon is reminiscent of what Satan saw on his flight: "And, fast by hanging in a golden chain, / This pendent world, in bigness as a star / Of smallest magnitude close by the moon" (*PL,* II, 1051–1053).

34–43 Blumenthal compared the grandeur of Lucifer's and Satan's flights through space (*PL,* II, 927–961, 1010–1055). Lucifer and Cain moved "like sunbeams onward" and floated "with more ease and composure" than did Satan, who dropped down ten thousand fathom and was saved only by a cloud that broke his fall (p. 5). Blumenthal might have noted too that Lucifer required no assistance while Satan needed Sin to open the gates of hell and later asked Chaos and Night for directions.

49–60 Bostetter stated that Cain was here painfully aware "of his body as the 'servile mass of matter' to which he is chained" (*The Romantic Ventriloquists,* pp. 266–267). But when Cain said that he felt the prophetic torture of Lucifer's truth, he referred not to an "agonized awareness" of sensuality nor to the "filthy cheat" and lure, and not here, as Bostetter declared, to "the futility of human effort," but to the climax of Lucifer's speech (59–60), "all foredoomed to be / As frail and few so happy," which repeated line 46, "all doomed to death and wretched." Cain's response in 60–71 to Lucifer was consistent with the despondency that he voiced on other occasions over his personal responsibility for "propagating death / And multiplying murder." It was not disgust with sensuality but anguish over his hideous role in bringing unhappiness to posterity that made Cain cry, "Here let me die."

Stavrou believed this passage (49–60) to be part of Lucifer's attempt "to indoctrinate Cain in positivism." The "subtle poison of his dialectic has infected" Cain's mind (p. 158). Stavrou did not support this statement. I do not detect in Cain's dialogue any reaction to the devil's derision of sensuality.

98–103 Eimer (pp. 99 ff., 215) and his predecessors collected references to the starry multitudes from Byron's contemporaries and earlier poets, e.g., "innumerable lights," "ten thousand worlds," in Edward Young's *Night Thoughts* (Night IX, 248, 250) and "thousand thousand stars" in *PL,* VII, 382–384. Eimer and other German readers were impressed by Shelley's use of "myriads" and other spatial and quantitative words in *Prometheus Unbound, The Witch of Atlas*, and "Ode to Heaven."

118–126 Cf. 28–43, where Cain noticed how the earth became smaller as they flew away from it.

Adam realized the smallness of the earth: "a spot, a grain, / An atom, with the firmament compared / And all her numbered stars . . ." (*PL,* VIII, 15–20).

Eimer quoted Young's *Night Thoughts* (Night IX, 277): "where is earth?" The resemblance of Cain's "Where is it?" to Young's question was probably coincidental.

Joseph cited Messac's article for Voltaire's reflection on the size of the earth in *Micromégas* (p. 119, n. 82).

130–132 Cf. III, 128–129, and the early "Prayer of Nature," stanza 11. "Thou, who canst guide the wandering star, / Through trackless realms of aether's space." The idea was a truism for the deists.

Gillardon: Cf. *The Deformed Transformed*, I, ii, 25–33, and various expressions by Shelley of a belief in the guiding power of Necessity: *Queen Mab*, VI, 197; *The Revolt of Islam*, IX, 27 (pp. 18–19).

174–175 Rainwater: The journey to the world of phantoms was similar to Plato's vision at the end of *The Republic*, to Ficino's Realm of Nature, and to Spenser's Garden of Adonis in *The Faerie Queene*. His Platonic interpretation pressed more into Byron's shadowy region of past existences than the poet put there: "It is the home of the Platonic reasons which produce the forms we know. It is at once the realm of birth and death, for all things have their origin and their reappearance there. The encouraging lesson it teaches is that death is but another form of life" (pp. 125–126).

Act II, Scene ii

44–62 Cf. II, i, 28–43; II, ii, 178–196, 357–365; III, 63–69, 176–184. In these passages Cain, though admiring the magnitude and splendor of the heavenly bodies and of past worlds and creatures, is at the same time perturbed by the inferiority of man and his earth.

Thomas Medwin: "I have reason to think that Byron owes to Shelley the platonic idea of the Hades,—the pre-adamite worlds, and their phantasmal shapes, perhaps suggested by Lucian's Icaro Menippus. Lord Byron had certainly a profound respect for Shelley's judgment" (*The Life of Percy Bysshe Shelley,* p. 334). In the flight of Menippus to the moon and then past the sun and among the stars to heaven, there is no foreshadowing of the phantasms of Byron's Hades. A few phrases on the littleness of the earth and "the faint shimmer of Ocean in the Sun" are barely germane to some images of Cain's journey ("Icaromenippus, an Aerial Expedition," *The Works of Lucian of Samosata,* translated by H. W. Fowler and F. G. Fowler, III, 126–144).

67–124 Lovell: World decay, "nature running down . . . had interested Englishmen as far back as Donne in his *Anatomie of the World* and Milton in 'Naturam non pati senium' " (p. 211).

Eimer gathered various literary allusions to cosmic destruction (pp. 125, 128, 221). Byron may have recalled Pope's couplet: "Atoms or systems into ruin hurl'd, / And now a bubble burst, and now a world" (*Essay on Man*, I, 89–90). Pope assumed a cycle of life and death; when one form of matter expired, its remains nourished other forms (*Essay on Man*, III, 15–20). Shelley's lyric in *Hellas*, "Worlds on worlds are rolling ever" (197 ff.), posited a cycle of generation, degeneration, and regeneration. Young in *Night Thoughts* had a vision, a "mighty shadow" of a departed world (Night IX, 228).

Byron acknowledged his indebtedness to Cuvier; see "Annotations," Preface, line 54.

In a passage of the "Detached Thoughts," written shortly after *Cain* was completed, Byron pondered the concept of the cycles of creation and destruction and merged it with a deistic commonplace on primal causation:

> If, according to some speculations, you could prove the World many thousand years older than the Mosaic Chronology, or if you could knock up Adam and Eve and the Apple and Serpent, still what is to be put up in their stead? or how is the difficulty removed? Things must have had a beginning, and what matters it *when* or *how*?
>
> I sometimes think that *Man* may be the relic of some higher material being, wrecked in a former world, and degenerated in the hardships and struggle through Chaos into Conformity—or something like it; as we see Laplanders, Esquimaux, etc., inferior in the present state, as the Elements become more inexorable. But even then this higher pre-Adamite supposititious Creation must have had an Origin and *a Creator*; for a *Creator* is a more natural imagination than a fortuitous concourse of atoms. All things remount to a fountain, though they may flow to an Ocean. (*LJ*, V, 459)

Medwin recorded some reflections that are germane here:

> *Do you imagine that, in former stages of this planet, wiser creatures than ourselves did not exist?* All our boasted inventions are but the shadows of what has been,—the dim images of the past—the dream of other states of existence. Might not the fable of Prometheus, and his stealing the fire, and of Briareus and his earth-born brothers, be but traditions of steam and its machinery? *Who knows whether, when a comet shall approach this globe to destroy it, as it often has been and will be destroyed,* men will not tear rocks from their foundations by means of steam, and hurl mountains, as the giants are said to have done, against the flaming mass?—and then we shall have traditions of Titans again, and of wars with Heaven. (p. 185, italics mine)

Destruction has been so frequent and has so indelibly impressed man's mind that he forgets his blessings and records only wars, droughts, plagues, earthquakes, and other calamities ("Detached Thoughts," *LJ*, V, 434).

Lines 80–85 and subsequent comments in *Cain* on cosmic destruction should therefore be associated with Byron's prolonged brooding over the fall of heroes, the decay of nations, and natural catacylsm. Annihilation was a topic in a few poems of 1805–1806. In "Translations from Horace," a ruthless deity, having blasted the earth with his lightning, beheld, unmoved, the "flames of an expiring world, / Again in crashing chaos rolled, / In vast promiscuous ruin hurled"; and then he smiled amidst "the wreck of earth" (*Poetry,* I, 81). Another possible forecast of the demolition in *Cain,* "A Version of Ossian's Address to the Sun" (*Poetry*, VII, 2–3) is a forgery, as Coleridge admitted (Theodore G. Ehrsam, *Major Byron. The Incredible Career of a Literary Forger* [New York: Charles S. Boesen, 1951], pp. 83–86. "Ossian's Address to the Sun in Carthon" (*Poetry*, I, 229–231), which is on the same subject, is probably authentic; the so-called Newstead MS of this piece is now in the Miriam Lutcher Stark Library of The University of Texas at Austin.

Ten years later he wrote "Darkness," a lurid nightmare of a dying world. Then Byron distributed through *Childe Harold* somber variations on the deterioration and collapse of Greece, Rome, Venice, Spain, and German feudalism. "Man marks the earth with ruin," and the ocean too was a mighty smasher: II, 53, 90; III, 46 ff.; IV, 11–15, 44–46, 79–82, 107–109, 179–182. In *Sardanapalus* a dynasty tumbled with a clatter of combat, a devastating flood, and a blazing pyre. In *Heaven and Earth* Byron gave to Japhet, to the malevolent Spirits, and to the Chorus of Mortals lamentations on the havoc of the deluge (iii, 1–310, 725 ff.).

In *Don Juan* Byron used Cuvier with colloquial zest and predicted that the earth would be burned or drowned, and, like all previous worlds, be hurled into the chaos it had come from; and then out of this wreckage there would arise a new earth. He also lightly assumed the past existence of giants and the steady deterioration of the species (IX, sts. 36–39). The skeptical images of the final stanza of Canto XV briefly restated the cycle: on the eternal surge of time, old bubbles burst and new emerge from the foam of ages.

89–103 Blumenthal (p. 5) compared Lucifer's revelation to Cain of by-gone times with the vision of future ages that Michael gave Adam in *PL*, Bks. XI, XII. See "Annotations," II, ii, 459–466 (Siegel, Thorslev).

132–144 Eimer (pp. 138–139, 222–225) made a whimsical anthology of leviathans, behemoths, and other monsters. Milton used them in *Paradise Lost* (VII, 409–416, 470–474). Young's "A Paraphrase on Part of the Book of Job" (*The Poetical Works,* II, 184–189) is possibly the longest and most fanciful passage in English verse on the behemoth and leviathan (here a prodigious crocodile)—103 lines plus several notes. See also Thomson's *Seasons,* Summer, pp. 708–714, Winter, pp. 1014–1019; *Endymion*, III, 133–136; Shelley's *Prometheus Unbound*, IV, 296–318; Coleridge's *Religious Musings*, lines 274–276.

Eimer omitted the references to the leviathan in the Bible and Shakespeare. Byron probably remembered the former along with Milton, as well as he did Young and Thomson: Job 3:8, 41:1; Pss. 74:14, 104:26; Isa. 27:1. The behemoth appeared in Job 40:15.

Byron referred to the behemoth only in *The Deformed Transformed*, III, 57, but he often used the mammoth and the leviathan, sometimes metaphorically: *Childe Harold*, IV, st. 181; *Marino Faliero*, III, 566; *Heaven and Earth*, I, 154; II, 81; *The Deformed Transformed*, I, 305; III, 55; *DJ*, VIII, st. 137; IX, st. 38; X, st. 52.

Joseph: Beckford's *Vathek* may have been one of Byron's sources. "At the end of the novel Eblis, who corresponds to Byron's Lucifer, offers Vathek and Nouronihar visions of the animals who lived before Adam and of the wealth of the Pre-Adamite sultans. The Muslin notion of Pre-Adamites seems to have blended with Buffon's assumption of a race of primitive giants . . ." (pp. 120–121). Joseph referred to *Vathek* in the Everyman *Shorter Novels*, III, 272, and to Buffon, *Oeuvres Philosophiques*, ed. Jean Piveteau (Paris: Presses universitaires de France, 1954), pp. 183–184.

148–152 In Shelley's *Queen Mab*, according to Ahasuerus, God told Moses that he planted the tree of evil so that man would eat and perish (VII, 110–111).

164–167 Lucifer talked like a Shelleyean Platonist when he suggested that death might be the gate to "highest knowledge." Cain was not convinced by this attempt to make death seem a blessing.

Miguel de Unamuno called *Cain* a stupendous poem and Lucifer a "great intellectual," but his reading of the latter's observation about death and knowledge seems eccentric and groundless: death leads to the highest knowledge—"that is to say, to nothingness" (*The Tragic Sense of Life in Men and in Peoples,* p. 103).

Northrop Frye saw a connection between Lucifer's supposition and

"Cain's own feeling that the understanding of death is his own ultimate victory," that is, "the converse principle that the highest knowledge leads to death" (*Fearful Symmetry: A Study of William Blake,* p. 199). I cannot follow this interpretation. Had Cain ever understood death, he would have regarded that understanding as a gain; but neither in Hades nor after the murder did he arrive at such an understanding. At one time in Hades he was gratified when he thought that death led to something definite, but he never achieved any sense of victory. Moreover, though he complained that the fruit of the tree of knowledge was death, he never asserted that the *highest* knowledge led to death.

Rainwater likewise seemed to derive from these lines a meaning Byron did not express. "Death leads to the highest knowledge in that to the Platonist it leads back to God the Source. Thus after all, the deadly tree of knowledge was true. It brought knowledge and death together. But in the end the latter leads to the former" (p. 130). Marshall also found here Shelleyean concepts that I could not discern: Cain accepted "the possibility of eternal intellectual life . . . Cain is disturbed by the seeming paradox that Man's death is requisite to his full intellectual freedom, that only through sorrow can Truth lead to Goodness" (p. 148).

242–245 Cain's intuitive confidence that beauty cannot die is an idea that Byron returned to in *Heaven and Earth.* Japhet, another sensitive hero, said that a beautiful being becomes "more so as it looks on beauty, / The eternal beauty of undying things" (ii, 6–8).

255–269 In *Paradise Lost* Eve told Adam that the sweet beauties of the world—the sunrise "with charm of earliest birds" and with the "orient beams, on herb, tree, fruit, and flower, / Glistering with dew," the fragrance of the earth after showers, the silent night with its "fair Moon" and "glittering star-light"—all these were sweet only if he were present (IV, 639–656). Havens (p. 232) listed the parallel passages, but did not discriminate the emotional experiences. Milton's Eve praised natural beauty to reveal her love of Adam, for his companionship was necessary for its enjoyment. Cain's eulogy of nature soared into transcendental exaltation in order to intensify the tribute to Adah's paramount beauty and to reveal his love for her.

274 Rudwin remarked on the not very common belief in the devil's sterility. Since Lucifer could have no offspring, his "brotherhood's with those who have no children." Rudwin also found this curiosity in Sir Thomas Browne's *Religio Medici* and in Balzac (pp. 227–228).

281–305 In giving Cain his longest discussion so far of the central theological paradox (God's goodness and man's evil) Byron had to stay within the compass of Cain's local experience. He could not borrow the spectacular and hypothetical situations that Bayle used to illustrate the theological problem.

> Here are two Princes, the one of whom suffers his subjects to fall into a wretched condition, that he may deliver them after they shall have suffered enough: the other keeps them constantly in a state of prosperity. Is not the latter a better Prince, is he not even more merciful than the former? . . . Nor need a man be a Metaphysician to understand this: the most ignorant country fellow knows most distinctly, that there is much more goodness in preventing a man's falling into a ditch, than in suffering him to fall into it, to help him out of it an hour after; and that it is much better to prevent an Assassin from committing murder, than to have him broke upon the wheel for the murders he was suffered to commit. All this should warn us, not to engage in a controversy with the Manicheans, unless we set down beforehand, the doctrine of *the exaltation of Faith, and the abasement of Reason.* (Paulicians, Note E, VIII, 217)

Cain's reply to Adam's sentimental, orthodox explanation of evil was an inference that could be drawn from Bayle's witty comment on an optimistic justification of providence:

> . . . if you assert, that God permitted sin with a design to show his wisdom, which appears with more glory, amidst the disorders, which men's wickedness occasions daily, than it would do in a state of innocence you will be answered, that this is comparing God either with the father of a family, who should suffer his children's legs to be broke, in order to shew what an able bone-setter he is; or with a King who should suffer disorders and seditions to rage throughout his dominions, that he might gain a great reputation by suppressing them. (Paulicians, Note E, VIII, 216)

320–322 Whether deliberate or not, Byron here followed Platonic tradition in having Cain define love as a desire for, or attachment to, something outside of self. Shelley and Goethe would have sanctioned these lines.

338 Egoism and the inability to love were also inherent in the negation of Mephistopheles, who could not understand altruism and refused to concede its existence. See, for instance, the following scenes: Forest and Cavern, Marthe's Garden, A Dismal Day. Part of the essence

of Milton's Satan was likewise the opposite of love—hate and destructiveness.

390 Rainwater noted that here as in *Manfred* and *Heaven and Earth* Byron presented the cosmos as limitless (pp. 117, 125, 130).

418–424 Cf. III, 63–74. Mephistopheles would have agreed with Lucifer's low evaluation of mortal man. In the second study scene of Part I, he tried to impress upon Faust the narrow limitations of man and the impossibility of progress.

Marjarum quoted *Manfred* I, ii, 37–47, as an expression of Byron's pessimism about the insignificance of man. He found it also in "Prayer of Nature," sts. 8, 10; "Adieu" st. 11; "Vision of Judgment," st. 40; *The Deformed Transformed*, I, ii, 320–329, and III, 71–81; *Don Juan*, IX, st. 13, and in various letters. The expression of this idea "gains steadily in volume until in *Cain* it is used as the motivation of the murder of Abel" (*Byron as Skeptic and Believer*, pp. 6–7).

One of the earliest antecedents of the second act of *Cain* was a sentence in a letter of June 18, 1813: "It was the comparative insignificance of ourselves and *our world,* when placed in competition with the mighty whole, of which it is an atom, that first led me to imagine that our pretensions to eternity might be over-rated" (*LJ*, II, 222).

In the next year, on March 3, he wrote to Miss Milbanke (*LJ*, III, 408): "In the midst of myriads of the living and the dead worlds—stars —systems—infinity—why should I be anxious about an atom?" On February 8, 1822, he wrote Murray (*LJ*, VI, 18), as the winter moon lighted the Arno, "so quiet and still: what Nothings we are! before the least of these Stars!"

Rivalling Lucifer's scorn is Caesar's sarcasm on the evasive nonchalance affected by the disappointed courtier, the outshone beauty, the heir whose sick father recovers, and the monarch who hears the truth. When they are asked, "What's the matter," they all reply, "Nothing." "And they themselves alone [are] the real 'Nothings'." (*The Deformed Transformed*, III, 2–36).

426–442 The resemblance here between Lucifer and Satan is closer than it has been in most speeches, except for I, 137–166. Here Lucifer shared Satan's pride and hate, his denial of God's superior force and defiance of it, his determination to contest it forever, his confidence in his power to endure and struggle indefinitely, and (463–466) to create an inner world independent of external existence.

Harroviensis (pp. 47–50) made an apt selection of five defiant speeches from *Paradise Lost* that were ancestors of Lucifer's belligerence, one by Moloch, and four by Satan to the host of fallen angels, to Beelzebub, and to the Archangel: I, 94–111; II, 94–105; IV, 105–113; V, 794–802; VI, 288–295. These Miltonic orations renounced fear, repentance, and remorse, accepted exile, urged strenuous effort to gain vengeance, promised unremitting strife, which Satan intended to win or which would turn heaven into hell. "All is not lost." "Evil be thou my good." Satan had confidence in his "unconquerable will . . . immortal hate, / And courage never to submit or yield." He claimed divided empire with heaven's king and equality in freedom and refused to acknowledge God's law or edict.

In Shelley's *Queen Mab* Ahasuerus began his "lonely and unending pilgrimage," "Resolved to wage unweariable war / With my almighty Tyrant . . . / Mocking my powerless Tyrant's horrible curse / With stubborn and unalterable will" (VII, 196–199, 256–257).

In Southey's *Thalaba* (1801) a tempter, Mohareb, used the Manichean dichotomy to explain the opposites in natural and human activities. He also argued that judgments of good and evil were the mandates of authority. Mohareb told the captive Thalaba in "sophistic speech" that "in Nature are two hostile Gods, / Makers and Masters of existing things, / Equal in power." Where the camel finds food, the viper sucks poison. Next door to a wedding festival, a mourner laments his dead. "Evil and Good . . . / What are they, Thalaba, but words? in the strife / Of Angels, as of Men, the weak are guilty; / Power must decide" (IX, 149–171).

Eimer (p. 213), who had briefly alluded to this antecedent of Lucifer's speech, also thought that he detected in Young's *Night Thoughts* some doubtful and trivial parallels to lines 436–437, e.g., "worlds on worlds" (Night VII, 167), "Orb above Orb" (Night IX, 258).

443–458 Lucifer's sophistry, the cynical axiom that power determined right and wrong, the denial that he was the fount of evil, the sardonic advice that Cain take a fresh look at God's gifts to him on earth, and base his evaluation of them on tangible results—all this was not unworthy a Satanic intelligence. It was more appropriate to Lucifer's sophisticated appeal to a man like Cain than it would have been to Satan's seduction of Eve.

459–466 Though Cain and Lucifer were negative most of the time, Byron ran through their gloom an undercurrent of idealism, an amalgam of stoic, Platonic, and Kantian ideas and of the eighteenth-century optimists like Hutcheson and Shaftesbury. These ideas supplied Cain and Lucifer with criteria for social criticism, a basis of individual discontent and rebellion, and a reservoir of inner strength that enabled the sufferers to endure adversity, to resist autocratic compulsion, and to form a new personal and spiritual order. This optimism provided the climax of Lucifer's farewell to Cain. For a discussion of Lucifer's idealism see the essay "An Apology for Revolt," and for a few parallels in Byron's poetry see the note on I, 213–216.

Paul Siegel cited a Shelleyean parallel to Lucifer's exhortation; Cythna urged Laon to look to the Paradise that his own heart could create within him (*Revolt of Islam*, IX, sts. 26–27). Siegel, in his comment on 459–466, gave Cain too much self-discipline. He thought that the space journey had enabled Cain to understand and therefore master "the immensity of the universe . . . and to rise above the dust of which he is composed. This is the inner world to be gained by obedience to the injunction: 'Think and endure' " ("A Paradise within Thee," p. 616). In contrasting the pious optimism that Adam learned from Michael (*PL*, XII) to the gloomy lessons Cain learned from Lucifer, Siegel erred in attributing Cain's awareness of human wretchedness almost entirely to Lucifer's instruction (pp. 615–616). Cain's pessimism had been dark before Lucifer's arrival, as Siegel later observed (p. 617).

Thorslev believed that Byron made an original addition here to Satanism with his stress on self-discipline. He noted the resemblance of (1) Lucifer's confidence in the mind's power to create its own reality to (2) Michael's promise to Adam that he would achieve a happier internal paradise (*PL*, XII, 586–587; "The Romantic Mind Is Its Own Place," pp. 266–267).

Act III

10–12, 17–18, 25–30 For the last time before Byron took his hero into the criminal catastrophe, he showed us three related attractive qualities: Cain's sensitivity to beauty, his gentleness, and his family affection.

53–62 Byron often used the concept of psychological time. "A slumbering thought is capable of years, / And curdles a long life into one hour" (*The Dream*, 25–26). Harold declared that he had "grown agèd in this world of woe, / In deeds, not years" (III, st. 5). On three occasions Manfred measured his life by an emotional clock. When he raved on the mountain about his torment, he felt that he had been "ploughed by moments, not by years / And hours" (I, ii, 71–74). To the Hunter, he looked scarcely middle-aged, but Manfred said that in his suffering he had lived many years and would have to live many more. Actions were man's epochs, and these had made his days endless (II, i, 44–54). Later he told the Abbot that some men become old in their youth and die before middle age (III, i, 138–140). Lucifer boasted that he had an elastic control of time; he could crowd eternity into an hour and stretch an hour into eternity (I, 535–538). Byron's broadest variation on the subjectivity of time occurred in *Heaven and Earth*, iii, 300–308. Time exists only when it can be experienced by the mind of man. The destruction of the earth would therefore reduce time to nothing. Just as Eternity would be a void without Jehovah, who created it, so the hours, without human life, have no significance; "without man, Time, as made for man / Dies with man . . ." A few other parallels were cited by Rainwater: *LJ*, II, 349; *The Giaour*, 261–272; *The Corsair*, 1624–1625; "To Time," *Poetry*, III, 60–61; *Don Juan*, II, st. 136; *Werner*, IV, i, 310–316; *The Island*, III, 118–120.

Rainwater related Byron's subjective view of time to Kant's idea that time "has no existence of itself," that its measurement by the clock and the calendar is arbitrary and artificial, and that the duration of time varies according to the intensity of individual experience (pp. 65–67).

Byron knew Shakespeare better than he did Kant, and he may have remembered Rosalind's descant on the idea that "Time travels in divers paces with divers persons," trotting, ambling, galloping, or standing, according to the moods or activities of different people—the maid about to be married, the priest who lacks Latin, the rich man without gout, the thief on his way to the gallows, and the lawyer on vacation (*As You Like It,* III, ii, 309–333).

Shelley wrote a long passage on the same notion:

> Time is our consciousness of the succession of ideas in our mind. Vivid sensation, of either pain or pleasure, makes the time seem long, as the common phrase is, because it renders us more acutely conscious of our ideas. If a mind be conscious of an hundred ideas during one minute, by the clock, and of two hundred during another, the latter of these spaces would actually occupy so much greater extent in the mind as two exceed one in quantity. . . . One man is stretched on the rack during twelve hours; another sleeps soundly in his bed: the difference of time perceived by these two persons is immense; one hardly will believe that half an hour has elapsed,

> the other could credit that centuries had flown during his agony. Thus, the life of a man of virtue and talent, who should die in his thirtieth year, is, with regard to his own feelings, longer than that of a miserable priest-ridden slave, who dreams out a century of dulness. (Note on *Queen Mab,* VIII, 203–207 in *Poetical Works,* 825, cited in part by Coleridge.)

Kenneth Neill Cameron, in *The Young Shelley* (p. 400), stated that Shelley borrowed his commentary on "the Humean doctrine" about time from William Godwin's *An Enquiry Concerning Political Justice*, I, 411–413.

85–91 Ten years before *Cain*, Byron wrote a criticism of the doctrine of the atonement in a letter to Hodgson, September 13, 1811 (*LJ*, II, 35).

> . . . the basis of your religion is *injustice*; the *Son* of *God,* the *pure,* the *immaculate,* the *innocent,* is sacrificed for the *Guilty.* This proves *His* heroism; but no more does away *man's* guilt than a schoolboy's volunteering to be flogged for another would exculpate the dunce from negligence, or preserve him from the Rod. You degrade the Creator, in the first place, by making Him a begetter of children; and in the next you convert Him into a Tyrant over an immaculate and injured Being, who is sent into existence to suffer death for the benefit of some millions of Scoundrels, who, after all, seem as likely to be damned as ever.

In Shelley's *Queen Mab* the Calvinist God, as described by Ahasuerus, devised the sacrificial atonement of Jesus only to save a few elect souls while he let millions die and suffer eternal torment, howling their tribute to his honor and justice (VII, 134–153).

99–103 In Act III Byron, like an expert craftsman, tried to tie his strands together. Here he neatly connected three psychological matters that he had dealt with earlier: Lucifer's iterated scorn of the angels, whose worship he thought pusillanimous, Cain's jealousy of Abel, and Cain's pride, which Byron had stressed and which Lucifer had pricked several times. Byron had prepared for the offerings back in I, 312–313, 324–332, and had referred to them in II, ii, 353.

125–126 The threat to Enoch is a dramatic forecast of Cain's murder of Abel. The two impetuous actions spring from the same fury over Jehovah's cruelty.

161 Those critics who have had reservations about Byron's motivation

of the murder need only look again at Cain's talk with Adah to see how carefully Byron in the 150 lines before Abel's entrance had his hero go over the seven matters that have long disturbed him: (1) his anger at his parents for their error (44, 75), (2) the loss of Eden (32–34), (3) his hard labor and struggle with the soil (109–113), (4) the injustice of undeserved punishment (24–25, 76, 88–89, 118–120), (5) the irrationality of making curiosity and knowledge sinful (91–92), (6) the limitations and insignificance of mortality (67–74, 114–116), and, above all, (7) the cruel plight of future generations (122–136). In this scene Byron also reminded us that Lucifer and the cosmic journey had aggravated some of these grievances, as Adah noticed and Cain himself admitted (45–51, 63–69).

182–183 Byron adapted to Cain's excitement the Pythagorean doctrine of the harmony of the spheres. Those planets that were nearer the central cosmic fire travelled more slowly and made deeper sounds; those that were farther from the center and orbited more rapidly rang higher notes.

Byron used the image three times in *Don Juan*: III, st. 28; XIV, st. 5; XV, st. 76. See also a Song, "Breeze of the night," st. 2.

Allusions to the concert of the celestial bodies were common in literature, e.g., "I had rather hear you to solicit that / Than music from the spheres," *Twelfth Night,* III, i, 112–113. See also *The Merchant of Venice,* V, i, 60–63. Dryden began *A Song for Cecilia's Day* with the cosmic harmony that attended the creation of the universe. In *Queen Mab* Shelley hoped that the earth would be a "dwelling place / Symphonious with the planetary Spheres" (VI, 40–41), and repeated the image in VIII, 18.

183–187 Abel's description of Cain's wild agitation, Cain's own awareness of his tension, and his five desperate pleas to be left alone (184, 188–190, 194–195, 206–207) remind us again of the shattering emotional impact of the journey and are a second foreboding in Act III of the imminent catastrophe.

Of doubtful relevance is Eimer's citation of a parallel (p. 174) from Young's *Night Thoughts* (Night IX, 246): "Canst thou descend from converse with the skies, / And seize thy brother's throat?"

255 For a discussion of the long series of "blood" images that begin here, see the essay on imagery.

279 Stage Directions. Bayle in the article on Abel regarded as traditional the fire that God sent from heaven as a sign of divine acceptance of Abel's offering. There was no mention of this fire in Genesis. "Milton imported the *propitious Fire* into the story from the many instances in the O.T. when fire from heaven consumes a sacrifice . . ." (*PL*, XI, 441 n., Merritt Y. Hughes edition). The whirlwind, which Gessner had also used to demolish Cain's altar, was in some later books of the Old Testament a manifestation of the divine presence. Bayle speculated on the reason why God rejected Cain's sacrifice and suggested that God intended us to imply that Cain's offering was unacceptable because Cain was an evil man.

> It is guess-work only, and beating the air, to spend one's time in seeking after the outward defects which might be in the offerings of Cain. Perhaps nothing was wanting in them in that respect: perhaps he forgot only the good dispositions of the heart, which are principally regarded by God. We see that St. Paul contributes to the faith of Abel alone the superiority which he had over his brother. (Cain, Note C, IV, 18)

Milton wrote that Cain's offering was not accepted because "his was not sincere" (*PL*, XI, 443).

Fabre d'Olivet: "The sacrifice of Cain is rejected . . . because it is presented in an improper manner." Cain is not in a reverent state of mind. "The volitive man, as long as he persists in his own will, and does not submit it to the universal will, ought not to approach the altar in office of pontiff" (p. 257).

286–316 Milton explained the cause of Cain's violence in Michael's speech to Adam: "the unjust the just hath slain, / For envy that his brother's offering found / From Heaven acceptance" (*PL*, XI, 455–457).

Byron carefully motivated the murder both in a letter and in the poem; see "Byron's View of His Play." Critics, however, have disagreed about his intentions. A sampling of these variations is here assembled. The interpretations of Talfourd, Goethe, Gerard, and Blumenthal can be found in Part III of this book.

Fabre d'Olivet: Cain was angered not at religion but at the form of worship. He refused to be constrained to a particular rite:

> . . . when he has made his prayer, which he finds good for himself, and when he has offered a sacrifice that he judges even purer than that of his brother, his irritation is at its height when it is said to him that his prayer is impious and that his sacrifice is an abomination. His pride revolts; all his passions

> are aroused; he believes himself persecuted and becomes persecutor. (p. 258)

Fabre d'Olivet generalized that religious wars were always caused by differences over forms of worship.

Stopford Brooke: The crime is done in a moment of impulse, "because there has been nothing left to revere . . . because when pride and hate and scorn are alone left in the soul, they multiply, till . . . all things are lashed to passion, and the smallest touch of opposition to the pride, and the smallest grain of anger, swell in a moment into murder" (p. 88).

Solomon Gingerich: Cain's recollection of his journey and Abel's description of his brother's abnormal excitement (177–188) explain the later violence. "Infected with the . . . spirit of Lucifer, flushed with a sense of new power and new knowledge, inspired by the immensities of eternal existence, he cannot adjust his mind to that of his commonplace, simple, and formalist brother." Abel's humble, stubborn persistence, Jehovah's approval of bloodshed, and his rejection of the fruit are the final exasperations. Cain "breaks out in a wild fury, not against Abel, but against Jehovah. . . ." Gingerich also thought that the law of original sin fatalistically worked through Cain's crime (pp. 269–270).

Lovell and Joseph briefly duplicated Gingerich's explication. Lovell attributed the fatal act to the hectic dissatisfaction that Lucifer had engendered in Cain. He accepted Byron's statement that Cain's violence was directed not solely against Abel but against life and against God (p. 212). Joseph similarly noted that the journey with Lucifer had bewildered Cain with a realization of man's insignificance in space and time. But Joseph did not clearly explain how Lucifer used this truth to "betray" Cain and to "trap" him into fratricide. His denotation of the immediate motive, however, was plain: God's preference of Abel's sacrifice aroused Cain's jealousy and incited him to denounce a God that savored a bloody sacrifice (p. 122).

Noel (*Essays,* p. 98) and Elze (p. 416) thought that Cain's tenderness caused his revulsion toward Abel's animal sacrifice. G. Wilson Knight, quoting lines 298–304, stated that hatred of animal sacrifice was the immediate cause of the murder ("The Two Eternities," p. 223). He repeated this narrow interpretation in *Lord Byron: Christian Virtues* (p. 247).

Hoxie Fairchild: Cain was less envious of his brother than "irritated beyond endurance" by Abel's submissive offering that showed "more of fear than worship." "The humility of others is hard for frustrated pride to bear" (p. 432).

Bonamy Dobrée: Cain "is goaded to smite his brother, by the injustice, as he sees it, of God, and by Abel's—not to say Adam's—hideous complacency" (*Byron's Dramas,* p. 9).

Bostetter: God's rejection of Cain's appeal to reason (his challenge that God should stop being a tyrant) enraged him and precipitated the murder (p. 575).

Frye: The origins of the murderous impulse were (1) Cain's vision that revealed death to be Cain's "true enemy," and Jehovah to be unworthy because of his malice and tyranny, (2) the dizzy enlightenment of the journey to older worlds, and (3) the state of mind that resulted (a) from Cain's feeling that the highest knowledge led to death, (b) possibly from Lucifer's suggestion that death led to the highest knowledge, and (c) from the two preceding experiences. Frye's phrasing of the third cause was confused and his whole exposition rather disconnected. See also the note on II, ii, 164–167.

Harold Bloom thought that the murder completed an act of knowledge, but he did not explain how it did so. Nor did he give a convincing exposition of how Cain, both as an artist and a deliberate criminal, sought the conditions for his art by violating the moral sanctions of his society, nor how Cain's imaginativeness flowered into murderousness but did not go far enough in merely negating the moral law (*The Visionary Company,* pp. 246–247).

Marshall: By the crime Cain "unwillingly offers support for his father's belief in a just God who is opposed only by evil" (p. 137). I cannot see that Byron implied that the murder was Cain's acknowledgment, willy-nilly, of Adam's belief in God's justice.

315–316 In the Bible, Bayle's *Dictionary,* and some of the Mysteries there was an interval between the offerings and the crime. In the Miltonic vision that Michael showed Adam, there was no time lapse between the sacrifices and the murder (*PL,* XI, 429–447).

319–320 Luke 23:34.

333–357 Cain's remorse and illumination, which continue in lines 371–379, 500–501, 510–515, 521–522, 531–533, 556–561, were a second subject in Act III that evoked a variety of comment. For the poet's own explanation, see "Byron's View of His Play." The first and longest contemporary analysis by Harroviensis has been included in "The Major Periodicals and Pamphlets."

Fabre d'Olivet: Cain's remorse "proves that he has no criminality in him, and that the crime he has committed is the effect of an irresistible fatality. This fatality falls back wholly upon Lucifer, who is its author" (p. 259).

Charles Kingsley: Cain's remorse and illumination expose the theme of the drama—a conflict with moral law, which Cain discovers only after struggle with it and after the crime. Cain's experience is a reflection of the poet's own discovery. Byron had an intense sense of this moral law, which is "independent of us, and yet the very marrow of our life, which punishes and rewards us by no arbitrary external penalties, but by our own conscience of being what we are." Byron and Cain had "tried to eradicate the sense of it by speculation." Sophistries had enabled them briefly to forget or deny it, but they finally concede that it exists and that they have broken it, and they are miserable. "If this be not the meaning of 'Cain,' and his awful awakening after the murder, not to any mere dread of external punishment, but to an overwhelming, instinctive, inarticulate sense of having done wrong, what is?" ("Thoughts on Shelley and Byron," pp. 44–45).

Gerard: Cain's remorse was a return of his normal family affection (p. 96).

Brooke: Rebellion is over. Cain in grief and humility admits that God has the right to punish and forgive sin. Previously Cain "had been conscious of his intellect, and its desires—a dreary dream—of home love, and the passions of human nature." After the crime he realizes that "he has been living . . . in shadows, in things like dreams" and that mortal life is a battlefield "of the eternal soul with evil." He also learns something about spiritual reality and about the nature of God. With this knowledge, he loses his horror of death (pp. 90–91). Brooke's didactic essay bestowed more wisdom on Cain than Byron gave him.

Oliver Elton: In the remorseful passages, Cain "is a living man, not merely a self-described personage. He is not merely a doubter who has read . . . Bayle's *Dictionary* . . . and who is inclined to criticise the curious bargain . . . between the good and evil principles . . .; he becomes august and tragic" (p. 165).

Gingerich: "Cain is stunned into a new sense of humanity." He cannot forgive himself and "is willing to undergo any punishment that may be meted out to him" (p. 270).

John W. Harrison: Cain did not know how he shared mankind's depravity until he killed Abel. Then he saw that death was "the fruit of his hand" and accepted his parents' symbol of sinfulness—the fruit of the tree—as his own (pp. 113–114).

Marshall: "Cain, who has seen only the spiritual effects of death, now witnesses it as a physical reality, an expression of the creative Principle in the universe rather than directly as the liberator of the intellectual spirit." He "has come to conceive of Death as an aspect of the realm of the material Principle which nevertheless is the instrument for Man's release to the intellectual Principle" (p. 154). I do not find that Cain had previously seen "the spiritual effects of death" nor that he now saw it as "a release to the intellectual Principle." And how can physical death be seen simultaneously as "an expression of the creative Principle" and as an "aspect of the material Principle"?

378–379 There has been some variation in the definition of the dreary dream that Cain awakened from. Gingerich wrote that in the presence of death, Cain's aspirations and his "knowledge of infinitude" seemed a nightmare (p. 270). This was close to Brooke's view (see above). Thorslev, to the contrary, believed that Cain referred "to the anger of frustration which had driven him to murder" (p. 182). According to Marshall, when Cain said that he had awakened from a dreary dream he repudiated the teaching of Lucifer (p. 154); this was similar to Bostetter's reading (see "Annotations" III, 506–561).

380–454 Gerard and Brooke described the effects of the crime on the family. See "The Victorian Approach to *Cain*" and "The Devout Stockade," n. 13.

382 The source of Adam's reproach of Eve, as Thorslev indicated, could be *Paradise Lost,* where Adam's first impulse after their awakening was to blame Eve (IX, 900–906, 921–925, 1067–1068, 1134 ff.).

408–443 For typical nineteenth-century abhorrence of this speech, see Uriel, Fabre d'Olivet, and Blumenthal in various sections of Part III of this book.

There were many differences and only a few similarities between Eve's speech and the curse that Southey had Kehama put on Ladurlad in Part II, st. 14 of *The Curse of Kehama.* A charm was to protect Ladurlad from sickness and time, from weapons, stone, wood, fire and flood, from the serpents and the beasts; but the earth was to deny him its fruits, water was to flee him, the winds were not to touch him, nor the dews to wet him. With a fire in his heart and brain, he was never to sleep nor to find release in death.

In the incantation that Byron published before *Manfred* and then included in that poem, the accursed was to be tormented by ineradicable thoughts. In the opening lines, the victim could sleep, but his spirit could not. Later in the poem both sleep and death were withheld from the sufferer.

467 For Byron's use of the Angel see "The Re-creation of Genesis."

477–482 Bayle speculated on the biblical Cain's fear of being murdered. If there were no inhabitants on earth other than Adam's progeny, whom did Cain fear? His brothers and nephews? Perhaps Cain only pretended fear to gain pity, or in his excitement he might have forgotten that there were no other people on earth. Did God's sign confirm the fear and imply that there were other people who might harm Cain? Bayle concluded that Cain's fear raised knotty problems (Cain, Note A, IV, 17).

Byron was not bothered by subtle difficulties. For comment on his transfer of the biblical Cain's fear to Adah see "The Re-creation of Genesis."

493–501 Bayle related various fantastic legends about the nature of the seal: it could have been one letter, three letters, the sign of the cross, leprosy, or a horn on his forehead (Cain, Note B, IV, 17–18). For Byron's use of the mark see the essay on imagery.

506–561 The last fifty lines of the play have stirred up much difference of opinion about Byron's final intentions, largely because of the apparent inconsistencies of Cain's speeches, which I discussed in "An Apology for Revolt."

Brooke: The old pride and the old anger recur when the Angel reproaches him, but they do not last. His theological problems evaporate in front of death. Brooke regarded lines 510–514 as "the birth of self-sacrifice," and Cain's speeches from 518 to 561 as proof that his heart was softened: the dread that Enoch will turn from him, the recollection of Abel's gentleness, the thought that Abel will forgive him, and the despairing question, "What place for me?" Since the crime will lead to ultimate good, Brooke saw an optimistic ending to the drama. The repentant "Cain is to be saved . . . from his pride . . . from his false scorn of life." He now sees "the difference between right and wrong" and submits to punishment as just. "He who goes quietly into the wilderness, thinking that the four rivers could not cleanse his soul . . . is very different from him who went, indignant, hard, with that pride in his own absolute right . . . into space with Lucifer." Cain has become "a conscious moral being" and is "for the first time, though he knows it not, capable of redemption." "Love is won in a terrible birth out of too late remorse." Some people attain knowledge of good only through doing wrong, and achieve salvation only after they have realized their selfishness by "some miserable exercise of it, as Cain learnt to love by slaying Abel" (pp. 90–94).

Gingerich: Byron shadowed his optimistic portrayal of domestic affection with a reminder of inescapable destiny: "Out of the general darkness there shines the love of Cain and Adah unsullied, and they . . . depart for the wilderness, not hopelessly. But to the last Cain asserts the fatality by which his career has been determined" (Quoted 506–510, p. 271).

Stavrou saw none of Brooke's optimism in the poem:

> It ends on a note that is anything but hopeful, showing the desperate and despairing fratricide, Cain, still sullen and resentful. Like our "grand parents" he has arrived at the realization that God has the right to punish and forgive sin, but he is not as sanguine as they are in contemplating the future. His state of mind is a disturbed one which harbors no reverence and adoration for the Maker. Like Raskolnikov he trudges off to his punishment with disbelief still gnawing at his heart, with his doubts and questionings still unresolved. (p. 154)

Stavrou, quoting III, 509–510, and 552–553, insisted that Cain was the same person who spoke the opening soliloquy:

> Nor is he at all daunted by the "Angel of the Lord" who visits him after his murder of Abel; he asks no mercy and, in fact, begs to die. The Cain at the end, I reiterate, is the identical Cain of the beginning—chastened to be sure by his crime, but still as contemptuous and defiant of the God who suffered Abel's death as he was of the God who placed man in Eden only in order to have the pleasure of later banishing him. (pp. 158–159)

Stavrou's interpretation overlooked the remorseful speeches that supported Brooke's pious view and that complicated Cain's emotional state: 371–379, 500–502, 510–515, 520–526, 528–544, 556–561. If one reads these one after the other, he surely cannot accept Stavrou's analysis as the whole truth.

Bostetter: Cain changes for the worse. He is a defeated intellectual, who had challenged social dogma and been banished by social authority and who at the end "abandons his right of reason, repudiates his trip with Lucifer as a 'dreary dream,' and intellectually submits to the values of the victor." Bostetter, concentrating on the repentant speeches, saw only surrender, and slighted those lines that revealed Cain's continuing resentment. He maintained, however, that Byron did not "concede the indestructibility of traditional values, or the futility of defiance." The manner in which God triumphed incites "further intellectual revolt"—in readers (p. 575).

Although Thorslev partly agreed with Stavrou, he continued to maintain Brooke's optimistic interpretation without the latter's piety. Thorslev saw Cain advancing beyond the defiance of Manfred and Lucifer, earnestly desiring to die if that would revive Abel, remorseful because he failed "in the positive human value of love," and leaving Eden "for a life of penance" (p. 182). Cain's remorse is "certainly a sign that he has learned to see what Camus calls 'the proper limits of rebellion'." *Cain* ends with an affirmation of love, "the one sure value in a world of irrational conflict" (p. 199).

Thorslev seemed misleading in regarding lines 509–510 as Cain's final summation of his position: "his view is not very different from that of Manfred: he can see the 'absurdity' of his situation in a world he did not make." Thorslev's main stress, however, was not on Cain's belligerent fatalism but on his final realization of "the value of his love for Adah, for his son, and for all of his posterity" (p. 183). Hence, lines 509–510, though typical of Cain's morose negation, are not a summation of his whole character.

Marchand: Cain, accepting his banishment as just, "subsides into the tragic gentleness of a broken spirit. None of the rebellious feeling but all of the fight has left him." Since he is remorseful and repentant, he no longer denounces Jehovah as a tyrant (pp. 86–90).

CAIN AND THE MYSTERIES

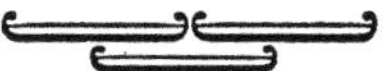

ONE CANNOT TAKE SERIOUSLY Byron's prefatory statement about the reason for his subtitle, "A Mystery." As earlier readers have observed, the only conformity to the old Mystery plays was Byron's "antient title." As he informed Murray, he used that word to indicate that he had written "a tragedy on a sacred subject," a biblical episode.[1] Though the Coventry and Chester plays had been published during Byron's time, he probably had not read a single play in these collections nor the French, Italian, or Spanish versions that he referred to in the Preface. He could have seen one or two historical accounts: Warton's *History of English Poetry* and Dodsley's *Old Plays*.[2]

In the past history of the Eden family, Byron and the Mysteries shared a few elements, some, but not all of which, were biblical. The mortality theme appeared in a Chester play. God reminded Adam that he and his kind were of the earth and must eventually return to it. In the Chester cycle the serpent was identified as the devil in disguise. In all the Mysteries that dramatized the fall, after Adam and Eve ate the fruit, they were doomed to a life of toil and trouble. In a Coventry play the seraphim

[1] *LJ*, V, 360. Chew and others have noted that the first sentence of Byron's preface wrongly identified the mystery and morality plays.

[2] *Poetry*, V, 200.

with a flaming sword, which also impressed Byron's hero, drove the guilty pair from Paradise.

All four cycles (Chester, Coventry, Towneley, and York) dealt with the murder of Abel, and here the behavior of the Cains differentiated them from Byron's concept of his hero. The treatment of the villainous brother seemed to follow a fixed tradition, though there were variations within the pattern. In all the Mysteries he was boisterous and in many respects unlike Byron's brooding and despondent intellectualist.

The Chester Cayme[3] was an arrogant and greedy peasant, refusing to offer the Lord the best corn, and grumbling that the fallen grain was good enough for Him and that if God did not reward him, He did amiss and was in Cayme's debt. After the flame descended on Abel's altar, as it did in *Paradise Lost* and in Byron's play, Cayme was envious of his brother, accepted God's challenge and killed Abell. In this play, as in Byron's, Cayme's grievance was against God; the murder of Abell was an act of defiance of the deity. After his banishment Cayme was rueful and frightened lest future harm befall him.

In the Coventry play,[4] Abelle's prayer acknowledged God's creative power and mercy. Caym was again greedy and arrogant, kept the best corn for himself and offered God inferior produce. God accepted Abelle's lamb with the descending fire but rejected Caym's stingy gift. When Abelle explained his brother's fault, Caym killed Abelle in anger.

The Towneley[5] Cayn (or Caym) was even further from Byron's hero—a profane roughneck, who was scornful of Abell's pious sermonizing and who cynically complained that his farthing was still in the priest's hand ever since he last gave it to him. Cayn was disgruntled with God, who he felt was responsible for the bad crops and other misfortunes. He did not want to stop ploughing to make an offering to an enemy. Byron's Cain and Lucifer were also hostile to God, but for other reasons. Byron did not give as much stress to the bad feeling between the brothers as the Mysteries did. Both the Towneley and the Coventry Caym regarded Abell as a fool for sacrificing a valuable sheep. The former kept the best produce for himself and thus cheated God. When his altar smoked and

[3] *The Chester Plays: A Collection of Mysteries Founded upon Scriptural Subjects, and Formerly Represented by the Trades of Chester at Whitsuntide*, ed. Thomas Wright, pp. 20–44.

[4] *Ludus Coventriae. A Collection of Mysteries, Formerly Represented at Coventry on the Feast of Corpus Christi*, ed. J. O. Halliwell, pp. 33–39.

[5] *The Towneley Plays*, eds. George England and Alfred W. Pollard, pp. 9–22.

choked him, and when Abell told him that he had made a bad offering, Cayn replied coarsely, and was insolent when God rebuked him: "God is out of hys wit." Even after the murder Cayn remained rude and defiant toward the deity. Byron complied with tradition in dramatizing Cain's wrath with Abel after God's rejection of the fruits, and there was a resurgence of the old sullenness in Byron's scene with the Angel.

The York[6] Cayme was a frivolous individualist, declaring he would work as he pleased, and preferring to have fun. He had a little of the Byronic Cain's intellectuality and used sophistry in his argument: if God is mighty, He needs no offering from man. It was fickle friendship to give back to God what he had given man. After the murder when the Angel appeared, the York rascal was drunk and insolent. This was the only one of the four plays to introduce the Angel into the final situation and the only one to retain, as Byron did, the episode of the mark. The Angel gave the outcast a token "printed so in thee, / That all men know thee certainly."

Byron's sensitive, affectionate, and aspiring murderer does not belong in the company of these crude peasants. There is no avarice in him, no coarseness, no petty cheating, and no flippancy. In spite of the major differences of purpose and conception between the primitive Mysteries and Byron's psychological drama, certain similarities in detail and situation (the stress on labor, the fiery sword, Abel's prayer, the flame, the quarrel, the appearance of the Angel) and the scattered resemblances between the older, simpler villains and Byron's hero (their pride, nonconformity and defiance, their antagonism toward the deity and their scorn of piety, their surliness and hot temper—these matters suggest that there may have been a continuous legendary tradition and that any writer on this biblical episode might be expected to draw upon it for a number of common traits and circumstances.

[6] *The York Cycle of Mystery Plays*, ed. J. S. Purvis, pp. 41–44. The play about Cayme, which was performed by the Gaunters (Glovers), is a fragment.

SOME POSSIBLE SOURCES AND PARALLELS FOR ACT II

I

MEDWIN SUPPLIED EIMER with a clue: "I remember what Fontenelle said of its [the moon's] having no atmosphere and the dark spots being caverns where the inhabitants reside" (p. 157). Scattered throughout the *Conversations on the Plurality of Worlds* were sensational details that Byron might have borrowed. Fontenelle described for his listener, the Marchioness, the great ring of Saturn, the bands around Jupiter, and the orbits of their several satellites (pp. 209 ff., 331, 338). The alternating expansion and contraction of Jupiter's belts indicated that enormous changes recurred on the surface of the planet when the oceans overflowed the land (p. 338). Jupiter's "long train of light" may have been caused by periodic conflagrations. On Mars, too, there were violent fluctuations as the seas surged over continents and then suddenly withdrew (p. 339). The planetary belts and rings, the orbiting moons, the oceans, and the great fires resemble the celestial phenomena that aroused Cain's wonder during the flight.

Fontenelle explained to the Marchioness that the fixed stars were suns, each being the center of a vortex and each having planets that revolved around it. He enjoyed the contemplation of infinite space, but the Marchioness was astonished and lost in the universe. "I no longer know where I am" (p. 265). The smallness of earth so humbled her that she thought she could not thereafter have a great desire for anything (p. 268). Here Fontenelle provided a precedent for Cain's despondency over his discovery of the littleness of earth.

Fontenelle also anticipated Lucifer's assurance that people lived on the heavenly bodies. He playfully suggested that the moon dwellers took shelter in the caverns (pp. 140 ff.) and later argued that the other planets were populated by creatures radically different from those on earth, with special mental and physical characteristics that adapted them to, or were caused by, the different environments on Venus, Mercury, and Saturn (pp. 188–191). He did not praise these people as superior in physique or intelligence to men on earth. But he did state that they were not children of Adam and surmised that this fact would disturb theologians (Preface, p. xiv). Fontenelle's fantasy was only a few steps away from the preadamites that Byron placed on the ghostly worlds in Hades. The edition of Fontenelle's book that I used was "translated by a gentleman of the Inner-Temple," London, 1767.

2

In the transit of Shelley's fairy through the ether (*Queen Mab*, I), there are a few similarities to Lucifer's later flight, but three of these are commonplace: just as Cain saw the light of the earth become smaller, so in *Queen Mab*, "Earth's distant orb appeared / The smallest light that twinkles in the heaven" (I, 250–251). Byron referred more often than Shelley did to the interminable expanse and to the innumerable stars. More striking are two images that have in common one word and a circling action, but are otherwise differently phrased and applied. Some of Byron's spheres were "begirt / With luminous belts and floating moons." Shelley's "immense concave" was "semicircled with a belt / Flashing incessant meteors" (I, 235–236). Byron's ambitious description of demolished worlds was more significant than Shelley's mention of some orbs that "dashed athwart with trains of flame, / Like worlds to death and ruin driven" (I, 260–261). The use the poets made of the sea was quite different. In *Queen Mab* it was a measure of the distance the Fairy and Ianthe travelled. At first they were so close to the tremendous ocean that they saw the stars mirrored in its still surface. Later they were so far away, it was indistinguishable (I, 222–240). The ocean that Cain wondered at in Hades, an "immeasurable liquid space / Of glorious azure," was a phantasm of a past world, and was one of the many phenomena that impressed on Cain the cruelty of God and the littleness of man. There were more differences than resemblances both in descriptive detail and in the psychological exploitation of the two journeys.

Gillardon (pp. 76–81) also hunted for parallels between Lucifer's journey and the flight of Shelley's magic car in *Queen Mab*. He listed lines from *The Revolt of Islam* (I, 49), *Prometheus Unbound* (I, i, 163), the "Ode to Heaven," and some fragments from *Hellas* that he thought similar to Byron's.

3

Chew mentioned another possible source: the journey to the moon in Ariosto's *Orlando Furioso*, Canto 34, sts. 66–87, but he did not support his opinion. Astolpho and St. John got to the moon in seven lines and the only phenomenon they encountered on the trip was a region of fire. Only one image is common to both flights: Ariosto saw the moon from the earth as a little circle or hoop. As Cain and Lucifer flew into space, they looked back at the blue circle of the earth and the purple circlet of the moon. After the two pairs of travellers reached their destinations, the experiences, moods, and purposes of their adventures were quite different. Ariosto's lunar topography duplicated that of the earth, except that the towns and houses were larger. In Byron's Hades, every phantom was tremendous and superior to its earthly counterpart. St. John, like Lucifer, was a guide, but his explanation was mainly implied and there was no discussion. St. John's purpose was to let Astolpho fetch for Orlando his vial of sanity and not to gratify his companion's curiosity nor to anger and humiliate him. Astolpho's only response was simple surprise. The tour through one moon valley that Ariosto described had a single principle in common with Byron's survey of Hades: both were filled with remnants of the past. Since Ariosto was interested in moral satire, the numerous objects in his moon valley were clever symbols of the manifold losses that men incur through vice and folly: time wasted in gambling, lost vows and reputations, frustrated plans, loves that ended unhappily, deceitful flatteries, the futile bribes of courtiers, and the work of counterfeiters. Flasks of liquor represented the wits lost in worldly enterprises. All infirmities were embodied in the valley except madness, which never left the earth. The closest that Ariosto's rapid inventory of allegorical objects came to Byron's ghosts of destroyed creatures were the ruined towns, that were symbols of ill-concealed conspiracies, and the mountain of swollen bladders, from which rose the shouts and tumult of the forgotten monarchs of vanished empires (sts. 76, 79).

The translations I read were those by William Stewart Rose (1915 edition) and Allan Gilbert (1954).

4

Chew (pp. 122–123) was convinced by Eimer that Byron borrowed from Richard Laurence's 1821 translation of the Book of Enoch. In the translations I read, Laurence's 1838 edition and one by R. H. Charles, and in the list of sentences Eimer compiled from Chapters 17–71 (pp. 27–29), I saw less similarity to the situations or diction of Byron's play than Eimer did. Several times Enoch was led to a high mountain where he saw, among many wonders, the firmament, "the likeness of the end of all things," "the power of the moon's light," several rivers, three great beasts, a fiery sword, the portals of heaven, a vast abyss, the prison of seven sinful stars, another place of chaos, a flaming area, the dungeon for sinful angels, which Enoch called horrible, and some smooth, deep hollows, where the souls of the dead assembled, waiting for judgment day. Enoch asked Raphael (or Rufael) about one lamenting spirit and was told that it was Abel, who would continue to complain about Cain "till his seed is destroyed from the face of the earth." There were references to whirlwinds, the trees of life and wisdom, and to the fall of Adam and Eve. Enoch told the angel that he would like to know everything, especially about the tree. This request was the only definite parallel to the dialogue of Byron's *Cain* that I could find. The details that Byron may have picked up from the confused Book of Enoch seem insignificant.

5

For still another speculation on parallels, see II, i, 174–175. One may assume that the broad concept of a space flight came from Milton. See "Annotations," II, i, 28–31, 98–117; II, i, 89–103. Perhaps Byron borrowed some physical details from other books. The vision of past worlds was derived from Cuvier and Milton. The religious discussion during the journey was influenced by his Calvinist boyhood and by his reading of Bayle and other rationalists. The critical, skeptical, psychological and dramatic use he made of his materials was directed by Byron's own temperament and by the rebellious attitudes shared by Blake, Shelley, and other writers of the age.

PART III

A SURVEY OF *CAIN* CRITICISM

"I shall have commentators enough by and by," said he, "to dissect my thoughts, and find owners for them."
(Medwin, *Journal,* p. 142)

THIS DIGEST IS REPRESENTATIVE of the explication and evaluation of *Cain* that has appeared in the past 145 years. Though selective, it covers the scope of varied opinion, most of the best that has been written about *Cain*, some of the worst, and a little that should never have been written at all. To assemble the complete literature on this disputatious drama would require several large reverberant volumes. More, I believe, was printed from 1821 to 1830 about the 1,800 lines of *Cain* than about the 20,000 of *Don Juan.*

Two general tendencies emerge in a survey of this massive material. First, there is a continuing tradition, a repetition of ideas, most of it unintentional. Many insights of Jeffrey, Harroviensis, and the reviewer of the *Monthly Magazine,* for instance, were perceived again by Gerard, Blumenthal, Brooke, and Chew; and then the critics since 1930 have made the discoveries all over again. Second, since methods and fashions do change, the passing generations have approached the play differently and have come to diverse conclusions about it, and our own time has continued to produce conflicting views about Byron's intentions and achievements in *Cain.* Or if later writers sometimes add little that is new, they express the familiar ideas in language that their generation prefers. Eccentric bias, from the very beginning to the present, has occasionally startled us with a fanatical or fantastic interpretation. Byron's romantic impulse might have been pleased by the wide divergence; his classical discipline might have mocked it, and his ego would have been alternately flattered and hurt.

Many reviewers of Byron's day understood much of what he was trying to do, and though their traditional prejudice compelled them to disapprove of his religious iconoclasm, they acclaimed his literary merits. Some liberal writers, moreover, who praised *Cain* because they liked its social or political implications did not hesitate to chide the poet for his artistic faults. We should therefore not assume that twenieth-century critics and scholars have a monopoly on vision and truth. A few recent commentators in their effort to minimize an obsolete theological controversy and to bring Byron up to date and force him to be subtle, profound, and intricate, have been as prone as their pious and conventional predecessors to find inferences in *Cain* that Byron did not put into his poem. These extremes are exceptional. Almost every critic has contributed some helpful insights.

THE OPINIONS OF BYRON'S SOCIAL AND LITERARY CIRCLE

". . . I THINK 'Cain' most wicked, but not without feeling or passion. Parts of it are magnificent, and the effect of Granville reading it out loud to me was that I roared till I could neither hear nor see."[1] Although no one else was quite as noisy as Harriet, Countess Granville, her mixed response was typical of the opinions of the nonprofessional reading public and of Byron's acquaintances and literary peers—frank entertainment over the novelty of the characters, admiration of some of the forceful language, misgivings about, and strong objection to, the heresy of many speeches and the author's pampering of the two heretics. Mrs. Piozzi thought that it would do more harm than Paine's *Age of Reason*: "you see there is a cheap edition advertised, in order to disseminate the poyson. Why, the yellow-fever is not half as mischievous."[2] *Cain* won unique attention when it was rumored that King George IV, a paragon of immorality and "the highest authority of the land," censured "the blasphemy and licentiousness of Lord Byron's writings," though it is hardly conceivable that His Majesty could ever have read the poem.[3]

1 Countess Harriet Granville, *Letters, 1810–1845*, I, 219.

2 Mrs. Hester Lynch Thrale Piozzi, *Autobiography, Letters and Literary Remains*, II, 454.

3 A letter to *The Examiner* (February 17, 1822, pp. 106–107) traced this rumor

Henry Crabb Robinson, who read the play twice (March 1 and December 20, 1822), was more thoughtful than the monarch and the women, and less disturbed by its content the second time, but also less impressed by its poetry and psychology:

> Cain has not advanced any novelties in the author's speculations on the origin of evil, but he has stated one or two points with great effect. The book is calculated to spread infidelity by furnishing a ready expression to difficulties which must occur to every one, more or less, and which are passed over by those who confine themselves to scriptural representations. The second act is full of poetic energy, and there is some truth of passion in the scenes between Cain's wife and himself. It is certainly a mischievous work calculated to do nothing but harm.
>
> . . . It offends me but little on a second perusal. At the same time I see not much to admire in it. All the commonplace topics against the commonplace religion are there embodied, and the objection to the character of the Supreme Being and the justice of punishment hereafter, from the existence of evil and the involuntariness of human existence, is well put. Strange that he omits altogether the dogma of necessity. It would perhaps have not suited the object of the poem. Why was Cain *originally* disposed to gloom and impious curiosity? Give him that original disposition, the motive for the murder is sufficiently apparent.[4]

One small voice that tried to speak as both a churchman and a man of letters, but that could not qualify for our circle by social rank and certainly not by talent, was that of Thomas Mulock. In a letter to *The Morning Post,* he reproached Byron for "attributing a softened sentiment of half-repentance to the first remorseless murderer," but found not a single blasphemy in the drama and justified his approbation with redundant nonsense: "Lord Byron has given expression to *the exceeding sinfulness of sin . . .*"[5]

---

to the *Literary Gazette* (January 19, 1822, p. 44). *The Gentleman's Magazine* alluded to it also (December, 1821, p. 613). *The Republican* ridiculed it (February 8, 1822, p. 192). See appropriate sections in "The Major Periodicals and Pamphlets," including note 2 of *The Examiner* for Richard Carlile's satire in *The Republican.*

[4] Henry Crabb Robinson, *Books and Their Writers,* I, 281, 352.

[5] *LJ,* V, 593. Byron and Moore were amused and bored by Mulock's absurdities (*LJ,* IV, 416; V, 131–132 and n.). He "went about the Continent preaching orthodoxy in politics and religion, a writer of bad sonnets, and a lecturer in worse

Byron's close friend of the London days, John Cam Hobhouse, expressed his disapproval of *Cain* in such strong terms that Byron called it gross invective. What Hobhouse recorded in his diary was decorous but no less decisive: "I think it has scarce one specimen of real poetry or even musical numbers in it. . . . Some will call it blasphemous, and I think the whole world will finally agree in thinking it unworthy." A few months later, after publication, when Murray told him about the possibility of a lawsuit and about the slow sale, Hobhouse was "more and more convinced of the correctness of [his] judgment concerning this publication."[6]

---

prose,—he tried to convert me [Byron] to some new sect of Christianity" (Medwin, p. 81).

[6] *LJ*, V, 483–485; *Correspondence*, II, 204–208. Byron replied with restraint (November 23 and December 16, 1821) but later (March 9, 1822) wrote that Hobhouse's criticism had given him more pain than all the other outcry. Hobhouse twice noted in his diary his qualms about his candid letter to Byron and reiterated his view that the play was "a complete failure." On December 9 he recorded Byron's displeasure with his letter. When Hobhouse visited Byron in Pisa, he wrote in his journal: "He also told me that my letter to him against 'Cain' had made him nearly mad. Madame Guiccioli confirmed this, but Byron confessed I was right" (*Recollections of a Long Life*, II, 172–179; III, 5).

Medwin recorded Byron's comment on Hobhouse's "furious epistle": "He contends . . . I should not have ventured to have put my name to [it] in the days of Pope, Churchill, and Johnson (a curious trio!) . . . he seems to have forgotten what poetry is . . . when he says my 'Cain' reminds him of the worst bombast of Dryden's" (p. 126).

Some of the phrases in this report were denounced by Hobhouse as the nonsensical invention of Medwin. His only objection to the words I have quoted was that he did not "join" Pope, Johnson, and Churchill. Hobhouse explained the meaning of his allusion: Byron would not have dared to expose *Cain* to the ridicule of these three critics and satirists. See Ernest J. Lovell's excerpt from Hobhouse's suppressed pamphlet "Exposure of the Mis-statements Contained in Captain Medwin's Pretended 'Conversations of Lord Byron' " (*Medwin's Conversations of Lord Byron,* p. 127, n. 300). Byron, however, thought Hobhouse meant that the poetry of *Cain* was inferior to the verse of Pope, Johnson, and Churchill. See Byron's reply to Hobhouse on November 23, 1821 (*Correspondence*, II, 205). In spite of Hobhouse's later protest, there is no doubt that the language of his letter condemning *Cain*—"*not* on a *religious* account"—had struck Byron as crudely violent: It was written "in such terms as make the grossest review in the lowest publication that ever I read upon any scribbler moderate in comparison" (*LJ*, V, 484).

Hobhouse thought that *The Corsair* and the fourth canto of *Childe Harold* were Byron's best works, but did not care much for Canto II of *Don Juan,* and by the time of Byron's death had not read the British cantos. His literary judgment was therefore characteristic of popular taste.

Thomas Moore, with whom Byron carried on a cordial and extensive correspondence, vacillated about *Cain.* He read the MS and wrote Byron about it on September 30. No one ever sent him warmer praise:

> Cain is wonderful—terrible—never to be forgotten. If I am not mistaken, it will sink deep into the world's heart; and while many will shudder at its blasphemy, all must fall prostrate before its grandeur. Talk of Aeschylus and his Prometheus!—here is the true spirit both of the Poet—and the Devil.[7]

Byron was gratified and within a few weeks (November 23) gloated to Hobhouse over the high opinion Henry Matthews and Moore held about his play. Hobhouse heard in London a report that Moore "says it is the best thing Byron ever wrote."[8] But then in December the dramas were published, the reviews were hostile, Murray's clique was upset, and Moore cooled off: "Cain, to be sure, *has* made a sensation; and grand as it is, I regret, for many reasons, you ever wrote it." In tactful language he preferred the "*poetry* of religion" to the "wisest results" of philosophy, cherished man's faith in immortality, and deprecated the influence that Shelley's atheism was having on Byron's mind and thereby implied that Shelley was responsible for the heterodoxy of the play. These inferences brought an assertion of belief in immortality from Byron and a long letter from Shelley to Horace Smith (see below).[9] Meanwhile, Moore confided to his diary his disapproval of *Cain*:

> Told them [the company at Holland House] about Lord Byron's "Cain," parallel with Milton: wrong for lovers of liberty to identify the principle of resistance to power with such an odious person as the devil. . . . I find (by a letter received within these few days, by Horace Smith), that Lord B. showed Shelley the letters I wrote on the subject of his "Cain," warning him

[7] Letter to Byron, September 30, 1821, Moore, V, 318.

[8] *Correspondence*, II, 204–205; Hobhouse, *Recollections*, II, 172.

[9] Letters to Byron, February 9 and 19, 1822, Moore, V, 318–320. "Moore says, that more people are shocked with the blasphemy of the sentiments, than delighted with the beauty of the lines" (Medwin, p. 127; *LJ*, VI, 23–24).

> against the influence Shelley's admiration might have over his mind, and deprecating that wretched display of atheism which Shelley had given into, and in which Lord B. himself seemed but too much inclined to follow him.[10]

In a letter, Moore assured Byron that he did not identify the author with "the blasphemies of Cain," but implored him nevertheless not to choose subjects that drew thunderbolts. Moore thought that Cuvier's book had a "desolating" effect, and that when Byron put this scientist's ideas into poetry that everyone read, he carried "this deadly chill, mixed up with your own fragrance, into hearts that should be visited only by the latter." This Moore begged him not to do again.[11]

Isaac D'Israeli mocked at the periodical censure and consoled Byron by assuring him of the validity of his pessimism. He was smart enough to pick a grim biblical sentence to confirm the poet's right to be gloomy:

> The bray of Assses which was returned among themselves on the publication of *Cain* was rather that of alarm and misconception. The dread of your "Mystery" is dying away; the perfect moral misery of Cain will now be found instructive for those who are capable of being instructed. Surely a Poet, like the dread Bard of Ecclesiasticus in the darkness of Nature, may show us how "A heavy yoke is upon the sons of Adam from the day that they go out of their Mother's Womb."[12]

Sir Walter Scott, to whom the work was dedicated, was enthusiastic in his reply to Murray, calling it a

> . . . very grand and tremendous drama. . . . I do not know that his Muse has ever taken so lofty a flight amid her former soarings. He has certainly matched Milton on his own ground. Some part of the language is bold, and may shock one class of readers, whose tone will be adopted by others out of affectation or envy. But then they must condemn the "Paradise Lost," if they have a mind to be consistent.[13]

[10] Entries for October 28, 1821, May 14, 1822, Thomas Moore, *Memoirs, Journal and Correspondence,* III, 295, 352–353.

[11] March 16, 1822, Moore, V, 321–322.

[12] Letter to Byron, July 19, 1822, *LJ,* VI, 84 n.

[13] December 17, 1821, John Gibson Lockhart, *Memoirs of the Life of Sir Walter Scott,* V, 150–151. Though the date that Coleridge gave was wrong (V, 206), I have used his reading "talks the language," instead of Lockhart's "takes the language," but retained the latter's "tone" instead of the former's "line."

In the same letter Scott explained, more clearly than Byron himself did, the dramatic necessity of making Lucifer a Manichean, though he wished that Byron had given God his due:

> I do not see how any one can accuse the author himself of Manicheism. The devil talks the language of that sect, doubtless; because, not being able to deny the existence of the Good Principle, he endeavours to exalt himself—the Evil Principle—to a seeming equality with the Good; but such arguments, in the mouth of such a being, can only be used to deceive and to betray. Lord Byron might have made this more evident, by placing in the mouth of Adam, or of some good and protecting spirit, the reasons which render the existence of moral evil consistent with the general benevolence of the Deity.

Scott also discerned the purposeful relationship that Byron had created for Cain and Lucifer: "The fiend-like reasoning and bold blasphemy of the fiend and of his pupil lead exactly to the point which was to be expected—the commission of the first murder, and the ruin and despair of the perpetrator." In a letter to William Stewart Rose, Scott repeated his praise of the conception of Lucifer but was more emphatic about his prediction that it would cause an uproar:

> He has been very great in his personification of the evil principle under the name of Lucifer, who speaks of course the language of the Manichean heresy. It is a most extraordinary piece of composition, and he seems to me in many places fairly to have drawn the bow of Milton. I think however the work will not escape censure, for it is scarce possible to make the Devil speak as the Devil without giving offence. . . . I question whether our noble friend has brought up his fiend sufficiently cleanly.[14]

The Shelley group—Percy, Mary, and Edward Williams—praised the play in general terms, and none of them left comment as specific as Scott's or D'Israeli's. Shelley wrote John Gisborne that Byron's volume of plays "contains finer poetry than has appeared in England since the publication of Paradise Regained.—Cain is apocalyptic—it is a revelation not before communicated to man." Some months later, he wrote Horace Smith that he had not influenced Byron or given him ideas that he used in the drama. "How happy should I not be to attribute to myself, however indirectly,

[14] December 18, 1821, *The Letters of Sir Walter Scott*, VII, 39.

any participation in that immortal work!"[15] Mary Shelley in two letters to Maria Gisborne was equally enthusiastic:

> You will be both surprised and delighted at the work just about to be published by him; his *Cain,* which is in the highest style of imaginative poetry. It made a great impression upon me, and appears almost a revelation, from its power and beauty. . . . perhaps by this time you have seen Cain and will agree with us in thinking it his finest production—To me it sounds like a revelation—of some works one says—one has thought of such things though one could not have expressed it so well—It is not this with Cain—one has perhaps stood on the extreme verge of such ideas and from the midst of the darkness which has surrounded us the voice of the Poet now is heard telling a wondrous tale.[16]

To some professional writers *Cain* was not an immortal revelation. Southey in a complaint about the *Quarterly* made a passing reference to the play that implied disapproval.[17] Thomas Campbell was too cautious

[15] January 26, April 11, 1822, *Letters of Percy Bysshe Shelley*, II, 388, 412. According to Medwin, Byron told him that Shelley, who was "no bad judge of the compositions of others," had been indignant at Hobhouse's critique and had praised *Cain* as the finest thing Byron had ever written and worthy of Milton (p. 126). Edward Williams echoed Shelley's praise (*Gisborne and Williams, Journals,* entries for November 4, 1821, January 24, 1822, pp. 109, 126–127). For the opinions of Shelley and Williams on Byron's use of the unities, see "Byron's Dramatic Theory."

[16] November 30, December 20, 1821, *The Letters of Mary W. Shelley*, edited by Frederick L. Jones, I, 150, 153. Copyright 1944 by the University of Oklahoma Press.

[17] Robert Southey, *Selections from the Letters*, III, 346. Had *Cain* been published when Southey wrote the Preface to his *Vision of Judgement*, he could have applied his castigation of *Don Juan* and the Satanic school to that drama. It too must have breathed for him the spirit of Belial and Moloch and "rebelled against the holiest ordinances of human society." Southey, though not referring to *Cain,* anticipated the modern view of the Byronic paradox: his pride and "audacious impiety" betrayed "the wretched feeling of hopelessness wherewith it is allied." Byron might hate religion but he could not disbelieve it (pp. xix–xxi). Southey's remarks here and in a letter to the *Courier* (January 5, 1822) implied that he, like some later readers, would have felt the political peril in *Cain.*

S. T. Coleridge published a narrative fragment, "The Wanderings of Cain," in *The Bijou; or Annual of Literature and the Arts*, pp. 17–23. John Wright in the

to take a position. *Cain* was not mentioned in his published letters, and no review appeared in the *New Monthly,* of which Campbell was editor.

Hazlitt in *The Spirit of the Age* hit the same demerits that the periodicals had trounced, but with more fanciful imagery. The plays lacked action, character, and "the essence of the drama," and were "gossamer tragedies spun out, and glittering, and spreading a flimsy veil over the face of nature." The humdrum egoism of the style deprived them of empathic power. They abounded in speeches and descriptions such as the poet "might make either to himself or others, lolling on his couch of a morning," and so the reader could never forget the author and live in the fictional situation. Not all of these clever shots struck *Cain.* He made one little jest, that was apposite, about the incongruity of dedicating this radical drama to the conservative Scott, "a pretty godfather to such a bantling." More significant was his protest that "speculative theory and subtle casuistry" were "forbidden ground" in poetry and that Byron wandered "into this ground wantonly, wilfully, and unwarrantably."[18]

Hunt

Our own generation has sometimes valued Hazlitt as a critic more highly than Leigh Hunt, but the latter's reflections on *Cain* are earnest and incisive. The long letter that he printed in the *Examiner* on June 2, 1822, "was written chiefly to set matters right respecting the moral and theological effects of the poem." He gave half a column to a comparison in the *Edinburgh Review* between "the moral effects of Lord Byron and Sir Walter Scott as public writers" (p. 340). Over four-fifths of his letter (four full columns) was a discussion of the following topics: the great mystery "why murder and other evils came into the world to disturb the otherwise beneficent results of our passions"; the significance of the Cain legend and the various problems it gave rise to; some pertinent opinions

---

1833 edition of Byron's *Works* erroneously thought that Coleridge's fragment had been written with Byron's poem in mind (XIV, 8). In a "Prefatory Note," not printed in *The Bijou,* but appearing with "The Wanderings of Cain" in the 1828 edition of the *Poetical Works,* Coleridge stated that the piece had been written in 1798, and scholars have accepted this as a fact. Cf. *The Complete Poetical Works of Samuel Taylor Coleridge,* ed. E. H. Coleridge, I, 285 n.

[18] William Hazlitt, *Complete Works,* XI, 74–77; XVII, 233. For the similarity between one of Hazlitt's opinions and Jeffrey's see the section on *The Edinburgh Review.*

cited by Bayle; and the perplexities one is confronted with when speculating about the relationship between worldly evil and a deity. All this was discussed from a liberal, urbane, and sophisticated point of view. Though there was no particular analysis of Byron's play, and the discussion remained abstract, Hunt did finally apply his reflections to *Cain*:

> The only real fault to be found with productions like the one before us, is that the poet either compliments or disregards the understandings of his readers a little too much; and by leaving them to gather his actual opinions on the subject for themselves, gives occasion to the weak and the hypocritical to charge him with something of this Cainite spirit. People are led to imagine that he has no other ideas of the Divine Being than the one which his drama puts in so disadvantageous a light; and not being able to take the real meaning of his hint, and work out his conclusion for themselves, they pay their unlucky faith the most unfortunate compliments, and complain bitterly of the atrocious and fiend-like person, who after all only lays before them a vigorous statement of their own proposition. (p. 340)

He thought that if Byron had written a few more "pithy prefatory sentences," he would have obviated "every objection on this score."

Hunt then proceeded to refresh us "after these polemics with a little of his Lordship's poetry." He filled one column with several extracts and his enthusiastic comments on them. Like most of the reviewers, however, he had reservations about the scope of Byron's dramatic imagination and remarked on his autobiographical habit of characterization: "Although the author's genius is not dramatic, . . . although he does not so much go out of himself to describe others, as furnish others out of himself, yet this is the most dramatic of all his productions" (p. 341). He made one keen observation on Byron's knowledge of humanity, declaring that two and a half lines on rationalization contained "the whole sum and substance of common theology": "man's vast fears and little vanity / Would make him cast upon the spiritual nature / His own low failing" (I, 221–223). He admired certain psychological passages: the description of Lucifer's initial appearance, Adah's feelings about Lucifer, the various reactions of Cain's family to death, and Cain's summary for Abel of his travel impressions (I, 80–98; 250–256, 509–519; III, 176–184). His highest praise not only agreed with Harroviensis and an earlier article on February 24 in *The Examiner,* but asserted the didactic value of *Cain.* "The noble-mindedness which flashes through the darkest and most mistakable parts of this drama, and the character of Adah alone, who makes a god of her affection, would be sufficient to lead thinking and sensitive minds to higher notions of the Deity . . ." (p. 341).

Hunt's later discussion of the drama in *Lord Byron and Some of his Contemporaries* was written after he had been soured by his residence in Italy. He regarded his Italian experience with Byron as so humiliating that five years afterward he was still bitter enough to write a book, whose hostility toward Byron had been exceeded only by Watkins's *Memoirs.* We should not, however, ignore Hunt's later commentary on *Cain,* for much of it was sensible, as well as astringent.

His report of what Byron said about *Cain* duplicated Byron's comments in the correspondence. His remarks on one of the themes of the play, on Byron's intellectual limitations and religious ambivalence are worth thinking about, as is his interpretation of Byron's purpose and self-defense. He gave a subtle explanation of Byron's stress on the principle of character consistency. A staunch liberal, he believed that Byron aimed to attack certain crude notions about the origin of evil. In this respect Hunt agreed with a few reviewers. The difference was that he commended the purpose, as Shelley would have: "Byron was a helper in a cause nobler than he was aware of." Though approving the goal, Hunt underrated Byron's technique and his mind, which he thought was too poorly trained and equipped, and his emotions too undisciplined, for him to carry out his purpose as effectively as Goethe might have done. The last paragraph of this excerpt is one of the most concise definitions of Byron's religious ambiguities and uncertainties that one meets in the mass of literature on that subject.

Hunt's answer to Byron's question about German morality led him into some rash generalizations about national character, but his main point—that the ordinary British audience was not at this time able to understand or accept a bold literary treatment of Lucifer and Mephistopheles—was probably true.

> Lord Byron's defence was, that "if 'Cain' was blasphemous, 'Paradise Lost' was blasphemous. 'Cain,' " said he, "was nothing more than a drama, not a piece of argument. If Lucifer and Cain speak as the first rebel and the first murderer may be supposed to speak, nearly all the rest of the personages talk also according to their character; and the stronger passions have ever been permitted to the drama."

This is not sincere. "Cain" was undoubtedly meant as an attack upon the crude notions of the Jews respecting evil and its origin. Lord Byron might not have thought much about the matter, when he undertook to write it; but such was his feeling. He was conscious of it; and if he had not been, Mr. Shelley would not have suffered him to be otherwise. But the case is clear from internal evidence. Milton, in his "Paradise Lost," *intended* nothing against the religious opinions of his time; Lord Byron did. The reader of the two poems feels certain of this; and he is right. It is true, the argumentative part of the theology of Milton was so bad, that a suspicion has crossed the minds of some in these latter times, whether he was not purposely arguing against himself; but a moment's recollection of his genuine character and history does it away. Milton was as decidedly a Calvinist at the time he wrote "Paradise Lost," and subject to all the gloomy and degrading sophistries of his sect, as he certainly altered his opinions afterwards, and subsided in a more *Christian* Christianity. Lord Byron, with a greater show of reason, and doubtless with a genuine wonder (for he reasoned very little on any thing), asks "What the Methodists would say to Goethe's 'Faust?' His Devil, says he, "not only talks very familiarly of heaven, but very familiarly in heaven. What would they think," he continues, "of the colloquies of Mephistopheles and his pupil, or the more daring language of the prologue, which not one of us will venture to translate? And yet this play is not only tolerated and admired, as every thing he wrote must be, but acted in Germany. Are the Germans then a less moral people than we are? I doubt it."

No: they are not: but they have got beyond us in these speculative matters; at least, as a nation. It is the case with other nations, to whom we set the example as individuals. We have something of the practical indecision of first thinkers about us. We start a point of knowledge and reformation, and then, out of the very conscience that has forced us to do it, shrink back from pursuing it through its consequences. Lord Byron may well question those as to their right of tolerating Goethe, who, without knowing him thoroughly, will put up with any thing he writes, because he is a foreigner, a great name, and a minister with orders at his buttonhole. But Goethe did not write, as Lord Byron did, without knowing his subject and himself, or without being prepared with a succedaneum for the opinions he was displacing,—one, too, that could reconcile those very opinions to the past condition of society, and even connect them and their very contradictions with the nobler views by which they are displaced. Lord Byron was a helper in a cause nobler than he was aware of, and he was not without the comforts of an instinct to that effect; but his unsubdued and unreflecting passions had not allowed him to be properly conscious of it. By the same defect he subjected himself to questions which he could not answer; and because he was not prepared with good arguments, resorted to bad and insincere ones, which deceived nobody.

The world have been much puzzled by Lord Byron's declaring himself a Christian every now and then in some part of his writings or conversations, and giving them to understand in a hundred others that he was none. The truth is, he did not know what he was; and this is the case with hundreds of the people who wonder at him. I have touched this matter before; but will add a word or two. He was a Christian by education: he was an infidel by reading. He was a Christian by habit; he was no Christian upon reflection. I use the word here in its ordinary acceptation, and not in its really Christian and philosophical sense, as a believer in the endeavour and the universality, which are the consummation of Christianity. His faith was certainly not swallowed up in charity; but his charity, after all, was too much for it. In short, he was not a Christian, in the sense understood by that word; otherwise he would have had no doubts about the matter, nor (as I have before noticed) would he have spoken so irreverently upon matters in which no Christian of this sort indulges license of speech. Bigotted Christians of all sects take liberties enough, God knows. They are much profaner than any devout Deist ever thinks of being; but still their profanities are not of a certain kind. They would not talk like Voltaire, or say with Lord Byron, that upon Mr. Wordsworth's shewing, "Carnage must be Christ's sister"![19]

Blake

The most challenging notice that Byron's contemporaries took of his drama came from William Blake. In *The Ghost of Abel* (1822), the

[19] Leigh Hunt, *Lord Byron and Some of His Contemporaries*, pp. 126–128. Twenty-two years later (1850) Hunt in his *Autobiography* regretted that he had published a syllable about Byron that "might have been spared." He had written the 1828 chapter on Byron while "agitated by grief and anger," and had been "goaded to the task by misrepresentations." Though in 1850 he repented the acrimony of 1828, he asserted his sincerity: "I wrote nothing which I did not feel to be true, or think so." The paragraphs on *Cain* were omitted in *The Autobiography*. He included a restrained criticism of some faults in Byron's character, disposition, and conduct, which he attributed to a bad environment, but admired his genius and did not reflect on the quality of Byron's thought (pp. 319–321, 353, 416).

last poem he published, he used *Cain* as an occasion for writing—or at least engraving—a playlet about God's forgiveness.[20] Our problem is not so much the interpretation of Blake's little dialogue as the determination of its relevance to *Cain*.[21] The latter can only be conjectural, since Blake was, as ever, laconic and cryptic.

The first few lines were a critical dedication:

> To LORD BYRON in the Wilderness
>
> What doest thou here, Elijah? Can a Poet doubt the Visions of Jehovah? Nature has no Outline, but Imagination has. Nature has no Tune, but Imagination has. Nature has no Supernatural, & dissolves: Imagination is Eternity.[22]

Though Blake addressed Byron as the prophet Elijah, he also rebuked him: why was he in the wilderness?[23] Was Byron, when he wrote *Cain,* lost in the wild and natural disorder of the forests of the night? The second question chided his skepticism: a poet should be certain of the Visions of Jehovah. The next three statements of the dedication, mingling a triad of antithetical abstractions with specific images of draughting, music, and chemistry, opposed Nature (the destructive, transitory, and material way of living and thinking) and Imagination (the creative, permanent, human-divine mind). Nature lacked what Imagination possessed: an outline (form, plan), a tune (a beautiful message or truth), and the supernatural that does not dissolve (spiritual permanence).

The two questions and the three antitheses indicate that Byron's drama

[20] I prefer the later theory that Blake wrote his poem in 1822 to the earlier one that he wrote it in 1788 and then thirty-four years later added the dedication and engraved it again. The earlier view evaporated the possibility that Blake wrote his dialogue with Byron's drama fresh in his mind. Even if this earlier opinion were correct, we could still maintain that he thought his poem offered a correction of Byron's mistaken ideas. The problem of dating arose because at the bottom of the second page Blake wrote "1822. W. Blake's Original Stereotype was 1788." Scholars now believe that the latter date referred to the year when Blake began his process of engraving with the *Songs of Innocence.*

[21] Blakean commentators offered little help. Either they ignored *The Ghost of Abel* or they gave no satisfactory explanation of the relationship of the poem to Byron's *Cain.* Some of them seemed not to know or understand Byron's drama.

[22] *The Prophetic Writings of William Blake,* I, 645–649.

[23] Surely Blake did not refer merely to Byron's exile in Italy, as one interpreter said.

did not give the older poet a satisfactory vision of the divine design, message, and eternity. Did he complain that Byron, Cain, and Lucifer trudged the dark, tangled, and ephemeral road of Nature and so missed the vision of Imagination? Perhaps Blake thought Cain and Lucifer too rational, skeptical, and worldly in their rebellion against Jehovah, and was disappointed because Byron's protest at the ignoble misconceptions of the deity, at the god of this world, that Blake also deplored, provided no vision of Divine Mercy. Though, as Bostetter explained, Byron had inverted the "conventional symbols of good and evil in much the same way" that Blake "had inverted them in *The Marriage of Heaven and Hell,*" Blake's "principal objection . . . would seem to be that [Byron] confused Jehovah with the God of this World" and thereby eliminated love from the divine nature.[24]

When Lucifer encouraged Cain to use his reason and judgment in determining right and wrong, he was far from Blake's position. Lucifer's manner of expression and the process he recommended were deliberative and intellectual, and could have smacked too much of pragmatic morality for Blake. He might have been sympathetic with Lucifer's exhortation that Cain use his mind to create a world, but since there was no divine permeation of this creative process, Blake would have passed it by. If he approved of Lucifer's telling Cain about the immortality of his soul, he would also probably have denied Lucifer's contention that their eternity consisted of pain, strife, and sorrow.

The dialogue of *The Ghost of Abel* begins after the murder. Cain is not present. Jehovah calls Adam and Eve, who are so grief-stricken that they are heedless and skeptical, lamenting that everything—including Jehovah—is vain delusion and that they will die as Abel did. Adam's reproach used a biblical decree that Byron ignored: "Is this [the murder of Abel] thy Promise, that the Woman's Seed / Should bruise the Serpent's head? Is this the Serpent? Ah!" Later Adam and Eve suddenly see the vision of the Father of Mercies and of Abel, terribly afflicted, but living. Though fallen and lost, they agree to believe Vision and they kneel before Jehovah.

Meanwhile the ghost of Abel has risen from the earth and demanded bloody vengeance, a life for a life. In Genesis, Jehovah, speaking to Cain after the rejection of his offering, told him that "unto thee shall be his [Abel's] desire, and thou shalt rule over him." Byron did not use this

[24] "Byron," p. 575 n.

speech in *Cain*. Blake adapted it to the evil of worldly man. Abel submitted to the rule of his angry brother when he requested justice and was unforgiving and therefore antagonistic to the merciful Jehovah ("I loathe thy Tabernacles"). Abel's implacable desire for blood payment was a parallel to the demand of Byron's Eve that the criminal Cain must suffer many torments.

When Abel sank into his grave, and Satan rose from the same earth,[25] Blake identified the avenger with the devil. The poet had already suggested this identity when he wrote that the Accuser had entered Abel's heart. Satan, the Accuser, rejected atonement, required human blood (i.e., the retributive justice of this world), and declared that since the Elohim lived on the sacrifice of men, Cain's city was built with human blood, and he, Satan, was therefore the God of Men. Jehovah must sacrifice on Calvary His humanity to the Satanic God of this earth. Then came the climax: Jehovah complied, because by means of His sacrifice Satan would die in self-annihilation. As a triumphant epilogue, the Chorus of Angels chanted the praise of the Great Altruist, the Divine Forgiver of sins. The heathen Elohim, who had sworn vengeance for sin, have been transformed, and Jehovah with His covenant of the forgiveness of sins has established each in his station by peace, brotherhood, and love.

This review of Blake's poem suggests that its hopeful resolution was his reply to Byron's gloom in *Cain*. Blake converted the doubting, despondent parents to a belief in God and eternity; he saw the Atonement as a subjugation of the evil in the human heart; and he subdued wrath and the cry for retribution with love and clemency. Perhaps Blake disliked Byron's many references to the punishments that Jehovah inflicted on mankind: the expulsion from Paradise and a life of toil, sorrow, and sinfulness, which Byron, Cain, and Blake abhorred as destructive vengeance. Blake may also have objected to Lucifer's demoralizing purpose in taking Cain through space and in showing him a vision of destruction in Hades, to Lucifer's fierce declaration of warfare, to Cain's rage and violence, to Eve's imprecation, to Adam's rejection of his son, to the Angel's banishment of the sinner, and to Cain's dejected conclusion that neither God nor his own soul could ever forgive him. All these actions,

[25] Whereas Byron distinguished the Eden serpent from Lucifer, Blake followed tradition and fused the devil and the snake: Adam recalled the serpent (lines 3–4), and Satan, the warrior God of earth, arose, armed with crown and spear and the glittering scales of a dragon-snake.

emotions, and speeches were manifestations of a pessimistic, worldly, and unforgiving temper. *The Ghost of Abel* with its stress on mercy was an optimistic counterpart to Byron's drama of guilt and punishment.[26]

We must note that if Blake remembered the younger poet's negations, he forgot that Byron had Abel forgive his slayer, that Cain was repentant and confident of his brother's forgiveness, that Adah pleaded with her parents not to curse and spurn her husband, begged the Angel for mercy, told Cain that the murder, which she shrank from, was a matter between him and God, and then demonstrated her tacit and practical forgiveness by accompanying the sinner into exile. In these feelings and actions Byron approached Blake's view of Christian forgiveness. But he also had Cain reject that atonement which was the climax of *The Ghost of Abel* (41–42). Uncertain as the relationship is between the two poems, at least Blake's criticism and continuation of *Cain* was vastly superior to the tedious rebuttals and versions of the parsons and poetasters who were drearily inspired or provoked by Byron's drama.

Goethe

Goethe left a longer record of opinions about *Cain* than did any other contemporary man of letters in England or abroad. Earlier works of the English poet had interested him, but the two religious dramas stimulated him to lavish praise, some of which reflected his own egotism: "Byron alone I admit to a place by my side; Walter Scott is nothing compared with him." Byron had been so successful with biblical subjects that Goethe expected him eventually to deal with the destruction of Sodom and Gomorrah, and he later told Crabb Robinson that Byron should have lived to dramatize the Old Testament. Even his reservations about the pessimism and intellectuality of *Cain* were complimentary. This play was excelled only by *Heaven and Earth*; the latter was "much more comprehensible and clearer than the first, which was too profound and too bitter, although sublime, bold and impressive."[27]

[26] Harried by his own sinfulness, and reprobated by a law he could not elude, and ever incapable of accepting the grace of forgiveness, Byron could have been one of Blake's mythical figures, lost in the wilderness, "Orc or Los, nailed to the rock of the ten commandments" (H. J. C. Grierson, *Lord Byron: Arnold and Swinburne*, pp. 17–18).

[27] For most of the incidental remarks on *Cain* that Goethe made to Eckermann and Müller I have used J. G. Robertson's translation in "Goethe and Byron"

The little essay he wrote on *Cain* is a disappointment, a casual piece, whose reflections were not commensurate with the author's reputation. The approach was devious, occasioned by a French defense that Goethe liked and quoted. The *Moniteur* reviewer justified the vehemence of Eve's curse by inventing for her a psychological history of deterioration and a painful view of her son as an image of her own depravity, all of which Byron had not included in his play. Goethe in his next to last paragraph seemed to accept the *Moniteur's* fanciful excursion. His own reminder that a presentiment of the coming of Christ ran through the play was another wayward overstatement.

In the few sentences of particular analysis, Goethe perceived that Byron had dramatized the emotional effect of a repressive theology by having Cain agonize over the mystery of death, both fearing and wanting it, and over the transmission of guilt to an innocent posterity. He also correctly defined the function of Lucifer's talk and journey as an exasperating experience that prepared for the murderous explosion. In one of the talks with Eckermann, Goethe repeated his admiration of Byron's motivation of the murder. "Its beauty is such as we shall not see a second time in the world."[28]

Goethe rightly surmised that in *Cain* Byron "sought to free himself from a doctrine that had been forced upon him" and that the drama thereby would antagonize the British clergy. This was more accurate than his remark that "there is nothing in the whole of 'Cain' which is not taught by the English bishops themselves."[29]

While Goethe's conversational opinions became a staple among later critics, his essay was not widely read. Goethe's reputation did not overawe men like Swinburne, who scoffed at Goethe's literary taste. A century later, W. P. Ker, who did not know the *Cain* essay, warmly defended Goethe's critical acumen.[30]

Although the *Moniteur's* defense, the first five paragraphs that Goethe

---

(pp. 72, 73, 77). For the remark made to Robinson, see the *Diary of Henry Crabb Robinson*, II, 77.

[28] Johann Wolfgang Goethe, *Conversations with Eckermann*, p. 215.

[29] The first comment made to Eckermann was quoted by Robertson (*Diary*, II, 77). The second also made to Eckermann appears in the 1901 translation cited above ("Goethe and Byron," p. 215).

[30] "Byron: An Oxford Lecture," pp. 2–5.

wrote, and the last three, are of minor consequence, the whole essay has here been reprinted.[31]

After having listened for almost a year to the most wonderful things about this work, I at last took it up myself, when it aroused in me astonishment and admiration, an effect which everything good, beautiful and great must produce on the genuinely receptive mind. I spoke of it with pleasure among my friends, and at the same time undertook to say something publicly about it. The deeper, however, one penetrates into the work of such a mind, the more one feels the difficulty of re-creating it in oneself, not to say, for others; and perhaps I should have said nothing at all about it—as about so much else that is excellent—had not a stimulus from without once more led me to it.

A Frenchman, Fabre d'Olivet, has translated the piece in question into rhymeless verse, and believes that he has refuted it in a series of philosophical and critical notes.[32] It is true, I have not seen this work, but the *Moniteur* of October 30, 1823 takes the poet's part, and as its opinions on certain parts and passages are in complete agreement with our own, it has vividly recalled our own reflections. This usually happens when, amidst many mediocre and confused voices, we at last hear one that appeals to us, and we are tempted to express our approval. Let us hear the advocate himself; he writes as follows:

"The scene which works up to Cain's being cursed by Eve, bears witness, in our opinion, to the vigour and depth of Byron's ideas; we recognise in Cain the worthy son of such a mother.

"The translator asks here, where may the poet have found his prototype? Lord Byron might answer him: in nature and the contemplation of nature, just as Corneille found his Cleopatra there, the ancients their Medea; as history shows us so many characters dominated by boundless passions.

[31] The essay was originally printed in February, 1824. The original German version can be found in *Gedenkausgabe der Werke, Briefe und Gespräche*, Vol. 14, *Schriften zur Literatur*, pp. 792–796. The translation here used was made by J. G. Robertson in "Goethe and Byron" (pp. 73–76). In addition to Robertson's monograph, there have been two more recent studies, by James Boyd and E. M. Butler, on the literary connections of Byron and Goethe, and both strive to find significance not only in Goethe's essay on *Cain* but also in the whole history of the relationship.

[32] See the section on Fabre d'Olivet.

"Whoever has carefully observed the human heart and seen how bewildered its manifold emotions can become—especially in women, who show themselves equally unrestrained in good and evil—will certainly not reproach Lord Byron for having sinned against truth or capriciously exaggerated it, although it is here the question of a newly created world and the very first family of all. He depicts nature depraved, as Milton was able, on the other hand, with entrancing freshness, to paint her in her beauty and original purity.

"At the moment of that terrible curse, for which the poet is blamed, Eve was no longer the paragon of perfection and innocence; she had already received from the tempter that poisonous leaven, whereby the splendid talents and emotions, which the Author of life had designed for so much better a purpose, were for ever degraded. Her pure, sweet self-content had already passed over into vanity, and into a curiosity incited by the enemy of the human race, which impelled her to fatal disobedience, belied the intentions of the Creator and distorted the masterpiece of His creation.

"Eve, in his preference for Abel, in her wild curses against the murderer Cain, appears entirely consistent in herself, the self she has now become. The weak but guiltless Abel, who is only a fallen Adam, must be the dearer to his mother, in so far as he less painfully recalls to her the humiliating memory of her false step. Cain, on the other hand, who has inherited far more of her own pride, and has retained that strength which Adam forfeited, stirs up at once in her all the memories, all the sensations of self-love; she is mortally wounded in the object of her motherly predilection, and her suffering knows no limits, although the murderer is her own son. It was for a powerful genius like Lord Byron to paint this picture in all its terrible truth; in this way he had to deal with it, or not at all."[33]

And so, without hesitation, we may repeat these words and apply generally what has here been said specifically: If Lord Byron would write a *Cain,* he had to deal with the subject in this way, or not at all.

The work itself is now, both in the original and in translation, in many hands, and needs on our part neither announcement nor recommendation; we feel, however, impelled to make some observations.

This poet who, with his burning spiritual vision, penetrates, beyond all conception, into the past and the present, and in their train, also into the

[33] Robertson's note: "*Le Moniteur universel,* No. 303, October 30, 1823, pp. 1277–1278. The above is translated, not from the original, but from the translation which Goethe prints."

future, has conquered here new domains for his unbounded talent; but what he will achieve in them is to be foreseen by no man. His method we can, however, in some measure, define more exactly.

He holds to the letter of the Biblical tradition. By making the first human pair barter their original purity and innocence for a guilt of mysterious origin, and by making the penalty which they thereby incur, be inherited by all their descendants, he lays an enormous burden on the shoulders of Cain as the representative of a dejected humanity, which had been plunged into deep misery without any transgression on its own part. This crushed, deeply incriminated first son of man is especially troubled by the thought of death, of which he has hitherto had no perception, and although he may wish the end of his present distress, to exchange it for a quite unknown condition seems to him still more repugnant. From this it is clear that the full burden of a dogmatic theology, expository, mediating, and always at variance with itself—a theology that still preoccupies us—has been placed on the shoulders of the first uneasy son of man.

These untoward experiences, which are not alien to human nature, surge in his soul and cannot be allayed by the resigned meekness of father and brother, or by the affectionate, soothing aid of his sister-wife. To aggravate them beyond endurance Satan appears, a powerfully seductive spirit, who first unsettles him morally, then leads him miraculously through all worlds, showing him the past as enormously great, the present as small and trivial, the future awe-inspiring and without consolation.

He returns to his own people, more excited but not worse than he was; he finds everything in his family's life as he had left it, and the importunity of Abel, who will compel him to take part in the sacrifice, becomes quite intolerable. We say no more than that the scene in which Abel is killed, is most exquisitely led up to; and what follows is equally great and inestimable. There lies Abel! This is death, of which we have heard so much, and the race of man knows just as little about it as before.

But we must not forget that through the whole piece there runs a kind of presentiment of the coming of a Saviour, and that in this as in all other points, the poet has been able to approximate to our interpretations and teaching.

Of the scene with the parents, where Eve finally curses the speechless Cain, a scene which our western neighbour has so admirably singled out for praise, there is nothing more to be said; we can only approach the close with admiration and reverence.

A gifted lady of our acquaintance, in sympathy with us in her high esteem for Byron, has expressed the opinion that everything that can be said religiously and morally in the world, is contained in the three last words of the piece.[34]

[34] Robertson's note: "'*Adah.* Peace be with him [Abel]! *Cain.* But with *me*!—' The lady was, no doubt, Ottilie."

THE MAJOR PERIODICALS AND PAMPHLETS (1821–1830)

JOHN WRIGHT in the 1833 edition gave abundant space to excerpts from seven contemporary reviewers of Cain, two selections from Brydges, and one each from Grant, Harness, and Kennedy; but Coleridge and Prothero (1898–1904) did not pay much attention to them, and the early critics have usually been discarded as obsolete. Byron had become so impatient with the journalists that soon after he posted the *Cain* MS to London (September 10, 1821), he wrote Murray not to send him any periodical,

> *No Edinburgh, Quarterly, Monthly,* nor any Review, Magazine, Newspaper, English or foreign, of any description. . . . Reviews and Magazines are at the best but ephemeral and superficial reading . . . if they regard *myself,* they tend to increase *Egotism*; if favourable, I do not deny that the praise *elates,* and if unfavourable, that the abuse *irritates* . . .[1]

He wrote Moore on August 8, 1822, that he had not for the past three years seen *Blackwood's Edinburgh Magazine,* except for extracts in *Galignani's Messenger.*[2] Since he continued to subscribe to this foreign journal, he did occasionally read its reprints of British criticism.

[1] September 24, 1821, *LJ*, V, 373–375.

[2] *LJ*, VI, 100.

His London friends told him about the conflagration over *Cain*, which ignited in December, 1821, and blazed for a year and then flared at intervals for a decade. "The parsons are all preaching at it from Kentish Town and Oxford to Pisa."[3] Murray sent him the first pamphlet, a *Remonstrance* by Oxoniensis, and he read it with scorn. He read and liked one other, the reply to the Oxonian. Though some of these pamphlets, those by Britannicus, Thomas Adams, and John Styles, were only museum oddities, a few grains of truth can, with patience, be winnowed from such folk as Uriel and Wilkinson.

Most of the major reviews, however, were not so inane as it has been customary to regard them. Though they were ruled by the fashions and prejudices of the day and were blind to some of the merits of *Cain* and saw defects that modern readers no longer worry about, yet they recorded a number of judgments that became traditional and that were challenged only by a small minority in the next 145 years. They had unanimously objected to the arbitrary and self-imposed handicap of the classical unities in Byron's historical dramas. Now they declared that too much introspection, ideological discussion, and scenic description, and too little action made the first two acts of *Cain* undramatic. They asserted that his range of characterization was narrow and lacked variety, that Cain and Lucifer were too much alike, and that Byron had little capacity for creative

[3] Letter to Moore, February 20, 1822, *LJ*, VI, 23–24. Prothero (*LJ*, VI, 9–10 n., 24 n.) mentioned two Kentish preachers: the Reverend John Styles and the Reverend Johnstone Grant. He cited Major Byron's *Inedited Works of Lord Byron* (p. 93) as a source for the latter name. The Kentish parson was probably Styles (Chew, *Byron in England: His Fame and After-Fame*, p. 99). The Oxford divine was Oxoniensis (the Reverend Henry John Todd). The Pisan clergyman was Dr. George Frederick Nott, who, according to Trelawny, "preached in a private room in the basement story of the house in Pisa" where Shelley was living (Edward John Trelawny, *Records of Shelley, Byron, and the Author*, II, 230–231). Byron retaliated with a lampoon—"The New Vicar of Bray." He charged that Nott, who roared against freethinkers, was himself a sinner. He "beguiled / His own Sovereign's child / To his own dirty views of promotion." Byron alluded to the scandal of Nott's alleged misconduct while he was subpreceptor to the Princess Charlotte, who became so fond of him she deeded to him "her library, jewels, and all other private property." Coleridge (*Poetry*, VII, 78 n.) cited, as an unreliable source for this gossip, Lady Anne Hamilton's *Secret History of the Court of England*, I, 198–207. Peter Quennell supposed that Byron rejoiced at the clerical and periodical fustian, because he preferred it to the indifference that had followed *Marino Faliero* (*Byron in Italy*, p. 206).

empathy and habitually transmitted his personal feelings and beliefs to his fictional people. They observed that he did not achieve progressive development, a gradual change or deterioration of character from the beginning to the end of the play, and that the minor roles, except for Adah, were thin and negligible. Adam and Abel were dull weaklings.

Their discussion of Byron's ideas, of the main traits of Cain, Lucifer, and Adah, of Lucifer's psychological purpose, and of Cain's motivation was often perceptive, though they were by no means in agreement on these matters. Some praised Adah's qualities, argued with Lucifer's audacity, were annoyed by Cain's discontented brooding, and protested that Byron's picture of man's mortal condition was too pessimistic. Others more tolerantly defined the causes of Cain's despair and of the crime, regarded Lucifer as a cunning deceiver, carefully assessed the damage he did, and charted the course of his conquest. They abhorred Eve's ferocity. It was so contrary to motherliness that they could not accept it as credible.

Some critics were puzzled by Byron's intentions in Act II—the journey through space and into the realm of the dead—and found it nonfunctional and irrelevant. A few mocked it as childish fantasy or were irritated because Byron had used geology as a basis for his description of never-ending degeneration. Some complained, as Cain did, that Lucifer's educational tour had a necessary vagueness about the nature of death. Others saw that Byron intended to have this trip exert a powerful influence on Cain's emotions.

The contemporary criticism of Byron's diction and versification we have discussed in the essays on metrics and language. Though many writers praised the "power and beauty" of certain long speeches, a few were worried because Byron's eloquence made the poetry an insidious spiritual danger.

The chief limitation of the early critics was their preoccupation with the moral and religious significance of the play, their insistence on interpreting *Cain* as subversive propaganda. One liberal writer attributed Byron's rebellion and lack of restraint to his aristocratic arrogance and his desire for novelty. Most of the reviewers had literal minds and could not accept the characters as fictitious but listened to them as heretical spokesmen of the author. Byron, they argued, had denied the benevolence of God and had even made Him a source of evil and destruction and had asserted the equal and eternal power of the Devil. They objected that the poet had drawn Cain and Lucifer too sympathetically, that he had not made Lucifer diabolical, but had granted him omniscience and other extraordinary powers. They charged that he had not demonstrated that Lucifer was genuinely evil and Cain completely wrong, but had instead written a potent defense of them. Since he had not allowed the Lord's side a fair showing, had not given Adam and Abel a full rebuttal of Cain's and Lucifer's blasphemies, the drama was therefore a social peril. Several commentators—Heber, Harness, the *Eclectic,* and Fabre d'Olivet—distinguished between genuine Manicheism and Byron's modification of it, which reversed the natures and functions of the two warring powers.

Dr. James Kennedy spoke for all of his brother clerics when he remonstrated with Byron:

> . . . they blame you . . . for not putting such sentiments into [the mouths] of Abel and Adam, as would have counterbalanced the effect of what Cain said. And they moreover urge, that the sentiments of Cain are carried too far, even to the height of blasphemy, and the effect of this is pernicious on many minds; especially when no counterbalancing effect is produced from the sentiments of the other characters: and, that being the case, it is naturally inferred, that many of the sentiments belong not so much to Cain, as to your lordship, and you have expressed them with all that force, vivacity, and energy, as coming from the heart. The subject was unhappy. . . . We know already that it has been productive of mischief.[4]

A few sober readers fretted lest the hero's continual upbraiding of Adam and Eve might weaken parental authority and encourage filial disobedience. Some were scandalized by the impropriety of Adah's naïve talk about incestuous love, but one writer defended it as harmless and appropriate to the context. Nobody fumed over Lucifer's ugly and disgusted assertion that God lured mankind with the pleasure of lust to the procreation of unhappiness. The most extreme reprobation by the righteous critics was that literature should not deal with theological or controversial matters, nor even with biblical subjects, and that *Cain* should never have been written or published.

More than one contemporary reviewer smiled at the wide-spread religious alarm, argued that skepticism was a healthy, universal experience, denied that Byron and the devil were identical, noted that the author had Adam, Abel, and especially Adah represent orthodox devotion, that the

[4] Kennedy, pp. 159–160. Byron relayed to Medwin a report that "the *he* and *him* not being in capitals, in full dress uniform, shocks the High-church and Court party" (p. 127). See "Byron's View of His Play," n. 20.

heterodox talk he gave Cain and Lucifer was natural for such embittered souls, that Byron made the murderer a repentant outcast, and that the drama was thus essentially moral and not a social menace.

Byron would have deprived the reviewers of much of their ammunition had he not written a Preface to *Cain.* Too many of them gave enormous space to this short essay, heaping up biblical texts to refute Byron's opinions that a serpent and not Satan had seduced Eve and that the Old Testament made no mention of immortality. Another favorite occupation of the commentators, which Byron had encouraged by his Preface, by a letter referring to Milton that Murray gave to the newspapers, and by the characterization of Lucifer, was a general and shallow comparison of Milton's and Byron's devils and of numerous passages in the two poems; and almost always Byron was judged inferior, not only artistically but also theologically. The commentators revered Milton for his piety and execrated Byron for impiety. Milton had taken his stand with the angels and had condemned Satan's deviltry, whereas Byron had sided with the devil and allowed him to speak without refutation.

Several in the pro-Milton group averred that *Cain* in conception and execution was so alien to *Paradise Lost* they scornfully denied that the later poem in any respect resembled, or could be indebted to, the Puritan epic. One heinous offense that deported Byron to a world foreign to Milton and that the orthodox reviewers pounced on was that many of Cain's and Lucifer's attitudes and assertions could also be found in Bayle's dictionary.

Not everyone was awed by Milton's hallowed reputation. A reviewer in the *Rambler's Magazine* (March 1, 1822, p. 119) had the audacity to prefer *Cain* to *Paradise Lost* and to tax Milton with blasphemy for putting "words into the mouth of the Almighty" and for letting Him wield the thunder of heaven and annihilate millions, "without giving them a moment for repentance." Lucifer's assault upon Omnipotence, however, afforded a nobler field for refutation. "We hold it allowable to make as free with the Devil as ever we please." The *Rambler's* final evaluation was inordinate: just as Dante risked torture from the Inquisition but was afterwards "nearly deified," so *Cain,* traduced in 1822, would eventually bring immortality to Byron and establish him as one of the ablest defenders of revealed religion.

The moral and religious critics inherited from the eighteenth century one assumption about the function of literature: Francis Jeffrey in the *Edinburgh Review,* Philo-Milton, as well as the clergymen like Bishop

Reginald Heber (*Quarterly*) and the Reverend Henry John Todd (Oxoniensis), all insisted that poetry must be didactic, must aim to improve the mind and to inculcate proper values and ideals. It was not an age that was receptive to skeptical pessimism.

A few reviewers caught Byron's political implications. In *Blackwood's* J. G. Lockhart consigned *Cain* to the Radicals with disdain, and E. E. Crowe, proudly confident that freedom was axiomatic in England, asserted that the politics of the poem were relevant only to conditions in Italy. The *British Critic* took the political message more seriously and feared that Byron was fomenting revolution. The *Examiner* charged that the opposition to *Cain* was mainly political.

A common practice of the *Cain* reviewers was profuse quotation, which ran to hundreds of lines, varying from one-fifth to almost a third of the play. Byron took the amount of quotation as a criterion for an evaluation of the book. Reviewers, he told Medwin, who disliked it printed few or no extracts.[5] The *Eclectic,* for instance, thought *Cain* a wicked poem and quoted only three lines. But this rule had exceptions. The *Edinburgh Review,* although unfavorable, offered its readers large chunks from the drama. Those reviewers that were careful about propriety avoided what they thought was offensive and reprinted the safe speeches, e.g., Cain's recollection of beautiful experiences on earth, his exclamation on the wonders of space, and Adah's affectionate words about Enoch. A few who wanted to horrify their readers and some who acknowledged the power of certain intense and strongly phrased speeches quoted Cain's soliloquy, Lucifer's first long speech, their various criticisms of God, the vistas of the phantoms, Lucifer's conclusion to Act II, Cain's altar address, and Eve's curse. As a whole, their selections reveal in one respect that critical taste has not changed, for the speeches they admired are those esteemed by modern readers of the poem.

Although there were many common characteristics and some repetition, the better reviewers were not imitative of each other, but wrote distinctive and thoughtful comments. Unfortunately for Byron's reputation, the favorable reviews, with two notable exceptions, were superficial and cursory, restricting themselves to a summary of the situation and a collection of splendid extracts. The unfavorable reviews were more detailed, had more particular analysis and more substantial ideas, and were more vigorously written.

[5] Medwin, pp. 121–122.

Since it is impossible to print the entire reviews, I have written a brief account of each and presented excerpts from several, with summary links in order to preserve the continuity of the article. I have eliminated from these excerpts all long quotations of speeches in the play and substituted references so that the passages could be quickly located.

The order is roughly chronological. I have, however, put six pamphlets (Oxoniensis through Uriel) in a group after the reviews.[6]

The reader who is interested in the changes of literary values and in the trends of modern scholarship should turn to the last two sections of the survey on the Victorians and the twentieth century. The ensuing exposition of some reviews and pamphlets of the 1820's was prepared for convenient reference.[7] It has brought together and evaluated a moderate number of materials from several libraries in this country and England. The portions on Harroviensis, *The London Magazine, The Edinburgh Review, Blackwood's, The Quarterly,* and *The Monthly* are the most rewarding; those on Grant and Fabre d'Olivet the quaintest. Since the review in *The European Magazine* combined pious chastisement with aesthetic appreciation, conventional judgment with unusual discernment, the few pages about this article offer a quick sampling of the varied facets of the contemporary reaction to *Cain.*

The Literary Gazette and Journal of Belles Lettres, Arts, Sciences, etc.:

"Cain, a Mystery: Sardanapalus, and The Two Foscari, Tragedies; by Lord Byron. Octavo, pp. 439. J. Murray," No. 257 (December 22, 1821), 808–812

[6] The reaction to *Cain* was expressed in still another form. People with no literary talent but with a determination that Byron's contortion of Genesis must be rectified wrote their own versions of the story. William Battine in May, 1822, published a prolix, theological play, *Another Cain,* to show that revelation and not reason was "the only infallible oracle." *The Literary Chronicle* mocked Battine's haste, presumption, and amateurishness, but granted that his pious purpose was entitled to forbearance (October 19, 1822, IV, 663–664). In 1829, J. E. Reade's *Cain the Wanderer* had many changes of scene and almost nothing in common with Byron's poem.

[7] I made no comments on about ten reviews that repeated attitudes already expressed in the magazines selected for discussion. The articles in *The Literary Speculum, The Ladies' Monthly Museum,* and in several others that I read were merely entered in the bibliography. The *Rambler's Magazine* was used in "History and Argument," *The Republican* in the section on *The Examiner.*

"Sardanapalus. The Two Foscari. By Lord Byron." No. 258 (December 29, 1821), 821–822

"Literature, Etc. Southey and Byron!" No. 261 (January 19, 1822) [Only p. 44 concerned *Cain.*]

"Literature, Etc. Lords—Authors—Publishers." No. 269 (March 16, 1822), 166–167

The review in the December 22 issue took up *Cain* first (though it was the last of the plays in the volume) "to get over the most painful part of our task at once, for none can look on Cain without feeling both pain and sorrow . . . a more direct, more dangerous, or more frightful production, than this miscalled Mystery, it never has been our lot to encounter" (p. 808). These introductory remarks set the tenor of the whole piece.[8]

The reviewer found no plagiarism from Milton because there was no resemblance between that poet's great and pious epic and Byron's play, which used every ingenious resource to advance "tenets of infidelity" and "to shake the faith of believers in revelation" (p. 811). He was sure that the poet, when he had Lucifer utter his blasphemies, had identified himself with the devil and was "for a season that which he imagines" (p. 809).

If Byron was pleased when the magazines gave copious extracts from his works, he would have had no complaint on that score with this one. Its quotation of 550 lines occupied fifty-five of the total ninety-four inches. The reviewer liked about a fifth of the quoted lines: the description of space and some passages "in which human passions are painted" and which were "the only truly admirable" ones—Cain's anguish because he must be the sire of wretched posterity, his aesthetic sensitivity, and his talk with Adah about the sleeping Enoch.[9] The bulk of the extracts formed an anthology of offensive passages. Such a collection was

[8] There seems to be some connection between this review and that in *The Gentleman's Magazine* for December, 1821 (XCI, 613–615). See the section on the latter. Robert W. Duncan, in his survey of the *Gazette's* treatment of Byron after 1817, assumed that the editor, William Jerdan, was the author of many of its reviews. In his paragraph on the review of *Cain,* Duncan did not definitely assign the authorship to Jerdan, who, he said, "recognized the fascination of the immoral, and his scruples, in spite of his indignation, did not prevent him from printing scandalous material." Duncan stated outright that Jerdan in 1830 wrote the review of Harding Grant's book on *Cain* ("Byron and *The London Literary Gazette,*" pp. 245–246, 248).

[9] II, i, 98–115, 177–190; I, 431–457; II, ii, 249–269; III, 10–34, 139–156.

almost unique among contemporary commentators: Cain's soliloquy, Lucifer's first declamation, several speeches that held God to be the source of evil, Lucifer's boast of his everlasting contest with his almighty foe, the assumption of equality between the two opposing forces, and Cain's curse of his father and of the creator of life.[10] The reviewer's comment on the vision of Hades identified a favorite form of Byron's pessimism: cosmic deterioration. He was outraged because Lucifer said that God's destructiveness was responsible for this decay. "*He* cannot create a second world so excellent as the first—the race of beings is inferior—the earth is debased" (p. 811). The reviewer then mentioned Milton's contrary view.

After a few slaps at Byron's diction, the reviewer wrote a synopsis, from the sacrifices to the point where Adah comforts Cain before their exile. He closed on the jibe that Adah's consolation must be the basis for the dedication of the play to Scott, "as it is the only sentiment in which one can trace any agreement between him and the author" (p. 812).

In the two weeks following this attack on *Cain* (December 29, 1821, and January 5, 1822), the reviewer discussed *Sardanapalus* and *The Two Foscari*. Only the opening paragraphs of the December 29 article had a slight bearing on *Cain*. They defended the harshness of the *Gazette's* treatment of Byron and returned to a favorite topic—the poet's habitual plagiarism. Then the reviewer agreed with the poet's scorn of the contemporary British theatre, but denied that Italy, Spain, France, Germany, or America provided the civilized, utopian paragon that Byron fancied. The *Gazette* was loyal to Nature and Shakespeare; they produced better dramas than Byron did with his neo-classical rules (p. 821).

Two weeks later (January 19, 1822) in an article on the quarrel between Southey and Byron, the *Gazette* reported the rumor that since the "highest authority" in Great Britain had been displeased by *Cain*, it would not be reprinted, or at least not by Murray. The King was also said to be surprised that "the two great Reviews of the day should have spared the immoral and pernicious works of Lord Byron." The *Gazette* expressed its satisfaction with the pamphlet written by Oxoniensis and was especially pleased because this writer had charged Byron "with plagiarism throughout his Cain" (p. 44).

On March 16, 1822, the *Gazette* appended to its publication of Byron's letter of February 8 to Murray ten stern and sardonic reproaches of

[10] The following are the passages he quoted and deplored as impious: I, 64–79, 127–163; II, ii, 13–25, 39–43, 175–214, 231–237, 363–382, 426–442; III, 68–94.

Byron's defense of *Cain* (p. 167). These contributed nothing new to the controversy.

The Gentleman's Magazine:

"Sardanapalus, a Tragedy; The Two Foscari, a Tragedy; Cain, a Mystery. By Lord Byron. pp. 439. Murray," XCI (December, 1821), 537–541 [Only p. 537 mentioned *Cain.*]

"Cain, a Mystery. By Lord Byron," XCI (December, 1821), 613–615

John Graham. "An Epistle to Lord Byron," XCII (March, 1822), 259

"Rhetoric of the Infidel School," XCII (December, 1822), 513–514

The first two paragraphs of a review of *Sardanapalus* generalized about the poet's decline of vigor in the entire 1821 volume. Though Byron had avoided extravagance by following a "matter-of-fact system," and though he had "gained in correctness and polish," and in "ease and facility of versification," he had also lost in brilliance, grandeur, and sublimity. *Cain* was "unquestionably the best" of the three dramas (537).

The other two articles in this magazine denounced *Cain* for its irreligion: "pernicious," "truly horrible," "wanton libels upon the Supreme Being." The earlier of the two, appearing in the month when Cain was published, briefly followed the mode of the day. It thought that *Cain* should never have been circulated and was erroneously pleased that, since a person of high rank had been disgusted by it, the play was suppressed and would "never more be reprinted."

It quoted Oxoniensis on Byron's plagiarism from Bayle and Voltaire and declared, "We have certaintly discovered great lack of originality in his Lordship's former writing" (p. 614). The only originality in this review was that it classified its quotations from Cain under two headings: "Hideous Blasphemy" and "Twaddle and Nonsense." In two passages of the first category (II, ii, 345–350, 363–382), the reviewer, garbling Byron's Preface, thought the poet had tried to make Lucifer talk like a clergyman and had written dialogue that had "hardly ever been equalled" in "wickedness and impiety." He deplored the "levelling of the Almighty to the Devil . . . [as] an outrage against decency and religion (p. 614). Other quotations in this group were II, ii, 14–19, 22–25. In the second classification, the reviewer selected verses that he considered to be stylistically bad, though he identified only a few specific faults: bad grammar, obscurity, and banality. Several samples were offered in a manner as if to say, "Now just look at this." Though other critics liked the descriptive passages of Act II, this writer even carped at these. From the words he italicized in his quotations from Act II, one may infer that he regarded the descriptive diction as inaccurate and whimsical.[11]

This review closely resembled one that appeared in *The Literary Gazette* on December 22, 1821. If two different people wrote them, one is indebted to the other. The two reviews selected the same passages for the same stylistic condemnation. Moreover, the article in the *Literary Gazette* included all the quotations used by the *Gentleman's Magazine* and made the same moral protests. The former was three times longer and contained more quotation and discussion.

The section dealing with *Cain* in the third *Gentleman's* article was somewhat more thoughtful than the first. It saw that "the deprecatory repinings of Cain" were "indicative of a restless and purturbed [*sic*] spirit" (p. 513). It also accurately defined Lucifer's animosity toward God. He was a defeated, but not subdued, leader, who hated his enemy as an embittered, defiant individualist would hate a tyrant. The writer recognized the power of Cain's and Lucifer's charge against the cruelty of a divine tyrant, who, they thought, took malevolent pleasure in the destruction of those myriads he himself had created.

Along with many contemporary and later critics, this writer dismissed Byron's philosophizing on the origin of evil as illogical, unoriginal, and presumptuous. He also chided Byron for citing Milton's Satan as a precursor of Lucifer, though he gave no evidence for his protest. He was content to assert that Satan was like Lucifer in arrogance and malignity, but unlike him in acquiescing in the justice of his doom and in not questioning "the moral attributes of Deity." The two latter ideas the author might have had difficulty in substantiating.

John Graham's short poem, that was printed in the March issue, reproved Byron's prefatory statement about the lack of testimony in the Old Testament on a future existence. Most of the couplets related some biblical evidence to the contrary. Graham attributed Byron's error to fear and insecurity, regretted the poet's deterioration, and begged him to repent and to shun the fate of Cain and Lucifer.

[11] The quotations placed under the heading "Twaddle and Nonsense" were I, 383–384, 474–476; II, i, 119–120, 177–189, 202–203; II, ii, 33–41 (misquoted), 59–60, 67–68, 123–124. There was one amusing comment: "This reminds us of a portion of one of Tilburnia's speeches in Sheridan's Critic: 'And then my Wiskerandos should'st be father / And mother, brother, cousin, uncle, aunt, / And friend to me!' " (p. 615).

The Examiner:

"Sardanapalus, a Tragedy. The Two Foscari, a Tragedy. Cain, a Mystery. By Lord Byron" (December 23, 1821), 808–810 [Signed "Q."]

"Lord Byron's Tragedies" (December 30, 1821), 827–828

"British Censorship of the Press" (February 17, 1822), 106–107 [A letter signed "Q.E.D."]

"Lord Byron's Cain (February 24, 1822), 120–121 [Signed "B."]

Leigh Hunt. "Letters to the Readers of the Examiner. No. 2—Lord Byron's Cain" (June 2, 1822), 338–341 [Signed with Hunt's hand symbol.[12]]

[12] The authorship of many articles in *The Examiner* has apparently remained unknown. Leigh Hunt signed much of his prose with a hand symbol, his verse with the pseudonym "Harry Brown." John Hunt published his political remarks over the name "Ch. Fitzpaine," and Robert Hunt acknowledged his column on the Fine Arts with the initials "R. H." The many other 1821 signatures seem not to have been identified: "G," "X," "Q," "G.R.," a reversed "C," "Traveller," a single asterisk, five asterisks, and a double plus, that appeared beneath the review of Cantos 2, 3, and 4 of *Don Juan* and many other articles. This double plus has been attributed to both John Hunt and to his son Henry Leigh. It is possible that one person used more than one signature and that different authors used the same one.

In 1821, "Q" contributed many "Literary Notices," including the review of *Marino Faliero,* a satiric series from August 26 to October entitled "Espionage," as well as a few "Political Examiners." From August 13 to the end of the year, "Q" wrote most of the "Theatrical Examiners." In 1822 and for some years thereafter he signed many reviews of books and of performances in the theatre.

After October 21, 1821, Leigh Hunt's hand symbol did not occur until the late spring of 1822. From November 15 to December 22 he and his family were trying to reach Italy and were twice forced back by storms to British ports. He was also afflicted with his wife's illness. It was therefore impossible for him to write the December article, for which "Q" apologized, because he had to read Byron's dramas and dash off a review in three days—between December 19, Murray's day of publication, and December 23. The prestige of Hunt's manual emblem was so high that its reappearance was announced in 1822, when he began to send letters from Italy. It seems unlikely that he wrote the February 24 article over the signature of "B."

John Hunt's authorship is also dubious. On February 21, 1821, he was convicted of libelling the House of Commons and after an appeal was sentenced to a year's imprisonment on May 28. Though "Ch. Fitzpaine" signed two pieces

The very size of the volume impressed the first reviewer with the fertility of Byron's genius. That genius could err in theatrical strategy. "Q" allowed that Byron's devotion to the unities was a "covert reproof of the extravagant license of the modern drama," but he doubted that their application was a remedy of this defect. Regularity was contrary to the taste of the British audience; it repressed more "beauty and nature" than it created.

The single paragraph that "Q" gave to *Cain* broached more ideas than some other articles were able to muster in three times that space. The conception of the poem was daring: since the hero *felt* the presence of evil in the world, he became a rebel against conventional faith. Lucifer fostered his doubts and plunged him into a grand and obscure question that has perplexed men for 2,000 years—the origin of evil, "admitting the union of omnipotence and benevolence." Though Byron put all his impiety into the mouths of Cain and Lucifer, the reviewer predicted that he would not escape the censure of the *Quarterly*.

"Q" admired the description of Hades. Here Lucifer, as always, promised more than he intended to perform, for he did not much increase Cain's knowledge, while fortifying his rebellion. In the devil's audacity and Cain's bitterness, Byron had scarcely exceeded the liberty taken by Milton. Indeed, since he followed Scripture so closely, the catastrophe and the mortal characters other than Cain were "somewhat ineffective." Nonetheless, this drama was "clearly the flower of the volume," and most characteristic of the author's genius. On December 30 a sequel to this first review printed quotations from *Cain* and *Sardanapalus*—from the former, III, 1–34, 245–279.

---

later in 1821, he could not have done "Q's" theatrical columns. He might have written "B's" February, 1822, essay on *Cain*. "B" signed many articles that year.

With John Hunt in prison and Leigh Hunt trying to reach Italy, *The Examiner* was probably turned over to Henry Leigh Hunt in the early fall of 1821. He may have been "Q" or "B." Another possibility for both signatures was Albany Fonblanque, a clever and thoughtful liberal, who had written for *The Examiner* before 1820 and who became steadily more active in the magazine's affairs. He was the major manager by 1826, and was given "sole and exclusive control" in 1830. See *The Life and Labours of Albany Fonblanque*, pp. 6–29. Leigh Hunt praised Fonblanque's wit and political knowledge (*The Autobiography*, p. 173). Although Fonblanque's biographer in 1874 published many selections from his contributions to *The Examiner* after 1827, he provided none written before that date. Nor did the excerpts from his letters identify the earlier articles.

The letter on censorship, written by "Q.E.D." on February 5, 1822, and printed in *The Examiner* on February 17, mocked the report in *The Literary Gazette* of the displeasure of "the highest authority in the kingdom" with *Cain* and the assumption that Murray would therefore not issue a second edition of the poem. "Q.E.D." jested about the identity of this highest authority. Could it be the Duke of Wellington or the Archbishop of Canterbury? If George IV had become the supreme judge of morality and literature, then "Q.E.D." urged the public to adopt certain fashions in dress, china, ornament, and architecture that he implied were typical of his Majesty's garishness. He concluded with a democratic slogan: "Now a days, a poet *may* damn a King, but I fear a King *cannot* crush a poet."[13]

In the week following this ridicule, an article submitted by "B" was more representative than the December review of the perceptive keenness and the political pungency of the Hunts and their associates. "B" was sarcastic about the clamor over blasphemy and protested the identification of Byron with Lucifer, arguing that no one equated Shakespeare with Iago or Milton with Satan. "It is likewise remarkable that authors are never likened to their amiable personages, but are forthwith invested with the evil attributes of the wicked people they have drawn" (p. 121).

Byron's defender, in arguing for the morality and "poetical justice" of the play, was inaccurate in his statement that Lucifer persuaded Cain to do evil, but he erred less on Byron's side than most other critics did in their opposition to the play:

> . . . it has been asserted, that Lord Byron has made the character of Lucifer the channel to pour forth his blasphemous tenets. . . . Lucifer

[13] Richard Carlile, a noted liberal, who issued a piratical edition of *Cain,* wrote a jeering page on the royal disapprobation of the poem in his paper *The Republican,* V (February 8, 1822), 192. "Kings are animals without intellect" and George IV was the "tool of his Ministers and Priests." Carlile would have been honored had the King disapproved of one of his writings. The "fourth Guelph's condemnation" was the complete finish of his character, "by adding to it the vice of hypocrisy . . . It is all over, Mr. Royal Reviewer, with your joint trade of King-craft and Priestcraft, and you had better yield silently to the improved knowledge of the People."

Carlile declared that Byron had borrowed the groundwork of the atheistical *Cain* from Shelley's *Queen Mab,* a far better poem. Then he tried to be ironical. Any honest impartial man would expect the Vice Society to attack Murray because Byron made Jehovah a murderous and implacable tyrant and Lucifer his

> tempts Cain; he succeeds in persuading him to do evil, and the immediate consequence is the severest and most hopeless misery. Surely a man of Lord B.'s talents . . . would not have shown such absurd want of skill as to represent his opinions leading at once to pre-eminent wretchedness, direct and self-caused. . . . It must, indeed, be an unreasoning mind which can be led to admire, far less adopt, tenets which thus immediately lead to such results. (p. 121)

The writer then tried a daring new defense; he compared the pattern of the biblical story with that of the play, just as Harroviensis was soon to do with *Cain* and *Paradise Lost*:

> . . . the serpent tempts Eve, as Lucifer, in this poem, tempts Cain. Eve fails, as does her son; the immediate consequence of the sin of both is punishment awarded by the Deity, and agony self-inflicted—can there be a closer parallel? The arguments of the serpent which corrupt Eve are given to the full, as much in detail, in proportion to the length of the story, as Lord Byron has made those of Lucifer which cause Cain to sin. The temptation precedes the crime; dire and immediate punishment follows it: this is natural progression and poetical justice,—this is, as I have proved, the practice not only of all profane writers, but of Moses himself. (p. 121)

The reviewer closed with some strongly phrased accusations that the opposition to *Cain* was politically inspired. He wanted to "show the besotted alarmists how hollow the means are by which the tools of Power have contrived to lead them by the nose. When literary envy joins itself to political ill-will, there is no meanness or malevolence of which it will not be guilty" (p. 121).

The long letter from Leigh Hunt, published on June 2, has been discussed, along with Hunt's later commentary, in "The Opinions of Byron's Social and Literary Circle."

The Literary Chronicle and Weekly Review:

"Cain. A Mystery. By Lord Byron," IV (January 5, 1822), 6–8

Six and a half columns of the eight in this article reprinted some of the

---

superior in virtue, manners, and knowledge. Byron's purpose was unmistakable. He had aimed a "ponderous blow at superstition," and "terrible and irrecoverable blows" at the Bible and its supporters. Byron called Carlile a fool and his writings trash (*LJ*, IV, 376–377; *Correspondence*, II, 131).

popular passages of *Cain*. Four were taken from Act II: Lucifer's sneer at the autocracy of "the other God," Cain's awe over a vista in space, his later amazement at the huge phantoms of Hades, and his rhapsody on the beauty of nature and of his sister. A sizeable selection from Act III included the parental concern for Enoch, Cain's acrimony over his troubled life, Adah's pleading, the sacrificial orations of the brothers, the murderer's frenzy, the agitation of the other members of the family, and the mother's malediction.[14] Though the reviewer did not object to these speeches, his cursory glance at the colloquy of the rebels in Act I, in which "the Majesty of heaven is insulted," implied his disapproval of that conversation. He concluded that the drama had more faults than merits and that it would be one of the least admired of Byron's works, if not the most condemned.

He was sidetracked by some of the poet's less consequential statements in the Preface and rebuked him for confusing the Mystery and Morality plays, for "touching a sacred subject with unhallowed hands," and for taking more impious liberties with the Bible than the medieval plays had dared. He was sure that Byron's metaphysics were unchristian. Like many of his contemporaries, he overemphasized the heterodoxy of the Preface. He was more illogical than most of them in deducing that its three "disputable assumptions" were the basis of the drama: that Eve was tempted not by the devil but by a serpent, that the Old Testament did not allude to a future state, and that the world had been destroyed several times. The reviewer did not perceive that these assumptions were not central in the dramatic development and that a writer as sensible as Byron would not have tried to "ground" a drama on three such unrelated ideas.

The European Magazine and London Review:

"Sardanapalus, a Tragedy; The Two Foscari, a Tragedy; Cain, a Mystery. By Lord Byron. 8vo. pp. 439. London, 1821," LXXXI (January, 1822), 58–70

[14] II, i, 1–43; II, ii, 1–14, 44–62; 252–269; III, 1–43, 109–160, 223–284, 321–357, 386–443.

In two preceding issues of the *Chronicle* (December 22 and 27, 1821, pp. 799–802, 815–817), the reviews of *Sardanapalus* and *The Two Foscari* likewise consisted of long quotations with summary links and with little critical comment. The only notice of *Cain* was a cursory explanation of its subtitle, "A Mystery." There was no evaluation of the volume as a whole. Instead, the first part of the first article reprinted much of Byron's appendix—especially the attack on Southey.

This reviewer, writing both as a literary critic and as a defender of the faith, tried, without success, to prevent his Christian qualm from overpowering his aesthetic judgment and pleasure. His remarks about the Preface were a mixture of quiet humor and stern disapproval. He accepted the inference that the poet had remembered little of *Paradise Lost,* for he saw almost no resemblance between Byron's first family and Milton's. He looked with some amusement at Byron's explanation that he could not make Lucifer talk like a clergyman and that he had endeavored to keep the devil within the bounds of politeness. This apology sounded so like a jest that it could be taken either as a palliation of the offense or as an aggravation. He rejected the argument that the speeches of Cain and Lucifer were consistent with their characters. No fictitious person could be permitted to curse his own father and God as Cain had done in lines 14–25 of Act II, Scene 2. Even worse were the sneers at the wisdom and the goodness of God, which qualified the play as the "legitimate offspring of the Satanic School." Twice the writer was reluctant to assert that Byron's blasphemy was intentional and to accuse him of "wilful perversion." He complained, however, that had Byron aimed to blast all religious principle, he could not have labored with greater ingenuity and diligence. The reviewer ultimately decided that the poet had deliberately tried to shake the confidence of believers in revelation and that the drama therefore deserved castigation because it would provide skeptics with a creed and might destroy the faith of thousands. He assumed that Cain's soliloquy and the talk with Lucifer expressed Byron's own ideas and that the poet had identified himself with Lucifer in order to impart verisimilitude to the diabolical conversation. Since Byron for a season became what he imagined, his fiction was so convincing that Cain and Lucifer in their original form could not have delivered "more shocking profanations."

If the writer's religious fervor condemned *Cain* as the worst of Byron's 1821 dramas, his critical taste admitted that its splendid poetry also made it the most powerful of them. The best parts were those that painted the passions. Lines 65–115 of Act I had "great impetuosity of sentiment and lofty daring." Lines 109–115 on Cain's suicidal impulse, "though not very new," were "given with great vigour and felicity of expression." The reviewer admired and quoted Adah's wonderment at Lucifer's brightness (I, 502–519), Cain's forecast of mankind's future wretchedness (I, 431–457), part of the talk about Enoch (III, 10–34, 139–156), Eve's curse, and the closing lines (III, 545–561), which included Adah's exhortation and Cain's final cry of remorse, and which were rarely awarded the attention they merited.

On the other hand, since Byron's genius was romantic (a provoking use of this word), it erupted "into long metaphysical disquisitions, usually combining at once all that is most dry in prose, most pernicious in morals, and most absurd in poetry." The reviewer considered puerile the description of the leviathans in Act II. He disliked the characterization of Lucifer and held it inferior to Milton's depiction of his mighty, degraded prince. Lucifer was a quibbling demon, who resembled "a mortal sinner in his sophistry" and impiety, repeating stale arguments about the cause of evil and "the punishment of inherited sin." Adah's character alone was "well preserved throughout," for she kept "to the last her gentleness and her love unshaken."

This reviewer was exceptional in the closeness and accuracy of some of his observations. He noticed that Cain's morose disagreement with his family in the sunrise encounter revealed a mind "prepared for the baneful workings of the Prince of Darkness." He questioned Adah's association of Lucifer's appearance with the stars, which looked as if they would be suns. The image was not "strictly appropriate" because it conveyed "a sense of the ambition of the fallen angel, far beyond the ken of Adah." Unlike several commentators, he recognized the function of Act II: the vision of former worlds intensified Cain's hostility and induced the catastrophe of the murder. His scrutiny of the crime and of Cain's remorse was unique. An excess of "short and smart dialogue" threw "a sort of wordy contest . . . about the act of blood." His objection to the psychology was contrary to the usual impression.[15] Byron, he thought, did not adequately describe "the operation of the hue and aspect of Death on the first murderer." When he had Abel forgive his brother long after he had been struck to the ground, he interrupted Cain's "grand and imposing contemplation of death." The *European* critic was the only one that I recall who praised Cain's supposition that Abel's silence was mockery and that his brother was sporting with him. He wished the poet had then passed "from this delusion, by slow gradations, to the dreadful certainty" that what Cain saw was death.

The article had too little analysis, for religious convention compelled the reviewer to recur to Byron's "indefensible tirades against the Al-

[15] The writer's judgment was erratic. He preferred *The Two Foscari* to *Sardanapalus.*

mighty." The good passages in *Cain* were only "the bright stars of a black night," glimmering through the stormy clouds, "lamps to a sepulchre," and "the dismal fires of a charnel-house." *Cain* was therefore the most "frightful production" the reviewer had ever read. He concluded by surmising that Sir Walter Scott as a poet would welcome the dedication, but that as a Christian "he must regret the distinction and shrink from the defilement."

The London Magazine:

Thomas Noon Talfourd[16] [unsigned]. "Sardanapalus, The Two Foscari, and Cain, By Lord Byron," V (January, 1822), 66–71

Talfourd's liberal politics, his religious decorum, and his journalistic competence produced one of the few complex articles that appeared in 1822 on Byron's dramas. He approved of the poet's "legitimate defiance" of "all established opinions and prejudices." Byron's "whole course has been one marvelous deviation from the beaten track of laureled bards." He was therefore ironical about Byron's conservative activities: his recent eulogy of Pope, his change "from the wild to the austere," and his playing "the rhetorician's part," as a patron of the unities and a "champion of dramatic coherence after the straitest sect in criticism." The change was not "the result of any principle harmonizing" the poet's faculties, but was a whimsical endeavor at a different style, undertaken, as Byron had done everything, with the pride and confidence of an aristocrat. The tame regularity of the historical tragedies should be no surprise after the irregular spirits of *Manfred*. This was the expected turn of a genius "with rank to sustain his excesses" and without self-discipline "to dispose into harmonious creations the vast elements within him."

The resentment of a commoner pervaded the first long paragraph of the article. Byron continually changed his poetic costumes, but all of them were those of a self-conscious aristocrat. The current one came from the courtly French stage. In an amusing survey of Byron's postures in the verse tales, *Childe Harold, Manfred,* and *Don Juan,* the reviewer everywhere saw an egotistical lord, "this Alcibiades of our literature," who had "little regard for the common sorrows of the people" but a haughty sensitivity to his own wrongs.

[16] William A. Coles discovered the authorship of this superior review ("Thomas Noon Talfourd on Byron and the Imagination," *K-SJ*, LX, Pt 2 [1960], 99). Though Coles was mainly interested in matters other than the section on *Cain,* he quoted one long passage from the introduction. My account of the *London* review was written before I read Coles' article.

His technical criticism of the plays was a general but severe expression of his dislike of the usual qualities of "those English tragedies which are badly modeled on the bad imitations of the Greeks by the French" (p. 67). His best observation was that which Orsino made about the Cenci family: they were addicted to garrulous introspection. Byron, he thought, too often relied on this sluggish method of characterization.

Talfourd admired two merits: the sympathetic and individual development of the women and the representation of natural grandeur, which he contrasted to Wordsworth's sensitive response to the "meanest flower" and the "lowliest path."

This introductory part of the review is superior in content and style to most of the 1822 notices of Byron's volume. In scope, in political bias, in the mingling of praise and blame, and especially in the witty imagery, the parallel structure, and the driving rhythm of its sentences, it resembles the critical writing of Hazlitt, and is here reproduced entire:

> "Once a jacobin, always a jacobin," was formerly a paradox; "but now the time gives it proof." "Once an aristocrat, always an aristocrat" might pass, with as little question, into a proverb. Lord Byron, who has sometimes sought to wrap himself in impenetrable mystery, who has worn the fantastic disguises of corsairs, giaours, and motley jesters, now comes out in all the dignity of his birth, arrayed in a court suit of the old French fashion, with the star glittering on his breast, and the coronet overtopping his laurels. The costume only has been changed, the man has been the same from the first. He has played off his most romantic vagaries from mere recklessness of will, in legitimate defiance of the world. When he sneered at human glory, at patriotism and virtue, put religion aside as an empty name, and scoffed at immortality as a "tale that is told," his rank gave him confidence and success. If he ranged over the mournful scenes of classic desolation, and called up the spirit of their old magnificence, he appealed almost exclusively to aristocratic sympathies. If he sought to represent the violence of passion as justifying its own excesses—to command admiration for the darkest spirits—or to bid a proud defiance to all established opinions and prejudices, he dared scarcely less as a lord than as a poet. In his very scorn of kings and rulers, there has been little regard for the common sorrows of the people; but a high feeling of injured dignity, a sort of careless ferocity, like that of Cataline amidst his hated foes and his despised supporters. On a lonely rock amidst the storm, in the moonlight shadows of the Colosseum, or pensively musing on the sad and silent shores of Greece, his nobility is ever with him. And now this Alcibiades of our literature, who has set all rules at defiance,

who thought it sport to drag the critics "panting after him in vain," whose whole course has been one marvelous deviation from the beaten track of laureled bards, comes forth with his eulogies on Pope, and is pleased to patronize the unities! He who breathed about "Manfred" its mighty mysticism, and there mingled in splendid confusion the spirits of various superstitions, now appears as the champion of dramatic coherence after the straitest sect in criticism. The "chartered libertine," who has made humanity a jest—who has scoffed not only at the forms and creeds of the pious, but at all which raises man above the dust on which he tramples—to whom the spirit of poetry even in himself has been a thing to mock at—now plays the rhetorician's part; discovers ethical poetry to be the finest thing in the world; and the author of that piece of shallowest philosophy, the Essay on Man, to be the first of ethic poets! This is the natural course of a man who has great powers, and great pride, with rank to sustain his excesses, and without that presiding and majestic faculty which would enable him to be master in his own heart, and to dispose into harmonious creations the vast elements within him. His present change, from the wild to the austere, is not the result of any principle harmonizing his faculties; but only a rash excursion into another style. Like a military adventurer drunk with glory, he rushes with half his forces into a strange country, trusting to his fortune and his name to defend him.

There are two of Lord Byron's characteristic excellencies which he never leaves behind in his most fantastic expeditions, and which he has accordingly brought into his new domain of classic tragedy. One of these is his intense feeling of the loveliness of woman—his power, not only of picturing individual forms, but of infusing into the very atmosphere which surrounds them the spirit of beauty and of love. A soft roseate light is spread over them, which seems to sink into the soul. The other faculty to which we allude is his comprehensive sympathy with the vastest objects in the material universe. There is scarcely any pure description of individual scenes in all his works; but the noblest allusions to the grandeurs of earth and heaven. He pays "no allegiance but to the elements." The moon, the stars, the ocean, the mountain desert, are endowed by him with new "speech and language," and send to the heart their mighty voices. He can interpret between us and the firmament, or give us all the sentiment of an everlasting solitude. His power in this respect differs essentially from that of Wordsworth, who does not require an over-powering greatness in his theme, whom the "meanest flower" can move to sweetest thoughts, to whom all earth is redolent with divinest associations, and in whose lowliest path beauty is ever present, "a simple product of the common day."

> We believe that we may safely refer to one or other of these classes of beauty and grandeur almost every passage in the tragedies before us which deserves a place in the memory. Excepting where these occur, the plays appear to us "coldly correct, and critically dull." They abound in elaborate antitheses, frigid disputations, stately common places, and all the lofty trifling of those English tragedies which are badly modeled on the bad imitations of the Greeks by the French. There is little strongly marked character, little picturesque grouping, and scarcely any action. For pages together of laboured dialogue, the fable makes no progress—but the persons develop their own characters with the most edifying minuteness. We almost wish the rule of our law, that no man shall be a witness for or against himself, were rigidly applied to the drama. In the French courts of justice, and on the French stage, the rule is otherwise; but we need not desire to imitate the taste of our neighbours in criminal jurisprudence or in tragedy.

Talfourd did not apply all these strictures to *Cain*, which he considered to be "of a higher order" than the classical tragedies. His column and a half[17] on the play is less impressive than the introduction. He conformed to the religious convention of his era: Byron conducted the theological argument and the "direct attacks on the goodness of God" with "frightful audacity" and these could not be reprinted. Though the language of *Cain* sometimes shocked him, he remained calm and joined the exceptional company of *The Examiner, The Monthly Magazine*, and Harroviensis, imputed no intentional impiety to the author, and was not apprehensive about its social peril. To the contrary, applying a phrase from Wordsworth's "Ode," he regarded Cain's "obstinate questionings" as a common experience of mature minds and a beneficial expression of the human yearning for immortality.

His main criticism was that Byron did not design a dramatic conflict but wrote a nondramatic dialogue, in which the people were desembodied abstractions, exponents of banal thoughts, describers of spatial landscapes,

[17] Wright reprinted a portion of these paragraphs on *Cain,* without indicating his omissions and with several inaccuracies (XIV, 106–107). He attributed the passage to "Mr. Campbell's Magazine," by which I think he meant *The New Monthly.* Thomas Campbell became its editor in 1821. Wright also assigned two passages that he quoted from *The Monthly Magazine* to "Mr. Campbell's Magazine" (see the section on *The Monthly Magazine*).

Though Elmer L. Brooks discussed many of the *London* articles on Byron, he only glanced at the reviews of the plays and did not mention the one on *Cain* ("Byron and the *London Magazine,*" *K-SJ,* V [1956], 49–67).

and spouters of impious discourse. Milton, on the other hand, with his "plastic power," had given a personal identity and a suitable environment to Satan and thus had surpassed Byron, who created only a speechmaker. Talfourd's reading must have been hurried for he ignored the varied traits that Byron developed in Cain and Lucifer.

He thought that Byron had restricted Cain's emotional range and had not "fulfilled our expectations of a gigantic picture of the first murderer; for there is scarcely any passion, except the immediate agony of rage, which brings on the catastrophe." Talfourd's summary of Lucifer's influence on Cain and of the vision of destruction in Act II contradicted this simple diagnosis of the homicidal motivation. The second clause in the following sentence also implied that Talfourd felt that strong undercurrents were at work in Cain, but he evidently missed them, for he was finally content with the immediate motive of fury: "He returns to earth, but his soul is unfitted for devotion; his prayers are impious, and his sacrifice is scattered to the winds; he rushes with wild rage to pull down the altar of his accepted brother, and kills him, because he resists his purpose" (p. 70).

The following excerpt contains the core of his objection to the characterization and to the metaphysics:

> This piece is essentially nothing but a vehicle for striking allusions to the mighty abstractions of Death and Life, Eternity and Time, for vast but dim descriptions of the regions of space, and for daring disputations on that great problem, the origin of evil. . . . The ground-work of the arguments, on the awful subjects handled, is very common place; but they are arrayed in great majesty of language, . . . They are not, perhaps, taken apart, bolder than some passages of Milton; but they inspire quite a different sensation, because, in thinking of Paradise Lost, we never regard the Deity, or Satan, as other than great adverse powers, created by the imagination of the poet. . . . The personal identity which Milton has given to his spiritual intelligences,—the local habitations which he has assigned them,—the material beauty with which he has invested their forms,—all these remove the idea of impiety from their discourses. But we know nothing of Lord Byron's Lucifer, except his speeches; he is invented only that he may utter them; and the whole appears an abstract discussion, held for its own sake, not maintained in order to preserve the dramatic consistency of the persons. He has made no attempt to imitate Milton's plastic power;—that power by which our great poet has made his Heaven and Hell, and the very regions of space,

sublime realities, palpable to the imagination, and has traced the lineaments of his angelic messengers with the precision of a sculptor. The Lucifer of "Cain," is a mere bodyless abstraction,—the shadow of a dogma; and all the scenery over which he presides is dim, vague, and seen only in faint outline. There is, no doubt, a very uncommon power displayed, even in this shadowing out of the ethereal journey of the spirit and his victim, and in the vast sketch of the world of phantasms at which they arrive; but they are utterly unlike the massive grandeurs of Milton's creation.

Talfourd then illustrated Byron's "uncommon power" of majestic language with two long quotations from Act II: i, 98–117; ii, 44–62.

The Monthly Review or Literary Journal:

"Art. IX. Sardanapalus, a Tragedy. The Two Foscari, a Tragedy. Cain, a Mystery. By Lord Byron. 8vo. pp. 439. 15s. Boards. Murray. 1821," XCVII (January, 1822), 83–98

This review, like the pamphlet by Oxoniensis, which preceded it by a few weeks, refused to go into detail about the content of *Cain.* After thirteen pages on the first two plays which included hundreds of lines from *Sardanapalus,* the writer allowed only two pages to the "aggravated horrors" of *Cain.* The three dramas were more than he could cope with. "The effect of all of them is rather grand, terrible, and horrific, than mollifying, subduing, or pathetic." He preferred tragedies that drew "floods of tears" to these of Byron that caused "shudders to stream along our backs" (p. 98).

The poet was a formidable giant in *Cain,* "for nowhere has he shewn more if so much imagination, boldness of character, subtilty of reasoning, or energy of dialogue." These merits were not widely acknowledged in 1822. Others in that year scoffed at the reasoning in *Cain* as superficial, objected to the characterization as unconvincing and monotonous, depreciated the dialogue as slow-moving and undramatic, and flouted the exploration of space and death as a juvenile fancy and a waste of words. The present reviewer belonged to that minority (e.g., Brydges) who praised the artistic values of *Cain* but deplored the subject of the drama and the author's destructive treatment of it. Though he wondered why Byron wrote "these pages of impiety," he was able to detach some beauty from their "revolting features" and to quote two, and only two, speeches. Adah's description of her child's joy (III, 140–156), and Abel's prayer before the altar (III, 223–244).

He was fairer than certain other moral critics, for he conceded that Byron had opposed the heterodoxy of Cain and Lucifer with the piety of his kinfolk and, better still, had wreaked justice on the murderer, adhered to "historic record," placed the mark on his forehead, and sent him "an outcast over the globe." But the spiritual damage of the drama was irrevocable: "the horrible career of the Evil Spirit and of Cain is unchecked, and their sad reasonings remain uncontroverted" (p. 97). There was thus more bad than good in the play, and the reviewer wished it had been written in sport, for to be in earnest made the offense more dreadful.

Without undertaking a comparison of *Cain* and *Paradise Lost*, he complained that Byron had failed to overcome the difficulties inherent in his subject, which Milton had eluded with skill and propriety. Byron's statement that he had not been as free with scripture as the medieval plays had been was unavailing, because "that which is wrong is wrong, though greater wrongs be done, and precedent is no plea for crime" (p. 97).

The reviewer wanted to hurry over this "war on Heaven" and would not discuss Eve's "powerful curse. . . . We are choaked with curses in the Mystery of Cain—Let the curtain drop, to rise no more upon such scenes!" (p. 98).

The Edinburgh Magazine and Literary Miscellany; a New Series of the Scots Magazine:

"Sardanapalus, a Tragedy—The Two Foscari, a Tragedy—Cain, a Mystery. By Lord Byron. 8vo. pp. 440," X (January, 1822), 102–114 [The comments on *Cain* are confined to pages 110–114.]

This reviewer used an arsenal of literary recollections but with only random polemical advantage. He quoted Shakespeare on suicide, Swift on freethinkers, Shelley on aerial fantasy, Latin authors five times, and Greek once; and all of them he aimed reproachfully at Byron. To his sophisticated taste, the irreligion of *Cain* was not only unscriptural and unphilosophical, but lacking in wit and novelty. Byron was not ingenious enough to rescue his "hackneyed walks" from disgust. Profanity was the easy occupation of shallow minds. The reviewer directed at the poet Swift's taunt that some intellectuals would never shine if Christianity were abolished, for then they would lose the only object they could rail at. He shrewdly surmised that Byron's attack on theology in *Cain* and on marriage in *Don Juan* proceeded from insecurity or, "evil conscience," and that this uneasiness might lead to an eventual change (p. 113).

Several passages drew particular disapproval. Cain's insolence toward his father should have been chastised (p. 110). The first soliloquy was perverse, and the conversation with Lucifer "a tissue of ignorance and vanity, of pretension and contradiction." How could Byron have published it had he read Milton since the age of twenty? The hero's loathing of the instinct of self-preservation (I, 109–115) was psychological nonsense. If misfortune caused a man to hate life, then the desire to die overcame the desire to live. The Romans never hesitated to quit the world when they hated it (p. 111).

The travels of the second act were a "gross and senseless piece of machinery." To transport a body through space snuffed out sublimity as quickly as when you sang "of a man tossed in a blanket. Flesh and bones must have standing ground" (p. 111). The critic preferred Hogg's "Pilgrims of the Sun, " that sent Mary Lee swinging through the ether. Our imagination could accept her flight because lightness, airiness, and fancifulness were feminine properties. Though the reviewer may have smirked at Hogg and Byron, he was serious—and among the periodical writers eccentric—in his praise of Shelley, whose name he misspelled. He set three passages from the spirit's flight in *Queen Mab* (I, 207–224; II, 68–82, 252–257) against two from the journey in *Cain* (II, i, 34–42, 98–109). Shelley was as musical as "Apollo's lute," while Byron labored to imitate Milton (p. 112).

The frivolity of this critic's disdain had the acrid savor of the "Noctes Ambrosianae" in *Blackwood's*. The sally into Hades seemed to him so absurd that the poet would have done better had he let Cain and Lucifer lie face down on the earth, "pressing their eyelids hard with their middle-fingers, and then rehearsing, in harsh lines of seeming verse, the wonderful apparitions of their inward eyes" (p. 112). Byron must not have believed in the existence of the Devil, or he would not have made him speak (I, 383–390) in blank verse that rattled "along like a coal-waggon." Indeed the verse in the whole volume was "almost as bad as possible." Our Scotsman even mocked the "watery words" of Adah's compassion (I, 517– 519): "That's a good child, now. Eat your bread and butter, and I'll give you a kiss" (p. 111).

The talk of father and son was ungracious and undramatic (I, 22–29), and nowhere in the drama could this reader find any poetry to atone for the unnatural situations and for the deformity of thought and feeling. The cause for the faults in style and substance was the subject itself. Byron had wasted his talent on repulsive material. Therefore the reviewer urged the poet to renounce his fantastical dreams, "be himself again," and work diligently lest through pride, haste, and negligence, he repeat the crude failure of Charles Churchill (pp. 113–114).

Blackwood's Edinburgh Magazine:

Siluriensis [John Matthews]. "Lord Byron," XI (February, 1822), 212–217 [For a list of the other articles in this magazine during 1822 see the Bibliography. Their authorship has been identified by A. L. Strout, *A Bibliography of Articles in Blackwood's Magazine, 1817–1825*, pp. 91–103.]

There is no more tangible evidence of the magic of Byron's name than the almost monthly disfavor that *Blackwood's* handed him during 1822. Some of the contributors were unusually tolerant, were opposed to censorship, and mocked at those who found the poem a social menace. The articles were remarkable (1) for their variety in tone, ranging from moral seriousness to witty capers and sarcastic and violent abuse of Byron's faults, and (2) for the variety of their judgments, two notices by Maginn being almost sympathetic. In J. G. Lockhart's unsigned January notice of "Lord Byron's Three New Tragedies," he grumbled about the attack on Southey that Byron had appended to *The Two Foscari,* and wrote only one damning sentence about *Cain*: it contained "five or six passages of as fine poetry as Lord Byron ever wrote," but was "a wicked and blasphemous performance, destitute of any merit sufficient to overshadow essential defects of the most abominable nature." The verse was lax and lumbering (XI, 91).

Lockhart returned to *Cain* in three later issues. At the end of the year ("Odoherty on Werner") he slapped at all the plays and was caustic about *Cain's* crude metaphysics, threadbare blasphemy, and puerile raving. It was an audacious but ineffectual insult to the faith of Christians. "Cain was abandoned to the Radicals" and was too dull to be popular among them. He tolerated the domestic passages and the occasional flashes of poetry in Cain's contemplation of the stars (XII, 711–712).

In July, over the signature of T. Tickler, he rejoiced because the piracy of *Cain* had depleted Murray's profit. Lockhart jeered at the *Quarterly*'s fuss over the Chancellor's judgment. He could not imagine what harm the "dreamy mysticism" of Cain would do (XII, 98–99).

Lockhart's cleverest article was a hoax in the first of the "Noctes Ambrosianae" in March. *Cain,* he wrote, had created little sensation because the parsons around Mr. Murray's shop were too tractable. He disagreed with the Lord Chancellor and denied that the play was blasphemous. If *Cain* were prosecuted, "the humbug of the age will then have achieved its most visible triumph." Then he printed a versified letter from Byron to Murray. The actual letter of February 8 Murray had sent to the newspapers. Lockhart pretended that Byron had written the verse and that one of Murray's parsons had turned it into prose for the papers. Later in this dialogue article, he awarded the palm to *Sardanapalus* and found *Cain* "sceptically disputatious" (XI, 357 ff.).

During the year, *Cain* was embalmed in two other bits of verse. In February, R. F. St. Barbe's doggerel, "Another Laddleful from the Devil's Punch Bowl," advised that Byron should have left Cain's "murderous fury" where he found it. Even Milton had faltered, and Byron did not have the talent to "play pranks" on Holy Writ ("Abstain from the topic," XI, 165, signed Blaise Fitztravesty). In the April "Critique on Lord Byron," John Matthews ("Palaemon") in a screed of alexandrines scoffed at the characters and situations of all the dramas. Those in *Cain* were painful and disgusting, and the metaphysics vile. A note chastised the prosody (XI, 459–460).

In the same issue a "Letter from Paddy" by Eyre Evans Crowe scorched *Cain* for two columns as stupid and influenced by Shelley's atheism, but marvelled that Oxoniensis took such schoolboy impieties seriously. Any university wrangler could squelch Lucifer, who was bad at logic, neither a noble nor a villainous fiend, who did nothing, had neither poetry nor character, and was a "sneaking, talking devil," inferior to Milton's Beelzebub. Crowe discerned that the plays had political implications. Such cant about liberty might go well in Italy but was passé in England, where freedom was "solid and substantial" (XI, 462–465).

In June, George Croly (P.P.P.) in "Cambridge Pamphlets," predicted that the *Quarterly* would make a scapegoat of *Cain*. Meanwhile he was gratified that the *Edinburgh* had flagellated Byron for his insolent and profane principles. Croly thought the tragedies a miserable failure without living characters, but he wrote nothing specific on *Cain* (XI, 740–741). Another minor editorial note, signed C. North (possibly John Wilson or Lockhart) and attached to a February "Letter from London," said that Cain was reprehensible, but less obnoxious than *Queen Mab,* the *Cenci,* and *Epipsychidion.* This note protested the Chancellor's rejection of Murray's petition because now Benbow would send *Cain* on "teapaper into the pot houses," where it would be misunderstood (XI, 237–238).

William Maginn contributed two animated articles. In the fourth "Noctes Ambrosianae" of July, Odoherty had a lively chat with Byron in

Pisa. The poet explained that Lucifer talked in character as Satan did in Book V of *Paradise Lost* and that critics were unfair in tearing speeches out of their context to prove what was contrary to the writer's intention (XII, 104). In December, Maginn ("Tickler on Werner") called Heber's criticism of *Cain* elegant humbug; the censure was too gentle and the theological refutation of such a book superfluous and perhaps insincere—"a puff collateral" (p. 785).

The principal article of the year, written by John Matthews, appeared in February. One of its distinctions was a criticism of Byron's inadequate motivation of the murder: Byron relied on innate depravity as a cause of the crime. Matthews did not take the journey to Hades seriously; the expedition was futile because Lucifer failed in his educational purpose, Cain being no better informed at the end than he was at the start.

The following excerpts represent the vigor and variety of Matthew's criticism:

> Our first parents, and their amiable son Abel, with their two daughters, are pleasingly drawn. The noble Lord has sufficient capabilities for this sort of painting . . . here it is introduced for the purpose . . . of giving contrast and relief to the favourite figures of Lucifer and Cain. . . . Cain is represented as innately, and inconceivably bad, though possessing a high degree of conjugal and parental affection. He violates the conclusions of probability and experience, which declare that bad men must gradually be drawn to the acme of wickedness. Adam is shewn to have inculcated good principles, and particularly a respectful veneration for the great Creator, into his offspring. His eldest son must therefore have been initiated, from his infancy, in offering this grateful adoration. Cain, however, boasts, that he never as yet bowed to his father's God. . . . what could be the writer's object in that part of the diabolical colloquy between these kindred spirits, in which the innocent Adah is made to join, when the present and future relation betwixt brother and sister is alluded to? Again, when the evil spirit throws out arguments to prove that the Creator delights in evil rather than in good, Cain receives his doctrine with silent acquiescence. . . .
>
> No poetical flight was ever more weak and impotent than the long progress which this *par nobile,* the dæmon and his pupil, take through the immense regions of space. Previous to this aerial excursion, Lucifer tells Cain—"If thou dost thirst for knowledge, I can satiate/ That thirst." All, however, that he imparts, is a view of the planetary orbs in motion, and a peep into the dark confines of Hades, where præ-adamite shadows are enveloped in

fog, so that they seem to be sights scarcely worth the trouble of so long a journey.

The only distinct object in this misty limbo is an immense snake, which seems espied from the sea serpent of good Bishop Pontoppidan. The crakan is, however, omitted, which might also have been as well employed to enliven his phantom of an ocean. If the travellers do nothing, and see little, they talk a good deal. . . . He employs the time in plying his companion with sceptical notions on the nature of the Deity, of his government, and his works, and on the nature of man. . . . These questions might perhaps have been as well mooted on terra firma, and the young traveller seems to have had but little satisfaction in his jaunt, or to have at all slaked his thirst for knowledge. . . . He therefore very naturally expresses his disappointment.

On descending to the terrestrial sphere the poet is now within his compass; but whether he ranges through unknown space, or treads the firm set earth, he is equally ready to throw his dart at revealed religion. Even in a conversation between Cain and his gentle Adah, he contrives to introduce a scoff at the Christian doctrine of atonement. On all occasions throughout this poem his end and aim appears to be to perplex his readers by starting doubts necessarily inexplicable to human understanding, and insinuating opinions derogatory to the veneration we owe to the Divine Being, and filling their minds with discontent at the nature which it has pleased Infinite Wisdom to bestow on mankind. (pp. 215–217)

Matthews expressed the common disapproval of Byron's metrical and verbal techniques:

Abundant, indeed, are the instances of lame and prosaic lines which are given, for the most part accurately measured into the length of blank verse. If his better skill had not been proved in many parts of these metrical dialogues, we should be tempted to believe that the poet conceived the counting of ten syllables on his fingers, was all that was required to constitute this species of rhythm [p. 214]. . . . the same slovenly haste may be detected in the Mystery as in the preceding compositions. The final adverbs, conjunctions, and prepositions, abound here as before, and the same occasional undignified modes of expression. In the prayer of Abel we have "but yet accept it *for*/ The thanksgiving of him who spreads it *in*/ The face of thy high heaven" [III, 240–242]. In the very finish of the fratricidal catastrophe, Adah, when she is labouring with an idea not very natural to her gentle bosom, observes rather familiarly, "If I thought that he would not, I would." (pp. 216–217)

Matthews closed by wishing that Byron would take more care in revision. Haste and heaviness "will perhaps gradually sink his fame to a more reasonable level, and thus will his errors do less mischief." If his mind were "imbued with better principles," he would be a benefit to the race, but, alas, he "labours under mental darkness of the most palpable obscurity."

The Edinburgh Review:

Francis Jeffrey or William Hazlitt[18] [unsigned]. "Art. V. Sardanapalus, a Tragedy. The Two Foscari, a Tragedy. Cain, a Mystery. By Lord Byron. 8vo. pp. 440. Murray, London, 1822," XXXVI, No. 72 (February, 1822), 413–452

Three months after this review appeared, Byron had not read it. He wrote Murray on May 17, 1822:

> I hear that the Edinburgh has attacked the three dramas, which is a bad business for *you*; and I don't wonder that it discourages you. However, *that* volume may be trusted to *Time*,—depend upon it. I read it over with some attention since it was published, and I think the time will come when it will be preferred to my other writings, though not immediately. I say this without irritation against the Critics or Criticism, whatever they may be (for I have not seen them); and nothing that has or may appear in Jeffrey's review can make me forget that he stood by me for ten good years, without any motive to do so but his own good will. . . .
>
> P.S.—If you think it necessary, you may send me the *Edinburgh*: should there be any thing that requires an answer, I will reply, but *temperately* and

[18] Since the authorship has been attributed to Hazlitt, P. P. Howe noted in his edition of the *Complete Works* that Hazlitt did submit to the *Edinburgh Review* an article on *Sardanapalus,* but that Jeffrey evidently rewrote it and claimed the essay in his *Contributions to the Edinburgh Review.* Howe could not assign particular passages to Hazlitt (XVI, 421). I surmise that parts of the introduction were derived from Hazlitt's ideas: the historical survey, the remarks on Byron's poetic style and characterization, and on the unsuitability of abstractions in poetry. Much of page 420 seems to be in Hazlitt's style. I doubt that the scolding of Byron's irreligion originated with Hazlitt. P. L. Carver argued against Jeffrey's authorship and was convinced by internal evidence that Hazlitt wrote the entire review, except "the first half of the second paragraph" ("Hazlitt's Contributions to *The Edinburgh Review,*" *The Review of English Studies,* IV [October, 1928], 387–389).

> *technically*: that is to say, merely with respect to the *principles* of the Criticism, and not personally or offensively as to its literary merits.[19]

On June 6, he wrote Murray he had read the article in Galignani's magazine and had not decided on a reply.[20] The review evoked some melancholy reflections in a letter to Isaac D'Israeli on June 10, 1822: "... all men—even to my grand patron Francis Jeffrey Esqre of the *E.R.* —have risen up against me and my later publications. Such is Truth! Men dare not look her in the face, except by degrees: they mistake her for a Gorgon, instead of knowing her to be a Minerva."[21] Hobhouse, who visited him in Pisa in September, recorded in his diary that Byron had been much hurt by the *Edinburgh* article.[22] The stanzas on Jeffrey in *Don Juan* (X, 16–17; XII, 16) and his later comment to Kennedy on the reviewer's fairness balanced the picture.[23]

Jeffrey began his critique with an historical survey of British drama and then depreciated the classical unities and Byron's desire to use them. Since the reviewer covered three plays, he generalized about their common poetic style, which he found diffuse, awkward, and labored. Then he made some strictures on the characterization that most later critics have accepted: Byron's people were monotonous, limited to a few types, which he had repeated in poem after poem. Jeffrey thought that this narrowness was due to Byron's inability or unwillingness to identify himself with diverse humanity.

Jeffrey denied that Byron could use literary precedent and the principle of dramatic consistency as a justification of Lucifer's attack on divine benevolence. This onslaught he regarded as the theme of the poem, and he regretted that Byron had provided no confutation, which the religious subject obligated him to do. The most thoughtful tenet that Jeffrey advanced in this section was one that Hazlitt maintained: philosophy and poetry were incompatible and abstractions made poor poetry. Byron's treatment of the origin of evil thus enlightened no one.

Jeffrey based most of his objections on the harm to the unreflecting public that the poem could do because it used emotional methods to com-

[19] *LJ*, VI, 64–65.

[20] *LJ*, VI, 76–77, 80–81. For his reply to Jeffrey's judgment that the plays were elaborate, see "Byron's View of His Play."

[21] *LJ*, VI, 89.

[22] John Cam Hobhouse, *Recollections of a Long Life*, III, 5.

[23] Kennedy, pp. 158–159.

municate bad ideas. *Cain* offended pious persons and perplexed simple minds. He expressed for all conservatives the dictum that poets should confine their poems "to the established creed and morality" or "to the *actual* passions and sentiments of mankind." He would never have admitted that these might include passions and sentiments contrary to law, convention, or the established creed. Since Cain's feelings were unorthodox and uncommon, the play should never have been written. Jeffrey would have banished from literature fantasy and individualism and all experimentation. In the community of modern letters this interdiction sounds as heretical as Byron's opinions did in 1822.

Jeffrey defined three qualities of Cain's mind: discontent, intellectual aspiration, and pessimism. He recognized Lucifer's dramatic function—the exacerbation of the "internal fury" that had long seethed in Cain. His most provocative comment was that Lucifer was "the personified demon" of Cain's own imagination. He concluded his general analysis with a consoling reflection on the moral of the play: pessimism had dreadful consequences.

Jeffrey's formidable reputation, the thoughtfulness of some of his remarks, and the facile dignity of his style merit publication of an extended excerpt (pp. 419–420, 437–439). According to R. A. Rice, this review has more historical importance than the others.[24] Jeffrey had praised Byron's earlier poems, even *Beppo.* His disapproval of the dramas may be taken as the turning point in the criticism of Byron's poetry in England. In spite of sporadic defenders, from now on until the 1870–1880's, his reputation among English critics went downward. *Cain* was Byron's Mont-St.-Jean, and Jeffrey fired one of the biggest guns at this literary Waterloo.

> . . . his late dramatic efforts have not been made carelessly, . . . they seem very elaborate and hard-wrought compositions; and this indeed we take to be their leading characteristic, and the key to most of their peculiarities.
>
> Considered as Poems, we confess they appear to us to be rather heavy, verbose, and inelegant—deficient in the passion and energy which belongs to the other writings of the noble author—and still more in the richness of imagery, the originality of thought, and the sweetness of versification for which he used to be distinguished. They are for the most part solemn, prolix, and ostentatious—lengthened out by large preparations for catas-

[24] Richard Ashley Rice, "Lord Byron's British Reputation," *Smith College Studies in Modern Languages,* Vol. 5, No. 2, pp. 14–16.

trophes that never arrive, and tantalizing us with slight specimens and glimpses of a higher interest scattered thinly up and down many weary pages of pompous declamation. Along with the concentrated pathos and home-struck sentiments of his former poetry, the noble author seems also, we cannot imagine why, to have discarded the spirited and melodious versification in which they were embodied, and to have formed to himself a measure equally remote from the spring and vigour of his former compositions, and from the softness and inflexibility of the ancient masters of the drama. There are some sweet lines, and many of great weight and energy; but the general march of the verse is cumbrous and unmusical. His lines do not vibrate like polished lances, at once strong and light, in the hands of his persons, but are wielded like clumsy batons in a bloodless affray. . . . it is apt, too, to fall into clumsy prose, in its approaches to the easy and colloquial style; and, in the loftier passages, is occasionally deformed by low and common images that harmonize but ill with the general solemnity of the diction. . . . the pieces before us are wanting in interest, character, and action:—at least we must say this of the last two of them—for *there is* interest in Sardanapalus—and beauties besides, that make us blind to its other defects. There is, however, throughout, a want of dramatic effect and variety; and we suspect there is something in the character or habit of Lord B.'s genius which will render this unattainable. He has too little sympathy with the ordinary feelings and frailties of humanity, to succeed well in their representation—"His soul is like a star, and dwells apart." It does not "hold the mirror up to nature," nor catch the hues of surrounding objects; but, like a kindled furnace, throws out its intense glare and gloomy grandeur on the narrow scene which it irradiates. He has given us, in his other works, some glorious pictures of nature—some magnificent reflections, and some inimitable delineations of character: But the same feelings prevail in them all; and his portraits in particular, though a little varied in the drapery and attitude, seem all copied from the same original. His Childe Harold, his Giaour, Conrad, Lara, Manfred, Cain, and Lucifer,—are all one individual. There is the same varnish of voluptuousness on the surface—the same canker of misanthrophy at the core, of all he touches. He cannot draw the changes of many-coloured life, nor transport himself into the condition of the infinitely diversified characters by whom a stage should be peopled. The very intensity of his feelings—the loftiness of his views—the pride of his nature or his genius, withhold him from this identification; so that in personating the heroes of the scene, he does little but repeat himself. It would be better for him, . . . if he would condescend to a more extended and cordial sympathy with his fellow-creatures; and we should have more variety of fine poetry, and, at all events, better tragedies. . . . it argues a poorness of genius to keep always to the same topics and persons; and that the world will weary at last of the most energetic pictures of misanthropes and madmen—outlaws and their mistresses! . . .

. . . though [*Cain*] abounds in beautiful passages, and shows more *power* perhaps than any of the author's dramatical compositions, we regret very much that it should ever have been published. It will give great scandal and offence to pious persons in general—and may be the means of suggesting the most painful doubts and distressing perplexities, to hundreds of minds. . . . It is . . . absurd . . . to observe, that Lucifer cannot well be expected to talk like an orthodox divine—and that the conversation of the first Rebel and the first Murderer was not likely to be very unexceptionable —or to plead the authority of Milton, or the authors of the old mysteries, for such offensive colloquies. The fact is, that here *the whole argument*—and a very elaborate and specious argument it is—is directed against the goodness or the power of the Deity, and against the reasonableness of religion in general; and there is no answer so much as attempted to the offensive doctrines that are so strenuously inculcated. The Devil and his pupil have the field entirely to themselves—and are encountered with nothing but feeble obtestations and unreasoning horrors. Nor is this argumentative blasphemy a mere incidental deformity. . . . It forms . . . the great staple of the piece—and occupies . . . not less than two-thirds of it;—so that it is really difficult to believe that it was written for any other purpose than to inculcate these doctrines . . . we do not think it fair, thus to argue [the origin of evil] partially and *con amore*, in the name of Lucifer and Cain; without the responsibility or the liability to answer that would attach to a philosophical disputant—and in a form which . . . doubles the danger. . . . Philosophy and Poetry . . . do not go very well together. It is but a poor and pedantic sort of poetry that seeks to embody nothing but metaphysical subtleties and abstract deductions of reason—and a very suspicious philosophy that aims at establishing its doctrines by appeals to the passions and the fancy. Though such arguments, however, are worth little in the schools, it does not follow that their effect is inconsiderable in the world. On the contrary, it is the mischief of all poetical paradoxes, that, from the very limits and end of poetry, which deals only in obvious and glancing views, they are never brought to the fair test of argument. An allusion to a doubtful topic will often pass for a definitive conclusion on it; and, clothed in beautiful language, may leave the most pernicious impressions behind. We therefore think that poets ought fairly to be confined to the established creed and morality of their country, or to the *actual* passions and sentiments of mankind; and that poetical dreamers and sophists who pretend to *theorise* according to their feverish fancies, without a warrant from authority or reason, ought to be banished the commonwealth of letters. In the courts of morality, poets are unexceptionable *witnesses*; they may give in the evidence, and depose to facts whether good or ill; but we demur to their arbitrary and self-pleasing summoning up; they are suspected *judges*, and not very often safe advocates, where great questions are concerned, and universal principles brought to issue. . . . We do not doubt that Lord Byron has written conscientiously, and that he is of opinion that the publication of his sentiments will not be disadvantageous to mankind. . . . we confess we think otherwise—and we too think it our duty to make public our dissent.

As to the question of the Origin of Evil, which is the burden of this misdirected verse, he has neither thrown any new light upon it. . . . It remains just where it was, in its mighty, unfathomed obscurity. His Lordship may, it is true, have recapitulated some of the arguments with a more concise and cavalier air, than the old schoolmen or fathers; but the result is the same. There is no poetical road to metaphysics. In one view, however, which our rhapsodist has taken of the subject, we conceive he has done well. He represents the temptations held out to Cain by Satan as constantly succeeding and corresponding to some previous discontent and gloomy disposition in his own mind; so that Lucifer is little more than the personified demon of his imagination: And farther, the acts of guilt and folly into which Cain is hurried are not treated as accidental, or as occasioned by passing causes, but as springing from an internal fury, a morbid state akin to phrensy, a mind dissatisfied with itself and all things, and haunted by an insatiable, stubborn longing after knowledge rather than happiness, and a fatal proneness to dwell on the evil side of things, rather than the good. We here see the dreadful consequences of not curbing this disposition (which is, after all, perhaps the sin that most easily besets humanity), exemplified in a striking point of view; and we so far think, it is but fair to say, that the moral to be derived from a perusal of this *Mystery* is a valuable one.

After this section Jeffrey quoted a generous number of samples, and wrote some expository, but few critical, remarks on them. He avoided offensive passages. The first part of the Cain-Lucifer dialogue he thought was "full of sublimity." Adah's account of the fascination Lucifer exercised over her was magnificent. But he apologized for quoting Cain's address to the Lord, venturing "on it, as the least obnoxious specimen of the prevailing tone of this extraordinary drama." Finally, Jeffrey acknowledged that the catastrophe was "brought about with great dramatic skill and effect."

The Manchester Iris; or, Literary and Scientific Miscellany:

Nemo. "*Cain,* a Mystery," I (February 23, 1822), 25–26

Nemo's ambivalence was similar to that of the *European Magazine,* but his praise was hackneyed, his discernment blurred, and his censure as portentous as that of the flustered clergymen, the *Literary Gazette, The Eclectic Review,* and *The British Critic.* Like Brydges, Philo-Milton, and *The Monthly Review,* he was bothered by a skittish contradiction: though *Cain* had artistic merit, it was poison to the soul. He crudely overstated Jeffrey's reluctant thesis: "I admire the genius of Byron; I lament its degradation." In his final sentence he recalled Ophelia's cry, "Oh! what a noble mind is here o'erthrown." The debasement of Byron's talents had begun with *Childe Harold* and continued with *Beppo* and *Don Juan,* a book that could be openly read only in a brothel. Here was a poet who might have been a blessing to the nation and to posterity, but who chose to become a calamity, and to demoralize all circles of society. The arrival of *Cain,* the *ne plus ultra* of libertinism, was a tribulation to all Christians and a savage triumph among infidels. The attacks of Hone and Carlile on the venerable institutions of England were impotent, but the Herculean powers of Byron could at least temporarily mislead unreflective minds. Disclaiming the malice and envy of other critics, Nemo reached for the rod only because Byron had assailed the sanctuaries of religion and morality.

When he began to look at *Cain* as literature, he saw little action or feeling. The virtuous people were as insipid as Cain himself said they were (I, 179–185). He accurately defined one purpose of the first act: Lucifer, the epitome of those metaphysical doubts that had disturbed men for ages, subtly and powerfully worked on Cain's discontent, but also shook the faith of readers who had not been "fortified against such attacks" (e.g., I, 137–147).

In his synopsis Nemo stepped gingerly along his checkered course, glancing at "poetical passages of the highest order [that were] mixed with revolting blasphemy." Unlike many of his contemporaries, when he came to Hades, he was not alarmed by Byron's use of Cuvier, nor contemptuous, and quoted without reprobation a few lines on cosmic destruction (II, ii,

80–86). With one exception, he skipped the utterances of the rebels that would be obnoxious to a pious public. His selection of purple patches was a blend of the familiar and a few that were not so popular with his colleagues. Among the former were Cain's quaking at the approach of Lucifer (I, 80–96), his delighted wonder at the stars (II, i, 98–113), and his love of natural beauty and of his sister (II, ii, 258–269); among the latter, Cain's dread of death (I, 269–281), his guilt for the woes of his descendants (I, 438–444), and Adah's tribute to Lucifer's splendor and her compassion for his unhappiness (I, 507–519). He reprinted the murder dialogue and part of Cain's exclamation of bewilderment, and then remarked that it would have been more natural for Eve to mourn over her son's guilt than to curse him. Adam's conduct was consistent and Adah's irreproachable.

Though Nemo noticed that the drama closed with Cain's remorse and despondency over the body of his brother, he nonetheless concluded that Byron had abused his genius "to render mankind as miserable as himself," and to wrest from them "that belief which is their . . . support under all the trials and sorrows of this world." Therefore every parent, fearing lest his daughters "meet with some impure thoughts, or naked image of pollution," must have shuddered when they heard that Byron had published another poem.

The Monthly Magazine:

"Sardanapalus a Tragedy; the Two Foscari, a Tragedy; Cain, a Mystery. By the Right Hon. Lord Byron," LIII (February, 1822), 10–15

"The Philosophy of Contemporary Criticism," LV (February, 1823), 33

The second of the two *Monthly* articles disagreed with the *Quarterly's* stress on Byron's irreligion:

> The review of Lord Byron's *Dramas* deserves great praise, as a piece of able, candid, and temperate criticism. . . . These productions of Lord Bryon are spoken of with respect, but his genius is not considered to be eminently dramatic, a truth which the noble lord seems to be determined to establish more strongly by every successive publication. We should have liked this article better, if the reverend critic had not, in his remarks on "Cain" yielded a little too much to the habits of his profession. His sermon, in confutation of the many heresies of that mystery, is well composed; but it is too long, and, we think, misplaced and uncalled for. That God is good, and that

virtue is better than vice, are doctrines which are in no danger of an overthrow from Lord Byron, and which call for no extraordinary aid even from the Quarterly Review. Lord Byron's "Cain" represents only one of the many moods of mind; one, it is true, which inclines us to take a gloomy view of things; but which can only exercise a partial and occasional influence, and cannot, by any possibility, be exalted into a system, or received as a standard of faith. When Lord Byron writes as a poet, it really appears to us to be somewhat ludicrous to answer him with sound divinity.

The longer article, a year earlier, had taken the same stand.

Lord Byron, after the outcry raised against the morality of Don Juan, could not lay his hand upon a sacred subject without exciting the horror of certain scrupulous critics, who have accordingly professed themselves thunderstruck with the impiety and blasphemy of the "Mystery of Cain." Such an accusation is sheer nonsense; and it deserves no other reply. The work is not free, to be sure, from allusions to questions of the greatest difficulty and moment; but when a poet, in the person of Cain or Lucifer, adverts to the old puzzles of necessity and free-will, the origin of evil, and other venerable and inevitable dilemmas, it is ridiculous to assume an inquisitorial tone, and to convert a few passages of a speculative metaphysical character, into a serious charge of blasphemy and irreligion. (p. 10)

The sophistries of Satan might have hurt Cain, but they could not affect "the mind of a sober reader. The church is in no danger from these" (p. 13).

Though generally favorable, the only noteworthy feature of this review was its lofty refusal to take seriously Byron's moral and religious ideas or to let such matters affect its literary judgment. Otherwise the review was thin and superficial, giving only four of its eleven and a half columns to discussion, the remainder consisting of extracts—about 340 lines from the play with summary links. Byron, however, was satisfied. He wrote Murray, "I have only seen one review of the book, and that was in Galignani's magazine, quoted from the *Monthly*. It was very favourable to the plays, as Compositions."[25]

The opening paragraph made the common criticism of Byron's dramatic limitations, though it did not speculate as carefully as some others did about the reasons for his monotony in characterization. Byron's genius

[25] March 15, 1822, *LJ*, VI, 41.

had force but no variety and was incapable of "entering into every diversity of passion and of character" that drama requires. Byron by perseverance might overcome his native limitations, but the reviewer recommended that he turn to the kind of poetry he did more easily. *Cain* was the best of the three works, because the "unity of passion and simplicity of action" were suitable to the poet's powers (p. 10).

The reviewer's analysis of the six characteristics of Cain's mind that were manifest in the first ninety lines of the play was more definite and perceptive than most contemporary comment:

> This passage affords a key to the temper and frame of mind of Cain throughout the piece. He disdains the limited existence allotted to him; he has a rooted horror of death, attended with a vehement curiosity as to his nature, and he nourishes a sullen anger against his parents, to whose misconduct he ascribes his degraded state. Added to this, he has an insatiable thirst for knowledge beyond the bounds prescribed to mortality, and this part of the poem bears a strong resemblance to Manfred, whose counterpart, . . . Cain seems to be. He continues intractable, and desires to be left alone. (p. 10)[26]

The reviewer's comparison of Satan and Lucifer was limited to a few figurative generalities. Though both were charged with "fierce and bitter spleen," Lucifer is inferior to Satan, who "still has a tinge of heaven," whose stature is vast and solemn, and whose passions are heroic and suited to the solitude of Eden. Lucifer is less dignified and more abrupt, has more worldly knowledge, and is "at home in the busy walks of men" (p. 11).

His brief discussion of the great flight in Act II was mildly sarcastic, but

[26] This excerpt and the one alluded to in the next paragraph, comparing Satan and Lucifer, were reprinted by Wright (XIV, 20, 24) and attributed to "Mr. Campbell's Magazine." Thomas Campbell assumed the editorship of *The New Monthly Magazine* in 1821. Although he had been friendly toward Byron before and after the latter left England in 1816, he merely announced the publication of the 1821 volume of plays without comment (VI [February 1, 1822], 74). For the whole year of 1822, *The New Monthly* reviewed only *Werner* in the December issue (pp. 553–555), and in April printed Byron's letter of February 8 to Murray (pp. 161–162). Wright therefore erred in ascribing his quotations from the *Monthly* article to "Mr. Campbell's Magazine."

For a general account of the *Monthly's* treatment of Byron's poetry, see Wilfred S. Dowden's article, "A Jacobin Journal's View of Lord Byron," *Studies in Philology*, XLVIII (January, 1951), 56–66. He has one paragraph on the review of Byron's volume of plays.

he discerned that one of Byron's purposes was to have Lucifer work on Cain's mind:

> . . . there are some departed spirits which we should hardly have looked for, amongst which are gigantic apparitions of mammoths, with tusks like trees; the soul of a sea-snake, with head "ten times higher than the haughtiest cedar," apparently the progenitor of that which has lately infested the Atlantic; and, above all, "the phantasm of an ocean" itself, which, Cain sagaciously remarks, "looks like water"—in which the "past Leviathans" are disporting themselves. This exhibition seems well calculated to answer Lucifer's purpose in confounding Cain's understanding; and, accordingly, when he thinks the mystification has been carried far enough, he returns . . . to business, and [arouses Cain's jealousy of Abel]. (p. 12)

This critic liked and defined clearly Byron's contrasts in the domestic scene of Act III:

> The opening of the . . . act presents a scene of tenderness and beauty, powerfully contrasted with the horrors of its close. . . . The dark discontent of the father's temper gives additional effect to these beautiful touches of natural affection. The proud spirit, which nothing else can tranquillize, is melted into tenderness by the presence of the lovely infant. (p. 13)

At the end of his article the reviewer went along with the majority in objecting to the prosody:

> . . . the author indulges in a license of versification beyond all fair limits; and which would almost lead us to conclude that he first sketches his subject in prose, and afterwards reduces the composition, by a summary process, into blank verse. In his finest passages, however, his measure always improves into smoothness and harmony; and we see no reason why, in any place, he should affect a prosaic ruggedness, which is quite inadmissible into any composition which purports to be governed by even the loosest laws of poetical rhyme. (p. 15)

The British Review and London Critical Journal:

William Roberts [unsigned].[27] "Art. IV.—Sardanapalus, a Tragedy. The Two Foscari, a Tragedy. Cain, a Mystery. By Lord Byron. 8vo. Murray, London, 1821," XIX (March, 1822), 72–102

[27] John Olin Hayden in his dissertation ("The Reviewers of British Romantic Literature 1802–24," pp. 81–82) cited the testimony of Roberts' son, Arthur, who stated that all the articles on Byron's works in *The British Review* were written

Like the article in *The Monthly Review,* this magazine gave more detailed comment to *Sardanapalus* and *The Two Foscari* than it did to *Cain* (only six of the thirty pages). Its criticism of Byron's versification, though aimed at the first play, was also relevant to *Cain.* Roberts had always doubted the "correctness of his lordship's poetical ear," had consistently found him "deficient in delicacy of perception, and fineness of tact." Now he declared that Byron had "retrograded into the flattest province of prose," had broken up the continuity of blank verse by "subdivisions of the dialogue" and robbed it of all rhythm. Along with a few others, he noted Byron's "predilection for a pronoun, or other familiar monosyllable, at the end of his line; and particularly the capital I is so frequently found in that place, that it seems as if its columnal shape recommended it as a proper terminus" (p. 78). He also objected to Byron's methods of enjambment, ending one line with a preposition and beginning the next "with the noun it governs; and the same divorce between the adjective and substantive is perpetually occurring." He listed a number of the words that Byron repeatedly used at the end of lines: *and, if, no, such, which, with, ay, both, is, his, 'tis, has.* Without specifying other mannerisms, the reviewer asserted that Byron had violated "every rule which the ear of harmony has established" (pp. 81–82).

His commentary on the substance of *Cain* was not so detailed as his discussion of the verse or of the characterization in the other plays. He was more detached than some other reviewers and did not attribute to Byron all the opinions of Cain and Lucifer, and noted without indignation that Byron had given them ingenious arguments without providing refutation. He did dislike some of Lucifer's attacks on the deity, which he identified as borrowings from Bayle and Voltaire.

Roberts admired the vigorous drawing of Cain's character and that part of Act III in which Cain contended with Adah, but thought that in the first two acts Byron had not given the devil his due and had sacrificed dramatic interest by reducing his diabolical nature and by making him a sympathetic character—"elegant, pensive, and beautiful, with an air of sadness and suffering that ranks him with the oppressed, and bespeaks our pity" (p. 96).

---

by his father (*The Life, Letters and Opinions of William Roberts* [London and St. Albans, 1850], pp. 37–38).

Wright (XIV, 43–44) incorrectly attributed to *The British Critic* a quotation from this article on the sympathetic characterization of Lucifer (p. 96).

He maintained in a jocular manner that though the distribution of the play in cheap editions ought to cause Byron some remorse, there should be no worry over the moral damage it might do, first because it was too dull to appeal to many readers and second because Byron's devil was such a melancholy aristocrat that the populace would not take to him.

Like all the Tories, Roberts could not deal humorously with Byron's Preface, and the chief defect of his discussion of *Cain* is that he shovelled up a heavy load of biblical texts to refute Byron's statement that the Old Testament did not allude to immortality. He also joined the company of his orthodox contemporaries in objecting to Byron's belief that it was the serpent and not Satan that seduced Eve.

As a whole this review was less severe with *Cain* than with the other plays and is exceptional mainly because it found a great deal more to condemn in them than in the religious play.

The Eclectic Review:

"Art. II. 1. Cain, a Mystery. By Lord Byron. 12 mo. London, 1822," XVII (May, 1822), 418–427 [The article also reviewed Robert Southey's *The Vision of Judgement.* The author was tentatively identified by John Wright as Robert Hall (XIV, 29).]

This reviewer reflected on Byron's reasons for publishing such an unorthodox work as *Cain* and flippantly concluded that Byron wanted to bait the Lord Chancellor and to test the freedom of the press. The principal topic that he discussed seriously was the familiar one of impiety. He deplored the lack of rebuttal of Lucifer's comments, the attractive qualities that Byron had given Lucifer, the wholesale falsification of religious truth, the repeated assertion of the prevalence and triumph of evil, and the denial of God's benevolence. In making poetry out of insoluble ethical problems, Byron was on the side of the devil, luring untrained minds to their ruination. One comment that revealed the reviewer's anti-intellectual bias concerned the damage that curiosity can do. He saw that the purpose of Lucifer's indoctrination of Cain was to prepare the young man for fratricide. But he objected to Byron's arousing our sympathy for the murderer and argued that, in his conception of an heroic victim, Byron was following the bad precedent of the Greek tragedians.

To impute motives to any writer, is seldom justifiable; and yet, it is impossible that the motives of the author of Cain . . . could be good. . . . we cannot help suspecting that his Lordship was disposed to put the liberty of the press in this country, in reference to irreligious works, to a fair trial. . . . For this purpose, he seems here to have thrown down the gauntlet to Mr. Attorney General; and we can easily imagine that he laughs in his sleeve at the silent consternation produced by his challenge; that he secretly enjoyed the solemn perplexity of the Lord Chancellor, when the application for an injunction against the pirated edition came before the Court, and when Cain was gravely paralleled with Paradise Lost; and that, most of all, he laughs at the awkward situation in which he has placed the Poet Laureat, as at once his rebuker and his fellow culprit. . . . who would envy him the utmost gratification he can derive from his diabolical joke? (p. 419)

But the impiety chargeable on this Mystery, consists mainly in this; that the purposeless and gratuitious blasphemies put into the mouth of Lucifer and Cain, are left unrefuted. . . . the arguments, . . . levelled against the wisdom and goodness of the Creator, are put forth with the utmost ingenuity. And it has been his Lordship's endeavour, to palliate as much as possible the characters of the Evil Spirit and of the first murderer; the former of whom is made an elegant, poetical, philosophical sentimentalist, a sort of Manfred; the latter an ignorant, proud, and self-willed boy. Lucifer, too, is represented as denying all share in the temptation of Eve. . . . It is not necessary to combat this monstrous absurdity with a serious argument. Lord Byron disbelieves the whole Scripture narrative. . . .

[The reviewer was aroused by I, 200–202 ("an insidious falsehood"), to sermonize on the danger of curiosity:]

Innocence is *not* the cause of curiosity, but has in every stage of society been its victim. Curiosity . . . has ruined greater numbers than any other passion; and as, in its incipient actings, it is the most dangerous foe of innocence, so, when it becomes a passion, it is only fed by guilt. . . .

Cain . . . is made, like the Faust of Goethe, to be the victim of curiosity; and a fine moral might have been deduced from it. . . . The Poet asserts again and again the prevalence and triumph of Evil; he imagines its having extended to former worlds; he seems to exult in the idea of its universal diffusion, as rolling on for ever, "A part of all things." He goes further than even the Manichean mystics. He . . . in the person of Lucifer, argues from the existence of Evil, against the benevolence of God. By this means, he prepares Cain . . . to become a fratricide; and he would fain beguile the reader into sympathy with him, as less a criminal than a victim. For all this, he might plead high Pagan precedents. To the old Grecian muse, this was the highest flight attainable—to soar above the vulgarities of Olympus, into the unfathomable darkness of metaphysical atheism, and there to shape to herself a blind, inert, implacable phantom deity under the name of Necessity or Fate. Lord Byron . . . has but attributed to their right author, the stale impieties of the old atheists. He has but put into the Devil's mouth the bewildering question, *Si Deus est, unde malum?* making poetry the organ of the dark and barren metaphysics of Bayle and Spinosa. But then he has done this in a manner which shews that he sides with the enemies of human happiness, and with the arch enemy who inspires and leads them on. He has summoned both fiction and falsehood to aggravate the philosophical difficulties . . . with which the young and inexperienced are ill able to grapple. These, this new apostle of infidelity has endeavoured to propagate in a shape the most adapted to make an impression on the imagination. In the very spirit of the fabled Sphinx, he propounds these dark enigmas, that those who fail to unravel them, may perish.

That this is a heinous offence against society, who will dare deny? . . . Lord Byron . . . is a blasphemer. (pp. 423–427)

The British Critic:

"Sardanapalus, a Tragedy. The Two Foscari, a Tragedy. Cain, a Mystery. By Lord Byron," XVI (May, 1822), 529–550

The introductory paragraphs were sarcastic about Byronic liberalism. The poet's eloquence about superstition and despotism was the Arcadian babbling of "a secure aristocrat" (p. 521). It was the reviewer's duty to tell the noble lord that nature and the wisdom of generations were not false and that "the reckless opinions of a few desperate young men" did not provide a good argument for a revolution in religion, laws, and manners.

There followed several moderately favorable paragraphs on *Sardanapalus,* a brief dismissal of the *Foscari,* some mockery of Byron's disclaimer of stealing an epithet from Lady Morgan, and two pages scolding Byron for his appendix on Southey.

The last ten pages were a disorganized and intemperate attack on the impiety of *Cain,* which the poet must have written "under the dominion of a temporary phrenzy" (p. 522). Though the reviewer's aim was to expose "the shallow sophistry, the gross ignorance, and the scandalous falsehoods" of the play, he refused to analyze it (that had been done in Chancery) or to comment on the nonsense of many parts (p. 530). He jumped on two statements in the Preface: Byron was wrong in maintaining (1) that the serpent was not the devil in disguise (e.g., Genesis never gave animals the gift of speech or of reasoning); and (2) that the Old

Testament said nothing about immortality (he quoted a few passages to prove that it did).

The one meagre contribution to literary criticism that the reviewer made was incidental to his attempt to refute Byron's defense that if he were blasphemous, Milton also was blasphemous. He wrote an incomplete and inexact exposition of the differences between *Cain* and *Paradise Lost.* Milton's purpose was "to assert Eternal Providence / And justify the ways of God to men." He gave three-fourths of his poem to praise of the deity. The reviewer used some excerpts to show that Milton had condemned Satan, whereas Byron approved of Lucifer as a friend to man and had him accuse God of being the source of human misery.

Overlooking some lines of *Paradise Lost,* he was inaccurate in stating that Lucifer's doubt of Jehovah's creativity was alien to Satan's thought. By a series of rhetorical questions, he pointed to other distinctions: Did Satan (like Lucifer) hesitate to appear and act as a tempter of Eve? Did he pretend to have a good motive for this temptation? Did he deny the goodness, justice, greatness, and happiness of God, as Lucifer did? Did Satan impute the evil of this world to God? Did he ascribe to himself the wish of diffusing good and happiness to mankind? Since Byron had Lucifer assert that he was co-eternal and co-equal with God and that he was a champion of freedom and waged everlasting conflict with the tyrant, Byron was clearly on the side of the devil. Why then did he object to being branded by Southey as a leader of the Satanic School (pp. 529, 535–537)?

And why did he make Cain so ignorant of matters he must have learned from Adam (e.g., that God created heaven and earth) that he could not debate with Lucifer about some of the latter's aspersions of Jehovah (p. 537)? These so agitated the reviewer that he was blind to Byron's psychological conception of Cain and utterly incapable of understanding his rebellion.

The article had nothing to say about *Cain* as literature. When the reviewer defended himself against the charge of bigotry and fastened that label on Byron, he unintentionally marked out the difference between them: "Is it no bigotry to set up the restless and disturbed imaginations of man before the undoubted testimony of God Almighty" (p. 537)? Byron and Cain were indeed afflicted with "restless and disturbed imaginations," and they did presume to question the rigid confidence of those who were certain about the testimony of supreme authority.

At the end of the article the writer returned to Byron's inconsistency:

he denied that he wanted revolution, but clearly hated England and did encourage it. The English people, however, would not be deceived or swayed by Byron's "effusions of misanthropy and sensuality," which were the consequence of a creed compounded of Manicheism and Epicureanism. For the public good, the court should have banned the book, and prosecuted and amerced the author and publisher.

The Quarterly Review:

Bishop Reginald Heber [unsigned]. "Art. X.—1. Marino Faliero, Doge of Venice, an Historical Tragedy.—2. Sardanapalus, a Tragedy.—3. The Two Foscari, a Tragedy.—4. Cain, a Mystery," XXVII (July, 1822), 476–524

"You had better not send me the *Quarterly* on *Cain,* as it can only be in the preaching style, and may make me answer or say something disagreeable."[28] Murray posted the magazine probably before he got Byron's letter. A month later (November 23) Byron sent it back unopened because he had decided not to read periodicals and gave the same reasons he had the preceding autumn.[29] Byron could not escape the *Quarterly,* however, for Galignani printed half of the piece (he had previously excerpted reviews from the *Monthly* and the *Edinburgh*). Byron wrote Murray that it was "extremely handsome, and any thing but unkind or unfair. . . . I liked what I read of the article much."[30] No comment appears in the correspondence on the second half, which Galignani planned to print in the next issue.[31] According to Medwin, Byron was caustic and cynical about Heber's essay and also about Murray's control of the magazine: as long as Murray published Byron's poetry, he kept the *Quarterly* from abusing his source of income. Byron predicted that after their rupture Murray would let the magazine attack him.[32] Murray was so angry

[28] Letter to Murray, October 24, 1822, *LJ,* VI, 130.

[29] See the introduction to this section.

[30] December 25, 1822, *LJ,* VI, 155–158. If he read only the first half, he had not yet seen the part on *Cain,* nor the section in which Heber preached about Byron's irreligion. Byron saw the remainder of the review and was discouraged by it. "I am the most unpopular writer *going*" (Medwin, p. 123). *Correspondence,* II, 223; *LJ,* VI, 171–173.

[31] No letter to Murray appears in the published correspondence for the year 1823. After the final break in their relationship (see letter of November 18, 1822, *LJ,* VI, 138), Byron seldom wrote to Murray.

[32] Medwin, pp. 169–171; *LJ,* VI, 143. Medwin and/or Byron were confused

at this and other things in Medwin's book that he issued his own reply. In it he denied that he ever exercised autocratic direction of the *Quarterly* and published a letter to show that he and Byron had remained on good terms.[33]

The review, a long one on *Marino Faliero* and the three plays in the 1821 volume, was written in a solemn, verbose, and ponderous style. Heber strongly objected to one of Byron's stylistic habits that others had also disliked:

> One source of feebleness . . . of frequent occurrence in all Lord Byron's plays, is his practice of ending his lines with insignificant monosyllables. *Of, to, and, till, but, from,* all occur in the course of a very few pages, in situations where, had the harmony or vigour of the line been consulted, the voice would have been allowed to pause, and the energy of the sentiment would have been carried to its highest tone of elevation. This we should have set down to the account of carelessness, had it not been so frequent, and had not the stiffness and labour of the author's general style almost tempted us to believe it systematic. A more inharmonious system of versification, or one more necessarily tending to weight and feebleness, could hardly have been invented. (p. 490)

Although he commented on Byron's dramatic theory, siding with the English in the dispute about the unities, his main interest in *Cain* was moral and religious. He preferred it to *Don Juan:*

> . . . the Mystery of Cain, wicked as it may be, is the work of a nobler and more daring wickedness than that which delights in . . . stimulating the

about the dates. According to Medwin, Byron said that three months after *Werner* was published the article in the *Quarterly* appeared. The latter came out in July, 1822, whereas *Werner* was not published until November, 1822. Indeed the copies of *Werner* and the *Quarterly* seem to have reached him at the same time in Italy. Though Byron's remarks about Murray were typical of him, they may be one of Medwin's unreliable reports. They vexed Murray, but the publisher's reply was not entirely convincing.

[33] *The Gentleman's Magazine,* XCIV (November, 1824), 438–442. Murray also printed his reply in a separate pamphlet of fifteen pages, a copy of which is in the Stark Library of The University of Texas at Austin. The letter referred to was that of December 25, 1822 (*LJ,* VI, 155–158). We should remember that when Byron wrote this letter, he had not seen the second half of the *Quarterly* article, and that Murray's use of the letter to demonstrate Byron's satisfaction with the review was misleading.

> evil passions, and casting a cold-blooded ridicule over all the lofty and generous feelings of our nature: and it is better that Lord Byron should be a manichee, or a deist,—nay . . . it is better that he should be a moral and argumentative atheist, than the professed and systematic poet of seduction, adultery and incest; the contemner of patriotism, the insulter of piety, the raker into every sink of vice and wretchedness to disgust and degrade and harden the hearts of his fellow-creatures. (p. 477)

Heber advanced through the play, summarizing, selecting "some of the finest and least offensive specimens," and writing more particular criticism of them and other passages than most of his contemporaries did.

He was unimpressed by the beginning of the drama. The family hymn had little merit and the "expostulation" over Cain's surliness was feeble. He also regarded two other major portions of the poem as artistic failures. The fantasy of Hades was a jumble of prehistoric mammals, "Preadamite giants," and phantoms of ruined worlds "with their mountains, oceans and forests, all . . . in a state of eternal suffering." This vision belonged to "that species of sublime, which is considerably less than a single step removed from the ridiculous." In Act III Heber found the sacrifice and quarrel scene "heavy and clumsily managed," and the commotion that followed, the Angel's charge, and the departure "hardly worth notice" (pp. 511–512).

Heber's belief that God required obedience and that conformity was therefore essential for happiness enabled him to agree with Byron's observation that God and society usually punished the rebel (I, 145–162): the "pervading *moral* . . . of the play" was that independent souls "are condemned by God to be wretched everlastingly" (p. 510).

His particular analysis raised many objections to Byron's psychology. He carped at the illogicality in having Cain exclaim about his ignorance of death and also talk about his brother's sacrifices at the altar, thus revealing that he did know "what was meant by the extinction of animal life" (p. 524). Heber was not able to follow Byron's complicated treatment of his hero. At the outset he accurately defined Cain's prevailing mood and its causes: anger and gloom because an existence embittered by toil and soon to be ended by death was the work of a deity who thereby deserved no thanksgiving (p. 509). But then he protested that Byron had not fully explained the causes of Cain's habitual gloom. Some circumstances were conducive to a contrary mood: his love of Adah and Enoch and the easy cultivation of the soil.

He found Byron's psychology muddled in the Hades section and argued that the effect of the trip on Cain would be awe or a decision to investigate the fortunes of God's friends, but certainly not to attack his brother, a fellow-sufferer. He did concede that Byron had prepared for Cain's sardonic abuse of the deity in Act III: "The spectacle [of Hades] has the effect of making Cain still more displeased with that God who creates in order to destroy . . . " (p. 512). But the motivation for the crime he thought unconvincing and declared that the murder would seem a surprise to one not already familiar with the story. Since Byron had not made Cain envious of, or hostile toward, his brother, the catastrophe was an incomprehensible shock. He approved only of the characterization of Adah.

The passage on incest Heber glossed over as neither worthy of, nor requiring, an answer (p. 510). He gave many pages to a confutation of Byron's irreligion. The play was an attack on providence. Byron had made God and the Devil exchange places, ascribing tyranny to the former and benevolence to the latter. Heber distinguished between true Manicheism and Byron's distortion of it: Byron had elevated the Evil Principle and relegated the Good. He complained with more fullness than others did that Byron had drawn Lucifer too sympathetically and had not provided any rebuttal to his arguments.

Though he did not accuse Byron of believing "the monstrous creed" he put into *Cain*, he did reproach him for wasting his talents libeling God. Heber was gratified, however, that the theological argument in Cain was "infirm and disjointed," based on the paradox that a benevolent creator would never have sanctioned the origin of evil and yet evil did exist. Heber dismissed the paradox and asserted simply that life was full of disagreeables.

The following extract is taken from pages 513–517 of his long article:

> . . . the event which is the catastrophe of the drama is no otherwise than . . . accidentally produced by those which precede it. Cain, whose whole character is represented in scripture as envious and malicious rather than impious;— this Cain, as painted by Lord Byron, has no quarrel with his brother whatever, nor, except in a single word, does he intimate any jealousy of him. Two acts and half the third are passed without our advancing a single step towards the conclusion; and Abel, at length, falls by a random blow given in a struggle of which the object is not *his* destruction but the overthrow of Jehovah's altar. If we could suppose a reader to sit down to a perusal of the drama in ignorance of its catastrophe, he would scarcely be less surprized

by its termination in such a stroke of chance-medley, than if Abel had been made to drop down in an apoplexy, and Cain to die of grief over his body.

Nor is it easy to perceive what natural or rational object the Devil proposes to himself in carrying his disciple through the abyss of space, to show him that repository, of which we remember hearing something in our infant days, "where the old moons are hung up to dry." To prove that there is a life beyond the grave was surely no part of his business when he was engaged in fostering the indignation of one who repined at the necessity of dying. And, though it would seem that entire Hades is, in Lord Byron's picture, a place of suffering, yet, when Lucifer himself had premised that these sufferings were the lot of those spirits who sided with him against Jehovah, is it likely that a more accurate knowledge of them would increase Cain's eagerness for the alliance, or that he would not rather have inquired whether a better fortune did not await the adherents of the triumphant side? At all events, the spectacle of many ruined worlds was more likely to awe a mortal into submission than to rouse him to hopeless resistance; and even if it made him a hater of God, had no natural tendency to render him furious against a brother who was to be his fellow-sufferer.

We do not think, indeed, that there is much vigour or poetical propriety in any of the characters of Lord Byron's Mystery. Eve on one occasion and one only expresses herself with energy, and not even then with any great depth of that maternal feeling which the death of her favourite son was likely to excite in her. Adam moralizes without dignity. Abel is as dull as he is pious. Lucifer, though his first appearance is well conceived, is as sententious and sarcastic as a Scotch metaphysician, and the gravamina which drive Cain into impiety are circumstances which could only produce a similar effect on a weak and sluggish mind, the necessity of exertion and the fear of death! Yet, in the happiest climate of earth and amid the early vigour of nature, it would be absurd to describe (nor has Lord Byron so described it) the toil to which Cain can have been subject, as excessive or burthensome. And he is made too happy in his love, too extravagantly fond of his wife and his child to have much leisure for those gloomy thoughts which belong to disappointed ambition and jaded licentiousness.

Nor, though there are . . . some passages in this drama of no common power, is the general tone of its poetry so excellent as to atone for these imperfections of design. The dialogue is cold and constrained. The descriptions are like the shadows of a phantasmagoria, at once indistinct and artificial. Except Adah, there is no person in whose fortunes we are interested; and we close the book with no distinct or clinging recollection of any single passage in it, and with the general impression only that Lucifer has said much and done little, and that Cain has been unhappy without grounds and wicked without an object. . . .

. . . It is not . . . a direct attack on Scripture and on the authority of Moses. The expressions of Cain and Lucifer are not more offensive to the ears of piety than such discourses must necessarily be, or than Milton, without offence, has put into the mouths of beings similarly situated. And though . . . the Atheists and Jacobins . . . circulate the work in a cheap form, among the populace, we are not ourselves of opinion that it possesses much power of active mischief, or that many persons will be very deeply or lastingly impressed by insinuations which lead to no practical result, and difficulties which so obviously transcend the range of human experience. . . .

The sarcasms of Lucifer and the murmurs of Cain are directed against Providence in general; and proceed to the subversion of every system of theology, except that . . . which holds out God to the abhorrence of his creatures as a capricious tyrant, and which regards the Devil . . . as the champion of all which is energetic and interesting and noble; the spirit of free thought and stern endurance, unbrokenly contending against the bondage which makes nature miserable.

This deification of vice; this crazy attachment to the worser half of Manicheism, we long since lamented to find . . . in some of the most powerful lines which have proceeded from Lord Byron's pen . . .

. . . if to represent, through three long acts, the Devil as sympathizing with the miseries of mankind and moralizing on the injustice of Providence; if to represent God as the unrelenting tyrant of nature; the capricious destroyer of worlds which he has himself created; the object of open flattery and of secret horror even to the celestial ministers of his will and minstrels of his glory; if this be not to transfer, from God to Satan and from Satan to God, the qualities by which, in the general estimation of mankind, they are most distinguished from each other, we must own ourselves very little skilled in the usual topics of praise or censure.

We should have done an essential wrong, however, to the most celebrated of ancient heretics, if we had designated this system as more than the worser half of the system of Manes. His followers,—though they imputed the prevalence of evil in the world to the inveterate and invincible obstinacy of that principle of darkness, which they supposed to share with God the empire of things, and to pervade and govern all material existence,—confessed, nevertheless, that the superior and supreme Intelligence was transcendantly wise and benevolent. They anticipated, in fullness of faith, the ultimate victory of this last over his malignant enemy, and looked forward to a future state of happiness and glory, where the souls of the good were to be delivered from the God of this world and the bondage of their corporeal prisons. But the theology of "Cain" is altogether gloomy and hopeless. His evil God is *the supreme*: his Hades exclusively a state of misery; the body of man is, on his system, ordained to nothing more than to labour, disease and death, and the soul is immortal only to be wretched. . . .

Of Lucifer, as drawn by Lord Byron, we absolutely know no evil: and, on the contrary, the impression which we receive of him is, from his first introduction, most favourable. He is indued not only with all the beauty, the wisdom and the unconquerable daring which Milton has assigned him, and which may reasonably be supposed to belong to a spirit of so exalted a nature, but he is represented as unhappy without a crime and as pitying our unhappiness. Even before he appears, we are prepared (so far as the poet has had skill to prepare us) to sympathize with any spiritual being who is opposed to the government of Jehovah. The conversations, the exhibitions which ensue are all conducive to the same conclusion, that whatever is is *evil*, and that, had the Devil been the Creator, he would have made his creatures happier. Above all, his arguments and insinuations are allowed to pass uncontradicted, or are answered only by overbearing force, and punishment inflicted not on himself but on his disciple. Nor is the intention less apparent nor the poison less subtle, because the language employed is not indecorous, and the accuser of the Almighty does not descend to ribaldry or scurrilous invective.

That the monstrous creed thus inculcated is really the creed of Lord Byron himself, we, certainly, have some difficulty in believing. As little are we inclined to assert that this frightful caricature of Deism is intended as a covert recommendation of that further stage to which the scepticism of modern philosophers has sometimes conducted them. We are willing to suppose, that he has, after all, no further view than the fantastic glory of supporting a paradox ably; of showing his powers of argument and poetry at the expense of all the religious and natural feelings of the world, and of ascertaining how much will be forgiven him by the unwearied devotion of his admirers. But we cannot, with some of our contemporaries, give him the credit of "writing conscientiously." We respect his understanding too highly to apprehend that he intended a benefit to mankind in doing his best to make them vicious and discontented; and we tell him, *"even more in anger than in sorrow,"* that the great talents which he has received are ill employed in writing a libel on his Maker, and that the dexterity which flings about firebrands in sport is no object of ambition to any but a mind perverted by self-opinion and flattery.

We return, however, to Cain, and it is some comfort to find that the argument, however plausibly put together, is as infirm and disjointed as poetic arguments are apt to be. It depends on the admitted fact that evil exists, and on the presumption that a wise and benevolent Deity would not have permitted its existence. And it is, consequently, levelled . . . not against the Mosaic account of the manner in which evil first appeared on earth, . . . but against the God by whom the present frame of things was constituted. It is not the Jehovah only, of the Christian or the Jew, against whom it may be alleged that he has created men to toil, to sicken and to die. If we admit a Creator at all, we must admit that he sends us into the world under this necessity; and any man, with whatever religious opinions, who dislikes these accompaniments of life more than he likes life with its countervailing advantages, may plead with Cain,—"I was unborn; / I sought not to be born, nor love the state / To which that birth has brought me!" (I, 67–69)

Oxoniensis [The Reverend Henry John Todd].[34] *A Remonstrance Addressed to Mr. John Murray, Respecting a Recent Publication.* London: F. C. & J. Rivington, 1822. 20 pp.

Byron soon heard about this tract and wrote to Kinnaird (February 6, 1822), "I know nothing of Rivington's remonstrance by the 'eminent Churchman,' but I suppose he wants a living." Two days later in a letter to Murray (February 8), he indicated that he had read the *Remonstrance,* for he quoted the Oxford gentleman's Miltonic phrase: "Evil, be thou my Good."[35] The dates of these letters and the fact that the December issue of the *Gentleman's Magazine* quoted from the pamphlet show that it was printed in December, 1821, perhaps before, or soon after, the offi-

[34] Todd received his B.A. from Oxford in 1784 and the M.A. in 1786. Appointed a royal chaplain in 1812, he was an active churchman and wrote "Original Sin, Free Will, and Other Doctrines" and a number of religious pieces. He was also interested in literary matters and produced editions of Milton, Spenser, and Johnson's dictionary. In 1822 he was Rector of Settrington in Yorkshire.

[35] *Correspondence,* II, 210–211; *LJ,* VI, 15–16. "An Oxonian has addressed a bullying letter to him [Murray], asking him how so moral a bookseller can stain his press with so profane a book?" (Medwin, p. 170).

cial publication date (December 19) of Byron's volume of plays. Its main merit was that its stimulated Harroviensis to a careful defense.[36]

The *Remonstrance*, which cannot be termed literary criticism, was given far more attention than it deserved, while the superior reply of Harroviensis was neglected. John Wright printed five paragraphs from it in the 1833 edition (XIV, 2–3), and these were retained in 1837. He ignored Harroviensis. Prothero gave another sample (the concluding paragraphs) in his edition of Byron's letters (VI, 14–15), but he did no more than identify Byron's queries about Harroviensis (VI, 48). Coleridge also paid Oxoniensis more respectful notice than he did the long analysis of Byron's play that it elicited (V, 202). Chew gave more space to the twenty pages of Oxoniensis than to the eighty-five–page defense of Harroviensis and made no relative evaluation of the two pamphlets.[37]

Isaac D'Israeli's scorn of Todd's "heavy labour" had some of Byron's power. He at first thought that the "dull and pompously insolent," "puffy giant," "with legs too weak to bear him up," must have been aborted by a country schoolmaster and was amazed to learn that a bishop, "a Doctor of the Sorbonne," had been the author of the "huffing" remonstrance, which "would have been more to the purpose in the Xth Cent^y^, when Excommunications were in vogue."[38]

The main weakness of Todd's poorly organized attack was its generality. This was the result of the author's unwillingness to stain his pages with quotations from the play, to comment on situations, speeches, and the characterization, and to explain Byron's main themes, though he did speculate about Byron's general purposes.

[36] Since this in turn provoked Philo-Milton's counterattack, the three pamphlets form a related sequence.

[37] *Byron in England,* pp. 80–84.

[38] Letter to Byron, July 19, 1822, *LJ*, VI, 84 n. D'Israeli wrote that Murray had told him that Todd was the author.

Others were also contemptuous of Oxoniensis. After *The Literary Chronicle* on January 5, 1822, had disapproved of *Cain,* a brief article in this weekly on January 19 trounced the bishop's pamphlet as "a mixture of bigotry, cant, and falsehood," a coarse, unmanly, malicious, slanderous, and ruffianly attack. It then printed a hefty section of the *Remonstrance* (IV, 39–40). Conservative journals, however, were pleased by Todd's pamphlet, e.g., *The Gentleman's Magazine,* XCI (December, 1821), 614; *The Literary Gazette* (January 19, 1822), 44.

Motivated by the conviction that *Cain* was socially obnoxious and full of "moral poisons," Todd was certain that it should be banned and that only the government's "cautious deference to the peculiar temper of the times" had protected it and Murray. He maintained that *Cain* would do great damage to "religion, morality, and law" and that the "blasphemous impieties . . . though nothing more . . . than the echo of often repeated sophisms, by being newly dressed and put forth in a form easy to be remembered, may produce considerable effect; that is, they may mislead the ignorant, unsettle the wavering, or confirm the hardened sceptic in his misbelief" (p. 13). The closest Todd came to spelling out the dangerous blasphemies was his charge that Byron quarreled with the very conditions of humanity, rebelled "against that Providence which guides and governs all things," and that Byron had arraigned "God's wisdom and goodness," caviled "at the condition under which the human race has been called into existence," and with "pestilent sophistries" and a "dastardly perversion of intellectual ingenuity" had tried "to mislead" "the weaker sex" (pp. 6, 14, 18). Todd never became more specific than that and did not track down these offenses in particular parts of the play.

Nor did he confine his attack to *Cain.* In a broad survey of Byron's personal and literary career, Todd found him controlled by pride, by an "all mastering self-love," which had cut him off from home and country, had caused him to throw away the tender feelings associated with man's solemn obligations, and had made him an enemy of civilized institutions, unable to allude to England without scorn and hatred. Although Todd no doubt had *Beppo* and *Don Juan* in mind, he did not name them. He did refer to *Childe Harold* and *The Giaour* in assaying the glamour of Byron's youthful reputation. This he thought exaggerated because Byron's admirers had mistaken promise for achievement. Todd deplored the moral gloom that hung over these early poems and that had spread through Byron's later writing, "involved his whole intellect," vitiated his talent, and kept him from becoming a great writer.

He specified two of Byron's literary defects: a mechanical versification, which he called "clumsy cuttings of ten syllables," and a lack of design, a "desultory style," and a "want of taste in the selection of incidents and of judgment in the conduct of a story" (pp. 10, 16). This he compared to La Rochefoucault's use of "detached reflections," which spared him "the labour of transition and arrangement, to which his powers were . . . unequal." His harshest literary criticism was that he found nothing original in *Cain,* "not a single passage,—not a point of sentiment, imagery, or incident, which he has not repeated from himself, or stolen from some other writer" (p. 12).

Todd was the first writer to advertise Byron's use of Bayle. He ticked off seven sections of the *Dictionary* that Byron must have read. Then he sternly lectured Murray for allowing Byron to cheat him, by offering him "obsolete trash, the very offscourings of Bayle and Voltaire, which he has made you pay for, as though it were first rate poetry and sound metaphysics" (p. 10).

He replied to Byron's prefatory statement that he had not recently read the *Death of Abel* and *Paradise Lost* by declaring that he should have studied them well, for Gessner "would have taught him, that the finest fancy may be made subservient to a devotional spirit; and from Milton he would have learned in what manner a really powerful mind grapples with those difficulties, which Bayle and Voltaire have taught him to consider as insurmountable" (p. 11).

The pamphlet included much petty, malicious, and irrelevant comment: allusions to Byron's marital troubles and departure from England; the assumption that Byron and Murray were primarily interested in the profit that they expected from such a work as *Cain* (Todd predicted that Murray was doomed to disappointment); the attempt to frighten Murray by declaring that he was responsible to the society he was helping to destroy and that the powerful people on whom he depended for his prosperity would punish him for publishing *Cain*; and the angry introductory remark that he (Todd) was writing to Murray because it was useless to appeal to Byron's reason or compassion.

The only shrewd comment that Todd made about *Cain* was his conjecture about Byron's purpose in writing the play. "He doubtless thinks it a fine thing to bully the bigots" and to calumniate their principles, outrage their feelings, and insult, "those from whom he differs both in faith and practice" (p. 14).

Harroviensis. *A Letter to Sir Walter Scott, Bart., in Answer to the Remonstrance of Oxoniensis on the Publication of Cain, a Mystery, by Lord Byron.* London: Rodwell & Martin, 1822. 67 pp.

In April, 1822, Byron learned about " 'an excellent defence' of *Cain* against 'Oxoniensis.' . . . If there be such 'a defender of the Faith,' you may send me his thirty nine articles." [39] A copy, already on the way, soon

[39] Letter to Murray, April 13, 1822, *LJ,* VI, 48–49 and note.

arrived and Byron thought the reply "conclusive," and he wrote Murray that if he understood his own interest, he would give it maximum circulation and print it as an appendix to the drama. This request he repeated in two later letters, and he also kept asking who the author was.[40] By June, Byron gave up coaxing, for Murray had implied how little he thought of the pamphlet by calling the author "a tyro in literature." Byron showed his displeasure with a jibe at Murray's commercialism: "I think both you and I are under great obligation to him; but I suppose *you* won't think so, unless his defence serves as an advertisement."[41]

The great obligation was due for several reasons. Byron had tried to justify Lucifer by citing Milton as a precedent and Murray's counsel Shadwell had used the same argument before the Lord Chancellor. Harroviensis located many passages in *Paradise Lost* in order to prove that Satan had spoken and acted just as Lucifer had done.

> . . . if we find in Milton many striking parallels for the demoniacal sentiments of Lord Byron's characters, then must candour pronounce that *Cain* is neither an impious nor an immoral poem, unless *Paradise Lost* fall under the same imputation.
>
> Let us then . . . examine those passages, against which "Oxoniensis" has thought fit to pronounce his anathema, considering them with reference to their own immediate tendency, and bringing them to the test of Milton's compositions. (p. 7)

The Miltonic analogues were of secondary importance. Harroviensis did Byron a greater service by considering many passages "with reference to their own immediate tendency." He clearly showed that the two rebels could not possibly speak the language of true angels or worshippers. Then he paged the play, interpreting the psychology of the speeches, following the interaction of the people on each other, in an attempt to clarify Byron's purposes, to account for Cain's ruin, and to support his thesis: Lucifer's corruption of Cain was achieved by aggravat-

[40] April 18, May 1, 4, 1822, *LJ*, VI, 49, 54, 60–61.

[41] Letter to Murray, June 6, 1822, *LJ*, VI, 76. Apparently Murray never divulged the identity of the author and he never complied with Byron's request. After Byron's death *Cain* was reprinted annually along with the other works, but Harroviensis was forgotten.

ing his skepticism and by destroying his confidence in divine goodness and mortal capability. This thesis Harroviensis pursued in speech after speech, intent on showing that Cain became a murderer only after and because Lucifer's cunning and powerful mind had accomplished his spiritual devastation. He explained the methods that Lucifer used to make himself seem impressive and the psychological tricks he resorted to in corrupting Cain: e.g., his pretense of sympathy for Cain's unhappiness, his assurance that he would have treated man more fairly and more generously than God had, and the denunciation of God's injustice and tyranny. Typical of his interpretive technique was the description of Cain's despondency and irritability in Act III after Lucifer had finished with him, and Cain had returned to earth.

Modern readers, bored and annoyed by the moral and sentimental preachment and by the verbose and exclamatory phrasing of the pamphlet, might miss its matter because of the manner of this literary novice. His enthusiasm in trying to prove that *Cain* had a religious purpose swept him into some statements as extravagent as those of the critics who damned the play for its irreligion. Some reviewers—Jeffrey, Talfourd, and those in the *Monthly* and the *Examiner*—wrote more gracefully and vigorously, and surpassed Harroviensis in generalizing about the characterization, but no one in his generation tried more earnestly and sympathetically to read the conversations of Cain, Adah, and Lucifer as psychological literature. His analytical approach and many of his ideas are by no means archaic. Harroviensis, with his continuous synoptic exposition and his focus on an emotional theme that unified various parts of the poem, was a windy and sentimental precursor of the New Critics.

Though Byron welcomed the pamphlet, since its defense came at a time when *Cain* was being heavily bombarded, we need not assume that he sanctioned all its interpretations. One part of his mind might have wondered how Harroviensis could be so sure that Cain's career demonstrated the spiritual damage that skepticism could cause.

Since this pamphlet is not readily accessible and has been long neglected and since much of its commentary has more merit than that of many of Byron's contemporaries, generous excerpts have been printed here. I have omitted the quotations from Milton and from *Cain*. In some places I have given a bracketed summary of the discussion.

I need not dwell upon the manifest absurdity there would have been in making Cain and Lucifer speak the language of angels, or true worshippers of the Deity; nor impress upon the mind of any reader . . . that they are creatures of the imagination, an ideal race of beings—not to be measured by the common standard applied to man, but by the great objects comprehended in the event of the Drama. When the characters were to be depicted by the poet, it would have been wholly impossible to represent them other than we have always considered them; Cain—as one, who, never having known "the calm of a contented knowledge," is ready to receive all impious impressions, who is afterwards a murderer, and of whom Lucifer says, "Hadst thou not been fit by thine own soul/ For such companionship, I would not now/ Have stood before thee as I am." Lucifer—as a vindictive Demon, who by subtle arguments is to break down all the great truths, revealed to fallen man for his consolation and guidance; ere he can lead his victim to imbrue his hands in his brother's blood, and thus make him the instrument, at once of his own revenge against the Highest, and of the confirmation of his dominion over the new world.

Such is the cast of characters necessary to work out the great moral of the "Mystery"; and if Lord Byron, or any other poet, may be charged with giving his own sentiments through the mouth of his fictitious characters; then Shakespeare, Milton—nay, the great moralists of all ages—must be treated as the abettors of evil; and examples of depravity are no longer to be considered as written for our instruction, but regarded as the emanation of a malignant temper in the authors who record them. (pp. 7–9)

[Harroviensis wrote the best commentary I have seen on the diplomacy that Lucifer used to ingratiate himself with Cain.] The fallen spirit first presents himself to Cain, as he is absorbed in the midst of a discontented sceptical train of thought. . . .

In order to establish an early influence over his mind, by inspiring an idea of his greatness and power, he comes to him in a shape "Like to the angels, mightier far than they, nor less beautiful." He tells him he is "master of spirits"; and excites his astonishment by showing him that he is acquainted with his most secret thoughts; flattering him, at the same time, with the assurance that those thoughts are worthy and noble;—"'Tis your immortal part,/ Which speaks within you"; declares to him that he has been deceived; —that he shall not die, but live;—seems to sympathise in his wretchedness, with which, if *he* had made him, he should not have been afflicted;—and having by these arts inspired Cain with such an awful sense of his attributes, that he exclaims, "Thou look'st almost a God," he insinuates that the angels of Heaven offer up a forced homage to the Deity. (pp. 9–10)

[Harroviensis quoted Lucifer's speeches (I, 133–163, 383–390), and averred that such sentiments arouse not approbation, but detestation of the spirit of evil (pp. 10–15).]

. . . I proceed to show the progress of Cain's seduction. Far from being shocked at Lucifer's impiety, he says, "Thou speak'st to me of things, which long have swum / In visions through my thoughts." He acknowledges that he is dissatisfied with the weight of daily toil, and the comparatively virtuous tenor of his father's life; and that, until he saw Lucifer, "he had never met aught to sympathise with him."

Encouraged by this declaration, Lucifer proceeds in his treacherous work. He has just instilled into the mind of Cain a sentiment of God's injustice and tyranny in the fall and punishment of man, which he contrasts with what he himself would have done for him [quoted I, 202–210]. (pp. 16–17)

Lucifer . . . disclaims having tempted Eve: he pretends to sympathise with mankind in their fall from happiness; and to have confessed that it was through his intervention that death came into the world, would have belied his own words, and have driven Cain from him in terror. When, therefore, he lets fall an expression, which excites the suspicion of Cain,—"Ah! didst *thou* tempt my mother?" he immediately answers, "I tempt no one, &c. . . . Here he craftily breaks off his discourse of immaterial things, the rather to increase Cain's desire of knowing their mysteries, and to watch the workings of his mind: "But I speak to thee of what thou know'st not." Cain's presumptuous spirit [exclaims that he thirsts for all the knowledge Lucifer can give him. Lucifer asks, "Dar'st thou to look on Death?"] Then follow those sublime and beautiful passages, descriptive of the feelings, which agitate the soul of Cain, when he contemplates the nature and the power of death. . . . [quoted I, 256–288, 298–301]. (pp. 18–20)

Lucifer, perceiving the intense interest to which he has excited his destined victim, takes advantage of such a moment to secure him in his toils; he promises to gratify his thirst after the higher knowledge to which he alludes; but upon one condition (and to this point we may observe his treacherous reasoning throughout has been directed) that he will pay him the tribute of his homage, and confess himself his votary [quoted I, 301–303]. (p. 21)

[Harroviensis then wrote a little essay on the universality of the drama, the applicability of Cain's seduction and downfall to the doubts and discontent in all men.]

Let us . . . inquire how Cain was to be seduced to the mission of his crime, . . . unless by such subtle arguments as . . . continued to exercise a fatal influence over so many of the sons of humanity. How otherwise was the mind of Cain to be inspired with the contempt and hatred of God's divine laws to which in the progress of events we see him conducted, a wretched blood-stained criminal; or by what less powerful agency hurried on to perdition, than by the fascination of the unrighteous spirit . . .? And if by such a being, how otherwise than by means which suited his character of a demon, and might best accomplish his malicious object? by creating a doubt of Heaven's mercy and goodness, by inculcating an awful admiration of the attributes of God's enemy, by inspiring a discontent of his own imagined wrongs, and a disbelief of those truths, which formed his surest safeguard, and the mainspring of his happiness? One or all of these are the daily and hourly causes of man's fall from virtue; they are the instruments, by which sin is permitted to operate upon our depraved nature; and though Cain and Lucifer express themselves in the strong language of poetry, and are bolder in their impiety,—the one a fiend, the other already an infidel, in his heart,—yet there are few of us, perhaps, who are not sometimes assailed by the whisperings of the same doubts, and of the same discontented spirit. The personages of the "Mystery" give utterance only to those feelings by which, though not openly pronounced, and perhaps never clearly defined, man always has been, and always will be, impelled to works of evil.

The demon, however, is foiled in his expectation of immediate conquest over Cain by that very pride of heart, which had first induced him to attempt his conversion: Cain refuses to worship the seducer, . . . [quoted I, 310–320]. (pp. 21–23)

We may hope that this, at least, is no pestilent doctrine, calculated to mislead the ignorant, but a confirmation of the natural train of inference, which I hope I shall hereafter prove to be deducible from the whole drama: it points out the danger of unsettled sceptical reasonings, which lead to the denial of the God who made us, and our consequent subjection to the influence of his declared enemy . . . (p. 23)

[Harroviensis commented on the contrast Byron drew between Adah and Cain, on her gentleness and beauty of character, her invulnerability to Lucifer's sophistry, and her perception and fear of his evil nature. He then pointed out how Lucifer, disappointed by his failure with Adah, retaliated by prophesying that her bosom carried the germ from which would come millions of sufferers.

He concluded his survey of Act I by defining the "edifying moral" that he thought was Byron's main objective: the unhappiness that has been caused by pride, independence, and skepticism.]

. . . Let him call to mind the relative influence, which the master-spirit of evil exercises over Cain and Adah, and he will see how forcibly the poet has pourtrayed the unhappy consequences of permitting even the approach of scepticism, . . . he will see a discontented and aspiring mind, relying rather on its own strength than on the benign influence of religion, which is no sooner assailed by the arguments of infidelity, than it yields to the congenial spirit, and is lost in its own self-love and vanity: on the other hand he may contemplate the calm and steadfast faith of a grateful heart, impressed with a sense of its own unworthiness, which either flies from the insidious attack of scepticism, or rests its hope on the divine assistance, as all-sufficient for its defence . . . (pp. 31–32)

[In his discussion of Act II, Harroviensis resumed his analysis of Lucifer's cunning effort to throw Cain into turmoil. For instance, in lines 43–49, Lucifer checked Cain's delight at the wonders of the cosmos and dispelled the veneration these might arouse by insinuating that God used his power to enfeeble, distress, and destroy mankind (p. 33). During the flight, Lucifer instilled the same impious thoughts by which he tempted Cain to the journey, "exciting his desire to know more than is permitted for mortals to know, yet unfolding only so much of the mysteries," as may confuse him, and "increase his discontent of his own fallen state," rather than inspire admiration of cosmic wonders. Having "by crafty appeals to his passions," bewildered Cain and rendered him a fit companion for the fallen host, Lucifer conducted him to the gates of Hell (pp. 36–37).

Harroviensis then described the result of Lucifer's psychological campaign.]

Cain no sooner plunges into the realm of death than he loses all reserve; every spark of remaining virtue seems blasted by the pestilential air he breathes in common with the Demonian spirits [quoted II, ii, 18–25. Cain's curse of God and Adam, as creators of his life climaxes his defeat and Lucifer's victory. Lucifer] has him in his toils: nothing now seems wanting to complete his victory; for Cain has cursed his God and his father, which is the seal of his doom! . . . (pp. 37–38)

Lucifer had first seduced Cain to tempt the "Abyss of Space" by representing to him the beauty of knowledge, which would place him beyond the reach of fear and above the groveling thoughts of earth, and lead him to happiness in the contemplation of celestial and unimaginable things. But now that he sees him securely in his power, he no longer conceals the misery, which this very knowledge will occasion him, as he predicts the future empire of sin throughout the world . . . [quoted II, ii, 215–253]. (p. 39)

The mind of the betrayed Cain now begins to be sensible to the danger of his situation: he has penetrated all the mysteries, which Lucifer could disclose: he feels that, so far from relieving his unquiet thoughts, or satisfying his desires, they have only led him to the foreknowledge of the wretchedness entailed on him, and on the successive generations of which he is the germ: he hears, above all, that it is the misery and debasement of sin, by which they shall suffer; and he now, for the first time, begins to doubt the purpose of Lucifer, and perceives the mercy of the Deity in having concealed from man the great dispensations of his providence.

But, alas! it is too late: his curse of God and his father has passed his lips irrevocably. He finds the tempter is about to leave him—as he ever has, and ever will leave his unhappy victims,—in utter hopelessness and despair. He reproaches him for having seduced him from earth, only to make him wretched. The demon, however, offers him no consolation, but malignantly endeavours to poison the only remaining source of comfort which is left to him,—his affection for Adah, his beloved Adah, by foretelling the decay of her beauty, and the consequent diminution of his love for her [quoted II, ii, 242–272; 323–332]. (pp. 41–42)

Though the unhappy victim's mind has been agitated by the sight of new worlds, and his imagination bewildered, and as it were set afloat on a tempestuous sea of uncertainty, by the tortuous reasoning of his seducer, yet the recollection of Adah and his parents lights up the last gleam of tender feeling in his heart; it cheers, and for a moment inspires him with affection for his family—"Adam and my mother both are very fair"; "I turn from earth and heaven to gaze on Adah's face." And he adds, "I pity thee, who lov'st nothing," for Lucifer had told him a little before, "Mortal, my brotherhood's with those who have no children." This last remnant of nature's softer mould, and the reproachful expression of a mortal's pity, excite all the malevolence of the fiend to expel the rising sentiments of love, lest Cain should find some resting-place for his heart, which might lead him to be thankful and to worship: he touches, therefore, another fatal chord, and wakes up fresh sounds of mischief in his heart—jealousy of his brother Abel, and hatred, its direful accompaniment. (pp. 43–44) [Quoted II, ii, 338–357.] The devil perceives that he has fixed his stamp on Cain and that everything works to the dreadful consumation of his fate. A brother . . . has been rendered the object of all the passions which raged in his bosom: the virtues of Abel, cherished of his kindred, and favoured of God, become, by the agency of hell, the source of crime and bloodshed. (pp. 44–46)

. . . The deadly purpose is effected, for the heart is poisoned: and Lucifer, exulting in his work, and confident of the certainty of its effect, proposes to dismiss his new creature to his native earth, which is too soon to be stained with the first murder. (p. 46)

[He quoted II, ii, 414–466, which he considered "dreadfully energetic" and suitable to the fiend, and also four of Satan's and one of Moloch's speeches, that resembled Lucifer's in thought and in vigor.

Then Harroviensis analyzed Lucifer's purpose in II, ii, 459–466. He forced this final speech of Act II to fit his thesis that Lucifer was a tempter. His interpretation, though wrong at this point, was ingenious. Lucifer's idealism was a subtle trap that climaxed his campaign and that used all of Cain's feelings to destroy him. The devil's parting exhortation confirmed Cain's presumptuous confidence in himself. He tried to persuade Cain that he could "form an inner world," but such an attempt will bring his victim to perdition. Lucifer knew that Cain's pride, his skepticism about things "beyond the capacity of his reason," the frustration of his longing for knowledge, his aversion to earthly life, his eager acceptance of Lucifer's assurance that man's soul was immortal, and his willingness to regard God as a malevolent tyrant—all these emotions, attitudes, and experiences had prepared Cain to follow Lucifer's final counsel to rely on and exercise his own reason, which Lucifer had succeeded in perverting (pp. 50–51).

At the outset of his discussion of Act III, Harroviensis described Cain's mood and related it to the events in Act II. His association with the devil has aggravated his passions and deepened his discontent to a denial of God's beneficence. Jealousy of Abel and hatred of his parents, who have robbed him of Paradise, are now cankering sores. Fear of death has become reckless despair. In this mood of suppressed tension he returns to Adah and sullenly addresses the sleeping child (pp. 54–55).]

. . . [Cain] seems to feel himself that the malignant spirit, whom he followed to the other world, has led him on to greater misery than he felt before [quoted III, 63–84]. (p. 56)

Cain now perceives two altars, built by Abel during his absence, for their intended sacrifice: he is stung with furious jealousy at this instance of his brother's piety,—of that piety, which has met the favour of Jehovah, and obtained for him the preference of their common parents. The insinuations of the fiend have worked their poisonous effects in his soul: his brother's offerings, he says, are made with base humility, showing more of fear than worship, and, for himself, *he* has *no* sacrifice to make [quoted III, 105–127]. (pp. 58–59)

Adah's gentleness, however, subdues the furious spirit of Cain. In language most beautiful, in tones of such tender sentiment as "fill our eyes with pleasant tears," she appeals to his feelings as a father and a husband, and, at length, by her soul-subduing eloquence, restores him to a momentary composure. When he says it were better Enoch never had been born, she answers him in all the strain of impassioned yet affectionate feeling, which such a reproach was calculated to excite in a mother's bosom, . . . [quoted III, 137–156]. Cain's rugged temper is for a moment softened [quoted III, 156–158]. (pp. 58–61)

From here on Harroviensis relied on a summary of events probably because he had already made his points and the remainder of the play required little interpretation.

His comment on Cain's illumniation was unique among contemporary critics:

Cain's sin stares him in the face in all its horror. He sees the gulf, into which he has been led by the arguments of Lucifer:—he has brought death into the world, and awakens from his fatal dream only to find, that he has himself accomplished "the heavy doom, so long forespoken" to man [quoted III, 371–379]. (p. 63)

Harroviensis turned to the other people, admired the family prayers of Act I, the portrayal of Abel's "piety, resignation and humility," and Adah's devotion, and briefly contrasted all these with Cain's career and again drew a moral: Cain's downfall is "a salutary warning of the nature and consequences of impiety."

He next puzzled over the accusation made by Oxoniensis that Byron had aimed to mislead "the weaker sex." Harroviensis replied that he had scanned the whole poem, but had found nothing obscene, nothing that may "not safely be read by the weakest of 'the weaker sex'." He then quoted I, 363–380 (p. 68), in which Adah talks about the love of brothers and sisters. His defense was again unique among his contemporaries:

Permit me to ask, Sir, if you perceive anything in this, framed to mislead either an ignorant or an innocent mind?—Adah is the sister of Cain as well as his wife, which, in them, was no offence; for, as there was only one family on the earth, their marriage was necessary to the fulfilment of God's wise purposes. Adah was as wholly unconscious of, as she was free from, sin in loving Cain, her brother; and it is expressly said by Lucifer, "you do not transgress, though it will be a sin in the generations which follow you:"

> alluding to those wise and salutary restrictions, afterwards introduced by the inspired lawgiver of the Hebrews, and adopted by all civilized nations, to prevent the intermarriage of near relatives, for reasons which would suggest themselves to every reflecting mind. In my apprehension, this is so far from appearing to "strike at the existence of society," that it is, in fact, one of the few occasions when Lucifer speaks the truth. (pp. 68–69)

He quoted II, ii, 196–215, and found nothing indecent there. He concluded that after a "calm and deliberate review of the whole scope of the drama, I can find no ground, on which to impugn its moral tendency" (p. 72). The rest of his pamphlet did not concern *Cain,* but was a general defense of Byron's character.[42]

Philo-Milton. *A Vindication of the Paradise Lost from the Charge of Exculpating "Cain," a Mystery.* London: Rivington, April, 1822. 60 pp.

Since the writer, in reply to Harroviensis, praised Milton as a defender of the faith and damned Byron as a heretic, he denied that the similarity of many passages in *Cain* and *Paradise Lost* proved that Byron's poem was no more harmful than Milton's. Extracts from both might cause readers to shudder, but Milton's context established the right point of view and reassured the reader that Satan and his tribe were evil. Byron provided no such context, never stepped in, as Milton did, to editorialize and condemn his devil and never assigned to other people in his play, as Milton did in his epic, speeches that combated the devil's heresies. For instance, he admitted that Satan's taunt to the Seraph came from a rebellious spirit (VI, 165 ff.).

> [But]the antidote is at hand; both in *word* and in *deed.* The soliloquy of Abdiel, which immediately precedes, and his reply to the apostate, nullify the mischief, as it regards *us*; and the Arch-Angel, . . . foiled in combat by the faithful Seraph, and the weight of reproof made valid upon his crest, is a glorious refutation of the vaunts just advanced. (p. 11)

Philo-Milton explained that Milton allowed more and more of Satan's base qualities to appear: "throughout the action of the poem, he uniformly continues to fall. . . . the last appearance he makes upon the scene,

[42] Other references to, or summations of, Harroviensis may be found in the following Annotations: I, 137–166, 352–357, 395–405, 441–450; II, i, 3; II, ii, 426–466. These are mainly Miltonic analogues.

brings the consummation to his disgrace" (p. 17). Byron on the other hand ascribed to Lucifer omniscience and other powers that did not deteriorate.

He countered Byron's attempt in his letter to Murray (*LJ,* VI, 13–18) to appeal to precedent by citation of Gibbon, Hume, Priestley, and Drummond, whose skeptical books had not been censored. Byron had professed surprise that his fiction could be considered more harmful than their histories and argumentation. Philo-Milton pointed out that just because *Cain* was fiction, it would reach a larger group of readers than Hume and Priestley could. No publisher would ever print them in cheap editions for the multitude, as Benbow had done with *Cain.*

> All will read such a work, because all will be captivated by the embellishments of its poetry; many, indeed, will fail to comprehend it, in its highest reaches; but many who have scanty or no resources of their own, will, at least find a commanding interest, and "a fastening attraction," generally pervading it;—and all this will be effected, solely because it is professedly a work of *fiction*, and not *of argument* or *history.* (pp. 40–41)

Hence Philo-Milton implied that *Cain* should be banned.

The author belonged to that large school who wanted literature to be didactic and to support Christian doctrine. Thus even when he made a literary comment it was given a moral and religious bias. Eve's "revolting imprecation" he acknowledged to be "an effort of powerful genius," but it was in bad taste and would "prove a plague of the first order let loose upon society" (p. 53). In general that was also his judgment upon the whole play.[43]

The Reverend William Harness. *The Wrath of Cain: A Boyle Lecture, Delivered at the Church of St. Martin's in the Fields, Wednesday, February 6, 1822.* London: Rivington, 1822. 109 pp.

Harness had liked Byron at Harrow, had written to him before and after the Mediterranean trip, had visited Newstead Abbey briefly in 1811, and had seen Byron intermittently thereafter in London. But since their habits and values diverged, they stopped corresponding long before 1821. Though Byron may never have read *The Wrath of Cain,* he seemed to know of its publication and was sentimental about it. "I hope he did not

[43] *The Literary Chronicle* conceded that the author was well intentioned but allowed him little talent and chided his conceit (IV, [October 19, 1822], 663).

abuse me personally, for that would be too bad, as we were school-fellows, and very good friends." His informant, a clergyman, assured him that Harness had been "fair and candid" in writing about what he thought were the poet's "mis-statements."[44]

The pamphlet was broadly conceived, firmly planned, and written with erudition, restraint, and dignity. He permitted himself only one sarcastic remark. If the opinions of Cain and Lucifer represented a new code, their disciples "should frame their actions by the example of Shylock; and study ethics in the maxims of Iago" (p. viii).

His conception of Cain's character in Genesis was almost as fictitious as Byron's: a villain, "obdurate in his transgression," delighting in wickedness, conscious of his guilt, and impenitent. When his pride was offended by the Lord's remonstrance, he murdered his brother (pp. 1–2). Had he thereafter been able to return to Eden, his bad disposition would have made him unhappy even in that garden of perfection (p. 61). Harness surmised that Cain later would have tried to palliate his crime to relieve his mind of the burden of guilt. Then as his sins multiplied, he would have become more skilled in casuistry and in justifying his offenses. He would have said that they were the result of irresistible impulses, "involuntarily excited by the accidents in which he had wickedly permitted them to be interested" (pp. 2–3).

Byron's poem vindicated the criminal with the deceitful arguments that guilty people always used to protect their esteem. Though Cain and Lucifer admitted that their sin had made them miserable, they gloried in it and remained arrogant and remorseless. The use of Bayle and the inversion of Manicheism were suitable to the development of such characters, but no less reprehensible. It was logical for Cain and Lucifer to call good evil and evil good. For them pride was a virtue, rebellion a duty. To exculpate themselves they had to say that God had made temptation efficacious, had delighted in the punishment of malefactors, and had rejoiced in the afflictions of his creatures. These attitudes were common to the diseased imagination of sinners who meditated on the attributes of deity and on human destiny (pp. 3–5).

Like Jeffrey and other sober writers who feared the emotional power

[44] "Lord Byron," *Blackwood's*, XV (June, 1824), 696. The anonymous author stated that his talk with Byron occurred in 1823.

A few journals gave Harness's book favorable notice; e.g., *The Literary Gazette*, No. 266 (February 23, 1822), 114.

of poetry, Harness warned that its danger derived not from the antiquated ideas of Bayle but from the manner of their presentation. The dramatic intensity and the enticement of Byron's poetry gave it wide circulation among people to whom literature was a form of dissipation. While it warmly infected them with demoralizing doubts, they would ignore a cold metaphysical essay that refuted its heresy (p. 6). The poem was especially dangerous because the zeal of Milton's time had vanished, and the skepticism of the present age encouraged men to listen to any apology for vice. They applied the words of Cain and Lucifer to the sickness of their own souls and welcomed this vicarious extenuation of their guilt (p. 7). Harness was worried about the poet's imaginative appeal, the empathic response of the audience, and its habit of rationalization. He would not have smiled had he heard Byron ask, "What poem ever harmed a sensible man?"

Harness calmly corrected not only the biblical mistakes that disturbed his fellow clergymen, but also some that the others had not caught. He explained how the narrative in Genesis had been validated by an accurate translation of the Hebrew text, by the geological theories of Cuvier, and by the hypothesis that light existed before the creation of the sun (pp. 9–18). The serpent, of course, was the devil. Adam had freely eaten the fruit of the tree of life before the fall. As a punitive measure, that tree (eternity) was barred to the flesh, but not to the spirit of man. The tree of knowledge could never have made man wise, as Cain should have inferred when he saw that his parents had learned nothing from it. This tree was a test of obedience and taught man only that to forbear was good, to indulge was evil. God's ban aimed to exercise man's restraint over his appetites, which was necessary for social stability. Hence the interdiction was consistent with God's kindly interest in human welfare and not an arbitrary decree (pp. 62 ff.). Without denouncing Lucifer's criticism of divine despotism, Harness tried to show that all the facts of Genesis testified to God's generosity to man, e.g., the bountiful environment he had created for Adam and Eve.

He accepted the axiom of original sin. Since observation of modern families showed that mental and moral traits were hereditary, Harness, by inference, agreed that Cain's fear was warranted, for Adam had transmitted to his children the corruption caused by his disobedience (pp. 74 ff.). He answered Byron's pessimism without identifying it and argued (1) that the benevolent deity had tried to prevent man's iniquity by incorporating in him good desires and faculties that battled against his wickedness, (2) that man therefore has always had the strength to resist evil, and (3) that sinning was a free act of the human will (pp. 65–78). In reply to one of Cain's and Bayle's contentions, again without quoting it, Harness conceded that God had the power to annihilate all evil in the world but had not done so because such compulsion would destroy the liberty of action (pp. 90 ff.).

In rebuttal of Cain's complaint that expulsion from Eden was cruel, Harness, still without reference to the poem, adopted Abel's view that since man's sin deserved death, the exile was a lenient punishment (pp. 95 ff.). Finally, he contradicted Byron's and Warburton's view that Cain was ignorant of immortality. He thought that every man had an inherent sense of his own eternity and also made the unusual statement that God's acceptance of Abel's sacrifice implied the truth of immortality (pp. 100 ff.).

Since the lecture purported to survey the whole range of truth in the second and third chapters of Genesis, Harness discussed many matters that Byron did not write about. He tried to rectify several common errors, e.g., the attempt at an allegorical reading (Genesis was a simple relation of fact [pp. 20–21]); the objection that God created man in his own image (a spiritual not a physical likeness) and talked to him (pp. 34–39); the ridicule of the creation of Eve from Adam's rib (p. 48); the protest that the punishment of the serpent was unjust (p. 49); and the refusal to believe that the devil was still active in human affairs (pp. 26–29).

Harness's pamphlet was a reasonable exposition of conventional doctrine, notable for its moderate tone and tact. He disputed Byron's ideas often without mentioning the poem, and when he did refer to *Cain,* it was without anger.

Britannicus. *Revolutionary Causes: With a Brief Notice of Some Late Publications; and a Postscript Containing Strictures on Cain, etc.* London: J. Cauthorne, 1822. Pp. 74–97

This writer recorded in exclamatory language how he had felt when he read *Cain* and wrote his marginal expostulations on it. He discussed the play with the greatest reluctance, as a moral and social duty, deplored the poet's abuse of his genius, and hoped to lead him back "to those paths where he [was] so brilliant." In the past he had prayed for his Lordship's conversion and now he strove to reclaim him for virtue and religion and begged him to desist from drama and to return to decency and to tenderness, which were his "forte." Britannicus admitted that there was beauty in the play, implied that this was confined to the tender passages of Act III, and lamented that they were lost among the horror (one of his favorite responses to *Cain*), "like two or three brilliants on a large dunghill."

He gave a disproportionate amount of space to the Preface. He tried to refute Byron's statement that Eve was tempted by the serpent *because* he was the most subtle of beasts. Britannicus accused Byron of careless quotation and illogicality and declared that the poet had inserted "because" into the biblical context. He also objected to Byron's view that there was no reference to immortality in the Old Testament and cited a few passages in refutation. He caught Byron's inconsistency in announcing that he was not going to use the New Testament and then drawing upon it occasionally in the poem, quoted two references to the New Testament, and concluded that Byron "knew not what he did."

He had some reservations about the principle of dramatic consistency and explained why he believed that Lucifer expressed the author's own views:

> There is no intention of disputing the rule of criticism, that the distinction of character is to be supported by appropriate language, sentiment, and action. But the rule cannot stand unqualified by another rule, equally, or still more imperative. If an author concentrates all his own powers of reasoning and eloquence in any character, in which he is to maintain the side of great enormities, of vice, of falsehood, he is bound to counteract it with superior eloquence. If he leave blasphemy, impiety, vice, triumphant in the personage he has introduced, without exposure, he brings upon himself the reproach of abetting the opinions, sentiments, and actions of that personage. (p. 84)

Britannicus reproached Byron for making a hero out of Lucifer, for writing the play "to justify the Devil," and hence for making "almost every line profane and blasphemous," "pregnant with mischief to mankind."

To support these judgments, Britannicus quoted some flagrant passages (including part of Cain's first soliloquy and Lucifer's first diatribe against God) and reproduced his marginal strictures on them. To relieve the oppression that "this insane composition" left, he offered a passage from *Paradise Lost,* in which Satan confessed that he regretted his fall, attributed it to "pride and worse ambition," and hailed God as "Heaven's matchless king," who had created him, who "deserv'd no such return," and whose service had not been hard (p. 89).

He paid only cursory attention to Act II, where the sole object was to demonstrate that "as evil exists, God cannot be good, and, dreadful to say! there is not the slightest opposition given to the Devil's arguments" (p. 91).

In Act III Britannicus misinterpreted the first scene: "Cain, having taken lessons from the Devil, sets to with all his might to corrupt his wife Adah" (p. 93). Abel's address to the Lord was "truly Miltonic," but "beautiful as it is, it makes no alteration in the ground of the condemnation of this poem" (p. 94). Though its pious resignation and thanksgiving were "necessary to mark his character," it did not refute the blasphemies of the heretics. Cain's oration at the altar he found disgusting and the lines on bloodshed "horribly expressed" (p. 99).

A minor criticism was one that Heber and Jeffrey also made: Cain said that he was ignorant of death; yet he knew about Abel's sacrifice of animals and thus "must have seen lambs die" (p. 97). This Postscript had more to say than Oxoniensis did, but it was still a flimsy essay, naïve, diffuse, and flustered.

Uriel. *A Poetical Address to the Right Honorable Lord Byron, Written on the Continent: With Notes, Containing Strictures on the Spirit of Infidelity Maintained in His Works. An Examination into His Assertion, that "If Cain is Blasphemous, Paradise Lost is Blasphemous." And Several Other Poems.* London: Hatchard and Son and Burton & Smith, 1822. 127 pp.

The 711 earnest lines of the *Poetical Address* combined a statement of conventional religious doctrine with a reproach of Byron's many faults: his immorality, lack of patriotism, skepticism, and infidelity. Uriel lectured him solemnly and begged Byron to search his soul, to leave the dissipated environment of Italy and return to the Christian fold.

Only a few stanzas concerned literary matters. Uriel approved *Hebrew Melodies* and requested the poet to write more of them. He detected "sentiments of scepticism" even in these lyrics, but also some gratifying orthodoxy. Half a dozen stanzas and their notes contained his objections to *Cain.* Byron had allowed Lucifer to blaspheme without refutation, whereas Milton had always balanced Satan's wickedness with corrective comment. Uriel had no sympathy with Cain's dissatisfactions, for man had no cause to complain about God's treatment of him. He saw no injustice in the punishment of man's disobedience.

He was distressed because Byron made Cain more evil than the Bible had done, by associating him with Lucifer and thus putting him beyond the hope of forgiveness. Uriel's concept of the biblical Cain was that he was a criminal tormented by guilt but not beyond redemption. A second cause of distress was Eve's execration. With her unnatural behavior, Byron had again worsened a biblical portrait.

Uriel began his prose discussion of *Cain* with a criticism of the Preface. He was confused by the term "mystery" and thought that Byron referred to Christian doctrines that were "stumbling blocks to the pride of human reason." He made the customary objection to Byron's statement that Eve was tempted by the serpent and not by a demon. Then he unloaded more biblical quotations than other commentators had done to prove that the Old Testament had alluded to immortality. He disparaged Warburton and related an anecdote to show how egotistical that bishop was.

Since he had read Cuvier's book, he quoted a passage in which he thought the scientist had substantiated Genesis.

> Cuvier states also this remarkable fact as the result of geological inquiries, that strata, incumbent upon each other, exhibit fossil remains in gradations, corresponding to the order of creation. It is however to be lamented, that some geologists attempt to subvert the truths of Revelation . . . (p. 111)

After these remarks on the Preface, Uriel posed three questions that he almost ignored in the rest of his article.

> I. Is the language, put into the mouth of Cain, such only as he may be supposed to have used in his unhappy situation?
>
> II. Are the impieties he utters, repelled by sound arguments, for the truth? or, are they suffered to rest unanswered on the mind?
>
> III. Is the powerful genius of Lord Byron most eloquently displayed on the side of infidelity, or in defence of the truth? (p. 112)

Having stated these criteria, he summarized Cain's complaints in the first scene and maintained that these tended "to weaken parental authority, and promote, filial disobedience" (p. 112). In Act II Cain's denunciation of Adam and God, his curiosity about the two principles, and his charge that God was the author of evil originated in the common depravity of man and encouraged dissension among families. Since men were imitative, the frequent presentation of vice in literature lessened their aversion to it and corrupted them. Thus if *Cain* were widely read, parental ties would be enfeebled (p. 113). Uriel saw no biblical precedent for Cain's disobedience. Both Cain and Eve were "strained beyond the record in Holy Writ" (p. 115).

Eve's repentance and Cain's love of Adah and Enoch were slight antidotes to the evil spoken by Lucifer and Cain. Act II rectified some of the damage because it referred to scriptural "maxims and miracles," to "the spiritual essence of the soul," to "a directing Providence," and to the misery of Lucifer, who was unable to love anyone (p. 114).

Uriel's survey of Act III was detailed and heavily moral. He rejoiced that Cain, though consistently defiant, proved that none are "so sunk in the blackness and horrors of guilt, but that they exhibit some emanation, however faint, of that primal purity, in which they were created . . ." Uriel thus saw Cain "somewhat softened by the sight of artless infancy" (p. 114). He commended Cain's admission of his own nothingness. His Calvinist bias, which applauded humility, caused him to misinterpret Byron's intent.

He was especially impressed by Adah, quoted some of her speeches, and wrote the best contemporary exposition of her conduct in Act III:

> Adah stands forth a bright example of maternal and conjugal virtues. Towards her child she is the affectionate parent . . . and towards Cain, the friend that was born for adversity; banished from Paradise, she murmurs not. In the allurements of a happy home and a contented mind, she urges Cain to seek refuge from the gnawing spirit that corrodes his peace; and tells him, . . . "Where'er thou art, I feel not / The want of this so much regretted Eden." [She] urges Cain to return her love, . . . reminds him what a blessing it is to be a parent, . . . She gently urges him to join in Abel's grateful offering as a means to recall him to peace and happiness: and even when atrocious guilt, a brother's murder, had banished him from a father's home, and rendered him an outcast from society, followed with a mother's curses; her affectionate regard cast a brightness through the overhanging gloom; she adds not to the chidings. When Cain inquires, if she fears not to dwell with him? She replies . . . [Uriel then quoted Adah's statement of stoical altruism, III, 462–466, 546–548]. (pp. 116–117)

He also noted that it was to Adah that Byron gave the hope of future atonement.

In the account of the sacrifice, quarrel, and murder, he described Cain's emotions accurately. The remaining nine pages of the essay attempted to rescue Milton from the accusation which Lord Byron had "unjustly brought against him." At intervals in his poetic commentary, Uriel had reminded the reader how remote *Cain* was from *Paradise Lost* by exclaiming, "Not in such strains as these hath Milton sung!" Now in concluding his essay, he tried to show that Milton's treatment of the biblical subject was superior to Byron's. Uriel gathered one group of quotations that presented Satan and his fellow rebels in an evil light, then a group that showed the fallen angels acknowledging God's power and goodness, and finally a third group of passages that presented the Deity reverently and that also gave pious utterance to Adam and Eve. This concluding section was so intent on defending Milton that it was only indirectly related to Byron's play. The exposition of Milton's achievement was an implied rebuke of Byron, who in differing from Milton, became morally culpable.

[John Watkins]. *Memoirs of the Life and Writings of the Right Honourable Lord Byron, with Anecdotes of Some of His Contemporaries.* London: Printed for Henry Colburn and Co., 1822. Pp. 370–388

On August 8, 1822, Byron wrote Moore that he had not seen the *Memoirs* and did not want to. "The price is, as I saw in some advertisements, fourteen shillings, which is too much to pay for a libel on oneself. Some one said in a letter, that it was a Dr. Watkins, who deals in the life and libel line." He asked for Moore's opinion about the feasibility of publishing part of his own *Memoirs* "to counteract the fellow" (*LJ*, VI, 100–101).

Although this book, during Byron's lifetime and afterward, has been ignored as biased and unreliable, its literary opinions are representative of the era, and a few show some acumen. Watkins started his chapter on *Cain* with scornful depreciation of the old mystery plays. "Sacred history" was not a suitable subject for secular drama. Fabrication of additional matter was necessary to fill out any play on a biblical story and this expansion encouraged error. No one had committed more heinous errors than Byron, for no one else had grafted upon biblical facts "such monstrous fictions as would destroy the credit of the whole" Bible. Watkins charged that Byron was insincere in associating his play with the medieval Mysteries and that, influenced by the odious Bayle, he used the term to refer to the incomprehensible and irrational aspects of religion. According to Medwin, Byron may have used the word as Uriel and Watkins asserted he did: the Cain story "is a grand mystery" (p. 129).

Watkins then chided Byron for forcing publication against the advice of Murray, Gifford, and Hobhouse, and for seeking favor by dedicating it to the popular Scott, whom he rebuked for accepting the dedication.

One of Watkins' blunders was his supposition that Byron had never read Cuvier. He also challenged Byron's opinion that the French scientist's theory confirmed, rather than invalidated, the Mosaic cosmogony. Watkins, following Oxoniensis and some early reviewers, asserted that Byron was indebted to Bayle. He quoted some sentences from the *Dictionary* that he regarded as the foundation of the entire development of the play.

Another criticism was aimed at the passage in which Adah talks about the love of brothers and sisters. Watkins inferred that Byron had presented incest in an attractive light and had used Adah and Lucifer to imply that the modern law prohibiting it was "an act of tyranny." He assumed that Cain and Lucifer were spokesmen for the author.

In the last five paragraphs of the chapter on *Cain*, Watkins rebuked Murray for publishing the play and was contemptuous of Byron's defense of February 8, 1822. He recounted Murray's attempt to stop Benbow's piracy, summarized Shadwell's argument, and declared that Milton could not be used to justify *Cain*.

> But if the Devil does not talk like a clergyman, the noble lord, by the help of Bayle and his ape Voltaire, has taken special care to make him prate with the cunning of a sophist, and he has managed the matter so well as to give even to the Devil's argumentation a colouring calculated to raise doubts in the minds of thousands. The noble lord and his advocates, if he has any, will perhaps pretend that the infidelity here brought forward is merely in character, and that the impiety belongs to Lucifer; but who has exhibited this being in a dramatic poem? and who made him utter what ought not to be written at all? Will Lord Byron, or any man, dare advance the position, that a poet has a right to create a character for the purpose of obtruding upon the world, through that fictitious organ, language which the author in his own proper person could not venture to publish? No man of common understanding can avoid seeing in the speeches of Cain and Lucifer, the sentiments of the dramatist himself; and to prove that this is not an unjust imputation, one passage alone will be sufficient . . . the diabolical justification of incest . . . the subject is thus introduced, for the purpose of showing that the connexion which then subsisted between brother and sister, would in the next generation become a sin by the arbitrary violation of the law of

nature [quoted I, 365–382]. Now this is not the delusive reasoning of a tempter, but conclusions put into the mouth of a child of nature, and so expressed as to make the reader believe that the law which prohibits certain connexions is an act of tyranny. To make the venom stronger, the author of this Mystery has made Cain and Adah twins. (pp. 375–378)

. . . Such is the morality of this poem; but it is only consequential of the principles of infidelity, for thus says Bayle, the oracle of the sect: "According to the rules of philosophy it may be maintained, that if it be repugnant to the nature of the Deity to produce sin, it is also repugnant to the same nature to produce creatures who will infallibly commit sin, under those circumstances in which he chose to place them: for according to our most distinct ideas, it is altogether the same thing to commit murder oneself, as to put a man into circumstances where we know he must inevitably be killed." Again: "If we depend only upon one cause, almighty, infinitely good, and infinitely free, and which disposes universally of all beings, according to the pleasure of his own will, we ought not to feel any evil, all our good ought to be pure, and we ought never to have any thing dangerous. The author of our being, if He is infinitely beneficent, ought to take a continual pleasure in making us happy, and preventing every thing that may disturb or diminish our felicity; for this is a property essentially inherent in the idea of supreme goodness." These are the fundamental positions ramified into dialogue, expanded into declamation, and worked up into action, throughout the Mystery of Cain. . . . (pp. 378–379)

[Watkins then argued that Byron's and Lucifer's Manicheism sank into atheism] since, if the moral government of the universe is limited and divided, there must be endless confusion and misery . . . consequently the idea of omnipotence is at an end. [This inference the author has] put into the mouth of Cain, who, when Lucifer says that "Jehovah and he both reign together, though their dwellings are asunder," answers him like an Epicurean, or one just fresh from reading Lucretius . . . (pp. 381–382)

Were this passage [II, ii, 459–466, which he quoted], and the same might be said of a great many others in the drama, printed as plain prose, no reader who then saw it for the first time would ever dream that it had been divided into the form of verse. . . . [Watkins quoted II, ii, 120–124 to illustrate the "beggarliness" of Byron's language.]

For [the] notion of a succession of worlds the noble author in his preface quotes the authority of Cuvier, and roundly asserts that the speculation is not contrary to the Mosaic account, but rather confirms it. Now having read the bible, he must know that the cosmogony of Moses directly maintains, and necessarily pre-supposes, a creation of the world in its original elements; and not the renovation of a decayed planet out of the old materials. But though Lord Byron pretends to call in the aid of Cuvier it is clear, that he never read the works of that great naturalist: and that he is indebted for this, as he is for all the rest of his machinery and sentiments, solely to Bayle, who has defended the notion at great length in various parts of his Dictionary. (pp. 380–381)

Thomas Adams. *A Scourge for Lord Byron; or "Cain a Mystery" Unmasked.* London: T. Adams, 1823. 33 pp.

Adams abhorred the play because he was both an obdurate optimist and a militant moralist. The laws and processes of nature, especially the cycle of the seasons and the annual renewal of life, had convinced him that everything was divinely ordained and controlled for the purpose of making mankind happy. God had also given man wisdom, all the essential rules for his guidance, and proofs of rewards hereafter. Men were intended to live happily together. Peace was centered in virtue, and vice never prospered. Since everything was perfect, one wonders why Adams found it necessary for an author to be didactic. The sole purpose of poets was to stimulate virtue, to nurture the mind and make it healthy, giving assurance to those who were unsettled, cheering and soothing the despondent, and enabling all men to obey God's laws and thereby to live in harmony.

Cain must have stunned a man who sincerely held such beliefs. *The Scourge* was his first attempt at verse, and he modestly admitted to a very limited education, but the lethargy of the great writers, who had not rallied against Byron, had stirred him to denounce the awful blasphemer, to rescue the moral education of youthful minds, and to preserve the purity of his own five infants. Adams had to do his duty for king, country, and family and save them all from disgrace.

He became almost frantic when he wrote about the damage Byron had done. Perhaps the Italian air had warped the poet's brains and hardened his heart, for he had taught youth to lie and swear, rob and murder. He had vitiated souls, dissipated friendship and connubial love, made virgins mourn and wives decay. The two most horrible crimes of the villainous poet were the destruction of the beauty and goodness of English womanhood and the corruption of the minds of innocent children.

Adams mentioned a few definite matters that he abominated in *Cain*: Byron's cowardice in using fictitious people to speak his own thoughts, his absurd notion that man should live in idleness and luxury and that he ought never to know death, his statement that after death man became extinct, his derision of Scripture, and his calling God a tyrant who made man to torture him. Anyone who wrote such stuff was a knave or a fool, a lunatic or a descendant of a Hottentot. Adams decided that Byron was a lunatic, for only a madman would have joined Satan, warred against reason and nature, and strewed poison around the world as Byron had done. To prove his indictment he quoted Lucifer's first long speech in Act I and Cain's reply (I, 136–191). On doomsday the poet will count the souls he had sent to Hell. Adams concluded that Byron was past redemption, and we may infer that he thereby admitted the futility of his twenty pages of incoherent couplets.

Adams also reproached Byron for attacking Southey and George III in the *Vision of Judgment*. The magnitude of this error was obvious: no one in the land except him had found a single fault in this kind, humane, wise, and venerable monarch.

Adams' fatuous pamphlet was one of the shortest of the religious attacks, and therefore somewhat less unpalatable than the writings of Britannicus, Grant, and their brethren.

Antoine Fabre d'Olivet. *Cain a Dramatic Mystery in Three Acts by Lord Byron Translated into French Verse and Refuted in a Series of Philosophical and Critical Remarks Preceded by a Letter Addressed to Lord Byron, upon the Motives and the Purpose of This Work.* [Paris] 1823. Trans. Nayán Louise Redfield. New York and London: C. P. Putnam's Sons, 1923

Cain was the first poem by Byron that Fabre d'Olivet read. He was a biblical and theological scholar, a linguist, and a moral and social philosopher, not a poet or literary critic. He had a low opinion of French poetry, but was astonished by the power of *Cain* and repeatedly praised its language. He was also dismayed by Byron's dangerous ideas, which the poet's skill made all the more imperative for him to combat. He thus fell in step with several English writers who admired the style of *Cain* but deplored its content.

In order to be fair to the poet and to know his drama thoroughly, Fabre d'Olivet translated it in fifteen days, and then analyzed its central fallacy in a long public letter. Byron, he wrote, took his biblical facts from the faulty King James translation, did not know the original Hebrew text, and hence committed many gross errors. For instance, Byron read Genesis, 3:1, thus: "Now the serpent was more subtil than any beast of the field, which the Lord God had made." Fabre d'Olivet's translation was extraordinary: "Now Nahash (cupidity) was an insidious passion (blind principle) in all elementary life which Yahweh Aelohim had made" (p. 24).

Fabre d'Olivet's version of Genesis turned all the people of the Eden narrative into allegorical figures, "cosmogonic beings," he called them. "Cain and Abel are the two primordial forces of elementary nature. . . . Cain can be conceived as the action of compressive force, and Abel as that of expansive force," and they are always hostile to each other (p. 27). Cain and Abel were not brothers and there was no fratricide. According to Fabre d'Olivet, Lucifer was not known to Moses, and when he did appear later in the Bible, Fabre d'Olivet called him Nahash, i.e., cupidity, original attraction, "radical egoism," "the blind passion of elementary animality" (pp. 29–30). From Fabre d'Olivet's point of view, Byron's story never existed in Genesis, and all his characters were "fantastic and deprived of truth . . . hypothetical . . . dissolved in thin air" (p. 31).

When Fabre d'Olivet considered Byron's characterization independently of his own version of Genesis, which he did very reluctantly, he found it inferior. Adam was too subservient to Eve, she was violent and vindictive, and Abel gentle but weak. Cain was "passionate but generous, capable of the highest virtues as of the greatest crimes . . . indomitable in his will, but susceptible to influence." That Fabre d'Olivet was unable to read Byron's drama exactly appears in his casual opinion that the portrayal of Adah was no more than the "rough outlines of a beautiful womanly character" (pp. 25–26). The American translator of Fabre d'Olivet's letter, Nayán Louise Redfield, thought his refutation brilliant and concluded her Foreward with Byron's alleged self-defense: he was "a poet and not a metaphysician" (p. ix).

Fabre d'Olivet in the numerous annotations that he wrote on particular speeches continually regarded Byron's people as not fictitious but historical persons (wrongfully conceived and developed), whose ideas must be seriously refuted. He wished that Byron had employed his great talent in elaborating a contrast between the "vain declamations" of Cain and Lucifer and the "magnificent expressions" of God. In the ancient Greek fashion he should have used a chorus, an "aerial choir," to warn Cain and reason with him. Byron had once dallied with the idea of including a chorus in the drama (*LJ*, V, 189), though he did not tell us what it was to chant. Fabre d'Olivet could not have read Byron's journal, nor was it likely that he knew he was following the recommendation of Jeffrey, Scott, and their orthodox contemporaries, when he supplied nine Adamical lectures totalling twenty-four pages, in which at intervals he soberly corrected the errors made by Cain and Lucifer. The first one was a long answer that Fabre d'Olivet thought Adam should have made to Cain's question about why life and knowledge were evil. The last one was an even longer addition to Adam's brief dismissal of his son in III, 444–446. Fabre d'Olivet, in effect, rewrote much of the play, explaining what Byron should have had Cain or Adam say, and even revising Zillah's prayer at the beginning of the poem. His favorite exercise was to debate with Lucifer. For instance, when Lucifer denounced God as a destroyer (I, 267), Fabre d'Olivet declared that such a charge only convicted Lucifer of ignorance. The devil surely knew that the soul was unalterable and that God did not destroy the body but only freed it in death for a new formation.

The annotations were thus almost exclusively concerned with moral and religious argument. The central ideological criticism arose from Fabre d'Olivet's optimism. He repudiated Manicheism because he assumed the existence of innate goodness and resolutely denied that evil was an independent inherent entity. He argued that every intelligent man had a distinct idea of absolute good, "whereas that of absolute evil can never enter his comprehension." Fabre d'Olivet used Cain's "thirst for good" and Lucifer's agreement (II, ii, 238–240) as evidence that the desire for good was universal and that no one desired evil. In turn, this universal desire suggested that "good [was] therefore the primordial, absolute principle; whereas evil [was] only an accident brought about by a cause known or unknown" (pp. 232–233). Lucifer's assumption that evil was a universal necessity (II, ii, 236–237) and his gloomy description of past and present conditions were thus contrary to fact. Fabre d'Olivet regretted that Byron assigned to Adam the trivial justification of evil as a mysterious source of good. He wondered if Byron had done this to weaken Adam's character and to "take away from him all his empire over his son" (p. 234).

Fabre d'Olivet could be unintentionally frivolous and inexact. Byron, he wrote, implied that the serpent had spoken only to Eve, and not to Adam, but the poet had not plainly stated so out of gallantry to womankind (p. 232). Actually Byron more than once referred to the serpent's temptation of both parents (I, 216, 224–227, 240–242). After we discount Fabre d'Olivet's occasional aberrations and subtract all of his allegorical theory and his abstruse disputation, we have left a large body of analytical interpretation that is still acceptable today. Only Harroviensis excelled him in the number of particular insights into the thought and feeling of Byron's people.

For instance, when Cain's parents evaded his question about why life and knowledge were evil, and Eve counselled work and resignation, Fabre d'Olivet wisely declared that quiet acceptance was not possible for a man like Cain. "It is not by sending him to labour and exhorting him to silence that one can satisfy his reason" (p. 181). He thought, however, that Cain's description of his family's attitudes toward death (I, 179–189) was unrealistic and that Byron erred in making Adam, who ought to be strong in this circumstance, the weakest person (p. 194). Fabre d'Olivet understood why Cain's feelings about death were variable and contradictory; it was the natural product of emotional disturbance (p. 220).

His most penetrating remarks concerned Lucifer. He held that Cain and the devil were identical "volitive spirits," though Byron was not aware of this duplication (pp. 186, 193). He, along with Harness and Heber, explained that Byron had reversed the powers of Satan and Jehovah, giving

> . . . to the Creator of the world the evil intention of keeping man in the ignorance to which he had created him, without revealing to him the goal of his existence, which is immortality. Contrariwise, he gives to his antagonist, Lucifer, in the work of creation, the praiseworthy design of making man emerge from that state of darkness and dependence, in causing the light of knowledge, of liberty and of eternal life to shine before his eyes. (p. 190)

Fabre d'Olivet made this comment on I, 207–210, and repeated it for II, ii, 452–455: Byron "transports to one principle that which belongs to the other. Lucifer speaks here as principle of good, and states as fact that which is in question" (p. 243). These comments could also be applied to I, 199–205, 266–267, 458–489.

Fabre d'Olivet, like Harroviensis, interpreted Lucifer's function as a crafty seducer, who belittled the universe, stressed mankind's worst vices, harped on its misery, advocated the past "at the expense of the present," and made gloomy predictions about the future—all to throw the blame on God and "to irritate the mind of Cain more and more, and bring it to an outburst." He even excited Cain's "indignation against the creator . . . by representing to him the suffering of animals as the height of injustice and barbarity" (pp. 213–214, 226–228, 242). After Lucifer had destroyed all other sentiments in Cain's heart, he undertook to destroy love, "by showing the frailty of its cause" (II, ii, 269–272, 323–332); for Lucifer, by inference, admitted only a physical love (pp. 233–234).

He traced Lucifer's torment of Adah:

> Now that Lucifer is sure of Cain, he attacks Adah . . . where he knows she . . . will be most easily moved. He brings her to think of love; he makes her uneasy concerning the future fate of her children, frightens her concerning the purity of her union with Cain, makes her foresee a crime in the future; brings her back to love, and makes her consider what the effect of knowledge is upon this sentiment. (pp. 204–205)

Like many commentators, Fabre d'Olivet was dissatisfied with the tour of Hades. Lucifer cheated Cain by not showing him death as he had promised to do. "The shadows of darkness are not death" (p. 220). He wittily declared that with Cain's question, "And to what end have I beheld these things?" (II, ii, 417), Byron summed up the criticism of his poem (p. 242).

Fabre d'Olivet was cheerful about the eternal war between good and evil and so was sure that Byron had not given Lucifer any possibility of victory: "it is his pride alone, his indomitable will, which precipitates him into this combat. . . . He fights with a blind fury, and the weapons he uses are those of weakness and of perfidy. . . . Lucifer, of his own confession, [is] ignorant and cowardly" (p. 240). Fabre d'Olivet attached this comment to line 388. It belongs also with lines 375 and 392 and is most applicable to lines 426–442.

He admired the psychology of the domestic scene with the sleeping Enoch, thought all of Act III good theatre, but joined the majority in condemning Eve's curse as so abnormal as to be implausible (p. 260). It was Fabre d'Olivet's objection that drew from the *Moniteur* an explanation of Eve's deterioration, and that in turn spurred Goethe to write his essay on *Cain.*[45]

Henry Wilkinson. *Cain, a Poem, Intended To Be Published in Parts, Containing an Antidote to the Impiety and Blasphemy of Lord Byron's Cain with Notes, etc.* Part I. London: Baldwin, Cradock, and Joy, 1824. 97 pp. [No further parts published.]

Over half of the ninety-seven pages of this hodgepodge had nothing to do with Byron. A Preface opened with the explanation that some years earlier the author had begun an epic on the life of Cain after the banishment. Then he read Byron's play and decided he must refute its "sophistry and ignorance." The next fifteen pages of the Preface dealt with poetical principles and practices and argued against Samuel Johnson but did not mention *Cain.* The language of the second section of the pamphlet, a brief apology for quoting from *Cain,* prepared us for the tone of Wilkinson's treatment of Byron: the drama was a weak, impious, and monstrous production of ridiculous and detestable falsehood and blasphemy.

The third part, the epic fragment, started with a long invocation of the muse, proceeded to even longer descriptions of Satan and of Death and the latter's speech and then to the serpent's talk with Eve. Wilkinson strained for a pompous Miltonic style and larded his clumsy verse with jabberwocky: *frothy unction, deeplier gloom'd, terrid, unwarped, emanient, glore, slured, cronius.*

After a description of Eden, Wilkinson, without transition, turned to the human demon who had recklessly tried to spread infidelity. He made the usual objections to Byron's Preface and then jumped on Act II, provided the reader with samples of it at the bottom of several pages, and sprinkled his own lines with many of Byron's words to show how "nonsense foaming in blank verse runs mad." Since he took Genesis to be a true account of creation, he disapproved of Byron's use of Cuvier's book, because it was contrary to holy writ. The prehistoric monsters of Act II were incredible, and the concept that worlds and people had existed and been destroyed before Adam was a false and impious derogation of the deity. He also deplored Cain's curse of the Creator.

The last section of the bulky pamphlet, twenty-three pages of prose in

[45] For other quotations on Cain's conduct see "Annotations," III, 279, 286–316, 333–357.

small print, began with another violent attack on Byron's Preface, and then concentrated on the "folly, grossness, distortion, and absurdity" of the "wild and extravagant flight" into Hades. Wilkinson surpassed all of Byron's antagonists in the detail of his scrutiny of Act II. He was also unique in the kind of attacks he made on its content and style. The subject of literature, he asserted, should be the possible and the probable, and Byron had gone beyond the bounds of both. He should have used a narrative rather than a dramatic form, and had Cain dream about the flight and then relate the fantasy to Adah. Wilkinson thought that Byron presented it as an actual experience, and so, with abundant display of scientific knowledge, he argued that the journey and everything the travellers saw and talked about were impossibilities. He quibbled about the manner of Cain's transportation, with much ado about the first four words of Act II ("I tread on air"). Did Cain tread or fly with wings or was he borne by Lucifer? Byron violated all "the rules of astronomy" as well as those of physics, chemistry, and physiology. Cain could not have breathed, much less talked, in the rarefied atmosphere of remote space. Nor could he have known about the luminous belts of Saturn because there were no telescopes in Eden. Taking a hint from the remark that Cain and Lucifer were travelling like sunbeams, Wilkinson made some mathematical calculations about the speed and distance of the flight and concluded that they were going too fast to see anything at all. Moreover they could have seen nothing after they reached Hades because of the darkness there. He surmised that since they spent an hour talking in Hades, they had only one hour to go there and return and that even if they went at the speed of light they could not have flown out of the solar system in thirty minutes. He protested, therefore, that the stars could not have receded and vanished.

Among the many pages Wilkinson gave to such scientific debunking of the fantasy, he occasionally paused to chastise the poet for the same offenses that had angered the theological critics. He tore into Lucifer's allusion to the New Testament episode of Peter walking on the waves and even complained that Cain's inspiration about a power guiding the star and firefly made God ludicrous.

Wilkinson's main literary criticism was his mockery of Byron's diction. Unaware that he had mangled some language in his own verse, he combed many passages of *Cain* phrase by phrase and scoffed at the poet's inaccurate, nebulous, and inappropriate words. What did he mean by "conditional creed," and "the roundest of the stars"? Wilkinson denied that the earth looked like a circle *swinging* in the ether, that other orbs *swung* in the upper air, that the star-lights *rolled like leaves* along a stream, and that a man could be *tossed on water drops.* He pelted so much of Byron's vocabulary that by chance he scored a few hits, e.g., the careless and excessive use of *things,* which Lucifer applied indiscriminately to ideas, to planets, and to the preadamites and other dead creatures. He also spotted one sentence that Byron had ruined by an inept repetition of *such* and by a verb of dubious meaning here (*inherit*): "but as I know there are / Such and that my sire's sin makes him and me / And all that we inherit liable / To such . . ." (II, i, 192–195).

Though his scientific approach had a certain freshness and ingenuity and though some of his jibes at Byron's phrasing were valid, Wilkinson's disorganization and verbosity, his laborious sarcasm and stylistic gaucherie were self-defeating. We may be thankful that he did not finish either the epic or the commentary on *Cain.*

The Reverend John Styles. *Lord Byron's Works, Viewed in Connexion with Christianity, and the Obligation of Social Life: A Sermon, Delivered at Holland Chapel, Kennington.* London: Knight and Lacey, 1824. 31 pp.

This clergyman's values were strictly ethical and religious: virtue and piety were more important to society than genius. A man's worth to the community lay not in his talent, but in his principles and in the moral influence they diffused. The meanest follower of Christ, who might have little more intelligence than an idiot, but who was humbly useful in menial service, was more glorious than Byron's wicked and destructive genius. Styles professed not to circumscribe the range of poetry—so long as it was moral. Literature had to be didactic to satisfy him. The end of poetry might be pleasure, but that pleasure must be pure and innocent.

Guided by these principles, Styles praised Byron as an unrivalled genius, a writer of exquisite poetry, but lamented, more emphatically than Philo-Milton, that his wonderful gifts made his offenses all the more odious. *Cain* was "the glory and disgrace" of English literature. The "greatest genius of the age" became the greatest enemy of man. Though Byron enriched our literature, he "impoverished our virtues" and, like Voltaire, Hume, and Paine, was a disintegrating force. Byron's poetry was insidious because its charm and beauty made evil attractive and increased its deleterious power. Since his speculations were atheistic and misanthropic, he confounded all moral distinctions, annihilated man's immortal hopes, and left him desolate. Byron was an Epicurean, an advocate of selfishness, and an infidel.

Most of the sermon was confined to such generalities and much of its condemnation was aimed at *Don Juan*. Styles made a single expository statement about Byron's drama: since Cain thought God was a tyrant, his discontent led to rebellion. The preacher's other comments on the play were broad expressions of religious and moral disapproval. Christianity was the poet's aversion. *Cain* was "a vehicle of all the sophistries and subtle objections" that impugned the character and government of the deity and that were designed to perplex the reader, to make him feel that God was an enigma and life a burden. The poet's purpose was "to inspire the wicked with the pride of depravity." Since the later works of this "denaturalized" poet, this cool fiend, were all "saturated with impurity" and opposed to the laws of God and the state, the clergyman exhorted the youth of his congregation to read only those poems that wise and good people had not denounced. What these rarities were he did not say.

Sir Egerton Brydges. *Letters on the Character and Poetical Genius of Lord Byron*. London: Longman, Hurst, Rees, Orme, Brown, and Green, 1824. Pp. 264–265, 366–368, 450

The author's moral and religious bias was conventional He cast aside as futile Byron's defense of his play and considered it no longer necessary to repeat the answers to Byron's "attack on the goodness of Providence." Brydges followed the crowd in briefly defining the differences between Milton's Satan and Byron's Lucifer. Milton "always brings forward a *good angel* to controvert triumphantly all the daring assertions and arguments of the Evil Spirit." Byron made no attempt to expose Lucifer's malevolence.

Brydges reached the apex of that ambivalence we have already noticed in *The Monthly Review,* Philo-Milton, and Styles: with his right hand he chastised the poem for its frightful impiety, and with his left he conferred the most lavish praise it ever received. Cain was "the more dangerous because it [was] one of the best written" of Byron's poems. But he soon contradicted himself and parted company with Philo-Milton and Styles, who had likewise warned their readers that the poetic beauty of *Cain* increased its peril. Brydges now cheerfully reasoned that since the style was beautiful, "the most enchanting and irresistible of all Lord Byron's works . . .," this beauty acted as an antidote to its moral poison.

> . . . the class of readers whom this poem is likely to interest are of so very elevated a cast, and the effect of the poetry is to refine, spiritualise, and illumine the imagination with such a sort of unearthly sublimity, that the mind of these, I am persuaded, will become too strong to incur any taint . . . (p. 368)

Except for quoting a few admirable passages (e.g., Cain's praise of Adah's beauty and of the sky and stars), Brydges confined his remarks to generalities. The most extravagant compliment put Byron beside Shakespeare: ". . . there are speeches in the mouth of *Cain* and *Ada* [*sic*], especially regarding their child, which nothing in English poetry but the 'wood-notes wild' of *Shakespeare* ever equalled" (pp. 450–451).

James and Edward Aston. "A Dissertation on Lord Byron, His Moral Character—*Don Juan—Cain*" in *Pompeii and Other Poems*. London: Longman & Co., William Benning, 1828. Pp. 169–183

The Astons set their six pages on *Cain* (pp. 175–181) within a frame of general and favorable evaluation of the poet's intentions and achievements. Byron, they maintained, stood among the first rank of English writers, "an epoch in the annals of our literature." Although his stupendous powers would sway future generations, his appeal was limited to those who "had sympathy with himself." They anticipated the propensity of the Victorians for comparing Byron with other poets. He excelled his contemporaries "with the storm of passion," and among his predecessors, only Shakespeare was superior in wit, fancy, and emotional insight, while Byron equalled him in natural description and "in developing the feelings which link the mind to 'mute and material' things" (p. 182). Shakespeare had a greater range as a dramatist, for Byron, with all his energy and intellect, created people in his own image.

Since the Astons assumed that Providence made genius benevolent and that men of unusual talents were also inherently virtuous, they tried to account for Byron's dissipation and pessimism and to show that his poetry was not immoral and corrupting. The lack of firm, gentle guidance in youth, the acquaintances who fostered his bitter contempt, an isolation that deprived him of the society of his intellectual peers and that encouraged pride, a sensitivity to the slightest irritation, an unhappy marriage, the severe criticism and calumny that had been heaped upon him—these conditions made him ill-tempered and misanthropic. One should not therefore be surprised to meet defiance of established opinions and prejudices in Byron's poetry. The Astons found his skepticism fluctuating and casual and declared that he never deliberately attacked those feelings that were "the firmest bulwark of domestic and social happiness" (p. 171).

Cain was "the boldest, and, in its poetry, one of the happiest" of his dramas. Though the play had shocked piety, it had no malignant ideas and his "indiscretion" bore "no proportion to the obloquy" it had met with" (p. 181). The charge that he had introduced the question of the origin of evil in order to criticize the Deity was unworthy of refutation. The Astons did, however, try briefly to refute it. Cain's discontent, they pointed out, was due to an inability to reconcile his unhappiness with divine benevolence and power. It was logical that Byron should present this intense feeling passionately. Moreover, the poet had provided in the drama a refutation of his "self-tortured sophist" with Adam's resignation, Abel's serenity, and Adah's loving sweetness and persuasiveness (they quoted two of her speeches in Act III about Enoch and family love). Byron had contrasted Cain's pride and asperity with Abel's "fraternal tenderness and pious humility" (p. 179). All this was proof that "happiness arose from an incorrupt and well regulated mind, and was therefore almost wholly in the power of the individual" (pp. 180–181).

The Astons did not think that the treatment of the murderer was too sympathetic. All writers bestowed redeeming qualities on their heroes, and Byron gave fewer to Cain than Milton had to Satan, an angel of "fortitude, valour, and sagacity," willing to sacrifice "every selfish principle, . . . to deliver his fellow sufferers from thraldom" (p. 177). Milton had thus put Satan in a more amiable light than Byron did Cain, who had only one agreeable trait—his love of Adah. His misguided aspirations were rash, and he easily became the tool of Lucifer, who appeased Cain's thirst of knowledge only to increase his discontent.

If the Astons overlooked a great deal, they also praised two passages extravagantly: (1) Milton rarely surpassed Cain's "apostrophe to the universe, from the abyss of space"; (2) Cain's stupefaction as he looked at the breathless form of Abel should be associated with Lear's grief over Cordelia, Macbeth's amazement at Duncan's murder, and Othello's astonishment after he had smothered Desdemona.

Just as the Astons maintained that *Don Juan,* "the most indefensible of

Byron's poems," was moral, because it revealed the consequences of vice and folly, so their criticism of *Cain,* like the more specific and thorough analysis made by Harroviensis, reflected the moral concern of the decade. Their praise and occasional discernment were merged with an incongruous optimism and the chary purpose of showing that *Cain* was not subversive.

The Athenaeum. Frederick Denison Maurice [unsigned]:
"Sketches of Contemporary Authors. No. XII.—Lord Byron" (April 11, 1828), 351–352
"Lord Byron's Monument" (September 24, October 1, 1828), 751–752, 767–768 [The two-part article was signed "M." The authorship of this and that of April 11 was identified by Leslie A. Marchand (*Athenaeum,* pp. 252–253). For three reviews of books about Byron see *The Athenaeum* in the Bibliography.]

Late in the decade, as books appeared about Byron by Leigh Hunt, James Kennedy, and Thomas Moore, *The Athenaeum*, along with other magazines, reviewed them, offered copious selections and sometimes commented on Byron as a man and a writer. On these occasions almost no attention was given to specific poems. Kennedy's book evoked some toleration of Byron's dislike of religious sham, but *The Athenaeum* concluded that he had read and thought little about religion and that his questioning was the kind that came to "every half-informed and reflective mind" (June 19, 1830, p. 369). The review of Moore's *Life* also asserted that Byron's mentality was not profound. But his letters showed that the Conrads and the Giaours did not constitute the whole of his mind. He was neither great nor altogether bad, but a man of many delusions and weaknesses (January 30, 1830, p. 49).

The first article by Maurice, that appeared shortly after the *Athenaeum* began publication, revealed the tenacity of the moral and religious aversion to Byron among the popular journalists of the 1820's. Though a powerful, psychological poet, Byron's anti-Christian and impure tendencies were degrading. He encouraged sexual promiscuity and a disbelief in providence. Just as bad was his cynicism; he had no sympathy with humanity, no confidence in its goodness, and no love of truth. The single mention of *Cain* hinted at a fresh approach that Maurice was to take within a few months: because the heroes of the early poems were gross exaggerations, *Childe Harold* would do more harm than *Cain,* "and either of them more than the parody of 'The Vision of Judgment'."

In September and October, 1828, Maurice somersaulted with the argument that Byron was entitled to a monument in Westminster Abbey. In supporting his recommendation, he maintained that Byron's poetry had been influential and not by any means harmful. The popular and superficial tales could not have encouraged crime in more than one or two people. The unpopular tragedies had far greater power. Those who read *Cain* were at first sadder and, thereafter, wiser men.

The defenders of the poem had obscured its merit by attempting to compare the blasphemies of Lucifer with those of Satan. Maurice, like his predecessors, observed that the enemy of God had been fully confuted. He assumed that the Satanic rebellion had occurred within the mind of Milton, who had fought with it until he achieved a calm, certain faith.

Although Byron had never won such a victory, his skepticism was an intellectual trial that had been shared by every genius before his character was consummated. To explain the poet's moral immaturity, Maurice went to the same environment that the Astons had described in accounting for Byron's saturnine temper. A bad education, certain dissolute circumstances, "the temptation to sensuality, and the means of gratifying it" had arrested his development. But even in *Cain* there were "intimations," "flashes of light," that indicated the possibility of an eventual triumph over his handicaps. The value of the drama, however, derived not from these hopeful glimpses but from the skepticism itself. Since Byron sincerely wanted to find a "haven of truth," *Cain* was good for those minds who were spurred by the same longing and troubled by doubts. The poem was also pungent medicine for the complacent slave of custom, for it might awaken a dormant sensibility, shake it out of indifference, the greatest sin of the present age, and prick it into strong affirmation. Smug people should read not *The Excursion* of Wordsworth but *Cain*. "Do you think it will make them sceptical? Thank God for that too. For that scepticism will terminate in religion and that misery will conduct to happiness." Maurice's trust that out of doubt and struggle came Christian serenity enabled him to skip over the process by which a skeptic arrived at peace.

His distinction between Hume's and Byron's skepticism was cloudy and metaphorical. Hume puzzled not about "the laws of his own being," but speculated on matters detached from self, whereas Byron found doubts within his own mind. One could read Hume comfortably, but nobody read *Cain* without discomfort. This discrimination was less helpful than the contention that skepticism was sane and salutary and that Byron's poem was therefore beneficial to all men, and so he deserved a monument in the Abbey.

Harding Grant. *Lord Byron's Cain, a Mystery: With Notes; Wherein the Religion of the Bible Is Considered, in Reference to Acknowledged Philosophy and Reason.* London: William Crofts, 1830. 432 pp.

One might reasonably assume that no man could surpass Fabre d'Olivet's extraordinary effort to inform Frenchmen about what Byron should have written in *Cain.* But this assumption fails to reckon with the dogmatic fervor that evangelical Calvinism exerted in Great Britain for combatting spiritual peril. In 1830 it produced a book that must still be the most perverse and cumbersome polemic ever directed against one of Byron's plays or poems. Harding Grant, a barrister and author of *Chancery Practice,* had become acquainted and displeased with *Cain* when he saw some excerpts in one of the 1822 reviews. Like Fabre d' Olivet, he never read even a part of another work of the poet. Nine years after the publication of *Cain,* he read the entire play and was stirred to battle for the Christian cause.

His book spaced the 130 pages of the text of the poem generously, but interlarded this with, and overwhelmed it by 125,000 words of Grant's turgid prose, 300 pages in small print. Most of this verbiage was heaped onto Act I and the second scene of Act II. The first eight lines of the play elicited 10 pages of Grant's lucubration on what Plato, Aristotle, Cicero, *et al.* had allegedly written to prove the existence of God and to define the nature of deity and of atheism. The twenty-one lines of Byron's conventional hymn were granted over 19 pages of such matter.

Some of the "Notes" are a tolerable paraphrase of Byron's text, which Grant restated fairly and accurately. But when he reflected on Byron's intentions and assumptions and when he religiously evaluated what was said in the play, he found truth in not one line in fifty of the first two acts. His Calvinistic criteria of truth were the omnipotence, omniscience, and universal benevolence of God. Anything that Cain and Lucifer said that cast the remotest doubt on divine perfection drew from Grant thirty awkward sentences and one thousand ponderous words. Cain was forever mistaken, illogical, fractious, and hence an impossible human being. Lucifer spewed one tricky irrationality after another, and Grant labored to disprove them all. Every one of Cain's and Lucifer's ideas was rejected as fallacious, and every expression of anger or resentment denounced as baseless and unjustified. Byron got almost nothing right.

Unlike some of his predecessors, who fought Byron with an array of biblical or Miltonic quotations, Grant used few scriptural citations, referred to no men of letters, and quoted no theologian or philosopher, though he occasionally dropped a few famous names like Plato and Bayle. He relied on a solid store of common Calvinist doctrine and tried to write theological, ethical, and psychological argument. He is unreadable today because his phrasing is too redundant and prolix, because he continually meandered far afield in speculation about the unexpressed thoughts and feelings of Cain and Lucifer, and because he always opposed the barest hint of unorthodoxy with enormous rebuttal. He liked to dwell on a minutia and so wasted two pages on a definition of one of Byron's epithets for Lucifer, "Master of Spirits" (I, 99, pp. 54–55). Chew was kinder with this book than he was with others. "In this stout, handsome, well-printed volume [he must have seen a different edition from the execrable one I dozed over] . . . the notes . . . are often acute, generally not uninteresting, and always quite charitable and tolerant in tone."[46]

Since the disconnected bulk of Grant's "Notes" makes a summary difficult, a few samples will represent his method. In the eight pages on Cain's soliloquy, he regarded all of Cain's dissatisfactions as the result of misinformation, faulty reasoning, and an incredibly bad disposition. Why, for instance, should a man complain about work when the soil and climate obviously made farming easy and productive (pp. 40–41)? Grant rebuked Cain for wanting to enjoy the fruits of earth without working for them (II, ii, 124–130). All aspects of his discontent were equally unreasonable. "As to his not being able to 'gratify his thousand swelling thoughts with knowledge,' he has not given us a very favourable specimen of his manner of thinking, nor shewn, to any rational mind, that his 'swelling thoughts' ought to be gratified, or were worth gratifying" (p. 252).

Grant was consistently unsympathetic with Byron's characterization of the proud, unhappy rebel. When Cain spurned "happiness / which humbles me and mine" (I, 465–466), Grant declared that this attitude involved an absurd contradiction: it was contrary to the nature of happiness for it to humiliate anyone (pp. 172–173). Cain's criticism of God

[46] Chew, p. 100.

was always illogical; for example, the supposition that God would lose if Adah's beauty vanished (II, ii, 334–336). Since it was "part of God's . . . plan that every thing human *do* decay and perish," man must accept the revelation that all human beauty will be resurrected "beyond the grave" (p. 310). How should Cain have received the revelation and why have been convinced by it? No doubt Adam had told him, and all children should trust the wisdom of parents. Grant was especially impatient with Cain's suicidal tendency. To want to die was abnormal. No good Christian could be sick of life, and Cain, moreover, had no cause to be sick of it (p. 248).

In similar fashion, Grant debated all of Lucifer's speeches, phrase by phrase. For instance, he challenged Lucifer's boast that he could range over all space (II, ii, 368). The devil must be excluded from those regions "from whence he was *expelled for ever*." His "pretensions of having the range of all space, therefore, must be disallowed, and he be confined to Hell, or to such excursion in *this* world, as . . . may be *permitted* to him by the Almighty" (p. 317). Lucifer's description of the cataclysm of worlds was wholly imaginary and false, and everything he showed Cain in Hades had not a scrap of truth (p. 242). Lucifer's charge that God was destructive was another lie because the nature of the deity excluded cruelty and destructiveness (p. 244).

Grant denied that Lucifer had much knowledge; this sham was assumed to impress Cain. Although Grant probably did not know Harroviensis (he referred to no previous critic), he agreed with him in regarding Lucifer's avowal of sympathy for mortal misfortune and his assurance of Cain's immortality as clever flattery (pp. 58–59). The twenty-four pages on Lucifer's first extended diatribe (I, 137–163) treated it as a bold collection of lies. The last one hundred lines of Act II required thirty-nine pages to contend with Lucifer's Manicheism, his claim to sovereignty, his promise of eternal warfare, and his counsel to Cain about the exercise of reason in the determination of good and evil.

Grant's orthodoxy was so strict that, even though he thought Adah amiable, he carped at her venial errors. She was wrong in saying that the tree was the source of knowledge and sorrow (I, 351–353), "for . . . *eternal* sorrow was by no means the inevitable effect of the tree being that of *knowledge*, as Lucifer always affects to call it, in odium of the Almighty, instead of the knowledge of good and evil:—a material difference . . ." (p. 149). He objected to Adah's list of human misfortunes (I, 357–361), because she could not have suffered them (pp. 150–151). He even chided her for thoughtlessness in denying that she could find happiness in solitude (466–476). Had she forgot God's constant presence (p. 174)?

Grant found something to approve in Act II—Lucifer's appeal to Cain's jealousy of Abel (ii, 338–356), but he wondered how Lucifer knew of Cain's past envy of his brother (ii, 355; pp. 311–312). In Act III so much was either appropriate or innocuous that Grant had relatively little to say about it. He thought Byron made excellent use of Adah: "At every step, we see the author's aim to correct this unreasonable Cain . . . in Adah's remonstrance . . . and her sharp animadversions" upon Lucifer, "to whom she attributes the evil impressions upon Cain's mind" (p. 364). We might expect a screed on Cain's altar speech, but Grant wrote only six pages on it. He had repeated his arguments so often that he had worn them out. He was dissatisfied with Abel's prayer. In lines 226–230, he objected that "God *cannot* . . . temper his justice with mercy in regard of the *salvation* of man." Before he finished with Abel's speech, he decided that some of its lines were more suitable to Cain and Lucifer than to Abel because they presented God in an unfavorable light (p. 389).

Grant admired the psychological realism of the quarrel after the whirlwind (280–315) and wrote four pages describing the unbrotherly emotions of the contestants. Cain was, of course, wildly at fault until after the murder, and then Grant was pleased with the criminal's repentance (336–357, 371–379): "one should hardly have thought Cain capable of harbouring" such sentiments. He was willing to overlook the possibility that the change might be implausible, because he rejoiced over Cain's new emotions, which he considered good in the sad circumstances. He showed unusual insight in surmising that grief and guilt were the causes of Cain's prolonged silence during his family's agitation, though he later thought that it might be due to his "taciturn and sullen character" (pp. 407–418).

Grant may "have treated the proceedings and speeches of Cain and Lucifer with the same earnestness as if they were existing and earthly personages" (p. xvi), but no one could regard as real the people his corrections created. His renovation destroyed the conflict, the catastrophe, and the whole drama. Grant's reconstituted hero never would have been unhappy, nor have listened to Lucifer for two minutes, nor have made a journey through space to Hades. He would have tilled the earth patiently and industriously, and since Grant insisted on the propriety of animal sacrifice, his cheerful Cain would have bought a dozen fat sheep from

Abel at double the going price, and rendered a rich and redolent offering, more acceptable to God than Abel's, and put his sluggish brother to shame. But in eighteen hundred lines Byron had made sixteen hundred blunders, and the damage was irremediable, even though the length to which Grant went to rectify each error was exceeded only by the distance that Cain and Lucifer had travelled through the universe in Act II.

Some Victorians evidently read and thought about Grant's "Notes." The copy in the Stark Library has fallen to pieces, and one nineteenth-century owner pencilled a few pious remarks here and there. He seemed to agree with the author, but could not determine if Grant had read Swedenborg. It would be hard for anyone to discover that Harding Grant had read anything except the Bible and *Cain,* and the latter at least he never understood.[47]

[47] A few periodicals reviewed the book. The *Literary Gazette* ([December 4, 1830], 783–784) and *Fraser's Magazine* (III, [April, 1831], 285–304) mocked it and were gentler with Byron than they were with Grant. Another review appeared in *The Monthly Magazine* (May, 1830).

THE VICTORIAN APPROACH TO *CAIN* (1831–1899)

PUBLIC COMMENT on *Cain* from 1821 to 1830 had come mainly from the periodical reviewers and the religious pamphleteers. Though obscure folk and rabid or sentimental hacks contined a flow of print, the major writers, the academic historians, and the humanistic critics after 1830 also began to publish their reflections. The appearance of seventeen volumes on Byron's life and works, prepared by Thomas Moore and John Wright in 1831–1833, the changes in tastes and habits, and the passing of time encouraged the discussion of four big topics. The critics tried (1) to evaluate Byron's mind and character and (2) to give more substance to the view that autobiography was an important element in his poetry. (3) Those who liked an historical approach explained how social and political ideas and tendencies influenced Byron. (4) Most critics were now eager to rank Byron among his contemporaries and in the whole of English and even world literature. Their judgment fluctuated with the barometer of his reputation, falling to a dismal low by 1850 and then rising moderately after 1880. Notable exceptions were Swinburne's frenetic onslaught in 1884 and Alfred Austin's intemperate sponsorship in 1882.

The critics of this period were so fond of generalizing that few of them gave much space to particular analysis. For one reviewer of Volume XIV of Wright's edition, *Cain* was sad, terrific, and sublime. He quoted Adah's lament on the woe that followed her mother's sin and the girl's dread of

Lucifer's hypnotic power (I, 395–419). His introduction to the passage was vapid: such "domestic loveliness" and feminine naturalness he could not readily find elsewhere.[1] Writers were reluctant to look more closely at the text than this reviewer did. In 1831 Thomas Babington Macaulay defined eight qualities of the typical Byronic hero—pride, moodiness, unhappiness, defiance, capacity for strong affection, cynicism, scorn of his fellow men, and revengefulness. All but the last three belong to Cain's personality, but Macaulay made no specific discrimination, nor did he try to prove that these traits could be variously found in any one hero.[2]

One advance was that few major critics railed at the poem as a horrendous outburst of skepticism and atheism. Allan Cunningham in 1834 upheld the moral disapproval of the twenties. He thought that Byron had written the drama for an evil purpose and that when the devil "adds metaphysics to his other terrors we detest and shun him." He was therefore perhaps glad that *Cain* was a failure: "It can never be understood by the world at large." John Genest condemned Lucifer's charge that myriads of atoms were animated "for the sake of being consigned to eternal agonies."[3] Owen Howell thought *Cain* so harmful to religion that in 1843 he published a play, *Abel,* to provide a countersummation of pious, optimistic doctrine.

In 1889, Mrs. Margaret Oliphant, however, marvelled that there had been an outcry after its publication. She heard no profanity in Lucifer's talk; it was just what we would expect from him. Indeed his boast that his power was equal to God's was more shallow than Satan's "nobler claim" and his failure to promise happiness as the reward for disobedience, as well as the "tragical issue," showed Byron's "moral tendency." John Morley (1887) can serve as the spokesman of those Victorian liberals who respected Byron's intentions: "*Cain* remains, a stern and lofty statement of the case against that theological tradition which so outrages, where it has not already too deeply depraved, the conscience of civilised man." George Brandes proffered a rational tenet to dispel the blasphemy of the drama. *Cain* did not attack God, but only the "belief that the order of

[1] *The Athenaeum* (February 9, 1833), 86.

[2] Thomas Babington Macaulay, "Moore's Life of Lord Byron" in *Critical, Historical, and Miscellaneous Essays,* p. 359.

[3] Allan Cunningham, *Biographical and Critical History of the British Literature of the Last Fifty Years,* p. 290; John Genest, *Some Account of the English Stage, from the Restoration in 1660 to 1830,* IX, 137.

nature is a moral order and that goodness, instead of being one of the aims of human life, is its postulate."[4]

Certain perceptive readers—Brandes, Edward Dowden, William Gerard, John Nichol, and Roden Noel—observed one paradox in *Cain* that many early reviewers had missed: Byron was bound by Calvinist dogma even while he condemned it. They were aware that the drama was born amid a long and painful strife within the poet. While his heart and his logic arraigned the cruelty and injustice of evangelicalism, at the same time he was unable to escape his upbringing and its rigorous lessons of mortal sinfulness and divine vengeance. These commentators saw that the hero suffered an inner conflict between the habitual man that had been saturated with Scottish piety and the reasonable man that repudiated its deformity. Nichol decided that since Byron was grappling with perplexities and with doctrine he could never wholly accept or reject, *Cain* was "a dialogue between two halves of his mind." Noel, though sensing that Byron sometimes appeared "to take the whole orthodox position for granted in sheer despair of finding anything better," simplified his interpretation of the drama by attending mainly to its revolt against harmful religious conventions.[5]

On the other hand, a few critics, looking backward from a pinnacle of enlightenment, waved aside Byron's religious protest as bland and obsolete, no longer germane to current problems. In 1875 the iconoclasm moved Brandes no more than "a disputation on the belief in werewolves." J. A. Symonds, fifty-nine years after the publication of the poem, wrote that though *Cain* had a scandalous success in its day, the "advance in religious toleration and freedom of speech has shorn its daring scenes of half their lustre." Likewise, the passage that early reviewers had denounced for its immorality now aroused little concern. Harriet Beecher Stowe quoted I, 363–379, to prove that Byron argued against the sinfulness of incest, while Austin in his *Vindication* (1869) rallied what evidence he could to refute the charge.[6]

If the major Victorians were not excited by the moral and theological issues that had exercised their predecessors, they did have many opinions

[4] Mrs. Margaret Oliphant, *The Literary History of England,* pp. 64–65; John Morley, "Byron" in *Critical Miscellanies,* p. 162; Brandes, p. 313.

[5] John Nichol, *Byron,* p. 142; Noel, *Life,* pp. 162–163.

[6] Brandes, pp. 312–313; J. A. Symonds, "Lord Byron" in *The English Poets,* p. 251; Harriet Beecher Stowe, *Lady Byron Vindicated*, pp. 433–434.

about *Cain's* literary faults and merits. Readers after 1830 objected to the same lapses in grammar, sentences, diction, and versification that the reviewers had scorned. An era that enjoyed the metrical niceties and euphonious phrasing of Keats, Shelley, Tennyson, Arnold, Rossetti, and Swinburne was repelled by Byron's technical crudities. Samples of these were spotted in *Cain* as quickly as they had been in 1822. Mrs. Oliphant objected to the grandiloquence that some 1822 reviewers had praised. She thought the words too big, high sounding, inappropriate for the substance, and not poetic.[7]

There was less agreement about the scope of Byron's art. Matthew Arnold and others insisted that Byron lacked architectural ability and that he was most effective in isolated outbursts or in the eloquent portions of the long poems. Swinburne, throughout his 1866 essay, and Symonds maintained, however, that he was at his best in long, multifarious poems, *Childe Harold* and *Don Juan,* and that it was unfair to *Cain* to offer selections from it in an anthology, as Arnold had done. W. P. Trent's compliment would have delighted Byron: though he was inferior to many poets in any one achievement, he excelled them all in versatility. *Cain* and *Heaven and Earth* were almost as different from *Marino Faliero* as they were from *Beppo.*[8] Critics no longer lectured on the dramatist's penchant for the unities. Cunningham, Nichol, and Friedrich Blumenthal were the rare exceptions who returned to this tiresome debate. But the majority still debarred the dramas from the stage because of their paucity of incident.

Though Cunningham agreed with this view, he heard a higher strain of poetry in the dramas than in Byron's other work. In 1832 Bulwer Lytton, a year after Macaulay's essay, regretted that an indiscriminate depreciation of Byron had begun. He was perhaps the first to insist that the dramas, though their style was less rich and musical, possessed higher genius, nobler conceptions, and a greater artistic mastery than the earlier, more popular poems. According to Bulwer, contemporary readers had been disappointed because they did not always find in the plays what they expected and wanted—Byron's exotic self-portrait, in which they had been accustomed to lose themselves. Byron had formerly addressed the prev-

[7] Oliphant, *History,* pp. 65–66.

[8] Arnold, "Byron" in *Essays in Criticism,* pp. 100, 118; Symonds, "Lord Byron," p. 251; W. P. Trent, "The Byron Revival" in *The Authority of Criticism,* pp. 223, 230.

alent sentiment of the time. Perhaps Shelley was responsible for the change, inducing him to meditate on metaphysical matters and to explore human motives. Whatever the cause, Byron in the dramas ceased to be exclusively egotistical and to reflect only the temper of the age. He now dealt with thoughts and passions common to all times. Bulwer was thus one of the first critics to combat a narrow autobiographical approach to Byron's plays.[9]

In *Cain* he saw the same excellent art as in the historical tragedies, but since it had "more of the early stamp of Byron's mind" (his egotism?), it was so well known and its merit so universally allowed that he need not praise "the Hercules none have blamed." After the hullabaloo of the 1820's, Bulwer's encomium revealed either an historical naïveté or a crotchety intent to capsize decorous persuasion in the manner of Samuel Butler and Bernard Shaw. A few decades later Gerard, Trent,[10] and several other critics strode out as champions of the dramas and awarded *Cain* a very high rank, not only among Byron's works but in all of English literature. Noel called it one of the finest poems in the language. Brandes and Dowden admired its emotional power and social significance, and A. E. Hancock closed his chapter on Byron with climactic praise of the "mystery." Nichol offered his readers longer quotations from *Cain* than from the other poems, gave it almost as much attention as *Don Juan*, and paired it with *The Cenci* as the two greatest dramatic poems in the nineteenth century, superior to the efforts of Wordsworth, Keats, Coleridge, Browning, Tennyson, and Swinburne.

This approbation was not unanimous, for many gave a low rating to the plays. Henry Taylor (1834) and Paul Elmer More (1898), for instance, agreed with Goethe and Leigh Hunt about Byron's intellectual poverty and declared that the cosmic and the abstract endeavors of *Cain* were beyond his shallow resources. The staunchest defenders of his mind were those who were impressed by his liberalism: Gerard, Noel, Charles Kingsley, and the continental writers—Brandes, Giuseppe Mazzini, Karl Elze, and Blumenthal. But even Gerard declared that Byron was unable to cope with philosophical abstractions.

Some doubted or, like Thackeray, denied his sincerity and called him a theatrical poseur: "That man *never* wrote from his heart. He got up rapture and enthusiasm with an eye to the public . . ." Though the verse

[9] Edward Bulwer Lytton, *England and the English,* pp. 72–96.

[10] *Ibid.,* p. 86; Trent, "Revival," p. 231.

narratives and *Childe Harold* drew most of this censure, *Cain* either by implication or outright assertion was at times included, but no scrutiny of the play buttressed this charge, and indeed Swinburne in his earlier essay, Arnold, Ruskin, Trent, and others insisted that sincerity was one of his virtues.[11]

Several acute critics restated Talfourd's perception of a weakness in Byron's characterization: he gave his people too much introspection and self-description and did not render their traits in action. Though they protested that there was excessive discussion in *Cain,* a few allowed that the dialogue was often lively. Macaulay and too many of his successors repeated the cliché about the narrowness and the monotony of Byron's characters. Bulwer Lytton allowed that this stricture was fairly applied to the tales, but maintained that it was an absurd fallacy if attached to the dramas. He and Noel took the trouble to display Byron's range and variety by succinctly differentiating not only Cain, Faliero, and Sardanapalus, but also Adah, Myrrha, and Marina. Nevertheless, Lucifer and Cain were still considered to be almost identical twins. Swinburne in his 1866 essay saw no difference between them "except in strength and knowledge," and Noel did not make a single qualification about their resemblance. Macaulay declared that the animated exchange between Cain and Lucifer was a dialogue only in form, a soliloquy in essence, "a debate carried on within one single unquiet and sceptical mind. The questions and the answers, the objections and the solutions, all belong to the same character."[12]

Though the Victorians did not appreciate Lucifer's wit and cleverness, their psychological insight was often sound and penetrating and opened the door to the complexity of the two principals of the drama. Gerard identified at least eleven attributes of Cain's personality, some of them contradictions: "a soul ardent to know, yet always baffled—conscious of error, yet haunted by a rankling sense of injustice—capable of hope, pity, love, but compelled to hate, rebellion, despair, and remorse." Whereas the 1822 reader was repelled by Cain as a peevish and perilous fellow,

[11] William Makepeace Thackeray, "Notes of a Journey from Cornhill to Grand Cairo" in *The Works,* p. 625; Algernon Swinburne, "Byron" in *The Complete Works,* XV, 121; Arnold, "Byron," pp. 114–117; John Ruskin, Letter to Charles Eliot Norton in *The Works,* XXXVI, 574; Trent, "Revival," p. 215.

[12] Bulwer Lytton, *England,* pp. 76–90; Noel, *Essays,* p. 102; Noel, *Life,* p. 138; Swinburne, "Byron," XV, 129; Macaulay, "Life," p. 361.

Gerard, Noel, Elze, and Blumenthal denied that Byron had painted him as a sour and heinous criminal. Gerard did not discuss all the qualities he saw in Cain, but did give some space to his tenderness, to that human sympathy which "is the ground-work of his character." Elze also stoutly defended him. "Cain is by no means wicked, either before or after the murder; he is not envious, nor unfeeling, nor hateful, nor revengeful. He is a loving husband and a tender father."[13]

The psychological approach, however, did not often lead into cheerful galleries, for Victorian readers, no less than those of the 1820's, were estranged by Byron's vehemence and despondency. On one page of Mrs. Oliphant's literary history, she was pleased because Cain was more credible than the "weird recluse" and the "mysterious bandit" that Byron had fabricated in other poems. The difficulties of the first skeptic and first rebel seemed reasonable to her. But on the next page, she slipped into the sharp antipathy of 1822: Cain's ingratitude for the gift of life, his churlish complaint that he was not consulted about his birth, his sulky, ill-tempered rebellion—all this might be a legitimate subject for literature, but it was not to her sunny and gaudy taste. She preferred the earlier Byronic hero that she need not take seriously. Cain as a primitive rebel and misanthrope required the drapery of the "melodramatic cloak and sable plume" and "the furniture of mystery."[14]

Fifty years before Mrs. Oliphant, Macaulay had listened with displeasure to Byron's dissonant dirge that was a monotone of anguish: unhappiness is normal and all desire ends in disappointment. His heroes (and Macaulay was surely thinking of Cain among others) war with society, defying to the last "the whole power of earth and heaven" and they all arrive "at the same goal of despair," supported only by their Satanic pride and Promethean will. Noel's optimisitic bias was likewise typical of one Victorian outlook. He expected spiritual uplift from literature and got none of it in *Cain.* He was downcast by the youth's chronic grumbling about "honest labour," by his testy impatience, stubbornness, and constant ire over the injustice he saw in everything. The tragedy was depressing because the desires and meditations of the hero were consistently discordant and baffled and because his plight was hopeless. He had not the power to overcome obstacles or to change his unhappy state, and re-

[13] Gerard, pp. 193, 194; Elze, p. 416.

[14] Oliphant, *History,* pp. 64–66.

mained incapable of transcending defeat by self-discipline that would reward him with an impregnable inner peace.[15]

Dowden and Hancock placed Cain among the numerous company of Byron's antisocial men like Conrad, Lara, and Manfred. Mazzini, though embracing the poet as a liberal comrade, lamented this sterile isolation as a fatal flaw of egotistical idealism. Cain and the other heroes, he wrote, may thirst for good and be intoxicated with eternity, but when they attained personal freedom by repulsing their fellow men and withdrawing from society, they were "nothing more than free," and of no use to themselves or to anyone else. Their faculties and circumstances were inadequate to their desires and conceptions because they achieved no comprehension of humanity and pursued no altruistic and constructive mission, and therefore were social failures. Mazzini, like Goethe and Shelley and the young Wordsworth, sought for spiritual growth through active participation in the vicissitudes of the brotherhood of man. Mazzini regretted that Byron portrayed only the emptiness and the aimlessness of the life and death of the solitary individual, the lonely, futile aspirant, and the egotistical rebel. Similarly, Noel judged that Cain's career showed a failure of idealism, an incapacity for stoicism.[16]

The psychological critics were interested in Act III, in the tense scene between husband and wife, in the underlying and immediate causes of the friction between the brothers and in the emotions of the entire family following the catastrophe. Gerard and Blumenthal made a careful analysis of Cain's feelings during the quarrel and after the crime. Elze and Noel conjectured that Cain's opposition to Abel's animal sacrifice was caused by his tenderheartedness. Kingsley merged Byron's with Cain's experience and wrote a zestful and introverted exposition of the aftermath of the murder.[17] Eve's curse was reproved for the usual reasons, but Adah's brave initiative was commended as a superb conception.

Arnold in his anthology of Byron's poetry selected two sustained passages from *Cain* that illustrated two talents admired by the Victorians: the psychological realism of the scene with Adah in Act III, 1–161, and

[15] Macaulay, "Life," p. 363; Noel, *Essays,* pp. 99, 102; Noel, *Life,* pp. 162–163.

[16] Wilfred S. Dowden, *The French Revolution and English Literature,* p. 264; A. E. Hancock, "Byron" in *French Revolution and the English Poets,* pp. 90–91; Giuseppe Mazzini, "Byron and Goethe" in *Life and Writings*, pp. 68–73; Noel, *Life,* p. 163.

[17] Elze, p. 416; Noel, *Essays,* 98. See "Annotations," III, 333–357 for Kingsley's comment.

the descriptive power of the journey through outer space (II, i, 26–195). Stephen Phillips extolled the vast scene painting of II, i, 173–200; it left on the mind "a deep sense of the illimitable," and proved that Byron's imagination, though inferior to Milton's, was of high quality. Genest thought the one serious objection to *Cain* was that "the second act might be totally omitted without any detriment to the story." Blumenthal also spurned the description and the colloquy of Act II as undramatic and non-functional.[18] Dowden was almost unique in his defense of the concord of its setting and discussion:

> The poem is deficient in material action, but its dialogue is filled with . . . acts of the intellect; and in the flight . . . through space . . . while daring doubts are ever proposed and are ever met by daring sophistries, a sense is conveyed to us of the grandeur and immensity of the universe, and at the same time a sense of the mysteries which encircle and baffle the human mind."[19]

In 1866 when Swinburne was publishing his Byron anthology, he suggested that the entire second act of *Cain* be added: "these two scenes hold the kernel of the poem and will stand, as a shorter poem in dialogue, by themselves . . ." The most fervid praise that any portion of the drama received was accorded by Roden Noel to the "tragic intensity and pathos" of all the situations in Act III.[20]

The significance of such tributes and of the psychological exegesis, general though it was, is that the Victorian critics were finding a deeper seriousness in *Cain,* a broader scope of achievement, than Byron's contemporaries had. Later generations recognized a universality, a range of human experience that the clergyman and reviewers in 1822 were unable to see or admit. For Gerard, Byron had written a tragedy of human relations, of loss and frustration, and thus "Cain is the race itself." Although Brandes was often extreme, he too sought for the universals. Byron's compassion for suffering, "which it is impossible to relieve, but equally impossible not to be conscious of," was as strong as his anger at a power that created only to destroy. Hence *Cain* dealt with "the source of all tragedy

[18] Stephen Phillips, "The Poetry of Byron," *The Cornhill,* LXXVII (January, 1898), 23–24; Genest, *Account,* IX, 137; Blumenthal, p. 11.

[19] Dowden, *Revolution,* p. 277.

[20] Algernon Swinburne, *The Swinburne Letters,* I, 148; Noel, *Essays,* pp. 97–98; Noel, *Life,* pp. 160–161.

—the fact that man is born, suffers, sins, and dies."[21] The partisan zeal of Brandes drove him to claim for the drama a vast and optimistic allegory, most of which was fanciful and utopian:

> Cain is thinking humanity, . . . [beholding] millions of spheres rolling in freedom, high above Jehovah's rattling thunder-chariot. Cain is working humanity, which is striving in the sweat of its brow to produce a new and better Eden . . . of knowledge and harmony; a humanity which, long after Jehovah has been sewn into His shroud, will be alive, pressing to its breast Abel, who has been restored from the dead.[22]

Some earnest Victorians were stimulated by Cain's aspiration. Gerard read it as a "drama of yearning intellect." Brandes took Lucifer's name as a guide to the author's lofty purpose and hailed the devil as a true "bringer of light, the genius of science, the proud and defiant spirit of criticism, the best friend of man . . . he opens Cain's eyes." C. H. Herford's hope of progress ignored Byron's conception of Cain's futility: "He is humanity working its way by force of intellect to its own intellectual inheritance." Noel had some reservations about Cain's intellectual zeal. The hero's aspiration was checked by the Calvinist interdiction that denied free initiative to mortals, by an inertia that was the result of skepticism and disillusionment, and by an apathy endemic in the era.[23]

Cain's and Lucifer's cherishing of physical and intellectual liberty, which had antagonized the Tory reviewers, was as joyfully received by certain Victorians as it had been by Shelley. Mazzini, Noel, Dowden, Hancock, and Brandes welcomed Byron as a revolutionary poet. They maintained that the rebellion of Cain and Lucifer epitomized the opposition of all oppressed men to Metternich and the Holy Alliance, to all usurpation of privilege, and to all restraint upon freedom. When Cain asked if to be powerful was to be good, Byron, these critics averred, was asking if political power was good when its social fruits were bitter. For these liberals, the drama advocated democracy in both politics and religion and affirmed the right of the individual to determine his own conduct without undue interference from paternalistic authority. Cain and Lucifer were foes of all entrenched and indurated customs that impeded progress.

[21] Gerard, p. 93; Brandes, pp. 313–314.

[22] Brandes, p. 317.

[23] Brandes, pp. 315–316; C. H. Herford, *The Age of Wordsworth,* p. 231; Noel, *Essays,* pp. 98–99.

Brandes called Lucifer "the spirit of freedom," who was "overthrown because he would not cringe or lie," but who remained inflexible because he was eternal. When the Danish historian bent the drama to fit his view of nineteenth-century politics, he distorted those speeches that urged resistance to tyranny: Lucifer represented "not the frank, open struggle for liberty, but the feeling which inspires gloomy conspirators, who seek their aim by forbidden ways—the feeling which prevailed among the despairing young friends of liberty in Europe in the year 1821." Brandes also overstated Cain's revolt.

> [The drama depicted] the struggle between suffering, searching, striving humanity and that God of hosts, . . . [and of violence], whose weakened arms are forced to let go a world which is writhing itself free from his embrace . . . [God tried to exterminate the rebellious world]; but Cain rises unscathed from the ashes of the fire, and flagellates the priests with undying scorn.[24]

R. W. Chambers protested that the Victorian liberals had a false notion of Tory politics in the early nineteenth century and had accepted uncritically Byron's and Shelley's abusive opposition to the Tories. He did not mention the Victorian opinion of *Cain,* nor discuss many critics, but struck mainly at Morley's essay, which Samuel Chew had admired, but which had slighted *Don Juan* and "The Vision of Judgment." Chambers maintained that John Ruskin, though he despised Liberalism, had a truer and broader appreciation of Byron's qualities than did most Victorians. During his long career Ruskin praised Byron exuberantly, but he left only a few passing remarks on *Cain*: a "truly religious" work, on which Byron had "done his best."[25]

Between 1831 and 1899 five critics gave the poem detailed consideration. Nichol, who rated it as the best of Byron's eight dramas, wrote a synopsis with much quotation and little analysis. Brandes combined an incomplete summary with comments that were sometimes discerning, but often inaccurate and hotly seasoned by his revolutionary gusto.[26] Noel on two occasions awarded Act III a panegyric and also wrote a vigorous, if

[24] Brandes, pp. 315, 317.

[25] R. W. Chambers, "Ruskin (and others) on Byron," *The English Association,* Pamphlet No. 62 (November, 1925), 3–28; Ruskin, "Fiction, Fair and Foul" in *The Works,* XXXIV, 347.

[26] Nichol, *Byron,* pp. 142–147; Brandes, pp. 310–318.

unsystematic, estimate of Byron's ideas. His reflections on *Cain* merit reproduction here, along with selections from Gerard and Blumenthal, whose books are no longer easily accessible.

Roden Noel. "Lord Byron and His Times" in *Essays on Poetry and Poets.* Pp. 50–113. London: Kegan Paul, Trench & Co., 1886 [Had appeared in *St. Paul's Magazine* (November, December, 1873), 555–577; 618–638. The 1886 version has a few omissions, additions, and minor revisions.]

Noel struck at those shortcomings in the first two acts that had been the targets of earlier critics: the verse was clumsy, the treatment of character static, the teacher and his pupil alike, their discourse shallow, and their journey lacking in grandeur. He denied, however, that Byron restricted himself to a self-portrait and praised his ability to render a single experience in an intense situation. In his rhapsody on Act III, he was warmly specific about the suffering of the whole family and, like a shrewd attorney, wrote a sympathetic brief for his client, advancing the most favorable extenuation possible for Cain's anger and violence during and after the sacrificial scene. The murder was the inevitable outcome of the hero's frustration, compounded of inner and outer burdens.

In a haphazard fashion, Noel attempted an expository evaluation of Byron's, Cain's, and Lucifer's intellectual and emotional revolt. His most unusual ideas were (1) a scolding of Cain's indolence, impatience, obstinacy, and lack of stoicism and ingenuity in mastering his environment, and (2) a detraction of Cain's skepticism as the weak brain child of a superficial era. Noel, however, properly valued the fiery independence of both rebels and their opposition to current theology.

To this disorganized discussion, I have added two short extracts; one lavished on Adah a rich hyperbole and the other damned Byron's verse with superlatives as harsh as those of the 1822 reviewers.

But although I hold with Shelley, Goethe, Scott, and Wilson, that "Cain" is one of the finest poems in our language, the early portion of the poem, wherein Byron may be said to enter into direct competition with Milton, is surely a failure. There is no soul-overwhelming grandeur at all in those queer regions of space to which he conducts Lucifer and Cain, while the verse halts terribly. In the long discourse of Lucifer with Cain we discern little difference between them, while we do painfully feel here, as elsewhere in Byron where thought is wanted, that if Byron had been a thinker like Dante, or Milton, or Goethe, he might have sat beside the three greatest poets of Europe—Homer, Dante, and Shakespeare; but the lucubrations of Cain and Lucifer lack vigour and point, as those of Faust and Mephistopheles never do. It is in the human element, however, that "Cain" is so magnificent, as a *great dramatic picture*. And I cannot but think that though Byron is not a great dramatist, he is a great dramatic painter. I believe it is Wilson who says, that his groups and personages are as statuesque bronzes cast in the fire. It is to be recollected that Goethe, who ought to be an authority, most highly praised his dramas. Certainly he has not the wonderful skill in dramatic dialogue of Landor; nor in dramatic monologue of Mr. Browning. But where Byron is effective in drama, it is by lyrically pouring the quintessence of his characters into the mould of one supreme situation, capable of realizing them with the utmost intensity.

. . . there is little Shakespearian development of character in Byron, yet I should maintain, as against the ordinary criticism, that Byron can realize characters of a type opposite to that one type most congenial to his genius, sufficiently to present these as truly and vitally influencing one another, especially in certain supreme scenes or situations. That is not so in "Manfred," which is a mere monologue; but it so in "Cain," "Marino Faliero," and "Sardanapalus." From the third act onward, Cain becomes and continues magnificent—from where Cain mutters forebodings over little Enoch, his own and his sister Adah's child, while she gently remonstrates, to where Cain is contrasted with Abel, as the spirit of revolt and denial with that of tranquil faith, rising to utmost heights of moral dignity and wrath, where Abel confronts the blasphemer who would overthrow the chosen altar of Jehovah, his own proud offering lying unaccepted, his own altar smitten to the dust. There is nothing in English poetry finer for tragic intensity and pathos, than the supreme scene where Cain strikes his brother dead with a brand snatched from the altar, then bows in horrified remorse over the corpse—he who so sullenly arraigned the fated Doom, fated through his own passions, half-righteous and half-evil, to bring himself that dreaded Doom into the world; Eve, the mother of all, cursing with terrific energy her own eldest-born, slayer of her well-beloved son; gentle Zillah, Abel's wife, lamenting over him; and Adah, one of the most perfect types of holy womanhood in literature—Adah, when the dark smitten murderer bids her leave him alone, only answering with troubled wonder, "Why, all have left thee!" Then Cain, the brand upon his brow, wanders forth with

Adah into the wilderness, she leading their little Enoch by the hand, kissing Abel's cold clay, and praying "Peace be with him!" to which Cain in the last words of this great poem responds, "But with *me!*" Byron's Cain is by no means a very wicked man; he is surprised as it were into the murder, and, as matters are here represented, we feel that he did well to be angry. He with becoming dignity makes an offering appropriate to him, according to his light, which he may well hope that the all-seeing, just God will accept; he is throughout half-doubtful about his God, half-defiant of what seems to himself evil in that God. His very objection to the sacrifice of innocent animals proves him to be humane, and a foe to all cruel oppression, as also his abhorrence of human vengeance, even in Deity, if it were true that Deity needed to be propitiated by bloody sacrifice. Need Christians any longer think this poem very blasphemous? That there are *"no ideas"* in Byron, moreover, Mr. Arnold in the face of this poem should scarcely maintain; and Goethe goes a little too far when he says, "He is a child when he begins to reflect." I conceive "Cain" to be the philosophico-imaginative consummation to which the "Tales," "Manfred," and "Childe Harold" tended. Together with "Manfred," moreover, it proves Mr. Browning's objection as to Byron's unduly exalting Nature over men, a somewhat unfortunate one. If you must judge a poet as you would a didactic philosopher, I should say that Byron's error is, on the contrary, in unduly exalting the individual human spirit; in a lack of humility and resignation. Cain, like Faust, is insatiably curious, and chafes against the limitations of human knowledge; yet he represents a faithless, desultory time, which ours still is, moreover; for in this region of the intellect, he rather seems angry at not knowing without being at the trouble of learning; he takes no laborious pains reverently to seek truth. In that, too, Byronism represents an age of rather shallow scepticism, that sneers and sighs over the insolubility of problems, which it is too weak and idle manfully to grasp—but with a doom overshadowing himself, his beloved ones, and all mankind, which seems to him unintelligible and unjust, he refuses to be meekly happy and content, even though he loves Adah and his child. He is the genius of speculative yearning, oppressed and overcharged with evil within, the curse of hereditary sin; morbidly sensitive to evil without; overclouding all past, present, and prospective good with the gloom of his own sullen frown, out of which must inevitably spring the lightning of his crime; even by the side of his own true wife and his own sweet boy, *alone!* In a fine sonorous invective Lucifer avers that God Himself, however powerful, must be most miserable of all—

for He is the most *alone.* Could He but annihilate Himself and all; but alas for His and our *immortality!* Of such a God—proud, capricious, revengeful, apart—had Byron heard from accredited teachers. Cain finds too that "the *tree of knowledge is not that of life.*" Byron's is the wail of baffled human understanding, without faith, hope, resignation, self-control, inward harmony.

Christianity has taught him discontent with this life, but he cannot accept the solutions of her theologians; Byron defies and rails against his Deity. But of course *he* had only a lingering notion that the popular representation might be true, and that there was really a Creator, who, having created immortal spirits, tyrannically forbids them, as Lucifer finely phrases it, "*to use their immortality*," their reason, their conscience, and their heart. It is against this God, formed in the image of priests and kings, that Lucifer and Cain rebel, rather than against the true Author and Essence of Things. Of this true Author and Essence of Things Byron had unfortunately, from the circumstances of his time, and his own want of philosophic grasp, very little idea; yet he believed in *a* God; and very naturally, however irrationally, confounded the true God with the current orthodox conception of Him, against which he inveighed—if vaguely, still with enlightened soul, knowing that God was by theology caricatured, and that the vulgar conception was monstrous, and to be fought against. But after all, this was a *dominant* conception, one that had always been dominant more or less; the force of education, authority, universal conviction, practically moulding all the relations of society, together with the poet's own ineffectual habit of thought, forced the idea on him as a kind of reality; but his better, yet audacious self, dared to wrestle with it, even on this basis of its dubious reality; . . . What makes Cain sound blasphemous is that Cain believes in Jehovah, yet defies him; this is precisely as Shelley's Prometheus defies Zeus; . . . Lucifer and Cain, like Prometheus, are champions of human liberty. Cain's sullen hatred of effort and labour, his want of patient faith, his obstinate self-will, his ignorance of how to conquer Fate by calmly accepting it, or circumventing it by fertility of resource, this is truly evil and folly, and miserable weakness; . . . Adah is not to be surpassed for heavenly, yet human, tender, unsullied perfection of womanliness—a perfect sister, mother, wife; she is not surpassed in Shakespeare, Victor Hugo, George Sand, Walter Scott; even the Marguerite of Goethe is only equal to her. . . . The blank verse of Byron's dramas is probably the worst ever written by a great poet; the lines end in the awkwardest of monosyllabic parts of speech, "ands," "ofs," etc. There is no harmonious flexibility and resonance in the metre at all; and there is a quantity of tedious prose cut up into lengths. His ear was indeed most uncertain.

Roden Noel. *Life of Lord Byron.* London: Walter Scott, 1890. Pp. 159–164

When Noel seventeen years later came back to *Cain* in his *Life of Lord Byron*, he again condemned the verse as all very bad, ignored the first two acts almost entirely, wrote a more concise eulogy of Act III, omitting many actions and feelings that he had earlier considered to be wonderfully presented, adding a metaphorical sentence of general praise at the outset and paying a new tribute to the handling of Abel.

Noel was now less favorable toward Byron's thought because it was predominately destructive. He valued Byron's portrait of the unhappy hero at war with himself and his external state, and acknowledged the importance of the author's political and social rebellion against autocracy and outmoded conventions. But Noel would have been happier had *Cain* inspired him with a positive, challenging, or fortifying vision of the mighty capacities of the human spirit to endure and conquer, to create and grow.

Because we rarely meet a critic taking a second careful look at *Cain*, it seems worthwhile to offer a selection from Noel's later view of the drama.

> . . . Byron's great dramatic poem is "Cain." The scene between Cain and Abel, prior to the murder, before the two altars, and those that follow, are tremendous, equal to anything in our literature. The terrible situation is wonderfully realized, and the protagonists start out before us, revealed as by a lightning flash, lurid and awful, in the supreme moment of their career, into which moment their whole life and character are, as it were, fused and concentrated—of colossal stature; so to speak, cast in bronze. From the third act onward to the end the work is grand. Cain embodies the spirit of revolt and denial, Abel that of tranquil, reverent faith; Cain is the outcast, the Denier, the Rebel, and Abel is as fine as Cain when he confronts the blasphemer, who would overthrow the chosen altar of Jehovah, his offering left unaccepted, his altar smitten to the dust. Then, having slain his brother with a burning brand, Cain bows in horrified remorse over the corpse, knowing himself fated—even he—to bring that heretofore unknown, dread doom of death into the world! Eve curses her firstborn, but Adah, his wife-sister, when the stricken murderer bids her leave him, only answers in troubled wonder: "*Why, all have left thee!*" So Cain wanders forth into the wilder-

ness with her, she leading their little Enoch, kissing Abel's cold clay, and praying: *"Peace be with him!"* to which Cain, in the last words of this great poem, responds with so much weight of meaning: *"But with me!"*

But this work raised such a storm of reprobation in England, that Murray was threatened with prosecution, and so Byron offered to come over and stand his trial as the author. It was thought very blasphemous; at which continental critics are surprised; but free thought had not then made much progress in this country. This is Byron's most important contribution to the discussion of religious problems, so far as they bear upon life and conduct; yet it is of small value in that respect. Byron had no metaphysical or speculative faculty. Still his powerful intellect brooded over these questions, but he remained always more or less of a sceptic. His was not a constructive period in speculative, or political questions, so far as England was concerned. . . . "Cain," therefore, so far as its contribution to thought is concerned, is chiefly important for its negation, and revolt against unworthy conceptions of religious truth. The inward disharmony and discontent of a nature not reconciled with itself is the psychological condition most powerfully depicted in the character of "Cain." He is one who overclouds all past, present, and future good with the shadow of his own sullen frown, out of which must inevitably spring the lightning of his crime. But there is no alchemy in "Cain" potent for the transmutation of suffering and endurance into richer life or deeper vision. Even honest labour seems to him a mere curse, unfruitful in blessing. All that happens is unjust, and evokes defiance; disappointment is never borne with the heroic fortitude that converts it into priceless self-education. How have we retrograded here from the serene and brave philosophy of Epictetus, and Marcus Aurelius! Yet there are such elements, it must be admitted, in the lovely patience and devotion of Adah, as also in the gentle and religious submission of Abel.

Cain, whatever the author might pretend, is felt to be a main channel for what is most characteristically personal in Byron. And the poem was an undoubtedly powerful protest against certain officially orthodox representations of the Divine Character, upon which so much that was immoral and unlovely in some of our most cherished institutions had long rested. Hence a great part of the loud horror, and shocked protest of our official and privileged classes against it. There are, indeed, two great ideas in Byron, though both Goethe and Matthew Arnold are disposed to deny him any; these are *Individuality*, and *Popular Freedom*—no patient fortitude does he teach; but aggressive energy, defiance, daring. . . . Therefore, both Lucifer and Cain (Lucifer is only a shadowy Cain) declaim passionately against a God who forbids a man to use his own inalienable spiritual inheritance, his reason and conscience, to develop his personality in his own way. Lucifer and Cain, like Prometheus, while rebelling against the established order, personified whether in Zeus, or Jehovah, even as Byron against the "Holy Alliance" of states and hierarchies for the benefit of usurping privilege, and for the oppression of peoples—are indeed champions of the true hidden God, of the Ideal, who manifests Himself progressively, who ever breaks up, and recasts, even the best customs, habits, and institutions which have served their purpose and become tyrannical, no longer protective of that expanding life within, but, on the contrary, imprisoning and fatal. Yet the earlier portions of this poem, imaginatively considered, where Byron competes with Milton, seem to me poor; while the verse often halts. With occasional hesitations, Byron did believe in God, and in the immortality of the soul. . . . But the poem is full of superficial objections, like the following:

> *Cain.* Then my Father's God did well
> When he prohibited the fatal tree.
> *Lucifer.* But had done better in not planting it!

The idea that from Discord may grow a higher Harmony was beyond its scope. It is a pity that Byron had recourse to evasions in defending his work against the almost universal chorus of objectors; but then he wavered in his own mind as to his own beliefs.

William Gerard [W. Gerard Smith].[27] *Byron Re-studied in His Dramas; Being a Contribution towards a Definitive Estimate of His Genius.* London: F. V. White & Co., 1886

If one has recently endured the preaching and turgid redundance of Grant and Fabre d'Olivet, he turns gratefully to Gerard's essay, which comes from the entirely different world of *belles lettres* and sweeps from one grand generality to another. Along with Bulwer Lytton, Arnold, Nichol, and Roden Noel, Gerard sought to check Victorian depreciation of Byron and to rehabilitate the poet's reputation. Though he may not have read Bulwer's 1832 praise of the dramas, Gerard grasped that critic's radical thesis and boldly tried to show that the dramas, one of the less respected of Byron's forms, were the supreme expression of his genius. In method and content Gerard's book belongs to a long British tradition

[27] Robert Escarpit (*Lord Byron: Un Tempérament Littéraire*, II, 295) referred to the author as Mrs. W. Gerard Smith. The British Museum catalogue did not note the pseudonym, though Chew did (*Byron in England: His Fame and After-Fame*, p. 400) and both implied that the writer was a man.

of literary appreciation that has flourished from the eighteenth century to the present. Only 50 of the 229 small pages discussed, with a modicum of detail, the particular themes and characters of the eight plays, allowing about 6 little pages for each play. The rest of the book assembled a host of imposing generalizations on dramatic topics, many of them couched in figurative and emotive language.

After a wide historical approach to his subject, Gerard worked toward broad theses about Byron's poetry and dramas. He conceded a large number of stylistic flaws and the usual limitations in design and characterization, but then exalted Byron as an important leader among a group of European writers who were trying to develop a new kind of drama that subordinated action and character to idea. Each of Byron's plays was "the evolution of an idea" (p. 155). He agreed with the customary opinion that a strong autobiographical pressure and the Promethean spirit of revolt controlled part of the writing of the dramas, but he also maintained that Byron went beyond egotism and personal rebellion to the complex emotional problems of humanity (pp. 64–67, 179). Gerard claimed for the plays a moral seriousness that many others had found lacking in Byron's poetry. The dramas dealt with common experience, with the great ideas and problems "dear to the heart of humanity," "with the inward meanings of things, not their mere outward shows and effects" (pp. 144, 151).

In the last section of his essay, Gerard's enthusiasm dashed into a series of comparisons between Byron and a select company of dramatists from Aeschylus to Goethe. He found that Byron, in spite of many defects, shared now one and now another of their varied talents and insights. Sophocles' sympathy for the nobility of man and his perception of fateful irony, Euripides' keen sense of pathos, Shakespeare's universality, Alfieri's and Schiller's presentation of man's aspirations, Goethe's conceptive power, "intuitive of the latest tendencies" of the present age, and his ability to articulate them and reveal the world to itself (pp. 200–202). Finally, Byron's dramatic achievements made him superior to Scott, Landor, Keats, Shelley, Coleridge, Leopardi, Musset, Lamartine, Hugo, Heine, and Tennyson, and enabled him to share poetic eminence with Wordsworth (pp. 202–210).

As evidence of Byron's humanism and probing gravity and as proof that he deserved high literary rank, Gerard described the tragic protagonist of the eight dramas, whom he called Dipsychus, a Faustian embodiment of the conflict between affirmation and negation, aspiration and despair, love and destructiveness (p. 78). Sometimes Dipsychus was split into two opponents: the suffering, loving soul and the renouncing, destroying soul. More often these opposites clashed within one turbulent personality. Gerard, speculating about Byron's interest in Tiberius as a tragic subject, thought that the outward degradation of the emperor and the ruin, turmoil, and despair of his powerful mind followed the pattern of Dipsychus (pp. 73–77).

This description of the bifurcated protagonist, together with three specific observations, was pertinent to *Cain*: (1) The nobler half of Dipsychus was a seeker for knowledge, "thirsting to enjoy"; the worse half touched Mephistopheles (pp. 79–81). (2) "The primary phase of Byron's dramatic genius [was] the delineation—born through self-suffering—of a soul spiritually at bay" (p. 227). (3) The Byronic woman always accompanied these opposing principles of good and evil as "a moral necessity of their existence" (pp. 78–79).

The following excerpt is Gerard's analysis of *Cain* (pp. 93–99). It should be read in the context of the preceding survey of this author's general aims and conceptions. At the beginning and end of the selection, pursuing his thesis of Byron's universality, Gerard made Cain representative of certain forces that persist in human experience. In his exposition, though he did not allude to Harroviensis and the early reviewers, some of his perceptions duplicated theirs and anticipated many that were to be made by Blumenthal, Brooke, Chew, and later twentieth-century commentators. The following ideas were common to them all: Cain's aspiration, disappointment, and revolt, his domestic tenderness, the identity of Cain and Lucifer, Adah's devotion, and the criminal's remorse. Since Gerard defined many of the artistic merits and defects of Byron's plays that Chew later discussed, the latter's judgment (1915) that the monograph was "almost worthless" was unwarranted. In 1924 Chew retracted his statement, praised the book, surveyed some of its content, but wrote nothing about the particular analysis of the plays.[28]

Gerard did not support his opinions and had only six citations in the pages on *Cain*. I have retained the first one.

> If Manfred was Byron and something more, Cain is a conception infinitely higher and opens immeasurable horizons. Manfred, as a Hamlet-like soul, is interesting to men, but Cain is the race itself, and his ruin the ruin of mankind. The poem is at once the mythus of the human mind that "looks

[28] Chew, Preface, n. 1; Chew, *Byron in England*, pp. 317–319.

before and after"; the tragedy of its aspiration that thirsts vainly for an apprehended good; the drama of its Paradise Re-lost. Dipsychus is here distributed between Cain and Lucifer. Cain as a mere incarnation of revolt is inexplicable and undramatic. But his revolt is the measure of his aspiration, and thus becomes clear and explicable and grandly dramatic.[29] Sympathy is the ground-work of his character; human affection pulses in him at full. To his parents he is not undutiful; to his brothers and sisters he can say, crossed as he is, "Your gentleness must not be harshly met." He is "wrought upon" by "Abel's earnest prayer." For Adah his love is such that "rather than see her weep" he would "bear all"; and the sight of his son Enoch awakes in him an inexhaustible tenderness. Akin to his human sympathy is his intellectual aspiration, which seeks indeed knowledge, but only as being "the road to happiness." Nor will he believe that evil must ever be a part of all things, for his own emphatic avowal is: *"I thirst for good."* The beginnings of the tragedy are by now apparent, but there is still hope. Cain's "mind of large discourse" apprehends an injustice in his fate, but may not a larger knowledge solve it? He would only be assured that all is not in vain. "A thousand swelling thoughts, a thousand fears" are within him; "knowledge" is his reiterated cry. At this point he meets Lucifer, who is but his complement—a Cain superhuman and immortal. His revolt begins where Cain's leaves off, and is based on defiant *hopelessness*. Byron, therefore, with perfect consistency represents him as capable of sympathizing with Cain, but unfeelingly, and as showing involuntary reminiscent touches of magnanimity and pity—the insidious traits of a spirit which by the very nature of its being seeks to involve others in its loss. Against this hopelessness clashes Cain's yet unquenched hope, and the tragedy is consummated. Cain is what he is. Were he weaker it were his salvation. But he cannot "think and endure" supinely as the fiend mockingly advises him. *Thinking,* he must hope, and, the hope destroyed, revolt. Aspiration, turned back on itself, creates an eddying madness in his brain, and he slays—not Abel, but injustice momentarily personified. The deed done, his human affections surge back; he feels horror, remorse, and would willingly give his own life for the brother he has loved and slain.

To Cain is given his counterpart Adah—the woman who feels and loves as fulfilment of the man who aspires and would know. The boundless desire of Cain is outbalanced by the noble comprehensiveness of her love and

[29] Gerard's own note: "Byron has, in this instance, clearly expressed his dramatic purpose. The despair and consequent murder arise, he explains, from Cain's 'rage and fury against the inadequacy of his state and his conception'."

sympathy. "Who," she exclaims, "could be happy and alone, or good?" Alone, she "could not nor *would* be happy." This unselfishness comes out in the tears she sheds for Lucifer, whom she mistrusts, and in the swift apostrophe when her parents are mentioned: "Would I could die for them so they might live." And how much wiser is her feeling than Cain's reasoning! Hers is no unreflecting love. Its note is clear-sightedness. It reasons, and therefore wisely will not reason. She cannot answer the "immortal thing" who yet, she feels, "steps between heart and heart," but, steadfast to her intentions, urges Cain to "choose love." Nor does her devotion blind her for a moment. Cain she would never leave though his God left him; yet while she clings to the murderer, shrinks from the deed that calls for her self-sacrifice. Nor, at the last, is she a mere clinging Medora, but a resolved woman. Henceforth her office is "to dry up tears and not to shed them"; and her last words have almost the sternness of an exhortation: "Now, Cain, I will *divide thy burden* with thee."

The idea of *Cain,* involving as it does the problem of man's being, demands to be shown in its relation to human lives in general. Hence the dramatization, which is effected by a small but adequate group of subsidiary characters. Abel and Zillah, in dramatic contrast to Cain and Adah, suggest the tranquillity of the life that is at one with itself. The deed of Cain dissipates this tranquillity and at once lets loose the anarchic discords it had but filmed. The remorse of the murderer himself, the sad resignation of Adam, the mute despair of Zillah, the crowning denunciation of Eve, attest, in an overwhelming climax, the complete disintegration of the human ideal; and the tremendous *"But with me!"* of Cain expresses not merely the burden of his own punishment but the burden of the mystery of the human spirit ever distracted between its aspiration and its destiny.

This drama moves in an atmosphere finely reflective of its spiritual meaning. It is a drama of the yearning intellect, and the starry world of space is opened as if to afford room for the spirit's utmost expansion; it is a drama of human relations, and the sway of the heart's emotion finds an outlet in reiterated passages of tenderness and beauty; it is a drama of loss, and yearning cadences as for some "regretted Eden" continually sigh through it like the moanings of an Æolian harp.

Friedrich Blumenthal. *Lord Byron's Mystery "Cain" and Its Relation to Milton's "Paradise Lost" and Gessner's "Death of Abel."* Oldenburg: Gerhard Stalling, 1891. 12 pp.

Blumenthal's short monograph is a sane and deliberate comparison; he was sentimental only in the discussion of two of the Eves. His exposition of the motivation, the personalities of Cain and Adah, and the limitations of the drama was perceptive and rationally balanced.

The first four of his closely printed pages are the longest and most objective synopsis of the play that I have seen among nineteenth-century commentators. When the author came to his announced topic, he was briefer and more thoughtful than Harroviensis and Philo-Milton in drawing parallels between *Paradise Lost* and *Cain.* All of these, as well as some that he did not mention, have been included in the Annotations, except for his observation that neither Satan nor Lucifer could feel fear and that neither was limited by any mortal weakness. Though Blumenthal overlooked most of the differences between these two great spirits, he did note that whereas Satan was given a formidable and monstrous body, Byron had tried to excite our sympathy for Lucifer by endowing him with celestial beauty, "a certain melancholy unhappiness," and a fascination that stirred Adah deeply.

The resemblances that he pointed out between Cain and Milton's Adam have likewise been recorded in the Annotations. In his remarks on the relationship between Gessner's characterization and Byron's, he described the former's mediocrity:

> The demon Anamelech . . . is an altogether inferior creature. . . . He is a devil of the lower order who wants to rise in rank above his companions in hell, by committing an infamous deed. He chooses Cain for his instrument, but instead of boldly making his appearance like Lucifer, he approaches him stealthily while asleep and inspires his dreaming victim with the thought of murder. When the fatal deed is done, he sneeringly delights in his success and shows his contemptible meanness by mocking the dead body of the pious Abel. He dares not openly brave the Almighty; as soon as the heavenly power attacks him, his cowardly nature is developed, he flees howling to hide himself in hell. (p. 6)

Blumenthal thought that the two Abels were similar in their meekness, piety, and affectionate nature. Byron's Abel was not quite "so soft and lachrymose" and energetically resisted Cain's attempt to destroy the altars (p. 9).

He likewise saw some resemblance between Adah and Gessner's Mehala.

> [The latter is] sad and melancholy, and her soft temper suffers severely

from her husband's stern and inflexible nature. In one or two instances, she reminds us of Adah, particularly when, after the murder, she implores Abel's wife Thirza not to curse her wretched husband and when, not heeding Cain's opposition, she insists on accompanying him into banishment to share his misery. But, all in all, her character is not so richly developed and is less distinctly marked. (p. 10)

Blumenthal was repelled by Byron's Eve.

[She is not only partial to Abel,] but unnaturally cruel in her bursts of passion against Cain. Although he stands before her, . . . contrite and unable to utter a word, she does not check her rage. Regardless of Adah's imploring words . . . [404–407] she pronounces such a deep malediction upon her miserable son that we must believe her destitute . . . of all womanly feeling. When she ends her imprecation . . . we turn away from her with disgust. Byron has not drawn a passionate woman, but an impossible character—for what mother could turn into such a horrible Fury? One might wish that the poet . . . had copied either the loving wife of Adam from "Paradise Lost" or Eve, as she is represented by Gessner. (p. 10)

His bias appeared in his approval of the maternal and devout ideal drawn by the emotional German:

In the latter we find a simple unpretending woman, whose aim it is to fulfill her duties to husband and children. Treating all the members of her family with equal kindness, she carefully tends Adam, while he is suffering, and she is anxious to banish from Cain's mind the gloomy thought, that he is less loved by his parents than his brother Abel. The sight of this son killed, fills her with violent grief, but instead of cursing the murderer, she accuses herself as the one who has first trespassed against God, and thus brought sin and death into the world. However, she does not abandon herself to sinful despair; the first painful agitation in her breast having subsided, her gentle soul finds consolation in praying to the Almighty. (p. 10)

Blumenthal mentioned Cain's sensitivity to beauty, his intellectual curiosity, his aversion to violence, his pity of the animals, his lack of jealousy of Abel, his love of his family, especially of Adah, to whose gentleness he quickly responded, and his compassionate resentment over Enoch's destiny. He wrote a long account of the murder, which he regarded as unpremeditated. When Cain entreated his brother not to urge him to sacrifice, but to leave him, "he must have had a presentiment of the fatal issue of the holy rite and therefore instinctively shrunk from it." His displeasure increased with Abel's persistence, but not wishing to offend him, he yielded to his brother's demand. When God refused Cain's worship, Blumenthal surmised that Cain recalled Lucifer's scornful statement that Abel's sacrifices were always acceptable and that Cain's wrath was thus kindled by his wounded pride. Abel's advice that his brother offer a new gift then seemed an insult, and Cain felt that he had to destroy the altars, which reminded him of his disgrace. Knowing that his passion had become dangerous, he cautioned Abel not to oppose him, but the latter was heedless and provoked the fatal blow (pp. 7–8). Blumenthal admitted that the influence of Lucifer was a preliminary cause of the murder, but he underestimated the extent of Lucifer's damage to Cain's mind. He did see that the murder was the climax of "Cain's resistance to the Almighty's will" (p. 3). Blumenthal stressed one part of Cain's emotional history that many of Byron's contemporaries had ignored—his remorse and repentance after the murder.

He was almost as eloquent as Noel in his admiration of Adah, whom he regarded as the best portrait in the play. "She is one of the most beautiful female characters that Byron has created and belongs entirely to his own conception. . . . Adah keeps our interest alive from the first moment when she appears to the very end of the play" (pp. 10–11). He described her intuition of Lucifer's evil nature and her resistance to it:

> Without knowing who he is she instinctively shrinks from the prince of hell, and warns Cain not to associate with him, for a true feeling tells her that, in spite of his dazzling beauty, this spirit is not an angel of light. Though his supernatual power may captivate her senses for a moment, she does not hesitate to free herself from this influence as soon as she perceives that it is an ungodly one. (p. 9)

Blumenthal praised her trustfulness, her ardent preference for love over knowledge, and her ability to soothe her husband. He dwelt upon her solicitude for him in Act III:

> When her husband is accused by Eve of the horrible deed, she is most anxious that he should clear himself from this guilt, and his crime being undeniable, she implores her mother not to curse him, and cries to heaven for mercy, when the angel has pronounced the Almighty's sentence which Cain, deeply moved, hears in mute resignation. While all the rest of the

> family leave the murderer to despair and misery, she clings to him as to her husband, whom she is willing to follow wherever he may lead . . . We are filled with the consoling thought that, however great the misery of Cain may be, it will not crush him, while he is guarded by this angelic companion. . . . It almost seems as if in painting Adah, Byron had combined all that is sublime and beautiful in woman . . . (pp. 9–10)

Blumenthal's discussion of the dramatic limitations of *Cain* was a summary of most of the strictures that earlier critics had made. Byron's concern for the unities was a pointless handicap. More serious was a persistent subjectivity that saturated the characters with Byron's own feelings and ideas and that produced lyrical, not dramatic, poetry. An even greater flaw was the lack of variety, especially the "fundamental resemblance between Cain and Lucifer." Both expressed "the same bitter indignation and implacable discontent" (p. 11). There was no character development; the people were complete when we first met them and did not change thereafter. He found the dialogue, with few exceptions, sluggish and too much involved with "metaphysical reflexions" to hold our attention. He underrated Act II:

> The description of those wild and supernatural regions is no doubt very beautiful, but it contains nothing really dramatic, there is no action and no life, and as for the development of the play the flight through the universe and the visit to Hades might have been left out altogether, so little do they contribute to bring on the catastrophe. (p. 11)

He did, however, touch on the psychological purpose of the journey: "Cain more and more gives way to the power of Satan, who rouses ambition and discontent in his soul and strengthens his doubts about the Almighty's goodness towards man" (p. 2). Blumenthal concluded that *Cain* was a memorable psychological poem—"rich in beautiful and masterly descriptions of the human heart and passions" (p. 12).[30]

[30] Additional references in the "Annotations" to the monograph concern Miltonic parallels: I, 441–450; II, i, 34–43; II, ii, 89–103.

CAIN IN THE TWENTIETH CENTURY

AN ESSAY BY W. M. Payne (1907), that had not a word on *Cain*, was almost a summation of the decade's understanding of Byron. Payne quoted the opinions of two dozen critics; wrote an analysis of Byronism; slighted its pride, sensuality, guilt, egoism, and flamboyance; mentioned some of the pressures on his character and writing, but missed Catherine Gordon, the lame foot, the Scottish elders, Augusta Leigh, the Alps, and a few other matters; accounted for the decline of Byron's British fame and the growth of his foreign popularity—and did all this in thirty pages. Payne and his colleagues were as general as the critics of Byron had been since the time of Macaulay. Arthur Symons stated that Byron did his best writing when he was stirred by the passion for liberty, the passion against injustice, the passion of the will to live, and the passion to know, which fretted against the bars of death and ignorance.[1] Three of these generalities were true of *Cain,* but Symons in his history of the Romantic movement did not pause to write a particular exposition of them.

In some respects, too, there was little difference before and after 1900 in the commentary on *Cain.* The views of Symons, P. E. More, Stopford Brooke, and W. J. Courthope were closer to nineteenth-century thought than to the tenor of Byronic criticism after 1940. One reason was that

[1] Arthur Symons, *The Romantic Movement in English Poetry*, p. 261.

some books published in the first twenty years of this century had been written in the 1890's. More's introduction to his 1905 edition of Byron was a fusion of two articles that had appeared in 1898 and 1901. Brooke's essay, "The Poetry of Byron," printed in 1920 in *Naturalism in English Poetry*, was written in 1887.[2] A more common reason why the year 1900 marked no boundary was that certain ideas that had settled in the minds of critics in the 1820's were continuously repeated for the next 145 years.

The preoccupation of *Cain* with theological problems was still regarded as mental autobiography. In 1910 Courthope entitled his chapter on Byron "The Poetry of Romantic Self-Representation" and assumed that Byron had used *Cain* as a vehicle of his own insurgence. Though Courthope accepted Matthew Arnold's verdict that Lucifer's Manicheism was inappropriate, if judged by the canon of credibility, he waived that requirement because he read the dramatic poem as a personal lyric.[3] One of the fixations of Byron criticism—an exclusively biographical approach to his writing—has persisted to the present day.

Most commentators have accepted the traditional exposition of the religious content of the play, and continued the toleration and condescension of the Victorians. Symons was annoyed that the poet had filled his dialogue "with exactly the same arguments that he used in his conversation with Dr. Kennedy." Byron's anti-Calvinism was usually stressed, not with the rancor of the 1822 clergymen but with approval. Samuel Chew, Stopford Brooke, E. W. Marjarum, and others have pointed out, as Harroviensis and a few of his contemporaries had done, that Byron had not denied the existence or the power of God, but had only opposed certain conceptions of Providence that he and they considered harmful.[4]

A few writers iterated the detraction that J. A. Symonds had made in the last decade of the nineteenth century. Byron's attack on a dead theology had built obsolescence into the work. More, in 1898, agreed with Arnold's low estimate of Byron's intellect and declared that his freethinking elicited little more than a smile. H. J. C. Grierson thought that

[2] Though his study of *Cain* appeared posthumously in the *Hibbert Journal* (1919), it may have been based on one of the many lectures Brooke gave from 1900 to 1913. One familiar topic that several critics returned to was Byron's use of the unities. For these comments see "Byron's Dramatic Theory."

[3] Courthope, VI, 270.

[4] Symons, *Romantic Movement*, p. 260; Chew, p. 132; Brooke, pp. 74 ff.; Marjarum, *Byron as Skeptic and Believer*, p. 33.

Byron's "childish orthodoxy and the scepticism of Bayle" were strangely blended and that "the glamour and the horror which invested *Cain* have both departed. Neither the orthodoxy which Byron learned from his nurse at Aberdeen nor the scepticism which he learned from Bayle can affect us to-day." Oliver Elton was derisive: "The sceptical audacities of *Cain* are now beatings at an open door. . . . Cain too often resembles an eighteenth-century heretic who rediscovers some elementary objections to the cruder forms of orthodoxy . . ."[5]

Sir Arthur Quiller-Couch looked at Lucifer's heresy from an historical perspective and granted it the significance it deserved: "even to venture a doubt that the Universe came into being in six days of twenty-four hours by the clock was to evoke every curse of the orthodox" and required the courage of a truly Promethean mind. But E. H. Coleridge at the beginning of the century declared that it was almost impossible for readers of his day to appreciate Byron's recklessness, and Leslie A. Marchand thought it even more difficult in 1965 to realize how radical *Cain* had seemed to an 1822 audience. In 1933 Ernest De Selincourt found it hard to understand the admiration it "excited among a few enlightened spirits" as well as "the storm of fear and horror it aroused among the pious."[6]

Like a few Victorians, most modern critics were certain that *Cain* revealed Byron's bondage to the religious doctrines he opposed. Brooke, Solomon F. Gingerich, and De Selincourt were only three among many who reiterated the judgment that Byron hated the dogma of original sin and its fatalistic manacles, but that he had never cut himself loose from them. Marchand observed that in the closing pages of *Cain* the poet's "sense of sin" weakened his skepticism.[7] Since Hoxie Fairchild saw in the dialogue a "reflection of Byron's spiritual predicament," he used that quandary as a weapon against both the man and the poet. He scoffed at the claim to dramatic objectivity as an insincere and timid rationalization: Byron denied responsibility for his thoughts because he did not want to admit "the full extent of his unbelief." Fairchild called the Preface a smoke screen; Byron had there introduced topics that he knew would stir

[5] More, "Biographical Sketch" in *The Complete Poetical Works of Byron,* p. xviii; H.J.C. Grierson, *Lord Byron: Arnold and Swinburne*, pp. 17–18; Elton, pp. 163–164.

[6] Quiller-Couch, "Byron" in *Studies in Literature,* pp. 18–20; *Poetry,* V, 202; Marchand, p. 85; De Selincourt, p. 116.

[7] Brooke, pp. 74–83; Gingerich, pp. 265–266, 275; De Selincourt, pp. 115–116; Marchand, p. 86.

up a controversy and divert attention from the real subject of the play, "man's hopeless defiance of God," which he shrank from announcing.[8] The Old Believers of the 1820's, who combatted Byron's little Preface with irate prolixity, would have been dumbfounded to learn that they had been gulled by a patent and cautious fraud.

Byron's upside-down Manicheism, that made God the destroyer and Lucifer the benefactor of man, and that Heber and Fabre d'Olivet had defined with dismay, was now identified with academic neutrality by Stavrou, Bostetter, Marchand, and others. Frank Rainwater and William H. Marshall rephrased the inversion to involve a Platonic refinement that Byron did not seem to imply: Lucifer represented the ideal principle and Jehovah the material principle.[9]

Since Byron had often turned to Deism on a religious peregrination that continued for over twenty years, Marjarum, Ernest J. Lovell, Jr., and M. K. Joseph spotted some deistic remnants in the poem:[10] the guidance of the stars by a supernatural power, the chasm between man and a remote God, and the solitude of Jehovah, who created world after world to occupy his loneliness and to lighten the onus of his eternal isolation.

Some critics struck at gaps in Byron's Christian creed and repeated a complaint of the parsons from 1821 to 1850. According to Marjarum:

> Byron missed entirely the significance of the teaching that by union with Christ there may follow a mystic participation in the crucifixion and resurrection; he never accepted the atonement as a timeless and universal act of expiation. The Platonic idealism upon which the doctrine was erected was utterly foreign to him . . .[11]

Fairchild, likewise noting that Byron rejected the atonement as a "repulsive example of divine unfairness," attributed this disapproval to Byron's egotism: "He feels that he would have been highly indignant if God had crucified *him* for the sins of other men. Unable to conceive of divine self-sacrifice, he cannot see in Genesis the first stages of a redemptive plan: it is merely an ugly tale of obscurantism and malice."[12] Fairchild did not reckon with causes other than egotism that might account for

[8] Fairchild, p. 429.

[9] Rainwater, p. 123; Marshall, pp. 150–151.

[10] Marjarum, *Skeptic,* p. 14; Lovell, p. 195; Joseph, p. 123.

[11] Marjarum, *Skeptic,* p. 11.

[12] Fairchild, p. 431.

Byron's rejection of the atonement and for his inability to recognize the beginning of "a redemptive plan" in Genesis.

Elton was more stringent than Jeffrey and Hazlitt had been in condemning the religious discussion in *Cain* as unpoetic and undramatic. Lucretius, Marlowe, and Milton might turn abstract controversy into poetry, but Byron had not the genius for it. *Cain* was "a mixture of cosmic pageantry, argumentation, and idyll" and depended too much on the second of these ingredients.[13]

A few critics revived the political allegory of Mazzini, Noel, Dowden, Brandes, and Hancock. Marjarum referred to it briefly, and Edward Bostetter developed it fully in an excellent essay. He noticed that a criticism of despotic authority pervaded many of Lucifer's speeches and was consolidated in the addresses of the two brothers to Jehovah. Abel's speech was "almost a parody of the behavior of the self-righteous, well-intentioned people who by their blind submission encourage the perpetuation of social tyranny and evil." Cain's address was the reasoning of a "nineteenth-century intellectual," who bids God cease to be a bloody tyrant and to become "the rational God that accepts the fruits of peaceful labor."[14]

The more detached temper of modern critics and the sobering effect of world struggles have enabled them to accept as reasonable and normal that which the reviewers, the clerics, and the Victorians deplored—the dour pessimism of the drama. Cain's discontent, bitterness, and dejection, Lucifer's negation and cynicism, Adah's sorrow, and the dominant mood of hopelessness have been seldom challenged since 1920.

For many years there was little advance in the understanding of Byron's characterization. Critics continued to recite the generalities of the past about the principal traits of Byron's first family. But the temerity of his favorable treatment of Cain and Lucifer now rarely evoked regret or reproach. Gingerich was almost alone in thinking that the author's sympathy for the murderer, "whose ideas are in harmony with Lucifer's," was still a scandal. Coleridge saw in Lucifer majesty, solemnity, and "a most life-like personality of his own," but he did not tell us what this uniqueness consisted of, for the qualities he mentioned he also found in Satan and Mephistopheles. Nor did he precisely describe the "new emotion" that he said Byron had given to the devil. Chew in fifteen pages on *Cain* allowed about three paragraphs to the characterization. Elsewhere

[13] Elton, p. 164.

[14] Marjarum, *Skeptic*, p. 35; Bostetter, p. 575.

he made it tangential to his discussion of the sources of the play, its Miltonic and Faustian analogues, and other topics. He seemed uncertain about, and uninterested in, Lucifer, who, he said, was "nearer to pure spirit, more of an abstraction than Satan." But two pages later he wrote that Byron had endowed Lucifer "with personality, even with sympathy."[15] Except for a few scattered clauses, Chew wrote almost nothing about that personality.

Practically all commentators, even those who did not read the poem primarily as a political allegory—Brooke, De Selincourt, Marjarum—went along with their liberal ancestors and respected Lucifer as a paragon of revolt against tyranny. To Joseph, he was both the archetypal rebel and the Antigod, who claimed an equal share of the universe and who was dedicated to an endless war against the opposite Principle. Thorslev regarded Lucifer's defiance as self-assertion, called him a titanic "yea-sayer," and made him more constructive than the text seems to warrant.[16] Most thoughtful readers have also accepted the interpretation of certain nineteenth-century writers that Byron had equated Lucifer not with evil but with intellect and knowledge.

Though Marchand granted that in Lucifer, Byron represented "the speculative mind of man," he diminished the knowledge that this mind had been able to accumulate. Marchand declared that Lucifer asked more questions than he answered, met his companion's queries with other queries, and was able to tell Cain only what the youth already knew, since Lucifer was really the creation of man's mind.[17] Marchand did not, however, make Lucifer a completely subjective entity, as Jeffrey and Hazlitt had done in terming him "the personified demon" of Cain's imagination.

Marchand's qualification of Lucifer's knowledge, though traditional, was not entirely compatible with Byron's aim and tactics. The rhetorical question was one mannerism that worked well in the devil's machination. When Lucifer met a question with another question, the latter was often a declarative statement converted into a taunting interrogation, and it had the desired effect of irritating or depressing Cain. Before we shrink Lucifer, as the speculative mind, down to Cain's bewildered ignorance, we should consider that in both answering and not answering Cain's ques-

[15] Gingerich, p. 265; *Poetry,* V, 201; Chew, pp. 124, 126.

[16] Joseph, p. 118; Thorslev, pp. 112, 178–179.

[17] *Poetry,* V, 87–88.

tions, Lucifer had the diabolical purpose of overwhelming his pupil with the conviction of mortal nothingness. If we regard Lucifer's questions as proof that he knew no answers, if we join in the mockery of the 1822 reviewers at Lucifer's ineffectiveness as a tutor and declare that Cain was no wiser after the devil's departure than he had been at the start of their conversation, then we ignore the poet's intentions. Moreover, Byron thought he had bestowed on Lucifer a knowledge of the past, present, and future and that Lucifer had revealed to Cain the extent of the cosmos, the history of past existence, and the nature of death, all of which Cain admitted he had not known before. But if, in spite of Byron's effort, Lucifer still seems to know too little to enlighten Cain, the difficulty may lie with Byron's intellectual and imaginative deficiencies, with his own inability to answer Cain's questions. Lucifer could not think more profoundly than Byron did. The poet's interest and capability in this area of inquiry was less penetrating than that of Plato, Dante, Milton, Goethe, and Shelley.

Chew, F. W. Moorman, H. J. C. Grierson, and too many others merged Cain and Lucifer into a single person. Fairchild, like Swinburne, discerned only one difference between them: Lucifer's extensive knowledge. Constantine N. Stavrou made a neat distinction: Cain doubted and Lucifer denied. For Peter L. Thorslev, Jr., the important difference was that the devil had no sensibility and was therefore incapable of love. Some, like Stavrou, differentiated between Cain and Lucifer by taking the position of Harroviensis and Fabre d'Olivet that the latter was a cunning tempter. Chew, who had objected that the mortal duplicated the immortal insurgent, inconsistently admitted that Lucifer, the principle of evil, systematically misled Cain, the human soul. More recently, Joseph asserted that this temptation was the central movement of the drama and that it culminated in a second Fall, during which Byron explored the mystery of the first one. Joseph's essay kept drifting to other topics and did not pursue closely and completely the devious and manifold involution of Lucifer's temptation, nor did he elucidate its similarity to the original Fall.[18]

Chew paid more attention to the humanity of Cain and Adah than he did to Lucifer's capacities. Earlier writers had anticipated every trait he mentioned, but his few eclectic paragraphs were the fullest discussion of

[18] Chew, pp. 126, 130–131; Moorman, p. 52; Grierson, "Byron and English Society," pp. 190–191; Fairchild, p. 431; Stavrou, pp. 156–157; Thorslev, p. 180; Joseph, pp. 117–122.

the characterization that our century produced. Brooke gave more space to Cain than Chew did, but he fixed his evangelical eye on the emotional experience of Act III.

Without denying the autobiographical compulsion, some readers of Byron's poem have recognized two other components: the literary fashions of the past and present and Byron's creative talent. A few have joined his Victorian advocates, who insisted that Byron was not confined to an egoistic mirror, but could conceive and animate universal qualities. This recognition of an ability, almost unanimously denied to Byron since 1817, opened the door to a more complete understanding of the complexity of the three personalities in the poem and of their involved relationships. Readers have begun to see many reasons for Cain's discontent, rebellion, and crime. Stavrou elaborated on Heber's explanation of Cain's several personal grievances. Gingerich saw Byron working with two forms of determinism. Using a Calvinist concept of human helplessness, Byron rendered Cain a victim of destiny; he was fated to commit murder. Then Byron drew upon his knowledge of people and his artistry to have fate operate convincingly in human affairs and so endowed his characters with those qualities, emotions, and attitudes that made the disagreement between the hero and his kinfolk and his every action, including the murder, seem unavoidable.[19]

A few scholars since the second world war have been cerebral and doctrinaire in their treatment of Byron's people. Specialists, who have been intent on an analysis of structure, or on the literary genealogy of Cain and Lucifer, or on their pertinence to the political scene of 1821, or on placing a few of their speeches in a history of this or that idea, have made valuable contributions to their particular topics, but in the process have sometimes dessicated and devitalized Cain and Lucifer. The professional mind of 1960 will smile indulgently at Harroviensis, Gerard, Noel, and Blumenthal as sentimentalists, and yet these men looked warmly at Byron's people as souls in tense situations, troubled with serious emotional problems; and these matters are surely the heart of literature.

A few Victorians had thought that Byron had firmly built his play around a major theme. Their successors placed even more importance on artistic unity, and many assumed that Byron had concentrated on a single idea, which they defined as some kind of struggle. Convinced that drama thrives on conflict, modern critics have tried to solve one problem Byron

[19] Stavrou, p. 158; Gingerich, pp. 265–269.

left them. He had excluded God from the cast and so had deprived Lucifer of his great opponent and the drama of a visible confrontation. To listen to Lucifer denounce an absent foe was not a thrilling substitute.

This complaint was a familiar one. The clergy and the periodicals of the 1820's, who cried that the poem was one-sided, wanted a stern contest between Cain and his family. Modern readers have been no less dissatisfied than their forbears with Adah's opposition in Act I and with the different kinds of resistance that she and Abel made to Cain's moods in Act III. They also slipped by the denouement where the parents, Zillah, and the Angel were aligned against the malefactor and Adah, who staunchly tried to ward off their blows. There was conflict, but it was intermittent, and apparently absent in Act II, except in retrospect.

Critics, with the usual formal, aesthetic, and theatrical canons in mind, would have enjoyed a continuous struggle between protagonists, with Cain, a strong, good man, forcing Lucifer to fight with trickery and temptation for his victory, probing for a fatal flaw and exploiting it. Cain should have wrestled some hours with the devil and deteriorated in clearly marked stages, until, incensed, he accomplished his own ruin. But Byron either could not or would not try to create a spiritual battle between a credulous Othello and a crafty Iago. Chew's criticism has been the stereotype: in handing the same ideas to Cain and Lucifer and in having the former too ready to accept the latter's criticism, Byron flubbed every opportunity for an exciting clash.[20] There was more friction than Chew saw, but his objection has prevailed.

In lieu of an external contest, our critics have looked for one within the hero. The variations on Gerard's Dipsychus that they defined imply that this internal division might have been more complex than any one critic thought it was. Coleridge's version of the conflict was one that earlier writers had described: Cain rebelled "against the limitations of the inexorable present." The hero was "capable of infinite satisfaction," but was doomed by the hovering menace of death to frustration. His view has been repeated many times by later writers. Chew's variant lifted a phrase from Byron's letter of November 3, 1821—"the inadequacy of his state to his conceptions"—and made it the central theme. A few pages later he declared that the "final message" was that an inquiring and independent skeptic insisted on the right to use his mind to find out if God had ordered events justly. Cain refused to surrender this right for the sake of "com-

[20] Chew, p. 131.

fortable acquiescence" and therefore rejected whatever seemed contrary to personal feeling and observation. Chew thus thought that an aggressive individualism was the cause for the hero's rebellion against autocracy.[21] Neither Coleridge nor Chew developed their generalities, which they probably considered to be self-evident.

Fairchild returned to Chew's second idea. Byron had dramatized a struggle between Cain's aggressive mind and the checks that God had imposed upon its ambitions. Pride fought with mortality. Cain's conceit would not let him believe in "an extrapersonal curb, but his sense of limitation" forced that belief on him. Fairchild asserted that "the inadequacy of his state to his conceptions" did "not express the tragedy of a character in a play"; it expressed "the personal tragedy of Lord Byron."[22]

Marchand complicated this biographical view: the talk between Cain and Lucifer was a projection of Byron's duality. His quest for an infinite world, that he "never quite believed in," was crippled by skeptical disillusion, which had been caused by the constrictions of finite existence. Marchand did not assign the first half of this dichotomy to Cain and the second to Lucifer, for he probably realized that Byron had mingled idealism and pessimism in both of them. Instead, he found a conflict between the moods of the two speakers, "a temperamental difference in their reaction to the cosmic picture." Lucifer's immortality permitted him to sustain a cold, logical detachment that the aspiring Cain, trapped and irked by mortality, could not achieve. "In this sense the conversation of the two characters did dramatize an inner conflict of the author."[23]

Brooke, Ruby, and Thorslev thought that the battle within Cain occurred between his love of Adah and his desire for Lucifer's knowledge. The decision to accept the devil's offer of "reason without love" was the turning point of the struggle and assured Cain's destruction. Since this decision came in Act I, the struggle was not continuous, but restricted to the single scene with Cain, Adah, and Lucifer. Another difficulty with this interpretation was that some later experiences in Acts II and III, including Cain's assault upon Abel, were very remote and indirect consequences of the choice Cain had made in Act I.

Brooke invented a sequence that Byron did not follow in the drama:

[21] *Poetry,* V, 200; Chew, pp. 128, 133.

[22] Fairchild, p. 432.

[23] *Poetry,* V, 86–90.

when the love of God has vanished, knowledge produced pride that resented interference, scorned and hated piety, and led to crime. I also doubt that Byron arranged Lucifer's conversation with Cain to show, as Brooke said, that science without love sapped man's moral strength and increased his power of doing wrong.[24] Brooke's interpretation was as pious as that of the early reviewers, but the outcome was reversed, since he thought Byron had preached a useful sermon.

Wade Ruby was close to Brooke's dread of the danger of intellectuality. Byron, he thought, demonstrated that Cain's thirst for knowledge was inordinate and that his inadequate adjustment to his environment brought catastrophe to himself, his family, and all the race. Ruby seemed to overlook the fact that Byron clearly attributed Cain's maladjustment and the catastrophe to a combination of forces and conditions, of which Cain's thirst for knowledge, whether excessive or not, was only one. Fairchild derided Cain's intellectual aspiration and repeated Noel's censure of its indolence.[25]

Thorslev related the conflict between intellect and emotion to his exposition of the types of eighteenth-century heroes. Cain was pulled in opposite directions by the longings of a Faustian mind and by the affections of a man of sensibility. Lucifer, though possessing the defiance and intellectual idealism of Satan and Prometheus, was incapable of the latter's altruism. Thorslev's exposition did not seem to clinch his theory (1) that Lucifer's inability to love was the crux of the play, (2) that the love-knowledge struggle within Cain provided the "eventual resolution," and (3) that the murder was "inherent in Cain's first climactic choice of knowledge over love." In his historical approach, Thorslev may have oversimplified the psychology, and his passing notice of two immediate causes for the murder implied that his analysis had omitted other conditions and pressures.[26]

Five times in lectures and essays from 1920 to 1945 Grierson rephrased his view that, in all of Byron's serious poems after 1816, the poet was troubled by an unresolved struggle "between the will of man and the will of God." Byron's pride and sense of justice were affronted by the illogi-

[24] Brooke, p. 87.

[25] Ruby, "A Study of the Influence of Mortality on Byron's Thought and Poetry," p. 38; Fairchild, p. 429.

[26] Thorslev, pp. 180–181.

cality of holding man responsible for his mistakes, his sins, and his misfortunes when these were not the results of his willful choice, and when initiative had been wrested from him by a higher power and he had been rendered a victim (1) of heredity, (2) of a nature not formed by himself but given to him by God, and (3) of every accident and adversity beyond his control.[27]

Three other definitions of Byron's primary intention did not focus on an inner heroic struggle. All three were novel and esoteric conceptions of the poet's thought and of his dramatic expression of it. G. Wilson Knight fancied that Byron, "at grips with the deepest problems of evil," concentrated "his challenge in terms of the suffering of animals." William H. Marshall maintained that Byron's inversion of Jehovah and Lucifer as the material and spiritual principles gave the play a structural unity. His method of synoptic commentary, effective for some of Byron's earlier poetry, did not explain for me how the irony of the inversion and the conflict inherent in it provided the themal unity of the drama.[28]

John W. Harrison tried to prove that the main movement was Cain's search for the meaning behind the symbols that his parents had used to explain the origin of evil. Cain accepted the fruit as a symbol of innate depravity when he realized after his crime that everyone had a potentiality for evil. Less convincing was the statement that Cain's recollection of the injured lamb was an explicit acceptance of "his parents' symbol of the serpent as evil tempter." The most unusual part of Harrison's exegesis was his comparison of Cain's career to a quest that Joseph Campbell described in *The Hero with a Thousand Faces*. This hero ventured into a supernatural region, achieved a fabulous victory, and returned to aid his fellow men. Byron's poem departed so often from this pattern that there were not many significant elements of the myth in the dialogue and action of *Cain*. In order to discover particular resemblances to the myth, Harrison occasionally seemed to stray from the plain meaning of the text.[29]

A sampling of opinion during the past sixty-five years about the flight through space into Hades encompasses the variety of interests, criteria, and judgments in our century's interpretation of *Cain*. The Victorians,

[27] Grierson, *Lord Byron,* p. 16; Grierson, "Byron and English Society," pp. 183–192.

[28] Knight, "The Two Eternities: An Essay on Byron," p. 223; Marshall, Chap. 7.

[29] Harrison, pp. 98–106, 109, 113–115.

partly because they had little patience with detail and partly because neither the science nor the religion disturbed them, had paid slight attention to Act II. The 1820's had ridiculed its scientific fantasy and denounced its religious heresy. Some modern critics also looked at the episode with disfavor, but for technical reasons, while others were interested in its psychological import.

Bonamy Dobrée declared that the journey was "unactable" and that the long dialogue would "drive an audience to distraction." Elton asserted that the "scenic-supernatural requires a great artist . . . like the author of the *Book of Job* or of *Faust*" and that Byron lacked the craftsmanship to manage it. Harrison thought Cain's experience in Hades "structurally disjointed," because the long discussion was unrelated to the setting. Gingerich was disappointed because Byron wasted a situation pregnant with "profound tragedy—experience and knowledge to be gained at certain fundamental spiritual risks!" The poet merely impressed us with the vastness of space, juggled a little with time, and presented "rather ineffectively a vague picture of past, present, and future worlds."[30]

Bostetter analyzed the effect that the scenic shifts of the three acts had on the reader's imagination and conjectured that Byron used them to imply a criticism of the respectable thought of his time. By moving out of the small biblical world into the cosmos of nineteenth-century scientific speculation and then back to the limited environs of Eden, Byron showed "the inadequacy of the traditional cosmology" while he revealed "its continuing power over the minds of men. . . . There is no place for the anthropomorphic deity of the first act" in the abyss of space.[31] Bostetter returned to Blumenthal's contention that Act II did not further the psychological deterioration of the hero and might therefore have been omitted.

> . . . Cain needs no trip with Lucifer to stir him up to the acts culminating in the murder of Abel. They have been directly and adequately prepared for in the first act. Cain's defiance, God's demonstration of his power both in overthrowing Cain's offering and in setting the mark upon and exiling him, a punishment which the broken Cain accepts as just—these follow logically upon the first act.[32]

[30] Bonamy Dobrée, *Byron's Dramas,* p. 9; Elton, p. 163; Harrison, pp. 102–103; Gingerich, p. 267.

[31] Bostetter, pp. 571–573.

[32] *Ibid.,* 574.

A large majority of readers, from Scott and Goethe to Marjarum, Lovell, and Marchand, have accepted Byron's own explanation: the journey stimulated Cain's yearning for the infinite and also aggravated his frustration and self-contempt.[33] Chew did his best writing when he dwelt on the abasement and dejection of the hero, who measured his world and himself "against the background of eternity" and the mighty creations of the past, and realized that mortal nothingness was the sum of human knowledge. Lovell traced Lucifer's continuous attack along the glittering flight through the cosmos and into the black region of the stupendous apparitions. He followed the prolonged gamut of eagerness, admiration, amazement, dejection, and mortification, as Cain saw his planet dwindle within the infinite universe, and then as he realized in Hades how inferior man and his earth were in beauty and grandeur to the colossal creatures and worlds that had preceded them.[34]

Joseph agreed with earlier readers that Lucifer during the journey annihilated Cain's ego. He returned to the familiar distinction between Lucifer's two comparisons that depressed his companion. For the first, Byron relied on a traditional diminution of the earth in cosmic space; for the second, the poet adapted a modern geological theory that abbreviated the age of Cain's earth among the aeons of many worlds now demolished. By distending space and time and diminishing humanity, Byron widened the gulf between God and man.[35]

Fairchild dilated the paradox that Byron had defined in his letters: the tour demoralized Cain "by making him feel at the same time excessively big and excessively little." Lucifer gratified "his victim's pride with huge draughts of knowledge, but he [crushed] that pride by demonstrating Cain's insignificance in relation to infinite space and time, the fleshly degradations of earthly existence, and the inevitable doom of death."[36]

Gingerich's description of the upheaval within the traveller involved still other emotions that hurled Cain toward the catastrophe.

> [The journey forced him to] be utterly discontent with his lot, almost hectic with longings to break with his environment, more deeply confirmed in his own half-formed disloyalty to his parents and in his hatred of

[33] See "Byron's View of His Play."

[34] Chew, pp. 129–130; Lovell, pp. 209–212.

[35] Joseph, pp. 119, 122.

[36] Fairchild, p. 431.

Jehovah, ready to do some wild deed of rebellion. When Abel inquires . . . what he had seen, he answers almost savagely, with flushed cheeks and with eyes flashing with unnatural light. . . . He is as one possessed.[37]

Stavrou pointed Cain's disenchantment toward the future: "When he returned from his cosmic flight . . . he knew . . . that Paradise was a dream and that men and women could only look forward to a grim struggle for survival amid an inimicable universe."[38]

To Brooke, the effect of the journey showed how Calvinist dogma obliterated all civilizing virtues: Cain came back to earth wildly indignant at a cruel God and furious at his own fate. "All reverence, gentleness, gratitude, humility, sense of sin has perished in him, all faith and love and hope. The one black upas of his belief in an inherited sin poisons the whole of life." Brooke stretched far to connect the space journey with inherited sin. Two recent interpretations also seem to veer from the text. Marshall made a subtle distinction that would have pleased Shelley and Leigh Hunt: in Act II Cain "moves from an absolute fear that God determines the nature of Right to the relative notion that Right must precede God" (p. 137). G. Wilson Knight strove for an ambitious Faustian allegory: at the end of the journey Cain was "European man overburdened by his own accumulating yet unsatisfying knowledge."[39]

Three aspects of Act III have drawn much discussion: the motivation for the murder, the criminal's remorse, and the author's ultimate view of his hero. The first two have been the object of explication ever since Byron himself stated his aims in his correspondence. The debate on the third topic has been confined to our century. Since the commentary on all three is focused on a small area of the drama, it has been assembled in the Annotations.

A few scholars have evaluated part of the store of opinion about the play that the preceding century had amassed. Coleridge minimized the views of Byron's contemporaries, listed several reviewers and pamphleteers, and briefly reported the court trial. Chew in his second book on Byron brushed aside most of the reviewers, quoted, as Coleridge had done, from Byron's literary peers, and summarized some of the ideas of the

[37] Gingerich, p. 268.

[38] Stavrou, p. 159.

[39] Brooke, p. 87; Marshall, p. 137; G. Wilson Knight, *The Golden Labyrinth. A Study of British Drama,* p. 234.

many amateurs and churchmen who had replied to *Cain* or written plays on the subject. Several scholars—Elmer Brooks, William A. Coles, Wilfred S. Dowden, Alan L. Strout, Robert W. Duncan, and others—in their useful surveys of the periodicals have recorded a little of the contemporary comment on *Cain*.

Coleridge's introduction and Chew's chapter on *Cain* in his earlier book took advantage of the industry of German scholars, who in the latter part of the nineteenth century had been hunting for sources of the play. Joseph, drawing mainly from Eimer, Chew, R. Messac, Henri Blaze de Bury, and Edward Sarmiento, dispersed among his exegesis of the poem the names of at least fifteen of Byron's creditors and antecedents, but he did not reproduce the particular resemblances.[40] The most fruitful result of Teutonic research was a more precise attention to the relationship between *Cain* and *Paradise Lost*, the definition of resemblances and differences between Lucifer and Satan, and the citation of analogous detail and phrasing. R. D. Havens, however, gave us little. His generalities about Byron's indebtedness in the description of space and Hades he might have found hard to document. His cursory comparison of the two devils belittled Lucifer, and a few of his parallel citations seemed inexact.[41] Stavrou's perceptive article argued that Byron had written an anti-Miltonic poem. He clearly distinguished Satan and Lucifer as manifestations of the differing philosophies of the two poets.

One of the most useful enterprises of modern scholarship has been to place *Cain* in its literary environment, to relate it to other writings of the author and to certain eighteenth-century and Romantic traditions. Recent studies have made more specific the general observation of Macaulay and the more careful reviewers that Cain and Lucifer belonged to the heroic family that Byron created in the verse narratives and the plays. We have already noted that Thorslev categorized Cain with Faust and with the literature of sensibility. Many readers since 1822 have seen Promethean qualities in Lucifer. Thorslev provided a compendium of the attitudes toward Satan and Prometheus in the eighteenth and early nineteenth centuries. Maximilian Rudwin's book enabled us to see that the character of Byron's devil was partly shaped for him by wide-spread conditions and concepts of the age. Rudwin also discovered that Lucifer's intellectuality

[40] Joseph, pp. 117–121.

[41] Havens, pp. 231–232.

was a traditional trait, which had been assigned to the devil by the medieval church as well as by certain nineteenth-century writers.[42]

Marjarum in his monograph on Byron's religious thought associated many of the ideas in *Cain* with Byron's expression of similar or contrasted ideas in the letters and poems. For instance, he observed that lines 116–119 of Act I were typical of the poet's dualism that "always treated mind and matter . . . as though they were mutually exclusive concepts."[43]

Marjarum also reminded us that Byron's discouragement about man's insignificance had recurred in several poems.[44] Lovell set *Cain* in a wide context of poems, letters, and conversations that lamented human and earthly nothingness and that deplored divine cruelty and universal destruction. Ruby considered the play to be "Byron's most effective treatment" of an idea that he often came back to—the limitations of mortality. Bostetter, using a phrase from Cain, "the servile mass of matter," as a title for one section of his book, suggested that Lucifer's slurs about sensuality were an outgrowth of Byron's homosexual tendencies and his disgust with carnality. Lucifer's unpleasant remarks were consistent with Byron's pessimism about the sway of body over mind, that I have traced in Cantos II and V of *Don Juan* and that frequently recurred in his poetry.[45]

Rainwater tried to show that Byron shared some of Shelley's ideas, that he differentiated between an ideal conception of an absolute God and the cruder view of a deity with human limitations. Byron, however, made no such distinction in *Cain*, for he did not there give us an explicit statement of a platonic ideal of divinity. Thorslev, in a thoughtful article on the idea that mind is reality, associated some of Lucifer's speeches with a similar expression of this subjective confidence in Milton, Blake, Shelley, and other English and continental poets. Fairchild linked Lucifer's idealism with Manfred's "conception of mind as a stronghold against life" and considered it a pose: "Byron's bosom was a chaos which, as he well knew, did not include the power to transform itself into a cosmos." Ward Pafford saw that Byron had oscillated between pessimism and optimism in *Man-*

[42] Thorslev, Chap. 8; Rudwin, pp. 271 ff., 246–247.

[43] Marjarum, *Skeptic,* pp. 63–64.

[44] See "Annotations," II, ii, 418–424.

[45] Lovell, pp. 209 ff.; Ruby, "Study," p. 37; Bostetter, *The Romantic Ventriloquists,* pp. 266–267; Steffan, *The Making of a Masterpiece,* pp. 192–196, 208–210.

fred and *Childe Harold,* and Marchand remarked that the poet returned to the same paradox in dramas other than *Cain:* "the defiant Promethean invincibility of the mind and will" was always countered by "the spirit's inevitable slavery to the limited human condition."[46]

Critics have said less about the style of *Cain* than about its content. In 1912, Ethel Mayne foretold the mixed evaluation of subsequent generations: the poem "has his energy, his sincerity . . . with its thousand errors of taste . . . with all this terrible welter of slovenliness and tunelessness, *Cain* is nevertheless a work which abides in the memory as a notable expression of the Byronic spirit . . . whatever modern criticism may deny it of importance in art."[47] In 1941 Peter Quennell, with disdain as caustic and patronizing as Swinburne's, tossed the dramas away as "scarcely readable." *Cain* was merely a "ponderous Biblical concoction." As we have seen almost everyone disapproved of the versification, and Bostetter damned the diction as an incongruous failure. Had the poetry been better, Oliver Elton concluded, it might have been "one of the great super-terrestrial dramas in the language; indeed, with all its faults, such it is."[48] A few recent studies have exposed an artistry in the writing of *Cain* that earlier readers had not seen. Harrison, W. Paul Elledge, and Ronald Gregg Coleman in their dissertations have showed that the imagery and symbolism of the poem are broadly functional, sufficiently complex, and carefully unified.

Performance

Boleslaw Taborski discussed the difficulties of production and suggested that Act II must be condensed and that the space journey could be depicted with skillful lighting. Though Adah's entrance in Act I enlivened the dramatic illusion and though Act III would move an audience today more readily than it would have in Byron's time, still there was too much philosophical talk and too little activity for success in the popular theatre.[49]

Taborski and Knight, writing before television, believed that the most suitable medium for *Cain* was the radio. Knight, an advocate of putting

[46] Rainwater, pp. 122–123; Thorslev, pp. 250–268; Fairchild, p. 432; Marchand, p. 75.

[47] Ethel Mayne, *Byron,* p. 378.

[48] Quennell, *Byron in Italy,* p. 205; Bostetter, p. 575; Elton, pp. 165–166.

[49] Boleslaw Taborski, "Lord Byron and the Theatre," pp. 106–107.

Byron on the boards, stated that the production in 1949 by the Rudolf Steiner School of Dramatic Art showed "what reserves of stage power are housed in Acts I and III." He regretted that the second act had been omitted but conceded that it would have to be curtailed for the theatre. John W. Klein, who attended the same performance, granted that the climax "was treated with the skill of a master of dramatic effect," but, as Byron and a large majority of readers would have predicted, found the rest of the poem more suitable for the closet than the stage.[50] Taborski disparaged this scholastic effort as not worth putting on the record.

Heinrich Straumann reported on a performance given four or five times by amateurs in April, 1951, at the University of Zürich. The German translation by Wilhelm Leyhausen, who made only a few cuts, "sounded well-suited" for the stage. The only scenery was the stone staircase of the building and a few curtains and screens. The lighting and costumes gave "a good deal of scenic effect." Attendance was poor; the reviews "fairly good." In the same year *Cain* was presented by another amateur group in St. Giles Cathedral, Edinburgh, presumably in its original form.[51]

The Times printed an account of a performance in April, 1960, at Lucerne. A revision by Heinrich Koch of Otto Gildenmesiter's translation made many cuts, including the talk about the morning star and the description of the prehistoric beasts, and brought together from different parts of the poem two of Cain's speeches about his longing for knowledge and death. The play was produced by Walter Oberer without interruption and took an hour and a quarter. The costumes for Lucifer and the Angel were "inspired by William Blake," and the family was clothed to represent humanity and not "our primitive forbears." A revolving centerpiece was used for the space flight. The spectator wished that the fruits and the lamb had been put on the altars and that "the flame of acceptance" had been included as well as the whirlwind. He commended the acting of Wolfgang Schwarz as Cain and Wolfgang Rottsieper as Lucifer.[52]

[50] G. Wilson Knight, "The Plays of Lord Byron," *The Times Literary Supplement,* February 3, 1950, p. 80; John W. Klein, "Byron's Neglected Plays," *Drama,* LXIII (Winter, 1961), p. 35.

[51] *K-SJ,* I, 121; Audrey G. Insch, "English Blank Verse Tragedy from 1790 to 1825," p. 367.

[52] This article also referred to a performance that had used the same adaptation eighteen months before at Frankfurt am Main.

Burns Mantle recorded a production of *Cain* on April 8, 1925, by the Manhattan

Ninety years before this experiment, an oratorio was made out of Byron's poem by Max Zenger and repeatedly performed in 1869–1870 at Frankfort.[53] In 1930 James Joyce tried to turn *Cain* into an opera. In September of that year he sent copies of the drama to the composer George Antheil and to John Sullivan, a tenor whom Joyce admired and who was to sing the leading part. Joyce wanted a second tenor for Abel, a baritone for Lucifer, and a bass for Adam. At first he did not know what voice to use for the Angel, suggested that the loud speaker in the Rouen Station be borrowed, and later found a male soprano for that role.

He urged Antheil to start on some themes and mentioned the sections that interested him: the opening sacrifice, the fire and whirlwind, Eve's malediction, and "the music around Enoch and Cain's exit." He and Antheil agreed that Acts I and III must be compressed, and at first he wanted a "figured intermezzo" for Act II but then decided that it should be choreographed. On November 25 he and Herbert Gorman were "at work pruning Act I of Cain." By December 7 he had learned that Ezra Pound did not care for the enterprise. Joyce asserted, however, that others liked it and that *Cain* was a magnificent subject, new to the operatic repertoire. Antheil's talent, Sullivan's remarkable voice, and "the work and name of a great poet" would create "an immense effect" and be "the greatest event in the artistic future." Joyce finished his condensation of Act I, offered to cut more from it, and asked for Antheil's opinion before he went on with Act III. According to Richard Ellman, Joyce made only a few small excisions and "would not allow his name on the programme." On December 22, Joyce wrote that Antheil at Pound's suggestion was "backing out of Byron" and that the composer wanted him to write "a peppy libretto." "I wired refusing and sending him a polite ultimatum either to go ahead with my adaptation or let me hand it over to Stravinsky, to which he has not yet replied." Antheil probably then sent a soothing note. From a letter to him on January 3, 1931, we learn that he was willing to provide

---

Little Theatre Club at the Lenox Little Theatre in New York. There were fourteen performances (*The Best Plays of 1924–25,* pp. 568, 604–605). In 1960 the play was put on in Poland (*K-SJ,* XV, 23).

[53] Elze, p. 417 n. The Dictionary Catalogue of the Music Collection of the New York Public Library Reference Department lists Zenger's work as "Kain [Oratorio] Nach Byrons Mysterium frei bearbeitet, von Theodor Heigel, Für Solostimmen, Chor und Orchester composiert von M. Zenger. Leipzig CFW Siegel [1867] 248 p."

music for the opera, but regarded Byron's play "as hopeless for the German stage" unless Joyce wrote the libretto. This the novelist again declined to do; he was ready to provide a scissors-and-paste job, but he would never have "the bad manners to rewrite the text of a great English poet." Furthermore, he did not want the music to be composed for German singers but in "the pure tenor tradition." If Antheil could not begin at once "with enthusiasm and with spiritual profit" and "without any consideration for the veering tastes of impresarios," he should say so, and Joyce would offer "poor Byron and poorer Sullivan" elsewhere. The plan then languished and four years later Joyce complained, "Antheil missed the chance of a lifetime when he did not write the opera on Byron's Cain for Sullivan. Maybe he wasn't capable of it. . . . He'll fly no more, the noisy butterfly."[54]

More recently two Italians, Felice Lattuada and G. Zambianchi, made an opera out of Byron's play, *Caino* (Milan, 1957).[55]

[54] Letters of September 7 and 23, and December 7, 1930, January 3, 1931, James Joyce, *Letters,* ed. Stuart Gilbert, pp. 287–298. Letters of November 25 and December 22, 1930, October 29, 1934, February 18, 1935, James Joyce, *Letters,* ed. Richard Ellmann, III, 207–209, 327, 344.

In February, 1935, Joyce stated that Antheil had written a splendid opera on *Cain.* He was probably mistaken. No composition with that title appears in Madeleine Goss's list of Antheil's works (*Modern Music Makers,* pp. 344–345), nor in several biographical sketches of Antheil that I consulted.

Antheil's account of his acquaintance with Joyce is confined to the middle 1920's, though a few remarks in Chapter 15 of his autobiography may refer to later events. "Joyce's madness was opera . . . Another [madness] . . . was Irish singers; almost any Irish singer traveling through Paris could be assured of Joyce's support . . ." Antheil reported that Joyce intended to write a libretto and that they often discussed it at Joyce's apartment, but Antheil did not date these plans. Though he often alluded to his operas in Chapters 24–26, that covered the years 1930–1934, he did not there or elsewhere mention *Cain* (*Bad Boy of Music,* pp. 153–154).

[55] The catalogue of the Music Collection of the New York Public Library also lists a composition by Franz Kessel, "Kain, phantastische Tondichtung nach Lord Byrons gleichnamigem Mysterium, für grosses Orchester. Hannover. 75 p."

BIBLIOGRAPHY

Adams, Thomas. *A Scourge for Lord Byron; or, "Cain a Mystery" Unmasked.* London: T. Adams, 1823.

Anderson, Gordon R. "The Form and Content of Byron's Historical Tragedies." Thesis, The University of Oxford, 1957.

Another Cain. A Poem. [A Reply to Lord Byron's "Cain."] London: Hatchard & Son, 1822.

Antheil, George. *Bad Boy of Music.* Garden City, New York: Doubleday, Doran & Company, Inc., 1945.

Ariosto, Lodovico. *Orlando Furioso.* Trans. William Stewart Rose. 2 vols. London: G. Bell & Sons, Ltd., 1913. [Canto 34, sts. 66–87.]

Ariosto, Lodovico. *Orlando Furioso.* Trans. Alan Gilbert. 2 vols. New York: S. F. Vannia, 1954. [Canto 34, sts. 66–87.]

Arnold, Matthew. "Byron" in *Essay in Criticism,* Second Series. Ed. S. R. Littlewood. London: Macmillan & Co., Ltd., 1954. [This was his introduction to the *Poetry of Byron* (London: Macmillan & Co., 1881).]

Ash, Charles Bowker [unsigned]. "A Layman's Epistle to a Certain Nobleman with Special Reference to Lord Byron's 'Cain' " in *The Poetical Works of C. B. Ash.* Vol. II. London: Longman, Rees, Orme, Brown, and Green, 1831. [Brought out as a pamphlet in 1824.]

Aston, James and Edward. "A Dissertation on Lord Byron" in *Pompeii and Other Poems.* London: Longman & Co., William Benning, 1828.

The Athenaeum [This magazine used various subtitles.]

Maurice, Frederick Denison [unsigned]. "Sketches of Contemporary Authors. No. XII.—Lord Byron" (April 11, 1828), 351–352.

———. "Lord Byron's Monument" (September 24, October 1, 1828), 751–752, 767–768. [Signed "M."]

"*Letters and Journals of Lord Byron; with Notices of his Life.* By Thomas Moore. 2 vols. 4to Vol. I, London, 1830. Murray. [Second Notice.]" (January 30, 1830), 49–50.

"*Conversations on Religion, with Lord Byron and Others, Held in Cephalonia, a Short Time Previous to His Lordship's Death.* By the late James Kennedy, M.D., 8vo. London, 1830. Murray" (June 19 and 26, 1830), 369–371, 390–391.

"*The Life and Works of Lord Byron.* Vol. XIV. London: Murray" (February 9, 1833), 86.

Austin, Alfred. "Byron and Wordsworth" in *The Bridling of Pegasus.* London: Macmillan and Co., Ltd., 1910. [Had appeared in *The Quarterly Review,* July, 1882.]

———. *A Vindication of Lord Byron.* London: Chapman and Hall, 1869.

Aycock, Roy Edwin. "Lord Byron and Bayle's *Dictionary.*" Thesis, University of North Carolina, 1952.

Babcock, R. W. "The Inception and Reception of Byron's 'Cain'," *The South Atlantic Quarterly,* XXVI (April, 1927), 178–188.

Bair, George Eldridge. "The Plays of the Romantic Poets: Their Place in Dramatic History." Dissertation, University of Pennsylvania, 1951.

Ball, P. M. "The Plays of Byron in Relation to the Dramatic Work of Other English Poets." Thesis, The University of Leeds, 1953.

Battine, William. *Another Cain, a Mystery.* [In verse] London: John Cahuac, 1822.

Bauer, Josephine. *The London Magazine, 1820–29* (*Anglistica,* Vol. I). Copenhagen: Rosenkilde and Bagger, 1953.

Bayle, Pierre. *A General Dictionary, Historical and Critical: In Which a New and Accurate Translation of That of the Celebrated Mr. Bayle, with the Corrections and Observations Printed in the Late Edition at Paris, Is Included; and Interspersed with Several Thousand Lives Never Before Published. The Whole Containing the History of the Most Illustrous Persons of all Ages and Nations, Particularly Those of Great Britain and Ireland, Distinguished by Their Rank, Actions, Learning, and Other Accomplishments. With Reflection on Such Passages of Mr. Bayle, as Seem To Favor Scepticism and the Manichee System.* By the Reverend Mr. John Peter Bernard, the Reverend Mr. Thomas Birch, Mr. John Lockman, and other Hands. 10 vols. London: Printed by J. Bettenham, 1734–1741. [The title pages of the volumes are not identical; e.g., different printers are listed.]

Blackwood's Edinburgh Magazine. [Though some of the authors used pseudonyms, all articles were unsigned.] Vol. XI:

Croly, George [P. P. P.]. "Cambridge Pamphlets—Irish Ball, etc." (June, 1822), 740–741.

Crowe, Eyre Evans. "Letter from Paddy" (April, 1822), 461–465.

Lockhart, John Gibson. "Lord Byron's Three New Tragedies" (January, 1822), 90–92.

———. "Noctes Ambrosianae, No. 1" (March, 1822), 375–377.

——— or John Wilson [C. North]. Note to a "Letter from London" (February, 1822), 237–238.

Matthews, John [Palaemon]. "Critique on Lord Byron" (April, 1822), 456–460.

——— [Siluriensis]. "Lord Byron" (February, 1822), 212–217.

St. Barbe, R. F. [Blaise Fitztravesty]. "Lord Byron's Combolio," part of "Another Laddleful from the Devil's Punch Bowl" (February, 1822), 165.

———. Vol. XII:

Lockhart, John Gibson. "Odoherty on Werner" (December, 1822), 711–712.

——— [T. Tickler]. "The Quarterly Review, No. LIII" (July, 1822), 98–99.

Maginn, William. "Noctes Ambrosianae, No. 4" (July, 1822), 104.

———. "Tickler on Werner" (December, 1822), 785.

———. Vol. XV:

"Lord Byron (June, 1824), 700. [Strout (*A Bibliography of Articles in Blackwood's Magazine, 1817–1825,* p. 121) doubtfully assigned the authorship to John Galt. Hunt (*Lord Byron and Some of His Contemporaries,* pp. 137–139) and certain implications in the article indicated that the writer was a clergyman, introduced to Byron by Hunt at Albaro. This was also Lovell's opinion (*His Very Self and Voice: Collected Conversations of Lord Byron,* p. 639 n. 14).]

Blake, William. "The Ghost of Abel" in *The Prophetic Writings of William Blake.* Eds. D. J. Sloss and J. P. R. Wallis. I, 645–649. Oxford: Clarendon Press, 1926.

Blaze de Bury, Henri. "Lord Byron et le Byronisme," *Revue des Deux-Mondes,* Paris, CI (1872), 513–550.

Bloom, Harold. *The Visionary Company.* Garden City, New York: Doubleday, 1961. [Pp. 246–248.]

Blumenthal, Friedrich. *Lord Byron's Mystery "Cain" and Its Relation to Milton's "Paradise Lost" and Gessner's "Death of Abel."* Oldenburg: Gerhard Stalling, 1891.

Bostetter, Edward E. "Byron and the Politics of Paradise," *PMLA,* LXXV (1960), 571–576.

———. *The Romantic Ventriloquists.* Seattle: University of Washington Press, 1963. [This book incorporates most of the earlier essay on *Cain.*]

Boyd, James. *Goethe's Knowledge of English Literature.* Oxford: Clarendon Press, 1932.

Brandes, George. *Main Currents in Nineteenth Century Literature.* London: William Heinemann, 1901–1905. 6 vols. [Volume 4 was originally written in 1875, though not translated by Mary Morison until 1905.]

Brighton Magazine. "Review of Books. 1. Cain, a Mystery.—By Lord Byron. Dec. 1821," I (January, 1822), 72–79.

Briscoe, Walter A. (ed.). *Byron, the Poet: A Collection of Addresses and Essays.* London: George Routledge & Sons, Ltd., 1924.

Britannicus. *Revolutionary Causes: With a Brief Notice of Some Late Publications; and a Postscript Containing Strictures on Cain, etc.* London: J. Cauthorne, 1822.

The British Critic. "Sardanapalus, a Tragedy. The Two Foscari, a Tragedy. Cain, a Mystery. By Lord Byron," XVI (May, 1822), 529–550.

The British Review and London Critical Journal. William Roberts [unsigned]. "Art. IV—Sardanapalus, a Tragedy. The Two Foscari, a Tragedy. Cain, a Mystery. By Lord Byron. 8vo. Murray, London, 1821," XIX (March, 1822), 72–102.

Brooke, Stopford. "Byron's Cain," *The Hibbert Journal. A Quarterly Review of Religion, Theology, and Philosophy,* XVIII (October, 1919–July, 1920), 74–94. [Reprinted in 1920 as Chapter XII of *Naturalism in English Poetry.* London: Dent & Sons. The first seven chapters of this book were lectures delivered in 1902.]

Brooks, Elmer L. "Byron and the *London Magazine,*" *K-SJ,* V (1956), 49–67.

Brydges, Sir Egerton. *Letters on the Character and Poetical Genius of Lord Byron.* London: Longman, Hurst, Rees, Orme, Brown, and Green, 1824.

Bulwer, Edward [Lytton]. *England and the English.* 2 vols. London: R. Bentley, 1833.

Butler, E. M. *Byron and Goethe.* London: Bowes & Bowes, 1956.

Byron, George Gordon Lord. *Cain, a Mystery.* With Introduction, Notes and Appendix by B. Uhlemayr. Nürnberg: C. Kock's Verlagsbuchhandlung, 1907. [Since this edition was prepared for German readers, the notes defined words, indicated their pronunciation, paraphrased some verses, and scanned a few of them oddly. The short introduction was derived mainly from Goethe, Elze, Noel, and Brandes; and the appendix quoted some selections from them.]

———. "Cain. A Mystery in Three Acts." [Original Manuscript, 1821]. The Stark Collection of the Miriam Lutcher Stark Library of The University of Texas at Austin.

———. *The Complete Poetical Works of Byron.* See More, Paul Elmer.

———. *The Poetical Works of Lord Byron.* London & New York: Oxford University Press, 1904, reprinted 1945.

———. *Sardanapalus, the Two Foscari, Cain.* London: John Murray, 1821.

———. *The Works of Lord Byron.* See Wright, John, and also Moore, Thomas, *Letters and Journals of Lord Byron.*

———.*The Works of Lord Byron. Complete in One Volume.* London: John Murray, 1837.

———. *The Works of Lord Byron.* 6 vols. London: John Murray, 1831.

———. *The Works of Lord Byron. Letters and Journals.* Ed. Rowland E. Prothero. 6 vols. Revised and enlarged edition. London: John Murray, 1898–1901.

———. *The Works of Lord Byron. Poetry.* Ed. Ernest Hartley Coleridge. 7 vols. Revised and enlarged edition. London: John Murray, 1904–1905.

Byron, Major George Gordon (ed.). *The Inedited Works of Lord Byron.* New York: G. Byron and R. Martin, 1849. Parts I and II.

"*Cain.* A Performance of the Play at the 13 Rows Theatre in Opole, Poland, in 1960," *K-SJ,* XII (1963), 127.

Calvert, William J. *Byron, Romantic Paradox.* Chapel Hill: University of North Carolina Press, 1935. [Reprinted by Russell and Russell, New York, 1962.]

Cameron, Kenneth Neill. *The Young Shelley. Genesis of a Radical.* New York: The Macmillan Company, 1950.

Campbell, Joseph. *The Hero with a Thousand Faces.* New York: Pantheon Books, 1949.

Carver, P. L. "Hazlitt's Contributions to *The Edinburgh Review,*" *The Review of English Studies,* IV (October, 1928), 385–393.

Chambers, R. W. "Ruskin (and Others) on Byron," *The English Association,* Pamphlet No. 62 (November, 1925), 3–28.

The Chester Plays: A Collection of Mysteries Founded upon Scriptural Subjects, and Formerly Represented by the Trades of Chester at Whitsuntide. Ed. Thomas Wright. London: Printed for the Shakespeare Society, 1843.

Chew, Samuel C. *Byron in England. His Fame and After-Fame.* London: John Murray, 1924.

———. *The Dramas of Lord Byron.* Gottingen: Vendenhoeck and Ruprecht, 1915, Baltimore, The John Hopkins Press. [Reprinted by Russell and Russell, New York, 1964.]

Coleman, Ronald Gregg. "Cosmic Symbolism in Byron's Dramas." Dissertation, Vanderbilt University, 1965.

Coleridge, Samuel Taylor. *The Complete Poetical Works Including Poems and Versions of Poems Now Published for the First Time.* Ed. with textual and bibliographical notes by Ernest Hartley Coleridge. 2 vols. Oxford: Clarendon Press, 1912.

———. "The Wanderings of Cain. A Fragment" in *The Bijou; or Annual of Literature and the Arts.* Pp. 17–23. London: William Pickering, 1828.

Coles, William A. "Thomas Noon Talfourd on Byron and the Imagination," *K-SJ,* LX, Pt. 2 (1960), 99–113.

Collins, J. Churton. "The Collected Works of Lord Byron" in *Studies in Poetry and Criticism.* London: George Bell & Sons, 1905.

Congregational Magazine. "*Cain, a Mystery.* By Lord Byron. London. 1821," V (April ,1822), 202–206.

Courthope, W. J. *A History of English Poetry.* 6 vols. London: Macmillan & Co., 1910.

Crowe, Eyre Evans [Paddy]. See *Blackwood's Edinburgh Magazine.*

Cunningham, Allan. *Biographical and Critical History of the British Literature of the Last Fifty Years.* Paris: Baudry's Foreign Library, 1834. [Previously published in *The Athenaeum* (December 28, 1833), 800–891.]

Cuvier, George Leopold. *Essay on the Theory of the Earth.* With Mineralogical Notes by Professor Jameson and Observations on the Geology of North America; Illustrated by Samuel L. Mitchell. New York: Kirk & Mercein, 1818.

Darley, George [John Lacy]. "A Fifth Letter to the Dramatists of the Day," *The London Magazine,* VIII (November, 1823), 533–538.

De Selincourt, Ernest. "Byron" in *Wordsworthian and Other Studies.* Pp. 105–128. New York: Russell & Russell, 1947, reissued 1964. [Originally an Oxford lecture, 1933.]

Dobrée, Bonamy. *Byron's Dramas.* The University of Nottingham, Byron Foundation Lecture, 1962.

Dowden, Edward. *The French Revolution and English Literature.* New York: Scribner's Sons, 1897.

Dowden, Wilfred S. "A Jacobin Journal's View of Lord Byron," *Studies in Philology,* XLVIII (January, 1951), 56–66.

Drinkwater, John. *The Pilgrim of Eternity, Byron—A Conflict.* London: Hodder and Stoughton, Ltd., 1925.

Duncan, Robert W. "Byron and the *London Literary Gazette,*" *Boston University Studies in English,* II (Winter, 1956), 240–250.

The Eclectic Review. "Art. II. 1. Cain, a Mystery. By Lord Byron. 12 mo. London, 1822," XVII (May, 1822), 418–427. [The author was tentatively identified by John Wright as Robert Hall (XIV, 29)].

The Edinburgh Magazine and Literary Miscellany; a New Series of the Scots Magazine. "Sardanapalus, a Tragedy—The Two Foscari, a Tragedy—Cain, a Mystery. By Lord Byron. 8vo. pp. 440," X (January, 1822), 102–114. [The review of *Cain* is confined to pages 110–114.]

The Edinburgh Review. Jeffrey, Francis or William Hazlitt [unsigned]. "Art. V. Sardanapalus, a Tragedy. The Two Foscari, a Tragedy. Cain, a Mystery. By Lord Byron. 8vo. pp. 440. Murray, London, 1822," XXXVI, No. 72 (February, 1822), 413–452.

Eimer, Manfred. "Byrons Beziehungen zur deutschen Kultur," *Anglia,* XXXVI, 442–443.

———. *Byron und der Kosmos. Ein Beitrag Zur Weltanschauung des Dichters und den Ansichten seiner Zeit.* Anglistische Forschungen, XXXIV. Heidelberg: Carl Winter, 1912.

———. "Das Apokryphe Buch Henoch und Byrons Mysterien," *Englische Studien,* XLIV (1911), 18–31.

Elledge, W. Paul. "Imagery and Theme in Byron's Cain," *K-SJ,* XV (Winter, 1966), 49–57.

———. "The Enkindled Clay: Imagery and Theme in Byron's Poetry." Dissertation, Tulane University, 1965.

Elton, Oliver. *Survey of English Literature, 1780–1830.* 2 vols. New York: The Macmillan Company, 1924. [First published by E. Arnold in 1912.]

Elze, Karl. *Lord Byron, a Biography with a Critical Essay on His Place in Literature.* London: John Murray, 1872.

Enoch, Book of. Trans. R. H. Charles. Oxford: Clarendon Press, 1893.

Enoch, Book of. Trans. Richard Laurence. 3rd ed. Oxford: J. H. Parker, 1838.

Erdman, David. "Byron's Stage Fright," *ELH,* VI (1939), 219–243.

Escarpit, Robert. *Lord Byron: Un Tempérament Littéraire.* 2 vols. Paris: Le Cercle du Livre, 1957.

The European Magazine and London Review. "Sardanapalus, a Tragedy; The Two Foscari, a Tragedy; Cain, a Mystery. By Lord Byron. 8vo. pp. 439. London, 1821," LXXXI (January, 1822), 58–70.

Evangelical Magazine and Missionary Chronicle. "Cain: A Mystery. By Lord Byron," XXX (May, 1822), 192–193.

The Examiner.

"Sardanapalus, a Tragedy. The Two Foscari, a Tragedy. Cain, a Mystery. By Lord Byron" (December 23, 1821), 808–810. [Signed "Q."]

"Lord Byron's Tragedies" (December 30, 1821), 827–828. [A sequel of the preceding article.]

"British Censorship of the Press" (February 17, 1822), 106–107. [This letter was dated "Newcastle-upon-Tyne, February 5, 1822" and signed "Q.E.D."]

"Thursday, February 7. Lord Byron's "Cain."—Murray v. Benbow (February 11, 1822), 90.

"Court of Chancery. Lord Byron's 'Cain'—Murray v. Benbow and Another" (February 17, 1822), 111.

"Lord Byron's Cain" (February 24, 1822), 120–121. [Signed "B."]

Hunt, Leigh. "Letters to the Readers of the Examiner. No. 2—Lord Byron's Cain" (June 2, 1822), 338–341. [Signed with Hunt's hand symbol.]

"Police Bow-Street" (October 19, 1823), 684.

Fabre d' Olivet, Antoine. *Cain a Dramatic Mystery in Three Acts by Lord Byron Translated into French Verse and Refuted in a Series of Philosophical and Critical Remarks Preceded by a Letter Addressed to Lord Byron, upon the Motives and the Purpose of This Work.* [Paris] 1823. Trans. Nayán Louise Redfield. New York and London: C. P. Putnam's Sons, 1923.

Fairchild, Hoxie Neale. *Religious Trends in English Poetry.* Vol. III: *1780–1830, Romantic Faith.* New York: Columbia University Press, 1961. [First printed in 1949 by the same press.]

Fonblanque, Albany. *The Life and Labours.* Ed. Edward Barrington de Fonblanque. London: Richard Bentley and Son, 1874.

Fontenelle, Bernard le Bovier de. *Conversations on the Plurality of Worlds. By a Gentleman of the Inner-Temple.* 2nd ed. London: T. Caslon, 1967.

Frye, Northrop. *Fearful Symmetry: A Study of William Blake.* Princeton: Princeton University Press, 1947.

Galt, John. *The Life of Lord Byron.* London: Colburn and Bentley, 1830.

Genest, John. *Some Account of the English Stage, from the Restoration in 1660 to 1830.* 10 vols. Bath: H. E. Carrington, 1832.

The Gentleman's Magazine.

"Sardanapalus, a Tragedy; The Two Foscari, a Tragedy; Cain, a Mystery. By Lord Byron. pp. 439. Murray," XCI (December, 1821), 537–541. [Only p. 537 mentioned *Cain.*]

"Cain, a Mystery. By Lord Byron," XCI (December, 1821), 613–615.

Graham, John. "An Epistle to Lord Byron," XCII (March, 1822), 259.

"Rhetoric of the Infidel School," XCII (December, 1822), 513–514.

Gerard William [W. Gerard Smith]. *Byron Re-studied in His Dramas; Being a Contribution towards a Definitive Estimate of His Genius.* London: F. V. White & Co., 1886.

Gessner, Salomon. *The Death of Abel.* Trans. Mrs. Mary Collyer. London: T. Heptinstall, 1797.

Gillardon, Heinrich. *Shelley's enwirkung auf Byron.* Karlsruhe: M. Gillardon, 1898.

Gingerich, Solomon Francis. "Byron" in *Essays in the Romantic Poets.* New York: The Macmillan Company, 1929. [First printed 1924.]

Gisborne, Maria, and Edward E. Williams. *Maria Gisborne and Edward E. Williams, Shelley's Friends. Their Journals and Letters.* Ed. Frederick L. Jones. Norman: University of Oklahoma Press, 1951.

Gleckner, Robert F. *Byron and the Ruins of Paradise.* Baltimore: The Johns Hopkins Press, 1967. [This book appeared after mine had gone to press.]

Godwin, William. *An Enquiry concerning Political Justice, and Its Influence on General Virtue and Happiness.* 2 vols. London: G. G. J. & J. Robinson, 1793.

Goethe, Johann Wolfgang. "Cain, a Mystery by Lord Byron." Trans. by J. G. Robertson as a part of his essay "Goethe and Byron" in *Publications of the English Goethe Society.* N.S. II, 73–76. London: Alexander Moring, 1925.

———. *Conversations with Eckermann.* Introd. Wallace Wood. Washington and London: M. Walter Dunne, 1901.

Goode, C. T. *Byron as Critic.* Weimar: R. Wagner Sohn, 1923.

Goss, Madeleine. *Modern Music-Makers, Contemporary American Composers.* New York: Dutton, 1952.

Grant, Harding. *Lord Byron's Cain, a Mystery: With Notes; Wherein the*

Religion of the Bible Is Considered, in Reference to Acknowledged Philosophy and Reason. London: William Crofts, 1830.
Granville, Countess Harriet. *Letters, 1810–1845.* Ed. F. Leveson Gower. 2 vols. London: Longmans, Green & Co., 1894.
Greef, A. "Byron's Lucifer," *Englische Studien,* XXXVI (1905), 64–65.
Grierson, H. J. C. "Address at the Presentation to Aberdeen Grammar School of a Statue of Lord Byron—1923" in *Essays and Addresses.* Pp. 1–18. London: Chatto and Windus, 1940.
———. "Byron and English Society," a Nottingham Lecture, March 17, 1922, amplified and printed in *Byron, The Poet. A Collection of Addresses and Essays.* Ed. Walter A. Briscoe. Pp. 55–85. London: George Routledge & Sons Ltd., 1924. [Reprinted in *The Background of English Literature, Classical and Romantic and Other Collected Essays and Addresses.* Pp. 167–199. London: Chatto and Windus, 1950. This book was often reprinted before and after 1950.]
———. *Lord Byron: Arnold and Swinburne.* London: Published for the British Academy by Humphrey Milford, Oxford University Press. n. d. [A Wharton lecture on English poetry read November 24, 1920.]
———, and J. C. Smith. "Byron" in *A Critical History of English Poetry.* Pp. 380–381. New York: Oxford University Press, 1946.
Guiccioli, Countess Teresa. *My Recollections of Lord Byron; and Those of Eye-Witnesses of His Life.* Trans. Hubert E. H. Jerningham. New York: Harper & Brothers, 1869.
Hall, Robert. See *The Eclectic Review.*
Hancock, A. E. "Byron" in *French Revolution and the English Poets.* Pp. 78–118. New York: Henry Holt & Co., 1899.
Harness, The Reverend William. *The Wrath of Cain: A Boyle Lecture, Delivered at the Church of St. Martin's in the Fields.* London: Rivington, 1822.
Harris, Audrey Louise. "English Tragedy in the Early Romantic Period 1790–1830." Thesis, University of London, 1954.
Harrison, John William. "The Imagery of Byron's Romantic Narratives and Dramas." Dissertation, University of Colorado, 1958.
Harroviensis. *A Letter to Sir Walter Scott, Bart., in Answer to the Remonstrance of Oxoniensis on the Publication of Cain, a Mystery by Lord Byron.* London: Rodwell and Martin, 1822.
Havens, Raymond D. *The Influence of Milton on English Poetry.* Cambridge: Harvard University Press, 1922.
Hawkes, Terence. "The Problems of Prosody," *A Review of English Literature,* III (April, 1962), 32–49.
Hayden, John Olion. "The Reviewers of British Romantic Literature 1802–24." Dissertation, Columbia University, 1965.
Hazlitt, William. *Complete Works.* Ed. P. P. Howe, after the edition of A. R.

Waller and Arnold Glover. 21 vols., London and Toronto: J. M. Dent and Sons, Ltd., 1930–1934. [See also *The Edinburgh Review.*]

Heber, Bishop Reginald. See *The Quarterly Review.*

Herford, C. H. *The Age of Wordsworth.* London: George Bell & Sons, 1901. [First published in 1897 by the same press.]

Hobhouse, John Cam, Lord Broughton. *Recollections of a Long Life.* Ed. Lady Dorchester. 6 vols. London: John Murray, 1909–1911.

Howell, Owen. *Abel. Written, but with Great Humility, in Reply to Lord Byron's Cain.* [In verse.] London: John Mardon, 1843.

Hunt, Leigh. *The Autobiography.* Ed. J. E. Morpurgo. London: The Cresset Press, 1948.

———. *Lord Byron and Some of His Contemporaries.* London: Henry Colburn, 1828.

"Icaromenippus, an Aerial Expedition," *The Works of Lucian of Samosata,* translated by H. W. Fowler and F. G. Fowler. Oxford: Clarendon Press, 1905.

The Imperial Magazine or Compendium of Religious, Moral, and Philosophical Knowledge. "Cain; a Mystery, by the Author of Don Juan," IV (April, 1822), 379.

Insch, Audrey G. "English Blank Verse Tragedy from 1790 to 1825." Dissertation, The University of Durham, England, 1958.

The Investigator; or Quarterly Magazine. "Review.—Licentious Productions in High Life: Lord Byron—Sir C. H. Williams— Percy B. Shelley," V (July and October, 1822), 315–371. [This review included a long general discussion of the prosecution of vicious books, paid some attention to Shelley's *Queen Mab*, to Cantos II–V of *Don Juan*, to *Cain* (pp. 342–360), and presented the criticism made by Uriel and by the pamphlet by Oxoniensis.]

Jack, Ian. *English Literature, 1815–1832.* Oxford: Clarendon Press, 1963.

Jeffrey, Francis. See *The Edinburgh Review.*

Jespersen, Otto. *Essentials of English Grammar.* New York: Henry Holt and and Company, 1933.

Joseph, Michael Kennedy. *Byron the Poet.* London: Victor Gollancz Ltd., 1964.

Joyce, James. *Letters.* 3 vols. Vols. 2 and 3 edited by Richard Ellmann. New York: Viking Press, 1966.

———. *Letters.* Ed. Stuart Gilbert. New York: Viking Press, 1957.

The Kaleidoscope or Literary and Scientific Mirror. "Lord Byron's Tragedies. Cain," II (February 19, 1822), 258.

Keats, John. *The Poems.* Ed. E. De Selincourt. London: Methuen, 1905. [Reprinted in 1961 by Methuen, London.]

Kennedy, James. *Conversations on Religion, with Lord Byron and Others, Held in Cephalonia, a Short Time Previous to his Lordship's Death.* London: John Murray, 1830.

Ker, W. P. "Byron: An Oxford Lecture," *The Criterion*, II (1923), 1–15. [Reprinted in *Collected Essays*. Ed. Charles Whibley. II, 207–223. London: Macmillan and Co., Ltd., 1925.]

Kingsley, Charles. "Thoughts on Shelley and Byron" in *Literary and General Essays*. Pp. 35–58. London: Macmillan and Co., 1890. [Published in *Fraser's Magazine*, XLVIII (November, 1853), 568–576.]

Klein, John W. "Byron's Neglected Plays," *Drama*, LXIII (Winter, 1961), 34–36.

Knight, G. Wilson. *Byron's Dramatic Prose*. Byron Foundation Lecture. Nottingham: University of Nottingham, 1953.

———. "Byron" in *The Golden Labyrinth. A Study of British Drama*. Pp. 229–239. New York: Norton, 1962.

———. *Lord Byron: Christian Virtues*. London: Routledge & Kegan Paul, Ltd., 1952.

———. "The Plays of Lord Byron," *The Times Literary Supplement*, February 3, 1950, p. 80.

———. "Shakespeare and Byron's Plays," *Shakespeare Jahr-Buch*, XCV (1959), 82–97.

———. *The Times Literary Supplement*, February 20, 1959, p. 97.

———. "The Two Eternities: An Essay on Byron" in *The Burning Oracle*. London: Oxford University Press, 1939.

The Ladies' Monthly Museum or Polite Repository. "Cain: A Mystery. By Lord Byron," XV (1822), 38–41.

Lady's Magazine and Museum of the Belles-lettres, III (March, 1822), 153. [The two short paragraphs on *Cain* are part of "Review of Lord Byron's Tragedy of The Two Foscari."]

The Leeds Correspondant, a Literary, Mathematical, and Philosophical Miscellany. "Sardanapalus, a Tragedy; the Two Foscari, a Tragedy; and Cain, a Mystery. By Lord Byron.—London, 8vo. pp. 439," IV (April, 1822), 110–116.

Lehman, B. H. "'Leadership' in the Romantic Poets," *PMLA*, XXXVII (1922), 655–660.

"A Letter of Expostulation to Lord Byron, on His Present Pursuits; with Animadversions on His Writings and Absence from His Country in the Hour of Danger," *The Pamphleteer*, XIX (London, 1822), 347–362.

The Literary Chronicle and Weekly Review.

"Sardanapalus, a Tragedy. The Two Foscari, a Tragedy. Cain, a Mystery. By Lord Byron. 8vo. pp. 439. London, 1821" (December 22, 1821), 799–802. [Page 799 has a cursory mention of *Cain*.]

"Cain. A Mystery. By Lord Byron," IV (January 5, 1822), 6–8.

"A Remonstrance addressed to Mr. John Murray, respecting a recent Publication. By Oxoniensis. 8vo. pp. 24. London, 1822," IV (January 29, 1822), 39–40.

"A Vindication of the Paradise Lost, from the Charge of Exculpating 'Cain,' a Mystery. By Philo-Milton. 8vo. pp. 60. London, 1822," IV (October 19, 1822), 663.

"Another Cain, a Mystery. By William Battine, Esq. L.L.D. 12 mo. pp. 64. London, 1822," IV (October 19, 1822), 663–664.

The Literary Gazette and Journal of Belles Lettres, Arts, Sciences, etc.

"Cain, a Mystery: Sardanapalus, and The Two Foscari, Tragedies; by Lord Byron. Octavo, pp. 439. J. Murray," No. 257 (December 22, 1821), 808–812.

"Sardanapalus. The Two Foscari. By Lord Byron," No. 258 (December 29, 1821), 821–822. [The final article in the series that appeared on January 5, 1822, had nothing on *Cain*.]

"Literature, Etc. Southey and Byron!" No. 261 (January 19, 1822). [Only p. 44 concerned *Cain*.]

"Literature, Etc. Lords—Authors—Publishers," No. 269 (March 16, 1822), 166–167.

"The Wrath of Cain: A Boyle Lecture delivered at the Church of St. Martin in the Fields, Wednesday, Feb. 6, 1822. By the Rev. Wm. Harness, A. M. Etc. Rivingtons," No. 266 (February 23, 1822), 114.

Literary Speculum. "Remarks on Lord Byron's Cain," I (February, 1822), 257–260.

Lockhart, John Gibson. *Memoirs of the Life of Sir Walter Scott, Bart.* 7 vols. Edinburgh, 1837. [See also *Blackwood's Edinburgh Magazine*.]

The London Christian Instructor. See *Congregational Magazine.*

The London Magazine. Talfourd, Thomas Noon [unsigned]. "Sardanapalus, The Two Foscari, and Cain, by Lord Byron," V (January, 1822), 66–71.

The London University Magazine. "The Poetry of Thought, No. 1.—Lord Byron's '*Cain*'," I (October–January, 1829), 144–157.

"Lord Byron's *Cain* Produced in Lucerne," *The Times*, London, April 12, 1960, p. 6.

Lord Byron's Correspondence Chiefly with Lady Melbourne, Mr. Hobhouse, the Hon. Douglas Kinnaird, and P. B. Shelley, with Portraits. 2 vols. Ed. John Murray. London: John Murray, 1922.

Lovell, Ernest J., Jr. *Byron: The Record of a Quest.* Austin: University of Texas Press, 1949. [Reprinted in 1966 by Archon Books, Hamden, Connecticut.]

——— (ed.). *His Very Self and Voice: Collected Conversations of Lord Byron.* New York: Macmillan, 1954.

Ludus Coventriae. A Collection of Mysteries, Formerly Represented at Coven-

try on the Feast of Corpus Christi. Ed. James Orchard Halliwell. London: Printed for the Shakespeare Society, 1841.

Macaulay, Thomas Babington. "Moore's Life of Lord Byron" in *Critical, Historical, and Miscellaneous Essays.* II, 324–367. New York: Hurd and Houghton, 1866. [Published anonymously as "Art. XI.—Letters and Journals of Lord Byron. With Notices of his Life. By Thomas Moore, Esq. 2 vols. 4to. London: 1830," *Edinburgh Review,* LIII (June, 1831), 544–572.]

The Manchester Iris; or, Literary and Scientific Miscellany. "Cain, a Mystery," I (February 23, 1822), 25–26. [Published over the pseudonym "Nemo."]

Mantle, Burns (ed.). *The Best Plays of 1924–25.* Boston: Small, Maynard & Co., 1925.

Marchand, Leslie A. *The Athenaeum. A Mirror of Victorian Culture.* Chapel Hill: University of North Carolina Press, 1941. [Especially pp. 250–255.]

———. *Byron. A Biography.* 3 vols. New York: Alfred A. Knopf, 1957.

———. *Byron's Poetry. A Critical Introduction.* Boston: Houghton Mifflin Co., 1965. [Pp. 84–91.]

Marjarum, Edward Wayne. *Byron as Skeptic and Believer.* New York: Russell and Russell, 1962. [This Princeton dissertation was published in 1938.]

Marshall, William H. *The Structure of Byron's Major Poems.* Philadelphia: University of Pennsylvania Press, 1962. [Pp. 136–154.]

Matthews, John. See *Blackwood's Edingburgh Magazine.*

Maurice, Frederick Denison. See *The Athenaeum.*

Mayn, George. *Ueber Lord Byrons Heaven and Earth.* Breslau, 1887. [Cf. *Englische Studien,* XI, 145.]

Mayne, Ethel Colburn. *Byron.* Second revised edition. London: Methuen & Co. Ltd., 1924.

Mazzini, Giuseppe. "Byron and Goethe" in *Life and Writings.* VI, 61–97. London: Smith, Elder and Co., 1891.

Medwin, Thomas. *Journal of the Conversations of Lord Byron: Noted during a Residence with His Lordship at Pisa in the Years 1821 and 1822.* London: Printed for Henry Colburn, 1824.

———. *The Life of Percy Bysshe Shelley.* London: Oxford University Press, 1913.

Medwin's Conversations of Lord Byron. Ed. Ernest J. Lovell, Jr., Princeton: Princeton University Press, 1966. [My references are to the 1824 edition only because this recent edition appeared after I had completed my book.]

Messac, R., "Caïn et le Problème du Mal dans Voltaire, Byron et Leconte de Lisle," *Revue de Littérature Comparée,* IV (1924), 620–652.

Milton, John. *Paradise Lost.* Ed. Merritt Y. Hughes. Garden City, New York: Doubleday, Doran & Company, Inc., 1935.

———. *The Poems of John Milton.* Ed. James Holly Hanford. Second edition. New York: Ronald Press Co., 1953.

The Monthly Magazine. "Sardanapalus, a Tragedy; the Two Foscari, a Tragedy; Cain, a Mystery. By the Right Hon. Lord Byron," LIII (February, 1822), 10–15.

———. "The Philosophy of Contemporary Criticism," LV (February, 1823), 33.

The Monthly Review or Literary Journal. "Art. IX. Sardanapalus, a Tragedy. The Two Foscari, a Tragedy. Cain, a Mystery. By Lord Byron. 8vo. pp. 439. 15s Boards. Murray. 1821," XCVII (January, 1822), 83–98.

Moore, Thomas. *Letters and Journals of Lord Byron.* 6 vols. in *The Works of Lord Byron.* 17 vols. London: John Murray, 1832.

———. *Memoirs, Journal and Correspondence.* Ed. Lord John Russell. 8 vols. London: Longman, Brown, Green, and Longmans, 1853.

Moorman, F. W. "Byron" in *The Cambridge History of English Literature.* Eds. A. W. Ward and A. R. Waller. XII, 34–62. New York: The Macmillan Co., 1933. [First published in 1917 by The Macmillan Company, New York.]

More, Paul Elmer. "Biographical Sketch," pp. xi–xxi, and "Dramas," pp. 447–478, in *The Complete Poetical Works of Byron.* Boston: Houghton Mifflin Company, 1905. [More prepared his edition and wrote the general introduction about ten years before the book was published. His introduction is a composite of two 1898 articles: "The Wholesome Revival of Byron," *Atlantic Monthly,* LXXXII (December, 1898), 801–809; "Lord Byron," *Independent,* LIII (October 3, 1901), 2359–2360.]

Morley, John. "Byron" in *Critical Miscellanies.* Pp. 125–173. London: Macmillan and Co., Ltd., 1923. [This essay had appeared under the same title in *The Fortnightly Review,* XIV (December, 1870), 650–673.]

Mortenson, Robert Lawrence. "Lord Byron's *Cain, A Mystery*: A Variorum Edition." Dissertation, University of Pennsylvania, 1964.

Mulock, Thomas. Letter to *The Morning Post,* quoted in *LJ,* V, 593.

Murray, John. "Notes on Captain Medwin's Conversations of Lord Byron." Unbound pamphlet. n.d. [1824]. [This was also printed in *The Gentleman's Magazine,* XCIV (November, 1824), 438–442.]

———. See *Lord Byron's Correspondence Chiefly with Lady Melbourne, Mr. Hobhouse, the Hon. Douglas Kinnaird, and P. B. Shelley, with Portraits.*

Nichol, John. *Byron.* New York: Harper & Brothers, 1880.

Noel, Roden. *Life of Lord Byron.* London: Walter Scott, 1890.

———. "Lord Byron and His Times" in *Essays on Poetry and Poets.* Pp. 50–113. London: Kegan Paul, Trench & Co., 1886. [Had appeared in *St. Paul's Magazine* (November, December, 1873), 555–577; 618–638. The 1886 version has a few omissions, additions, and minor revisions.]

Norman, Arthur M. "Dialogue in Byron's Dramas," *N&Q*, N.S. I (July, 1954), 304–306.

Oliphant, Mrs. Margaret (Wilson). *The Literary History of England.* London: Macmillan and Co., 1889.

Oxoniensis [The Reverend Henry John Todd]. *A Remonstrance Addressed to Mr. John Murray, Respecting a Recent Publication.* London: F.C. & J. Rivington, 1822.

Pafford, Ward. "Byron and the Mind of Man: *Childe Harold* III–IV and *Manfred*," *Studies in Romanticism*, I (Winter, 1962), 105–127.

Payne, William Morton. "George Gordon Byron" in *The Greater English Poets of the Nineteenth Century*. Pp. 64–95. New York: H. Holt and Company, 1907.

Pedrini, Lura Nancy, and Duilio T. Pedrini. "Serpent Imagery and Symbolism in the Major English Romantic Poets: Blake, Wordsworth, Coleridge, Byron, Shelley, Keats," *Psychiatric Quarterly Supplement,* XXXIV (1960), 189–244; XXXV (1961), 36–99.

Phillips, Stephen. "The Poetry of Byron," *The Cornhill,* LXXVII (January, 1898), 16–26.

Philo-Milton. *A Vindication of the Paradise Lost from the Charge of Exculpating "Cain," a Mystery.* London: Rivington, April, 1822.

Piozzi, Mrs. Hester Lynch Thrale. *Autobiography, Letters and Literary Remains.* Ed. A. Hayward. 2 vols. Boston: Ticknor and Fields, 1861.

Pönitz, Arthur. *Byron und die Bibel.* Inaugural-Dissertation zur Erlangung der Koktorwürde Universität Leipzig, 1906.

The Quarterly Review. "Cases of Walcot v. Walker; Southey v. Sherwood; Murray v. Benbow, and Lawrence v. Smith," XXVII (April, 1822), 123–132.

———. Heber, Bishop Reginald [unsigned]. "Art. X.—1. Marino Faliero, Doge of Venice, an Historical Tragedy.—2. Sardanapalus, a Tragedy.—3. The Two Foscari, a Tragedy.—4. Cain, a Mystery," XXVII (July, 1822), 476–524.

Quennell, Peter (ed.). *Byron A Self-Portrait. Letters and Diaries 1798 to 1824. With Hitherto Unpublished Letters.* 2 vols. London: John Murray, 1950.

———. *Byron in Italy.* New York: Viking Press, 1941.

Quiller-Couch, Sir Arthur. "Byron" in *Studies in Literature.* Second Series. Pp. 3–31. New York: G. P. Putnam's Sons, 1922. [The first Nottingham lecture, 1918.]

Rainwater, Frank. "Lord Byron: A Study of the Development of His Philosophy, with Special Emphasis upon the Dramas." Dissertation, Vanderbilt University, 1949.

Rambler's Magazine or Man of Fashion's Companion. "Cain, a Mystery. By Lord Byron," I (March 1, 1822), 119.

Read, Herbert. "Byron" in *The True Voice of Feeling*. Pp. 288–319. New York: Pantheon, 1953.

Reade, John Edmund. *Cain the Wanderer; A Vision of Heaven; Darkness; and other Poems*. London: Whittaker, Treacher and Co., 1830.

"Remarks on Cain." n.d. [1826?] 12 pp. [These remarks are a religious and psychological defense. They are preceded by a dedication "To the sister 'whom he loved'," and a "Preface to the Second Edition" of selections from Byron's poetry. On the first prefatory page is written "Not published." This item was No. 400 on page 61 of *Byron and Byroniana*, London: Elkin Mathews, 1930. The copy of the "Remarks" that I consulted is in the Houghton Library of Harvard University.]

The Republican. Richard Carlile [unsigned]. "Queen Mab; Cain, a Mystery; and a Royal Reviewer," V (February 8, 1822), 192. [Signed "Editor."]

Rice, Richard Ashley. "Lord Byron's British Reputation," *Smith College Studies in Modern Languages*. Vol. 5, No. 2. Northampton, Mass.: Smith College, 1924.

Roberts, William. See *The British Review*.

Robertson, J. G. "Goethe and Byron," *Publications of the English Goethe Society*, N. S., Vol. II. London: Alexander Moring, 1925.

Robinson, Henry Crabb. *Books and Their Writers*. Ed. Edith J. Morley. 3 vols. London: J. M. Dent and Sons, Ltd., 1938.

———. *Diary, Reminiscences, and Correspondence*. Ed. Thomas Sadler. 2 vols. London and New York: Macmillan & Co., 1872.

Ruby, Wade. "A Study of the Influence of Mortality on Byron's Thought and Poetry" in *Abstracts of Dissertations*. Pp. 36–39. Los Angeles: The University of Southern California, 1944.

Rudwin, Maximilian. *The Devil in Legend and Literature*. Chicago: The Open Court Publishing Co., 1931.

Ruskin, John. "Fiction, Fair and Foul [Parts] III, IV" in *The Works*. Eds. E. T. Cooke and Alexander Wedderburn. XXXIV, 347, 361–362. London: George All, 1908. [Previously published in *Nineteenth Century*, VII (September, November, 1880), 394–410, 748–760.

———. Letter to Charles Eliot Norton, July 11, 1869, *The Works*, Eds. E. T. Cooke and Alexander Wedderburn. XXXVI, 574. London: George All, 1908.

Russell, Bertrand. "Byron and the Modern World," *Journal of the History of Ideas*, I (1940), 24–37. [Partially reprinted in *A History of Western Philosophy*. Pp. 746–752. New York: Simon and Schuster, 1945. The long quotations of poetry and most of the last six pages of the earlier essay were omitted.]

Saintsbury, George. "The Prosody of the Nineteenth Century" in *The Cambridge History of English Literature*. XIII, Chap. 7. New York: The Macmillan Company, 1933. [First published in 1917 by The Macmillan Company, New York.]

Sarmiento, Edward. "A Parallel between Lord Byron and Fray Luis de León," *Review of English Studies*. IV (1953), 267–273.

Schaffner, Alfred. *Lord Byrons Cain und seine quellen*. Strassburg: K. J. Trübner, 1880. [Cf. *Englische Studien*, IV, 335.]

The Scots Magazine. See *The Edinburgh Magazine*.

Scott, Sir. Walter. *The Letters*. Ed. H. J. C. Grierson, assisted by D. Cook, W. Parker, and others. 12 vols. London: Constable & Co., 1934.

Shelley, Mary W. *The Letters of Mary W. Shelley*. Ed. Frederick L. Jones. 2 vols. Norman: University of Oklahoma Press, 1944.

———. *Mary Shelley's Journal*. Ed. Frederick L. Jones. Norman: University of Oklahoma Press, 1947.

Shelley, Percy Bysshe. *The Complete Poetical Works of Percy Bysshe Shelley*. Ed. Thomas Hutchinson, with Introduction and Notes by Benjamin P. Kurtz. New York: Oxford University Press, 1933.

———. *The Letters of Percy Bysshe Shelley*. Ed. Frederick L. Jones. 2 vols. Oxford: Clarendon Press, 1964.

Siegel, Paul. "'A Paradise within Thee' in Milton, Byron, and Shelley," *Modern Language Notes*, LVI (December, 1941), 615–617.

Smiles, Samuel. *A Publisher and His Friends: Memoir and Correspondence of the Late John Murray*. 2 vols. London: John Murray, 1891.

Southey, Robert. *The Complete Poetical Works*. New York: D. Appleton & Co., 1860.

———. *Life and Correspondence*. Ed. Charles Cuthbert Southey. 6 vols. London: Longman, Brown, Green, and Longmans, 1849.

———. Preface to *A Vision of Judgement*. London: Longman, Hurst, Rees, Orme, and Brown, 1821.

———. *Selections from the Letters*. Ed. John Wood Warter. 4 vols. London: Longman, Brown, Green, and Longmans, 1856.

Stanhope, Leicester F. C. *Greece in 1823 and 1824*. London: Sherwood, Gilbert, and Piper, 1825.

Stavrou, Constantine N. "Milton, Byron, and the Devil," *The University of Kansas City Review*, XXI (March, 1955), 153–159.

Steffan, Truman Guy. *The Making of a Masterpiece*. Vol. I of *Byron's Don Juan*. Austin: University of Texas Press, 1957.

Stout, George Dumas. *The Political History of Leigh Hunt's Examiner. Together with an Account of "The Book."* Saint Louis: Washington Universsity Studies—New Series, No. 19, 1949.

Stowe, Harriet Beecher. *Lady Byron Vindicated*. Boston: Fields, Osgood and Co., 1870.

Strout, Alan Lang. *A Bibliography of Articles in Blackwood's Magazine, 1817–1825.* Lubbock: Texas Technological College, 1959.

Styles, The Reverend John. *Lord Byron's Works, Viewed in Connexion with Christianity, and the Obligation of Social Life: A Sermon, Delivered at Holland Chapel, Kennington.* London: Knight and Lacey, 1824.

Swinburne, Algernon Charles. "Byron" in *The Complete Works.* Ed. Sir Edmund Gosse and Thomas James. XV, 129–139. London: William Heinemann, 1926. [This appeared in 1866 as a preface to a selection of Byron's poetry.]

———. "Wordsworth and Byron," *ibid.* XIV, 155–244. [This later essay first appeared in *The Nineteenth Century,* XV (April, May, 1884), 583–609, 764–790.]

———. *The Swinburne Letters.* Ed. Cecil Y. Lang. 6 vols. New Haven: Yale University Press, 1959.

Symonds, J. A. "Lord Byron" in *The English Poets.* Ed. T. H. Ward. IV, 244–255. New York: The Macmillan Co., 1907. [First published in 1880.]

Symons, Arthur. *The Romantic Movement in English Poetry.* London: Archibald Constable and Co., Ltd., 1909.

Taborski, Boleslaw. "Lord Byron and the Theatre." Master's thesis, The University of Bristol, England, 1952–1953.

Taine, H. A. *History of English Literature.* Trans. Henri van Luan. New York: A. L. Burt Co., n.d. [First edition in 1911.]

Talfourd, Thomas Noon. See *The London Magazine.*

Taylor, Henry. "Preface" to *Philip Van Artevelde.* London: Henry S. King & Co., 1877. [The Preface was dated May, 1834.]

Thackeray, William Makepeace. "Notes of a Journey from Cornhill to Grand Cairo" in *The Works.* X, 624–625. New York and London: Wiley and Putnam, 1903. [First printed in 1846.]

Thompson, James Roy. "Studies in the Drama of Lord Byron." Dissertation, University of Cincinnati, 1964.

Thorslev, Peter L., Jr. *The Byronic Hero.* Minneapolis: University of Minnesota Press, 1962.

———. "The Romantic Mind Is Its Own Place," *Comparative Literature,* XV (Summer, 1963), 250–268.

The Times Literary Supplement, February 20, 1959, p. 97.

The Towneley Plays. Eds. George England and Alfred W. Pollard. London: Published for the Early English Text Society by Kegan Paul, Trench, Trübner & Co., 1897.

Trelawny, Edward John. *Records of Shelley, Byron, and the Author.* 2 vols. London: B. M. Pickering, 1878.

Trent, W. P. "The Byron Revival" in *The Authority of Criticism.* Pp. 205–

236. New York: Scribner's Sons, 1899. [Appeared in *The Forum*, XXVI (October, 1898), 242–256.]

Uhlemayr, B. See Byron, George Gordon Lord.

Unamuno, Miguel de. *The Tragic Sense of Life in Men and in Peoples.* Trans. J. E. Crawford Flitch. London: Macmillan and Co., Ltd., 1921.

Uriel. *A Poetical Address to the Right Honorable Lord Byron, Written on the Continent: With Notes, Containing Strictures on the Spirit of Infidelity Maintained in His Works. An Examination into His Assertion, that "If Cain is Blasphemous, Paradise Lost is Blasphemous." And Several Other Poems.* London: Hatchard and Son and Burton & Smith, 1822.

Warburton, William. *The Divine Legation of Moses Demonstrated on the Principles of a Religious Deist, from the Omission of the Doctrine of a Future State of Reward and Punishment in the Jewish Dispensation.* 3 vols. London: Fletcher Gyles, 1741.

Watkins, John [unsigned]. *Memoirs of the Life and Writings of the Right Honourable Lord Byron, with Anecdotes of Some of His Contemporaries.* London: Henry Coburn and Co., 1822.

Wenzel, G. "Miltons und Byrons Satan," *Archiv für das Studium der neueren Sprachen und Litterturen*, LXXXIII (1889), 67–90.

West, Paul. *Byron and the Spoiler's Art.* New York: St. Martin's Press, 1960.

White, Newman I. "The English Romantic Writers as Dramatists," *Sewanee Review,* XXX (April, 1922), 206–215.

Wilkinson, Henry. *Cain, a Poem, Intended To Be Published in Parts, Containing an Antidote to the Impiety and Blasphemy of Lord Byron's Cain; with Notes, etc.* Part I. London: Baldwin, Cradock, and Joy, 1824. [No further parts published.]

Wright, John (ed.) [unsigned]. *The Works of Lord Byron.* Vols. VII–XVII. London: John Murray, 1832–1833. [Prepared in conjunction with Thomas Moore's *Letters and Journals of Byron,* Vols. I–VI.]

The York Cycle of Mystery Plays. Ed. J. S. Purvis. London: The Society for Promoting Christian Knowledge, 1957.

Young, Edward. *The Poetical Works.* Vol. I, "Night Thoughts"; Vol. II, "A Paraphrase of Part of the Book of Job," pp. 169–189. London: Bell and Daldy, n.d. [The Aldine Edition.]

Zall, Paul M. "Lord Eldon's Censorship," *PMLA,* LXVIII (June, 1953), 436–443.

INDEX

The subject matter of the drama has not been indexed. Byron's development of his main ideas can be found in the documentation of the essays. For instance, the occurrence in the poem of Cain's antipathy toward his parents is recorded in note 13 on page 41. Numbers that refer to lines of the text of *Cain* are italicized in the Index to distinguish them from page numbers.